THE COUNTY WICKLOW DATABASE

432 AD TO 2006 AD

THE COUNTY WICKLOW DATABASE

432 AD TO 2006 AD

BRIAN WHITE

NONSUCH

First published 2006

Nonsuch Publishing
73 Lower Leeson Street
Dublin 2
Ireland
www.nonsuch-publishing.com

© Brian White, 2006

The right of Brian White to be identified as the Author
of this work has been asserted in accordance with the
Copyrights, Designs and Patents Act 1988.

All rights reserved. No part of this book may be reprinted
or reproduced or utilised in any form or by any electronic,
mechanical or other means, now known or hereafter invented,
including photocopying and recording, or in any information
storage or retrieval system, without the permission in writing
from the Publishers.

British Library Cataloguing in Publication Data.
A catalogue record for this book is available from the British Library.

ISBN 1 84588 551 1
ISBN-13 978 1 84588 551 9

Typesetting and origination by Tempus Publishing Limited
Printed in Great Britain

Contents

Foreword	7
Section One: Data by Date	9
Section Two: Data in Alphabetical Order	245
Section Three: Index	363

Foreword

My interest in Local History began in 1972 when the Bray Camera Club undertook to make a film tracing the History of Bray. I fell in love with doing research for the project and I realised that the recording of the history of Bray and County Wicklow had been neglected for years, except for a few writers.

The birth of any book takes a considerable time and this book is no exception. I can trace the origins of this book back to a November evening in 1974. When I had a chance conservation with my landlord, John O'Callaghan of Quigles Point in County Donegal. John and myself were discussing the similarity of County Donegal and County Wicklow.
I asked John if there was a single reference book about County Donegal. In return John posed the same question about County Wicklow. Over the next few weeks we discussed a length what should be included in such a book.

We came up with the terms of reference 'Transport', 'Education', 'Religion', 'Human Endeavour', 'Sport', 'Flora and Fauna' and 'Achievements' On my return to Wicklow the following year I began working on the project, first as a paper record and in 1994 I took it to the next stage a computerised record. It would not have been possible for one person to create such a reference book or database about County Wicklow without help and assistance.

The help and encouragement shown by the staff of the Bray Public Library and the County Library Service, especially Eileen Murray, Michael Kellegher, Rita Morrissey, Robert Butler and Brendan Martin.

The first public reference to the database was carried in the Wicklow People newspaper in 1978 when Jim Brophy made reference to it in his column 'Man on the Corner'. Jim kept the readers of the Bray People / Wicklow People up to date with developments of the database. I followed his advice was to make it a County database instead of just a Bray database.

Walking the towns and villages of Wicklow on a Sunday afternoon took on a new purpose. Jotting down the dates of buildings, visiting graveyards and historic houses. Sometimes been mistaken as a property developer.

The research took me to the Office of Public Works, National Library, National Archive, National Art Gallery and Museum both in Dublin and London. The Hunt Museum, Limerick. I also must acknowledge the assistance given by the Princess Grace Library in Monaco, and the Congressional Library in the USA. for access to newspapers, photographs, books, pen images and private papers with a County Wicklow interest.

The Royal Hibernian Academy, The Royal Irish Automobile Club, Scouting Ireland for assistance and verification of dates.

I must mention three well known County Wicklow local historians Christy Brien, Joe Loughman and Colbert Martin who are no longer with us. They would dole out snippets of information each a gem in its own right. Soon other historical societies heard of my goal to make a reference book for a reader to find out additional information about County Wicklow or the amateur historian to find a starting point for his/her research.

Additional information was provided by Val Byrne, Mary Davies, Bob Montongmery, Pat Hunt, Christian Corlett, Daithi O'Hogain, Jim Rees, Michael Murray, Moran and Elizabeth O'Sullivan, Arthur Flynn, Marie and John Megannety, Rob Goodybody, Claire Crowther, Kathleen Kinsella, Liam Clare, Jim Lynch, Padraig Laffan, Aideen Ireland, Seamus O'Maithiu, Henry Cairns, Fergal McGarry, Eamon de Buitlear, Derek Paine, Brendan O'Leary, Jim Scannell, Earl of Meath, Dr. Tom Curtis, Terry Kiely, Vaughan Dodd, Noel Keyes, Wicklow 400 Committee, and The Committee and members of the Bray Cualann Historical Society and all who provided assistance, in Ireland and overseas.

To Adrienne, David, Aoife and Cormac for allowing me to open the gate and explore the 'Garden of Ireland' County Wicklow. I would like to thank Nonsuch Publishing for taking the publication to the final stage in this the 400 anniversary of the shirring of Wicklow as a County

I hope you enjoy the Book, and if you discover something that should have been included, no doubt we will make room for it in Volume II.

Brian White
January 2006

Section One: Data by Date

A-Z Reference	Day	Date	Month	Year	DATA
Palladius				431	Pope Celestine sends his deacon St. Palladius to Ireland as its first bishop. Palladius lands at Arklow, Co. Wicklow
Glendalough				617	Ecclesiastical settlement founded at Glendalough Co. Wicklow by St. Kevin
Glendalough				618	The death of St. Kevin of Glendalough
Bell			circa	800	Hunt Museum, Limerick. Exhibit (HCA 621) 9th Century Irish Bronze Bell. Listed as Bronze Bell from Bray, Co. Wicklow
Glenmama. Battle of				998	Blackhill near Dunlavin the site of the Battle of Glenmamma
Toole. King Mac				1010	An inscription on a grave slab at Glendalough "Behold the resting-place of the body of King Mac Toole, who died 1010
Delgany				1022	The Battle of Delgany
Dublin Archdiocese				1028	The Roman Catholic Archdiocese of Dublin constituted
Ferghaile. Donnall Ua				1043	Donnall Ua Ferghaile, King of Fortuatha, killed at Termonn Coengin (Trooperstown) near Glendalough
Glendalough				1061	Some of the buildings in Glendalough destroyed by fire
Glendalough				1084	Some of the buildings at Glendalough were destroyed by fire
O'Toole. St Laurence				1128	St. Laurence O'Toole born
Dioceses of Dublin				1137	The limits of the Dioceses of Dublin and Glendalough set out in a papal bull by Pope Alexander
Baltinglass				1148	An Abbey established at Baltinglass, Co. Wicklow
Sacrobosco. Johannes			circa	1150	Johannas Sacrobosco (a philosopher and mathematician) born Hollywood, Co. Wicklow
O'Toole				1153	St. Laurence O'Toole appointed Abbot of Glendalough
Military Road				1170	Anglo-Norman military road constructed between Bray and Blacklion (Greystones). Ref. "A Garden and a Grave" by Fr. J. Masterson
Delgany				1172	Delgany Church appears in Strongbows charter as Deirgni
Arklow				1172	King Henry II granted Theobald Walter the lands and castle of Arklow
Ballyman				1172	Ballyman Church appears in Strongbows charter as Glenmuneri
de Riddelsford. Walter				1173	Richard de Clare, Earl of Pembroke granted the Manor of Bray to Walter de Riddelsford
de Riddelsford. Walter				1174	Walter de Riddelsford built at castle on the Southside of the river near St. Paul's Church, Bray, Co. Wicklow
O'Toole. St Laurence	Fri	14	11	1180	St. Laurence O'Toole died at Eu in Normandy, France
de Riddelsford. Walter				1181	Walter de Riddelsford built a castle at Kilkea near Athy, Co. Kildare
Comyn. John				1185	Archbishop of Dublin John Comyn granted half the lands of the abbey of Glendalough, The manor of Bellmore, Blessing ton
Marissa. Jordan de				1190	An Anglo-Norman mote built at Donard by Jordan de Marissa
Chapman. Robert				1200	Robert Chapman bailiff of Bray Town

Section One: Data by Date

Subject	Weekday	Day	Month	Year	Event
Meagan. Peter				1200	Philip Meagan Dean of Bray
Carleton				1204	Matthew Javanese owner of lands at Balicurtld (Curtlestown)
Wexford				1210	County Wexford shirred
Dublin				1210	County Dublin shirred
Carlow				1210	County Carlow shirred
Comyn. John	Thu	25	10	1212	Archbishop John Comyn died
de Riddelsford. Walter				1213	Walter de Riddelsford married Emeline (von Ulster) de Burgh
Castlekevin				1216	Fortification (Anglo-Norman) built at Castlekevin near Annamoe, Co. Wicklow
de Riddelsford. Walter				1220	Ela Longspee daughter of Walter de Riddelsford and Emeline de Burgh, born
Castlekevin				1225	Archbishop Henry was granted the rights to hold a weekly market at Castlekevin
Dermot				1225	The Song of Dermot and the Earl, lines" 3092 -3095" reference to Bray and Co. Wicklow
Delgany				1225	Kindlestown Castle probably built by Walter de Bendevill who owned land in Delgany
O'Toole. St Laurence				1226	Saint Laurence O'Toole was canonized
Newcastle Mill				1228	Mill established at Newcastle, Co. Wicklow
Baltinglass				1228	Baltinglass Abbey was home to 36 Cistercian Monks and 50 lay brothers
O'Toole. St Laurence				1230	The heart of St. Laurence O'Toole was returned from France to Christ Church, Dublin
Sacrobosco. Johannes				1235	Johannas Sacrobosco died in Paris and is buried in the Convent of St. Maturine
Delgany				1241	The lands of Delgany were held by Henry Prudum, from Archbishop of Dublin
Glencree				1244	84 Deer were sent from the Royal Forest at Chester to the King's Park at Glencree, Co. Wicklow
de Riddelsford. Walter				1244	Walter de Riddelsford died
Wicklow Ale				1244	Wicklow Ale sold at the Donnybrook Fair
Marisco. Geoffery de				1260	Geoffery de Marisco (Norman knight) granted lands at Hollywood and Donard in West Wicklow.
de Riddelsford. Walter				1276	Emeline (Von Ulster) de Burgh wife of Walter de Riddelsford died
Wicklow Friary				1279	Franciscan Friary was founded in Wicklow Town. The ruins now form part of a Park opposite the Grand Hotel, Wicklow
Glencree				1280	John de Walhope was granted 7 oak trees from the Royal Forest of Glencree to build a house at Sandyford Co. Dublin
Fitz Walter, Theobald	Wed	26	09	1285	Theobald Fitz Walter, of Arklow died
Glencree				1296	King Edward I of England gave Eustace Le Poer of Wicklow a present of 12 Fallow Deer
Kildare				1296	County Kildare first shirred

A–Z Reference	Day	Date	Month	Year	DATA
Delgany				1301	Albert de Kenleye, who was Sheriff of Kildare was granted lands near Bray, these lands today are called Kindlestown
Mathew. John				1305	John Mathew appointed Royal Forester of Glencree, Co. Wicklow by King Edward I of England
Glencree				1305	According to the Justiciary Rolls of Edward I. Thomas de Sandely a carpenter was charged with stealing timber at Glencree
Castlekevin				1308	The fortification at Castlekevin near Roundwood was attacked and burned by the O'Toole clan
Roche. de la George				1308	George de la Roche received a third share of the barony of Wicklow
Bray. Castle	Thu	16	04	1310	The O'Byrne and the O'Toole Clans attack the Castle at Bray and destroy it
Lawless. Hugh				1314	Sir Hugh Lawless was appointed by the crown as Constable of Bray Manor
O'Byrnes	Fri	16	04	1316	The O'Byrne clan from Glenmalure invade the towns and villages of North Wicklow, destroyed the castle at Bray
Cramp. Geoffery				1335	Goffery Cramp was given lands at the Manor of Oldcourt, Bray, Co. Wicklow
de Mareys. Adam				1352	Sir Adam de Mareys appointed Vicar of Bray
Dublin				1355	Dublin City employed the O'Toole Clan from West Wicklow to protect the city from attack by the O'Byrne Clan from East Wicklow
Danyell. Laurence				1355	Laurence Danyell commanded 16 foot soldiers at Wicklow Castle, Wicklow
Ballymore Eustace				1373	The Archbishop of Dublin appointed Sir Thomas Fitz Eustace as Constable of Castle Ballymore
Harold. Thomas			09	1374	Thomas Harold appointed constable of the Parish of Newcastle
O'Byrne clan				1374	The O'Byrne Clan attacked two Royal Castles in Wicklow, at Newcastle and Wicklow Town
Wicklow Town				1375	The Black Castle at Wicklow harbour its fortifications were enhanced
O'Byrne Clan	Sat	20	07	1398	The O'Byrne and Nolan clans of Wicklow attacked the Lord Lieutenant's forces at Kellistown, Co. Carlow
Sunnybank				1402	The Battle of Bloodybank now Sunnybank Little Bray
Dublin				1402	John Drake, Mayor of Dublin led the British forces in a skirmish against the Wicklow Clans at Sunnybank, Bray, Co. Wicklow
Act				1420	Subsidized Castles Act, Gave a grant £10 towards building a strong house or castle
O'Byrne Clan				1428	The Viceroy mustered a force of Dublin men at Bray, and led an attack on the O'Byrne Clan
Bray. Castle				1440	Castle built in the grounds of Oldcourt estate, Bray
Tommnafinnoge				1444	Timber from trees cut at Tommnafinnoge Wood near Shillelagh used in the building of King's College, Cambridge
Mulso. Sir Edward				1450	Parliament granted Sir Edward Mulso permission to establish a borough on the present site of Powerscourt Demesne
Mulso. Sir Edward				1463	Sir Edward Mulso died
Crosbie. Francis				1510	Francis Crosbie of Crosbie Park, Baltinglass, Co. Wicklow born

Section One: Data by Date

Name	Year				Event
Sacrobosco, Johannes	1518				Johannas Sacrobosco work "De Sphaera" was published in Venice in 1518
Brabazon. Sir William	1534				Sir William Brabazon of Dublin was appointed Vice Treasurer and General Receiver of Ireland
Brabazon. Sir William	1535				Fassaroe Castle near Bray was built for Sir William Brabazon Vice Treasurer and General Receiver of Ireland
Parish Schools	1537				Parish Schools were established for the education of the lower classes
O'Toole Art	1540				King Henry VIII granted Art O'Toole the Manor of Castlekevin
Baltinglass	1541				The title Viscount Baltinglass of 1st creation was granted to the Eustace family
Wicklow County Shirred	1542	07	Tue	04	Thady O'Birne of Wynde Gates, Bray made the first petition to King Henry VIII to Shire Co. Wicklow. Shirred 23/01/1606
O'Byrne. Feagh McHugh	1544				County Wicklow chieftain Feagh McHugh O'Byrne was born
Seymour. Mary	1547				Mary Seymour the daughter of Edward Seymour 1st Duke of Somerset and niece of Jane Seymour wife of King Henry VIII. born
Blessington	1547				The English and the O'Toole Clan defeated the Fitzgeralds at ThreeCastles North of Blessington, Co. Wicklow
Brabazon. Sir William	1550	02	Sun	02	Sir William Brabazon appointed Lord Justice for Ireland
Kiltimon Castle	1550	circa			Kiltimon Castle, Dunran Demesne built
Brabazon. Sir William	1552	07	Sat	09	Sir William Brabazon Vice Treasurer and General Receiver of Ireland, died
Glen of the Downes	1552				A road way was made through the Glen of the Downes
Baltinglass	1556				Sir Edmund Butler granted the Abbey at Baltinglass
Glencap	1557	07			The Glencap freeholders brought a case Feagh McArt Oge and Phelim O'Toole of Powerscourt about applying levies
Glencap	1557	07			Lord Deputy heard the case of the Glencap freeholders, He ruled that Glencap came under the sheriff of Dublin.
Seymour. Mary	1560				Mary Seymour 1st Married Andrew Rodgers, 2nd married Henry Peyton and 3rd Married Francis Crosbie of Crosbie Park, Wicklow
Wicklow Castle	1566	04	Thu	04	Thomas Fitz Williams appointed constable of Wicklow Castle
Byrne. Hugh	1567	05	Thu	08	Hugh Bryne of Ballymanus granted a royal pardon
Morgan. Major	1567	06	Tue	10	Major Morgan M.P. for Wicklow speaks out in the English Parliament against more taxes on Ireland
Seymour. Mary	1570	01	Wed	18	Mary Seymour died and was buried at Glendalough, Co. Wicklow
Hill.Moyes	1573				Sir Moyes Hill a military officer with the Earl of Essex
Harrington. Sir Henry	1574				Sir Henry Harrington of Wicklow knighted at Christ Church, Dublin
Wicklow Town	1578				Queen Elizabeth granted a permit to establish a spytle house/maudlens (Leper Hospital) in Wicklow Town
Wicklow County Shirred	1578				A Royal Commission under Sir W. Drury, Lord Justice set about to draw up the boundaries of County Wicklow. Shirred 23/01/1606
Carnew Castle	1578				Carnew Castle built for Sir Henry Harrington rent £13.6s.8d.

A-Z Reference	Day	Date	Month	Year	DATA
Glenmalure, Battle of	Thu	25	08	1580	Fiach Mac Hugh O'Byrne defeated the forces of Lord Grey de Wilton at Glenmalure, Co. Wicklow
Crosbie. Francis	Thu	25	08	1580	Francis Cosbie of Crosbie Park, Wicklow died at the Battle of Glenmalure
O'Dalaigh. Aonghus				1580	Aonghus MacDaire O'Dalaigh (poet) born Co. Wicklow
Brabazon. Sir Edward				1585	Sir Edward Brabazon, Lord Ardee was M.P. for Co. Wicklow
Baltinglass				1585	The title Viscount Baltinglass of 1st creation granted to the Eustace family became extinct
O'Donnell. Hugh			12	1590	Red Hugh O'Donnell 1st escaped from Dublin Castle and took refuge in the Wicklow Mountains, but recaptured
Kennedy. George				1590	George Kennedy obtained a grant of the manor of Newtown (Mount Kennedy) on being knighted by King Charles II
O'Neill/O'Donnell	Fri	24	12	1591	Art O'Neill and Red Hugh O'Donnell escaped from Dublin Castle and took refuge in the Wicklow Mountains
O'Neill. Art	Sat	25	12	1591	Art O'Neill died in the Wicklow Mountains. Local tradition has it that he is buried in Old Connaught Graveyard, Bray
Deputies Pass				1594	A road way was made at Deputies Pass, Glenealy
Crosbie. Alexander	Wed	19	05	1596	Alexander the eldest son of Francis Crosbie and Mary Seymour died at the battle of Stradbally, Laois, Ireland
O'Byrne. F	Sun	08	05	1597	County Wicklow chieftain Feagh McHugh O'Byrne was killed and his head was displayed on the battlements of Dublin Castle
Dunganstown Castle				1597	Dunganstown Castle near Kilbride south of Wicklow Town was granted to Sir John Hoey
Arklow	Thu	21	06	1599	The Lord Lieuntant Essex defeated in a skirmish at Arklow Co. Wicklow.
Glenmalure				1599	A battalion of English soldiers under the command of Sir Henry Harrington defeated at Glenmalure by Phelim O'Byrne
Parnell. Tobais			02	1600	Tobais Parnell born, later became Mayor of Congleton, Chershire, England in 1625
Old Connaught				1600	The Parish of Old Connaught contained the following town lands Little Bray, Ballyman, Conna, Corke, Phrompstown
O'Donnell. Hugh				1602	Red Hugh O'Donnell died in Spain
Wingfield. Sir Richard	Wed	20	04	1603	Sir Richard Wingfield of Wicklow appointed Knight Marshal of Ireland
Powerscourt	Thu	27	10	1603	Powerscourt, Enniskerry, Co. Wicklow was granted to Sir Richard Wingfield by King James I of England
Wicklow County Shirred			12	1605	Sir Arthur Chichester Lord Deputy of Ireland passed an order to shire Wicklow with effect from 23/01/1606
O'Byrne. Feagh McHugh	Thu	16	01	1606	An Inquisition was held at Ballinacor to determine the estate of Feagh McHugh O'Byrne
Wicklow County Shirred	Thu	23	01	1606	Wicklow shirred as a County. Dublin extended from Gormanstown to a point just North of Arklow
Grand Jury				1606	Between 1606 and 1634 the Wicklow Grand Jury looked after bridges and roads
Brabazon. Sir William			02	1607	Sir William Brabazon the son of Sir Edward Brabazon married Jane Bingley
Woodenbridge Inn				1608	The Woodenbridge Inn established, one of the oldest in Ireland
Roundwood				1609	John Wakeman given the O'Toole's land at Castlekevin, Roundwood

Section One: Data by Date

Name	Day	Date	Month	Year	Event
St. Paul's, Bray				1609	St. Paul's Church Bray built
Wolferston, John				1609	John Wolferston appointed sheriff of County Wicklow
Rathmichael				1609	Edmund Walsh of Rathmichael and Phrompstown died and is buried at Tully
Maps				1610	John Speeds Map of Leinster
Burne, Moris				1610	Moris Burne a Reading Minister and Vicar of Bray
Carnew Castle				1610	Constable Richard McHew and 12 soldiers were stationed in Carnew Castle
Byrne, Gerald				1612	Gerald Byrne appointed sheriff of County Wicklow
Borough of Wicklow	Tue	30	03	1613	Borough of Wicklow created by Royal charter
Eustace, James				1613	James Eustace appointed sheriff of County Wicklow
Belyng, Sir Henry				1614	Sir Henry Bellng appointed sheriff of County Wicklow
Brabazon, Sir Edward	Fri	19	07	1616	Sir Edward Brabazon was given the title Baron of Ardee
Brabazon, Killruddery				1616	The yearly rent for Killruddery House, the Brabazon family home near Bray was £8-6s-8d
Pilsworth, Philip				1617	Philip Pilsworth appointed sheriff of County Wicklow
Brabazon, Sir William			08	1618	Killruddery Estate, Bray County Wicklow granted to Sir William Brabazon
Chambre, Calcot				1618	Calcot Chambre appointed sheriff of County Wicklow
Grehan, Sir Richard				1618	Sir Richard Grehan appointed sheriff of County Wicklow
Grehan, Sir Richard				1619	Sir Richard Grehan appointed sheriff of County Wicklow
Carnew Castle				1619	Carnew castle was granted to Mr. Colcott Chamber
Fitzwilliam, W. 1st	Fri	01	12	1620	William Fitzwilliam elevated to the Irish Peerage as 1st Baron Fitzwilliam
Powerscourt/Religion				1620	Richard Wingfield of Powerscourt built a Church near his manor house Enniskerry, Co. Wicklow
Grehan, Sir Richard				1620	Sir Richard Grehan appointed sheriff of County Wicklow
Walker, Robert				1621	Robert Walker appointed sheriff of County Wicklow
Potts, John				1622	John Potts appointed sheriff of County Wicklow
Petty, William				1623	Sir William Petty born. Responsible for mapping Ireland 1650-1670
Leigh, Edward				1623	Edward Leigh appointed sheriff of County Wicklow
Daniel, Thomas				1624	Thomas Daniel appointed sheriff of County Wicklow
Brabazon, Sir Edward	Sun	07	08	1625	Sir Edward Brabazon died and was succeeded by his son Sir William 1st earl of Meath
Brabazon, Mary	Tue	23	08	1625	Mary Smyth wife of Sir Edward Brabazon died
Parnell, Thomas			12	1625	Thomas Parnell born Congleton, Cheshire

A-Z Reference	Day	Date	Month	Year	DATA
Cavanagh, Bryan				1625	Bryan Cavanagh appointed sheriff of County Wicklow
Clonegal				1625	Huntington Castle, Clonegal Co. Wicklow built
Brabazon. Edward	Sun	16	04	1627	William Brabazon the son of Lord Ardee Edward Brabazon was given the title the 1st Earl of Meath
Baltinglass				1627	The title Viscount Baltinglass of 2nd creation was granted to the Roper family
Brabazon. Edward	Sun	31	03	1628	Charles I authorised the Governor of Ireland to grant the Earl of Meath the Lordship and Manor of Bray
Sexton. Pierse				1628	Pierse Sexton appointed sheriff of County Wicklow
Borough of Carysfort				1628	The Borough of Carysfort was created at Mecredin in Co. Wicklow near the town of Aughrim.
Royal School				1629	Royal School was established in County Wicklow
Weather				1630	Great Storm at Bray
Plunket. William				1630	The Rector of Bray was William Plunket Esq. Vicar of Bray
Old Connaught School				1630	Garret Warren school master for Roman Catholic families of Old Connaught
Sandford. Francis				1630	The writer Francis Sandford was born near Carnew, Co. Wicklow
La Touche				1632	Jacques La Touche born at Sarraltroff near Moselle, France
Ware. James				1632	Sir James Ware Auditor General of Ireland stayed in Avoca and Arklow Castle one of the homes of the Earl of Ormond
Brabazon. Edward				1632	Edward Brabazon 2nd Earl of Meath married Mary Chambre
Loftus. Samuel				1633	Samuel Loftus appointed sheriff of County Wicklow
Grand Jury				1634	From 1634 the Grand jury handed over control of Bridges to Parish select vestry committees and Magistrates
Brabazon. Edward				1634	Edward Brabazon 2nd Earl of Meath, M.P. for Athlone 1634-35
Election				1634	William Usher and James Byrne returned as M.P.'s for borough of Wicklow
Carnew Forge				1635	A Forge established at Carnew by Calcott Chambre
Ironworks				1635	Carnew Ironworks founded by Calcott Chambre
Howard. John				1636	John Howard married Dorothea Hassells
Castlekevin				1636	Sir John Coke Knight, Secretary of State was granted 1,544 acres and the Castle at Castlekevin near Roundwood, Co. Wicklow
Survey				1636	The Wentworth Survey of Ireland
Coolross House				1637	Coolross House near Tinahealy built for Lord Stafford
Iornworks			circa	1638	Ironworks founded at Ballard/Minmore by Sir Thomas Wentworth
Mining				1638	The ironworks at Minmore near Carnew Co. Wicklow founded by Sir Thomas Wentworth

Section One: Data by Date

Name	Year	Weekday	Day	Month	Event
Carnew Castle	1638				Carnew passed to Lord Malfont, the Marquis of Rockingham
Fitzwilliam. W. 2nd	1638				William Fitzwilliam 2nd Baron Fitzwilliam married Jane Perry
Books	1639				The Antiquities of Ireland by Sir James Ware
Dillon. Sir. James	1639				Sir James Dillon, Member of Parliament of County Wicklow from 1639–1642
Hollywood	1640				The Protestant Church at Hollywood Co. Wicklow built
Talbot. Bernard	1640				Bernard Talbot appointed sheriff of County Wicklow
O'Byrne Clan	1641	Fri	12	11	The O'Byrne Clan of Wicklow lay siege to Carysfort Co. Wicklow
Coote. Charles	1641	Wed	01	12	The O'Toole Clan defeated by Sir Charles Coote's army at Kilcoole Co. Wicklow.
Coote. Charles	1641	Tue	02	12	Sir Charles Coote was appointed Governor of Dublin City
Dillon. Sir. James	1641				Sir James Dillon fled to France and founded an Irish regiment and held the post of Field Marshal of France
Wicklow Town	1641				The O'Toole Clan attack the Black Castle in Wicklow Town
Domvile. William	1641				Sir William Domvile, Attorney General of Ireland granted lands at Loughlinstown
Farrell. Kathleen	1641				Kathleen Farrell was arrested at Killincarrig, Greystones as a spy, taken to Dublin Castle, and sentenced to be hanged
Ironworks	1641				Carnew Ironworks ceased
Survey	1641				The book of Survey and Distribution of County Wicklow published
Molyneux. Thomas	1642				Thomas Molyneux Governor of Wicklow, died
Fitzwilliam. 1st Earl	1643	Sat	29	04	William Fitzwilliam born, 3rd Baron Fitzwilliam, and in 1716 created 1st Earl Fitzwilliam of Ireland
Kennedy. Robert	1643				Robert Kennedy appointed sheriff of County Wicklow
Fitzwilliam. W. 1st	1643				William Fitzwilliam 1st Baron Fitzwilliam died and he was succeeded by his son William Fitzwilliam
Howard. John	1643				John Howard died
Hassells. Dorothea	1643				Dorothea Howard nee Hassells marries her 2nd cousin Robert Hassells first owner of Shelton, Co. Wicklow
Brabazon. Jane	1644	Thu	19	12	Jane Brabazon the wife of Sir William Brabazon 1st earl of Meath died
Killruddery	1645				Killruddery House destroyed during the civil war
Loftus. Edward	1645				Edward Loftus appointed sheriff of County Wicklow
Fitzsimons. Richard	1648				Rev Richard Fitzsimons born
Killincarrig	1649				Killincarrig (fortified house) near Greystones was attacked by Cromwell's forces on their march from Dublin to Wexford.
Cromwell. William	1649				Cromwell attacked CastleKevin Castle near Roundwood The owner Luke O'Toole captured and executed.
Putland	1650				Thomas Putland Snr, born

A–Z Reference	Day	Date	Month	Year	DATA
Kilcroney				1650	Kilcroney House, Bray built (original).
Chammey. John				1650	John Chammey born, the son of the Forge master (blacksmith), Shillelagh
Brabazon. Edward	Fri	19	12	1651	William Brabazon died and was succeeded by his son Edward Brabazon 2nd Earl
Porter. John			circa	1651	John Porter – quartermaster of the Army of Charles II (1630 – 1685) granted land at Ferrybank, Arklow
Killruddery				1651	Killruddery House rebuilt by Sir Edward Brabazon, 2nd Earl of Meath
Petty. William				1654	William Petty conducted the Down Survey of Ireland 1654-1658
Flora-Fauna				1654	The Government appointed a head wood reeve, four assistants and a clerk to look after the Forestry in Wexford and Wicklow
Ponsonby. John				1655	John Ponsonby appointed sheriff of County Wicklow
Petty. William				1655	William Petty Survey of Co. Wicklow published
Parish Records				1655	Earliest Record of Births in Church of Ireland Parish Wicklow Town
Coddington. William				1656	William Coddington appointed sheriff of County Wicklow
Dargle River				1657	Work began on the first Bray Bridge over the Dargle River (see 1666, 1856)
Hutchinson. Daniel				1657	Daniel Hutchinson appointed sheriff of County Wicklow
Fitzwilliam. W. 2nd	Sun	21	02	1658	William Fitzwilliam 2nd Baron Fitzwilliam died and was succeeded by his son William Fitzwilliam 1st Earl of Fitzwilliam
Coote. Chidley				1658	Chidley Coote appointed sheriff of County Wicklow
Population Bray				1659	Population of Bray 300 ★not a census year★
Act				1660	Act of Indemnity & Oblivion -restored some of the lands confiscated by Cromwell's Army
Boyle. Michael	Sun	27	01	1661	Michael Boyle created bishop of Dublin at St. Patrick's , Dublin
Molyneux. Sir Thomas	Sun	14	04	1661	Sir Thomas Molyneux (Physician and Philosopher) born in Dublin
Jones. Theophilus	Mon	27	05	1661	Sir Theophilus Jones appointed Governor for Counties of Meath and Wicklow
Hassells. Robert				1661	Robert Hassells appointed sheriff of County Wicklow
Royal Order				1661	Royal Order controlled by regulation the felling and use of timber in the woods at Shillelagh, Co. Wicklow
Matthews. William				1662	William Matthews appointed sheriff of County Wicklow
Parish Records				1662	Earliest Record of Marriage in Church of Ireland Parish Newcastle
Hackett. John				1663	John Hackett appointed sheriff of County Wicklow
Parish Records				1663	Earliest Record of Deaths in Church of Ireland Parish Newcastle
Boyle. Michael				1663	Michael Boyle appointed Archbishop of Dublin

Wingfield. Cromwell				1664	Cromwell Wingfield appointed sheriff of County Wicklow
Abdey. Humphrey				1665	Humphrey Abdey appointed sheriff of County Wicklow
Buckley. Richard				1666	Richard Buckley appointed sheriff of County Wicklow
Markets				1666	Markets held weekly in Bray and Fairs twice yearly
Dargle River				1666	The first Bray Bridge erected over the Dargle River
Burton. John				1666	John Burton appointed Vicar of Bray 1666–1693
Parish Records				1666	Earliest Record of Marriage in Church of Ireland Parish Delgany
Parish Records				1666	Earliest Record of Deaths in Church of Ireland Parish Delgany
Parish Records				1666	Earliest Record of Marriage in Church of Ireland Parish Bray
Parish Records				1666	Earliest Record of Deaths in Church of Ireland Parish Bray
Oldcourt. Bray				1666	The lands of Oldcourt, Bray granted to the Edwards Family
Parish Records				1666	Earliest Record of Births in Church of Ireland Parish Delgany
Parish Records				1666	Earliest Record of Births in Church of Ireland Parish Bray
Reeves. William				1667	William Reeves appointed sheriff of County Wicklow
Howard. Ralph	Thu	16	07	1668	Ralph Howard of Dublin married Katherine the daughter of Roger Sotheby, M.P. for Wicklow
Edwards. Richard				1668	Richard Edwards appointed sheriff of County Wicklow
Fitzwilliam. 1st Earl	Mon	10	05	1669	William Fitzwilliam married Anne Cremor
Dillon. Sir. James				1669	Sir James Dillon died
Boyle. Michael				1669	The Manor of Blessington was created for Michael Boyle, Archbishop of Dublin by King Charles II
Loftus. John				1669	John Loftus appointed sheriff of County Wicklow
Blessington				1669	The Sovereign, Bailiffs and Burgesses of the Borough and Town of Blessington was incorporated by charter
Boswell. John				1670	John Boswell appointed sheriff of County Wicklow
Fitzwilliam. W. 2nd			04	1671	Jane Fitzwilliam nee Perry died
La Touche				1671	David Digues La Touche born near Blois, France
Brabazon. William				1671	William Brabazon 3rd Earl of Meath married Elizabeth Lennard
Boswell. John				1671	John Boswell appointed sheriff of County Wicklow
Graham. Thomas				1672	Thomas Graham appointed sheriff of County Wicklow
Baltinglass				1672	The title Viscount Baltinglass of 1st creation granted to the Roper family became extinct
Moore. James				1673	James Moore appointed sheriff of County Wicklow

20   *The County Wicklow Database: 432 AD to 2006 AD*

A–Z Reference	Day	Date	Month	Year	DATA
Blessington House				1673	Blessington House built
King. John				1674	John King appointed sheriff of County Wicklow
Howard. Hugh	Tue	16	02	1675	Hugh Howard the son of Ralph and Katherine Howard baptized at Shelton Abbey, Wicklow
Brabazon. William	Thu	25	03	1675	Edward Brabazon 2nd Earl of Meath died by drowning and was succeeded by his son William Brabazon 3rd Earl
Ballymurrin House			circa	1675	Ballymurrin House, Ballymurrin Lower, Kilbride built
Byrne. John				1675	John Byrne appointed sheriff of County Wicklow
Heyden. Alexander				1676	Alexander Heyden appointed sheriff of County Wicklow
Parish Records				1677	Earliest Record of Births in Church of Ireland Parish Newcastle
Stratford. Robert				1677	Robert Stratford appointed sheriff of County Wicklow
Usher. Christopher				1678	Christopher Usher appointed sheriff of County Wicklow
Books				1678	Strange and Wonderful News from County Wicklow by Dr. Moore
Boyle. Michael				1678	Rev. Michael Boyle appointed Primate of Ireland
Whale			01	1679	Sir Robert Southwell FRS. Reported that a whale of great bigness was cast up 17 miles south of Dublin on the Wicklow coast
Ships/Yachts				1679	The vessel "Santa Cruz" carrying 200 chests of Gold shipwrecked between the Welsh and Wicklow Coast
Warren. John				1679	John Warren appointed sheriff of County Wicklow
St Kevin's Church			circa	1680	St Kevin's Church, Knockroe, Hollywood built
Ballyarthur House			circa	1680	Ballyarthur House, Ballyarthur, Woodenbridge built
Warren. John				1680	John Warren appointed sheriff of County Wicklow
Hodson. Laurence				1681	Laurence Hodson appointed sheriff of County Wicklow
Brabazon. Killruddery				1682	The gardens at Killruddery House, the Brabazon home near Bray were designed and laid out by a Frenchman called Bonet.
Fitzsimons. Richard				1682	Rev Richard Fitzsimons ordained a priest
Brabazon. Chambre				1682	Chambre Brabazon 5th Earl of Meath married Juliana Chaworth
Hayden. Alexander				1682	Alexander Hayden appointed sheriff of County Wicklow
St. Mary's Blessington	Fri	24	08	1683	St. Mary's Church, Blessington consecrated
Howard. Robert	Mon	24	09	1683	Robert Howard the son of Ralph and Katherine Howard born
Cradock. Philip				1683	Philip Cradock appointed sheriff of County Wicklow
Parish Records				1683	Earliest Record of Deaths in Church of Ireland Parish Blessington

Subject	Year				Event
Parish Records	1683				Earliest Record of Marriage in Church of Ireland Parish Blessington
St. Mary's Blessington	1683				St. Mary's Church of Ireland, Blessington built
Hoey. William	1684				William Hoey appointed sheriff of County Wicklow
Hassells. Dorothea	1684				Dorothea Hassells died and was buried at Kilbride, Co. Wicklow
Brabazon. William	1685	Sun	01	03	William Brabazon 3rd Earl of Meath died and was succeeded by his brother Edward Brabazon the 4th Earl of Meath
Talbot. Richard	1685	Sat	20	06	Richard Talbot of Malahide was given the title Baron of Talbotstown and Viscount Baltinglass and Earl of Tyrconnell
Stockton. John	1685				John Stockton appointed sheriff of County Wicklow
Hodson	1686	Sun	14	02	Rev John Hodson Bishop of Elphin died
Parnell. Thomas	1686				Thomas Parnell born in 1625 died 1686
Brabazon. Chaworth	1686				Chaworth Brabazon 6th Earl of Meath born
Kennedy. Robert	1686				Sir Robert Kennedy appointed sheriff of County Wicklow
Putland	1686				Thomas Putland Jnr, born
O'Meara. Francis	1687				Francis O'Meara appointed sheriff of County Wicklow
Byrne. Thady	1688				Thady Byrne appointed sheriff of County Wicklow
Foot Regiment, Meath	1689				The Earl of Meath Foot Regiment established
Parish Records	1689				Earliest Record of Marriage in Church of Ireland Parish Mullinacuff, Tinahely
Byrne. Thady	1689				Thady Byrne appointed sheriff of County Wicklow
Sheet/British Library	1689				The indictment and arraignment of J. Price with other Protestants at Wicklow by the Receiver General of Ireland
Fitzsimons. Richard	1690				Rev Richard Fitzsimons appointed Parish Priest of Delgany, Powerscourt, Kilmacanogue and Bray
La Touche	1690				David Duiges La Touche fought at the Battle of Boyne in General Caillemote's Regiment
O'Meara. Francis	1690				Francis O'Meara died at the Battle of the Boyne
Wall. Ambrose	1690				Ambrose Wall appointed sheriff of County Wicklow
Brabazon. Edward	1691			11	Edward Brabazon 7th Earl of Meath born
Price. John	1691				John Price appointed sheriff of County Wicklow
Pub/Tavern/Inn	1691				Killppeder Inn established
Brabazon. Chambre	1692			11	Juliana Brabazon nee Chaworth the wife of the Chambre Brabazon the 5th Earl of Meath died
Stafford. Robert	1692				Robert Stafford appointed sheriff of County Wicklow
Bray. Barracks	1692				Bray barracks built

A–Z Reference	Day	Date	Month	Year	DATA
Porter. William	Thu	30	03	1693	William Porter son of John Porter of Arklow married Marion sharp of Wexford
Howard. Katherine				1693	Katherine Howard the daughter of Ralph and Katherine Howard, married 1st Bart of Castle Dillon Sir Thomas Molyneux
King. John				1693	John King appointed Vicar of Bray 1693-1695
Matthews. William				1693	William Mathews appointed sheriff of County Wicklow
Hill. Trevor				1693	Trevor Hill born
Ships/Yachts	Thu	20	12	1694	The vessel "Drake" shipwrecked between the Welsh and Wicklow Coast
Hoey. William				1694	William Hoey appointed sheriff of County Wicklow
Hinton. John				1695	John Hinton appointed Vicar of Bray 1695 -1703
Parish Records				1695	Earliest Record of Births in Church of Ireland Parish Blessington
Whitshead. John				1695	John Whitshead appointed sheriff of County Wicklow
Foot Regiment, Meath				1695	The Earl of Meath Foot Regiment ceased as an Irish Regiment
Burrows. Thomas				1696	Thomas Burrows appointed sheriff of County Wicklow
Shelton Abbey				1697	Ralph Howard of Dublin acquired from the Duke of Ormond an estate North of Arklow
Price. Evan				1697	Evan Price appointed sheriff of County Wicklow
Howard. Ralph				1697	Ralph Howard son of Dorothea Hassells acquired from the Duke of Ormond, the estate of North Arklow, which is Shelton Abbey
Kilmacurragh House				1697	Kilmacurragh House, Rathdrum built for Thomas Acton
Parish Records				1697	Earliest Record of Births in Church of Ireland Parish Dunlavin
Powerscourt				1697	Richard 1st Viscount Powerscourt born
Parish Records				1698	Earliest Record of Births in Church of Ireland Parish Mullinacuff, Tinahely
Eccles. Hugh				1698	Hugh Eccles appointed sheriff of County Wicklow
Parish Records				1698	Earliest Record of Marriage in Church of Ireland Parish Dunlavin
Parish Records				1698	Earliest Record of Deaths in Church of Ireland Parish Dunlavin
Stratford. John				1698	John Stratford born, later 1st Earl of Albborough, M.P. for Baltinglass, Sheriff of Co Wicklow, 1st Baron of Baltinglass
Archer. Anthony				1699	Anthony Archer appointed sheriff of County Wicklow
La Touche				1699	David Duiges La Touche married Marthe Judith Biard and had two sons David and James and one daughter
Stratford. Robert				1699	Robert Stafford, M.P for County Wicklow. died

Section One: Data by Date

Name	Day			Year	Event
Jones. Owen				1700	Owen Jones appointed sheriff of County Wicklow
Roberts. Lewis				1700	Lewis Roberts lived in Old Connaught, Bray, Eldest son of the M.P. of Dungarvan Co. Waterford
Leeson	Tue	11	03	1701	Joseph Leeson of Russborough House, Blessington. 1st Earl of Milltown born
Hoey. John				1701	John Hoey appointed sheriff of County Wicklow
Boyle. Michael	Thu	10	12	1702	Michael Boyle Archbishop of Dublin died aged 93 years
Brabazon. Edward				1702	56 St. Stephens Green, Dublin built for Edward Brabazon 4th Earl of Meath
Edwards. Richard				1702	Richard Edwards appointed sheriff of County Wicklow
Wicklow Gaol				1702	Wicklow Town Gaol built
Bridge House Inn				1702	The Bridge House Inn established in Wicklow Town
Jenney. C				1703	Christophilus Jenney appointed Vicar of Bray 1703–1706
Graydon. Robert				1703	Robert Graydon appointed sheriff of County Wicklow
Brabazon. Edward	Wed	12	07	1704	The 1st wife of Edward Brabazon 4th Earl of Meath, Cecila Brereton died
Brabazon. Edward	Fri	22	09	1704	Edward Brabazon the 4th Earl of Meath married Dorothea Stopford of Tara Hall, Co. Meath
Lovett. John				1704	John Lovett appointed sheriff of County Wicklow
La Touche				1704	David Digges La Touche born, son of David and Marthe La Touche
Monck	Tue	23	10	1705	Charles Monck married Agenta, sister and heir of Sir John Stephens, alias Hitchcock, of Charleville, Co. Wicklow
Parnell. Rev Thomas				1705	Thomas Parnell (1625) his son the Rev Thomas Parnell appointed Archdeacon of Clogher
Charleville House				1705	The Monck family became the owners of Charleville Estate, Enniskerry, Co. Wicklow
West. Tichbourne				1705	Tichbourne West appointed sheriff of County Wicklow
Stratford. Edward				1706	Edward Stratford appointed sheriff of County Wicklow
Iredall. Benjamin				1706	Benjamin Iredall appointed Vicar of Bray 1706–1728
Brabazon. Edward	Sat	22	02	1707	Edward Brabazon the 4th Earl of Meath died and was succeeded by his brother Chambre Brabazon the 5th Earl of Meath
Fownes. Sir William				1707	Sir William Fownes appointed sheriff of County Wicklow
Percy. Henry				1708	Henry Percy appointed sheriff of County Wicklow
Allen. Joshua				1709	Joshua Allen appointed sheriff of County Wicklow
Putland				1709	John Putland born the son of Thomas Putland Jnr
Stewart. Robert				1710	Robert Stewart appointed sheriff of County Wicklow
Dawson. Joshua				1710	Joshua Dawson became Secretary to the Lord Lieutenant of Ireland

A-Z Reference	Day	Date	Month	Year	DATA
Bushe. Letitia				1710	Letitia Bushe (artist) born in Co. Kilkenny
Mount Kennedy House				1710	Sir Richard Kennedy of Mount Kennedy House, NewtownMountKennedy died following a duel.
Howard. Ralph				1710	Ralph Howard died and was succeeded by his son Hugh Howard of Shelton Abbey, Wicklow
Acton. William				1711	William Acton the son of Thomas Acton builder of Kilmacurragh House was born
Acton. Thomas				1711	Thomas Acton appointed sheriff of County Wicklow
Grand Jury				1712	The Wicklow Grand Jury Query Books for the period 1712-1782 destroyed by fire in the Public Records Office, Dublin in 1922
Nixon. Abraham				1712	Abraham Nixon appointed sheriff of County Wicklow
Sterne. Laurence	Tue	24	11	1713	Laurence Sterne (writer) was born in Clonmel, Co. Tipperary
Powerscourt				1713	Wingfield House, Kilmacanogue built. Henry Grattan lived in it from 1782-1784
Hodson				1713	The grandson of Rev John Hodson a William Hodson of Tuitstown, Co. Westmeath died
Fownes. Kendrick				1713	Kendrick Fownes appointed sheriff of County Wicklow
Herman Molls Map				1714	Herman Molls Map of County Wicklow showed 27 Bridges in County and 211 Miles of Statute Road
Reeves. Thomas				1714	Thomas Reeves appointed sheriff of County Wicklow
Brabazon. Chambre	Fri	01	04	1715	Chambre Brabazon the 5th Earl of Meath died and was succeeded by his son Chatworth Brabazon the 6th Earl of Meath
Molyneux. Sir Thomas				1715	Sir Thomas Molyneux (Physician and Philosopher) appointed State Physician and held the post until 1730
Arklow Barracks				1715	Arklow Military barracks established
Boswell. John				1715	John Boswell appointed sheriff of County Wicklow
Powerscort Arms Hotel				1715	The Powerscourt Arms Hotel, Enniskerry built
Fitzwilliam. 1st Earl	Sat	04	02	1716	Anne Fitzwilliam nee Cremor died
Acton. Thomas	Mon	13	02	1716	Thomas Acton obtained from Viscount Rosse the lease of the lands at Kilmacurragh, Rathdrum Co Wicklow
Acton. Thomas	Thu	10	05	1716	Thomas Acton obtained a 2nd lease from Viscount Rosse for land at Rathdrum, the lease renewable forever.
Fitzwilliam. 1st Earl	Sat	21	07	1716	William Fitzwilliam elevated to the title 1st Earl of Fitzwilliam of Ireland and Viscount Milton
Parnell. Rev Thomas				1716	Rev Thomas Parnell appointed vicar of Finglas
Saunders Grove				1716	Saunders Grove, Baltinglass was built for Morley Saunders M.P.
La Touche				1716	David Duiges La Touche and Nathaniel Kane formed a Bank in Dublin
Hayes. John				1716	John Hayes appointed sheriff of County Wicklow
Aghold				1716	A church erected at Aghold, near Shillelagh

Section One: Data by Date

Name	Day	Date	Month	Year	Event
Hill. Trevor	Wed	21	08	1717	Trevor Hill created 1st Viscount Hillsborough
Mitchelburne. Richard				1717	Richard Mitchelburne appointed sheriff of County Wicklow
Parnell. Rev Thomas				1717	Rev Thomas Parnell died
Rathnew				1717	Fr William Cavanagh of Rathnew, Co. Wicklow died
Hill. Willis	Fri	30	05	1718	Willis Hill 1st Marquis of Downshire born
Fitzwilliam. 2nd Earl	Wed	17	09	1718	John Fitzwilliam 2nd Earl Fitzwilliam married Anne Stringer
Stephens. John				1718	John Stephens appointed sheriff of County Wicklow
Molyneux. Sir Thomas				1718	Sir Thomas Molyneux (Physician and Philosopher) appointed Physician-General of the Army and held the post until 1733
Fitzwilliam. 3rd Earl	Thu	15	01	1719	William Fitzwilliam 3rd Earl Fitzwilliam born
Fitzwilliam. 1st Earl	Mon	28	12	1719	William Fitzwilliam 1st Earl of Fitzwilliam died and was succeeded by his son John 2nd Earl Fitzwilliam
Putland				1719	Bridget Putland born
Hodson. Laurence				1719	Laurence Hodson appointed sheriff of County Wicklow
Porter. Rev. William				1719	William Porter, later Rector of Hollywood, Co Wicklow. Born in Arklow in 1719
Tober House			circa	1720	Tober House, Dunlavin built
Sterne. Laurence				1720	Laurence Sterne (writer) while staying with relatives fell into the mill race at Annamoe, Co. Wicklow, escaped unhurt
Brabazon. Edward				1720	Edward Brabazon the 7th Earl of Meath married Martha Collins of Warrick, England
Parish Records				1720	Earliest Record of Births held by Church of Ireland Parish Donoghmore
Parish Records				1720	Earliest Record of Deaths in Church of Ireland Parish Castlemacadam, Avoca
Parish Records				1720	Earliest Record of Births in Church of Ireland Parish Castlemacadem, Avoca
Parish Records				1720	Earliest Record of Marriage in Church of Ireland Parish Castlemacadam
Parish Records				1720	Earliest Record of Marriage in Church of Ireland Parish Donoghmore
Parish Records				1720	Earliest Record of Deaths in Church of Ireland Parish Donoghmore
Collins. William				1720	William Collins born Co. Wicklow 1720, father of William Collins 1788 and grandfather William Wilkie Collins born 1824
Goowdin. Simon				1720	Simon Goowdin appointed sheriff of County Wicklow
Howard. Katherine				1720	Katherine Howard nee Sotheby died
Brabazon. Anthony			02	1721	Anthony Brabazon the 8th Earl of Meath born
Putland	Tue	30	03	1721	Thomas Putland Jnr died
Powerscourt	Tue	01	08	1721	Richard 1st Viscount Powerscourt 1st married Anne Usher of Dublin
Hodson				1721	William Hodson a grandson of William Hodson of Tuitstown, Co. Westmeath born

A–Z Reference	Day	Date	Month	Year	DATA
Wingfield. Richard				1721	Richard Wingfield appointed sheriff of County Wicklow
Stratford. John				1721	John Stratford elected M.P. for Baltinglass 1721
Leland. Dr. Thomas				1722	Thomas Leland born in Dublin
Saunders. Robert				1722	Robert Saunders appointed sheriff of County Wicklow
Putland	Sun	14	02	1723	Thomas Putland Snr died
Avoca Handewavers				1723	Handweavers mill at Avoca established. The oldest surviving working mill in Ireland.
White. John				1723	John White appointed sheriff of County Wicklow
Reade. Richard				1724	Richard Reade appointed sheriff of County Wicklow
Parish Records				1724	Earliest Record of Deaths in Church of Ireland Parish Powerscourt
Sheet/British Library	Tue	22	12	1725	Murder upon murder, Or the account of the execution committed on the body of Mr. R. W. Warrerman by his wife at Glanely
Delgany				1725	Delgany Church furnished with new pews
La Touche				1725	David La Touch the son of David Duiges La Touche married Marie Canasaille and they had three sons David, John, and Peter
Baldwin. Arthur				1725	Arthur Baldwin appointed sheriff of County Wicklow
Powerscourt			circa	1726	Anne the wife of the Richard 1st Viscount Powerscourt died
Percy. Robert				1726	Robert Percy appointed sheriff of County Wicklow
Howard. Robert				1726	Robert Howard born 1683 appointed Bishop of Killala
Powerscourt	Thu	13	04	1727	Richard 1st Viscount Powerscourt 2ndly married Dorothy Rowley of Summerhill Co. Meath
Parnell. John	Fri	07	07	1727	Thomas Parnell (1625) his son John Parnell died
Parish Records				1727	Earliest Record of Marriage in Church of Ireland Parish Powerscourt
Dawson. Joshua				1727	Joshua Dawson died , Member of Parliament for Wicklow
Chapel. Richard				1727	Richard Chapel appointed sheriff of County Wicklow
Sheepwalk House				1727	Sheepwalk House, Arklow built for the Earl of Wicklow
Parish Records				1727	Earliest Record of Births in Church of Ireland Parish Powerscourt
Fitzwilliam. 2nd Earl	Wed	28	08	1728	Anne Fitzwilliam nee Stringer died
Hume. William				1728	William Hume appointed sheriff of County Wicklow
Sheet/British Library				1728	The case of R. J. and W. W. with their objections against the Bill of sale of the estate of Sir R. Kennedy
Candler. William				1728	William Candler appointed Vicar of Bray 1728 – 1730

Pub/Tavern				1728	Pub/Tavern established in Aughrim – now Phelan's Bar
Powerscourt	Thu	23	10	1729	Edward 2nd Viscount Powerscourt born
Parish Records				1729	Earliest Record of Marriage in Church of Ireland Parish Wicklow Town
Howard. Robert				1729	Robert Howard born 1683 appointed Bishop of Elphin
Heighington. John				1729	John Heighington appointed sheriff of County Wicklow
Parish Records				1729	Earliest Record of Deaths in Church of Ireland Parish Wicklow Town
Dublin				1729	The Irish Parliament Buildings at College Green cost £40,000 built of Wicklow granite
La Touche				1729	David (Diuges de) La Touche (Banker) born, grandson of David La Touche born 1671
Powerscourt	Thu	24	12	1730	Richard 3rd Viscount Powerscourt baptised
Hawkshead. Thomas				1730	Thomas Hawkshead appointed sheriff of County Wicklow
Leeson				1730	Joseph Leeson Jnr. of Russborough House, Blessington was created 2nd Earl of Milltown born
Fortgranite House				1730	Fortgranite House, Baltinglass built for the Saunders Family
Powerscourt				1730	Work began on the building of Powerscourt House, Enniskerry
Clara				1730	The stone bridge at the village Clara, Co. Wicklow erected
Bushe. John				1730	John Bushe appointed Vicar of Bray 1730 – 1746
Putland				1730	John Putland got a loan of £1,500 from Dean Jonathan Swift (1667-1745) at rate of five and one-third percent
Clermont House				1730	Clermont House, Rathnew built
Brabazon. Chaworth	Mon	13	12	1731	Chaworth Brabazon the 6th Earl of Meath married Juliana Prendergast
Eaton. Thomas				1731	Thomas Eaton appointed sheriff of County Wicklow
Barret. George				1732	George Barret Landscape Artist painted views of Powerscourt
Archer. Richard				1732	Richard Archer appointed sheriff of County Wicklow
Molyneux. Sir Thomas	Fri	19	10	1733	Sir Thomas Molyneux (Physician and Philosopher) died
Westby. William				1733	William Westby appointed sheriff of County Wicklow
Clara				1733	Stone bridge erected over the River Avonmore at Clara Co. Wicklow
Reeves. William				1734	William Reeves appointed sheriff of County Wicklow
Leeson	Sat	20	12	1735	Brice Leeson of Russborough House, Blessington. 3rd Earl of Milltown born
Pender. George				1735	George Pender appointed sheriff of County Wicklow
Acton. William	Thu	04	03	1736	William Acton born in 1711 married Jane Parsons the daughter of Sir Lawrence Parsons of Birr Castle
Stratford. John	Fri	21	05	1736	John Stratford created 1st Baron of Baltinglass Co. Wicklow of the third creation

A–Z Reference	Day	Date	Month	Year	DATA
Bushe. Letitia				1736	Letitia Bushe painted a view of Bray. Co. Wicklow
Stratford. John				1736	John Stratford appointed sheriff of County Wicklow
Annacarter School			12	1737	Annacarter School Roundwood opened
Hayes. John				1737	John Hayes appointed sheriff of County Wicklow
Act	Wed	01	02	1738	The Wool Act, Controls placed the exportation of Wool from Wicklow and other counties in Ireland
Chammey. Joseph				1738	Joseph Chammey appointed sheriff of County Wicklow
Howard. Hugh				1738	Hugh Howard the son of Ralph and Katherine Howard died and was succeeded by his brother the Right Rev Robert Howard
National Archives				1738	Business Records Survey Wicklow No. 03. Fogarty Family & Aughrim Mill 1738 to 1903
Enniskerry Bridge	Tue	11	09	1739	A road bridge at Enniskerry destroyed in a storm
Parish Records				1739	Earliest Record of Deaths in Church of Ireland Parish Preban, Tinahely
Parish Records				1739	Earliest Record of Marriage in Church of Ireland Parish Preban, Tinahely
Carroll. James				1739	James Carroll appointed sheriff of County Wicklow
Parish Records				1739	Earliest Record of Births in Church of Ireland Parish Preban, Tinahely
Howard. Robert	Thu	03	04	1740	Rev Robert Howard, Bishop of Elphin died
Smith. Sir Michael	Sun	07	09	1740	Sir Michael Smith born, became 1st Baron Cusack Smith and Master of the Rolls of Ireland
Fitzsimons. Richard				1740	Rev Richard Fitzsimons died
Dillon. John Talbot				1740	John Talbot Dillon born Lismullen Co. Meath
Blessington				1740	Building of Russborough House, Blessington started
Nixon. Abraham				1740	Abraham Nixon appointed sheriff of County Wicklow
Hodson				1740	William Hodson born 1721 married Eleanor Adair of Hollybrooke, Bray four children Robert, Mary, Jane, Anne
Lowe. Christopher				1740	Christopher Lowe born at Templecarrig, Delgany
Goodwin. William				1741	William Goodwin appointed sheriff of County Wicklow
Smith. John				1741	John Smith appointed sheriff of County Wicklow
Books				1741	A full and true account of the barbarous murder of Robert Usher of Rathdrum on 9th August 1741 by Matthew Fountain
Ireland				1741	Famine
Dargle River				1741	Bray Bridge over the Dargle River carried away in a storm
Fitzwilliam. 3rd Earl	Mon	19	04	1742	William Fitzwilliam 3rd Earl Fitzwilliam elevated to the UK peerage as Lord Fitzwilliam

Section One: Data by Date

Name	Day			Year	Event
Goodwin, William				1742	William Goodwin appointed sheriff of County Wicklow
Powerscourt				1743	Powerscourt House Enniskerry completed
Chamney, Edward			02	1743	Edward Chamney appointed sheriff of County Wicklow
Wingfield, Baron	Sat	04	02	1744	The title Baron Wingfield created as an Irish peerage title
Powerscourt, Viscount	Sat	04	02	1744	The title Viscount Powerscourt created as an Irish peerage title
Fitzwilliam, 3rd Earl	Fri	22	06	1744	William Fitzwilliam 3rd Earl Fitzwilliam married Lady Anne Watson Wentworth
Baldwin, Robert				1744	Robert Baldwin appointed sheriff of County Wicklow
Mozeen, Thomas				1744	Thomas Mozeen wrote the poem "A Description of a Fox-Chase" better known as "The Killruddery Hunt"
Allen, John	Fri	26	04	1745	John Allen (3rd Viscount Allen), former MP for Carysfort, Co. Wicklow. Kills a solider in a brawl in Eustace Street, Dublin
Allen, John			07	1745	John Allen (3rd Viscount Allen) son of Robert Allen M.P. for the Borough of Carysfort in Co. Wicklow died
Parnell, Sir John				1745	Sir John Parnell married Anne Ward daughter of the 1st Viscount Bangor, Co. Down
Putland				1745	George Putland Snr, of Bray born
La Touche				1745	David Duiges La Touche died in Dublin
Acton, Henry			07	1745	Henry Acton appointed sheriff of County Wicklow
Grattan, Henry	Tue	03		1746	Henry Grattan born
Monck, Henry				1746	Henry Monck appointed sheriff of County Wicklow
Bushe, John				1746	Rev John Bushe Vicar of Bray died at Cork Abbey, Bray he was the youngest son of Mr. Arthur Bushe M.P.
Lyon, John				1746	John Lyon appointed Vicar of Bray 1746-1764
Hill, Willis	Sun	01	03	1747	Willis Hill 1st Marquis of Downshire married Margaretta daughter of the Earl of Kildare
La Touche	Mon	24	08	1747	William George La Touche (Banker) born in Dublin. The grandson of David Digges La Touche
O'Keeffe, John				1747	John O'Keeffe playwright born in Dublin
Whaley, R.C				1747	Richard Chapell Whaley of Whaley Abbey Co. Wicklow represented Wicklow as M.P. 1747-1760
Hume, William				1747	William Hume born at Humewood Castle, Wicklow
Steele, Laurence				1747	Laurence Steele appointed sheriff of County Wicklow
Parish Records				1748	Earliest Record of Births in Roman Catholic Parish Wicklow Town
Parish Records				1748	Earliest Record of Marriage in Roman Catholic Parish Wicklow Town
Fitzwilliam, 4th Earl	Mon	30	05	1748	William Fitzwilliam 4th Earl Fitzwilliam born
Onge, Samuel				1748	Samuel Onge appointed sheriff of County Wicklow
Putland				1748	John Putland born in 1709 was acting as Sheriff of Dublin County in 1748

A-Z Reference	Day	Date	Month	Year	DATA
Templestown	Mon	30	01	1749	A school inspector's report for the Charter School at Templestown, Co Wicklow. 2 boys farming, Girls knit stockings
Howard. Ralph				1749	Ralph Howard appointed sheriff of County Wicklow
Acton. Thomas	Tue	02	01	1750	Thomas Acton died
Perkins. Deborah			's	1750	The Poem "On Deborah Perkins of county Wicklow" writer Anonymous-Page 303 of A Carpenter book of 18th cent verse in Ireland
Hodson				1750	William Hodson born 1721 married Harriet Hutchinson and had two son's William born 1757 , Hartley born 1759
Allen. Elizabeth				1750	Elizabeth Allen sister of John Allen married John Proby
Roberts. L				1750	Reference Roberts 1765. 38,00 Trees planted at Old Connaught, Bray
Ships/Yachts				1750	The vessel "Prince Frederick" carrying Tobacco shipwrecked of the Wicklow Coast
Adair. Foster				1750	Forster Adair appointed sheriff of County Wicklow
Glenart Castle				1750	Glenart Castle near Arklow built
Powerscourt	Mon	21	10	1751	Richard 1st Viscount Powerscourt died
Bond. Henry				1751	Henry Bond appointed sheriff of County Wicklow
Calendar				1752	Ireland adopts the Gregorian calendar and suppressed the days 3 to 13 September 1752
Proby. John				1752	John Proby created Baron of Carysfort Co. Wicklow
Symes. Richard				1752	Richard Symes appointed sheriff of County Wicklow
Stephens. Sir John				1752	Sir John Stephens died and Charleville House, Enniskerry inherited by Agenta Monck
Smuggling	Tue	27	02	1753	Joseph Cudworth Custom's Surveyor at Arklow, seized Spirits and Tobacco at Arklow
Hill.Arthur-2nd	Sat	03	03	1753	Arthur Hill 2nd Marquis of Downshire born
Brabazon. Chaworth			03	1753	The 6th earl of Meath became a patron of the Meath Hospital, Dublin
Sliver Mines	Tue	01	05	1753	Silver Mines discovered in Co. Wicklow – Reported in the Belfast Journal
Fitzimons	Fri	04	05	1753	A person named Fitzimons was killed at Callarah. Co. Wicklow. When he was stabbed with a penknife and his throat cut
Ballynaclash	Fri	21	12	1753	The bridge at Ballynaclash, Co. Wicklow destroyed by floods
Rathnew				1753	Rev. Stephen Kavanagh of Rathnew Co. Wicklow died
Wicklow Harbour				1753	Between 1753 and 1767 the Irish Parliament granted £6,850 towards the construction of a harbour at Wicklow Town
Wicklow Harbour				1753	The Irish Parliament grant aided Wicklow Harbour by £6,850 in the period 1753-67
La Touche				1753	The La Touche family acquire land around Delgany from Rev Dr. Corbert.
Smith. Thomas				1753	Thomas Smith appointed sheriff of County Wicklow

Keyword	Day	Date	Month	Year	Event
Herrings	Tue	20	08	1754	Tents/Sheds for the salting of Herrings erected at Greystones and Wicklow Head
Marsden.William	Sat	16	11	1754	William Marsden born at Vervale, Co.Wicklow. Son of John Marsden and Alice Crampton
Monck			circa	1754	Charles Stanley Monck born, later 1st Viscount Monck
Bellevue House				1754	Bellevue House, Delgany built for Dublin banker David la Touche
Eccles.Thomas				1754	Thomas Eccles appointed sheriff of County Wicklow
Wicklow.Earl of	Mon	11	08	1755	Ralph Howard 1st Earl of Wicklow married Alice Forward
Eaton.J				1755	J. Eaton appointed sheriff of County Wicklow
Ships/Yachts				1755	The vessel "Dan" shipwrecked of the Wicklow Coast
Crosbie.Richard				1755	Richard Crosbie the son of Sir Paul Crosbie born at Crosbie Park, near Baltinglass, Co.Wicklow
Leeson	Wed	05	05	1756	Joseph Leeson owner of Russborough House, Blessington became Baron Russborough
Fitzwilliam. 3rd Earl	Tue	10	08	1756	William Fitzwilliam 3rd Earl Fitzwilliam died and was succeeded by his son William Fitzwilliam 4th Earl Fitzwilliam
Newrath	Fri	19	11	1756	A man was shot dead at Newrath Bridge, Co.Wicklow
Hickey.John				1756	John Hickey (sculptor) born completed the La Touche memorial in Delgany Church in 1789
Baldwin.Richard				1756	Richard Baldwin appointed sheriff of County Wicklow
Mining				1756	The ironworks at Minmore near Carnew Co.Wicklow ceased
La Touche				1756	Bellevue House, near Delgany completed for David La Touche a Dublin Banker
Ironworks				1756	The Ironworks at Ballard/Minmore ceased production 1638 - 1756
Bushe.Letitia	Thu	17	11	1757	Letitia Bushe (artist) died in Dublin
Hodson				1757	William Hodson born
Saurin.William				1757	William Saurin born in Belfast
Hoey.Robert				1757	Robert Hoey appointed sheriff of County Wicklow
Campbell.John Henry				1757	John Henry Campbell (artists) born
Brabazon.Anthony	Sat	20	05	1758	Anthony Brabazon the 8th Earl of Meath married Grace Leigh of Wexford
Brabazon. Chaworth	Tue	12	12	1758	Juliana Prendergast the wife of the Chaworth Brabazon the 6th Earl of Meath died
Saunders. Morley				1758	Morley Sanuders appointed sheriff of County Wicklow
Falkiner. Daniel	Fri	26	01	1759	The M.P. for Dublin and Baltinglass Daniel Falkiner died
Crosbie. Sir Warren	Tue	30	01	1759	Sir Warren Crosbie the father of Sir Paul Crosbie of Crosbie Park , Wicklow died
Hodson				1759	Hartley Hodson of Old Connaught, Bray born
Edwards.James				1759	James Edwards appointed sheriff of County Wicklow

A–Z Reference	Day	Date	Month	Year	DATA
Arklow				1759	The Nineteen Arches Bridge at Arklow designed by Andrew Noble
Baltinglass				1759	Edward Augustus Stratford, 2nd Earl of Aldborough elected M.P. for Baltinglass from 1759 to 1768
Military			03	1760	1st Battalion Royal Scotch stationed in Bray
Powerscourt	Sun	07	09	1760	Richard 3rd Viscount Powerscourt married Amelia, daughter of 1st Earl of Aldborough
Leeson	Mon	08	09	1760	Joseph Leeson of Russborough House, Blessington was created Viscount Russborough
Shillelagh			circa	1760	Ballyraheen House near Shillelagh built
Carroll. James				1760	James Carroll appointed sheriff of County Wicklow
Dargle River				1760	Oil painting by John Butt with title Poachers:View in the Dargle
Maps				1760	Rocques Map of Dublin sponsored by George Putland of Bray
Tulfarris House				1760	Tulfarris House, Blessington built
Maps				1760	Wicklow Grand Jury commissioned Jacob Nevill to make a map of County Wicklow
Callaghan. Christopher				1760	Fr. Christopher Callaghan Parish Priest of Bray born at Finglas, Dublin in 1760
Walker. Joseph C.				1761	James Cooper Walker (antiquarian) born in Dublin
Grattan. James				1761	Henry Grattan's father James was elected M.P. for Dublin City
La Touche				1761	David La Touche born in 1729, became M.P. for Dundalk in 1761
Hume. Dennison				1761	Dennison Hume appointed sheriff of County Wicklow
Quin				1761	John Quin owner of Quins Coaching Inn, (Royal Hotel) born at Galtrim, Co. Meath
Brabazon. Edward	Sat	24	04	1762	Martha Brabazon nee Collins wife of Edward Brabazon the 7th Earl of Meath died
Powerscourt	Fri	29	10	1762	Richard 4th Viscount Powerscourt born
Pound				1762	Bray Town Pound House erected near the site of the present Town Hall
Wingfield. Hon. Richard				1762	Hon. Richard Wingfield appointed sheriff of County Wicklow
Holt. Joseph				1762	Joseph Holt was born in Co. Wexford
La Touche	Tue	10	05	1762	David La Touche married Elizabeth Marlay the daughter of George Marlay, Bishop of Dromore
Leeson	Sat	14	05	1763	Joseph Leeson of Russborough House, Blessington was created 1st Earl of Milltown
Brabazon. Chaworth				1763	Chaworth Brabazon the 6th Earl of Meath died and was succeeded by his brother Edward Brabazon the 7th Earl of Meath
Newspapers	Sat	10	09	1763	Freeman's Journal Newspaper first edition
Tarrant. Charles				1763	Charles Tarrant of Greystones appointed draughtsman to the Board of Ordinance of the City of Dublin

Name	Day	Date	Month	Year	Event
Brownrigg, Henry				1763	Henry Brownrigg appointed sheriff of County Wicklow
Powerscourt	Sun	06	05	1764	Edward 2nd Viscount Powerscourt died. Unmarried and was and was succeeded by his brother Richard 3th Viscount Powerscourt
Mail	Tue	04	09	1764	The King's Mail carrier was stopped on a road in Co. Wicklow and he was shot in the shoulder with pistol shot
Powerscourt	Fri	26	10	1764	Reports of a robbery at Powerscourt House, Enniskerry. Co. Wicklow appeared the newspapers
La Touché				1764	Marley House Rathfarnham built for the La Touche Family
Powerscourt				1764	Six Bronze urns discovered in a mound near Powerscourt
Beresford, William				1764	William Beresford appointed Vicar of Bray 1764-1767
Usher, John				1764	John Usher appointed sheriff of County Wicklow
Plunket			07	1765	William Coyngham Plunket of Old Connaught, Bray born
Ships/Yachts	Mon	30	09	1765	The vessel "St Peter" shipwrecked of the Wicklow Coast
Act				1765	Public Health Service Act - establishment of hospital/infirmary in every county
Eccles, Isaac				1765	Issac Eccles appointed sheriff of County Wicklow
Roberts, L.				1765	Mr. Lewis Robert's of Old Connaught, Bray received the Dublin Society Gold Medal for preserving 38,000 trees at Old Connaught
Smith, Sir Michael				1765	Sir Michael Smith married Mary Anne Cossack of Ballyronan, Kilcoole, Co. Wicklow
Mining				1765	The value of Copper extracted from the Cronebane Mine (between Avoca and Redcross) was £17,260
Smith, Sir W.C.	Thu	23	01	1766	Sir William-Cusack Smith son of Sir Michael and Mary Smith born
Parnell, Sir H.B.	Thu	03	07	1766	Sir Henry Brooke Parnell 4th Baronet Congleton, 1st Baron Congleton and grand uncle of Charles S Parnell born
Nairne, Carolina	Sat	16	08	1766	Carolina Oliphant (Scottish Poet and Song Writer) born
Parnell, Sir John	Mon	03	11	1766	Sir John Parnell of Ratleague, High Sheriff of Queens County created a Baronet Congleton of Ireland
Clanwilliam, Viscount	Mon	17	11	1766	The title Viscount Clanwilliam created as an Irish peerage title
Smuggling	Wed	19	11	1766	Arklow Revenue Officers seized counter band at Wicklow, but one officer was wounded
Whaley, Thomas (Buck)	Mon	15	12	1766	Thomas Whaley son of Richard Whaley born in Dublin
La Touche				1766	An Octagan was built on the La Touche property in Delgany
Population				1766	The estimated Catholic population of Bray, Powerscourt, Curtlestown, Enniskerry and Kilmacanogue was 2,177
Ships/Yachts				1766	The vessel "Stag" shipwrecked between the Welsh and Wicklow Coast
Infirmary County				1766	A County Infirmary was established in Wicklow Town by the Grand Jury
Grattan, James				1766	James Grattan died
Population Bray				1766	The population of Bray Parish and Little Bray was 560

The County Wicklow Database: 432 AD to 2006 AD

A-Z Reference	Day	Date	Month	Year	DATA
Leslie. Charles				1766	Charles Leslie appointed sheriff of County Wicklow
Hempenstall. Edward				1766	Edward L Hempenstall born at Upper Newcastle. Co. Wicklow
Rathdrum Fair	Sat	21	02	1767	John McNally and Daniel McNally arrested for using counterfeit guineas at Rathdrum Fair
Smuggling	Tue	18	08	1767	The sloop Gottenburg with a cargo of brandy is seized of Bray Head, the crew is taken to Dunleary by Custom officer George Glover
Symes. Mitchelburne				1767	Mitchelburne Symes appointed sheriff of County Wicklow
Burgage Bridge				1767	The Burgage Bridge, Blessington built
Grattan. Catherine				1767	Henry Grattan's sister Catherine died
Morrison. Sir Richard				1767	Richard Morrison (architect) born
Leland. Dr. Thomas				1767	Dr Thomas Leland (historian) was appointed rector of Bray 1767-1773
Woodenbridge				1767	Some small fragments of gold was found in the streams that flow from Croghan Kinsella Mountain. Co. Wicklow
Bernard. Rev W.H.				1767	The Rev William Henry Bernard born Co. Derry
Sterne. Laurence	Thu	17	03	1768	Laurence Sterne (writer) died in London
Murray. Daniel	Mon	18	04	1768	Daniel Murray born at Sheepwalk, Arklow. Archbishop of Dublin (see 1823)
Hill. Willis	Fri	14	10	1768	Willis Hill 1st Marquis of Downshire married Mary Stawell
Mozeen. Thomas				1768	Thomas Mozeen died.
Smith. John				1768	John Smith appointed sheriff of County Wicklow
Harristown				1768	Harristown House, Co. Kildare was bought by the La Touche family
Hodson				1768	William Hodson born 1721 died 1768
Grattan. Mary				1768	Henry Grattan's mother Mary Marlay died
Brabazon. William	Thu	06	07	1769	William Brabazon 9th Earl of Meath born
Fitzwilliam. 3rd Earl	Tue	29	08	1769	Lady Anne Fitzwilliam nee Watson Wentworth died
Shee. Martin Archer	Wed	20	12	1769	Martin Archer Shee (artist) born in Dublin
Rossmore				1769	Lord Rossmore bought some land at Newtown Mount Kennedy
Hume. William				1769	William Hume appointed sheriff of County Wicklow
Mount Kennedy House				1769	Lt. General Robert Cunningham bought Mount Kennedy House, Newtown Mount Kennedy
Fitzwilliam. 4th Earl	Wed	11	07	1770	William Fitzwilliam 4th Earl Fitzwilliam married Lady Charlotte Ponsonby
Meath Hospital	Wed	10	10	1770	Lord Brabazon of Killruddery, Bray laid the foundation stone of the Meath Hospital in the Coombe, Dublin

Section One: Data by Date

Key	Year	Month	Weekday	Day	Description
Shelton Abbey	1770				Shelton Abbey near Arklow was built for Ralph Howard 1st Earl of Wicklow
Woodstock House	1770				Woodstock House, Kilcoole built for John Stratford son of the Earl Aldborough
St. Paul's. Bray	1770				St Paul's Church Bray extended and repaired
Powerscourt	1770				Bamberg Gate dates from
Fairbrother. William	1770				William Fairbrother appointed sheriff of County Wicklow
Tighe. William	1771	02			William Tighe appointed sheriff of County Wicklow
Tarrant. Charles	1771	04			Charles Tarrant granted the lands of Rathdown just North of Greystones
Ships/Yachts	1771				The vessel "Hibernia" carrying Timber shipwrecked of the Wicklow Coast
Ships/Yachts	1771				The vessel "Providence" shipwrecked of the Wicklow Coast
Pobje. Henry	1771				Henry Pobje born England
Dillon. John Talbot	1771				John Talbot Dillon elected member of parliament for County Wicklow
Lowe. Christopher	1771				Christopher Lowe entered the priesthood
Carroll. Grorge	1772	02			George Carroll appointed sheriff of County Wicklow
Brabazon. John	1772	04	Thu	09	John Chambre Brabazon 10th Earl of Meath born
Mount Kennedy House	1772	06	Thu	04	Major Cunningham had plans drawn up to remodel Mount Kennedy House, Newtown Mount Kennedy
Tighe. Mary	1772	10	Fri	09	Mary Tighe writer born
Proby. John	1772	10	Sun	18	John Proby Baron Carysfort died
Brabazon. Edward	1772	11	Tue	24	Edward Brabazon the 7th Earl of Meath died and was succeeded by his son Anthony Brabazon the 8th Earl of Meath
Grattan. Henry	1772				Henry Grattan called to the Irish Bar
Woodenbridge	1772				A stone bridge was erected at Woodenbridge and it replaced a wooden bridge that was destroyed in a storm in 1770
Proby. John Joshua	1772				John Joshua Proby succeeded his father John Proby as Baron Carysfort
Dwyer. Michael	1772				Michael Dwyer (insurgent leader) born at Camara near the Glen of Imaal
Hume. W.H.	1772				William Hoare Hume born
Tottenham. Robert P.	1773	09	Sun	05	Robert Ponsonby Tottenham born
Leland. Dr. Thomas	1773				Dr Thomas Leland (historian) was appointed rector St. Anne's Parish Dublin
Putland	1773				John Putland born in 1709 died in 1773
Weaver Thomas	1773				Thomas Weaver owner of the Luganure Mine, Glendalough, born in England
Hayes. Samuel	1773				Samuel Hayes appointed sheriff of County Wicklow
Domville. Benjamin	1773				Benjamin Domville appointed Vicar of Bray 1773-1774

A-Z Reference	Day	Date	Month	Year	DATA
Weaver. Thomas				1773	Thomas Weaver (Mine Developer) born in England
Stylebawn House				1773	Stylebawn House, Delgany. Co. Wicklow built
Leland. Dr. Thomas				1773	Dr Thomas Leland published "History of Ireland from the invasion of Henry II
Parnell. Sir John	Tue	19	07	1774	Sir John Parnell 2nd Baronet Congleton married Lettia Charolette Brooke
Bayly. Henry	Sat	26	11	1774	Rev Henry Lambert Bayly born
Kyan. John Howard	Sun	27	11	1774	John Howard Kyan born in Dublin, the son of a Co Wicklow Mine owner
Weld. Isaac				1774	Isaac Weld born in Dublin
Powerscourt				1774	Work began on Powerscourt Town House at William Street, Dublin
Oldcourt Castle, Bray				1774	A drawing of Oldcourt Castle, Bray by Major John Corneille held in the National Library of Ireland
Boyd. Patrick				1774	Patrick Boyd appointed sheriff of County Wicklow
Cradock. Thomas				1774	Thomas Cradock appointed Vicar of Bray 1774-1776
Meath Hospital				1774	The Meath Hospital, Dublin renamed the County Dublin Infirmary
Parnell. Sir J. A.			05	1775	Sir John Augustus Parnell 3rd Baronet Congleton and granduncle of Charles S. Parnell born
Grattan. Henry	Mon	11	12	1775	Henry Grattan elected M.P. for the constituency of Charlemont
Potato			circa	1775	The Red nosed Kidney potato variety, syn. Wicklow Bangers (in Dublin) is introduced in Great Britain
Reeves. Thomas				1775	Thomas Reeves appointed sheriff of County Wicklow
Byrne. Billy				1775	Billy Byrne of Ballymanus born
Clanwilliam. Earl	Sat	20	07	1776	The title Earl Clanwilliam created as an Irish peerage title
Stratford. John	Mon	22	07	1776	John Stratford created 1st Viscount Aldborough of Belan Co. Kildare
Old Connaught House				1776	Old Connaught House, Bray was destroyed by fire
Putland. George				1776	George Putland Snr appointed sheriff of County Wicklow
Kilcommon Parish				1776	Rev. Bryan Byrne of Kilcommon Parish, Rathdrum died
Torrens. Thomas				1776	Thomas Torrens appointed Vicar of Bray 1776-1791
Old Connaught				1776	Old Connaught House leased by Alderman William Lightbourne
Ships/Yachts				1776	The vessel "Eagle" shipwrecked of the Wicklow Coast
Quin				1776	Qunis Coaching Inn established in Bray (now Royal Hotel)
Stratford. John	Sun	09	02	1777	John Stratford created 1st Earl of Aldborough, of the Palatinate of Upper Ormond [Ireland]

Section One: Data by Date

Stratford.John	Sun	09	02	1777	John Stratford created 1st Viscount Amiens [Ireland]
Byrne. Dr	Mon	14	04	1777	On the road between Burgage and Blessington villains attacked Dr Byrne of Blessington and his watch was stolen
Tea & Coffee	Mon	09	05	1777	Bags of Tea and Coffee were stolen from the Military Stores at Bray, Co. Wicklow
Crampton. Sir Philip	Sat	07	06	1777	Sir Philip Crampton born in Dublin
Stratford.John	Sun	29	06	1777	John Stratford, 1 Earl of Aldborough died
Kemmis. William	Thu	23	10	1777	William Kemmis 3rd son of Thomas Kemmis born at Ballinacor, Co. Wicklow
Nugent. Count Lavall			11	1777	Count Lavall Nugent born at Ballincor, County Wicklow
Putland				1777	George Putland Snr MP for Rathoat Co. Meath 1777 to 1784
Dolan. Bridget				1777	Bridget Dolan the leading anti-heroine of the 1798 rebellion was born at Carnew, Co. Wicklow
Parnell				1777	Avondale House was built for a Samuel Hayes a barrister and M.P. for Wicklow in the Irish House of Commons
Westby. Nicholas				1777	Nicholas Westby appointed sheriff of County Wicklow
Parish Records			10	1778	Earliest Record of Marriage in Roman Catholic Parish Avoca
Parsons. William				1778	William Parsons appointed sheriff of County Wicklow
Putland				1778	William Putland a brother of George Putland Snr married Anne Evans
Skinners Map				1778	Skinner's Road Map of Ireland
Moore. Thomas	Fri	28	05	1779	Thomas Moore (poet) born in Dublin
Putland				1779	George Putland Sir married Catherine (Kitty) Evans
Avondale House				1779	Avondale House near Rathdrum completed
Doyle. James				1779	Rev James Doyle born in the Parish of Rathdrum
St. Paul's. Bray				1779	A gallery was added to St. Paul's Church, Bray
Derrybawn Bridge				1779	Derrybawn bridge near Laragh built
Saunders. Morley				1779	Morley Saunders appointed sheriff of County Wicklow
Acton. William				1779	William Acton born in 1711 died in 1779
Parnell. Charles S			08	1780	William Parnell Hayes, brother of John A Parnell and Sir Henry and grandfather Charles S. Parnell born
Ballinacor House				1780	Ballinacor House, Rathdrum, Co. Wicklow built
Hodson				1780	Sir Robert Hodson 1st Bart. married Anne Adair of Hollybrooke, Bray
Devlin. Anne				1780	Anne Devlin born at Cronebeg near Aughrim. She was associated with Robert Emmet and her cousin Michael Dwyer.
Baltinglass				1780	Cooke family appointed at sub-postmaster of Baltinglass

A-Z Reference	Day	Date	Month	Year	DATA
Proby, John (2nd)				1780	John Proby the son of John Joshua Proby 1st Earl of Carysfort born
Dwyer, Mary				1780	Mary Dwyer nee Doyle wife of insurgent leader Michael Dwyer born at Glen of Imaal
Roundwood				1780	The Prince of Wales Hotel, Roundwood established
Woodstock House				1780	Arthur Knox bought Woodstock House and Estate from John Stratford
Ballycoog				1780	St. Kevins Church at Ballycoog near Arklow was renovated
Murray, Andrew				1780	Andrew Murray appointed sheriff of County Wicklow
Acton, Thomas				1780	Thomas Acton the son of William Acton and Jane Parsons married Sidney Davis the daughter of Dublin barrister Joshua Davis
Lighthouse	Thu	01	09	1781	A Lighthouse established on Wicklow Head
Ships/Yachts	Fri	12	04	1782	The vessel "Trusty" shipwrecked of the Wicklow Coast
Parnell, Sir John	Sun	14	04	1782	Sir John Parnell 1st Baronet Congleton died
Grattan, Henry			06	1782	Henry Grattan voted £50,000 by house of commons
Scott, Hopton				1782	Hopton Scott appointed sheriff of County Wicklow
Rawson, George				1782	Geroge Rawson M.P. for County Armagh lived at Belmont House, Bray
Putland				1782	George Putland Jnr born
Aughrim				1782	Smelting works and forge established at Aughrim, County Wicklow on a site donated by Lord Powerscourt
Mount Kennedy House				1782	Work began on building Mount Kennedy House for Lord Rossmore at Newtown Mount Kennedy
Carnew castle				1782	Carnew Castle and the Barony of Shillelagh passed to the Earl of Fitzwilliam
Tinnehinch House				1782	Henry Grattan purchased Tinnehinch Coaching Inn near Enniskerry. He did not take up residence until 1784
Grattan, Henry				1782	Henry Grattan married Henrietta Fitzgerald
Leeson	Thu	02	10	1783	Joseph Leeson of Russborough House, Blessington. 1st Earl of Milltown died
Edwards, Col.				1783	Colonel Edwards of Oldcourt, Bray was commander of the Rathdown Cavalry
Putland				1783	Mary Putland nee Bligh born
Hutchinson, Sir F.				1783	Sir Frances Hutchinson, High Sheriff of Dublin and MP for Jamestown, Co. Letrim lived in Old Conna later moved Palermo House
Hutchinson, Sir F.			/	1783	Sir Francis Hutchinson appointed sheriff of County Wicklow
Enniskerry				1783	Francis Wheatley painted a pencil and watercolour of Enniskerry
Parnell, Sir John				1783	Sir John Parnell 2nd Baronet Congleton elected M.P. for Queen's County 1783-1801
Marsden, William				1783	William Marsden published a "History of Sumatra"

Section One: Data by Date

Subject	Day	Date	Month	Year	Event
Old Connaught				1783	Old Connaught House bought by Rev William Gore, Bishop of Limerick
Shee. Martin Archer				1783	Martin Archer Shee parents died and Martin moved to the Cliff Road Windgates, Bray to live with an Aunt
Hawkins. Sir William				1783	Sir William Hawkins, Ulster King of Arms lived at Bolton Hall later Ravensewell House, Bray
Peacock. Joseph				1783	Joseph Peacock (artists) born
Wingfield. Hon. R.				1784	Hon. Richard Wingfield appointed sheriff of County Wicklow
Mount Kennedy House				1784	Mount Kennedy House completed for Lord Rossmore at Newtown Mount Kennedy
Dwyer, John				1784	John Dwyer the father of Michael Dwyer bought a farm at Eadstown four miles from Camara
Ships/Yachts				1784	The vessel "Liberty" shipwrecked of the Wicklow Coast
Ships/Yachts				1784	The vessel "Perserverance" shipwrecked of the Wicklow Coast
Monck				1784	Charles Stanley Monck married Anne Quin (his cousin)
Crosbie. Richard	Wed	19	01	1785	Richard Crosbie of County Wicklow made the first balloon ascent in the British Isles by a UK subject from Ranelagh , Dublin
Parish Records			01	1785	Earliest Record of Births in Roman Catholic Parish Tomacork, Carnew
Whaley, Thomas (Buck)	Thu	10	02	1785	Thomas Whaley elected to the Irish House of Commons for Newcastle, Co. Wicklow
Wicklow. Earl of	Wed	22	06	1785	Ralph Howard was given the title Viscount Wicklow
Fires	Fri	01	07	1785	Fires lit on the Wicklow Mountains on 23rd June to mark the feast of St John was a danger to shipping, reported in the Belfast Journal
Powerscourt	Thu	21	07	1785	Dorothy the wife of the Richard 1st Viscount Powerscourt died
Monck	Tue	26	07	1785	Henry Stanley Monck born, later 2nd Viscount Monck
Ships/Yachts				1785	The vessel "Reserve" shipwrecked of the Wicklow Coast
La Touche				1785	The La Touche property at Delgany was inherited by Peter La Touche the son of David La Touche
Putland				1785	Charles Putland Snr born
La Touche				1785	David La Touche died, son of David and Marthe La Touche
Tynte. Sir James S.				1785	Sir James Stratford Tynte appointed sheriff of County Wicklow
Callaghan. Christopher				1785	Fr. Christopher Callaghan ordained a priest, later Parish Priest of Bray
Leland. Dr. Thomas				1785	Thomas Leland died
Fitzwilliam. 5th Earl	Tue	04	05	1786	Charles Fitzwilliam 5th Earl Fitzwilliam born
Wesley, John	Sun	25	06	1786	John Wesley the Methodist leader stayed at Rosanna, Ashford the home of the Tighe family when he visited Co. Wicklow
Wesley, John	Sat	25	06	1786	John Wesley preached in Ashford
Wesley, John	Mon	26	06	1786	John Wesley preached in Wicklow Town Courthouse

The County Wicklow Database: 432 AD to 2006 AD

A–Z Reference	Day	Date	Month	Year	DATA
Hill. Arthur–2nd	Thu	29	06	1786	Arthur Hill 2nd Marquis of Downshire married Mary Sandys
La Touche				1786	Rebecca La Touche died
Hodson. Robert				1786	Robert Hodson appointed sheriff of County Wicklow
Watson. John				1786	John Watson of Ballydarton House, Carlow is reputed to have hunted and killed the last Irish Wolf at Baltinglass, Co. Wicklow
Duel	Tue	20	02	1787	Mr Trant and Sir John Colhurst had a duel at Bray. Co. Wicklow. Mr Trant was wounded by gun shot.
Bray River				1787	Lime Kiln built at river quay just off Seapoint Road, Bray
Hamilton. Archibald				1787	Archibald Hamilton appointed sheriff of County Wicklow
Bray River				1787	The Bray River dredged yearly in order to keep the riverside quay open.
Ships/Yachts				1787	The vessel "Darnall" shipwrecked between the Welsh and Wicklow Coast
Ships/Yachts				1787	The vessel "Mersey" shipwrecked between the Welsh and Wicklow Coast
Ships/Yachts	Sun	02	02	1788	The vessel "Neptune" shipwrecked of the Wicklow Coast
Wicklow. Earl of	Wed	13	02	1788	William the 4th Earl of Wicklow born
Wicklow Ale	Thu	24	04	1788	A song. "Wicklow Ale" was sung in a new opera by Signor Marhinisine. The song starts with the line O' Wicklow Ale So Brisk and Pale
Powerscourt	Fri	08	08	1788	Richard 3rd Viscount Powerscourt died and was succeeded by his son Richard 4th Viscount
La Touche	Thu	28	08	1788	James Digges La Touche (banker) born in Dublin, the son of William George La Touche
Hill. Arthur–3rd	Wed	08	10	1788	Arthur Hill 3rd Marquis of Downshire born
Falkener. Samuel				1788	Samuel Falkener appointed sheriff of County Wicklow
La Touche				1788	Peter La Touche married Rebecca La Touche sister Elizabeth
Hayes. Samuel				1788	Samuel Hayes MP for Wicklow proposed the following Bill " An Act for Encouraging the Cultivation and Better Preservation of Trees".
Collins. William				1788	William Collins (landscape painter) born, London
Lucas's Directory				1788	Richard Lucas's Directory of traders in Arklow, Bray and Wicklow
La Touche				1788	Peter La Touche married Rebecca Vicars and the lived at Merrion Square Dublin
Hayes. Samuel				1788	Samuel Hayes of Avondale represented Wicklow in the Irish House of Commons
Meade. Anne				1788	Anne Meade married John Whaley of Whaley Abbey, Rathdrum. County Wicklow
Ships/Yachts				1789	The vessel "Speedwell" shipwrecked of the Wicklow Coast
Wicklow. Earl of	Fri	26	06	1789	Ralph Howard 1st Earl of Wicklow died
Powerscourt	Tue	30	06	1789	Richard 4th Viscount Powerscourt married Catherine, 2nd daughter of the 1st Earl of Clanwilliam

Section One: Data by Date

Name	Day	Date	Month	Year	Event
Hill.Willis	Thu	20	08	1789	Willis Hill created 1st Marquis of Downshire
Hodson	Fri	28	08	1789	Sir Robert Hodson created a Baronet of Ireland
Proby.John Joshua	Mon	28	12	1789	John Joshua Proby created 1st Earl of Carysfort
Horndrige.Richard				1789	Richard Hornridge appointed sheriff of County Wicklow
La Touche				1789	The La Touche statue by John Hickey in Delgany Church
Coins				1789	The Cronebane halfpenny first issued
Delgany				1789	A new Church of Ireland, Church at Delgany built. Peter La Touche gave a large donation
Crosbie.Sir Paul				1789	Sir Paul Crosbie father of Richard Crosbie (first balloonist in Ireland) was barrack-master in Bray
Mail Coaches				1789	The introduction of Mail Coaches in Ireland to service all major towns including Bray
Acton.William				1789	Wiliam Acton born elected MP for Wicklow 1841
Blessington.Countess				1789	Margurite Power Countess Blessington born in Knockbrit. Co.Tipperary
Grattan.Henry Jnr				1789	Henry Grattan son Henry was born
Hacketstown				1789	Capt Hardy killed defending Hacketstown
Brabazon.Anthony	Mon	04	01	1790	Anthony Brabazon the 8th Earl of Meath died and was succeeded by his son William Brabazon the 9th Earl of Meath
Powerscourt	Sat	11	09	1790	Richard the 5th Viscount Powerscourt born
Patrickson.William				1790	William Patrickson appointed sheriff of County Wicklow
Grattan.Henry				1790	Henry Grattan elected M.P. for Dublin City for first time
Luggala				1790	The land around Luggala, Roundwood Co.Wicklow bought by Peter La Touche
Delgany				1790	Horse and Hound Inn Delgany built
Mail Coach				1790	Tobias Toole established a mail coach service to and from Bray
Whaley.R.C	Sun	16	01	1791	Richard Chapell Whaley of Whaley Abbey Co.Wicklow died
Parish Records			06	1791	Earliest Record of Births in Roman Catholic Parish Avoca
Monck	Tue	12	07	1791	Charles Joseph Monck born, later 3rd Viscount Monck
Pobje.Henry				1791	Henry Pobje married Mary Towning
Wolfe.Charles				1791	Charles Wolfe born Blackhall, Co. Kildare
Ships/Yachts				1791	The vessel "Precedent" shipwrecked of the Wicklow Coast
Plunket				1791	William Coyngham Plunket married Catherine MCausland
Bernard.W.H.				1791	William Henry Bernard appointed Vicar of Bray 1791-1796
La Touche				1791	Elizabeth La Touche of Delgany laid the foundation stone of the Kirwan's Orphanage, North Circular Road, Dublin

A–Z Reference	Day	Date	Month	Year	DATA
Knox.Arthur				1791	Arthur Knox appointed sheriff of County Wicklow
Glenealy				1792	Church of Ireland Glenealy built
Stratford on Slaney				1792	Printing Works established at Stratford on Slaney
Charleville House				1792	Charleville House, Enniskerry destroyed by fire
King.William				1792	William King appointed sheriff of County Wicklow
Murray.Daniel				1792	Daniel Murray ordained a priest and appointed to St Paul's Church Arran Quay, Dublin
Cunningham.R.A.G				1792	Robert A. Gun Cunningham born
Plunket				1792	Thomas Plunket of Old Connaught, Bray born
La Touche				1792	John David La Touche commissioned a marble statue of Amorino (Cupid)
Hayes.Samuel				1792	Col. Samuel Hayes of Avondale Co. Wicklow designed the Market House in Monaghan. The market House was built in 1792
Powerscourt	Tue	08	01	1793	A fire destroyed some rooms at Powerscourt House
Act	Tue	09	04	1793	Catholic Relief Act
Falkner.Thomas	Fri	19	04	1793	The proprietor of the Dublin Journal (newspaper) Thomas Falkner died at Bray. Co. Wicklow
Wicklow Militia	Mon	10	06	1793	The Wicklow Regiment of Militia established
Parish Records			06	1793	Earliest Record of Marriage in Roman Catholic Parish Tomacork, Carnew
Hill.Willis	Mon	07	10	1793	Willis Hill 1st Marquis of Downshire died and was succeeded by his son Arthur
Nugent. Count Lavall	Fri	01	11	1793	Count Lavall Nugent appointed an cadet in the Austrian engineer corps
Crosbie.Sir Paul	Tue	23	11	1793	Sir Paul Crosbie of Bray died
Wicklow.Earl of	Thu	05	12	1793	Alice Howard wife of 1st Earl of Wicklow was created Countess Wicklow
Wicklow.Earl of	Thu	05	12	1793	The title Earl of Wicklow created as an Irish peerage title
King.Thomas				1793	Thomas King appointed sheriff of County Wicklow
Wicklow Militia				1793	The sermon by Rector Edward Bayly preached at Arklow Church, before a General Meeting of the Militia of County Wicklow
Tighe.Mary				1793	Henry Tighe of Rossanna House, Ashford and Woodstock House, Inistioge Co. Kilkenny married Mary Blachford
Plunket				1793	John Plunket of Old Connaught, Bray born
Cullen.Luke				1793	Historian Luke Cullen born in Bray
Flannel Hall				1793	Flannel Hall built in Rathdrum
Luggala				1793	Peter La Touche built a shooting Lodge at Luggala, Roundwood

Section One: Data by Date

Powerscourt				Catherine the wife of the 4th Viscount Powerscourt died	1793
Crosbie. Sir William	Sun	18	05	Sir William Crosbie of Crosbie Park, Wicklow born	1794
Parish Records			05	Earliest Record of Deaths in Roman Catholic Parish Tomacork, Carnew	1794
Mail	Tue	15	08	Bray man robbed 14 letters from post bags on the road between Wicklow and Wexford.	1794
Smith. Sir W.C.				Sir William-Cusack Smith M.P. for Lanesborough Co Longford 1794-1797	1794
Ball. Teresa				The foundress of the Loreto Order Frances Mary Teresa Ball born in Dublin	1794
Callaghan. Christopher				Fr. Christopher Callaghan appointed Parish Priest of Bray	1794
Carnew				The Catholic Church for Carnew, built in the town land of Tomacork, about 1.3 miles outside the village	1794
Monck. Charles				Charles Stanley Monck appointed sheriff of County Wicklow	1794
Tarrant. Charles				Charles Tarrant of Greystones appointed Colonel	1794
Hayes. Samuel				Samuel Hayes published "A Practical Treatise on Planting and Management of Woods and Coppices"	1794
Rathdrum				St Saviours Church Rathdrum built	1794
Fitzwilliam. William	Sun	04	01	William the 4th Earl of Fitzwilliam sworn in as Lord Lieutenant of Ireland	1795
Parish Records			01	Earliest Record of Births in Roman Catholic Parish Rathdrum	1795
Wicklow Militia	Wed	01	07	The Wicklow Militia finished a 15 month tour of duty in Strabane, Co. Tyrone	1795
Hickey. John				John Hickey (sculptor) died	1795
Military				Col. Leith's Company of Aberdeen Fencebles stationed in Bray	1795
Military				Essex Fencebles Regiment stationed in Bray	1795
Parnell. William				William Parnell, grandfather of C.S. Parnell inherited Avondale Estate, Rathdrum, Co. Wicklow	1795
Gore. Robert				Robert Gore appointed sheriff of County Wicklow	1795
Military				Downshire Regiment stationed in Bray	1795
Smith. Sir W.C.				Sir William-Cusack Smith M.P. for Donegal 1795	1795
Marsden. William				William Marsden appointed secretary of the Admiralty in London	1795
Darley. George				George Darley born in Dublin but brought by relatives in Springfield House now Kilternan Hotel	1795
Military				Londonderry Regiment stationed in Bray	1795
Bernard. Rev W.H.				The Rev William Henry Bernard (artist) lived in Bray	1795
Avondale House				Samuel Hayes of Avondale died. The house and lands passed to his cousin of John Parnell	1795
Ships/Yachts				The vessel "Anna" shipwrecked of the Wicklow Coast	1795
Inglis. Henry D				Henry D. Inglis born in Edinburgh	1795

A-Z Reference	Day	Date	Month	Year	DATA
Police/Garda				1795	John Hayes Hatton born at Newcastle. Co. Wicklow
Wicklow Militia	Sat	07	05	1796	The Wicklow Militia finished a 15 month tour of duty in Strabane, Co. Tyrone
Rossmore. Lord	Wed	19	10	1796	Lt. General Robert Cunningham of Mount Kennedy House, Newtown was given the title Lord Rossmore of Monaghan
Military				1796	Aberdeen Fencebles stationed in Bray
Hugo. Thomas				1796	Thomas Hugo appointed sheriff of County Wicklow
O'Keeffe. John				1796	The John O'Keeffe play The Wicklow Mountains sometimes goes under the title The Lad from the Hills
Airs/Music				1796	The Wicklow Mountains composed and compiled by W. Sheild, based on poetry of John O'Keefe
O'Keeffe. John				1796	John O'Keeffe wrote an opera called The Wicklow Gold Mine
O'Brien. John				1796	John Thomond O'Brien born Co. Wicklow. He was Aide-de-camp to Jose de San Martin, the liberator of Argentina
Donegal Militia				1796	Donegal Militia stationed in Bray
Kilpedder				1796	Trees felled at Tinnapark for making of bobbins for use in the manufacture of clothing in Scotland
Ormsby. J.W				1796	James Wilmot Ormsby appointed Vicar of Bray 1796-1800
O'Keeffe. John				1796	John O'Keeffe the opera The Wicklow Gold Mine was transformed into a play called The Wicklow Mountains
Military				1796	Inverness Fencebles stationed in Bray
Brabazon. William	Sat	20	05	1797	William Brabazon 9th Earl of Meath died as a result of gun shot to the upper leg and the infection that followed
Brabazon. William	Fri	26	05	1797	William Brabazon 9th Earl of Meath was succeeded by his brother John Chambre Brabazon 10th Earl
Brabazon. William			05	1797	William Brabazon 9th Earl of Meath and Capt. Gore had a duel near the Eagle Gate, Powerscourt. The earl died a few days later
Wicklow Militia	Sun	20	08	1797	The Wicklow Militia finished tour of duty in County Westmeath
McCormick. William	Mon	21	08	1797	The Lord Lieutenant proclaims a reward for the apprehension of the persons for murdering William McCormack at Blessington
Antrim Militia			09	1797	Major Joseph Hardy took over command of the Antrim Militia in County Wicklow
Monck	Thu	23	11	1797	The Irish peerage created the title 1st Baron Monck
Monck. Baron	Thu	23	11	1797	The title Baron Monck created as an Irish peerage title
Barony of Talbotstown			11	1797	The Barony of Talbotstown placed under martial law
Grattan. Henry				1797	Henry Grattan withdraws from the house of commons and declines to stand for re-election
Parish Records				1797	Earliest Record of Deaths in Church of Ireland Parish Mullinacuff, Tinahely
Charleville House				1797	Charleville House, Enniskerry built for 1st Viscount Monck

Keyword	Year	Month	Weekday	Day	Description
La Touche	1797				Peter La Touche appointed sheriff of County Wicklow
Ships/Yachts	1797				The vessel "Dublin" shipwrecked between the Welsh and Wicklow Coast
Military	1797				Londonderry Regiment stationed in Bray
Military	1797				Donegal Regiment stationed in Bray
Military	1797				Louth Regiment stationed in Bray
Military	1797				Tyrone Regiment stationed in Bray
Military	1797				Royal Artillery Regiment stationed at Loughlinstown Camp
Military	1797				Romney Horse Regiment stationed in Bray
Hempenstall. Edward	1797				Lieutenant Edward L Hempenstall married Miss Leonard. Hempenstall stood 7ft fall and was known as "Walking Gallows"
Martial Law	1798	03			Martial law proclaimed in County Wicklow.
Orange Lodge	1798	04	Mon	09	The first meeting of The Grand Orange Lodge of Ireland took place in Dublin
Rebellion 1798	1798	05	Sun	13	The Crown issues an ultimatum for surrender of arms in Co. Wicklow
Tinahely	1798	05	Sun	20	The Battle of Tinahely
Carnew	1798	05	Fri	25	The Battle of Carnew
Dunlavin	1798	05	Fri	25	The brutal execution by Crown forces of 28 prisoners at Dunlavin Co. Wicklow
Armstrong's Hotel	1798	05	Wed	30	Armstrong's Hotel Newtown Mount Kennedy destroyed by fire
	1798	05	Wed	30	Battle of Newtown Mount Kennedy part of 1789 Rebellion
Gore. Robert	1798	06	Mon	04	Robert Gore died
Newspaper	1798	06	Tue	05	A report of the 1798 rebellion in Wicklow appeared in the Belfast News-Letter Newspaper
Crosbie. Sir Edward	1798	06	Tue	05	Edward Crosbie the son of Sir Paul was executed in Carlow for alleged complicity with the rebels, later his innocence was proved
Arklow. Battle of	1798	06	Sat	09	Fr. Michael Murphy led the insurgents at the Battle of Arklow
Smith. Mary	1798	06	Sat	23	Mary Smith nee Cusack died
Byrne. W.M.	1798	07	Wed	25	William Martin Byrne of the Glen of the Downes was executed at Newgate Prison, London
Farrell	1798	08	Tue	07	A man named Farrell was apprehended at Crinken, Bray Co. Wicklow in possession of a blunderbuss
Newspapers	1798	10	Mon	08	The Times Newspaper had an article about Wicklow. County Wicklow are infested with bands of lawless depredators.
Hume. William	1798	10	Mon	08	William Hume of Humewood Castle murdered
Dwyer. Michael	1798	10	Tue	16	Michael Dwyer married Mary Doyle
Holt. Joseph	1798	11	Sat	10	The insurgent leader Joseph Holt surrendered and transported to Australia
Holt. Joseph	1798	11			Gen. Joseph Holt insurgent leader surrender and deported to Australia

A–Z Reference	Day	Date	Month	Year	DATA
Books				1798	A minute description of the battles of Gorey, Arklow and Vinegar Hill by Archibald McClaren
Madden. Richard				1798	Richard Robert Madden (historian) born in Dublin (see 1855)
Nugent. Pat				1798	Pat Nugent schoolmaster of Enniskerry killed on Bray Common
Louth Militia				1798	Louth Regiment of Militia stationed in Bray
Moore. John				1798	John Moore was hanged on a tree for his part of the murder of William Hume
Military				1798	15th Dragoons Regiment stationed in Bray
Military				1798	Bray Cavalry was under the command of the Earl of Meath
Military				1798	Bray Infantry was under the command of Capt. John Edwards
O'Neill. Henry				1798	Henry O'Neill (artist) born Clonmel, Co. Tipperary
Military				1798	Powerscourt Infantry was under the command of Capt. Viscount Powerscourt
Military				1798	Wingfield Cavalry was under the command of Lord Powerscourt
Cavan Militia				1798	Cavan Regiment of Militia stationed in Bray
Military				1798	Powerscourt Cavalry was under the command of Capt. Charles S. Monck
Saunders Newsletter				1798	Described Wicklow as "a wilderness as impenetrable as the jungles of the Amazon"
Ballyboy House				1798	Ballyboy House, Gelnmalure home of William Critchley a Yeoman Captain
Downshire House				1798	Downshire House, Blessington the seat of the Earls of Downshire was destroyed during the 1789 rebellion
Carroll. Walter				1798	Walter Carroll appointed sheriff of County Wicklow
Clelland. Hugh	Mon	21	01	1799	Mr Hugh Clelland surgeon of Fermanagh Militia died at Roundwood. Co. Wicklow
Ashford	Fri	25	01	1799	A chapel at Ashford was burned
Ships/Yachts	Tue	29	01	1799	The vessel "Jenny" wrecked off Arklow
Leeson	Mon	11	02	1799	Joseph Leeson of Russborough House, Blessington. 4th Earl of Milltown born
Dwyer. Michael	Fri	15	02	1799	Michael Dwyer and Samuel McAllister took refuge in a cottage at Derrynamuck
Dargan. William	Thu	28	02	1799	William Dargan (Pioneer of Irish Railways) born
Glenealy			02	1799	A chapel at Glenealy was burned
Ships/Yachts	Wed	10	04	1799	The vessel "Lord Mulgrave" shipwrecked of the Wicklow Coast
Wicklow Town	Fri	12	07	1799	The house of the Parish Priest of Wicklow was destroyed
Byrne. Billy	Thu	26	09	1799	Billy Byrne of Ballymanus executed for his part in the 1798 Rebellion
Ships/Yachts				1799	The vessel "Lord Ludgate" shipwrecked of the Wicklow Coast

Section One: Data by Date

Name	Year	Month	Day	Date	Description
Hodson	1799				Sir Robert Hodson 1st Bart. married Jane Neville of Dublin and had four children Robert, George, Helena Jane, Jane
Clara	1799				The Catholic Church of St. Patrick and St. Killian in Clara Co. Wicklow erected
Saurin. William	1799				William Saurin became M.P. for Blessington. Co. Wicklow and opposed the Act of Union
Parnell. Sir John	1799				Sir John Parnell was dismissed from his post as Vice-Treasurer of Ireland
Arklow	1799				Fr. Ryan Parish Priest of Arklow was shot dead in his home. The PP of Wicklow Fr. O'Toole had a similar fate
Donnellan. Michael	1799				Rev Michael Donnellan Parish Priest of Valleymount 1799-1810
Archer. Thomas	1799				Thomas Archer appointed sheriff of County Wicklow
Roundwood	1799				The Catholic Church in Roundwood destroyed by fire
Dublin City Militia	1800	01			480 men from the Dublin City Militia stationed in Arklow
North Cork Militia	1800	01			560 men from the North Cork Militia stationed in Wicklow Town
Military	1800	01			490 men from the Duke of York's the 40th Foot stationed in Bray
Grattan. Henry	1800	02	Sat	15	Henry Grattan and Issac Corry fought a duel at Ballsbridge, Dublin
Military Road	1800	02			A petition was made to the Lord Lieutenant of Ireland to build a road over the Dublin and Wicklow Mountains
Lloyd. Humphrey	1800	04	Wed	16	Humphrey Lloyd (Physicist and Educationalist) born in Dublin
Roundwood	1800	05	Fri	30	Yeomen from Powerscourt are attacked at Roundwood, Co. Wicklow
Act	1800	07	Wed	02	Act of Union . Merged the Irish Parliament with that of Great Britain
Dwyer. Michael	1800	07	Thu	03	The Government offered 500 guineas for the capture of Michael Dwyer
Henniker. Sir John	1800	07	Wed	30	Sir John Henniker of Stratford upon Slaney created Lord Henniker
Military Road	1800	08	Tue	12	Work began on the Military Road from Rathfarnham to Aghavanagh
Whaley. Thomas (Buck)	1800	11	Sun	02	Thomas Buck Whaley died at Knutsford, Cheshire, England
Darby. John Nelson	1800	11	Tue	18	John Nelson Darby born in England
Parish Records	1800	11			Earliest Record of Marriage in Roman Catholic Parish Killaveny,Tinahely
Parish Records	1800	11			Earliest Record of Births in Roman Catholic Parish Kilvaveny,Tinahely
Monck	1800	12	Mon	29	The Irish Peerage created the title 1st Viscount Monck
Campbell. John Henry	1800	circa			John Henry Campbell painting "Sugar Loaf Mountain, Co. Wicklow"
Smith. Sir W.C.	1800				Sir William-Cusack Smith appointed Solicitor General of Ireland
Grattan. Henry	1800				Henry Grattan elected M.P. for borough of Wicklow
Archer. Thomas	1800				Thomas Archer appointed sheriff of County Wicklow
Mangin. Edward	1800				Edward Mangin appointed Vicar of Bray 1800-1803

A–Z Reference	Day	Date	Month	Year	DATA
Gahan				1800	Mr. Gahan M.P. for Wicklow died
Shanaganagh Castle				1800	Shanaganagh Castle, Shankill Co.Dublin bought by Sir General George Cockburn
Act	Thu	01	01	1801	The Act of Union, comes into effect
Monck.Viscount	Mon	05	01	1801	The title Viscount Monck created as an Irish peerage title
Monck	Mon	05	01	1801	Charles Stanley Monck given the title 1st Viscount Monck
Parnell. Sir H.B.	Tue	17	02	1801	Sir Henry Brooke Parnell married Caroline Elizabeth the daughter of the Earl of Portarlington
Hempenstall. Edward			04	1801	Lieutenant Edward L Hempenstall a much hated man in Co. Wicklow "Human scaffold"; "Walking Gallows" died in Dublin
Rossmore. Lord	Thu	06	08	1801	Lt. General Robert Cunningham of Mount Kennedy House, Newtown died without issue
Hill.Arthur-2nd	Mon	07	09	1801	Arthur Hill 2nd Marquis of Downshire died and succeeded by his son Arthur
Leeson	Fri	27	11	1801	Joseph Leeson Jnr. of Russborough House, Blessington 2nd Earl of Milltown died
Parnell. Sir John	Sat	05	12	1801	Sir John Parnell 2nd Baronet Congleton died and left Avondale House, Rathdrum to his son William Parnell
Brabazon.John	Thu	31	12	1801	John Chambre Brabazon 10th Earl of Meath married Melosina Adelaide daughter of John 1st Earl of Clanwilliam
Books				1801	General view of agriculture and mineralogy; present state and circumstances of County Wicklow by Robert Frazer
Coollattin House				1801	Coollattin House, Shillelagh remodelled by 4th (William) Earl of Fitzwilliam It replaced a house burnt in 1789
Ships/Yachts				1801	The vessel "Mary & Peggy" shipwrecked of the Wicklow Coast
Wicklow County				1801	Statistical Survey of County Wicklow by Robert Fraser for the Dublin Society now the Royal Dublin Society (RDS)
Proby.John Joshua				1801	John Joshua Proby created a UK peer with the title Baron Carysfort of the Norman Cross
Mount Kennedy House				1801	Jean Gordon a daughter of one of Major Cunningham's sisters inherited Mount Kennedy House, Newtown Mount Kennedy
Elections–Polling Day				1801	William Hoare Hume elected M.P. for Wicklow at the General Election
Eccles. William				1801	William Eccles appointed sheriff of County Wicklow
Annamoe				1801	Chapel built in Annamoe, Roundwood, Co. Wicklow
La Touche				1801	Elizabeth La Touche opened an orphanage and school for female children in the grounds of Bellevue, Delgany
Downshire. Marquis of				1801	The Marquis of Downshire was paid £15,000 for the loss of franchise of Blessington granted in 1669
St. Columba Church				1801	St. Columba Church, Greenane, Rathdrum Co. Wicklow erected
Military Road	Fri	25	01	1802	The Lord Lieutenant of Ireland and the Chief Secretary Charles Abbott visited the Glencree area to view progress of Military road

Roads	Wed	10	02	1802	Major Taylor estimated that £1,900 would have to be spent on bridges between Glendalough and Aughvanagh
Roads	Wed	10	02	1802	Major Taylor reported to Wicklow Grand Jury that £1,500 was spent on 86 bridges and water pavements in Co. Wicklow
Roads	Wed	10	02	1802	Major Taylor reported to Wicklow Grand Jury that £9,400 was spent on the 15 miles of road between Rathfarnham and Glendalough
Hodson	Sun	14	03	1802	Sir Robert Adair Hodson 2nd Bart. born
Wicklow Militia	Sun	23	05	1802	The Wicklow Militia disbanded
Monck	Wed	09	06	1802	Charles Stanley Monck, 1st Viscount Monck died and was succeeded by his son Henry Stanley Monck 2nd Baron
Elections-Polling Day	Thu	22	07	1802	William Hoare Hume and George Ponsonby elected M.P.'s. for Wicklow at the General Election
Roads				1802	Castle Street, Bray was laid out as a thoroughfare
Kilquade				1802	The R.C. Church Kilquade Co. Wicklow was constituted from Newcastle c1400 and Kilcoole c1179
Ships/Yachts				1802	The vessel "John & Edward" shipwrecked of the Wicklow Coast
Ships/Yachts				1802	The vessel "Three Friends" shipwrecked of the Wicklow Coast
Kilquade				1802	The R.C.Church in Kilquade built
Critchley. James				1802	James Critchley appointed sheriff of County Wicklow
Ships/Yachts				1802	The vessel "Adventure" shipwrecked of the Wicklow Coast
Flora-Fauna				1802	A Blue Whale got stranded on the beach near Arklow
Police/Garda				1802	Anthony Thomas LeFroy born
Military Road				1802	A painting by T.S. Roberts shows Scottish highland soldiers building the Military Road.
Military Road				1802	The 1802 painting by T.S. Roberts of the Military Road. property of Leger Galleries London
Tarrant. Charles				1802	Charles Tarrant of Greystones appointed Major General
Glencree Barracks	Wed	02	02	1803	Tenders invited to build 5 Military Barracks at Glencree, Drumgoff(Glenmalure), Aghavanagh, Leitrim (Glen of Imaal) and Liffey Head
Henniker. Sir John	Mon	18	04	1803	Lord Henniker of Stratford upon Slaney died
Wicklow Militia	Wed	25	05	1803	The Wicklow Militia reformed
Brabazon. William	Tue	25	10	1803	William Brabazon the 11th Earl of Meath born
Lowe. Christopher			10	1803	Rev Christopher Lowe died and is buried at Kilmacanogue
La Touche	Mon	07	11	1803	William George La Touche (Banker) died
Dwyer. Michael	Wed	14	12	1803	Michael Dwyer surrenders to Col. Hume M.P. for County Wicklow
Ormsby. J.W				1803	James Wilmot Ormsby starts 2nd term as Vicar of Bray 1803-1811 First term 1796-1800
Plunket. William				1803	William Plunkett 1st Baron Plunket of Old Connaught, Bray. Chief prosecutor at the trial of Robert Emmet

The County Wicklow Database: 432 AD to 2006 AD

A-Z Reference	Day	Date	Month	Year	DATA
Heighington. William				1803	William Heighington appointed sheriff of County Wicklow
Drumgoff Barracks				1803	Drumgoff Military Barracks in Glenmalure completed
Aghavanagh Barracks				1803	Aghavanagh Barracks built, later shooting lodge of Parnell Family and also used as Youth Hostel
Glen of Imaal				1803	The British War Office built a military barracks at Leitrim near the Glen of Imaal
Barter. Dr. Richard				1803	Dr. Richard Barter was born. He built the Turkish Baths in Bray
Arklow				1803	A Chapel built at Johnstown, Arklow
Valleymount Church				1803	St Josephs Church Valleymount built
Moore. Thomas				1803	Thomas Moore (poet) appointed registrar of the Admiralty Court in Bermuda
Ships/Yachts			04	1804	The vessel "Aid" shipwrecked of the Wicklow Coast
Act	Tue	10	07	1804	Stamp (Ireland) Act, 1804
Whiteside. James	Sun	12	08	1804	James Whiteside born in Delgany
Martello				1804	3 Martello Towers built in Bray (1) Southern end of Bray Prom (2) near the Harbour (3) Corke Abbey Each cost £1,800
Synge				1804	Glanmore Castle designed by Francis Johnston. Built for Francis Synge the great grandfather of J.M.Synge
Kyan. John Howard				1804	John Howard Kyan died his father was a Mine Manager in Avoca
Ships/Yachts				1804	The vessel "Justina Maria" shipwrecked of the Wicklow Coast
Parish Records				1804	Earliest Record of Deaths in Church of Ireland Parish Strafford on Slaney
Grene. W.F				1804	William Francis Grene appointed sheriff of County Wicklow
Hume. W.H.				1804	William Hoare Hume of Humewood Castle, Wicklow married Charlotte Ann Dick
Parish Records				1804	Earliest Record of Marriage in Church of Ireland Parish Stratford on Slaney
Crampton. Sir J.F.T.	Tue	13	08	1805	Sir John Fiennes Twisleton Crampton the son of Sir Philip Crampton born
Hume. William.W.F	Mon	28	10	1805	William Wentworth Fitzwilliam Hume born
Ships/Yachts				1805	The vessel "The Little Sisters" shipwrecked of the Wicklow Coast
Dillon. John Talbot				1805	John Talbot Dillon died
Tighe. Mary				1805	Mary Tighe published her poem Psyche
Wicklow Ale				1805	The song "Old Jolly Dog" contains the line "What wine can equal Wicklow Ale"
Grattan. Henry				1805	Henry Grattan elected to Westminster for the English constituency of Malton
Scott. J.M				1805	John Middleton Scott appointed sheriff of County Wicklow
Military				1805	North Downshire Regiment stationed in Bray

Section One: Data by Date

Subject	Year	Month	Day	Weekday	Event
Tottenham. Charles	1805				Ballycurry House, near Ashford designed by Francis Johnston for Charles Tottenham
Mail Coach	1805				Mail Coach Road (Ireland) Act 1805
Cookson. Geroge James	1805				George James Cookson born
Dwyer. Michael	1806	02	18	Tue	Michael Dwyer Arrived in Port Jackson N.S.Wales after deportation for Ireland ref. 1798
Nairne. Carolina	1806	06	02	Mon	Carolina Oliphant married Baron William Murray Nairne
Kemmis. William	1806	06	11	Tue	William Gilbert Kemmis born
Fitzwilliam. 5th Earl	1806	07	08	Tue	Charles Fitzwilliam 5th Earl Fitzwilliam married Mary Dundas
Education Inquiry	1806	07	21	Mon	The Irish Education Inquiry Commission, the Wicklow members were Henry Grattan, and William Parnell
Monck	1806	07	28	Mon	Henry Stanley Monck 2ndViscount Monck married Frances la Poer Trench daughter of 1st Earl Clancarthy
La Touche	1806	09	06	Sat	Charlotte Cornwallis married Peter (Marlay) La Touche they had 14 children only 3 sons William, Ashley and Octavius married
Hodson	1806	10	25	Sat	Sir George Frederick John Hodson 3rd Bart of Hollybrooke, Bray born
Elections-Polling Day	1806	11	15	Sat	William Hoare Hume and William Tighe elected M.P's. for Wicklow at the General Election
Grattan. Henry	1806				Henry Grattan elected M.P. for Dublin City
Crampton. Selina	1806				Selina Crampton a sister of John Crampton born in Dublin
Pobje. Charles	1806				Charles F. Pobje the son of Henry Pobje and Mary Pobje, born in Bray
Pobje. Henry Jnr	1806				Henry Pobje born the son of Henry Probje and Mary Pobje
Westby. Edward	1806				Edward Westby appointed sheriff of County Wicklow
Arklow	1806				A Chapel built at Castletown, Arklow
Leeson	1807	01	10	Sat	Brice Leeson of Russborough House, Blessington. 3rd Earl of Milltown died
Wicklow. Earl of	1807	03	07	Sat	Robert Howard 2nd Earl of Wicklow succeeded his mother Countess of Wicklow
Bayly. Edward S	1807	04	09	Thu	Edward Symes Bayly son of Henry and Selina Bayly , of Ballyarthurh House, Co. Wicklow, born
Elections-Polling Day	1807	05	23	Sat	William Hoare Hume and William Tighe elected M.P's. for Wicklow at the General Election
Parish Records	1807	05			Earliest Record of Births in Roman Catholic Parish Baltinglass
Parish Records	1807	06			Earliest Record of Births in Roman Catholic Parish Glendalough
Tollemache. Laura	1807				Lady Laura Maria Tollemache born
Wall. James	1807				James Wall appointed sheriff of County Wicklow
Forge Road Enniskerry	1807				The Forge Road Enniskerry was laid out by Lord Powerscourt
Military	1807				Royal Artillery Regiment stationed in Bray

A-Z Reference	Day	Date	Month	Year	DATA
Military				1807	Fermanagh Regiment stationed at Cork Abbey, Bray
Weaver. Thomas				1807	Thomas Weaver developed the Luganure Mine at Glendalough
Woodenbridge				1807	Thomas Moore wrote the verse "The Meeting of the Waters", Avoca
Quin				1807	John Quin of Quins Coaching Inn Bray bought Fairy Hill from John Donnellan and renamed the house "Galtrim" in 1860
Ships/Yachts				1807	The vessel "Anne" shipwrecked off the Wicklow Coast
Ships/Yachts				1807	The vessel "Duncan" shipwrecked off the Wicklow Coast
Ships/Yachts				1807	The vessel "Lune" shipwrecked off the Wicklow Coast
Luganure Mine				1807	Thomas Weaver started the Luganure Mine, in the Glendalough Valley
Saurin. William				1807	William Saurin appointed Attorney General a post he held until 1822
Parish Records			01	1808	Earliest Record of Marriage in Roman Catholic Parish Glendalough
Nelsons Pillar	Mon	15	02	1808	The foundation stone of Nelson's Pillar, Dublin laid by Duke of Richmond. Column 134 ft made of Ballyknockan granite cost £6,857
Doyle. James	Sat	11	06	1808	Fr. James Doyle ordained a priest
Tottenham. Charles J.	Mon	27	06	1808	Charles John Tottenham born at Woodstock House, Kilcoole
Smith. Sir Michael	Wed	17	08	1808	Sir Michael Smith died
Putland				1808	John Putland son of William Putland and the husband of Mary Bligh died
Ballycurry House				1808	Ballycurry House, Ashford remodelled for Charles Tottenham M.P.
Military				1808	1st Garrison Battalion Royal Artillery stationed in Bray
Airs/Music				1808	In Wicklow by the Sea (words by W. Guernsey) music by John Liptrot Hatton
Smythe. William				1808	William Barlow Smythe born, the son of Ralph Smythe and Elizabeth Lyster of Newpark. Co. Westmeath
Blachford. John				1808	John Blachford appointed sheriff of County Wicklow
Military				1808	2nd Garrison Battalion Royal Artillery stationed in Bray
Blake. William H.	Fri	10	03	1809	William Hume Blake born Kiltegan, County Wicklow, famous lawyer in Toronto, Canada
Parish Records			05	1809	Earliest Record of Births in Roman Catholic Parish Arklow
Militia Act 1809	Mon	19	06	1809	The Militia (Ireland) Act 1809, List of Military Regiments in each County in Ireland
Powerscourt	Wed	19	07	1809	Richard the 4th Viscount Powerscourt died and was succeeded by his son Richard 5th Viscount
Hodson	Wed	19	07	1809	Sir Robert Hodson 1st Bart. died
Hodson	Wed	19	07	1809	Sir Robert Adair Hodson succeeded his father as 2nd Baronet
Knox. John				1809	John Knox appointed sheriff of County Wicklow

Section One: Data by Date

Keyword	Entry	Year	Mo	Wk	Day
Military Road	The 45 miles of the Military Road from Rathfarnham Co. Dublin to Aghavanagh Barracks Co. Wicklow completed. Cost £43,587	1809			
Hempenstall. Edward	The image of Lieutant Hempenstall "The Walking Gallows" first appeared in Watty Cox's Irish Magazine	1810	01		
Wicklow Militia	The Wicklow Militia finished a 24 month tour of duty in Drogheda. Co. Louth	1810	02	Wed	28
Parish Records	Earliest Record of Marriage in Roman Catholic Parish Valleymount and Blackditches	1810	02		
Parish Records	Earliest Record of Marriage in Roman Catholic Parish Baltinglass	1810			
Tighe. Mary	Mary Tighe of Rosanna, Ashford died	1810	03	Sat	24
Parish Records	Earliest Record of Births in Roman Catholic Parish Valleymount and Blackditches	1810	06		
Parnell. Charles S	Charles S. Parnell grandfather William Parnell married Frances Howard daughter of the Earl of Wicklow, Col. Hugh Howard	1810	10	Mon	01
Walker. Joseph C.	James Cooper Walker died at St.Valarie, Bray, Co. Wicklow	1810	10	Fri	12
Dennis. T.S.	T.S.Dennis married Katherine Saunders	1810			
Charleville House	Charleville House, (present house) Enniskerry built	1810			
Cronebane Lodge	Robert Howard (1757-1815) 1st Earl of Wicklow bought Cronebane Lodge, Avoca from the Associated Mining Company	1810			
Drought. G.M.J	George M.J. Drought appointed sheriff of County Wicklow	1810			
Airs/Music	La Retour de Wicklow, Waltz for harp and piano by T.T. Bennison	1810			
Fortgranite House	Fortgranite House, Baltinglass remodelled by T.S.Dennis	1810			
Cassidy. Peter	Peter Cassidy murdered at Hollywood, Co. Wicklow	1810			
Bull. George P.	George P. Bull established a printing works in Roundwood, Co. Wicklow	1810			
Putland	Mary Putland nee Bligh married Maurice O'Connell of Kerry	1810			
Parnell. Charles S	Charles S. Parnell father John Henry Parnell born	1811	08	Sun	04
Hill. Arthur-3rd	Arthur Hill 3rd Marquis of Downshire married Maria eldest daughter of the Earl of Plymouth	1811	10	Fri	25
Kish Lighthouse	The Commissioners of Irish Lights purchased the Galliot "Veronia Gesina" and placed it on the Kish Bank	1811	11	Sat	16
Powerscourt	Powerscourt Town House in Williams Street Dublin sold to the Commisioners of Stamp Duty for £15,000	1811			
Knox. Edmond	Hon Edmond Knox appointed Vicar of Bray 1811-1817	1811			
Moore. Thomas	Thomas Moore (poet) married Bessy Dyke	1811			
Post	A new mail coach service from Dublin to Wexford established. With stops in Bray, Wicklow and Arklow on route	1811			
Bray. Barracks	The report of Military Barracks in Ireland. In 1810, Bray had Three Officers and Sixty Four soldiers of various ranks	1811			
Putland	Geroge Putland Snr died	1811			

A–Z Reference	Day	Date	Month	Year	DATA
Eccles. Isaac				1811	Isaac A. Eccles appointed sheriff of County Wicklow
Military				1811	Royal Artillery Garrison stationed in Bray
Lackan				1811	The Church of Our Lady of Mount Carmel built at Lackan, Co. Wicklow
Lee. Walter				1811	Rev Walter Lee born
Dispensary. Bray				1811	The Gentry of Bray established a Dispensary in Bray
Putland				1811	The Putland family bought part of Col. Edwards land at Oldcourt, Bray
Wakefield				1811	Statistical Survey of Ireland Mining
Ships/Yachts	Mon	16	03	1812	The vessel "Duncan II" shipwrecked of the Wicklow Coast
Ships/Yachts	Tue	24	03	1812	The vessel "Hector" shipwrecked of the Wicklow Coast
Wicklow Militia	Mon	20	07	1812	The Wicklow Militia finished a 18 month tour of duty in Drogheda. Co. Louth
Parnell. Sir J. A.	Thu	30	07	1812	Sir John Augustus Parnell 3rd Baronet Congleton and grand uncle of Charles S. Parnell died
Hill. Arthur–4th	Thu	06	08	1812	Arthur Hill 4th Marquis of Downshire born
Elections–Polling Day	Sat	17	10	1812	William Hoare Hume and William Tighe elected M.P's. for Wicklow at the General Election
Brabazon. Anthony	Fri	23	10	1812	Grace Brabazon nee Leigh the wife of Anthony Brabazon the 8th Earl of Meath died
Marsden. William				1812	William Marsden published "A Dictionary and Grammar of the Malayan Language"
Putland				1812	Charles Putland Snr married Constance Massy
Parish Records				1812	Earliest Record of Births in Church of Ireland Parish Stratford on Slaney
Tottenham. Charles				1812	Charles Tottenham appointed sheriff of County Wicklow
Castle Howard				1812	Castle Howard the seat of the Earl of Wicklow was redesigned in 1812
Powerscourt	Sat	06	02	1813	Richard, 5th Viscount Powerscourt married Frances Roden daughter of the 2nd Earl of Roden
Putland	Mon	25	10	1813	Charles Putland Jnr born
Archer. William				1813	Rev. William Archer Rector of Newcastle 1813–1844
Weld. Isaac				1813	Isaac Weld M.P. bought Ravenswell House, Little Bray
Lough Bray				1813	Sir Philip Crampton granted Lough Bray by Lord Powerscourt
Peacock. Joseph				1813	Joseph Peacock painting "The Festival of St. Kevin" of Glendalough, held in Ulster Museum, Belfast
Carnew				1813	The Church (COI) in Carnew was enlarged
Howard. Robert				1813	Robert Howard appointed sheriff of County Wicklow

Section One: Data by Date

	Day	Date	Month	Year	Event
Grand Jury				1813	The Wicklow Grand Jury Presentment Books for the period 1813–1887 destroyed by fire in the Public Records
Donard House				1813	Donard House, Dunlavin built for William Heighington
Wicklow Militia	Tue	02	08	1814	The Wicklow Militia disbanded
Parnell. Frances	Thu	11	08	1814	Frances Parnell the wife of William Parnell died
Police/Garda				1814	Peace Preservation established the fore runner of the RIC and the Garda
Hornridge. John				1814	John Hornridge appointed sheriff of County Wicklow
Ballymore Eustace				1814	Ballymore Eustace Enclosure Act
Aghold				1814	The Glebe house at Aghold, near Shillelagh built
Aghold				1814	The church at Aghold, near Shillelagh enlarged
Books				1814	The Wicklow Gold Mines:, or the Lads of the Hills by John O'Keefe
Leeson. Anne				1814	Anne Leeson murdered at Kilballyowen, Co. Wicklow
O'Brien. John				1814	John Thomond O'Brien emigrated to Argentina
Powerscourt	Wed	18	01	1815	Richard 6th Viscount Powerscourt born
Wicklow Militia	Thu	25	05	1815	The Wicklow Militia reformed
Gray. Sir John	Thu	13	07	1815	John Gray born Claremorris, Co. Mayo
Westby. Nicholas	Fri	25	08	1815	Nicholas Westby of Thornhill, Bray marries Lady Emily Waldgrave dau of William Waldgrave 2nd son of 3rd Earl of Waldgrave
Barrington. Sir William	Wed	04	10	1815	Sir William Barrington born
Fitzwilliam. 6th Earl	Thu	12	10	1815	William Fitzwilliam 6th Earl Fitzwilliam born
Wicklow. Earl of	Mon	23	10	1815	William Forward Howard became 3rd Earl of Wicklow succeeded his brother Robert 2nd Earl of Wicklow
Wicklow. Earl of	Mon	23	10	1815	Robert Howard 2nd Earl of Wicklow died
Parish Records			10	1815	Earliest Record of Births in Roman Catholic Parish Dunlavin
Hume. W.H.	Wed	15	11	1815	William Hoare Hume died
Napoleonic Wars				1815	Napoleonic Wars
Parish Records				1815	Earliest Record of Births in Church of Ireland Parish Ballynure
Enniskerry				1815	William Smith stayed in Enniskerry. He reported that a rat gnawed a candle and his shoes
Book				1815	The Irish Tourist
Thompson. Dr C.				1815	Dr Christopher Thompson born in Dublin
Saunders. Maj.Gen.J.S				1815	Major General John Stratford Saunders appointed sheriff of County Wicklow
Corke Lodge				1815	William Henry Mangan of Bray Commissioned Corke Lodge, Shankill Road, Bray to be built between 1815 –1820

A–Z Reference	Day	Date	Month	Year	DATA
Putland				1815	Charlotte Christian first wife of Charles Putland Jnr born
Carnew Castle				1815	Repairs carried out to Carnew Castle
Moyne Church				1815	Moyne Church built
Military				1815	1st Royal Lancashire Regiment stationed in Bray
Hodson				1815	William Hodson born 1757 died in 1815
Elections-Polling Day	Tue	13	02	1816	Hon. Granville Leveson Proby elected M.P. for Wicklow at the By-Election caused by the death of William Hoare Hume
Health	Fri	01	03	1816	Dr. Heffernan appointed Medical Superintendent of Bray Dispensary 1816-1836 with a salary of 100 guineas per annum
Elections-Polling Day	Fri	19	04	1816	Rt. Hon George Ponsonby elected M.P. for Wicklow at the By-Election caused by the death of William Tighe
Parish Records			11	1816	Earliest Record of Marriage in Roman Catholic Parish Rathdrum
Putland			11	1816	George Putland Jnr married Anna Dorothea (Nancy) Evans
Bayly. Henry				1816	Rev H.L. Bayly published No. III Parish of Arklow.
Ireland				1816	A Parochial Survey of Ireland. An unmarried woman of 20 years...is rarely to be met in country parts of Ireland.
St. Pauls. Bray				1816	Plans adopted to extend and repair St. Paul's Church Bray
Dunlavin				1816	St Nicholas Church, Stephen's Street Dunlavin built
Proby. Hon. G.L				1816	Granville Levenson Proby 3rd Earl of Carysfort , M.P. for Wicklow 1816 to 1829
King. Daniel M				1816	Daniel M. King appointed sheriff of County Wicklow
Nugent. Count Lavall				1816	Count Lavall Nugent commanded the Austrian Troops at the Battle of Naples
Parnell. Charles S				1816	Charles S. Parnell mother Delia Tudor Stewart born
Exchequer	Sun	05	01	1817	Exchequers of Ireland and Great Britain united
Grattan. Henry	Fri	09	05	1817	Henry Grattan's M.P. who lived in Enniskerry His motion in Parliament for Catholic Emancipation defeated
Elections-Polling Day	Tue	12	08	1817	William Hayes Parnell elected M.P. for Wicklow at the By-Election caused by the death of George Ponsonby
Monck	Sat	29	11	1817	Charles Joseph Monck married Bridget Willington
McCarthy. Joseph				1817	Joseph McCarthy who designed St.Kevins Parish Church Glendalough was born
La Touche				1817	David (Dinges de) La Touche (Banker) died the grandson of David La Touche born 1671
Nun's Cross, Ashford				1817	A church erected at Nun's Cross, Ashford by local landlord F. Synge
Wolfe. Charles				1817	Charles Wolfe wrote the ballad "Farewell to Lough Bray"
Hoey. Francis				1817	Francis Hoey appointed sheriff of County Wicklow

Section One: Data by Date

Fever hospital				1817	Fever Hospital established at Strafford on Slaney
Knox. Charles				1817	Hon Charles Knox appointed Vicar of Bray 1817–1825
Parnell. William				1817	William Parnell M.P. for Co Wicklow 1817–1820
Grand Jury				1817	The Wicklow Grand Jury Query Books for the period 1817–1882 destroyed by fire in the Public Records Office, Dublin in 1922
Parish Records			01	1818	Earliest Record of Marriage in Roman Catholic Parish Arklow
Acton. William	Tue	16	06	1818	William Acton the son of Thomas and Sidney Acton married Caroline Walker daughter of Thomas Walker Master in Chancery
Elections–Polling Day	Mon	29	06	1818	William Hayes Parnell and Hon. Granville Leveson Proby elected M.P's. for Wicklow at the General Election
Proby. Hon. G.L				1818	Granville Levenson Proby 3rd Earl of Carysfort married Isabella Howard granddaughter of 1st Earl of Wicklow
Bernard. Rev W.H.				1818	The Rev William Henry Bernard (artist) died
Parish Records				1818	Earliest Record of Deaths in Church of Ireland Parish Ballynure
Parish Records				1818	Earliest Record of Marriage in Church of Ireland Parish Killiskey
Lewins. Phil				1818	Thomas Lewins of Kilmacoo, Co. Wicklow was murdered by his son Phil Lewins
Lewins. Phil				1818	Phil Lewins was hanged in Wicklow for his fathers death
Monck. Emily				1818	Emily Monck born
Parish Records				1818	Earliest Record of Marriage in Church of Ireland Parish Ballynure
Fever hospital				1818	The Earl of Meath purchased the Barracks of Bray for a Fever Hospital for £100
Tarrant. Charles				1818	Charles Tarrant daughter Alice Brabazon inherited Charles Tarrant lands at Rathdown, Greystones
Hospital. Fever				1818	Fever Hospital established at Arklow
Lighthouse				1818	The new lighthouse was built on Wicklow Head
Parish Records				1818	Earliest Record of Births in Church of Ireland Parish Killiskey
Enniskerry				1818	Powerscourt National School Enniskerry built
Tarrant. Charles				1818	Charles Tarrant of Rathdown, Greystones died
Gun. George				1818	George Gun appointed sheriff of County Wicklow
Shanaganagh Castle				1818	Shanaganagh Castle was remodelled by Sir George Cockburn
Humphreys. C.F.				1818	Cecil Frances Alexander nee Humphreys born Co. Wicklow, daughter of Major Humphreys land agent to the Earl of Wicklow
Dunlavin				1818	A Bronze Age Food vessel was found at Lemonstown, near Dunlavin, West Wicklow
St. Pauls. Bray				1818	St Paul's Church Bray enlarged with a loan of £1020 from the Boards of First Fruits
Lemonstown				1818	A Bronze-Age food vessel was found in a mound at Lemonstown near Dunlavin

A–Z Reference	Day	Date	Month	Year	DATA
Bewley.Joshua	Tue	19	01	1819	Joshua Bewley one of the co-founders of Bewley Café's in Dublin was born
Ashford	Thu	06	05	1819	Ashford was granted the status of a Post town
Monck. Charles	Sun	10	10	1819	Charles Stanley Monck born, Later 4th Viscount of Charleville House, Enniskerry
Plunket	Tue	26	10	1819	Thomas Plunket of Old Connaught, Bray married Lousia Jane Foster
Castlemacadam				1819	The church at Castlemaccadam granted £291 for repairs by the Ecclesiastical Commissioners
Hacketstown				1819	The Glebe House in Hacketstown erected
Conran.John				1819	John Conran of Borklemore, County Wicklow, born
Synge.John				1819	John Synge appointed sheriff of County Wicklow
Elections–Polling Day	Fri	17	03	1820	William Hayes Parnell and Hon. Granville Leveson Proby elected M.P's. for Wicklow at the General Election
Powerscourt	Wed	10	05	1820	Frances Roden wife of Richard, 5th Viscount Powerscourt died
Grattan. Henry	Sun	04	06	1820	Henry Grattan M.P. who lived in Enniskerry died in London and was buried in Westminster Abbey, London
Bray School	Thu	20	07	1820	Roman Catholic School at Seapoint Road, Bray founded and blessed, Bray's Boys National School later called St Cronan's BNS
Mackintosh. C.H.			10	1820	Charles Henry Mackintosh born at Glenmalure Barracks, County Wicklow. Son of Captain Mackintosh, Glenmalure Barracks
Mecredy. Rev James	Tue	10	12	1820	Rev James Mecredy born
The school house			circa	1820	The school house at Killougher, Ashford, Co. Wicklow. built
Grattan. Henry			circa	1820	National Gallery of Ireland 567 Oil on Canvas. Portrait of Mrs Henry Grattan by Maria Spilsbury (Taylor) 1777–1823
Roundwood School			circa	1820	Watercolour of the Interior of John Synge's School at Roundwood by Maria Spilsbury (Taylor) 1777–1823
Coach House.			's	1820	The Coach House Inn Roundwood built
Inglis. Henry D				1820	Henry D Inglis was editor of a newspaper in Derbyshire and the Channel Islands 1820–1835
Powerscourt				1820	The church in the grounds of Powerscourt demesne was enlarged with a grant of £1000 from the Board of First Fruits
Boucicault. Dion				1820	Dion Boucicault actor and playwright born
Acton. William				1820	William Acton appointed sheriff of County Wicklow
Charleville House				1820	Charleville House Enniskerry rebuilt after the house was destroyed by fire in 1792
Ships/Yachts				1820	The vessel "Friends" shipwrecked of the Wicklow Coast
Pobje. Henry				1820	Henry Pobje carried out the stucco ceilings at Killruddery House, Bray
Brabazon.Killruddery				1820	Killruddery House, Bray the home of the Brabazon Family remodelled by William and Richard Morrison for the 10th Earl of Meath
Brabazon.John			02	1821	John Brabazon 10th Earl of Meath was appointed a Knight of the Order of St. Patrick

Plunket	Wed	14	03	1821	Catherine Plunket nee M'Causland died
Parnell. William	Mon	02	04	1821	William Parnell died and left Avondale to his son John Henry Parnell the father of Charles Stewart Parnell
Population Arklow	Mon	28	05	1821	Population of Arklow Urban 3,808 or 3.44% of the County Population
Population	Mon	28	05	1821	Population of Bray 2,029 or 1.84% of the County Population
Population County	Mon	28	05	1821	Population of County Wicklow 110,767 persons, 55,203 Males (49.8%) 55,564 Females (50.2%)
Population Wicklow (t)	Mon	28	05	1821	Population of Wicklow Town 2,046 or 1.84% of County Population
Population Greystones	Mon	28	05	1821	Population of Greystones & Delgany 570 or 0.52% of County Population
Royal Visit	Sun	12	08	1821	King George IV pays a visit to Ireland between 12th August and 3rd September
Powerscourt	Tue	14	08	1821	King George IV visits Powerscourt during the Royal visit to Ireland
Population of Brockagh				1821	The estimated population of the Electoral District of Brockagh in 1821 was 950 persons
Ships/Yachts				1821	The vessel "Higson" shipwrecked off the Wicklow Coast
Carroll. Alexander				1821	Alexander Carroll appointed sheriff of County Wicklow
Brocas. Samuel				1821	"Bray Head" a painting by Samuel Frederick Brocas –now in the National Gallery of Ireland
Dun Laoghaire				1821	King George IV leaves Ireland on 03/09/1821 at DunLeary renamed Kingstown in his honour
Pobje. Charles				1821	Charles F. Pobje married Anne Baggerley
Books				1821	The Cavern in the Wicklow Mountains, or the fate of the O'Brien family. A tale founded on facts
Pobje. Henry Jnr				1821	Henry Pobje Jnr married Jane Ivy
Monck	Sat	12	01	1822	Henry Stanley Monck created 1st Earl of Rathdowne
Fitzwilliam. 4th Earl	Mon	13	05	1822	Lady Charlotte Fitzwilliam nee Ponsonby died
Young. William	Sun	25	08	1822	Rev. William Young preached the Education sermon, Some 400 children attended schools in Bray
Wicklow Militia	Tue	24	12	1822	The numbers in the Wicklow Militia were reduced
Byrne. James (Pt.)				1822	James Byrne (Private) 86th Regiment Royal Irish Rifles born at Newtown MountKennedy, County Wicklow
Saunders. Robert				1822	Robert Saunders appointed sheriff of County Wicklow
National Archives				1822	Business Records Survey Wicklow No. 19 Building Accounts of Prebawn Church and School 1822-1829
La Touche				1822	John La Touche died
Grattan. Henry				1822	The publication of the speeches of Henry Grattan 4 vols
Young. William				1822	Rev William Young was a curate in Bray 1822-1831
Books				1822	"Guide to Wicklow" Illustrated by Petrie. by Rev George N Wright. Published in London 1822 – 1827
Police/Garda				1822	The Irish Constabulary force established (IC)

A–Z Reference	Day	Date	Month	Year	DATA
Meath Hospital				1822	Meath Hospital built at Heyesbury Street, Dublin
Police/Garda				1822	Irish Constabulary formed. Royal was added to its title in 1861
Murray. Daniel	Sun	11	05	1823	Daniel Murray appointed as Archbishop of Dublin 1823–1852
Quins Hotel	Wed	18	06	1823	A fire at Quin's Hotel (Royal Hotel) one person died
Fitzwilliam. 4th Earl	Mon	21	07	1823	William Fitzwilliam 4th Earl Fitzwilliam married Lady Louisa Ponsonby
Lube. Andrew	Sun	27	07	1823	Rev Andrew Lube preached the Education sermon. £100-16s-4d collected for Bray Schools
Powerscourt	Tue	09	08	1823	Richard, 5th Viscount Powerscourt died and was succeeded by his son Richard 6th Viscount
O'Callaghan. Rev	Mon	17	11	1823	Canon O'Callaghan died and is buried in Kilmacanogue Church
Doyle, James	Tue	25	11	1823	Fr. James Doyle appointed Parish Priest of Bray
O'Callaghan. Rev	Mon	01	12	1823	An article in "The Connaught Journal" newspaper published in Galway
Monck	Sat	20	12	1823	Anne Monck nee Quin died
O'Byrne. W.R				1823	William Richard O'Byrne born, lived at Cabinteely Co. Dublin
Hugo. Thomas				1823	Thomas Hugo appointed sheriff of County Wicklow
Parish Records				1823	Earliest Record of Births in Church of Ireland Parish Ballintemple, Arklow
Books				1823	Shamrock Leaves, or the Wicklow Excursion published in London
Roundwood				1823	The bridge at Oldbridge near Lough Dan, Roundwood erected
Wolfe. Charles				1823	Charles Wolfe died in Queenstown
Books				1823	The Novel "St. Ronan's Well" there is reference made to outdoor Theatre events at Killruddery
Parish Records				1823	Earliest Record of Marriage in Church of Ireland Parish Ballintemple, Arklow
Truell. Robert H	Fri	05	03	1824	Robert Holt Truell appointed sheriff of County Wicklow
Plunket	Mon	05	04	1824	John Plunket married Charlotte Bushe daughter of Lord Chief Justice Charles Kendal Bushe
Bray & Kilternan	Thu	17	06	1824	Bray and Kilternan Parish Act, set out the limits of Bray and Kilternan Parishes
Parish Records			08	1824	Earliest Record of Deaths in Roman Catholic Parish Valleymount and Blackditches
Healy, James	Wed	15	12	1824	Fr. James Healy born at Bluebell, Dublin one of twenty three children
Hornridge. George			12	1824	William Wallace murdered by Grorge Hornridge of Burgage, Co. Wicklow
Mason. G.H. Monck				1824	G.H. Monck Mason born, the son of Captain Thomas Mason (Royal Navy), and Mary, of Co. Wicklow
Kilmacanogue				1824	Roman Catholic Church at Kilmacanogue built
Mining Co. of Ireland				1824	The Mining Company of Ireland established in Dublin by wealthy Irish Gentry and Merchants

Ships/Yachts				1824	The vessel "Hope" shipwrecked of the Wicklow Coast
Ships/Yachts				1824	The vessel "Marquis of Wellington" shipwrecked of the Wicklow Coast
Books				1824	The Angling Excursions of Gregory Greendrake in County Wicklow
Collins. William W.				1824	William Wilkie Collins (novelist) born, Maryleborne, London
Brabazon. John				1824	Lord Brabazon laid the foundation stone of the Catholic Church of Our Lady of Refuge, Rathmines
Courthouses				1824	The County Courthouse built in Wicklow Town
J. Pigot's Directory				1824	J. Pigot's Directory of Arklow, Baltinglass, Blessington, Bray, Newtown , Rathdrum and Wicklow
Brabazon. John				1824	The Earl of Meath gave a site 2acres, 2 roods and 38 perches on Rathmines Road, for the Church of Our Lady of Refuge (Catholic)
Holy Redeemer, Bray				1824	A new chapel built at the Holy Redeemer Main Street Bray at cost £1,600
Parish Records				1824	Earliest Record of Deaths in Church of Ireland Parish Killiskey
Alexander. William				1824	William Alexander born Co. Derry
Bray Head				1824	Watercolour (Ref: PAD1476) Bray Head by Thomas McLean-Publisher- held in National Maritime Museum Greenwich, London
Nicol. Erskine			07	1825	Erskine Nicol (artists) born in Leith, Scotland
Dwyer. Michael	Tue	23	08	1825	Michael Dwyer insurgent leader died in Sydney, Australia In 1815 he appointed High Constable of Sydney, Australia
Scott. Walter			08	1825	Sir Walter Scott over-nighted at (Lough Bray) Lough Breagh House, with Sir Philip Crampton
Scott. Walter			08	1825	Sir Walter Scott over-nighted at Old Connaught House, Bray with Lord Plunkett
Parish Records			10	1825	Earliest Record of Births in Roman Catholic Parish Enniskerry
Murray. Daniel	Mon	14	11	1825	Archbishop of Dublin Daniel Murray opened St. Marys Metropolitan Chapel (Pro-Cathedral) Marlborough Strret, Dublin
Parish Records			11	1825	Earliest Record of Marriage in Roman Catholic Parish Enniskerry
Marsden. William				1825	William Marsden published "Numismata Orientalia 1823-1825
Parish Records				1825	Earliest Record of Deaths in Church of Ireland Parish Glenealy
Parish Records				1825	Earliest Record of Births in Church of Ireland Parish Glenealy
Ships/Yachts				1825	The vessel "Comus" shipwrecked of the Wicklow Coast
Plunket. William				1825	William Plunket of Old Connaught, Bray. held the post of Attorney General
Parish Records				1825	Earliest Record of Marriage in Church of Ireland Parish Glenealy
Luganure Mine				1825	The Luganure Mine, Glendalough was sold to the Mining Company of Ireland
Mining Accident				1825	Two miners trapped by a rock fall at the Luganure Mine, Glendalough for 33 hours before being released
Annacurra				1825	A school-house built in Annacurra by George Coates Esq.

A-Z Reference	Day	Date	Month	Year	DATA
Darby. John Nelson				1825	John Nelson Darby forms the Darbyites and Plymouth Brethern
Plunkett. W.C				1825	William Conyngham Plunkett appointed Vicar of Bray 1825-1857
Hodson. Sir Robert				1825	Sir Robert Hodson appointed sheriff of County Wicklow
Irish Mile	Thu	05	01	1826	The Irish mile ceased to have legality on 05/01/1826, English Statue Mile 1,760 yards, Irish Mile 2,240 yards
Hennessy. Henry	Sun	19	03	1826	Henry Hennessy (Physicist and Mathematician) born in Cork
Holt. Joseph	Sat	06	05	1826	Joseph Holt died
Elections-Polling Day	Wed	21	06	1826	James Grattan and Hon. Granville Leveson Proby elected M.P.'s for Wicklow at the General Election
Doyle. James			06	1826	Fr. James Doyle died
Roche. Alexandra	Mon	24	07	1826	Rev. Alexandra Roche was appointed Parish Priest of Bray and Killmacanogue
Parish Records			08	1826	Earliest Record of Marriage in Roman Catholic Parish Kilquade and Kilmurray
Parish Records			08	1826	Earliest Record of Births in Roman Catholic Parish Kilquade and Kilmurray
Grattan. Henry Jnr	Thu	05	10	1826	Henry Grattan Jnr married Mary Harvey of Portobello, Dublin
Luganure Road				1826	A road along the shore of the Upper Lake Glendalough built to service the Luganure Mine
Meade. Anne				1826	Anne Whaley nee Meade died
Curtlestown				1826	A school established in Curtlestown, near Enniskerry
Lifeboats				1826	Arklow Lifeboat Station established.
Darby. John Nelson				1826	John Nelson Darby appointed rector of Calary Church 1826 – 1828
Ships/Yachts				1826	The vessel "Mary" shipwrecked of the Wicklow Coast
Crampton. Sir J.F.T.				1826	Sir John Fiennes Twisleton Crampton appointed ambassador to Turin, Italy 1852-1856
Acton. Thomas				1826	Thomas Acton son of William and Caroline Acton born
Dempsey. Denis (Pt.)				1826	Denis Dempsey born Rathmichael, Bray. Co. Dublin
Carroll. Henry				1826	Henry Carroll appointed sheriff of County Wicklow
Rents				1826	Rents from Catholics in County Wicklow amounted to £174:14s:7d
Luganure Mine				1826	A mine road was opened between Luganure Mine and Glendalough
Rathmichael				1826	The Parish of Rathmichael was part separated from Union of Bray
Currency				1826	Irish Currency linked to Sterling ir£=stg£ (see 1979)
Westby. WJ	Thu	15	02	1827	William Jones Westby Jnr. appointed sheriff of County Wicklow

Section One: Data by Date

Name	Day	Date	Month	Year	Event
Holt. Ester	Sun	24	06	1827	Ester Holt died, wife of Joseph Holt
Bayly, Henry	Wed	25	07	1827	Rev. Henry Lambert Bayly died
Woodstock House				1827	Woodstock House bought by Rt. Rev. Lord Robert Tottenham, Bishop of Clogher
Parish Records				1827	Earliest Record of Births in Church of Ireland Parish Rathdrum
British Parliamentary Reports				1828	British Parliamentary Report " Report of Sums granted by Government for marking Mail-Coach Roads in Co Wicklow
Campbell, John Henry				1828	John Henry Campbell (artists) died
Higginbottam. Edward	Wed	23	09	1829	Mary Doyle of Arklow, murdered by Edward Higginbottam
Carnew School				1829	The Earl of Fitzwilliam built the school titled The Earl of Fitzwilliam Endowed School" in Carnew
Bray School				1829	Infant school erected in Bray with a grant from Viscount Powerscourt
Conran. Margaret				1829	Margaret Conran born
La Touche	Thu	11	02	1830	Peter (Marlay) La Touche of Bellevue, Delgany, Co. Wicklow died
Crosbie. Sir William	Tue	30	03	1830	Sir William Crosbie married Dorothea Walsh the grand-daughter of Sir Paul Crosbie
Pobje. Henry	Sun	20	06	1830	Henry Pobje died at Bray aged 59 years
Act	Sat	26	06	1830	Carriers (Luggage and Parcels) Act
Nairne. William	Fri	09	07	1830	Baron William Murray Nairne died
Elections–Polling Day	Tue	10	08	1830	James Grattan and Ralph Howard elected M.P's. for Wicklow at the General Election
Rathmines	Sun	15	08	1830	Archbishop Murray dedicated the church of Our Lady of Refuge, Rathmines
Darley. Sir FM	Sun	18	09	1830	Sir Frederick Matthew Darley born at Wingfield, Wexford Road, Bray. Son of John Henry Darley
Fitzwilliam. 5th Earl	Mon	01	11	1830	Mary Fitzwilliam nee Dundas died
Nairne. Carolina				1830	Between 1830 and 1845 Baroness Carolina Nairne lived in Enniskerry
Crampton.Sir J.F.T.				1830	Sir John Fiennes Twisleton Crampton painted a view of St. Petersburg, held by British Museum
British Parliamentary				1830	Report of the Archbishop of Dublin on Union of Parish of Wicklow
Lifeboats				1830	Arklow Lifeboat Station closed
La Touche				1830	When Peter (Marlay) La Touche died the Delgany estate was inherited by his son Peter David La Touche.
Shillelagh				1830	Shillelagh Farming Society established
Plunket				1830	William Coyngham Plunket elevated to the peerage as 1st Lord Plunket and appointed Lord Chancellor of Ireland
Acton. Charles				1830	Charles Acton son of William and Caroline Acton born
Parish Records				1830	Earliest Record of Deaths in Church of Ireland Parish Crosspatrick and Kilcommon
Parish Records				1830	Earliest Record of Births in Church of Ireland Parish Crosspatrick and Kilcommon

A–Z Reference	Day	Date	Month	Year	DATA
Hutchinson. F.S				1830	Francis Synge Hutchinson appointed sheriff of County Wicklow
Shelton Abbey				1830	Shelton Abbey near Arklow another home of the Earl of Wicklow was remodelled in 1830
Darley. F.M				1830	Sir Frederick Matthew Darley, Australian Statesman born in Co. Wicklow
Enniskerry				1830	Ballyman Castle removed and Ballyman House built
Killruddery				1830	The ceilings of Killruddery House designed by Richard Morriosn and executed by Henry Pobje
St. Peters. Bray				1830	St Peters Church Little Bray building started
Parish Records				1830	Earliest Record of Marriage in Church of Ireland Parish Crosspatrick and Kilcommon
Parish Records			02	1831	Earliest Record of Marriage in Roman Catholic Parish Dunlavin
Wicklow Coastguard	Wed	02	03	1831	Wicklow Coastguard Lieutenant Dabine R.N. was awarded the RNLI Silver Medal in recognition of his bravery on 02/03/1831
Wicklow Coastguard	Wed	02	03	1831	Wicklow Coastguards rescued four crewmen from the schooner "Jane" off Wicklow Head
Elections–Polling Day	Tue	10	05	1831	James Grattan and Ralph Howard elected M.P's. for Wicklow at the General Election
Population of Brockagh	Mon	30	05	1831	The estimated population of the Electoral District of Brockagh in 1831 was 1,200 persons
Population County	Mon	30	05	1831	Population of County Wicklow 121,557 persons. 61,052 Males 60,505 Females
Population Arklow	Mon	30	05	1831	Population of Arklow Urban 4,383 or 3.61% of the County Population
Population Greystones	Mon	30	05	1831	Population of Greystones & Delgany 356 or 0.29% of County Population
Population Wicklow (t)	Mon	30	05	1831	Population of Wicklow Town 2,472 or 2.04% of County Population
Population	Mon	30	05	1831	The Population of the Rathdrum area was 1,054
Population	Mon	30	05	1831	Population of Rathmichael 1,296
Population Bray	Mon	30	05	1831	Population of Bray. 3,758 or 3.09% of County Population
Population	Mon	30	05	1831	Population of Kingstown (Dun Laoghaire) 5,736
Howard. Catherine	Tue	23	08	1831	Catherine Howard daughter of 4th Earl of Wicklow born
Coronation Plantation			08	1831	The fencing of the Coronation Plantation (500 acres of trees) was under taking by the Marquis of Downshire
Railways	Tue	06	09	1831	An Act was passed establishing the Dublin & Kingstown Railway Co.
Education	Fri	09	09	1831	Primary Education system introduced in Ireland
Brabazon. John	Sat	10	09	1831	John Chambre Brabazon the 10th Earl of Meath was also given the title Baron Chaworth in the UK Peerage
Godkin. Edwin	Sun	02	10	1831	Edwin Lawrence Godkin, editor and author "Godkin Lectures" established at Harvard University. Born at Mayne Co. Wicklow
Stratford. Amelia	Tue	11	10	1831	Amelia Stratford daughter of the 1st Earl of Aldborough died

Section One: Data by Date

Keyword	Day			Event	Year
Powerscourt	Tue	11	10	Amelia the wife of the 3rd Viscount Powerscourt died	1831
Hodson	Wed	19	10	Sir Robert Adair Hodson 2n Bart. died and was succeeded by his brother Sir George Frederick John Hodson 3rd Bart.	1831
Carnew				The Church of Ireland Church in Carnew enlarged	1831
Ships/Yachts				The vessel "Bess" shipwrecked off the Wicklow Coast	1831
Prince William Seat				Prince William Seat Mountain to the west of Enniskerry, named at the time of the coronation of King William IV in 1831	1831
National Archives				OPW 5HC/6/0402 Proposed Road Roundwood to Blessington. engineer William Dargan, surveyor T.D.Moclair	1831
British Parliamentary				Memorial to Lord Lieutenant of Ireland from the Parishioners of Union of Wicklow	1831
Proby. Hon. G.L				Hon. Grenville Levenson Proby appointed sheriff of County Wicklow	1831
Cookson. Catherine	Fri	08	06	Catherine Teresa Murray the daughter of P. Murray of Wicklow married George James Cookson	1832
Elections–Polling Day	Fri	21	12	James Grattan, Ralph Howard, William Acton and John Humphreys elected M.P's. for Wicklow at the General Election	1832
Scalp				The road at the Scalp, Co. Wicklow was re-aligned	1832
Pearce. Thomas				Thomas Pearce born in Shillelagh. County Wicklow	1832
Smythe. William				William Barlow Smythe appointed High Sheriff of Co. Westmeath.	1832
Kyan. John Howard				John Howard Kyan discovered a way of preserving timbers. He patented his product as Kyanised	1832
Books				4th Edition. The Angling Excursions of Gregory Greendrake in County Wicklow	1832
Hoey. W.P				William Parsons Hoey appointed sheriff of County Wicklow	1832
Books				The Angling Excursions of Gregory Greendake in Counties of Wicklow, Meath, Westmeath, Longford, Cavan. Published in Dublin 1832	1832
Flora-Fauna				Yellow billed Cuckoo obtained near Bray, Presently part of the Bird collection University College Museum Cork	1832
Flora-Fauna				A Red footed Falcon shot in Co Wicklow "List of Birds of Ireland" by National Museum	1832
Health				Cholera epidemic in Ireland and parts of Co. Wicklow	1832
Blake. Edward	Sun	13	10	Edward Blake born 1833, son of William Hume Blake, Edward an expert on the Canadian Constitution	1833
Health			11	Outbreak of Cholera in Bray 25 persons die	1833
O'Keeffe. John				John O'Keeffe playwright died see 1796	1833
Parish Records				Earliest Record of Births in Church of Ireland Parish Shillelagh	1833
Kemmis. William				William Gilbert Kemmis appointed sheriff of County Wicklow	1833
Manor Kilbride				St. John the Baptist Church at Cloughleagh, Manor Kilbride built	1833
Parish Records				Earliest Record of Marriage in Church of Ireland Parish Shillelagh	1833
Parish Records				Earliest Record of Deaths in Church of Ireland Parish Shillelagh	1833

A–Z Reference	Day	Date	Month	Year	DATA
Kyan. John Howard				1833	John Joward Kyan patented a ship propulsion system using jet of water ejected at the stern of a ship
Killincarrig				1833	Coins of William III era discovered at Killincarrig
Ballygahan Mine				1833	The Ballyghan mine, belonging to Viscount Powerscourt was re-commenced by the Royal Irish Mining Company
Maps				1833	The first edition of six inch Ordnance Survey Maps 1833-1846
Brabazon Family	Thu	23	01	1834	Mary Aikenhead opened St.Vincents Hospital for Sick Poor at 56 St. Stephens Green, the former home of the Brabazon Family
Wicklow. County			04	1834	William Hampton became the first county surveyor to County Wicklow
Grattan Mary Anne	Tue	09	09	1834	Mary Anne Grattan the daughter of Henry Grattan married Thomas 8th Earl of Carnwath
Newspapers	Sat	20	12	1834	The Leinster Independent and Carlow, Kildare, Wicklow, Kilkenny, King's and Queens Counties General, first edition
Marsden. William				1834	William Marsden collection of 3447 oriental coins was presented to the British Museum
Calary Church				1834	Calary Church, Roundwood built
Inglis. Henry D				1834	Henry D Inglis wrote "A journey through Ireland during the Spring, Summer and Autumn of 1834"
Railways				1834	The Railway line between Dublin and Kingstown (Dun Laoghaire) was opened
Hollybrook House				1834	Hollybrook House, Kilmacanouge, Bray built. The family seat of Hodson Family
Curtlestown				1834	A National school was established in Curtlestown, Enniskerry
Loreto Convent Bray				1834	The Conservatory erected by the Putland family at San Souci now Loreto Convent Bray
Kilbride				1834	A saving's bank established at Kilbride near Redcross Co. Wicklow
Hodson. Sir. G.F				1834	Sir George Frederick Hodson appointed sheriff of County Wicklow
Parish Schools				1834	There were 9 Poor or Charity Schools in the area that included Bray, Enniskerry, Curtlestown, and Kilmacanouge
Crampton.Sir J.F.T.				1834	Sir John Fiennes Twisleton Crampton appointed ambassador to Brussels, Beligum 1834-1839
Luganure Mine				1834	A new water wheel installed at Luganure Mine, Glendalough
Carnew				1834	Dispensary established in Carnew
Wicklow Town				1834	County Infirmary and Fever Hospital erected in Wicklow Town
The school house				1834	The school at Knockanarrigan, Donard, Co. Wicklow built
Derralossary Church				1834	Derralossary Church built
Elections–Polling Day	Mon	19	01	1835	James Grattan and Col. Ralph Howard elected M.P's. for Wicklow at the General Election, Number of electors 1566
Ireland	Mon	18	03	1835	Thomas Drummond Under Secretary for Ireland 1835 - 1840

Wicklow Coastguard	Sat	11	04	1835	Lieutenant T.D.J Dabine left Bray Coastguard Station for an appointed to Kingstown (Dun Laoghaire) Coastguard Station
Parnell. Charles S	Tue	31	05	1835	John Henry Parnell (father of Charles S. Parnell) married Delia Stewart at Grace Church, New York
Bayly, Edward S	Sat	20	06	1835	Edward Symes Bayly of Ballyarthurh House, Co. Wicklow married Catherine FitzGerald daughter of the Knight of Kerry
Act	Mon	31	08	1835	Peace Preservation (Ireland) Act
Leeson	Sun	09	10	1835	Edward Nugent Leeson of Russborough House, Blessington. 6th Earl of Milltown born
Pub/Tavern				1835	Murphy's Hotel Tinahealy established
Devil's Glen				1835	A walkway was laid out in the Devil's Glen, Ashford by some local landlords
O'Neill. Henry				1835	Fourteen Views in Co. Wicklow by Henry O'Neill
Putland				1835	Workmen while building a gate pillar for George Putland find roman remains near Bray Seafront
Books				1835	"Guide to County of Wicklow" New Edition. Curry published in Dublin in 1835
Skeletons				1835	Skeletons and Roman Coins found near Bray Seafront.
Cookson. Catherine				1835	Catherine Teresa Cookson botanical illustrator published "Flowers Drawn and Painted after Nature, in India" published in London 1835
Books				1835	St. Kevin's Bed. A descriptive poem of various scenery in County Wicklow by Major Cosby. Published in Dublin 1835
Inglis. Henry D				1835	Henry D.Inglis died
Books				1835	Kevin's Bed. the legendary tales of St. Kevin by Major Cosby
Dunlavin				1835	Market House erected in Dunlavin
Beresford. William				1835	William Beresford appointed sheriff of County Wicklow
Blake. Samuel H.				1835	Samuel Hume Blake born, son of William Hume Blake, Samuel a Toronto Judge
Powerscourt	Mon	25	01	1836	Richard 6th Viscount Powerscourt married Lady Elizabeth Frances Charlotte Jocelyn
Halpin.Robert Charles	Tue	16	02	1836	Captain Robert Charles Halpin born in Wicklow Town
Parnell. William	Wed	09	03	1836	Charles S Parnell brother William born 09/03/1836 but died within a few weeks of birth
Grattan Harriet	Wed	06	04	1836	Harriet Grattan the daughter of Henry Grattan married Rev Richard W. Wake of Courteenhall, Northamptonshire
Putland	Thu	16	06	1836	Charles Putland Jnr married Charlotte Christian daughter of Capt. Christian R.N, In St Peter's Church Dublin
Manor Kilbride	Sun	26	06	1836	St.John the Baptist Church at Cloughleagh, Manor Kilbride. First consecrated
Act	Sat	20	08	1836	The Municipal Corporation (Ireland) Act, 1836
Smith. Sir W.C.	Sun	21	08	1836	Sir William–Cusack Smith died
Marsden. William	Thu	06	10	1836	William Marsden died at his home Aldenham, Hertfordshire, England
Powerscourt	Thu	13	10	1836	Mervyn 7th Viscount Powerscourt born

A–Z Reference	Day	Date	Month	Year	DATA
Lighthouse	Wed	19	10	1836	The Lighthouse on Wicklow Head struck by lighting, and fire destroyed the interior of the building
Cochrane. Henry	Wed	21	12	1836	Henry Cochrane, of Woodbrook, Bray born
				1836	St. Matthew's (COI) Church Newtownmountkennedy built
Population				1836	Poor Inquiry Commission set up following the 1836 census of Population
Blessington. Countess				1836	A portrait of Lady Blessington appeared in Revue de Paris Vol. 28 Page 137, in 1836
Teachers Salary				1836	The Average salary of Teachers was £16.13s.7d per annum
Ships/Yachts				1836	The vessel "Countess of Mansfield" shipwrecked of the Wicklow Coast
Boewn. Edward				1836	Edward Bowen was executed in Wicklow for the murder of his father, Thomas Bowen of Ashford
Health				1836	Mr Lenny replaced Dr. Heffernan as Superintendent of Bray's Dispensary
Parish Records				1836	Earliest Record of Deaths in Church of Ireland Parish Moyne
Parnell. John				1836	John Parnell appointed sheriff of County Wicklow
Glendalough School				1836	The Rev George O'Connor P.P. of Glendalough submitted an application to build a national school at Glendalough.
Parish Records				1836	Earliest Record of Births in Presbyterian Parish Bray
Population Bray				1836	Population of Bray, 3,500 *not a census year*
Railways				1836	Royal Commission to examine Irish Railways called "Drummond Commission on Railways and Communications in Ireland"
Leeson	Sun	22	01	1837	Henry Leeson of Russborough House, Blessington. 7th Earl of Milltown born
Fitzwilliam. 4th Earl	Wed	08	02	1837	William Fitzwilliam 4th Earl Fitzwilliam died and was succeeded by his son Charles Fitzwilliam
Smythe. William			02	1837	William Barlow Smythe married Lady Emily Monck of Enniskerry
Parnell. Delia			05	1837	Delia Parnell a sister of Charles S. Parnell born
Elections–Polling Day	Fri	11	08	1837	James Grattan, Ralph Howard, elected M.P's. for Wicklow at the General Election, Number of electors 1679
Hill.Arthur–4th	Wed	23	08	1837	Arthur Hill 4th Marquis of Downshire married Caroline Stapleton
Wicklow Street	Wed	18	10	1837	Part of Exchequer Street, Dublin was renamed Wicklow Street
Smythe. Emily	Wed	08	11	1837	Emily Smythe born to William Smythe and Lady Emily Monck
Monck. Emily	Wed	22	11	1837	Emily Smythe nee Monck died
Brabazon. William	Thu	23	11	1837	William Brabazon the 11th Earl of Meath married Harriot Brooke
Map				1837	Lewis Map of County Dublin
Survey				1837	Lewis Topographical Dictionary of Ireland

Police/Garda				1837	Police station built for the R.I.C near the Royal Hotel, Bray
Bray Hunt				1837	Sir John Ripton Master of Bray Hunt
Baltinglass Workhouse				1837	The building of Baltinglass Workhouse begun, The Building Cost £5,750 Fittings £1,050
Imports/Exports				1837	Wicklow Town Port: Exports 16,000 tons value £85,000- Imports 8,000 tons value £15,000
Guinness. R. W.				1837	Rev Robert Wyndham Guinness, Rector of Rathdrum. Co. Wicklow was born
Rathdrum				1837	St Saviours Church Rathdrum rebuilt
Peacock. Joseph				1837	Joseph Peacock (artists) died
Loughlinstown				1837	The building of Rathdown Workhouse begun, The Building Cost £6,500 Fittings £1,100
Imports/Exports				1837	Arklow Port: Exports 900 tons value £3,500- Imports 4,000 tons value £6,500
Bayly. Edward S				1837	Edward Symes Bayly appointed sheriff of County Wicklow
St. Peters. Bray				1837	St. Peter's Church Little Bray built to replace a church at Crinken
Railways				1837	A committee was formed to report on the advantages of running a railway line from Bray to Dublin
Rathdrum Workhouse				1837	The building of Rathdrum Workhouse begun, The Building Cost £6,600 Fittings £1,200
Avoca				1837	The Copper and Lead mines at Avoca produced 12,500 tons of ore with a value of £35,000
Mining				1837	The lead mines at Glendalough produced 2,500 tons of ore with a value of £38,000
Shillelagh Workhouse				1837	The building of Shillelagh Workhouse begun, The Building Cost £5,300 Fittings £1,000
Woodburn. William	Sat	14	04	1838	William Woodburn born in County Wicklow
Act	Tue	31	07	1838	Poor Law Act – 130 Poor Law Districts were established in Ireland
Act	Tue	14	08	1838	Railways (Conveyance of Mails) Act
Fitzwilliam. 6th Earl	Mon	10	09	1838	William Fitzwilliam 6th Earl Fitzwilliam married Lady Frances Douglas
Ships/Yachts	Tue	27	11	1838	The vessel "Le Nouveau Destin" shipwrecked of the Wicklow Coast, Report in Freeman's Journal 01/12/1838
La Touche				1838	Peter David La Touche appointed sheriff of County Wicklow
Brookey's Bridge				1838	The architect of Brookey's Bridge was William Rourk
Population				1838	Population of Rathdrum 1,054
Cookson. Geroge James				1838	George James Cookson died
Brookey's Bridge				1838	A bridge near Derrybawn House bears the inscription Erected by William Brokey at his own expense on changing the road
Cullen. Luke				1838	98145.451
98145.451				1838	Earliest Record of Births in Church of Ireland Parish Moyne
Curry, Eugene				1838	Eugene Curry survey of Antiquities of County Wicklow

A–Z Reference	Day	Date	Month	Year	DATA
Maps				1838	Bray Head, Greystones and Kilcoole, NewtownMount Kennedy surveyed by Ordnance Survey 6inches to Mile Map
Barton.T.J.				1838	Glendalough House, Annamoe, Co. Wicklow was bought by T.J. Barton from Hugo family
Parnell. Hayes				1838	Hayes Parnell a brother Charles S Parnell born
Flora-Fauna				1838	Honey Buzzard was sited at Killruddery Estate –The home of the Earl of Meath
Weather	Sun	06	01	1839	The night of the "Big Wind", Strong winds sweep over Ireland causing widespread devastation
Wicklow Coastguard	Thu	21	02	1839	Wicklow Coastguard Capt.. Jones awarded the RNLI Silver medal for bravery. Saving Six crew from Le Nouveau Destin on 27/11/1837
Avoca			05	1839	In five weeks 2,300 tons of ore was extracted at the Crone bane Mines, near Avoca
Rathdown Union	Fri	09	08	1839	The Rathdown Union was formally established
Tottenham. Charles	Wed	11	09	1839	Isabella Cornwallis daughter of 3rd Viscount Hawarden married Lieut. Col. Charles Tottenham of Woodstock House, Kilcoole
Tottenham. Charles J.	Wed	11	09	1839	Charles John Tottenham of Woodstock House, Kilcoole married Isabella Cornwallis
Wicklow. Earl of	Tue	05	11	1839	Charles Francis Arnold 5th Earl of Wicklow born
Baltinglass	Thu	21	11	1839	The Poor Law Union of Baltinglass established
Sugarloaf Common	Tue	03	12	1839	The partition deed of Sugarloaf Common signed by the Earl of Rathdowne, Viscount Powerscourt and Sir George Hodson
Grattan. Henry				1839	Memoirs of the life and times of the Rt. Hon Henry Grattan 5 vols (1839-46) by Henry Grattan Jnr.
Arklow School				1839	A Boy's National School opened on the Coolgraney Road, Arklow
Hodson				1839	Hartley Hodson of Old Connaught, Bray died
Parish Records				1839	Earliest Record of Births in Church of Ireland Parish Ballinaclash, Rathdrum
Delgany, School				1839	School house built at Delgany on lands donated by Peter La Touche
de Robeck. Bart.J.M.H				1839	John M.H. Baron de Robeck appointed sheriff of County Wicklow
Newrath Bridge				1839	A Bridge (Newrath) constructed over the River Vartry on the coast road near Rathnew.
Murphy.James				1839	James Murphy born in Dublin later became a teacher in Bray
Police/Garda				1839	Anthony Thomas Lefroy Chief Constable of the Irish Constabulary in Rathdrum
Saurin. William				1839	William Saurin died
Ships/Yachts				1839	The vessel "Avon" shipwrecked of the Wicklow Coast
Ships/Yachts				1839	The steamer "St. Patrick" shipwrecked of the Wicklow Coast
Crampton. Sir Philip				1839	Sir Philip Crampton knighted by Queen Victoria
Crampton.Sir J.F.T.				1839	Sir John Fiennes Twisleton Crampton appointed ambassador to Vienna, Austria 1839-1844

Police/Garda				1839	Anthony Thomas Lefroy appointed the first Chief Constable of Gloucestershire. He held the post between 1839 -1865
Lefroy. Anthony Thomas				1839	Anthony Thomas Lefoy was the first appointment of a Chief Constable to a county constabulary in England
Thompson. Dr C.				1839	Dr. Christopher Thompson qualified as a medical doctor from Trinity College, His address was 26 Upper Mount Street, Dublin
Crampton. Sir J.F.T.				1839	A drawing of Lord Enniskillen playing a Harp by John Crampton
Newspapers	Sat	18	04	1840	The Leinster Independent and Carlow, Kildare, Wicklow, Kilkenny, King's and Queens Counties General, last edition
Police/Garda			04	1840	John Hayes Hatton was appointed the first Chief Constable East Suffolk Constabulary
Maps			05	1840	County Wicklow 6 inch Map published
Lawrence. William	Sun	05	07	1840	William Mervin Lawrence (photographer) born
Act	Mon	10	08	1840	The Municipal Corporation (Ireland) Act
Laragh School			circa	1840	Laragh school built
			circa	1840	St. Michael's Church, Newtownmountkennedy built.
Trudder Lodge			's	1840	Trudder Lodge House near Newcastle built
Avoca			's	1840	Matthaew Johnston establishes a Copper Mine at Avoca, over 1,000 men employed
Land Use				1840	56% of the 782 sq miles of County Wicklow used for arable farming
Barton. T.J.				1840	Thomas Johnston Barton appointed sheriff of County Wicklow
Police/Garda				1840	Constabulary Barracks in Ashford established
Wicklow Ale				1840	List of Brewers in Ireland. Mr Colworthy Dobbin's Wicklow Spiced Ale. Strenght 4.9%
Woodstock House				1840	Woodstock House remodelled by Rt. Rev. Lord Robert Tottenham, Bishop of Clogher
Manifold. Francis				1840	Francis Manifold one of the founders of the Irish Christian Brothers, died. He was born in Arklow
Cricken Church				1840	St Jame's Church Crinken, built
O'Connell. Daniel				1840	Daniel O'Connell launched a campaign for Repeal of the Union with Britain
Woodbrook House				1840	Woodbrook House, Bray built for Cochrane family
Population County	Sun	06	06	1841	Population of County Wicklow 126,143 persons. 63,489 Males 62,654 Females
Population Wicklow (t)	Sun	06	06	1841	Population of Wicklow Town 2,794 or 2.21% of County Population
Population Arklow	Sun	06	06	1841	Population of Arklow Urban 3,254 or 2.58% of County Population
Population Bray	Sun	06	06	1841	Population of Bray 3,169 or 2.51% of County Population
Arklow Barony	Sun	06	06	1841	The Population of the Arklow Barony 25,263
Shillelagh Barony	Sun	06	06	1841	The Population of the Shillelagh Barony 14,057

A–Z Reference	Day	Date	Month	Year	DATA
Population Enniskerry	Sun	06	06	1841	Population of Enniskerry urban 448 or 0.36% of County Population
Population Greystones	Sun	06	06	1841	Population of Greystones & Delgany 380 or 0.30% of County Population
Talbotstown Upr Barony	Sun	06	06	1841	The Population of the Talbotstown Upper Barony 17,825
Talbotstown Lwr Barony	Sun	06	06	1841	The Population of the Talbotstown Lower Barony 15,444
Rathdown Barony	Sun	06	06	1841	The Population of the Rathdown Barony 11,423
Newcastle Barony	Sun	06	06	1841	The Population of the Newcastle Barony 16,444
Ballinacor Nth. Barony	Sun	06	06	1841	The Population of the Ballinacor North Barony 10,196
Ballinacor Sth. Barony	Sun	06	06	1841	The Population of the Ballinacor South Barony 15,491
Elections–Polling Day	Sat	17	07	1841	Ralph Howard, William Acton elected M.P's. for Wicklow at the General Election, Number of electors 1503
Brabazon. Reginald	Sat	31	07	1841	Reginald Brabazon the 12th Earl of Meath born
Rathdown Union	Tue	12	10	1841	The first admission to the Rathdown Union facility at Loughlinstown now Loughlinstown Hospital
Loughlinstown	Tue	12	10	1841	The Rathdown Union Workhouse at Loughlinstown opened
Baltinglass Workhouse	Thu	28	10	1841	The First admission to the Baltinglass Workhouse
French. Robert	Thu	11	11	1841	Robert French born, in Dublin (see Lawrence)
Putland			11	1841	George Putland Jnr died and his property passed to his brother Charles
Wicklow Gaol				1841	Wicklow Gaol housed 350 inmates
Parnell. Emily				1841	Emily Parnell a sister of Charles S. Parnell born
Court House. Bray				1841	Court House now Bray Tourist Office and Heritage Crentre, built
Synge. John				1841	John Synge appointed sheriff of County Wicklow
Irish Penny Magazine				1841	Irish Penny Magazine described Enniskerry as. "Enniskerry is famed for its roses, which can be smelt a long way off"
Books				1841	The Fate of Cathleen. A Wicklow story published in London
Parish Records				1841	Earliest Record of Marriage in Church of Ireland Parish Moyne
Population of Brockagh				1841	The estimated population of the Electoral District of Brockagh in 1841 was 1,563 persons
Powerscourt				1841	Picture of "Powerscourt Waterfall" engraved by J.T.Willmore
Books				1841	Ireland, It's Scenery and Character by T Creswick
Gray. Sir John				1841	John Gray became editor of the Freeman's Journal
Carnew				1841	Protestant school constructed in Carnew
Shillelagh Workhouse	Fri	18	02	1842	The First admission to the Shillelagh Workhouse

Keyword	Day			Year	Description
Wingfield. Lewis S.	Fri	25	02	1842	Lewis Strange Wingfield (artist and writer), son of the 6th Viscount Powerscourt born in London
Burnaby. F.G.	Thu	03	03	1842	Frederick Gustavus Burnaby born at Sombery Hall, Leicestershire
Rathdrum Workhouse	Tue	08	03	1842	The First admission to the Rathdrum Workhouse
Wicklow. Earl of	Tue	26	04	1842	Cecil 6th Earl of Wicklow born
Parnell. Sir H.B.	Wed	08	06	1842	Sir Henry Brooke Parnell died
Police/Garda			12	1842	John Hayes Hatton was appointed the first Chief Constable of the Staffordshire Police Force
Mason. G.H. Monck				1842	Captain. G.H. Monck Mason joined the Bengal Army
Books				1842	Co Wicklow featured in William Makepeace Thackeray book "The Irish Sketch Book 1842"
Books				1842	"Guide to County Wicklow" by James Frazer. Published in Dublin 1842 –1845
Tynte. Joseph P.				1842	Joseph Pratt Tynte appointed sheriff of County Wicklow
Cemetery St. Peter's				1842	New Cemetery opened at St.Peters Little Bray.
Darley. Cecil W.				1842	Cecil West Darley born at Wingfield, Bray. County Wicklow
Parish Records				1842	Earliest Record of Deaths in Church of Ireland Parish Ballinclash, Rathdrum
Military Road				1842	The Wicklow Grand Jury took over the maintenance of the Military Road in Wicklow
Kish Lighthouse				1842	The first attempt to erect a lighthouse on the Kish Bank, destroyed in winter storms
Putland				1842	Constance Putland nee Massy died
Wicklow Harbour				1842	Wicklow Harbour Act
Books				1842	Guide to the County of Wicklow by James Fraser
Marine House				1842	The Marine House, Wicklow Town built, now the Wicklow Bay Hostel
Synge. Frances Mary				1842	Frances Mary Synge born at Glanmore Castle, Co. Wicklow
Smythe. Emily				1842	Emily Smythe died
Hime. Sir Albert H.				1842	Albert Henry Hime born at Kilcoole, Co. Wicklow
Parnell. J.H.				1842	John Howard Parnell a brother of Charles S Parnell born
Matthew. Fr				1842	The Temperance Apostle Fr. Matthew paid a visit to Glendalough
Enniskerry	Fri	17	03	1843	The Fountain and Town Clock Enniskerry was erected by Lord Powerscourt to mark the 100 anniversary of Powerscourt House
Haskins. James	Sat	18	03	1843	James Haskins the last man to be executed at Wicklow Gaol
Haskins. James	Sat	18	03	1843	James Haskins was executed for the murder of John Pugh
Anderson. James Arthur	Mon	31	07	1843	James Arthur Anderson born at Baltinglass, Co. Wicklow. Later Chief engineer with the Bengal Railway Company
Repeal Meeting	Sun	06	08	1843	A Repeal Meeting held in Baltinglass Co. Wicklow estimated attendance 150,000

A–Z Reference	Day	Date	Month	Year	DATA
Powerscourt			10	1843	The terraces at Powerscourt House, Enniskerry were commenced by Richard 6th Viscount.
Pobje. Bessie	Sat	14	11	1843	Bessie Pobje the daughter of Herny Pobje Jnr and Jane Ivy born
Monck	Wed	22	11	1843	Frances Monck nee La Poer Trench died
Mackintosh. C.H.				1843	Charles Henry Mackintosh wrote "The Peace of God"
Mackintosh. C. Herbert				1843	Charles Herbert Mackintosh was born at London, (Ontario) Canada, the son of Captain William Mackintosh of Wicklow
Hodson. Richard				1843	Richard Hodson appointed sheriff of County Wicklow
New York				1843	In 1843 a town near New York called Eight Mile Tree changed its name to that of Avoca
Wicklow Infanticides				1843	The number of Infanticides in County Wicklow was 4
Wicklow Homicides				1843	The total number of Homicides, including Manslaughter and Murders in County Wicklow , 2
Tinahely				1843	Tinahely Courthouse built
Monck				1843	Bridget Monck nee Willington died
National Archives				1843	OPW 5HC/6/0401 Proposed road at Roundwood & Blessington, Engineer Brassington & Gale
Parish Records				1843	Earliest Record of Marriage in Church of Ireland Parish Ballinclash, Rathdrum
Ships/Yachts				1843	The vessel "Peggy & Jane" shipwrecked of the Wicklow Coast
Ships/Yachts	Tue	16	04	1844	The vessel "Penryn" shipwrecked of the Wicklow Coast
Monck	Tue	23	07	1844	Charles Stanley Monck, 4th Viscount married his cousin Elizabeth Monck daughter of 2nd Viscount Monck
Proby. Elizabeth	Wed	07	08	1844	Lady Elizabeth Proby the 2nd dau. of 3rd Earl of Carysfort married James Hamilton 1st Duke of Abercorn
Powerscourt	Sun	11	08	1844	Richard 6th Viscount Powerscourt died and was succeeded by his son Mervyn 7th Viscount
Post Office	Sat	21	09	1844	Bray Post Office allocated serial number 72 official sorting code
St.Patrick's. Wicklow	Sun	13	10	1844	The Catholic Church St. Patrick's in Wicklow Town, dedicated by Archbishop Murray of Dublin
Powerscourt	Wed	04	12	1844	Lady Julia Coke born
Hill.Arthur-5th	Tue	24	12	1844	Arthur Hill 5th Marquis of Downshire born
Ships/Yachts				1844	The vessel "Georgia" shipwrecked of the Wicklow Coast
Wicklow Homicides				1844	The total number of Homicides , including Manslaughter and Murders in County Wicklow , 0
Books				1844	"Illustrated Handbook of the County Wicklow" by Irwin O'Malley. Published in London in 1844
Carmelite Convent				1844	A Carmelite Convent established in Delgany
Flora–Fauna				1844	A Goshawk (Accipiter gentilis) was shot by the gamekeeper at Killruddery Co. Wicklow (Ref: List of Irish Birds 1961 edition)

Synge. Francis				1844	Francis Synge appointed sheriff of County Wicklow
Dunstone Hall				1844	Buckingham House now Dunstone Hall near Torquay, Devon built for the Earl of Wicklow
Books				1844	The illustrated Hand book of the County Wicklow by George O'Malley Irwin
Crampton. Sir J.F.T.				1844	Sir John Fiennes Twisleton Crampton appointed ambassador to Berne, Switzerland 1844-1845
Sweetman. James				1844	James Sweetman born. M.P. for East Wicklow 1892-1895. Chairman of Meath County Council 1902-1908
Wicklow Infanticides				1844	The number of Infanticides in County Wicklow was 1
Tottenham. C.R.W	Fri	21	02	1845	Charles Robert Worsley Tottenham born at Woodstock House, Kilcoole
Hill. Arthur-3rd	Sat	12	04	1845	Arthur Hill 3rd Marquis of Downshire died and was succeeded by his son Arthur
Armstrong. G.F.S	Mon	05	05	1845	George F.S. Armstrong born in County Down
Bayly. Richard	Fri	20	06	1845	Richard Bayly son of Edward and Catherine Bayly was born
Pobje. Mary	Thu	04	09	1845	Mary Pobje nee Towning died at Bray aged 73 years
Delgany, School	Wed	15	10	1845	National School opened at Delgany
Nairne. Carolina	Mon	27	10	1845	Baroness Carolina Nairne died. Wrote the song "A hundred pipers", poems "Charlie is my Darling" and "The Land of the Leal"
Schoolhouse				1845	The schoolhouse at Rathmeigue, near Knockananna. County Wicklow. Built
Parnell. Sophia				1845	Sophia Parnell a sister of Charles S. Parnell born
Crampton. Sir J.F.T.				1845	Sir John Fiennes Twisleton Crampton appointed ambassador to Washington 1845-1856
Wicklow Infanticides				1845	The number of Infanticides in County Wicklow was 6
La Touche				1845	Colonel Robert La Touche died
Flora-Fauna				1845	Belted Kingfisher (Ceryle alcyon) was shot at Lough Dan. Co. Wicklow (Ref; List of Birds of Ireland 1961 edition)
Matthew. Fr				1845	The Temperance Apostle Fr. Matthew paid a visit to Glendalough
Hume. William. W.F				1845	William Wentworth Fitzwilliam Hume appointed sheriff of County Wicklow
Wicklow Homicides				1845	The total number of Homicides , including Manslaughter and Murders in County Wicklow , 1
Health				1845	Great Famine 1845-1847
Inquiry				1845	Devon Commission-inquiry into the state of the law and practice in respect to the Occupation of land in Ireland
National Archives 1846	Wed	28	01	1846	RLF3/1/417 Letter from J.M. Barry Wicklow to Relief Commission re advice on the course of action if potato crop failure
Act	Thu	05	03	1846	Public Works (Ireland) (No 1) Act
National Archives 1846	Sat	21	03	1846	RLF3/1/878 Rev M Morgan of Dunlavin requesting immediate introduction of Indian Corn
National Archives 1846	Wed	25	03	1846	RLF3/1/954 G Hodson of Bray requested copies of instructions for the formation of relief committees

A–Z Reference	Day	Date	Month	Year	DATA
National Archives 1846	Mon	30	03	1846	RLF3/1/1080 J.M. Barry Wicklow requesting information re price and distribution of meal.
National Archives 1846	Wed	08	04	1846	RLF3/1/1307 Rev Daly of Kilbride regarding distress within his parish and price of Indian Meal.
National Archives 1846	Sat	11	04	1846	RLF3/1/1417 G. Hodson of Bray regarding the formation of relief committee for the Bray District.
National Archives 1846	Sat	11	04	1846	RLF3/1/1399 A. Jones of Delgany requesting Public Works to be under taken in the barony of Newcastle
National Archives 1846	Thu	16	04	1846	RLF3/1/1516 Rev J. Cumine of Preban applying to purchase Indian Corn at first cost for resale to the poor
National Archives 1846	Fri	17	04	1846	RLF3/1/1541 T.De Renzy of Carnew listing magistrates for relief districts of Shillelagh and Ballinacor South
National Archives 1846	Sat	18	04	1846	RLF3/1/1577 R. Chaloner of Tinahely seeking information on the procedure for establishing relief districts
National Archives 1846	Sun	26	04	1846	RLF3/1/1812 E. Bayly of Rathdrum Lists the relief committee for Arklow and requested provision of Indian meal
National Archives 1846	Mon	27	04	1846	RLF3/1/1860 R. Bates of Tinahely.Shillelagh relief district should look after Poor Law Union area, and not the Barony of Shillelagh
Powerscourt	Thu	30	04	1846	The 6th Lord Powerscourt died on 11/08/1844 and His wife Lady Elizabeth Married the 4th Marquis of Londonderry on 30/04/1846
National Archives 1846	Mon	01	06	1846	RLF3/1/2756 R. Chaloner seeking donation to match £600 spent by Lord Fitzwilliam of Coolatin on seed potatoes
National Archives 1846	Tue	02	06	1846	RLF3/1/2771 Capt. W. Neame That revenue cutters were available to carry corn to Courtown, Wicklow, Wexford, and Gorey
Laragh Church	Wed	03	06	1846	Fr Matthew the Temperance Priest blessed the foundation stone of Laragh Church
Glendalough	Wed	03	06	1846	The foundation stone laid for St. Kevin's Church Glendalough designed by James Joseph McCarthy(1817–1882)
National Archives 1846	Thu	04	06	1846	RLF3/1/3070 The Barony of Talbotstown Lower seeks £356 for Public Works
National Archives 1846	Wed	10	06	1846	RLF3/1/3074 J.C. Walker of OPW that there was great distress in Arklow and immediate public works should be undertaken
National Archives 1846	Thu	11	06	1846	RLF3/1/3126 Rev Brownrigg, Arklow applying for 3 tons Oatmeal and 10 tons Indian Meal to be stored in the Barracks Arklow
National Archives 1846	Sat	13	06	1846	RLF3/1/3226 Perrin & Nolan corn millers of Wicklow threatening to cease importing corn if price levels drop
National Archives 1846	Mon	15	06	1846	RLF3/1/3268 Rev Brownrigg requested 20 tons Indian Meal and 5 tons of oatmeal to replenish stocks requested 11/06/1846
National Archives 1846	Fri	19	06	1846	RLF3/1/3245 Rev Brownrigg requested 20 tons of Indian Meal and 5 tons of Oatmeal to be sent to Arklow by Revenue Cutter
Railways	Wed	24	06	1846	An Act was obtained to construct a railway line from Bray through Dundrum to Dublin
Parnell. Charles S	Sat	27	06	1846	Charles Stewart Parnell born
National Archives 1846	Sun	05	07	1846	RLF3/1/4011 R. Stephens reported to the Central Board of Health on his inspection of Wicklow Fever Hospital
National Archives 1846	Tue	21	07	1846	RLF3/1/4595 J.C. Walker enquiring about the extent of potato failure in Rathdown Barony and the town land of Templecarrig

Category	Day	Date	Month	Year	Description
National Archives 1846	Thu	23	07	1846	RLF3/1/4646 G.Hodson of Bray describing his efforts to relieve the local poor and fifty day labourers at Templecarrig
National Archives 1846	Wed	29	07	1846	RLF3/1/4870 J.C. Walker The OPW had approved works for the Parish of Delgany
National Archives 1846	Sat	01	08	1846	RLF3/1/5007 W.D. Browne describes the work by the Bray Relief Committee with donations of £180 and requests £80 grant
National Archives 1846	Thu	06	08	1846	RLF3/1/5127 A.S. Bride of Ashford describes an increase in fever in the area and failure of potato crop and a request a grant
Railways				1846	An act was obtained to extend the Dublin & Kingstown Line to Bray Bridge
Wicklow Homicides				1846	The total number of Homicides, including Manslaughter and Murders in County Wicklow , 1
Wicklow Infanticides				1846	The number of Infanticides in County Wicklow was 3
Darley. George				1846	George Darley died
Slater's Directory				1846	Slater's Directory of Arklow, Baltinglass, Blessington, Bray, Newtown, Delgany, Rathdrum and Wicklow
O'Kelly Edward Peter				1846	Edward P. O'Kelly M.P. born
Dock Terrace				1846	A storm destroyed some cottages at Dock Terrace Bray.
Dublin Gas Company				1846	The Dublin Consumers Gas Co. amalgamates with the Alliance Gas Co. and is renamed The Alliance & Dublin Consumers Gas Co.
Wicklow. County				1846	James Boyd succeeded William Hampton as County Surveyor
Delgany, School				1846	A national school opened at the Carmelite Monastery, Delgany
Tottenham. Charles				1846	Charles Tottenham appointed sheriff of County Wicklow
Railways				1846	The Dublin, Dundrum and Rathfarnham Railway founded
Railways				1846	The Waterford, Wexford, Wicklow and Dublin project was launched
Pobje. Charles				1846	Charles F. Pobje died in New South Wales
Ships/Yachts				1846	The vessel "Glenalvon" shipwrecked of the Wicklow Coast
Wicklow. County				1846	John McMahon became the clerk to County Wicklow
Ships/Yachts				1846	The vessel "Amicitea" shipwrecked of the Wicklow Coast
Act	Tue	19	01	1847	Post Office (Duties) Act
Employment			01	1847	2,383 men employed on Public Works in Co. Wicklow, 170 of the men were from Bray
Act	Thu	18	03	1847	The Poor Relief (Ireland) Act
Hart, Henry C.	Thu	29	07	1847	Henry Chichester Hart born, Rahney Co. Dublin see Lugnaquilla Walk
Elections-Polling Day	Sat	07	08	1847	William Acton and Viscount Milton (William T.S.W. Fitzwilliam) elected M.P's. for Wicklow at the General Election
Grattan. Rt.Hon.James	Sat	07	08	1847	Rt. Hon. James Grattan of Tinnehinch, Enniskerry married Laura Maria Tollemache
Railways	Wed	25	08	1847	The sod cutting ceremony for the railway line around Bray Head

A–Z Reference	Day	Date	Month	Year	DATA
Railways	Mon	29	08	1847	Work began on laying the railway tracks around Bray Head, 500 men undertook the work.
Railways	Sat	02	10	1847	A transfer deed to the Waterford, Wexford, Wicklow and Dublin Line to construct a railway line to Bray Bridge
Halpin.James	Sun	10	10	1847	James Halpin father of Robert Charles Halpin died
Act	Mon	20	12	1847	Crime & Outrage (Ireland) Act
Wicklow Infanticides				1847	The number of Infanticides in County Wicklow was 2
National Archives				1847	OPW,5HC/6/0112 Proposed Bridge at Bray by James Boyle, Civil Engineer
Rathdangan				1847	A St Mary's Church built at Killamote, Rathdangan, Co. Wicklow
Wade. Robert C				1847	Robert Craven Wade appointed sheriff of County Wicklow
Arklow				1847	5,000 troops deployed to combat an upsurge in crime, as landlords seek rent from penniless tenants. ref Crime & Outrage Act
Collins.William				1847	William Collins born 1788 died 1847
Synge				1847	Rev Robert Traill of Schull, Co.Cork died, his daughter Kathleen married John Hatch Synge
Putland				1847	Charlotte Putland nee Christian died
Murphy.James				1847	Rev. James Murphy Parish Priest of Tomacork, Carnew 1847–1872
Wicklow Homicides				1847	The total number of Homicides, including Manslaughter and Murders in County Wicklow , 0
Parnell. Fanny	Mon	04	09	1848	Fanny Parnell sister of C.S. Parnell born as per Parish records in Rathdrum
Monck	Wed	20	09	1848	Henry Stanley Monck, 2nd Viscount and Earl of Rathdowne died and was succeeded by his brother Charles Joseph Monck
Ships/Yachts	Fri	22	12	1848	The vessel "Enterprise" shipwrecked off the Wicklow Coast
Wicklow Gaol				1848	Wicklow Gaol housed 780 inmates in 77 cells, 6 day rooms, 4 exercise yards, 1 kitchen and some administration rooms
Killruddery				1848	Lord Brabazon appointed sheriff of County Wicklow
Humphreys. C.F.				1848	Cecil Frances Alexander nee Humphreys published "Hymns for Little Children and Verses for Holy Season"
Parish Records				1848	Earliest Record of Deaths in Church of Ireland Parish Ballintemple, Arklow
Railways				1848	The Waterford, Wexford, Wicklow and Dublin Railway Co changed its name to Dublin and Wicklow (sanctioned in 1851)
Books				1848	"Glendalough – Glendalough or the Seven Churches" poem by an Ex-Moderator T.C.D. Published in Dublin in 1848
Wicklow Infanticides				1848	The number of Infanticides in County Wicklow was 3
Kilmacurragh House				1848	Kilmacurragh House, Rathdrum remodelled by Lt. Col. William Acton M.P.
Wicklow Homicides				1848	The total number of Homicides , including Manslaughter and Murders in County Wicklow , 3

Section One: Data by Date

Keyword	Day	Date	Month	Year	Event
Monck	Mon	08	01	1849	Henry Power Charles Monck born, later 5th Viscount Moncks
Ships/Yachts			01	1849	The vessel "Britannia" shipwrecked of the Wicklow Coast
Newspapers	Sat	03	02	1849	The Kildare and Wicklow Chronicle, first edition published in Athy, Co. Kildare
Newspapers	Sat	17	02	1849	The Kildare and Wicklow Chronicle, last edition published in Athy, Co. Kildare
Blessington. Countess	Fri	02	03	1849	Margurite Power Countess Blessington died
Monck	Fri	20	04	1849	Charles Joseph Monck, 3rd Viscount died and was succeeded by his son Charles Stanley Monck
Patterson, James	Tue	24	04	1849	James Patterson was ordained minister of the Presbyterian Church Bray
Barrington. R.C	Tue	22	05	1849	Zoologist, Botanist, Climber Richard Manliffe Barrington lived at Old Fasaroe House near, Bray 1849-1915.
Act	Sat	28	07	1849	The Encumbered Estates Act-made it easier to sell estates to pay their debts.
Power. George	Sun	26	08	1849	Rev George Beresford Power, born
Powerscourt	Wed	10	10	1849	Graphite print (Ref:PAE5569) of Powerscourt by Edward William- held in National Maritime Museum Greenwich, London
Dargle River	Wed	10	10	1849	Graphite print (Ref:PAE5570) of the River Darlge, Bray by Edward William -held in National Maritime Museum Greenwich, London
Morrison. Sir Richard	Wed	31	10	1849	Sir Richard Morrison (architect) died, buried in Mount Jerome Cemetery, Dublin
Nugent. Count Lavall			11	1849	Count Lavall Nugent appointed an Austrian field-marshal
Ships/Yachts	Fri	07	12	1849	The vessel "Wanderer" wrecked off Greystones
Woodburn. William				1849	William Woodburn emigrated to the USA
The School house				1849	The schoolhouse, Parkbridge, Shillelagh, Co. Wicklow built
O'Byrne. W.R				1849	William Richard O'Byrne wrote "The Naval Biography 1849-1854"
Books				1849	A Three Days' Tour in the County of Wicklow
Glencree				1849	The Catholic Church near Glencree reformatory built
Putland				1849	Charles Putland Jnr married Georgina Anderson
Cunningham. R.A.G				1849	Robert A. Gun Cunningham appointed sheriff of County Wicklow
Glendalough				1849	St. Kevin's Church Glendalough designed by James Joseph McCarthy (1817-1882)
Wicklow Infanticides				1849	The number of Infanticides in County Wicklow was 3
Crampton. Selina				1849	Selina Crampton painted a view of Lough Bray, Co. Wicklow held in National Library of Ireland reference PD 3094TX63
Blessington				1849	Blessington Fever Hospital established
Wicklow Homicides				1849	The total number of Homicides, including Manslaughter and Murders in County Wicklow , 3
Act				1849	Cock-fighting made illegal in Ireland

A-Z Reference	Day	Date	Month	Year	DATA
Royal Visit				1849	H.R.H. Queen Victoria first visit to Ireland
Books				1849	"A Three Day's "Tour in County Wicklow" published in London in 1849
Kyan. John Howard	Wed	09	01	1850	John Howard Kyan died in New York
Ships/Yachts	Tue	12	01	1850	The vessel "Hottinguer" shipwrecked of the Wicklow Coast
Tottenham. Robert P.	Fri	26	04	1850	Robert Ponsonby Tottenham, Bishop of Clogher died
Ships/Yachts			04	1850	The vessel "Edouard Marie" shipwrecked of the Wicklow Coast
Loreto Convent Bray	Sat	10	08	1850	The Loreto Nuns buy (price region £8,000) San Souci House the home of the Putland family for a convent and boarding school
Shee. Martin Archer	Mon	19	08	1850	Sir Martin Archer Shee died in Brighton, England
Loreto Convent Bray	Fri	22	11	1850	The first mass in the Loreto Convent, Bray and Mother Conception Lopez a native of Spain appointed superior of the convent
Parnell. H.T.			12	1850	Henry Tudor Parnell a brother of Charles S Parnell born
Coollattin Hunt			's	1850	The Coollattin Hunt established by the Earl Fitzwilliam
Nicol. Erskine			's	1850	Erskine Nicol painted a landscape view of Bray Seafront
Wicklow Homicides				1850	The total number of Homicides , including Manslaughter and Murders in County Wicklow , 2
Wicklow Infanticides				1850	The number of Infanticides in County Wicklow was 1
Alexander. William				1850	Cecil Frances Humphreys married William Alexander was a curate from Co. Tyrone
Ball. Teresa				1850	Teresa Ball foundress of the Loreto Order establishes a convent in Bray
Glendalough School				1850	A private Protestant National School was established in Glendalough
Brooke. R.H				1850	Richard Howard Brooke appointed sheriff of County Wicklow
Bray Hunt				1850	Bray Fox & Hounds Hunt became known as Bray Harriers
Trade				1850	Allen's Menswear established at Mains Street,
Lloyd. Humphrey				1850	Kilcroney House, Bray built for Mr Humphrey Lloyd who later became Provost of Trinity College Dublin.
Holy Redeemer, Bray				1850	The Holy Redeemer Church Bray was enlarged by the addition of 33ft to the nave and a Tower erected
Main Street				1850	Houses in front of the Holy Redeemer Church Bray purchased and demolished
British Parliamentary				1850	Return of Share Capital of Waterford, Wexford, Wicklow and Dublin Railway Company
Ships/Yachts	Wed	15	01	1851	The vessel "Wilson" shipwrecked of the Wicklow Coast
Brabazon. John	Sat	15	03	1851	John Chambre Brabazon the 10th Earl of Meath died and was succeeded by his son William Brabazon the 11th Earl of Meath
Arklow Barony	Sun	30	03	1851	The Population of the Arklow Barony 21,922

Ballinacor Nth. Barony	Sun	30	03	1851	The Population of the Ballinacor North Barony 9,469
Ballinacor Sth. Barony	Sun	30	03	1851	The Population of the Ballinacor South Barony 11,045
Rathdown Barony	Sun	30	03	1851	The Population of the Rathdown Barony 9,499
Talbotstown Lwr Barony	Sun	30	03	1851	The Population of the Talbotstown Lower Barony 11,438
Talbotstown Upr Barony	Sun	30	03	1851	The Population of the Talbotstown Upper Barony 12,487
Shillelagh Barony	Sun	30	03	1851	The Population of the Shillelagh Barony 10,326
Newcastle Barony	Sun	30	03	1851	The Population of the Newcastle Barony 12,793
Population County	Sun	30	03	1851	Population of County Wicklow 98,979 persons. 50,230 Males 48,749 Females
Population Enniskerry	Sun	30	03	1851	Population of Enniskerry urban 380 or 0.39% of County Population
Population Greystones	Sun	30	03	1851	Population of Greystones & Delgany 410 or 0.41% of County Population
Population Arklow	Sun	30	03	1851	Population of Arklow Urban 3,306 or 3.34% of County Population
Population Bray	Sun	30	03	1851	Population of Bray 3,156 or 3.18% of County Population
Population Wicklow (t)	Sun	30	03	1851	Population of Wicklow Town 3,141 or 3.18% of County Population
Elliston. Henry	Sun	29	06	1851	Henry Elliston was born at Newcastle. Co. Wicklow
Devlin. Anne	Thu	18	09	1851	Anne Devlin died in Dublin
Ships/Yachts			09	1851	The vessel "Fame" shipwrecked of the Wicklow Coast
Ships/Yachts			12	1851	The vessel "Pilgrim" shipwrecked of the Wicklow Coast
Wicklow Infanticides				1851	The number of Infanticides in County Wicklow was 2
Wicklow Harbour				1851	Wicklow Harbour Act
Books				1851	2nd Edition. Guide to the County of Wicklow by James Fraser
Wicklow Homicides				1851	The total number of Homicides , including Manslaughter and Murders in County Wicklow , 2
Railways				1851	The Dublin, Dundrum and Rathfarnham Railway changed its name to the Dublin and Bray Railway in 1851
Whiteside. James				1851	James Whiteside elected M.P. for Enniskillen
Loreto Convent Bray				1851	Loreto Nuns open a school on the Vevay Road, Bray
Lifeboats				1851	The Arklow Lifeboat between 1851 and 1981 saved 327 lives
Act				1851	An Act changed the title of the Dublin, Dundrum and Rathfarnham Railway to the Dublin and Bray Railway Company
Hodson. George				1851	George Hodson appointed sheriff of County Wicklow
				1851	The Presbyterian Church Newtownmountkennedy built
Act	Tue	03	02	1852	Common Law Procedure Act

A–Z Reference	Day	Date	Month	Year	DATA
Moore. Thomas	Sun	22	02	1852	The poet Thomas Moore died. and is buried at Bromham, Wiltshire, England
Murray. Daniel	Thu	26	02	1852	Daniel Murray Archbishop of Dublin died
Parish Records			02	1852	Earliest Record of Marriage in Roman Catholic Parish Blessington
Griffith's Valuation	Tue	13	04	1852	Griffiths Primary Valuation for the Barony of Rathdown, County Wicklow completed
Parish Records			04	1852	Earliest Record of Births in Roman Catholic Parish Blessington
Parnell. Anna	Thu	13	05	1852	Catherine Anna Parnell sister of C.S. Parnell born
Elections–Polling Day	Sat	17	07	1852	W.W.F Hume and Viscount Milton (W.T.S.W. Fitzwilliam) elected M.P's. for Wicklow at the General Election, Electors 3350
Hodson	Wed	15	09	1852	Sir George Frederick John Hodson 3rd Bart of Hollybrooke, Bray married Meriel Neville of Clonpriest, Cork and had 4 children
Earthquake	Wed	10	11	1852	An earthquake occurred in Ireland at 04:10 a.m.
Ships/Yachts	Fri	12	11	1852	The cargo ship "Lady Harriet" was wrecked off Bray
Ships/Yachts	Wed	17	11	1852	The vessel "Seaflower" shipwrecked of the Wicklow Coast
Ships/Yachts	Tue	23	11	1852	The vessel "Emma" shipwrecked of the Wicklow Coast
John Quin (Elder)	Wed	01	12	1852	John Quin Bray Hotelier died
Killruddery				1852	Conservatory added to Killruddery House the home of the Brabazon family
Windgates				1852	Twenty six families registered living in the town land of Windgates, Bray
Wicklow Homicides				1852	The total number of Homicides , including Manslaughter and Murders in County Wicklow , 1
Grattan. Rt.Hon.James				1852	Rt. Hon James Grattan appointed sheriff of County Wicklow
Whiteside. James				1852	James Whiteside appointed Solicitor General for period 1852-1857
Bill				1852	Tenant Compensation (Ireland) Bill
Wicklow Infanticides				1852	The number of Infanticides in County Wicklow was 3
Booth. Denton				1852	Denton Booth born in County Wicklow
Forge, Blessington				1852	The Forge at Blessington built
Royal Visit	Fri	02	09	1853	Queen Victoria and Prince Albert visited Powerscourt Estate. Co. Wicklow
Grattan Mary Anne	Thu	22	09	1853	Mary Anne Grattan died
Hodson	Thu	29	09	1853	Sir Robert Adair Hodson 4th Bart. Born
Books				1853	"pleasure Tour in the Environs of Dublin and the County Wicklow" published in Dublin in 1853
Books				1853	"Handbook to Dublin and Wicklow" by Mr and Mrs S.C. Hall. Published in London in 1853

Murphy. James				1853	James Murphy appointed teacher and Assistance Principal in Bray Male National School
Flora–Fauna				1853	White-tailed Eagle was sited at Bray Head Co. Wicklow.
Exhibition				1853	The great industrial exhibition of Ireland, held in the grounds of Leinster House.
Railways				1853	Bray Railway station built.
Royal Visit				1853	H.R.H. Queen Victoria visit to Ireland
Wicklow. County				1853	Henry Brett became County Surveyor
Howard. Sir Ralph				1853	Sir Ralph Howard appointed sheriff of County Wicklow
Parnell. Theodosia				1853	Theodosia Parnell a sister of Charles S. Parnell born
Fitzwilliam. 9th Earl				1853	Eric Spencer the 9th Earl of Fitzwilliam born
Maps				1853	Wicklow Sheet Map 121 engraved 1853
Books				1853	Pleasure tours to the environs of Dublin and County of Wicklow
Wicklow Infanticides				1853	The number of Infanticides in County Wicklow was 8, that accounted for 6% of infanticides in Ireland
Wicklow Homicides				1853	The total number of Homicides , including Manslaughter and Murders in County Wicklow , 0
Plunket. William	Sun	05	01	1854	William Plunket 1st Lord Plunket of Old Connaught, Bray died and succeeded by his son Thomas Plunket 2nd Baron
Railways	Fri	17	03	1854	William Dargan contractor to the WWW&D signed a deed to construct the line between Dalkey & Wicklow within certain limits
Railways	Mon	10	07	1854	The first train from Bray Railway Station
Act	Thu	10	08	1854	The Town Improvements (Ireland) Act
Grattan. Rt. Hon. James	Sat	21	10	1854	Rt. Hon James Grattan died
Hodson	Sun	26	11	1854	George Frederick John Hodson brother of Robert 4th Bart born
Act				1854	Common Law Procedure Act
Railways				1854	The Dublin and Bray Railway Company was absorbed into the Dublin and Wicklow Railway Company in 1854
Wicklow Infanticides				1854	The number of Infanticides in County Wicklow was 4
Books				1854	Black's Guide to Dublin and the Wicklow Mountains published by Charles Black of Edinburugh
Quinsborough Road				1854	Quinsborough Road Bray laid out. Also known locally as the Forty Foot Road.
Holy Redeemer, Bray				1854	Work started on addition to the nave and Tower at the Holy Redeemer Church Bray. The work cost £2,000
Powerscourt				1854	Lord Powerscourt appointed Alexander Robertson a Scottish gardener to look after the gardens at Powerscourt (1854-1860)
Howard. Catherine				1854	Catherine Howard published "The Chapel Bell" in Dublin
Railways				1854	Dublin & Wicklow and Dublin and Kingstown Railway Acts

A–Z Reference	Day	Date	Month	Year	DATA
Parnell. Hayes				1854	Charles S Parnell brother Hayes Parnell died following a hunting accident
Wicklow Homicides				1854	The total number of Homicides, including Manslaughter and Murders in County Wicklow , 2
Brennan. John				1854	John Brennan appointed sheriff of County Wicklow
Arklow				1854	The Arklow Marine Society for the Prevention of Wrecking and Preservation of Life from Shipwrecks founded
Arklow			02	1855	Dr. Robert Augustus L'Estrange appointed District Medical Officer for Arklow.
Railways			02	1855	Dublin & Wicklow & Wexford Railway Co. undertook to carry mailbags for the Post Office between Dublin and Bray
Howard. Catherine			07	1855	Catherine Howard married Hon. Arthur Petre
Railways			08	1855	Kiloughter Railway Station opened
Railways	Fri	13	10	1855	Wicklow Town Railway station opened
Greystones	Tue	30	10	1855	The official opening of Greystones Railway Station by the Lord Lieutenant of Ireland
Lees. Kilcoole				1855	Lees Pub Kilcoole established
Forge Enniskerry				1855	The Forge and Blacksmith's house Enniskerry was built. The Forge cost £150 while the house cost £200
Madden. Richard				1855	Richard Madden published "A life of Countess Blessington (Marguerite Power)
Murphy. James				1855	James Murphy appointed Principal teacher in Bray Male National School (1855-1864)
Weld. Isaac				1855	Mr Isaac Weld was one of the trustee of the "Society for bettering the condition of the poor in Ireland"
Antler Hotel				1855	Antler Hotel Bray Seafront built
Sidmonton Cottage				1855	Sidmonton Cottage, Sidmonton Road Bray built
Kiernan. Thomas				1855	Thomas Kiernan was appointed the first railway station master of Kilcoole
Putland. George				1855	George Putland son of Charles Putland Snr appointed sheriff of County Wicklow
Weaver Thomas				1855	Thomas Weaver owner of the Luganure Mine, Glendalough, died
Railways				1855	Greystones Railway Station built.
Brunker. James P.				1855	James P. Brunker born
Wicklow Harbour				1855	The Packet Pier built at Wicklow Harbour
Weaver. Thomas				1855	Thomas Weaver (Mine Developer) died
Maps				1855	Wicklow Sheet Map 121 engraved 1853, published 1855
Griffith's Valuation				1855	The most common first name in Co Wicklow for females was Mary (3205) of 13937 recorded first names
Griffith's Valuation				1855	The most common first name in Co Wicklow for males was John (2369) of 13937 recorded first names

Section One: Data by Date

Category	Day	Date	Year	Event
Griffith's Valuation			1855	The top 5 family names in the County Valuation was Byrne (1108), Doyle (522), Murphy (285), Kavanagh (236), Cullen (208)
Turnpike Trust			1855	An Act of Parliament abolished the Turnpike Trust established to maintain the Dublin to Baltinglass Road
Pearce, Thomas			1855	Thomas Pearce moved to Toronto, Canada, began teaching at Toronto Central School
Turnpike Roads			1855	Dublin and Other Roads Turnpike Abolition Act 1855
Wicklow Homicides			1855	The total number of Homicides, including Manslaughter and Murders in County Wicklow, 0
Ships/Yachts			1855	The vessel "Lord Mostyn" carrying potatoes shipwrecked of the Wicklow Coast
Proby, Hon. G.L			1855	Granville Levenson Proby 3rd Earl of Carysfort succeeded his brother John Proby 2nd Earl of Carysfort
Proby, John (2nd)			1855	John Proby 2nd Earl of Carysfort died
Wicklow Infanticides			1855	The number of Infanticides in County Wicklow was 1
Rathdrum	Tue	03	1856	The foundation stone laid for the Church of St. Mary's and St. Michael's Rathdrum
Weld, Isaac	Wed	18	1856	Margaret Alexa Weld wife of Isaac Weld died
Weld, Isaac		08	1856	Mr Isaac Weld of Ravenswell House, Bray died and was buried in Mount Jerome cemetery, Dublin
Redmond, John E.	Mon	01	1856	John Edward Redmond (nationalist leader) born Ballytrent, Co. Wexford
Ships/Yachts	Sun	28	1856	The vessel "Higgeson" carrying timber shipwrecked of the Wicklow Coast
Lifeboats	Sat	18	1856	Capt Ward a Lifeboat Inspector visited Wicklow Town with the aim of forming a Lifeboat Station
Hodson	Mon	01	1856	Richard Edmond Hodson brother of Robert 4th Bart.born
Wicklow Homicides			1856	The total number of Homicides, including Manslaughter and Murders in County Wicklow, 1
Dargle River			1856	Bray Bridge over the Dargle River designed by David Edge.(2)
Wicklow Infanticides			1856	The number of Infanticides in County Wicklow was 4
Delgany			1856	Wicklow Arms Inn, Delgany established (1)
Christian, Jonathan W.			1856	Rt. Hon. Jonathan Whitby Christian the First Justice of Appeal in Ireland lived at Ravenswell House, Bray
Books			1856	"The Mines of Wicklow" published in London in 1856
Books			1856	Black's Guide to Dublin and the Wicklow Mountains published by Charles Black of Edinburgh
Slater's Directory			1856	Slater's Directory of Delgany, Kilcoole, Rathdrum, Wicklow and Ashford
Report			1856	The Weldons lived at the Vevay and a few small houses along that part of the road formed the village of Newtown Vevay, Bray
Brabazon, William			1856	The remainder of Mr Kynaston Edwards estate at the Vevay, Bray was bought by William Brabazon the 11th Lord Meath
Herbert Road			1856	Herbert Road, Bray laid out by Lord Herbert
Roads			1856	The Lower Road from Bray to Enniskerry was completed. Pre 1856 The Back Dargle via Powerscourt Gates to the Village

A-Z Reference	Day	Date	Month	Year	DATA
Byrne. A.W				1856	Andrew W. Byrne appointed sheriff of County Wicklow
Slater's Directory				1856	Slater's Directory of Arklow, Baltinglass, Blessington, Bray, Enniskerry, Newtown Mount Kennedy
Books				1856	"Pictorial Handbook of County Wicklow" by D. E. Heffernan. 2nd Edition published in London in 1856
Lifeboats				1856	Arklow Lifeboat station re-opened
Le Fanu. William R.	Thu	15	01	1857	William R. Le Fanu married Henriette Barrington
Railways			03	1857	Heavy rock fall onto the railway line at Bray Head
Elections–Polling Day	Thu	16	04	1857	Capt. Richard Monck elected M.P. for Wicklow
Elections–Polling Day	Thu	16	04	1857	W.W.F. Hume ,Viscount Milton (W.T.S.W. Fitzwilliam) elected M.P's. for Wicklow at the General Election
Mason. G.H. Monck	Mon	08	06	1857	Lieutenant George Henry Monck Mason was killed at Awah, in India
Dempsey. Denis (Pt.)	Wed	12	08	1857	Denis Dempsey (reg. No. 322) held the rank of Private in the 1st Battalion, 10th Regiment (Lincolnshire Regiment)
Lifeboats			09	1857	The 30ft Dauntless Lifeboat stationed at Wicklow Harbour
Plunket. William			09	1857	Rev. William Conyngham Plunket rector of Bray died
Lifeboats			09	1857	Wicklow Town Lifeboat station established
Fitzwilliam. 5th Earl	Sun	04	10	1857	Charles Fitzwilliam 5th Earl Fitzwilliam died and was succeeded by his son William Thomas Spencer Fitzwilliam
Town Commissioners	Fri	09	10	1857	The First meeting of Bray Town Commissioners held in the Court House, Bray
Lifeboats	Sat	10	10	1857	The first call out of the Dauntless lifeboat was to a Brig "Avondale" of the Wicklow coast
St. Mary's. Enniskerry	Fri	13	11	1857	Richard 6th Viscount Powerscourt gave the site for St. Mary's Church Enniskerry
Powerscourt				1857	The income from rents to Lord Powerscourt from his County Wicklow Estates amounted to £18,350
Powerscourt				1857	Lord Powerscourt increased rents on his Wicklow estates by 23%
Luganure Mine				1857	A crushing mill was built in the Glendalough Valley by the Mining Company of Ireland
Acton. Thomas				1857	Thomas Acton appointed sheriff of County Wicklow
Le Fanu. William R.				1857	The Railway Engineer William R Le Fanu reported to the Railway on the proposal to place Bathing Boxes on Bray Seafront
Barlow. Jane				1857	Jane Barlow (writer) born in Clontarf, Dublin
Luganure Mine				1857	The Mining Company of Ireland planted 150,000 tree, mainly Larch and Fir trees in the Glendalough Valley
Pub/Tavern				1857	Glen of Imaal Bar established
Lifeboats				1857	New lifeboat station built at Arklow
Wicklow Homicides				1857	The total number of Homicides , including Manslaughter and Murders in County Wicklow , 1

Section One: Data by Date

Wicklow Infanticides				1857	The number of Infanticides in County Wicklow was 2
Kilbride, Bray				1857	The Church of Ireland at Kilbride, Bray built
Putland				1857	Nancy Putland nee Evans of Portrane, Dublin died
Lifeboats				1857	Cahore Lifeboat Station established
Newspapers				1857	Wicklow Newsletter and County Advertiser Newspaper first edition
Byrne. H.J.				1857	H.J.Byrne & Co (Property Agents) establish in Bray
Wheatly. E.W				1857	Edward William Whately appointed Vicar of Bray 1857-1862
Lighting				1857	Public Lighting 22 lamps erected in Bray. Main Street (17) Seymour Road (2) Quinsborough Road (2)
La Touche				1857	Peter David La Touche died and the property was inherited by his brother William
Proby. Hon. G.L				1857	Granville Levenson Proby 3rd Earl of Carysfort held the rank of Admiral in Royal Navy
Lifeboats				1857	The Wicklow Town Lifeboat between 1857 and 1981 saved 252 lives
Killiskey School				1857	The school in Killiskey village near Ashford built
Maps	Thu	28	01	1858	A 6 inch map produced by the Ordnance Survey for the Dublin + Kingstown and Bray railway
Parish Records			01	1858	Earliest Record of Births in Roman Catholic Parish Kilbride and Barndarrig
Parish Records			02	1858	Earliest Record of Marriage in Roman Catholic Parish Kilbride and Barndarrig
Dempsey. Denis (Pt.)	Sun	14	03	1858	Pt. Denis Dempsey was awarded the Victoria Cross for valour shown on 12/08/1857 and 14/03/1958
Crampton.Sir J.F.T.	Wed	31	03	1858	Sir John Fiennes Twisleton Crampton appointed ambassador to St. Petersburg, Russia 1858-1860
Byrne, James (Pt.)	Sat	03	04	1858	At Jhansi, India, Pt. Byrne under heavy fire. Went to the aid of a fellow officer who was severely wounded. Pt. Byrne was wounded
Cunningham. George E.	Thu	29	04	1858	George Ernest Cunningham the son of Robert and Agnes Cunningham born
Power. Jenny Wyse			05	1858	Jenny Wyse Power born in Baltinglass
Crampton. Sir Philip	Thu	10	06	1858	Sir Philip Crampton died and buried in Mount Jerome Cemetery, Dublin
Scharff. Robert F.	Fri	09	07	1858	Robert Francis Scharff (Naturalist) born in Leeds
Act	Fri	23	07	1858	Franchise Act -simplified procedures and gave county vote to £12 rated occupiers
Wicklow Hotel	Tue	27	07	1858	The Wicklow Railway and Marine Hotel opened for business
Act	Mon	02	08	1858	The Cheap Trains Act
St Andrew's. Bray	Sun	12	09	1858	St.Andrew's Presbyterian Church Quinsborough dedicated
Bray Gas Works	Mon	04	10	1858	The Countess of Meath laid the foundation stone of Bray Gas Works at 2.P.M. on 04/10/1858
Ships/Yachts	Sun	14	11	1858	The vessel "Nestorian" shipwrecked of the Wicklow Coast
Glencree				1858	The military barracks at Glencree was converted into St Kevin's Reformatory run by the Oblate Fathers

A–Z Reference	Day	Date	Month	Year	DATA
Salkeld. Joseph				1858	Joseph Salkeld appointed sheriff of County Wicklow
Wicklow Infanticides				1858	The number of Infanticides in County Wicklow was 0
Ravenswell. Bray				1858	Mr Matthew O'Reilly Dease M.P. for Louth bought Ravenswell House, Bray.
Crampton. Sir J.F.T.				1858	Sir John Fiennes Twisleton Crampton appointed ambassador to Hanover, Germany 1857
Arklow				1858	Work commenced on the Catholic Church in Arklow St.Mary & St Patrick
Whiteside. James				1858	James Whiteside appointed Attorney General for period 1858-1859
Wicklow Homicides				1858	The total number of Homicides, including Manslaughter and Murders in County Wicklow, 0
Bray Gas Works	Thu	24	02	1859	The opening of Bray Gas Works
Barrington. Sir William	Mon	14	03	1859	Sir William Barrington married Elizabeth Darley of Wingfield, Bray
Cunningham. George E.	Tue	26	04	1859	George Ernest Cunningham the son of Robert and Agnes Cunningham died
Elections-Polling Day	Mon	09	05	1859	W.W.F. Hume and Lord Proby elected M.P.'s. for Wicklow at the General Election, Number of electors 3368
Parnell. Delia	Sat	11	06	1859	Delia Parnell married James Thomson
Parnell. Delia	Sat	11	06	1859	Delia Parnell a sister of Charles S. Parnell married James Thomson
Parnell. Charles S	Sun	03	07	1859	Charles S. Parnell father John Henry Parnell died
Grattan. Henry Jnr	Sat	16	07	1859	Henry Grattan's son Henry Grattan Jnr died
Roche. Alexandra	Sun	31	07	1859	Rev. Alexandra Roche died and was buried at Kilmacanogue
Railways	Mon	08	08	1859	The Gorey (Railway) Extension Act given Royal Assent
St. Mary's. Enniskerry	Thu	08	09	1859	St. Marys Parish Enniskerry was constituted by Cardinal Cullen
Turkish Baths	Sun	02	10	1859	The Turkish Baths in Bray were opened to the public
St. Mary's. Enniskerry	Wed	12	10	1859	Construction work on St. Mary's Church Enniskerry completed
Turkish Baths	Sat	15	10	1859	The Turkish Baths in Bray were officially opened by the Earl of Meath
Byrne. James (Pt.)	Fri	11	11	1859	Private James Byrne awarded the Victoria Cross. Reported in the London Gazeted
Hodson	Wed	07	12	1859	Gilbert Neville Hodson brother of Robert 4th Bart. born
Putland	Sun	25	12	1859	Charles Putland Snr died
Marine Hotel. Wicklow				1859	Marine Hotel, Wicklow Town opened
Keane. Joseph B				1859	Joseph B. Keane died, he designed Glendalough House, near Annamoe, Co Wicklow
Fitzwilliam Estates				1859	The rents on the Fitzwilliam Estates in Wicklow increased by 15% in the period 1859-1880
Wingfield Estates				1859	The rents on the Wingfield Estates in Wicklow increased by 23% in the period 1859-1880

Power. John Wyse				1859	John Wyse Power born Co. Waterford. 1884 – 1887 General Secretary of the GAA
Wynne. George				1859	George Wynne appointed Secretary of Wicklow Grand Jury 1859 -1882
Tottenham. Lt.Col. C.J				1859	Lt.Col. Charles J. Tottenham appointed sheriff of County Wicklow
St.Patricks Enniskerry				1859	St. Patrick's Church Enniskerry built
Act				1859	Bray Common Enclosure Act
Whiteside. James				1859	James Whiteside elected M.P. for Dublin
Cullen. Luke				1859	Historian Luke Cullen died
Miley. John J				1859	Rev John Joseph Miley D.D. appointed Parish Priest of Bray and Greystones
Turkish Baths				1859	Turkish Baths Quinsborough Road, Bray built for Dr Richard Barter
O'Dwyer. Thomas				1859	Rev Thomas O'Dwyer appointed Parish Priest of St. Mary's, Enniskerry
Miley. John J				1859	Rev John Miley Parish Priest of Bray 1859-1861
Ships/Yachts				1859	The vessel "Exchange" carrying railway iron shipwrecked of the Wicklow Coast
Wicklow Homicides				1859	The total number of Homicides , including Manslaughter and Murders in County Wicklow , 2
Duncairn Terrace. Bray				1859	Duncairn Terrace, Bray built
Cogan. Denis J.				1859	Denis J. Cogan born
Conran. John				1859	John Conran and Margaret Conran of Borklemore. Co. Wicklow, married
Wicklow Infanticides				1859	The number of Infanticides in County Wicklow was 1
Dempsey. Denis (Pt.)	Fri	17	02	1860	A report of Pt. Denis Dempsey, Victoria Cross citation appeared in the London Gazetted
Bernard. John Henry	Fri	27	07	1860	John Henry Bernard (Church of Ireland Archbishop and academic) born and educated in Bray
Crosbie. Sir William	Wed	03	10	1860	Sir William Crosbie died at Bray
Bewley. Ernest	Wed	14	11	1860	Ernest Bewley the son of Margaret and Joshua Bewley of Bray born
Crampton.Sir J.F.T.	Tue	11	12	1860	Sir John Fiennes Twisleton Crampton appointed ambassador to Madrid, Spain 1860-1869
Sea Park House			Circa	1860	Sea Park, Wicklow built for the Ellis Family
Rathdrum Corn Mill			circa	1860	Rathdrum Corn Mill built
Shillelagh Courthouse			circa	1860	Shillelagh Courthouse built
Carnew			circa	1860	All Saints Church, Carnew built
Proby. Hon. William				1860	William Proby married Charlotte the daughter of Rev. Robert Booshy.
Railways				1860	Dublin, Wicklow, and Wexford Railway (Enniscorthy Extension) Act changed of title to Dublin, Wicklow and Wexford Railway Co.

A–Z Reference	Day	Date	Month	Year	DATA
Books				1860	The Official Railway handbook to Bray, Kingstown, the coast and the County Wicklow by George Rennie Powell
Photo Collection				1860	Stero Pairs Photographic Collection 1860–1883. Photo No. 887 Glendalough
Westby. Nicholas				1860	Nicholas Westby M.P. for Wicklow died
Railways				1860	Dublin & Kingstown Railway Act
Parnell Bridge				1860	The Parnell Bridge, at the Mall, Wicklow Town constructed by Mssr's Clarke, Wicklow (Timber bridge)
Powerscourt				1860	Lord Powerscourt had a number of farm sheds and estate cottages built adjacent to Powerscourt House, Enniskerry
French. Robert				1860	Robert French joined the Irish Constabulary and after training sent to Glenealy, Co. Wicklow.
Housing				1860	Laxton House Novara Road Bray built
Enniskerry				1860	The dome designed by Sir George Moyers was added to the fountain in Enniskerry (ref 1843)
Greystones				1860	Carrig Eden Hotel, Greystones built
Vance & Wilson				1860	Vance & Wilson Chemist established Main Street, Bray
Water – Vartry				1860	The Hawkshaw Commission recommended the construction of Vartry Reservoir, Roundwood, Co. Wicklow
La Touche				1860	Wiliam Robert La Touche appointed sheriff of County Wicklow
Rathdrum				1860	The catholic church at Rathdrum built to a design by J.J. McCarthy. The Parish of Rathdrum was constituted
Baltinglass				1860	The Catholic Church in Baltinglass built
Lawlor: Hugh Jackson				1860	Hugh Jackson Lawlor born in Dublin
Powerscourt				1860	Lord Powerscourt had a number of Estate cottages built at Kilmolin near Enniskerry
Blacklion				1860	St. Kilians Church Blacklion, Greystones built
LeFoy. Thomas				1860	Thomas LeFoy Q.C. bought some land from the Earl of Pembroke and built Ardmore House, Bray
Dargan. William				1860	William Dargan lived at Fairy Hill House, Bray
Powerscourt				1860	The Steward and Head Gardener at Powerscourt Alexandra Roberston died
Wicklow Infanticides				1860	The number of Infanticides in County Wicklow was 2
Wicklow Homicides				1860	The total number of Homicides, including Manslaughter and Murders in County Wicklow , 1
Darley. Sir F.M				1860	Sir Frederick Matthew Darley married Lucy Forest and they had two sons and four daughters
Ships/Yachts	Sat	09	02	1861	The vessel "Tonquin" carrying coal shipwrecked of the Wicklow Coast
Kilcoole	Sat	09	02	1861	The railway line at Kilcoole was washed away in a storm
Ships/Yachts	Sat	09	02	1861	The vessel "William" carrying coal shipwrecked of the Wicklow Coast

Ships/Yachts	Mon	11	02	1861	The vessel "Mary Drapers" carrying coal shipwrecked of the Wicklow Coast
Ships/Yachts	Mon	11	02	1861	The vessel "Elizia" carrying coal shipwrecked of the Wicklow Coast
Ships/Yachts	Mon	11	02	1861	The vessel "Endeavour" carrying coal shipwrecked off Bray in a gale
Ships/Yachts	Mon	11	02	1861	The vessel "Robert Seamour" shipwrecked of the Wicklow Coast
Bray Head			03	1861	Charles Putland opened up public access to Bray Head
Population Arklow	Sun	07	04	1861	Population of Arklow Urban 4,706 or 5.44% of County Population
Population Greystones	Sun	07	04	1861	The Protestant of population of Greystones & Delgany was 423 equal 70% of the Census return of 605
Population County	Sun	07	04	1861	Population of County Wicklow 86,479 persons. 44,122 Males 42,357 Females
Population Wicklow (t)	Sun	07	04	1861	Population of Wicklow Town 3,448 or 3.98% of County Population
Population Greystones	Sun	07	04	1861	Population of Greystones & Delgany 605 or 0.69% of County Population
Population Enniskerry	Sun	07	04	1861	Population of Enniskerry urban 374 or 0.43% of County Population
Population Bray	Sun	07	04	1861	Population of Bray 4,182 or 4.8% of County Population
Ballinacor Nth. Barony	Sun	07	04	1861	The Population of the Ballinacor North Barony 8,192
Talbotstown Upr Barony	Sun	07	04	1861	The Population of the Talbotstown Upper Barony 9,946
Shillelagh Barony	Sun	07	04	1861	The Population of the Shillelagh Barony 7,773
Arklow Barony	Sun	07	04	1861	The Population of the Arklow Barony 20,444
Ballinacor Sth. Barony	Sun	07	04	1861	The Population of the Ballinacor South Barony 8,806
Newcastle Barony	Sun	07	04	1861	The Population of the Newcastle Barony 11,760
Rathdown Barony	Sun	07	04	1861	The Population of the Rathdown Barony 9,614
Talbotstown Lwr Barony	Sun	07	04	1861	The Population of the Talbotstown Lower Barony 9,916
Lee.Walter	Fri	19	04	1861	Rev Walter Lee D.D appointed Parish Priest of Bray and Greystones
Cricket Club, Bray	Tue	30	04	1861	Bray Cricket Club founded
Mecredy. Richard J.	Sat	18	05	1861	Richard James Mecredy the son of Rev. James Mecredy, born Ballinsloe, Co. Galway
Ball.Teresa	Sun	19	05	1861	The foundress of the Loreto Order Frances Mary Tersea Ball died
La Touche	Wed	05	06	1861	John David Digues La Touche, born at Tours, France
Newspapers	Sat	15	06	1861	Bray Gazette established
Water – Vartry	Mon	22	07	1861	The Vartry Water Bill given Royal Ascent to build a reservoir at Roundwood
Luganure Mine			07	1861	Net Profit from the Luganure Mine for first six months of 1861 amounted £2,661
Act	Tue	06	08	1861	Offences Against the Person Act

A–Z Reference	Day	Date	Month	Year	DATA
Railways	Sat	10	08	1861	A train collided with a locomotive at Greystones Railway Station
Arklow	Sun	18	08	1861	The Catholic Church Arklow St Mary & St Patrick was dedicated
Railways	Tue	20	08	1861	Rathdrum Railway viaduct completed
Monck. Charles	Mon	28	10	1861	Charles Monck 4th Viscount appointed 1st Captain General and Governor-in-chief of Canada, Governor-General of British America
Barnes. E				1861	E. Barnes in 1861 published half-yearly report to Wicklow Copper Mine Company.
Police/Garda				1861	The Irish Constabulary changed its title to The Royal Irish Constabulary (RIC)
O'Brien. John				1861	John Thomond O'Brien died in Lisbon, Portugal
Newspapers				1861	Bray Gazette Newspaper first edition
Thompson. Henry				1861	Henry Thomson the son of Delia Parnell and James Thompson born
St. Mary's. Enniskerry				1861	Seating in the church of St. Mary's Enniskerry supplied by Hearnes & Co, Waterford
Fitzsimons. C.				1861	Christopher O'Connell Fitzsimons appointed sheriff of County Wicklow
Dwyer. Mary				1861	Mary Dwyer wife of Michael Dwyer insurgent leader died
Wicklow Infanticides				1861	The number of Infanticides in County Wicklow was 1
Ships/Yachts				1861	The vessel "Roland" carrying coal shipwrecked of the Wicklow Coast
Whitshed. E.A.F.H.				1861	Elizabeth Alice Frances Hawkins–Whitshed born in London dau of Sir St. Vincent Hawkins–Whitshed
Ships/Yachts				1861	The vessel "Margaret Mortimer" carrying coal shipwrecked of the Wicklow Coast
Carysfort Arms				1861	William Rudd's Inn at Kinsella's Lane, Arklow renamed "Carysfort Arms"
Wicklow Homicides				1861	The total number of Homicides , including Manslaughter and Murders in County Wicklow , 4
Railways				1861	The Brabazon (railway) footbridge built at Bray Head
Housing				1861	Work began on building Prince of Wales Terrace, Bray
Bray Harbour				1861	Mr.O'Reilly Dease of Bray offered £1,000 towards the construction of a Harbour around the River Mouth. If built in 1861
Housing				1861	Building of Fitzwilliam Terrace, Bray began
Christ Church, Bray				1861	The foundation stone for Christ Church, Bray was laid
Brabazon. William				1861	William Brabazon the 11th Earl of Meath donated a site on the Rock of Bray for the building of Christ Church, Bray
St. Mary's. Enniskerry				1861	St. Mary's Church Enniskerry completed except the spire
Powerscourt				1861	Lord Powerscourt introduces into Ireland Sika Deer (Cervus nippon) from Japan
Miley. John J				1861	Rev.John Joseph Miley D.D. died and is buried at the South Transept of Holy Redeemer Church, Bray

Section One: Data by Date

Keyword	Weekday	Day	Month	Year	Event
Ships/Yachts				1861	The vessel "William Campbell" shipwrecked of the Wicklow Coast
Railways	Thu	13	02	1862	Dublin & Wicklow & Wexford Railway Co. accepted plans for Arklow Railway Station
Ships/Yachts	Sun	16	02	1862	The vessel "Crisis" shipwrecked of the Wicklow Coast
International Hotel	Mon	19	05	1862	John Brennan opened the International Hotel, Quinsborough Road. Bray
Railways	Fri	18	07	1862	Rathdrum Railway Station & Railway Hotel opened
Nugent. Count Lavall	Thu	21	08	1862	Count Lavall Nugent died at Bosiljero, near Karlstadt
Parnell. Sophia	Sat	13	09	1862	Sophia Parnell married Alfred McDermott
Carlisle Grounds			09	1862	Carlisle Spotrs Grounds Quinsborough Road Bray opened by the Lord Lieutenant of Ireland Lord Carlisle
Oldtown School	Mon	13	10	1862	Oldtown Schoolhouse near Roundwood opened
Water – Vartry			11	1862	The foundation stone for the Vartry Water Works, Roundwood was laid
Needham. George	Thu	25	12	1862	The Rev George rector of Ballynure Co. Wicklow and Termonfeckin Co. Louth died. He is buried in Termonfeckin.
Barrington. Charlotte				1862	Carlotte Jessy Barrington the daughter of Sir William Barrington and Elizabeth Darley was born, in 1901 married George Digby Scott
Stillorgan				1862	The first stone of the Prince of Wales Reservoir Stillorgan laid. The reservoir fed by the Vartry Water supply
Annacurra				1862	The Catholic Church at Annacurra near Aughrim built
International Hotel				1862	Work began on building the International Hotel, Quinsborough Road, Bray for Mr John Brennan
Bray Head Hotel				1862	John Lacey Owner of Bray Head Hotel in 1862 Post Office Directory
Wicklow Homicides				1862	The total number of Homicides , including Manslaughter and Murders in County Wicklow , o
Lloyd. Humphrey				1862	Humphrey Lloyd (Physicist and Educationalist) appointed Vice Provost of Trinity College, Dublin
Putland				1862	Sydenham Villas, Putland Road, Built
Carroll. C.A				1862	Coote A. Carroll appointed sheriff of County Wicklow
Railways				1862	Dublin & Wicklow & Wexford Railway Co. gave approval of Shillelagh Branch Line
French. Robert				1862	Robert French resigned from the Irish Constabulary
Wicklow Infanticides				1862	The number of Infanticides in County Wicklow was 3
Railways				1862	Dublin & Wicklow & Wexford Railway Co proposed the closure of Kiloughter Railway Station because of a new station at Rathnew
Avoca				1862	The Church of St. Mary's and Patrick's Avoca, built
Aravon School				1862	Aravon School, Bray founded
Callow Hill	Sun	04	01	1863	The Callow Hill (Roundwood) Water Tunnel was completed this allowed the Vartry System be pumped to Stillorgan, Co. Dublin
Roundwood	Wed	10	06	1863	The River Vartry was deflected into the Roundwood Reservoir

A-Z Reference	Day	Date	Month	Year	DATA
Plunket. William	Thu	11	06	1863	Anne Guinness daughter of Sir Benjamin Lee Guinness married Rev. William Plunket, 4th Baron Plunket of Old Connaught, Bray
Roundwood	Tue	30	06	1863	The Vartry Water tunnel at Roundwood between the reservoir and the filter beds opened
Railways	Sat	18	07	1863	Arklow Railway Station opened
Christ Church, Bray	Sat	25	07	1863	Christ Church Bray was consecrated by Bishop Fitzgerald
Cricket	Tue	04	08	1863	The Bray Cricket Club played South Wicklow Cricket Club, C.S. Parnell played for South Wicklow Club
Hodson	Mon	10	08	1863	Jane Hodson the daughter of Sir Robert Hodson 1st Bart, died
St. Patricks Enniskerry	Tue	15	09	1863	St. Patrick's Church Enniskerry officially opened
French. Robert	Tue	01	12	1863	Robert French married Henrietta Jones, a farmers daughter from Newcastle, Co. Wicklow at St. Peter's Church, Dublin.
Cogan. W.H.F				1863	William H.F. Cogan appointed sheriff of County Wicklow
Wicklow Homicides				1863	The total number of Homicides , including Manslaughter and Murders in County Wicklow , 3
Scott. J.G.				1863	Rev James George Scott appointed Rector of Bray, Christ Church Parish
Ships/Yachts				1863	The vessel "Samuel" shipwrecked of the Wicklow Coast
Act				1863	Trustee Savings Bank Act
Tyrrell. Kate				1863	Kate Tyrrell of Arklow born
Tottenham. Lt Col C. G.				1863	Lt. Col. C. G. Tottenham elected M.P. for New Ross 1863 -1868
French. Robert				1863	Robert French joins William Lawerence Photographic Studio, Dublin
Wicklow Infanticides				1863	The number of Infanticides in County Wicklow was 1
Housing				1863	Milton Terrace, Seapoint Road Bray built
Rathmichael				1863	Rathmichael Church built
Act				1863	Births and Deaths Registration Act
Housing				1863	Alexandra Terrace, Novara Road, Bray built
Gray. Sir John				1863	John Gray Chairman of Dublin Corporation Waterworks, proposed the Vartry Water Scheme at Roundwood. Co. Wicklow
Powerscourt	Tue	26	04	1864	Mervyn 7th Viscount Powerscourt married Lady Julia Coke
Jones. William	Thu	12	05	1864	William Jones born Co. Wicklow. Killed in Action at Spotsylvania, Virginia, USA
Jones. William	Thu	12	05	1864	William Jones held the rank of First Sergeant, Company A, 73rd New York Infantry
Manor Kilbride	Tue	28	06	1864	St. John the Baptist Church at Cloughleagh, Manor Kilbride. Consecrated for a second time
Kemmis. William	Wed	20	07	1864	William Kemmis 3rd son of Thomas Kemmis of Ballinacor, Co. Wicklow died

Section One: Data by Date

Keyword	Day			Year	Description
French School Bray	Mon	01	08	1864	French School Bray founded by Madame de Mailly
Casement. Roger	Thu	01	09	1864	Roger Casement born to Roger Casement Snr and Anne Jephson
Parish Records			09	1864	Earliest Record of Births in Roman Catholic Parish Ashford
Parish Records			10	1864	Earliest Record of Marriage in Roman Catholic Parish Ashford
Jones. William	Thu	01	12	1864	William Jones was posthumously awarded the Congressional Medal of Honour
Rathmichael	Mon	12	12	1864	Rathmichael Church consecrated by Archbishop of Dublin Rev. Richard Chenevix Trench
Plunket	Mon	19	12	1864	William Lee Plunket of Old Connaught, Bray born
Railways				1864	Railway Locomotive Number 25 built and Named Glenart, Withdrawn from service 1925
Tyrrell, John				1864	John Tyrrell & Sons Ltd, Ship & Boat Builders established in Arklow
Mining Accident				1864	One man died in an earth fall at the Luganure Mine, Glendalough
Lifeboats				1864	A RNLI Inspector visited the Wicklow Lifeboat Station and proposed the building of a new lifeboat station
Hume. W.H.				1864	Charlotte Ann Hume nee Dick died
Wicklow Homicides				1864	The total number of Homicides , including Manslaughter and Murders in County Wicklow , 0
Pearce. Thomas				1864	Thomas Pearce appointed principal of Toronto Central School.
Jones. William				1864	William Jones was buried at Fredericksburg National Military Park. Grave 2488(MH)
Howard. Catherine				1864	Catherine Howard published "SacredVerses" in London
Greystones				1864	St. Patrick's Church, Greystones consecrated by Archbishop of Dublin Rev. Richard Chenevix Trench
Wicklow Infanticides				1864	The number of Infanticides in County Wicklow was 0
St Andrew's. Bray				1864	St. Andrew's Methodist Church, Florence Road, Bray built
Millward Terrace				1864	Millward Terrace, Meath Road Bray built
Wicklow Friary				1864	The Franciscan Friary at Wicklow Town was granted to Henry Harrington
Putland				1864	Mary Putland nee Bligh died
Murphy. James				1864	James Murphy appointed Professor of Mathematics at Catholic University of Dublin
Ashford				1864	Ashford Roman Catholic parish constituted into a separate parish from Wicklow Town
St Patrick's School				1864	The Royal Drummond Institution (a school for soldiers daughters) was founded by Alderman John Drummond with sum of £20,000
Putland. Charles				1864	Charles Putland Jnr appointed sheriff of County Wicklow
Tyrrell Shipping				1864	John Tyrrell & Sons Ltd, Ship & Boat builders established in Arklow
Alexandra Bridge				1864	Alexandra Bridge near the source River Liffey, built in 1864 in honour the Princess who married the Prince of Wales in 1863
Boucicault. Dion				1864	"Arrah na Pogue" or "The Wicklow Wedding" a political melodrama by Dion Boucicault

The County Wicklow Database: 432 AD to 2006 AD

A-Z Reference	Day	Date	Month	Year	DATA
Kilmacanogue				1864	Glencormac House, Kilmacanogue built for James Jameson
Mackintosh. C. Herbert				1864	Charles Herbert Mackintosh became chief editor of the Hamilton Times newspaper
Grattan Harriet	Mon	02	01	1865	Harriet Grattan died
Ships/Yachts	Fri	24	02	1865	The vessel "Armenian" shipwrecked of the Wicklow Coast
Railways	Sat	25	03	1865	The 5.00 pm down train overran the signals and collided with some wagons at Bray Station
Railways	Sun	23	04	1865	Train derailment at Bray Head
Cochrane. Henry	Wed	10	05	1865	Henry Cochrane, of Woodbrook, Bray married Margaret Gilchrist
Railways	Mon	22	05	1865	Dublin & Wicklow & Wexford railway line was completed as far as Shillelagh
Green. Harry Plunket	Sat	24	06	1865	Harry Plunket Greene (singer and author) born in Old Connaught House, Bray
Lightship	Fri	30	06	1865	The lightship "Wicklow Swash" was put into service of Wicklow Head
Elections–Polling Day	Wed	19	07	1865	W.W.F. Dick and Lord Proby elected M.P.'s for Wicklow at the General Election, Number of electors 3537
Beit. Otto John	Thu	07	12	1865	Otto John Beit born
Blessington Fountain			12	1865	A fountain erected in Blessington to mark the coming of age of Arthur Hill, Lord Hillsborough and 5th Marquis of Downshire
Lawrence. William				1865	William Lawrence Photographic Collection 1865 -1914 includes 40,000 negatives held in National Library
Ships/Yachts				1865	The vessel "Anna" carrying coal shipwrecked of the Wicklow Coast
Railways				1865	Dublin, Wicklow and Wexford Railways Act
Lloyd. Humphrey				1865	Kilcroney House, Bray sold by Mr Humphrey Lloyd to Mr Matthew Peter D'Arcy M.P. for Offaly
Leland. Dr. Thomas				1865	Thomas Leland appointed Vicar of Bray
Water - Vartry				1865	Water from the Vartry Reservoir was turned on by the Earl of Carlisle, Lord Lieutant of Ireland
St. Joseph's Newtown				1865	St. Joseph's Church Newtown Mount Kennedy built
International Hotel				1865	International Hotel, Quinsborough Road, Bray completed for Mr John Brennan at cost of £24,000
St. Patrick's Church				1865	The spire was added to St. Patrick's Church Enniskerry
Mackintosh. C. Herbert				1865	Charles Herbert Mackintosh began the Strathroy Dispatch newspaper
Martello Terrace				1865	Martello Terrace, Bray completed
Wicklow Homicides				1865	The total number of Homicides, including Manslaughter and Murders in County Wicklow , 1
Wicklow Infanticides				1865	The number of Infanticides in County Wicklow was 3
Moore. J.S				1865	Joseph Scott Moore appointed sheriff of County Wicklow

Section One: Data by Date

	Weekday	Day	Month	Year	
Leeson	Wed	31	01	1866	Joseph Leeson of Russborough House, Blessington, 4th Earl of Milltown died
Brabazon, John	Mon	26	03	1866	Lady Melosina Brabazon nee Adelaide the wife of the John Chambre Brabazon the 10th Earl of Meath died
Monck	Thu	12	07	1866	1st Baron Monck was created in UK Peerage
Act	Mon	23	07	1866	Bray Township Act established the town boundaries
Railways	Sat	01	09	1866	Rathnew Railway Station opened
Lifeboats	Fri	07	09	1866	The naming ceremony of the Lifeboat Robert Theophilus Garden took place at Wicklow Lifeboat Station
Callow Hill			09	1866	The 2nd Callow Hill (Roundwood) Water Tunnel was commissioned
Plunket	Fri	19	10	1866	Thomas Plunket 2nd Baron died and was succeeded by his brother John Plunket 3rd Baron
Harmon	Thu	01	11	1866	Count Louis Le Warner Harmon otherwise known as The Great Cherio a clairvoyant was born in Bray in 1866
Lawrence, William	Wed	14	11	1866	William Mervin Lawrence married Fanny Henrietta Greatbatch at St. Philip and St. James Church Oxford
Kay, Dorothy	Mon	03	12	1866	The artist Dorothy Kay was born in Greystones, Co. Wicklow
Lifeboats				1866	New lifeboat Station built at Wicklow Harbour
Bayview				1866	Methodist Church built at Bayview, Wicklow town
Wicklow Infanticides				1866	The number of Infanticides in County Wicklow was 1
Putland				1866	Caroline Putland a dau. of Chas. Putland married William Bernard Shaw and uncle of George Bernard Shaw at Christ Church, Bray
Wicklow Homicides				1866	The total number of Homicides, including Manslaughter and Murders in County Wicklow, 1
Humewood Castle				1866	Humewood Castle, Kiltegan, Co. Wicklow designed by William White
Act				1866	Bray Township Act raised funds for Roads, Sanitary, and Water Supply
Christ Church, Bray				1866	The tower and spire was added to Christ Church, Church Road, Bray
St. Bridgets				1866	St. Bridget's (County Hospital) run by the Sisters of Mercy was established at Rathdrum Co. Wicklow
Lighthouse				1866	A dome was add to the old Lighthouse on Wicklow Head
Proby, Hon. William				1866	Hon. Willaim Proby appointed sheriff of County Wicklow
Railways				1866	Dublin and Kingstown (Lease) Act
Lifeboats	Sat	05	01	1867	The first service for the lifeboat Robert Theophilus Garden was to a sloop "Shamrock" of the Wicklow coast
Dargan, William	Thu	07	02	1867	William Dargan pioneer of Irish Railways died
Fenian Rebellion	Tue	05	03	1867	The Fenian Rising took place in Wicklow, Dublin, Tipperary, Limerick, Clare, Louth and Cork
Weather			03	1867	Flooding took place in Glenmalure when the Avonbeg River peaked at 15ft above normal level
Railways	Mon	01	04	1867	Killoughter Railway Station closed
Parnell, Emily	Tue	30	04	1867	Emily Parnell 1st married Capt Robert Munro Dickinson

A–Z Reference	Day	Date	Month	Year	DATA
Monck. Charles	Tue	04	06	1867	Charles Stanley Monck declared as 1st Governor-General of the Dominion of Canada
Railways	Fri	09	08	1867	Derailment at Bray Head (Brandy Hole Accident)
Donnelly. James	Sun	22	09	1867	James Donnelly injured in the Bray Head Rail accident in August 1867. Died at his home in Gorey, Co. Wexford
Lightship	Thu	10	10	1867	The lightship "Wicklow Swash" was withdrawn from service off Wicklow Head
Montague. Daniel	Tue	22	10	1867	Daniel Montague born County Wicklow.
Ships/Yachts				1867	The vessel "Scotia Queen" shipwrecked of the Wicklow Coast
D'Ombrain. Ernest A.				1867	Ernest Arthur D'Ombrain born Rathdrum Co. Wicklow
Wicklow Infanticides				1867	The number of Infanticides in County Wicklow was 2
La Touche				1867	William Robert La Touche married Ellen Henn
Laragh				1867	St. John's Church Laragh was dedicated
Lightship				1867	The lightship "Codling" was put into service off Wicklow
Lightship				1867	The lightship "North Arklow" was put into service off Wicklow
Books				1867	Photographs of Co. Wicklow by F.H. Mares published in Dublin and Glasgow
Whitshead. S.V.B.H				1867	St. Vincent B. Hawkins Whitshed appointed sheriff of County Wicklow
Massy. Anne L.				1867	Anne L. Massy (Marine Scientist and Conservationist) born Enniskerry. Co. Wicklow
Lloyd. Humphrey				1867	Humphrey Lloyd (Physicist and Educationalist) appointed Provost of Trinity College, Dublin
Books				1867	"Photographs of County Wicklow" with descriptive letterpress. Published in Glasgow in 1867
Humewood Castle				1867	Humewood Castle, Kiltegan, Co. Wicklow built for W.W.F. Hume Dick M.P.
Wicklow Homicides				1867	The total number of Homicides , including Manslaughter and Murders in County Wicklow , 0
Glenealy School				1867	Gleanealy Parochial School built
Darley. Cecil W.				1867	Cecil West Darley arrived in Sydney and joined Public Works Department
Dargle River				1867	The River Dargle broke its banks and flooded, Little Bray
Turkish Baths				1867	The Turkish Baths on Quinsborough Road, Bray was converted into Assembly Rooms
Barre. W.J.				1867	William J Barre, died (Architect) of Kilbride Church, Bray
Trams				1867	The City of Dublin Tramway Company was established
Lighthouse	Sat	04	01	1868	The Lighthouse on Wicklow Head was converted to oil gas, the gas was made in a small gas works attached to the lighthouse
Brabazon. Reginald	Tue	07	01	1868	Reginald Brabazon the 12th Earl of Meath married Lady Mary Jane Lauderdale

Section One: Data by Date

Railways	Mon	17	02	1868	Collision of a passenger train with some ballast freight wagons at Bray Railway Station
St. Joseph's Church	Thu	19	03	1868	The foundation stone was laid for St. Joseph's Church Glenealy. The church was built of granite from the Ballyknocken quarries, Blessington
Mackintosh. C. Herbert	Tue	07	04	1868	Charles Herbert Mackintosh married Gertrude Cook and they had nine children
Cochrane. Richard	Tue	26	05	1868	Richard Cochrane born 1st son of Sir Henry Cochrane, of Woodbrook, Bray
Connolly. James	Fri	05	06	1868	James Connolly born at 107 Cowgate, Edinburgh
Wingfield. Lewis S.	Tue	16	06	1868	Lewis Strange Wingfield married Emily Fitzpatrick the daughter of Lord Castletown
Hill. Arthur-4th	Thu	06	08	1868	Arthur Hill 4th Marques of Downshire died and was succeeded by his son Arthur
Elections–Polling Day	Tue	24	11	1868	W.W.F. Dick and W.H. W. Fitzwilliam elected M.P.'s for Wicklow at the General Election, Number of electors 3613
Henry. Grace				1868	Grace Henry nee Mitchell (artist) born in Scotland
Wicklow Homicides				1868	The total number of Homicides , including Manslaughter and Murders in County Wicklow , 0
Railways				1868	Wooden Footbridge at Bray Railway Station replaced with a steel structure
Avoca Bridge				1868	The bridge at Avoca village built
Proby. G.L				1868	Granville Levenson Proby 3rd Earl of Carysfort was succeeded by his son Granville Levenson 4th Earl
Books				1868	"Whammmd's Illustrated Guide to Dublin, Wicklow with historical sketches. Published in Dublin 1868
Ellis. R.F				1868	Robert F. Ellis appointed sheriff of County Wicklow
Proby. Hon. G.L				1868	Granville Levenson Proby 3rd Earl of Carysfort died
INTO				1868	Irish National Teachers Organisation founded
Water – Vartry				1868	The Vartry (Water) Scheme was completed at Roundwood
Killruddery				1868	The Prince and Princess of Wales visited Killruddery
Wicklow Infanticides				1868	The number of Infanticides in County Wicklow was 1
Walpole				1868	The Walpole Family purchased the old mill and one acre at Mount Usher, Ashford, Co. Wicklow
Gray. Sir John				1868	John Gray knighted by Lord Lieutenant of Ireland
Railways				1868	There was 39 Railway Companies operating in Ireland
Wicklow. Earl of	Mon	22	03	1869	William the 4th Earl died and was succeeded by his nephew Charles
Pim. Joshua	Thu	20	05	1869	Joshua Pim Wimbledon born Milward Terrace Bray
Halpin. Robert Charles	Thu	03	06	1869	Captain Robert Charles Halpin given command of the S.S. Great Eastern
Act	Mon	12	07	1869	Public Parks (Ireland) Act
Act	Mon	26	07	1869	Irish Church Act

A-Z Reference	Day	Date	Month	Year	DATA
Avoca Bridge	Wed	01	09	1869	The bridge at Avoca open to public traffic
Glenealy. St. Josephs	Mon	04	10	1869	St. Josephs Church, Gleanealy wad dedicated for worship
St. Joseph's Church	Mon	04	10	1869	Cardinal Cullen dedicated St. Joseph's Church Genealy
Brabazon. Reginald	Wed	24	11	1869	Reginald Brabazon the 13th Earl of Meath born
Powerscourt				1869	The Winged Horses (Pegasi) at the Pond at Powerscourt was made in Berlin by Professor Hagen
Bray Bye Laws				1869	Hackney Cars & Carriages Regulations – Bray and four mile radius
Wicklow Homicides				1869	The total number of Homicides, including Manslaughter and Murders in County Wicklow, 1
Arklow				1869	A jar found during the excavations for the Methodist Church Arklow is now in the British Museum, London
Bayly. Lancelot				1869	Lancelot Bayly (artist) born Nenagh Co. Tipperary
St. Pauls. Bray				1869	Alterations made to St. Paul's Church, Bray
Wicklow Infanticides				1869	The number of Infanticides in County Wicklow was 1
Arklow				1869	The Methodist Church Arklow was built
O'Mahony. Daniel				1869	Daniel O'Mahony appointed sheriff of County Wicklow
Glenart Castle				1869	Glenart Castle near Arklow was enlarged
Lacken School				1869	Lacken National School, near Blessington built
Bewley. Joshua				1869	Joshua Bewley took a lease on part of the Assembly Rooms, Quinsborough Road Bray
Masonic Lodge	Mon	21	02	1870	The Right Hon. Mervyn Viscount Powerscourt was appointed first Provincial Grand Master of Masonic Lodge of Wicklow & Wexford
Masonic Lodge	Mon	21	02	1870	The inaugural meeting of the Provincial Grand Lodge of the Freemasonry took place in the Assembly Rooms, Quinsborough Rd. Bray
Le Fanu. Henry	Fri	01	04	1870	Henry Frewen Le Fanu the son of Wiilam R Le Fanu of Abington, Bray born
Westby. Nicholas	Tue	05	04	1870	Emily Westby nee Walgrave of Thornhill, Old Connaught, Bray died (Reference Clare Journal Newspaper Mon. 11/04/1870)
Powerscourt	Wed	27	04	1870	The Holy Trinity Castlemacadam near Avoca was consecrated. The land was donated by Lord Powerscourt
Dominican Convent	Mon	20	06	1870	Dominican Convent and school established in Wicklow town
Hill. Arthur-5th	Tue	26	07	1870	Arthur Hill 5th Marquis of Downshire married Georgina Balfour
Act	Mon	01	08	1870	Landlord and Tennant (Ireland) Act
Act	Wed	10	08	1870	Glebe Loan (Ireland) Act
Lifeboats	Fri	02	09	1870	The Arklow Lifeboat Arundel Venables went to the aid of the Schooner "Dove" of Barrow sunk off Arklow
Lifeboats	Fri	02	09	1870	The Coxswain of the Arklow Lifeboat John Cummings was awarded a Silver Medal by the RNLI for the rescue of 02/09/1870

Section One: Data by Date

Barter. Dr. Richard	Mon	03	10	Dr. Richard Barter died	1870
Blake. William H.	Thu	17	11	William Hume Blake died	1870
Boghall Brick			's	Boghall Brick Company established at Brickfield, Killarney Road, Bray	1870
Maps				Bray Town surveyed 1-500 scale map	1870
Act				Elementary Education Act	1870
Castlemacadam				Lord Powerscourt donated the site of the Church of the Holy Trinity at Castlemacadam, near Avoca, Co. Wicklow	1870
Monck. Charles				Charles Stanley Monck 4th Viscount Monck, Charleville, Enniskerry appointed Commissioner for National Education in Ireland	1870
Thompson. Dr C.				Dr Christopher Thompson fought an outbreak of Cholera in Bray. Dr Thompson lived at 9 Duncairn Terrace, Bray	1870
Water – Vartry				Bray linked to the Vartry Water Supply Scheme	1870
Meath Road, Bray				Mount Coleman House, Meath Road, Bray built	1870
Christ Church, Bray				Spire completed on Christ Church, Church Road, Bray	1870
Greystones				Greystones Harbour built	1870
Wicklow Infanticides				The number of Infanticides in County Wicklow was 0	1870
Young, Bernard				Bernard Young an inmate of St Kevin's Reformatory, Glencree was found dead on Featherbed Mountain, Co. Dublin	1870
Synge. Frances Mary				Frances Mary Synge married Rev. James Ownes of Cheltenham Collage	1870
Darley. J. C.				John Evelyn Carmichael Darley was born to Wellington and Anna F Darley at Violet Hill, Bray	1870
Burnaby. F.G.				Painting (NPG 2642) of Frederick Gustavus Burnaby by James Jacques Tissot is held in National Portrait Gallery, London	1870
Delahunt. S.V.				S.V.Delahunt general hardware store established in Wicklow Town	1870
Tinakilly House				Tinakilly House, Rathnew built for Captain. Robert Charles Halpin	1870
Books				A collection concerning the family of Yarner of Wicklow by the family Yarner	1870
Wicklow Homicides				The total number of Homicides , including Manslaughter and Murders in County Wicklow , 0	1870
Thompson Dr C.				Dr Christopher Thompsom became a member of the Obstetrics Society	1870
Fortgranite House				Fortgranite House, Baltinglass remodelled by M.C.Dennis	1870
Segrave. O'Neill				O'Neill Segrave appointed sheriff of County Wicklow	1870
Childers. R. E				Robert Erskine Childers born in England, but reared at Glendalough House, Co. Wicklow the home of his cousin Robert Barton	1870
Putland				Charles Putland Jnr held 484 Acres in Bray, Co. Wicklow	1870
Slater's Directory				Slater's Directory of Arklow, Baltinglass, Blessington, Newtown, Rathdrum and Wicklow Town	1870
Act	Sun	01	01	Irish Church Act came into effect on 1/1/1871	1871

The County Wicklow Database: 432 AD to 2006 AD

A–Z Reference	Day	Date	Month	Year	DATA
Hopper. Nora	Mon	02	01	1871	Nora Hopper born
Population Enniskerry	Sun	02	04	1871	Population of Enniskerry urban 381 or 0.48% of County Population
Population Greystones	Sun	02	04	1871	Population of Greystones & Delgany 619 or 0.78% of County Population
Population Wicklow (t)	Sun	02	04	1871	Population of Wicklow Town 3,164 or 4.02% of County Population
Population Arklow	Sun	02	04	1871	Population of Arklow Urban 5,178 or 6.57% of County Population
Population County	Sun	02	04	1871	Population of County Wicklow 78,697 persons. 39,496 Males 39,201 Females
Newcastle Barony	Sun	02	04	1871	The Population of the Newcastle Barony 9,714
Population Bray	Sun	02	04	1871	Population of Bray 6,087 or 7.73% of County Population
Talbotstown Upr Barony	Sun	02	04	1871	The Population of the Talbotstown Upper Barony 9,148
Ballinacor Nth. Barony	Sun	02	04	1871	The Population of the Ballinacor North Barony 6,992
Talbotstown Lwr Barony	Sun	02	04	1871	The Population of the Talbotstown Lower Barony 9,101
Rathdown Barony	Sun	02	04	1871	The Population of the Rathdown Barony 10,082
Ballinacor Sth. Barony	Sun	02	04	1871	The Population of the Ballinacor South Barony 8,015
Shillelagh Barony	Sun	02	04	1871	The Population of the Shillelagh Barony 7,138
Arklow Barony	Sun	02	04	1871	The Population of the Arklow Barony 218,507
Leeson	Sat	08	04	1871	Joseph Henry Leeson of Russborough House, Blessington. 5th Earl of Milltown died
Synge	Sun	16	04	1871	John Milligton Synge born
Plunket	Sun	16	04	1871	John Plunket 3rd Baron Plunket died and was succeeded by his son William Coyngham Plunket 4th Baron
Hill.Arthur-6th	Sun	02	07	1871	Arthur Hill 6th Marquis of Downshire born
Cochrane. Richard	Tue	04	07	1871	Richard Cochrane, of Woodbrook, Bray died
Cochrane. H.J.	Sun	13	08	1871	Henry John Cochrane born 2nd son of Sir Henry Cochrane, of Woodbrook, Bray
Roundwood	Sun	13	08	1871	St. Laurence O'Toole Church, Roundwood dedicated
Yeats, Jack B.	Tue	29	08	1871	Jack B.Yeats (artist) born in London
Railways			08	1871	Dublin & Wicklow & Wexford Railway Co. gave approval for building of permanent Railway Station at Shillelagh
Truell. Henry P				1871	Henry P.Truell appointed sheriff of County Wicklow
O'Nolan. Shaun				1871	Shaun O'Nolan (song writer) born at Baltinglass Co. Wicklow
Aravon School				1871	Roger Casement educated at Aravon School, Bray

Category	Description	Year			
Lifeboats	Greystones Lifeboat service established the first boat Sarah Tancred came into service on 3/8/1872	1871			
Act	Trade Union Act	1871			
Wicklow Infanticides	The number of Infanticides in County Wicklow was 0	1871			
Ships/Yachts	George Putland of Bray won the Edinburgh Cup with his yacht "Enid" 56 tons at Kingstown Regatta	1871			
Books	"Dublin and the County Wicklow" How to see them for 44 Guineas by John Bradbury. Published in London in 1871	1871			
Books	"History and Antiquities of Glendalough" by Joseph Nolan. Published in Dublin in 1871	1871			
Pearce. Thomas	Thomas Pearce appointed a school inspector in Canada serving Waterloo County 1871-1912	1871			
Mackintosh. C. Herbert	Charles Herbert Mackintosh wrote the book "The Chicago Fire"	1871			
Wicklow Homicides	The total number of Homicides, including Manslaughter and Murders in County Wicklow, 0	1871			
Maps	The 1870 survey map 1-500 of Bray Town, published (zincographed)	1871			
Ships/Yachts	The vessel "Lily" shipwrecked of the Wicklow Coast	1872	01	Wed	10
Newspapers	Bray Gazette Newspaper final edition	1872	01	Sat	27
Newspapers	Kingstown and Bray Gazette Newspaper first edition	1872	02	Sat	03
Rathmichael	The separation of the Parishes of Bray and Rathmichael was completed	1872	06	Mon	17
Barrington. Sir William	Sir William Barrington died	1872	07	Sun	14
Fitzwilliam. 7th Earl	William Fitzwilliam 7th Earl Fitzwilliam born	1872	07	Thu	25
Lifeboats	Lifeboat (33ft) Sarah Tancred funded from a legacy of J J Tancred of Dublin. Lady Meath of Bray launched the lifeboat	1872	08	Sat	03
Railways	The boiler of Locomotive No 4 exploded at Bray Railway Station	1872	09	Mon	16
Ships/Yachts	The vessel "Fanny Palmer" shipwrecked of the Wicklow Coast	1872	11	Fri	29
Byrne. James (Pt.)	Private James Byrne (reg No.162) died in Dublin	1872	12	Fri	06
Wicklow Homicides	The total number of Homicides, including Manslaughter and Murders in County Wicklow, 1	1872			
Druhan. Loughlin	Rev. Loughlin Druhan Parish Priest of Tomacork, Carnew 1872-1879	1872			
Wicklow Infanticides	The number of Infanticides in County Wicklow was 0	1872			
Brabazon. Reginald	Meath Protestant Industrial School and Destitute Protestant Boy's Aid Fund was founded by the Reginald the 12th Earl of Meath	1872			
Lifeboats	Lifeboat Sarah Tancred served at Greystones Lifeboat Station from 1872 to 1886 launched 3 times saved 4 lives	1872			
O'Byrne. W.R	William Richard O'Byrne appointed sheriff of County Wicklow	1872			
Tozer. Mr	Mr. Tozer became Stationmaster at Bray Railway Station	1872			
Proby. Hon. William	Granville Levenson 4th earl of Carysfort died and was succeeded by his brother William Proby	1872			
Lifeboats	Greystones Lifeboat Station established	1872			

A-Z Reference	Day	Date	Month	Year	DATA
Synge, John Hatch				1872	John Millington Synge father John Hatch Synge died in Dublin
Act				1872	Ballot Act
Books				1872	The Tourist's Picturesque Guide to Wicklow and Dublin by George Rennie Powell
Bray Hunt Club				1872	The Bray Hunt Club founded
Polo				1872	The first recorded Polo match in Ireland was in County Carlow in 1872
Ships/Yachts	Mon	27	01	1873	The vessel "Pensiero" went aground north of Bray
Ships/Yachts	Sat	01	02	1873	The vessel "John Scott" shipwrecked of the Wicklow Coast
Newspapers	Sat	29	03	1873	Kingstown and Bray Gazette Newspaper final edition
Ships/Yachts	Thu	10	04	1873	The vessel "Dromedary" shipwrecked of the Wicklow Coast
Railways	Sat	26	04	1873	A footbridge at Rathdrum Railway Station collapsed under the weight of the crowd on it
Ships/Yachts	Sun	10	08	1873	The vessel "Charles" shipwrecked of the Wicklow Coast
Cochrane, Ernest	Thu	12	09	1873	Sir Ernest Cecil Cochrane 2nd Bart born The 3rd son of Sir Henry Cochrane 1st Bart, of Woodbrook, Bray
Smithson, Annie	Fri	26	09	1873	Annie Smithson born in Dublin
Railways				1873	Railway Locomotive Number 32 built and named Glenmalure, Withdrawn from service 1925
Mackintosh, C. Herbert				1873	Charles Herbert Mackintosh wrote "The Financial Panic in the U.S and its causes"
Lifeboats				1873	The 1857 lifeboat house at Arklow sold and a new lifeboat station was built on the south side of the river.
O'Toole, Luke				1873	Luke O'Toole born Co. Wicklow. 1901-1929 General Secretary of the GAA
Charleville House				1873	Sale of some of the contents of Charleville House, Enniskerry
Healy, John				1873	John Healy born at Kilbride, Co. Wicklow
Railways				1873	Railway Locomotive Number 33 built and named Glendalough, Withdrawn from service 1925
Parnell, Delia				1873	Delia Parnell inherited £1,000 from Sir Ralph Howard, Earl of Wicklow
Powerscourt				1873	The English Gate in the grounds of Powerscourt House, Enniskerry was purchased in London by Lord Powerscourt
Thompson, Dr C.				1873	Dr. Christopher Thompson, Bray became a Fellow of the Royal College of Surgeon's of Ireland.
Brabazon, Reginald				1873	The Earl of Meath built a forge and Market House at Aughrim, Co. Wicklow
Dargle River				1873	Storms and Flooding at Bray Seafront and the River Dargle broke its banks
Wicklow Homicides				1873	The total number of Homicides, including Manslaughter and Murders in County Wicklow, 2
Mackintosh, C. Herbert				1873	Charles Herbert Mackintosh appointed managing editor of the Chicago Journal of Commerce

Name	Description	Year			
Dennis.M.C	Meade C.Dennis appointed sheriff of County Wicklow	1873			
Kearon and Tyrrell	Kearon and Tyrrell shipping company established in Arklow	1873			
Ships/Yachts	The vessel "Copernicus" shipwrecked of the Wicklow Coast	1873			
Wicklow Infanticides	The number of Infanticides in County Wicklow was 1	1873			
Elections-Polling Day	The first time the Ballot Act (secret voting) was first used	1874	02	07	Sat
Elections-Polling Day	W.R. O'Byrne, W.W.F. Dick, elected M.P's. for Wicklow at the General Election, Number of electors 3579	1874	02	07	Sat
Hill.Arthur-5th	Arthur Hill 5th Marquess of Downshire died	1874	03	31	Tue
Monck	Henry Power Charles Monck married Edith Scott daughter of the Earl of Clonmell	1874	07	23	Thu
O'Connor. Peter J.	Peter J. O'Connor (athletics) born at Ashtown near Rathnew, Co. Wicklow	1874	10	18	Sun
Tottenham. C.R.W	Charles Robert Worsley Tottenham of Woodstock House, Kilcoole married Dorothea Cornwall	1874	11	05	Thu
La Touche	Charlotte La Touche nee Cornwallis died	1874	12	03	Thu
Hagan.John	Rev. John Hagan born at Ballycoog near Arklow	1874			
St. Peters School	St. Peter's School built in the grounds of St Peter's Church, Little Bray, built	1874			
Parnell. Charles S	Charles S. Parnell joined the Home Rule League	1874			
Kilbride, Bray	Church of Ireland church at Kilbride, Bray built	1874			
Cripples Home, Bray	The Cripples Home on the Lower Dargle Road was founded by Lucinda O'Sullivan	1874			
Parnell. Charles S	Charles Stewart Parnell appointed sheriff of County Wicklow	1874			
Books	The Dublin & Wicklow Manure Company's Almanac	1874			
Mining Accident	One man received a spinal injury in an accident at the Luganure Mine, Glendalough	1874			
Polo	The All Ireland Polo Club (Dublin) was founded	1874			
Mecredy. Rev James	Rev. James Mecredy died	1874			
Wicklow Infanticides	The number of Infanticides in County Wicklow was 3	1874			
Tottenham. Lt Col C. G.	Lt. Col. C. G. Tottenham elected M.P. for New Ross 1874	1874			
Parnell.J.H.	J. H. Parnell elected M.P for Wicklow 1874	1874			
Wicklow Homicides	The total number of Homicides , including Manslaughter and Murders in County Wicklow , 2	1874			
Beatty.Sir A. C.	Alfred Chester Beatty was born in New York City	1875	02	07	Sun
Woodburn.William	William Woodburn elected to the US Congress for Nevada - 04/03/1875 – 03/03/1877	1875	03	04	Thu
Roundwood	A woman named Byrne of Roundwood lost in a snowstorm, her body was found by John McCann an employee of the Water Works	1875	03	09	Tue
Rifle Contest	A meeting held in Wicklow to organise an International Rifle Contest on the Murrage, Wicklow in June 1876	1875	03	25	Thu

A–Z Reference	Day	Date	Month	Year	DATA
Gray. Sir John	Fri	09	04	1875	Sir John Gray died in Bath, England
Kearney. Teresa	Mon	12	04	1875	Teresa Kearney born at Knockenrahan, Arklow, Co. Wicklow
Parnell. Charles S	Mon	19	04	1875	Charles S. Parnell elected to the House of Commons on behalf of County Meath
Books				1875	2nd Edition. Gems of Home Scenery, Views of Wicklow and Killarney compiled by William John Loftie. Published in London in 1875
Bray Bye Laws				1875	Bray Fore-shore and Esplanade Bye laws,
Powerscourt				1875	The formal gardens at Powerscourt Estate, Enniskerry were completed
Act				1875	Public Health Act
Bray. Seafront				1875	Bray Improvement Committee was formed see 1883
Wicklow Infanticides				1875	The number of Infanticides in County Wicklow was 1
Brabazon. Reginald				1875	The Meath Protestant Industrial School for Boys was established in Blackrock by Reginald 12th Earl of Meath
Guinness. P.W				1875	Percy Wyndham Guinness the son of Rev Robert Guinness and Dora Boxwell born
Parnell. H.T.				1875	Henry Tudor Parnell a brother of Charles S Parnell sold all the property in Carlow inherited from his father in 1859
Sheet/British Library				1875	Evidence given in the case of O'Keeffe v McDonald at the Wicklow Assizes, 1875 by Rev. W. J. Walsh, R.C. Archbishop of Dublin
Books				1875	Wildfoot, the Wanderer of Wicklow by Edwin J. Brett
GFS				1875	The Girls Friendly Society of England was established in London
Grattan. Henry				1875	Essex Bridge over the River Liffey renamed Grattan Bridge after Henry Grattan
Esmond. Sir John				1875	Sir John Esmond appointed sheriff of County Wicklow
Wicklow Homicides				1875	The total number of Homicides , including Manslaughter and Murders in County Wicklow , 1
Grattan. Henry	Fri	07	01	1876	A statue to Henry Grattan was unveiled in Dame Street, Dublin
Ships/Yachts	Thu	13	01	1876	The vessel "Vesper" shipwrecked of the Wicklow Coast
Henry. Paul	Tue	11	04	1876	Paul Henry RHA was born in Belfast
Wilson. James	Mon	17	04	1876	James Wilson from Wicklow, 1 of 6 prisoners sprung from Freemantle Jail, and taken to America on the whaling ship "Catalpa"
Ships/Yachts	Sat	30	09	1876	The vessel "Leonie" capsized near Bray Harbour
Putland			10	1876	Charles Putland Jnr died
Guinness	Thu	02	11	1876	Ernest Guinness born
Railways	Sat	09	12	1876	Due to a landslide the railway services south of Killiney suspended for 5 days
Thompson. Dr C.	Sat	16	12	1876	Dr. Christopher Thompson, of Bray died

Section One: Data by Date

Category	Weekday	Day	Month	Year	Description
Police/Garda				1876	County Wicklow RIC Sgt. John O'Brien RIC was killed.
Railways				1876	The Brabazon Tunnel was bypasses by two short tunnels
Railways				1876	2nd Royal Commission established to examine Irish Railways
Whiteside. James				1876	James Whiteside died in Brighton, England
Tighe. James S				1876	James Stuart Tighe appointed sheriff of County Wicklow
Aravon School				1876	John Holdbrook– Head Master of Aravon School, Bray
Glendalough				1876	The east window in Teampil na Skellig (Rock Church) at Glendalough was replaced
Newspapers				1876	Bray Herald and Kingstown and Dalkey Advertise first edition
Glendalough				1876	A conical cap was placed on the round tower at Glendalough, construction work was done by the Board of Works.
Newspapers				1876	Bray Herald and South Dublin Herald Newspaper first edition
Lifeboats				1876	John Doyle of Greystones. Coxswain of Greystones Lifeboat 1876 -1892
Railways				1876	From rock fall and erosion the railway line around Bray Head had to be diverted in the following years 1876, 1879, 1888, 1917.
Wicklow Homicides				1876	The total number of Homicides, including Manslaughter and Murders in County Wicklow, 3
Books				1876	"A ride to Khira" by Frederick Gustavus Burnaby published
Wicklow Infanticides				1876	The number of Infanticides in County Wicklow was 1
Plunket. William				1876	Rev William Plunket grandson of W. Plunkett who died in 1854, appointed Bishop of Meath, His wife was Anne Guinness
Bray Coastguard				1876	Bray Coastguard station built off the Putland Road, Bray
Cunningham. Agnes E.	Mon	22	01	1877	Agnes Emma Gun Cunningham the wife of Robert A Cunningham died
Thompson. Dr C.	Fri	26	01	1877	At the meeting in Quin's Hotel was Sir Robert Stewart, Rev J.G. Scott, J.R. Sutcliffe, Captain Mostryn, and Dr. Wise all from Bray
Thompson. Dr C.	Fri	26	01	1877	Meeting held in Quins Hotel proposed to build a memorial to Dr. Thompson
Cunningham. R.A.G	Thu	07	06	1877	Robert A. Gun Cunningham died aged 85 years, memorial in the Church of Holy Trinty, Matlock, Derbyshire
Cochrane. Stanley	Wed	19	09	1877	Sir Stanley Herbert Cochrane born. The 4th son of Sir Henry Cochrane 1st Bart, of Woodbrook, Bray
Gladstone. William	Wed	17	10	1877	William Gladstone (1809-1898) paid a visit to Ireland. He visited the Earl of Meath at Killruddery, Bray
Gladstone. William	Tue	01	11	1877	William Gladstone given the freedom of the City of Dublin
Wicklow. Earl of	Mon	24	12	1877	Ralph Francis Howard 7th Earl of Wicklow born
Casement. Julius				1877	Julius Casement appointed sheriff of County Wicklow
Railways				1877	New station building built at Woodenbridge Railway junction by Dublin & Wicklow & Wexford Railway Co.
GFS				1877	The first meeting of the Girls Friendly Society of Ireland took place in Bray, County Wicklow

A–Z Reference	Day	Date	Month	Year	DATA
Wicklow Infanticides				1877	The number of Infanticides in County Wicklow was 5
Gladstone. William				1877	William Gladstone gave £5 towards the bells for Christ Church, Bray
Wicklow Homicides				1877	The total number of Homicides , including Manslaughter and Murders in County Wicklow , 0
Dublin Gas Company				1877	The Alliance of Dublin Gas (Bray Supply) Act
Wicklow Gaol				1877	Wicklow Gaol lost its status as County Gaol. Its functions were transferred to the Bridewell in Dublin
Parnell. Sophia				1877	Sophia Parnell died of scarlet fever contracted from her sick child
Thompson Dr C.				1877	Dr Thompson Memorial Committee members Sir Robert Stewart, Rev J.G. Scott, Mr.J.R.Sutcliffe, Captain Mostryn and Dr.Wise
Bray School	Sun	26	05	1878	Meeting held in the Holy Redeemer Church, Bray to establish a fund to build a new school.
Act	Thu	08	08	1878	Public Health (Ireland) Act
Galvin. Rev Richard	Fri	22	11	1878	The Rev Richard Galvin Parish Priest of the Church of St. Mary's and St. Michael's Rathdrum. died
Tottenham. Isabella	Tue	17	12	1878	Isabella Tottenham nee Cornwallis died
Books				1878	"Shaw's Tourists' Guide to Wicklow and Dublin" Published in London in 1878
Wicklow Homicides				1878	The total number of Homicides , including Manslaughter and Murders in County Wicklow , 0
Wicklow Infanticides				1878	The number of Infanticides in County Wicklow was 1
Tottenham. Lt Col C. G.				1878	Lt. Col. C. G. Tottenham elected M.P. for New Ross 1878 – 1880
Wilde. Oscar				1878	Oscar Wilde appeared in Bray Courthouse
Darley. Sir F.M				1878	Sir Frederick Matthew Darley was appointed Queen's Council
Wicklow Regatta				1878	1st Wicklow Regatta
Bray School				1878	Messrs O'Neill & Byrne given the contract to build a new Bray National School
Moorhead. Dr. Thomas G.				1878	Thomas Gillman Moorhead born at Benburb Co. Tyrone and educated at Aravon School , Bray and Trinity College, Dublin
Books				1878	Shaw's Tourist's Picturesque Guide to Wicklow and Dublin by George Shaw publisher
Wynne. Gladys				1878	Gladys Wynne (artist) daughter of the Archdeacon of Aghadoe born
St.John Whitty,Sophia				1878	Sophia St.John Whitty born in Dublin
Maps				1878	The 1870 survey map 1–500 of Bray Town updated and revised, published (zincographed)
Trams				1878	The Dublin Southern Districts Tramway Company established
Arklow School				1878	A Protestant School established in Arklow
Act				1878	Intermediate Education Act –payment to aid private secondary schools

				1878	Bray Town Commissioners proposed to build a Baths and Changing Rooms on the seafront
Bray. Seafront				1878	Bray Town Commissioners proposed to build a Baths and Changing Rooms on the seafront
Trams				1878	The Dublin Central Tramway Company established
Saunders. R.J.P				1878	Robert J. P. Saunders appointed sheriff of County Wicklow
Hodson	Wed	22	01	1879	George Frederick John Hodson (Lieut. 24 Foot) brother of Robert 4th Bart. killed in action at Isandula, South Africa.
Acton. Caroline	Fri	11	04	1879	Caroline Acton nee Walker died
Burnaby. F.G.	Wed	25	06	1879	Elizabeth Hawkins-Whitshed of Greystones married Frederick Gustavus Burnaby in London
Power. George	Thu	10	07	1879	Rev George Beresford Power, married Constance Putland 2nd dau of Charles Putland Jnr of Bray Head House, Co. Wicklow
Campbell. Joseph	Tue	15	07	1879	Joseph Campbell (poet) born in Belfast
Ships/Yachts	Wed	01	10	1879	The schooner ME Johnson launched it was built by Messrs W Ashburner & Sons, England
Arklow Convent	Sun	05	10	1879	The foundation stone laid for Arklow Convent
Harty.H.H	Thu	04	12	1879	Herbert Hamiltom Harty born at Hillsborough, Co. Down
Davidson. Lillian				1879	Lillian Lucy Davidson (artist) born
Putland				1879	Charlotte Mab Putland married Rev John West Neligan
Court Case				1879	Legal case re building on the Seafront. AG v Bray Town Commissioners
Clara				1879	The Forge in the village of Clara Co. Wicklow erected
Tombe. Gordon E				1879	Gordon E. Tombe appointed sheriff of County Wicklow
Arklow				1879	A very bad outbreak of smallpox in Arklow
Wicklow Infanticides				1879	The number of Infanticides in County Wicklow was 2
Ships/Yachts				1879	The vessel "Wicklow Head" (1st) built (1,453 Tons)
Baltinglass, Convent				1879	The Presentation Convent founded in Baltinglass
Books				1879	"My Lords of Strogue" by Lewis Strange Wingfield
Pobje. Henry Jnr				1879	Henry Pobje Jnr died
Sinnott. Walter				1879	Rev. Walter Sinnott Parish Priest of Tomacork, Carnew 1879 -1911
Bray. Town Hall				1879	Bray Town Hall designed by Guy Dawber
Wicklow Homicides				1879	The total number of Homicides , including Manslaughter and Murders in County Wicklow , 0
Books				1879	Ward and Lock's Tourist's Picturesque Guide to Dublin and Wicklow 5th Edition by Ward and Lock, London
Elliston. Henry			02	1880	Henry Elliston married Henrietta Kean
Ships/Yachts	Mon	29	03	1880	The vessel "Peter" shipwrecked of the Wicklow Coast
Baltinglass			03	1880	Fr. D. Kane of Baltinglass objected to Thomas McCoan standing as an M.P. for Wicklow

A-Z Reference	Day	Date	Month	Year	DATA
M.P.s for Wicklow	Fri	02	04	1880	Mr W.J. Corbett and Thomas McCoan elected as M.P.s for Wicklow
Elections–Polling Day	Tue	06	04	1880	W.J. Corbet, J.C McCoan, W.W.F. Dick elected M.P.s for Wicklow at the General Election, Number of electors 3212
Burnaby. H.S.V.G.			05	1880	Elizabeth Burnaby gave birth to Harry St. Vincent Gustavus Burnaby
Powerscourt	Fri	16	07	1880	Mervyn Richard Wingfield 8th Viscount Powerscourt born
Parnell. Theodosia	Wed	21	07	1880	Theodosia Parnell married Commander Claude Paget
Bray School	Thu	14	10	1880	Bray Boys National school established in the Little Flower Hall beside the Holy Redeemer Church, Bray
Parnell. Charles S	Tue	02	11	1880	Charles S. Parnell granted the Freedom of Limerick under Municipal Privileges Act 1875
Parnell. Charles S	Mon	06	12	1880	Charles S. Parnell granted the Freedom of Waterford City under Municipal Privileges Act 1875
Hamilton. Gladys Mary	Fri	10	12	1880	Gladys Mary Hamilton the daughter of the Earl of Abercorn born Duddingston House, Edinburgh
Wicklow. Earl of	Fri	10	12	1880	Lady Gladys Howard nee Hamilton born, Wife of the 7th Earl of Wicklow
Synge			circa	1880	1880 Synge family spent their summer holidays at "Uplands" near Annamoe
Lawrence. William			circa	1880	Robert French becomes chief outdoor photographer for William Lawrence (see French)
Wicklow. County			's	1880	Carter Draper became County Surveyor and first surveyor for Wicklow County Council in 1898
O'Neill. Henry				1880	Henry O'Neill (artist) died
Wicklow Homicides				1880	The total number of Homicides , including Manslaughter and Murders in County Wicklow , 0
Wicklow Harbour				1880	The east pier at Wicklow Harbour constructed
Bray Harbour				1880	15,000 tons of coal landed at Bray
Little Flower Hall				1880	The Little Flower Hall, Bray was constructed at a cost of £1,200-8s-2d
McCoan. J.C.				1880	J.C. McCoan elected M.P. for Drogheda in a by-election 1880
Parnell. Fanny				1880	Fanny Parnell published The Hovels of Ireland (New York, 1880)
Bray School				1880	The first class in Little Flower Hall, School, Bray had 21 pupils
Sea Baths				1880	Bray Sea Baths opened at Bray Harbour
Glendalough House				1880	Glendalough House was renovated
Burial Society				1880	St. Kevin's Catholic Tontine Burial Society founded in Bray
McCoan. J.C.				1880	J.C. McCoan elected M.P. for Wicklow 1880 – 1885
Wicklow Infanticides				1880	The number of Infanticides in County Wicklow was 0
Brooke. R.H				1880	Robert Howard Brooke appointed sheriff of County Wicklow
Grattan. Henry				1880	A Memorial drinking fountain to Henry Grattan unveiled at St. Stephen's Green, Dublin

	Day	Date	Month	Year	Event
Land League	Sat	01	01	1881	The Wicklow Branch of the Land League established at a meeting in Town Hall, Wicklow Town
Meath. Lady	Thu	20	01	1881	The Meath Convalescent Home, Dublin Road, Bray was instituted by Lady Meath
Land League, Ladies	Sun	30	01	1881	Ann and Fanny Parnell sisters of C.S. Parnell establish a ladies section of the Land League in Ireland
Parnell. Charles S	Tue	01	02	1881	Charles S. Parnell granted the Freedom of Drogheda under Municipal Privileges Act 1875
Barton. Robert	Mon	14	03	1881	Robert Barton and his twin brother Hugh Barton was born at Glendalough House, Co. Wicklow
Barton. Hugh	Thu	17	03	1881	Hugh Barton died
Arklow Convent	Thu	17	03	1881	The convent at Arklow opened
Parnell. Fanny			03	1881	An article by Fanny Parnell appeared in the North American Review, March Issue "The Irish Land Situation"
Population Wicklow (t)	Sun	03	04	1881	Population of Wicklow Town 3,391 or 4.81% of County Population
Population Bray	Sun	03	04	1881	Population of Bray 6,535 or 9.28% of County Population
Population County	Sun	03	04	1881	Population of County Wicklow 70,386 persons. 35,101 Males 35,258 Females
Population Enniskerry	Sun	03	04	1881	Population of Enniskerry urban 324 or 0.46% of County Population
Population Greystones	Sun	03	04	1881	Population of Greystones & Delgany 529 or 0.84% of County Population
Population Arklow	Sun	03	04	1881	Population of Arklow Urban 4,777 or 6.78% of County Population
Queen Victoria	Wed	25	05	1881	Prince Leopold, son of Queen Victoria created Baron of Arklow
Wicklow. Earl of	Mon	20	06	1881	Charles Francis 5th Earl of Wicklow died and was succeeded by his brother Cecil
Kemmis. William	Wed	10	08	1881	William Gilbert Kemmis died
Parnell. Charles S	Thu	13	10	1881	Charles S. Parnell and other prominent members of the Land League arrested and sent to Kilmainham Gaol
Land League			10	1881	A branch of the Land League was formed in Bray. Called the Michael Davitt Branch.
Parnell. Charles S			12	1881	Charles S. Parnell granted the Freedom of Wexford under Municipal Privileges Act 1875
Wicklow Regiment				1881	Col. George Tottenham appointed commanding officer of Wicklow Artillery Regiment
Wicklow Homicides				1881	The total number of Homicides , including Manslaughter and Murders in County Wicklow , 0
Christ Church, Bray				1881	A set of eight bell erected and first rung in Christ Church, Bray
Slater's Directory				1881	Slater's Directory of Arklow, Blessington, Bray,Delgany,Donard,Dunlavin, Enniskerry, Greystones,Newtown,Rathdrum,Wicklow
Town Hall. Bray				1881	The foundation stone for the Town Hall and Market Place, Bray was laid by the Earl of Meath
Land Commission				1881	Land Commission established
People's Park				1881	The People's Park and Park Lodge presented as a free gift to Bray Town Commissioners by Lord and Lady Meath
Books				1881	Black's Guide to Dublin and the Wicklow Mountains published by Charles Black of Edinburgh
Darley. Cecil W.				1881	Cecil West Darley worked on Newcastle Harbour and Sydney breakwater between 1867-1881

A–Z Reference	Day	Date	Month	Year	DATA
Books				1881	Black sand, in the drift North of Greystones, Co. Wicklow (From the scientific proceedings of Royal Dublin Society)
Wicklow Infanticides				1881	The number of Infanticides in County Wicklow was 1
Act				1881	Bray Township Act raised funds for the sea wall
Town Hall. Bray				1881	Work began on building the Town Hall and Market Place, Bray. The site was donated by the Earl of Meath
Act				1881	Protection of Person and Property (Ireland) Act
Act				1881	Land Law (Ireland) Act.
Parnell. Charles S				1881	Charles S. Parnell imprisoned in Kilmainham Gaol Dublin 1881-1882
St. Mary Convent. Arklow				1881	St. Mary's Convent Arklow established
Monck. Charles				1881	Viscount Monck sold 7,800 acres of his County Wicklow Estates.
Furlong				1881	Furlong's Forge established in Bray
Tottenham. Charles G				1881	Charles George Tottenham appointed sheriff of County Wicklow
Arklow Harbour Act	Mon	19	06	1882	Arklow Harbour Act passed
O'Kelly. Sean T	Fri	25	08	1882	Sean T O'Kelly born at Capel Street, Dublin
Parnell. Charles S	Mon	11	12	1882	A banquet given to Charles S. Parnell in Dublin, he was presented with a testimonial of £38,000
Howard. Catherine	Wed	27	12	1882	Catherine Petre (nee Howard) died
Wicklow Homicides				1882	The total number of Homicides , including Manslaughter and Murders in County Wicklow , 0
Mackintosh. C. Herbert				1882	Charles Herbert Mackintosh appointed Mayor of Ottawa 1882- 1887
Mecredy. Richard J.				1882	Richard James Mecredy founded the Champion Bicycle Club
Mecredy. Richard J.				1882	Richard James Mecredy founded the Irish Cyclist Association
Mackintosh. C. Herbert				1882	Charles Herbert Mackintosh elected Member of Parliament for Ottawa 1882-1887 and 1890 -1893
La Touche				1882	John David Digues La Touche of Kiltymon, Newtown Co. Wicklow. Appointed to the Imperial Maritime Customs Service, China 1882
Wicklow Infanticides				1882	The number of Infanticides in County Wicklow was 1
Dargle River				1882	The River Dargle broke its banks and flooded, Little Bray
Wingfield. Maurice	Thu	21	06	1883	Maurice Wingfield of Enniskerry born
Ships/Yachts	Fri	29	06	1883	The vessel "Kestrel" shipwrecked of the Wicklow Coast
Allgood. Sara	Wed	31	10	1883	Sara Allgood (actress) born in Dublin
Synge. Frances Mary				1883	Frances Mary Owen died
Wicklow Infanticides				1883	The number of Infanticides in County Wicklow was 2

Railways					1883	Railway Locomotive Number 61 built and named Earl of Wicklow, Withdrawn from service 1917
Brabazon. Reginald					1883	Lord Brabazon appointed sheriff of County Wicklow
Parnell. Emily					1883	Emily Parnell husband Capt Robert Munro Dickinson died
Bray Seafront					1883	The Bray Improvement Committee renamed Bray Amusements Committee see 1875
Act					1883	Labourers (Ireland) Act
St Matthwe's School					1883	The Gun Cunningham of Mount Kennedy gave the land for the building of St. Matthew's school at Newtown Mount Kennedy
Meath Road					1883	Killisk House, Meath Road, Bray built
Wicklow Homicides					1883	The total number of Homicides , including Manslaughter and Murders in County Wicklow , 2
Cullen. Fr. John					1883	Fr. John Cullen born Co. Wicklow, A priest in Tasmania along with his brothers Arthur and Joseph
Tinakilly House					1883	Tinakilly House, Rathnew completed
Wynne. Edward					1883	Edward Wynne appointed Secretary of Wicklow Grand Jury
Parnell. Charles S	Fri	11	01		1884	£796:6s:8d collected in County Wicklow in aid of Charles S. Parnell
Smyth. Algernon	Fri	11	01		1884	Capt. Algernon Bersford Smyth born in Bray Head House, Bray
Bray Town Hall	Mon	19	05		1884	The first meeting of Bray Town Commissioners in new Town Hall
Parnell. Charles S	Fri	22	08		1884	Charles S. Parnell granted the Freedom of Cork City under Municipal Privileges Act 1875
Tobin. James	Tue	26	08		1884	James Tobin executed in Wexford Gaol for the murder of Eliza Moore in Rathdrum, Co. Wicklow
Powerscourt	Tue	02	09		1884	Lady Elizabeth wife of 4th Marquis of Londonderry died
Bayly. Edward S	Wed	26	11		1884	Edward Symes Bayly of Ballyarthur House, Co. Wicklow died
Books					1884	[reprinted] The Wicklow Gold Mines:, or the Lads of the Hills by John O'Keeffe
Knockanarrigan					1884	Knockanarrigan Parochial Hall built
Wicklow Infanticides					1884	The number of Infanticides in County Wicklow was 2
Wicklow Railway Stn.					1884	Wicklow Town railway station built
Railways					1884	Railway Locomotive Number 63 built and named Earl of Carysfort, Withdrawn from service 1916
de Robeck. Baron					1884	Baron de Robeck appointed sheriff of County Wicklow
Town Hall. Bray					1884	The Town Hall and Market Place, Bray completed
O'Byrne. John					1884	John O'Byrne legal adviser and attorney general born Seskin Co. Wicklow
Synge					1884	J.M.Synge educated at Aravon School, Bray
Wicklow Homicides					1884	The total number of Homicides , including Manslaughter and Murders in County Wicklow , 1
Wicklow Harbour					1884	A Lighthouse established on the East pier, Wicklow harbour

A-Z Reference	Day	Date	Month	Year	DATA
Woodenbridge Golf Club				1884	Woodenbridge Golf Club established
Burnaby. F.G.	Sat	17	01	1885	Frederick Gustavus Burnaby died in the battle of Abu-Klea near Khartoum
Ships/Yachts	Wed	28	01	1885	The vessel "Giorgina" shipwrecked of the Wicklow Coast
Woodburn. William	Wed	04	03	1885	William Woodburn elected to the US Congress for Nevada – 04/03/1885 – 03/03/1899
Act	Fri	14	08	1885	Land Purchase (Ireland) Act
Ships/Yachts	Fri	30	10	1885	The vessel "Alhambra" carrying coal shipwrecked between the Welsh and Wicklow Coast
Elections-Polling Day	Sat	28	11	1885	W.J. Corbett elected M.P. for Wicklow East at the General Election, Number of electors 5569
Elections-Polling Day	Fri	04	12	1885	G.M. Byrne and W.W.F. Dick elected M.P.'s. for Wicklow West at the General Election, Number of electors 5226
Wicklow Infanticides				1885	The number of Infanticides in County Wicklow was 2
Wicklow Homicides				1885	The total number of Homicides , including Manslaughter and Murders in County Wicklow , 0
Tottenham. Lt Col C. G.				1885	Lt. Col. C. G. Tottenham elected M.P. for Wicklow East 1885
Dwyer. Michael				1885	The Bray Branch of the Irish National Foresters the Michael Dwyer branch established
Bray Seafront				1885	Seawall built at Bray to protect the Esplanade and Housing along the Seafront
Act				1885	Ashbourne Land Act-enabled Irish tenants to buy their holdings
Booth. George				1885	George Booth appointed sheriff of County Wicklow
Wicklow GAA				1885	Bray Emmets GAA Club established
Maps				1885	Arklow Town surveyed 1-500 scale map
Railways				1885	Railway Locomotive Number 59 built and named Earl of Fitzwilliam, Withdrawn from service 1917
Ships/Yachts				1885	The vessel "Holyhead" carrying cattle shipwrecked between the Welsh and Wicklow Coast
Books				1885	The Dublin & Wicklow Manure Company's Almanac
Wicklow Militia				1885	An outline of the history of the County Wicklow Regiment of Militia by Edward Benjamin Evans
Flora-Fauna			05	1886	Melodious Warbler (Hippolais polyglotta) was recorded at Coolattin, County Wicklow
Lugnaquilla Walk	Sun	20	06	1886	Henry Chichester Hart and Sir F. Cullinan walked from Terenure, Dublin to Lugnaquilla Mountain and back in 23 hours 50 min
Elections-Polling Day	Thu	08	07	1886	W.J. Corbett elected M.P. for Wicklow East at the General Election, Number of electors 5569
Elections-Polling Day	Mon	12	07	1886	G.M. Byrne elected M.P. for Wicklow West at the General Election, Number of electors 5226
Plunket	Sat	11	09	1886	Charlotte Plunket nee Bushe died
Ships/Yachts	Sat	23	10	1886	The schooner "Sarah Jane" wrecked off Greystones

Section One: Data by Date

Name	Day	Date	Month	Year	Description
Glenart Castle	Tue	09	11	1886	Shoot held at Gelnart Castle 9-12 Nov 1886. 1,687 Pheasants, 68 Woodcock, 2 hares and 97 rabbits were shot
Crampton. Sir J.F.T.	Sun	05	12	1886	Sir John Fiennes Twisleton Crampton died at Bushey Park, Enniskerry Co. Wicklow
Darley. Sir F.M	Tue	07	12	1886	Sir Frederick Matthew Darley was appointed Chief Justice of New South Wales
Wicklow GAA	Sun	26	12	1886	The first Convention of GAA Clubs in County Wicklow held in Town Hall, Wicklow Town
Brennan. Thomas				1886	Thomas Brennan born
Tottenham. Lt Col C. G.				1886	Lt. Col. C. G. Tottenham elected M.P. for Wicklow East 1886
Barrington. R.M.				1886	The first Lug Walk was a wager of fifty guineas between R.M. Barrington of Bray and C.H. Hart and F. Cuillinan
Wicklow GAA				1886	Aindreas O'hAolain Chairman of Wicklow GAA 1886 - 1895
Wicklow GAA				1886	Andrew Hyland of Barndarrig held the post of first Chairman of the County Wicklow GAA Board 1886-1895
Books				1886	Dublin and the County of Wicklow; how to see them for four and a half guineas by John Bradbury
Hime. Sir Albert H.				1886	Albert Henry Hime was made a CMG
Lifeboats				1886	Lifeboat Richard Robert Brown served at Greystones Lifeboat Station from 1876 to 1896
Madden. Richard				1886	Richard Robert Madden (historian) died
Act				1886	Bray & Enniskerry Light Railway Company Act.
Maps				1886	The 1885 survey map 1-500 of Arklow Town, published (zincographed)
Cunningham. Capt. C.				1886	Capt. C.R.D. Gun Cunningham appointed sheriff of County Wicklow
Railways				1886	The first attempt to link Bray & Enniskerry by railway was the establishment of Bray & Enniskerry Light Railway Co.
Whitshed. E.A.F.H.				1886	Elizabeth (Hawkins-Whitshed) Burnaby married J.F.Main
Wicklow Infanticides				1886	The number of Infanticides in County Wicklow was 0
Books				1886	Stories of Wicklow by George Francis Savage Armstrong
Wicklow Homicides				1886	The total number of Homicides , including Manslaughter and Murders in County Wicklow , 0
Armstrong. G.F.S				1886	Stories of County Wicklow published in London by George F.S.Armstrong
Allgood. Molly	Wed	12	01	1887	Molly Allgood (actress) also known as Marie O'Neill was born in Dublin
O'Dwyer. Thomas	Mon	14	03	1887	Rev.Thomas O'Dwyer Parish Priest of Enniskerry died
Brabazon. William	Thu	26	05	1887	William Brabazon the 11th Earl of Meath died and was succeeded by his son Reginald Brabazon 12th Earl of Meath
Joyce, George Alfred	Mon	04	07	1887	George Alfred Joyce a brother of James Joyce was born at 1 Martello Terrace, Bray
Joyce, George Alfred	Thu	14	07	1887	George Alfred Joyce was christened in the Holy Redeemer Church, Bray
St. Andrew's School	Sat	20	08	1887	The Earl of Meath laid the foundation stone for St. Andrew's School, Bray

A–Z Reference	Day	Date	Month	Year	DATA
Act	Tue	23	08	1887	Land Law (Ireland) Act
St. Mary's, Wicklow	Thu	08	09	1887	St.Mary's Preparatory College for boys established at the Dominican Convent, Wicklow Town.
Cullen. Augustus				1887	The legal firm Augustus Cullen & Sons was established in Church Street, Wicklow by Frank Kennedy
Monck. Hon. Henry				1887	Hon. Henry P.C.S. Monck appointed sheriff of County Wicklow
D&BST				1887	An Act established The Dublin & Blessington Steam Tramway Company
Act				1887	Savings Bank Act
Darley. Sir F.M				1887	Sir Frederick Matthew Darley was knighted
St.Andrew's School				1887	St.Andrew's School, Florence Road, Bray built
Patterson. M				1887	Rev M. Patterson became Parish priest of Enniskerry
Dargle River				1887	The River Dargle broke its banks and flooded, Little Bray
Aughrim				1887	The Earl of Meath commissioned Ardee Row, Jubilee Row and Meath Terrace, Aughrim. Built by Mr. Kelly at £80 per house
Brabazon. Reginald				1887	The 1st Public Children's Playground in Ireland was opened in Pimlico, Dublin by Reginald Brabazon the 12th Earl of Meath
Monck Family Estates				1887	The bulk of the Monck Family Estates in County Wicklow sold to the Land Commission between 1887–1889
Bray Furniture				1887	Bray Furniture Industry founded by Miss Faulkner
Scharff. Robert F.				1887	Robert Francis Scharff (Naturalist) appointed Assistant Keeper of the Natural History Museum, Dublin. And lived in Bray
Bray School				1887	J.M.Moore Principal of Bray Parish School
Maps				1887	County Wicklow was surveyed and the 1840 map revised for the edition of 1-2500 scale maps by the Ordnance Survey
Joyce, Family				1887	The Joyce family leased 1 Martello Terrace, Bray from Mrs Kelly the widow of Joseph Kelly builder of the terrace in 1859/60
Bray Head				1887	W.G.Morris chairman of a committee to erect an obelisk on Bray Head to mark the Jubilee of Queen Victoria.
Mecredy. Richard J.				1887	Richard James Mecredy married Catherine Anna Hopkins
Putland				1887	Charlotte Mab Neligan nee Putland died
Wicklow Homicides				1887	The total number of Homicides, including Manslaughter and Murders in County Wicklow, 0
Synge. Frances Mary				1887	Frances Mary Owen (nee Synge) Essays and Poems was posthumously published privately in London in 1887
Wicklow Infanticides				1887	The number of Infanticides in County Wicklow was 0
Wicklow Coastguard	Sat	17	03	1888	Two Wicklow Coastguards Fred Roncliffe and Thomas Mumford drowned of Five Mile Point and both are buried at Newcastle graveyard

Section One: Data by Date

Keyword	Day	Day	Month	Year	Description
Hodson	Mon	02	04	1888	Sir George Frederick John Hodson 3rd Bart of Hollybrooke, Bray died and was succeeded by his son Robert 4th Bart.
Life Saving	Fri	04	05	1888	C. Goodwyn (Architect) was given the Bronze Royal Humane Society Medal for a rescue at Bray Head. Co. Wicklow
Joyce, James	Tue	26	06	1888	James Joyce was one of the cast in a concert in Bray Boat House
Grattan. Lady Laura	Thu	12	07	1888	Lady Laura Grattan the wife of James Grattan. died
Trams	Wed	01	08	1888	The Dublin & Blessington Tram Company (DBST) first day of operation
Life Saving	Wed	08	08	1888	L. H. Goodbody was given the Bronze Royal Humane Society Medal for a rescue at Greystones. Co. Wicklow
Lifeboats			09	1888	A new lifeboat Robert Theophilus Garden II stationed at Wicklow Harbour
Lifeboats			09	1888	A new lifeboat house built at Wicklow Harbour at the cost of £628
Post Office				1888	A sub Post Office of Bray established at Brennan's Parade, Bray
Moneystown				1888	A school opened at Moneystown, Roundwood
Tottenham. Maj.C.R.W				1888	Major C. R. W. Tottenham appointed sheriff of County Wicklow
St Andrew's School				1888	St Andrew's School Bray opened
Kilcarra House				1888	Kilcarra House, Woodenbridge built
Ballynockan				1888	Local land lord agent named Cullen evicted a woman and blind sister. Local people built them a house in a single day
Act				1888	Probate Duties (Scotland and Ireland) Act
Canon Robinson				1888	Canon Robinson rector of Delgany 1888–1896
Synge				1888	John Millington Synge passes entrance examinations for Trinity College, Dublin
Act				1888	The Railway and Canals Act
Lovett. Richard				1888	Richard Lovett published his prints "Irish Pictures" including a number of views of County Wicklow
Roundwood				1888	The population of Roundwood dropped by 35% after the Reservoir Extension was completed
Wicklow Infanticides				1888	The number of Infanticides in County Wicklow was 0
Wicklow Homicides				1888	The total number of Homicides, including Manslaughter and Murders in County Wicklow, 1
Ships/Yachts				1888	Picture in the Royal St.George Yacht Club Dun Laoghaire of "Primula" owned by F.B.Jameson of Kilmacanogue at Kingstown
Joyce, Eileen	Tue	22	01	1889	Eileen Isbella Joyce a sister of James Joyce was born at Bray
Bewley. Thomas Arthur	Mon	28	01	1889	Thomas Arthur Bewley of Seapatrick, Greystones, Co. Wicklow died aged 45 years
Parnell. Charles S	Tue	23	04	1889	The City Fathers of Edinburgh voted to give Charles S. Parnell the Freedom of Edinburgh
St.Patrick's. Wicklow	Thu	28	11	1889	During the placing of the Bell in the belfry at St.Patrick's Church, Wicklow. It crashed on the floor of the porch
Hackett Hall				1889	Hackett Memorial Hall on the Bray Road, near Shankill built

The County Wicklow Database: 432 AD to 2006 AD

A–Z Reference	Day	Date	Month	Year	DATA
Wicklow Homicides				1889	The total number of Homicides, including Manslaughter and Murders in County Wicklow, 0
Christ Church, Bray				1889	The Great West Window of Christ Church Bray was completed
Elliston. Henry				1889	Henry Elliston appointed to the US Senate for Kanas USA
Boyle. Ina				1889	Ina Boyle singer and composer born at Bushey Park House, Enniskerry
Battley.Col.D'Oyly				1889	Col. D'Oyly Battley appointed sheriff of County Wicklow
D&BST				1889	The Dublin and Blessington Tramway Company incorporated
Collins. William W.				1889	William Wilkie Collins died, buried Kensal Green, London
La Touche				1889	A painting of David La Touche by Hugh Hamilton was purchased by the National Gallery of Ireland (NGI 7237) in Christie's London
Wicklow Infanticides				1889	The number of Infanticides in County Wicklow was 0
Joyce, Mary	Sat	18	01	1890	Mary Cathleen Joyce a sister of James Joyce was born at Bray
Connolly, James	Fri	30	04	1890	James Connolly married Lillie Reynolds from Carnew, Co. Wicklow at Perth in Scotland
Leeson			05	1890	Edward Nugent Leeson of Russborough House, Blessington. 6th Earl of Milltown died
French. Percy	Sat	28	06	1890	Song writer Percy French married Susan Ethel Kathleen Arimatage Moore at St Bartholemews Church, Conary Co.Wicklow.
Bestic. Albert A.	Tue	26	08	1890	Albert A. Bestic born Dublin
Deverell. Averill	Tue	01	11	1890	Averill Deverell, the first Irishwoman to practice as a barrister
Parnell. Charles S	Tue	16	12	1890	A motion was passed to remove Charles S. Parnell name from the register of Honorary Burgesses of the City of Edinburgh
Hopper. Nora			circa	1890	Poem "Wicklow Hills (To W.Y. Fletcher)" by Nora Hopper
Deverell.Averill			circa	1890	Averill Deverell born Greystones, Co. Wicklow
Casement. Julius			s	1890	Bellair House built for Julius Casement the building is now a hotel
Mc Mahon J. H.			's	1890	Rev J.H.Mcmahon Chaplin to the Lord Lieutenant's of Ireland. His daughter Ella wrote novel "Irish Vignettes"
Smithson. Annie			's	1890	Annie Smithson lived at Dargle Road, Bray
Everett. James				1890	James Everett born
Pennefather. Capt. C				1890	Capt. C. E. Pennefather appointed sheriff of County Wicklow
Act				1890	Housing for the Working Classes Act. the foundation statute for urban public housing
Aughrim				1890	The Catholic Church at Aughrim Co.Wicklow was constituted into a separate parish
Kilcroney				1890	Kilcroney House near Bray was sold to Alfred C. West
Cuddihy. C				1890	Rev C.Cuddihy became Parish priest of Enniskerry parish

Section One: Data by Date

Boucicault. Dion				1890	Dion Boucicault died
Act				1890	An act was obtained to construct at Harbour at Bray at cost of £45,000
Act				1890	Bray Township Act raised funds for General Purposes
Wicklow Homicides				1890	The total number of Homicides, including Manslaughter and Murders in County Wicklow, 2
Police/Garda				1890	Anthony Thomas Lefroy died
Wicklow Infanticides				1890	The number of Infanticides in County Wicklow was 0
Queen of Rumania				1890	The Queen of Rumania visited Lord and lady Meath at Killruddery, Bray
Mecredy. Richard J.				1890	Richard James Mecredy founded the Irish Road Club (Cyclist)
Newspapers				1890	Arklow Reporter Newspaper first edition
Assembly Hall				1890	The Assembly Hall, The Mall Wicklow Town, built
Mecredy. Richard J.				1890	Richard James Mecredy won 3 English Cycling titles 1mile, 5mile and 25 mile
Mecredy. Richard J.				1890	Richard James Mecredy set the endurance record for tandem cycling 204 mile
Proby. Hon. William				1890	William Proby 5th Earl of Carysfort appointed Lord Lieutenant of Wicklow 1890 - 1909
O'Toole Clan				1890	"History of the Clan O'Toole" by Rev P. L O'Toole. Published in Dublin in 1890
Luganure Mine				1890	The Mining Company of Ireland sold the Luganure Mine, Glendalough to the Wynne family for £3,364
Killruddery				1890	Carmen Sylva, the Queen of Rumania visited Killruddery
Scharff. Robert F.				1890	Robert Francis Scharff (Naturalist) appointed Keeper of the Natural History Museum, Dublin. And lived in Bray
Pim, Joshua				1890	Joshua Pim won the Wimbledon Tennis Champion (doubles) with fellow Irishman Frank Stoker
Flora-Fauna	Tue	17	02	1891	Lesser kestrel was shot near Shankill Co. Dublin. Specimen now in Natural History Museum, Dublin
Daly. Edward	Wed	25	02	1891	Edward Daly born in Limerick
Leeson	Tue	24	03	1891	Henry Leeson of Russborough House, Blessington. 7th Earl of Milltown died
Arklow Barony	Sun	05	04	1891	The Population of the Arklow Barony 13,432
Ballinacor Sth. Barony	Sun	05	04	1891	The Population of the Ballinacor South Barony 6,117
Newcastle Barony	Sun	05	04	1891	The Population of the Newcastle Barony 7,550
Rathdown Barony	Sun	05	04	1891	The Population of the Rathdown Barony 9,893
Talbotstown Lwr Barony	Sun	05	04	1891	The Population of the Talbotstown Lower Barony 7,108
Talbotstown Upr Barony	Sun	05	04	1891	The Population of the Talbotstown Upper Barony 7,185
Shillelagh Barony	Sun	05	04	1891	The Population of the Shillelagh Barony 6,076
Population, Blessington	Sun	05	04	1891	The Population of Blessington was 1,188

The County Wicklow Database: 432 AD to 2006 AD

A-Z Reference	Day	Date	Month	Year	DATA
Population Arklow	Sun	05	04	1891	Population of Arklow Urban 4,172 or 6.71% of County Population
Ballinacor Nth. Barony	Sun	05	04	1891	The Population of the Ballinacor North Barony 4,775
Population Enniskerry	Sun	05	04	1891	Population of Enniskerry urban 256 or 0.41% of County Population
Population Wicklow (t)	Sun	05	04	1891	Population of Wicklow Town 3,273 or 5.26% of County Population
Population Bray	Sun	05	04	1891	Population of Bray 6,888 or 11.08% of County Population
Population County	Sun	05	04	1891	Population of County Wicklow 62,136 persons. 31,054 Males 31,082 Females
Population Greystones	Sun	05	04	1891	Population of Greystones & Delgany 708 or 1.13% of County Population
Population Bray	Sun	05	04	1891	The Catholic population of Bray 3,395 *not a census year*
French. Susan	Fri	05	06	1891	Susan French nee Arimatage Moore died
Parnell. Charles S	Thu	25	06	1891	Charles S. Parnell married Katherine Wood the former wife of Capt. William O'Shea
Wicklow. Earl of	Fri	24	07	1891	Cecil 6th Earl of Wicklow died and was succeeded by his son Ralph
GFS			07	1891	A branch of the Girls Friendly Society was founded in Delgany, Co. Wicklow
Bray Harbour	Mon	03	08	1891	Work began on building Bray Harbour when Bray Town Commissioners signed contract with W.J.O'Doherty
Act	Wed	05	08	1891	Purchase of Land (Ireland) Act
Parnell. Charles S	Sun	20	09	1891	Charles S. Parnell addressed a large crowd at Deansgrange, Co. Dublin
Parnell. Charles S	Tue	06	10	1891	Charles S. Parnell died at Brighton England
Mecredy. Richard J.	Sat	10	10	1891	Richard Mecredy of Bray devised the rules for cycle polo and a pioneer match was held at the Scalp. Co. Wicklow
Cycle Polo	Sat	31	10	1891	Richard Mecredy published the rules cycle polo in "Cycling Ireland"
Wingfield. Lewis S.	Thu	12	11	1891	Lewis Strange Wingfield died in London
Joyce, Eva	Thu	26	11	1891	Eva Mary a sister of James Joyce was born at Bray
Redmond. John E.	Wed	23	12	1891	John Edward Redmond elected M.P. for Waterford 1891-1918
Joyce, Family			12	1891	The Joyce Family moved from Bray to 23 Carysfort Avenue, Blackrock.
Wicklow Infanticides				1891	The number of Infanticides in County Wicklow was 0
Elliston. Henry				1891	Henry Elliston appointed to the US Senate for Kanas USA
Act				1891	Stamp Act
Hodson. Sir R.A				1891	Sir Robert Adair Hodson appointed sheriff of County Wicklow
Browne. Maurice				1891	Fr. Maurice Browne born . Author of several novels

Railways				1891	A railway embankment of 200 yards was constructed by the Bray River for the Bray-Enniskerry Light Railway Co.
Armstrong. G.F.S.				1891	George F.S.Armstrong lived at Beech Hurst, Bray. County Wicklow between 1891 and 1905
Electricity				1891	Bray Electricity Light Company established at the Mill Race, Bray
Curtlestown				1891	St. Partick's Church Curtlestown built replacing an existing structure
Wicklow Homicides				1891	The total number of Homicides , including Manslaughter and Murders in County Wicklow , 1
Avondale House				1891	The Parnell family sold Avondale House and Estate, Rathdrum
Sheet/British Library				1891	Charge of the Lord Chief Baron on the trial, at the Leinster winter assizes, held at Wicklow, December 1890, James Redmond etc
Meade. Joseph				1891	Joseph Meade of Bray appointed Lord Mayor of Dublin 1891-1892
Books				1891	"The Maid of Honour" by Lewis Strange Wingfield
Ships/Yachts	Sat	20	02	1892	The vessel "Patriot" shipwrecked of the Wicklow Coast
Cochrane. H.J.	Fri	15	04	1892	Henry John Cochrane, of Woodbrook, Bray died
Hodson	Wed	08	06	1892	Richard Edmond Hodson married Margaret Pemberton
Monck	Thu	16	06	1892	Elizabeth Monck died
Roundwood P.P.	Sun	19	06	1892	Parnellism is a simple love of adultery and all those who profess Parnellism profess to love and admire adultery.
Elections–Polling Day	Thu	07	07	1892	James Sweetman elected M.P. for Wicklow East at the General Election, Number of electors 4583
Tottenham. Charles J.	Mon	11	07	1892	Charles John Tottenham of Woodstock House, Kilcoole died
Elections–Polling Day	Wed	13	07	1892	James O'Connor elected M.P. for Wicklow West at the General Election, Number of electors 4853
Hume. William. W.F	Thu	15	09	1892	William Wentworth Fitzwilliam Hume died
Ships/Yachts	Wed	05	10	1892	The vessel "Mersey" shipwrecked of the Wicklow Coast
Whitshed. E.A.F.H.				1892	J.F.Main husband of Elizabeth (Hawkins-Whitshed Burnaby) Main died
O'Byrne Clan				1892	"History of the Clan O'Byrne" by Rev P. L. O'Toole. Published in Dublin in 1892
St. Pauls. Bray				1892	The chancel of St.Paul's Church, Brinay was improved by building chancel arch and the arch enclosing the east window
La Touche				1892	William Robert La Touche died and was succeeded at Bellvue by his brother Octavius
Kiernan. Kitty				1892	Kitty Kiernan fiancée of Michael Collins born Granard Co. Longford. educated at Loreto Convent, Bray
La Touche				1892	When Octavius La Touche took over the property at Delgany. He was a widower with three daughters and one son Peter
Act				1892	Education Act
Armstrong. G.F.S.				1892	George F.S.Armstrong appointed Professor of History & English at Queen's College Cork.
Brabazon. Reginald				1892	The building of the Meath Industrial School for Girls was completed on a site given by the Earl of Meath

A-Z Reference	Day	Date	Month	Year	DATA
Tynte. Lieut. Col.FJ				1892	Lieut. Col. FJ Tynte appointed sheriff of County Wicklow
Newcastle Hospital				1892	Newcastle Hospital near Newtown Mount Kennedy built
Airs/Music				1892	County of Wicklow quick step. arrangement by A. Morelli
Parnell, J.H.				1892	J.H. Parnell elected M.P. for Wicklow West 1892
Books				1892	Stories of Wicklow 2nd Edition by George Francis Savage Armstrong
Wicklow Infanticides				1892	The number of Infanticides in County Wicklow was 0
Wicklow Homicides				1892	The total number of Homicides , including Manslaughter and Murders in County Wicklow , 0
Hanley. Daniel				1892	Daniel Hanley was executed in Wexford Gaol for the murder of Mary Lyons of Barndarrig in 1890
Crampton. Selina	Thu	05	01	1893	Selina Crampton a sister of John Crampton died
Plunket	Sat	14	01	1893	Lousia Plunket nee Foster died
Hodson	Wed	22	03	1893	Sir Edmond Adair Hodson 5th Bart born Son of Richard Edmond Hodson and nephew of Robert 4th Bart.
Conran. Margaret	Tue	16	05	1893	The murders took place of Margaret Conran and housekeeper Mary Farrell at Borklemore, Co. Wicklow
Conran. John	Mon	28	05	1893	John Conran was charged with the murders of Margaret Conran and housekeeper Mary Farrell
Hill.Arthur-6th	Thu	22	06	1893	Arthur Hill 6th Marquis of Downshire married Katkerine Hare daughter of the Earl of Listowel
Life Saving	Wed	12	07	1893	W.G.Doyle (Teacher) was given Bronze Royal Humane Society Medal ,saving Samuel M. Crombie from drowning at Greystones
Life Saving	Thu	10	08	1893	Bernard Collins (RIC) officer was given Bronze Royal Humane Society Medal , saving Lucy Kavanagh from drowning at Arklow
Mackintosh. C. Herbert	Tue	31	10	1893	Charles Herbert Mackintosh appointed the first and only Premier (Lieutenant Governor) of the Northwest Territories
Conran. John	Wed	06	12	1893	The murder trial of Margaret Conran and housekeeper Mary Farrell begins in Wicklow Courthouse
Conran. John			12	1893	John Conran found guilty of the murders of Margaret Conran and housekeeper Mary Farrell
Synge				1893	John Millington Synge sonnet "Glencullen" published
Barn Owls				1893	The National Museum of Ireland has a Northern Long Eared Owl found in the Glen of the Downes donated by R.G. Pilkington
Newspapers				1893	Arklow Reporter Newspaper final edition (incorporated with Bray Herald)
Wood Carving				1893	Wood Carving School established by Gertrude Bailey of Bray
Lee. Walter				1893	Rev. Walter Lee died and buried in Glasnevin Graveyard, Dublin
Kilbride, Bray				1893	An church organ made by Conacher of Huddersfield, England installed in Kilbride Church, Bray
Railways				1893	The Court orders the sale of the assets of Bray & Enniskerry Light Railway Co.
Mound				1893	Workmen discover a mound with human skeletons on Lord Plunkett land at Old Connaught, Bray

Pim. Joshua				1893	Joshua Pim won the Wimbledon Tennis Champion (doubles) with fellow Irishman Frank Stoker
Airs/Music				1893	The Wicklow Postman (words and Music by B.H. Janssen)
Comerford. Marie				1893	Marie Comerford born in Rathdrum, Co. Wicklow
Power. Jenny Wyse				1893	Jenny Wyse Power founder member of the Irish College, Ring Co. Waterford
Scott. G.D				1893	Rev George Digby Scott appointed Rector of Christchurch, Bray 1893-1943
Segrave. Capt. H				1893	Capt.H. Segrave appointed sheriff of County Wicklow
Booth. Denton				1893	Denton Booth was captain of the Dublin Metropolitan Police Tug of War team the won the world championship
Wicklow Infanticides				1893	The number of Infanticides in County Wicklow was 0
Wicklow Homicides				1893	The total number of Homicides, including Manslaughter and Murders in County Wicklow , 2
Lamb. Charles Vincent				1893	Charles Vincent Lamb (artist) born in Co. Armagh
Pim. Joshua				1893	Joshua Pim won the Wimbledon Tennis Champion (singles) 1893
Donnelly. N	Mon	01	01	1894	Rev. N. Donnelly appointed Parish Priest of Bray, Greystones and Little Bray 1894-1904
Halpin.Robert Charles	Sat	20	01	1894	Captain Robert Charles Halpin of Tinnakilly House near Wicklow Town, died
Conran. John			01	1894	John Conran death sentence was commuted to penal servitude for life
Hill.Arthur-7th	Sat	07	04	1894	Arthur Hill 7th Marquis of Downshire born
Plunket	Mon	04	06	1894	William Lee Plunket married Lady Victoria Hamilton-Temple Blackwood
Bower. Robert	Sat	09	06	1894	Robert Bower was born, the son of Sir Robert Bower and Annette Norah Head of Thornhill, Bray
Le Fanu. William R.	Sat	08	09	1894	The railway engineer William R. Le Fanu died
Healy. James	Wed	28	10	1894	Fr James Healy Parish Priest of Ballybrack and former priest in Bray died
Monck. Charles	Thu	29	11	1894	Charles Stanley Monck 4th Viscount Monck died and was succeeded by his son Henry Power Charles Monck
Railways				1894	Travelling Post Office Rail Vans built for the Dublin & Wicklow & Wexford Railway Co.
Flora-Fauna				1894	A pair of Wood Larks (Lullula arborea) bred in Co. Wicklow near Enniskerry
Greystones				1894	The Grand Hotel, Greystones established now the La Touche Hotel
Moore. Fletcher				1894	Fletcher Moore appointed sheriff of County Wicklow
Slater's Directory				1894	Slater's Directory of Traders, police, teachers, farmers and private residence for the towns and villages of the county
Saul.Capt. P				1894	Captain Patrick Saul born in Dublin
Co. Wicklow Tennis				1894	98145.451
98145.451				1894	Signal Cabin built at Bray Railway station
Le Fanu. Henry				1894	Henry Frewen Le Fanu ordained an Anglican Minister, appointed chaplain to the Bishop of Rochester

A–Z Reference	Day	Date	Month	Year	DATA
Pim, Joshua				1894	Joshua Pim won the Wimbledon Tennis Champion (singles) 1894
Railways				1894	Railway Locomotive Number 50 built and named Arklow, Withdrawn from service 1930
Harty.H.H				1894	Herbert Hamilton Harty aged 16 appointed organist at Christ Church, Bray.
Wicklow Homicides				1894	The total number of Homicides, including Manslaughter and Murders in County Wicklow, 0
Powerscourt				1894	Powerscourt Arms Hotel, Enniskerry destroyed by fire
Newcastle Hospital				1894	Newcastle Hospital near Newtown Mount Kennedy completed
Breen. Dan				1894	Dan Breen (Revolutionary and T.D.) born Co.Tipperary
Moorhead. Dr.Thomas G.				1894	Dr. Thomas G. Moorhead father Dr. William Robert Moorhead had a practice in Bray at 1 Prince of Wales Terrace.
Lifeboats				1894	Edward Archer of Greystones Coxswain of Greystones Lifeboat 1894–1896
Wicklow Infanticides				1894	The number of Infanticides in County Wicklow was 0
Yeats, Jack B.				1894	Jack B.Yeats married Mary Cottenham White from Devon
Books				1894	"Morluinents of the Ancient Family of Wingfields" by Mervyn 7th Lord Powerscourt. Published in London in 1894
Allen. Francis				1894	Francis Allen born at Dunlavin, Co. Wicklow
Elections–Polling Day	Fri	26	04	1895	Edward P. O'Kelly elected M.P. for Wicklow East at the By-Election caused when James Sweetman resigned
D&BST	Wed	01	05	1895	The first tram on the Dublin & Blessington Tramway line ran from Terenure to Blessington
Hodson	Tue	21	05	1895	Gilbert Stanley Hodson brother of Edmond 5th Bart., born
Fitzwilliam. 6th Earl	Sun	16	06	1895	Lady Frances Fitzwilliam nee Douglas died
Elections–Polling Day	Wed	17	07	1895	James O'Connor elected M.P. for Wicklow West at the General Election, Number of electors 4576
Elections–Polling Day	Mon	22	07	1895	W.J. Corbett elected M.P. for Wicklow East at the General Election, Number of electors 4461
Humphreys. C.F.	Sat	12	10	1895	Cecil Frances Alexander nee Humphreys died in Derry where her husband William Alexandra was a curate
Greystones Golf Club				1895	Greystones Golf Club established
Tottenham. Lt Col C. G.				1895	Lt. Col. C. G. Tottenham elected M.P. for Wicklow East 1895
Wicklow Infanticides				1895	The number of Infanticides in County Wicklow was 0
Kynoch of Arklow				1895	Kynochs Munitions factory opened at Arklow
Ashford				1895	The Grand Jury invited tenders to paint and repair the iron bridge at Ashford
Synge				1895	John Millington Synge enrols at the Sorbonne, Paris, France
Railways				1895	The Brabazon (railway) footbridge removed at Bray Head

Section One: Data by Date

Subject	Year	Month	Weekday	Day	Description
Wellesley. E.H	1895				Edward H. C. Wellesley appointed sheriff of County Wicklow
Railways	1895				Railway Locomotive Number 62 built and named Earl of Meath, Withdrawn from service 1916
Books	1895				Official Tourist Guide of Dublin, Wicklow and Wexford Railway by A. T. Hennessy
Esplanade Hotel	1895				Esplanade Hotel built on the site of the old Coastguard Station
Maps	1895				Wicklow surveyed using a scale 1:1056
Greystones	1895				A temporary R.C. Church built in Greystones
Cochrane. Stanley	1895				Sir Stanley Cochrane bought Bailieborough Castle, Co. Cavan from Lady Lisgar
Railways	1895				Railway Locomotive Number 55 built and named Rathdowne, Withdrawn from service 1929
Parnell. J.H.	1895				J. H. Parnell elected M.P. for Meath South 1895 -1900
Wicklow Homicides	1895				The total number of Homicides , including Manslaughter and Murders in County Wicklow , 1
Act	1895				Housing of the Working Class Act
Trams	1895				The Dublin & Blessington Tram extended to Pouluphouca
Newspapers	1895				Wicklow Star Newspaper first edition
Dempsey. Denis (Pt.)	1896	01	Fri	10	Pt. Denis Dempsey died at Toronto, Canada
Drumm. James	1896	01	Sat	25	James Drumm (Battery Train) born at Dundum, Co Down
Nursing Association	1896	03			Fr Healy Nursing Association was founded in Bray
O'Halloran. PJ.	1896	05	Fri	15	Patrick Joseph O'Halloran born Co. Galway
Fitzwilliam. 7th Earl	1896	06	Wed	24	William Fitzwilliam 7th Earl Fitzwilliam married Lady Maud Dundas
Act	1896	08	Fri	14	Light Railways Act
Shilelagh Flower Show	1896	08	Wed	19	Shilelagh Flower Show held in Shilelagh
Mackintosh. C.H.	1896	11	Mon	02	Charles Henry Mackintosh died
Mackintosh. C.H.	1896				Charles henry Mackintosh wrote "The God of Peace"
Ballygannon Hse.	1896				Ballygannon House, Kilcoole was sold by the Land Commission to William Digby Evans
Wicklow GAA	1896				Seosmah MacCearuil Chairman of Wicklow GAA 1896 - 1897
Lifeboats	1896				Greystones Lifeboat Station closed
Holy Redeemer, Bray	1896				The Holy Redeemer Church, Main Street Bray enlarged and decorated 1896 -1898 at cost £12,000
Wicklow Homicides	1896				The total number of Homicides , including Manslaughter and Murders in County Wicklow , 2
Trams	1896				The Tram Station at Poulaphaca, Co. Kildare built for Dublin and Blessington Steam Tram
Wicklow Infanticides	1896				The number of Infanticides in County Wicklow was 0

A–Z Reference	Day	Date	Month	Year	DATA
Maps				1896	The 1895 Wicklow surveyed map using a 1:1056 published
Electricity				1896	Bray Township Electric Lighting Order,1896
O'Byrne. W.R				1896	William Richard O'Byrne died
Irish Naturalist				1896	The "Irish Naturalist"Vol.V.,1896, page 155 deals with the submerged forest at Bray's North Strand.
Railways				1896	Railway Locomotive Number 58 built and named Rathdrum, Withdrawn from service 1940
Alexander. William				1896	William Alexander became Archbishop of Armagh and Protestant Primate of Ireland
Barrington. R.M.				1896	Between 1896 and 1916 R. M. Barrington of Bray donated 10 Barn Owls to the Irish National Museum of Ireland
Hume.William.H				1896	William H. Hume appointed sheriff of County Wicklow
Darley, Cecil W.				1896	Cecil West Darley appointed Chief Engineer for New South Wales Public Works Department 1896-1901
DUTC				1896	The Dublin United Tramway Company was founded
Bray Sailing Club				1896	Bray Sailing Club founded
Barrington. R.M.				1896	The naturalist R.M. Barrington and John A Harvie Browne led an expedition to Rockhall Island on a scientific field study
Grand Hotel				1896	The Grand Hotel established in Wicklow Town
Sisters of Charity				1896	The Sisters of Charity establish a home and school in Bray at Rack Rent House, Dublin Road
Railways				1896	Railway Locomotive Number 57 built and named Rathnew, Withdrawn from service 1933
Plunket	Thu	01	04	1897	Archbishop William Plunket, 4th Baron Plunket of Old Connaught, Bray died and was succeeded by his son William Lee 5th Baron
William Plunket	Thu	01	04	1897	William Plunket of Old Connaught died
Convent. Kilcoole	Fri	14	05	1897	St. Patrick's Convent established in Kilcoole
Arklow	Fri	14	05	1897	The cutting of the first sod on the site of St Saviours COI Church Arklow
Arklow	Thu	10	06	1897	The foundation stone laid for St Saviours COI Church Arklow
Conran, John	Tue	20	07	1897	John Conran died at Maryboro Gaol (Portlaoise)
Railways			07	1897	An act sought to establish The Central Wicklow and Glendalough (Seven Churches) Light Railway and Tramway Company
Railways			07	1897	A public notice appeared in Irish Times. Proposed to link the Dublin & Blessington Tramway with Glendalough & Rathdrum
Wicklow Harbour	Fri	06	08	1897	Wicklow Harbour Advances Act 1897
Royal Visit	Tue	19	08	1897	Prince George as Duke of York and his consort paid three week, Royal visit to Ireland to mark the Diamond Jubilee of the Queen
Flora-Fauna	Fri	20	08	1897	Robert Lloyd Praeger carried out fieldwork in the Newcastle and Killoughter area for Census of British Plants published in 1901

Keyword	Day	Date	Month	Year	Event
Powerscourt	Tue	24	08	1897	Prince George as Duke of York and his consort paid a visit to Powerscourt Estate
Bray Harbour	Wed	01	09	1897	Notice to Mariners–a Lighthouse at Bray Harbour 750 candle power light set to come into use 01/10/1897
Bray Harbour	Fri	01	10	1897	Lighthouse at Bray Harbour came into use. The light 30 flashes per minute, each flash lasting 1.5 seconds. Radius 5 miles
Halpin.Robert Charles	Sat	23	10	1897	Robert Charles Halpin Memorial unveiled at Fitzwilliam Sq. Wicklow Town
Brabazon. Reginald	Sat	13	11	1897	Letter from the Reginald Brabazon the 12th Earl of Meath Published in Irish Times about the clothing of destitute children in Dublin.
Railways				1897	An Act of Parliament established Bray & Glendalough Light Railway Company. Route Bray, Kilmacanogue, Kilmurry, Roundwood
Cochrane. Sir Henry				1897	Sir Henry Cochrane, of Woodbrook, Bray appointed sheriff of County Wicklow
Bray Golf Club				1897	Bray Golf Club formed
Housing				1897	Meath Villas, Meath Road, Bray
Bray Harbour				1897	Work on Bray Harbour completed
La Touche				1897	Octavius La Touche died and was succeeded by his son Peter a Major in the Royal Dublin Fusiliers
Booth. Evelyn Mary				1897	Evelyn Mary Booth born in Co. Wicklow
Wicklow Infanticides				1897	The number of Infanticides in County Wicklow was 0
Darley. Sir F.M				1897	Sir Frederick Matthew Darley was created K.C.M.G.
Books				1897	Report on a Pretoria Burial near Newcastle Co. Wicklow by G. Coffey, C. Browne and T.J. Westropp
Wicklow Homicides				1897	The total number of Homicides, including Manslaughter and Murders in County Wicklow, 0
School. Kilcoole	Mon	10	01	1898	A national school was established in Convent at Kilcoole,
Ships/Yachts	Thu	24	03	1898	The vessel "Magpie" shipwrecked of the Wicklow Coast
Parnell. Charles S	Sun	27	03	1898	Charles S. Parnell mother Delia Tudor Stewart died
Railways	Wed	11	05	1898	A train derailment took place at Tinahely
Montague. Daniel	Thu	02	06	1898	Daniel Montague held the rank of Chief Master at Arms of the US Navy
Montague. Daniel	Thu	02	06	1898	Daniel Montague displayed extraordinary heroism at the harbour of Santiago de Cuba
De Valois. N	Mon	06	06	1898	Dame Ninette De Valois (Edris Stannus) founder of Sadler's Wells Ballet School born in Baltyboys. Co. Wicklow
Cochrane. Ernest	Wed	08	06	1898	Sir Ernest C. Cochrane 2nd Bart, of Woodbrook, Bray married 1st Ethel Amy Davis
Hatton. Bridget	Wed	13	07	1898	Bridget Hatton died, She donated the St. Laurance O'Toole window to the Catholic Church, Roundwood
Act	Fri	12	08	1898	The Local Government (Ireland) Act saw the establishment of County Councils
Flora-Fauna	Sun	14	08	1898	Robert Lloyd Praeger carried out fieldwork in the Blessington area for Census of British Plants published in 1901
Bray. Castle	Thu	01	09	1898	An article about Little Bray Castle by E.R.MaC.Dix appeared in The Irish Builder

The County Wicklow Database: 432 AD to 2006 AD

A-Z Reference	Day	Date	Month	Year	DATA
Railways	Tue	27	12	1898	A train inspector Bernard Lynch accidentally killed at Bray Station
Lawlor. Hugh Jackson				1898	Hugh Jackson Lawlor appointed curate in Bray Co. Wicklow and Professor of Ecclesiastical History in Trinity College Dublin
Dick. Capt. Q				1898	Capt. Q. Dick appointed sheriff of County Wicklow
Wicklow Infanticides				1898	The number of Infanticides in County Wicklow was 0
Murphy. Michael				1898	The Fr. Michael Murphy Monument in Arklow erected
Wicklow GAA				1898	C. MacSuibhne Chairman of Wicklow GAA 1898 – 1901
D'Ombrain. Ernest A.				1898	Ernest Arthur D'Ombrain invented an instrument for the removal of the tarsal plate in trachoma.
Wicklow Homicides				1898	The total number of Homicides , including Manslaughter and Murders in County Wicklow , 0
Kearney. Teresa				1898	Teresa Kearney became a nun with Franciscan Order in London. When she took her vows she took the name Kevin
Act				1898	Local Government (Ireland) Act; Establishes county government on a representative basis
Photo Collection				1898	Thomas J. Westropp Antiquities Albums 1898–1921. Vol. 9 Counties, Cork, Dublin, Meath, Wexford and Wicklow 1902–1921
Marlborough Hall				1898	Marlborough Hall, Arklow built by 5th Earl of Carysfort
Wicklow County	Mon	22	04	1899	The first General meeting of Wicklow County Council held
Elections–Polling Day			04	1899	The first elections for Wicklow County Council
Flora-Fauna	Sat	03	06	1899	Robert Lloyd Praeger carried out fieldwork in the Shillelagh area for Census of British Plants published in 1901
Flora-Fauna	Sun	04	06	1899	Robert Lloyd Praeger carried out fieldwork in the Coolkenna area for Census of British Plants published in 1901
Flora-Fauna	Mon	05	06	1899	Robert Lloyd Praeger carried out fieldwork in the Avondale area for Census of British Plants published in 1901
Plunket	Wed	12	07	1899	Terrance Coyngham Plunket of Old Connaught, Bray born
Byrne. Billy	Thu	27	07	1899	The foundation stone was laid for the Billy Byrne memorial in Wicklow town
Arklow	Sat	12	08	1899	St Saviours COI Church Arklow was dedicated. The Church was a gift of William Proby 5th Earl of Carysfort
Life Saving	Sun	13	08	1899	Patrick Daly was given Bronze Royal Humane Society Medal , saving Mary Cleary from drowning at Poulaphuca Falls
County Councils	Tue	22	08	1899	The inaugural meeting of the Irish County Councils General Council. Wicklow represented by E.P. O'Kelly and D.J. Cogan
Anderson. James Arthur	Mon	25	09	1899	James Arthur Anderson chief engineer with the Bengal Railway Company died in India
Parnell Monument	Sun	08	10	1899	The foundation stone laid for the Parnell Monument Sackville (O'Connell) Street, Dublin
Montague. Daniel	Thu	02	11	1899	Daniel Montague awarded Spanish–American War Medal of Honour
Montague. Daniel	Thu	02	11	1899	Daniel Montague awarded the Congressional Medal of Honour

Name	Day	Date	Month	Year	Description
Guinness. Anne	Wed	08	11	1899	Anne Plunket nee Guinness died
BTIC	Wed	20	12	1899	Bray Technical Instruction Committee established
O'Dea. Jimmy				1899	Jimmy O'Dea (comedian) was born in Lower Bridge Street, Dublin. Educated at the Holy Faith Convent, Kilcoole Co.Wicklow
La Touche				1899	A painting of David La Touche by Hugh Hamilton was purchased by the National Gallery of Ireland (NGI 491)
Le Fanu. Henry				1899	Henry Frewen Le Fanu appointed chaplain to Guy's Hospital London. 1899 – 1901
Hime. Sir Albert H.				1899	Sir Albert Hime appointed Prime Minister of Natal 09/06/1899 to 17/08/1903
Wicklow Infanticides				1899	The number of Infanticides in County Wicklow was 0
Books				1899	Leigh of Lara; a romance of a Wicklow vale by Brian McDermott
Wicklow Homicides				1899	The total number of Homicides , including Manslaughter and Murders in County Wicklow , 0
Cycle Routes				1899	Cyclist Touring Club (CTC) Road book of Ireland published in two volumes 1899 and 1900
Bray Bye Laws				1899	Hackney Cars plying from Bray
O'Kelly Edward Peter				1899	Edward P. O'Kelly first Chairman of Wicklow County Council 1899 -1914
Powerscourt				1899	Mervyn Wingfield 7th Viscount Powerscourt member of Wicklow County Council 1899-1902
Railways	Wed	14	02	1900	A train from Bray to Harcourt Street Station crashed through the buffers at Harcourt Street Station
O'Faolain. Sean	Thu	22	02	1900	John Francis Whelan (Sean O'Faolain) Irish short-story writer born in Cork
Royal Visit	Tue	03	04	1900	H.R.H.Queen Victoria visits Ireland from 3rd to 26th April 1900
Proby. Elizabeth	Sun	24	06	1900	Lady Elizabeth Hamilton (nee Proby) wife of James Hamilton 1st Duke of Abercorn died,
Life Saving	Sun	01	07	1900	D. Chambers (RIC) and R. W. Anderson was given Bronze Royal Humane Society Medal , saving a child from drowning at Poulaphuca
Glen of Imaal	Mon	23	07	1900	The British War Office acquired 5,948 acres in the Glen of Imaal for use as artillery range
Railway	Mon	30	07	1900	Royal assent to the Dublin, Wicklow and Wexford Railway Act.
Act	Mon	06	08	1900	Intermediate Education (Ireland) Act
Bewley. Joshua	Fri	21	09	1900	Joshua Bewley of Dunore, Sidmonton Road, Bray died, and was buried in the Friends Burial Ground, Blackrock, Co. Dublin
Hodson	Mon	01	10	1900	Cecil George Hodson brother of Edmond 5th Bart, born
Elections–Polling Day	Thu	04	10	1900	Denis Joseph Cogan elected M.P. for Wicklow East at the General Election, Number of electors 4827
Elections–Polling Day	Fri	05	10	1900	James O'Connor elected M.P. for Wicklow West at the General Election, Number of electors 4671
Wilde. Oscar	Fri	30	11	1900	Oscar Wilde died in Paris, France
Hodson	Wed	05	12	1900	Gilbert Neville Hodson married 1st Etheldreda Bridges of Kettering, England
Mecredy. Richard J.			circa	1900	Richard James Mecredy founded the Irish Motoring News
Newspapers				1900	Wicklow Star Newspaper final edition

A–Z Reference	Day	Date	Month	Year	DATA
Railways				1900	A railway platform constructed at Bray Cove Baths
Wicklow Gaol				1900	Wicklow Gaol was closed
Collis.J.S				1900	John Stewart Collis (writer and naturalist) born in Dublin educated at Aravon School, Bray
Railways				1900	Dublin & Wicklow & Wexford Railway Act
Books				1900	Wildfoot, the Wanderer of Wicklow by Edwin J. Brett
Powerscourt				1900	The Venetian Gates erected in Powerscourt Gardens
La Touche				1900	Major Peter La Touche fought in the Boer War with the Royal Dublin Fusiliers
Books				1900	Excursions in and about Dublin and Wicklow by John Owens
Dromin House				1900	Dromin House, Delgany built
Cogan. Denis				1900	Denis Cogan M.P. for East Wicklow 1900 – 1907
Hime. Sir Albert H.				1900	Albert Henry Hime was knighted
Whitshed. E.A.F.H.				1900	Elizabeth (Hawkins–Whitshed, Burnaby) Main married Francis Bernard Aubery Le Bond
Barrington. R.M.				1900	R. M. Barrington of Bray published "Migration of Birds at Irish Lighthouses and Lightships" published in Dublin and London
Connolly. Roderick	Fri	11	01	1901	Roderick Connolly the son of James and Lillie Connolly born
Hennessy. Henry	Fri	08	03	1901	Henry Hennessy (Physicist and Mathematician) died at Bray. Co. Wicklow
Population Greystones	Sun	31	03	1901	Population of Greystones & Delgany 1,063 or 1.74% of County Population
Population of Brockagh	Sun	31	03	1901	The estimated population of the Electoral District of Brockagh in 1901 was 500 persons
Population Wicklow (t)	Sun	31	03	1901	Population of Wicklow Town 3,288 or 5.40% of County Population
Population Bray	Sun	31	03	1901	Population of Bray 7,424 or 12.26% of County Population
Population	Sun	31	03	1901	According to the Census of population 28% of the population of Ireland lived in an Urban area
Population County	Sun	31	03	1901	Population of County Wicklow 60,824 persons. 30,584 Males 30,240 Females
Population Arklow	Sun	31	03	1901	Population of Arklow Urban 4,944 or 8.12% of County Population
Population Enniskerry	Sun	31	03	1901	Population of Enniskerry urban 235 or 0.38% of County Population
Conacher. Lionel	Fri	24	05	1901	Lionel Conacher (Ice Hockey player) was born in Toronto Canada. His grandmother Elizabeth Black came from County Wicklow
Scott. G.D	Tue	04	06	1901	Rev. George Digby Scott Rector of Bray married Charlotte Jessy Barrington
Cormer. Frederick J.	Sat	06	07	1901	Frederick J. Cromer born in Middlesex, England
O'Connor. Peter J.	Sun	28	07	1901	Peter O'Connor jumped 24ft 11 and half inches in the long jump at Annacurra. Co Wicklow

Section One: Data by Date

Index	Day	Date	Month	Year	Event
O'Connor. Peter J.	Mon	05	08	1901	Peter J.O'Connor (athletics) set a long jump record at Ballsbridge Dublin of 24ft 11"
O'Connor. Peter J.	Mon	05	08	1901	Peter O'Connor set a World and Irish Long Jump record in the RDS, Dublin with a jump of 24ft 11 and three quarters inches
Chichester. Sir. F	Tue	17	09	1901	Francis Chichester born at Barnstaple, Devon
Cycle Polo	Sat	28	09	1901	The first international cycle polo match between Ireland and England took place at Crystal Palace London (Irl. 10. G.B. 5)
Carnew Castle			09	1901	Fire destroys Carnew Castle Co ... icklow the home of Lord and Lady Milton
Oranmore. Lord	Mon	21	10	1901	Baron Dominick Geoffrey Edward Browne born
Ships/Yachts	Sat	12	11	1901	The vessel "Forest Deer" shipwrecked of the Wicklow Coast
Cochrane. Margaret	Sat	07	12	1901	Margaret Cochrane, of Woodbrook, Bray died
Maps				1901	Wicklow Sheet Map 121 engraved 1853, published 1855, republished 1901
Wicklow GAA				1901	Luke O'Toole of Wicklow appointed the first full time Secretary of the GAA 1901-1929
Somerville-Large. P.				1901	Philip Townsend Somerville-Large (engineer) born in Bray
Greystones				1901	Building started on the Burnbay Estate, Greystones
Harty.H.H				1901	Herbert Hamilton Harty organist at Christ Church, Bray left for London.
Findlater. Alex				1901	Alex Findlater & Co, wine and spirit merchants and grocers opened at shop in Bray
Ravenswell. Bray				1901	The Sisters of Charity establish Ravenswell School, Little Bray
VEC. Bray				1901	Vocational School at Brighton Terrace, Bray
Reform Association				1901	The international conference of the Philanthropic Reform Association was held at Killruddery, Bray
Darley. Sir F.M				1901	Sir Frederick Matthew Darley was created G.C.M.G
Hopper. Nora				1901	Nora Hopper married Wilfrid Hugh Chesson
Hamilton. Gladys Mary	Tue	14	01	1902	Gladys Mary Hamilton the daughter of the Earl of Abercorn married Ralph Francis Howard 7th Earl of Wicklow in London
Wicklow. Earl of	Tue	14	01	1902	Ralph Howard 7th Earl of Wicklow married Lady Gladys Mary Hamilton dau of James 2nd Duke of Abercorn
Fitzwilliam. 6th Earl	Thu	20	02	1902	William Fitzwilliam 6th Earl Fitzwilliam died and was succeeded by his grandson William Fitzwilliam 7th Earl Fitzwilliam
Royal Inn Glendalough			02	1902	Royal Hotel Glendalough destroyed by fire
La Touche	Tue	01	04	1902	Major Peter la Touche of Bellevue, Delgany married Sophia Dora Elizabeth Tottenham
Stuart. Francis	Tue	29	04	1902	Henry Francis Stuart(writer) born Townsville, Australia
Ships/Yachts	Mon	02	06	1902	The vessel "Hematite" shipwrecked of the Wicklow Coast
Dwyer. Michael	Sun	15	06	1902	The foundation stone laid for the memorial to Michael Dwyer and Sam McAllister at Baltinglass
British Empire Day	Mon	21	07	1902	British Empire Day instituted by Reginald Brabazon 12th Earl of Meath, to encourage schoolchildren to become good citizens

132 The County Wicklow Database: 432 AD to 2006 AD

A-Z Reference	Day	Date	Month	Year	DATA
Hime. Sir Albert H.	Sat	26	07	1902	Wicklow man Sir Albert Henry Hime given the Freedom of the City of Edinburgh
Fitzgerald. John	Thu	31	07	1902	John Fitzgerald born Co. Westmeath
Wicklow. Earl of	Thu	30	10	1902	William Cecil 8th Earl of Wicklow born
Industrial School	Wed	03	12	1902	91 names were on the roll of The Meath Protestant Industrial School (for Girls)
Books				1902	History of the County of Dublin by Francis E. Ball 1st vol...... published 1902. Completed 4 vols in 1906
Act				1902	Licensing (Ireland) Act
Pim. Joshua				1902	Joshua Pim played on the Davis Cup Tennis team
Putland				1902	Rev John West Nehgan died
St Patrick's School				1902	An extension was added to the Meath Industrial School, Bray.
St.John Whitty.Sophia				1902	Sophia St. John Whitty was employed, as a teacher of woodwork, at Bray Technical School & Bray Furniture
Hime. Sir Albert H.				1902	Sir Albert Henry Hime was made a Privy Councillor
Wicklow GAA				1902	Mait Mac Muireartaih Chairman of Wicklow GAA 1902- 1905
Tottenham. C.R.W	Thu	08	01	1903	Charles Robert Worsley Tottenham of Woodstock House, Kilcoole died
Beit. Alfred	Mon	19	01	1903	Sir Alfred Beit born
Greystones	Thu	26	02	1903	The roof is blown off the temporary R. C. Church Greystones during a storm
Ships/Yachts	Fri	27	02	1903	The vessel "1902 Brackley" shipwrecked of the Wicklow Coast
Feis	Thu	21	05	1903	The first Wicklow County Feis started on 21/05/1903 and was held in Rathdrum, Co. Wicklow
Milne. Charles Ewart	Mon	25	05	1903	Charles Ewart Milne (poet, sailor) born in Dublin, educated at Nun's Cross school, Ashford.
Powerscourt	Tue	09	06	1903	Mervyn Richard Wingfield 8th Viscount Powerscourt married Sybil Bouverie
Gordon Bennett Race	Thu	02	07	1903	Camille Jenatzy won the Gordon Bennett Road race in a Mercedes Registration No GY 5145
Books	Mon	06	07	1903	Bray & Environs by A. L. Doran Price 1/-s
Act	Fri	14	08	1903	Motor Car Act, required motor vehicles to be registered and licensed
Henry. Grace	Thu	17	09	1903	Grace Mitchell married Paul Henry (artist)
Cochrane. Henry	Thu	08	10	1903	Sir Henry Cochrane, of Woodbrook, Bray created 1st Baronet Cochrane
Photo Collection				1903	Valentine Collection held in National Library (Photos 1903 -1950) Photo JV 8419s Glendalough
Railways				1903	The affairs of the Bray & Enniskerry Light Railway Co. wound up by the Courts
Synge				1903	In the Shadow of the Glen, a one act play by John Millington Synge set in Co. Wicklow
Connolly. James				1903	Mona Connolly the eldest child of James Connolly and Lillie Reynolds killed in an accident

Section One: Data by Date

Health				1903	Henry Raverty was Medical Officer for Bray
Population Bray				1903	Population of Bray 7,424 *not a census year*
Books				1903	A Description and History of Powerscourt by M. Wingfield
Monck Family Estates				1903	The remainder of the Monck Family Estates in County Wicklow, excluding Charleville House sold to the Land Commission
Railways				1903	Dublin, Wicklow and Wexford Railway Act
Childers. R. E				1903	Robert Erskine Childers wrote The Riddle of the Sands
Free Mason's Hall				1903	The Free Mason's Hall at Ferrybank, Arklow built
Bewley, Ernest				1903	The first Jersey Cows were imported into Ireland from Jersey Island by Ernest Bewley in 1903.
Speed limit				1903	The national speed limit for cars was set at 20 mph
Parnell. J.H.				1903	J. H. Parnell elected M.P. for Meath South 1903
Arklow				1903	(17)'98 Memorial unveiled at Arklow
Cars	Fri	01	01	1904	The Motor Car Act came into operation
Alcock. Dr. N.	Mon	04	04	1904	A plaque on an outcrop at Ballyman, Enniskerry in memory to Dr. Nathaniel Alcock who died on April 4 1904
La Touche	Wed	13	04	1904	Major Peter La Touche died.
Dwyer. Michael	Sun	08	05	1904	Memorial to Michael Dwyer and Sam McAllister unveiled at Baltinglass
Powerscourt	Sun	05	06	1904	Mervyn Wingfield 7th Viscount Powerscourt died
Harty.H.H	Fri	15	07	1904	Herbert Hamilton Harty married Agnes Helen Nicholls an operatic soprano and concert singer
Cochrane. Henry	Sun	11	09	1904	Sir Henry Cochrane died and was succeeded by his son Ernest 2nd Bart, of Woodbrook, Bray
Wicklow Golf Club	Fri	14	10	1904	Wicklow Golf Club established
Wicklow GAA				1904	Bray Emmets (Dublin Selection) won the all Ireland Football (GAA) title (referred to 1902)title
Cars				1904	Muriel E. Bland the first woman granted a car licence by Wicklow County Council
Post Office				1904	The Post Office on the Quinsboro Road, Bray built.
Plunket				1904	1904-1910 William Lee Plunket, 5th Baron Plunket held the post of Governor and Com. in Chief of the Dominion of New Zealand
Fitzwilliam. 10th Earl				1904	William Thomas George Fitzwilliam born
O'Gorman. Tiomthy				1904	The Very Rev. Tiomthy O'Gorman appointed Parish Priest of Bray, Little Bray and Greystones 1904-1912
Kilternan				1904	Kilternan Dairies established by the Verney family in 1904
Avondale House				1904	The State buys Avondale estate from William Boylan of Phisboro, Dublin
Cars				1904	Michael J. Rahilly of Wilford Cottage, Bray held the first Motor Vehicle licensed by Wicklow County Council
La Touche				1904	When Major Peter La Touche died, sister Frances Cecilia and her husband Dr Archer moved into Bellevue, Delgany

A-Z Reference	Day	Date	Month	Year	DATA
Avondale House				1904	The Department of Agriculture and Technical Instruction bought Avondale House, Rathdrum once the home of C.S. Parnell
Childers. R. E				1904	Robert Erskine Childers married Mary Ellen Osgood
St. Pauls N.S.				1904	Work began on St Pauls National School, Herbert Road Bray
Boylan. Dom Eugene				1904	Dom Eugene Boylan (Atomic Physicists, Monk, Writer) born in Bray
Hagan. John				1904	Rev John Hagan appointed vice-rector of the Irish College in Rome
Nicol. Erskine				1904	Erskine Nicol died
Cars				1904	The death of the first Irish Car passenger occurred at Marlton Hill, Wicklow
Le Faun. Henry				1904	Henry Frewen Le Fanu married Margery Ingle
Elections-Polling Day	Mon	16	01	1905	Elections to Bray Urban District Council took place
Brabazon. Reginald	Thu	13	04	1905	Reginald Brabazon the 12th Earl of Meath, Killruddery, Bray invested into the Order of St...... Patrick at Dublin Castle
Glen of Imaal			05	1905	The British War Office acquired an additional 1,262 acres at the Glen of Imaal
Powerscourt	Tue	22	08	1905	Mervyn Patrick Wingfield 9th Viscount Powerscourt born
Dargle River	Thu	24	08	1905	The River Dargle broke its banks and flooded, Little Bray
Weather	Fri	25	08	1905	In a 24 hour period 5.5 inches of rain fell in the Rocky Valley, near Bray
Life Saving	Fri	25	08	1905	J.W. Reigh was given Bronze Royal Humane Society Medal. With the help of others he conveyed persons to safety in Bray Flood
Wicklow GAA	Wed	15	11	1905	The Arklow Gaelic Pastimes Club founded
Childers. E.H	Mon	11	12	1905	Erskine Hamilton Childers born in London
Monck	Mon	11	12	1905	Henry Wyndham Stanley Monck, later 6th Viscount Monck born
Books				1905	Wildfoot, the Wanderer of Wicklow by Edwin J. Brett
Pobje. Bessie				1905	Bessie Pobje died in Dublin
Cochrane. Stanley				1905	Stanley Cochrane purchased the Mercedes that won the Gordon Bennett Race of 1903; Car given Road Registration IK 183
Arklow				1905	Arklow Vocational School established
Bray Golf Club				1905	Bray Golf Club won the Barton Cup
Bray Laundry				1905	Bray Laundry opened at the Dargle Road, Bray
Moorhead. Dr. Thomas G.				1905	Thomas Gillman Moorhead appointed a member of the Royal College of Physicians of Ireland
Bray Ball				1905	Bray Commercial Ball held in Town Hall, Bray
Glen of the Downes				1905	National School at Downs, Fairgreen

Section One: Data by Date

Subject	Description	Year	Month	Day	Weekday
Bray Furniture	Bray Art Furniture Industry established	1905			
Parnell. Anna	Anna Parnell published "The Tale of a Great Sham'" in Dublin in 1905	1905			
Newspapers	Wicklow Press Newspaper first edition	1905			
Synge	The Well of the Saints a play by J.M. Synge set in Co. Wicklow	1905			
Bray Furniture	Celtic Alter Cross by John Burke of Bray was exhibited in Dublin	1905			
Railways	Railway Locomotive Number 21 built and named Kilcoole, Withdrawn from service 1925	1905			
Muldoon. John	John Muldoon elected M.P. for Donegal North 1905-1906	1905			
Le Fanu. Henry	Henry Frewen Le Fanu appointed Canon of St. John's Cathedral, Brisbane, Australia 1905-1915	1905			
Cars	The first multiple death in a road traffic accident occurred at Balgrad Beg, Co. Wicklow when the chauffer and passenger were killed	1905			
Ships/Yachts	The vessel "Speranza" carrying coal shipwrecked of the Wicklow Coast	1906	01	03	Wed
Elections-Polling Day	Denis Joseph Cogan elected M.P. for Wicklow East at the General Election, Number of electors 4954	1906	01	15	Mon
Elections-Polling Day	James O'Connor elected M.P. for Wicklow West at the General Election, Number of electors 4406	1906	01	16	Tue
Hodson	Meriel Hodson nee Neville died	1906	03	17	Sat
Ships/Yachts	The coal vessel the Velenheli ran aground near Bray Harbour. Captain Hollingsworth	1906	03	20	Tue
Hopper. Nora	Nora Hopper died	1906	04	14	Sat
La Touche	An Executors sale took place at Bellevue, Delgany following the death of Major Peter La Touche	1906	05	09	Wed
Lighthouse	The Lighthouse on Wicklow Head was converted from gas to incandescent paraffin	1906	08	21	Tue
St. David's School	The Holy Faith Sisters opened a junior school in Greystones (St. David's)	1906	09	03	Mon
Bewley. Joshua	Margaret H Bewley the wife of Joshua Bewley died.	1906	11	27	Tue
Act	Town Tenant's Act	1906	12	21	Fri
Armstrong. G.F.S	George F.S. Armstrong died in County Down	1906			
O'Connor. Peter J.	Peter J. O'Connor (athletics) won the Gold Medal at the Intercalated Games held in Athens for the triple jump	1906			
Bus	The first public bus service commenced in Dublin	1906			
Railways	Dublin and Wicklow and Wexford Act changed of title to Dublin & South Eastern Railway Co with effect 1/1/1907	1906			
O'Connor. Peter J.	Peter J. O'Connor (athletics) won the Silver Medal at the Intercalated Games held in Athens for the long jump	1906			
Brabazon. Reginald	Above the entrance to the stable yard at Killruddery there is a clock built 1906-1909	1906			
Convent, Greystones	The Holy Faith Convent established in Greystones	1906			
Brabazon. Reginald	The water clock in the front courtyard at Killruddery built by the Reginald Brabazon the 13th Earl of Meath	1906			
Glen of the Downes	The Office of Public Works carried out repairs to St. Mary's Abbey, Glen of the Downes.	1906			

A–Z Reference	Day	Date	Month	Year	DATA
Act				1906	The Dogs Act
Act				1906	The Trade Disputes Act
Moorhead. Dr. Thomas G.				1906	Thomas Gillman Moorhead appointed a fellow of the Royal College of Physicians of Ireland
Synge				1906	John Millington Synge published "The Vagrants of Wicklow"
Photo Collection				1906	Pictures in colour of Counties Dublin and Wicklow by W. Lawrence
Kinsella. Tommy				1906	Tommy Kinsella Born
Corke Lodge				1906	Sir Stanley Cochrane acquired Corke Lodge, Shankill Road, Bray
Wicklow GAA				1906	Labhras O Pleimeann Chairman of Wicklow GAA 1906 – 1909
Railways	Tue	01	01	1907	The Dublin, Wicklow & Wexford Railway changed its name to the Dublin & South Eastern Railway
Cricket	Thu	02	05	1907	All Ireland Cricket Team played Yorkshire Cricket Team at Woodbrook, Bray
Barrington. Elizabeth			05	1907	Elizabeth Barrington nee Darley died
Wicklow GAA	Sun	28	07	1907	Leinster 2nd Division Football Final GAA. Wicklow 1-11 Westmeath 0-0
Elections–Polling Day	Mon	29	07	1907	John Muldoon elected M.P. for Wicklow East at the By-Election caused when Denis J Cogan resigned
Ships/Yachts	Fri	09	08	1907	The Arklow Schooner Celtic ran aground and broke up in Skaill Bay, Orkney Islands.
Cricket	Mon	12	08	1907	South African Cricket Touring Team played Sir Stanley Cochrane's X1 Cricket team at Woodbrook
Bayly. Richard	Fri	11	10	1907	Lt-Col Richard Bayly died
Needham. Mary	Thu	07	11	1907	Mary P Needham (writer) died, Mary was born at Ballynure, Co. Wicklow where her father was rector.
Wynne. Gladys				1907	Gladys Wynne (artist) daughter of the Archdeacon of Aghadoe (Kerry) lived at the Lake Cottage, Glendalough
Health Association				1907	Women's National Health Association founded by Lady Aberdeen, with branches in Co. Wicklow
Moorhead. Dr. Thomas G.				1907	Thomas Gillman Moorhead married Mai Quinn.
Sheep				1907	102,206 Sheep dipped in County Wicklow
Rooney. Philip				1907	Philip Rooney born Colooney, Co. Sligo
Births				1907	The Notification of Births Act, Local medical officers had to be notified of any birth within 36 hours
Books				1907	Rambles in Eirinn by William Bulfin
Wicklow Harbour				1907	Building work began on the new pier at Wicklow Harbour, total cost of the harbour £93,000
Bray School				1907	The Bray School in Castle Street closed and transferred to the Herbert Rd (Headmaster Mr. Moore)
Synge				1907	John Millington Synge published "At a Wicklow Fair" in the Manchester Guardian
Doran. Johnny				1907	Johnny Doran (uilleann pipe player) born in Rathnew. County Wicklow

Section One: Data by Date

Category	Day	Date	Month	Year	Event
Books				1907	Black's Guide to Dublin and the Wicklow Mountains published by Charles Black of Edinburgh
Bray Furniture				1907	Bray Art Furniture Industry opened a shop at 81 Main Street, Bray.
Sheep				1907	The Sheep Dipping (Ireland) Order required each local authority to set up sheep dips between 15th June and 31st Aug each year
Allgood. Molly				1907	Sara Allgood (actress) and her sister Molly Allgood (actress) lived in Glencree, Co. Wicklow
Railways				1907	Railway Locomotive Number 31 built and named Glen of the Downes, Withdrawn from service 1923
Bray Golf Club				1907	Bray Golf Club won the Barton Cup
Reynolds. B				1907	The Very Rev. B. Reynolds became Parish Priest of Enniskerry
Whitshed. E.A.F.H.				1907	Elizabeth (Hawkins-Whitshed, Burnaby, Main) Le Bond founder of the Ladies Alpine Club, President 1907–1934
Muldoon. John				1907	John Muldoon elected M.P. for Wicklow East 1907-1911
Barn Owls				1907	The National Museum of Ireland has a Barn Owl donated S. Cregan location Co. Wicklow
Brabazon. Reginald	Wed	12	02	1908	Reginald Brabazon 13th Earl of Meath married Lady Aileen Wyndham Quin
Sport	Fri	17	04	1908	Delgany Golf Club founded. The course was opened on Good Friday 1908
Cycle Polo			07	1908	Cycle Polo competition in the Olympic games. Ireland beat Germany in the final (3–1) held at Shepard's Bush Stadium London
Hart, Henry C.	Fri	07	08	1908	Henry Chichester Hart died, Carrablagh, Co. Donegal
Ships/Yachts	Tue	06	10	1908	The steamer "Amethyst" shipwrecked of the Wicklow Coast
Synge	Mon	26	10	1908	John Millington Synge mother Kathleen Synge nee Traill died
Sport	Sat	26	12	1908	Clem Robertson scored a round of 77 of a handicap of 15 at the new Delgany Golf Course
Powerscourt				1908	The Japanese Gardens at Powerscourt designed by the 8th Viscount and his wife Sybil
Railways				1908	The Railway and Canal Commission established
Act				1908	The Children's Act
Water – Vartry				1908	Work began on the North Reservoir of the Vartry Water Supply at Roundwood. The work took place between 1908-1925
La Touche				1908	Dr Archer became first President of the Golf club established at Bellevue Estate
Costal Erosion				1908	A Royal Commission on Coast Erosion held a meeting in Bray
Synge				1908	John Millington Synge published "In Wicklow. On the Road" in the Manchester Guardian
Bayly. Catherine				1908	Catherine Bayly died
Maps				1908	Bray Head, Greystones and Kilcoole, NewtownMount Kennedy surveyed by Ordnance Survey 6inches to Mile Map
Scouting				1908	1st Wicklow Scout Troop Greystones Founded. The Greystones troop and one in Dundalk were the first formed in Ireland.
Greystones				1908	Work began on the building of the Holy Rosary Church, Greystones

A–Z Reference	Day	Date	Month	Year	DATA
Act				1908	The Old Age Pensions Act
Mackintosh. C. Herbert				1908	Charles Herbert mackintosh wrote "Potential Resources of British Columbia
Saunders. Robert				1908	Robert Joseph Pratt Saunders died, former High Sheriff of Wicklow
Campbell. Christopher				1908	Christopher Campbell (artist) born in Dublin
Synge	Wed	24	03	1909	John Millington Synge died at Elpis Nursing Home, Dublin and was buried in Mount Jerome Cemetery, Dublin
Ships/Yachts			04	1909	The schooner ME Johnson bought by Captain Frank Tyrrell and Thomas Price of Arklow
Elliston. Henry	Sat	29	05	1909	Henry Elliston died
Proby. Hon. William	Sat	04	09	1909	William Proby 5th Earl of Carysfort died, as the Earl had no children the Earldom ceased.
Cricket	Fri	17	09	1909	First Class Cricket match Sir Stanley Cochrane XI v Australians at Woobrook, Bray
Goulding. Basil Sir	Thu	04	11	1909	Sir Basil Goulding born
Campbell. Arthur	Tue	09	11	1909	Arthur Campbell (Photographer and Artist) born in Belfast, brother of Frederick George Campbell
Corbett. W.J.	Mon	01	12	1909	W.J. Corbett M.P for Wicklow died
Joyce. James	Mon	20	12	1909	Volta Cinema, Dublin first custom built cinema in Ireland. Manager James Joyce
Roads				1909	The Galtrim Road extended to join the Adelaide Road, Bray
Greystones				1909	Dr. Walsh Archbishop of Dublin solemnly opened the Catholic Church, The Holy Rosary, Greystones
Housing				1909	Building of Connolly and St.Kevins Square (Purcells fields) Bray
Wicklow Regiment				1909	The Wicklow Artillery Regiment disbanded
Synge				1909	The Tinkers Wedding a play by J.M.Synge set in Co. Wicklow
Ivers. M				1909	Very Rev M.Ivers became Parish Priest of Enniskerry
BUDC				1909	Patrick Bateman appointed Rate Collector by the Bray Urban District Council
Glen of Imaal				1909	The British War Office purchased the additional 1,262 acres it acquired in 1905 at the Glen of Imaal
Darley. Sir F.M	Tue	04	01	1910	Sir Frederick Matthew Darley died in London
Elections–Polling Day	Mon	17	01	1910	John Muldoon elected M.P. for Wicklow East at the General Election, Number of electors 4710
Elections–Polling Day	Tue	18	01	1910	James O'Connor elected M.P. for Wicklow West at the General Election, Number of electors 4417
Wicklow GAA	Sun	23	01	1910	Leinster Junior Football Championship Final GAA Wicklow 1-10 Westmeath 1-3
Guinness	Tue	22	02	1910	Oonagh Guinness daughter of Ernest Guinness born
Scouting			02	1910	1st Bray Scout Troop established
Elections–Polling Day	Tue	29	03	1910	Edward P. O'Kelly elected M.P. for Wicklow West at the By-Election caused by the death James O'Connor

Arklow District Council	Sat	01	10	1910	Arklow Urban District Council established
Campbell, Joseph	Sun	23	10	1910	Joseph Campbell married Nancy Maude and both lived at Lackendarragh, Glencree. Co. Wicklow.
Brabazon. Anthony	Thu	03	11	1910	Anthony Brabazon the 14th Earl of Meath born
Elections–Polling Day	Tue	06	12	1910	Edward P. O'Kelly elected M.P. for Wicklow West at the General Election, Number of electors 4417
Elections–Polling Day	Mon	12	12	1910	John Muldoon elected M.P. for Wicklow East at the General Election, Number of electors 4710
Fitzwilliam. 8th Earl	Sat	31	12	1910	William Fitzwilliam 8th Earl Fitzwilliam born
Crimmins. PJ				1910	Very Rev P.J. Crimmins became Parish Priest of Enniskerry
Scott. G.D				1910	Rev. G.D.Scott elected Canon of Christ Church Dublin
Greystones				1910	Greystones Electric Light and Power Co, formed taken over by the ESB in 1927.
Moorhead. Dr.Thomas G.				1910	Thomas Gillman Moorhead appointed President of the Royal College of Physicians of Ireland
Library. Greystones				1910	Greystones Library established
Photo Collection				1910	The Eason collection of photographic negatives 1910 to 1930 held in the National Library
Synge				1910	In Wicklow and West Kerry, a travel book by John Millington Synge
Darley. FM				1910	Sir Frederick Matthew Darley, Australian Statesman, died
Yeats, Jack B.				1910	Jack B.Yeats lived between 1910-1917 at Redford House, Greystones
Childers. R. E				1910	Robert Erskine Childers wrote War and the Arme Blanche
St. Pauls. Bray				1910	Repairs carried out at St.Pauls Church Bray.
Wicklow GAA				1910	C.M. O Broin Chairman of Wicklow GAA 1910 – 1918
Cochrane. Stanley				1910	Sir Stanley Cochrane sold Bailieborough Castle, Co. Cavan to his cousin W. B. Cochrane a solicitor from Bailieborough
Barn Owls				1910	The National Museum of Ireland has 2 Barn Owls donated by Williams. Location of find Co. Wicklow
Masonic Lodge				1910	The Tynte 236 Masonic Lodge, Baltinglass was established in 1910
Woodenbridge	Thu	02	02	1911	A great storm sweeps Ireland. Tom Moore's tree at Woodenbridge up rooted.
O'Dalaigh. Cearbhall	Sun	12	02	1911	Cearbhall O'Dalaigh born at 85 Main Street, Bray. 1974 became President of Ireland
Lifeboats	Fri	03	03	1911	A new 40ft Motor Lifeboat Robert Theophilus Garden IV arrived at Wicklow Lifeboat Station
Lifeboats	Fri	03	03	1911	The Lifeboat Robert Theophilus Garden IV stationed at Wicklow was the first motor lifeboat in Ireland
Population Bray	Sun	02	04	1911	Population of Bray 7,691 or 12.66% of County Population
Population County	Sun	02	04	1911	Population of County Wicklow 60,711 persons, 31,113 Males 29,598 Females
Population Arklow	Sun	02	04	1911	Population of Arklow Urban 5,042 or 8.30% of County Population
Population Enniskerry	Sun	02	04	1911	Population of Enniskerry urban 221 or 0.36% of County Population

The County Wicklow Database: 432 AD to 2006 AD

A-Z Reference	Day	Date	Month	Year	DATA
Population Greystones	Sun	02	04	1911	Population of Greystones & Delgany 1,449 or 2.38% of County Population
Population Wicklow (t)	Sun	02	04	1911	Population of Wicklow Town 3,243 or 5.34% of County Population
Hodson	Thu	20	04	1911	Sir Robert Adair Hodson 4th Bart. married Emily Beresford of Waterford
Royal Visit	Mon	10	07	1911	The Prince of Wales and Princess Mary visited Lord and Lady Meath at Killruddery
Elections-Polling Day	Thu	13	07	1911	Capt. Anthony J. C. Donelan elected M.P. for Wicklow East at the By-Election caused when John Muldoon resigned
Cochrane. Ernest	Tue	12	09	1911	Sir Ernest C. Cochrane 2nd Bart., of Woodbrook. Bray married 2nd Elsa Schumacher
Parnell. Anna	Wed	20	09	1911	Catherine Anna Parnell (Cerisa Palmer) drowned off Ilfracombe, Devon, England
Parnell. Charles S	Sun	01	10	1911	A statue to Charles S. Parnell was unveiled by Mr. John Redmond M.P. at Upper Sackville Street now O'Connell Street
Parnell. Street	Mon	02	10	1911	Great Britain Street, Dublin renamed Parnell Street.
Ships/Yachts	Sat	21	10	1911	The vessel "Champion of the Seas" shipwrecked of the Wicklow Coast
Trade Union				1911	The Bray branch of the I.T.W.U. (Irish Transport Workers Union) formed
St. Paul's. Bray				1911	Repairs carried out on St.Pauls Church Bray
Cars				1911	The Public Road (Ireland) Act set the Maximum speed for motor cars at 20 MPH
Library. Bray				1911	William Burke appointed as head of Bray Library service.
Christ Church, Bray				1911	New organ for Christ Church Bray built by Conachar of Huddersfield
Allgood. Molly				1911	Molly Allgood married George Herbert Mair
Enniskerry Library				1911	Enniskerry Public Library built at Church Road, Enniskerry
Library. Bray				1911	Bray Public library built on Florence Road at a cost of £2,000
Books				1911	In Wicklow, West Kerry and Connemara by John Millington Synge
Childers. R. E				1911	Robert Erskine Childers wrote The Framework of Home Rule
Alexander. William				1911	William Alexander died in Torquay
Marriage Rate				1911	In the period 1851 – 1911 County Wicklow was the only east coast county to show an increase in the Marriage rate
Prandy. James				1911	Rev. James Prandy Parish Priest of Tomacork, Carnew 1911-1948
Muldoon. John				1911	John Muldoon elected M.P. for Cork East 1911– 1918
Scott. J.G.	Fri	12	01	1912	Canon James George Scott died, father of Canon George Digby Scott
De la Salle			01	1912	The De la Salle community establish a school in Wicklow Town
Montague. Daniel	Sun	04	02	1912	Daniel Montague died and is buried at Annapolis, Virginia, USA

St. Pauls. Bray	Sat	17	02	1912	St.Pauls Church reopens after repairs
Glen of Imaal			03	1912	The British War Office bought Coolmoney House in the Glen of Imaal from Adelaide Margaret Tighe
Foot & Mouth	Mon	01	07	1912	A serious outbreak of foot & mouth disease effects Dublin, Wicklow, Meath and Kildare. Strict movement of Cattle
Bray Electric Works	Wed	10	07	1912	Accident at Bray Electric Light Works, Christopher Coates was killed and 1 man injured
Cricket	Mon	22	07	1912	First Class Cricket match Woodbrook Club and Ground v South Africans held at Woodbrook, Bray.
Cricket	Thu	25	07	1912	First Class Cricket match Ireland v South Africans held at Woodbrook, Bray.
Cricket	Thu	12	09	1912	First Class Cricket match C.B, Fry's XI v Australians held at Woodbrook, Bray.
Maguire. Thomas	Sat	14	12	1912	Police Sergeant Thomas Maguire was stabbed by William Burke at Aughrim, Co.Wicklow
COI. Carnew				1912	Messers Geroge Benson of Manchester build an organ for the Parish Church at Tourmakeady, Co Mayo
Colahan. Richard				1912	Rev Richard Colahan appointed Parish Priest of Bray, Little Bray and Greystones.
Meceedy. Ralph				1912	Ralph Mecredy of Bray represented Ireland in cycling at the 1912 Olympic Games held in Stockholm
Bill				1912	Home Rule Bill
Aughrim				1912	Aughrim Community Hall built
Blake. Edward				1912	Edward Blake died, M.P. for South Longford in the House of Commons
Books				1912	Black's Guide to Dublin and the Wicklow Mountains published by Charles Black of Edinburgh
Lifeboats				1912	The slipway at the Arklow Lifeboat station was adapted for a motor lifeboat.
Christ Church, Bray				1912	Celtic Cross erected in memory of Canon Scott in Front of Christ Church Bray
Scouting				1912	1st Bray Sea Scouts Troop established in Bray
St.Joseph's Wicklow				1912	St.Josephs College Wicklow Town established
Books				1912	[updated] In Wicklow, West Kerry and Connemara by John Millington Synge
Pipe Band				1912	St Kevins Pipe Band, Bray founded
Kelleher. John				1912	Rev.John Kelleher born in Bray
Bewley. Victor				1912	Victor Bewley the son of Ernest Bewley was born in Dublin
Wednesday	Tue	03	06	1913	Wednesday is fixed as early closing day under the Shops Act of 1913
Bradshaw. Harry	Thu	09	10	1913	Harry Bradshaw (The Brad) golfer born Delgany Co.Wicklow
Dublin Lock Out	Fri	17	10	1913	Dockers clash with the police at Bray Harbour, when a coal boat for Heitons is off loaded, during the Dublin lock out of 1913
Arklow Cinema	Mon	17	11	1913	The Cosy Picture House (Cinema) opened on the South Quay, Arklow
Tuberculosis				1913	Tuberculosis (Ireland) Order
Leland. Dr.Thomas				1913	An oil painting of Dr.Thomas Leland acquired by the National Gallery of Ireland (NGI 655)

A-Z Reference	Day	Date	Month	Year	DATA
Books				1913	The Stones of Bray by Canon George Digby Scott
O'Toole. Luke				1913	Luke O'Toole. 1901-1929 General Secretary of the GAA and played a major role in the purchase of the Croke Park site
La Touche				1913	The Archers left Bellevue estate and moved into a smaller house in Delgany Village
Railways				1913	Work on the Long Tunnel, Bray Head to a design by C.E. Moore, the work was done by Naylor's of Huddersfield
Murphy. James				1913	James Murphy died at Dun Laoghaire Co. Dublin
Kilcoole				1913	The Forresters Hall in Kilcoole built
Nolan. Winifride				1913	Winifride Nolan born in Wales, lived on a farm near Aughrim, Co. Wicklow
Elections-Polling Day	Thu	15	01	1914	Elections to Bray Urban District Council took place
BUDC			04	1914	Partick McDonnell Town Clerk of Bray Urban District Council died. He lived at Beechfield, Bray
O'Kelly Edward Peter			07	1914	Edward P. O'Kelly M.P. for West Wicklow died in London
Kilcoole	Sat	01	08	1914	The Irish National Volunteers land 5,000 rifles at Kilcoole, Co. Wicklow
Goulet. Yann Renard	Thu	20	08	1914	Yann Renard Goulet (sculptor and artist) born St. Nazaire, Brittany, France
Redmond. John E.	Sun	20	09	1914	John E. Redmond M.P. at Woodenbridge near Arklow calls in the Irish Volunteers to fight for England in the Great War 1914-18
Smyth. Algernon	Sun	15	11	1914	Capt. Algernon Bersford Smyth of Bray Head House, Bray was killed in the Battle of Ypres
Dunphy. Fr. James			11	1914	Fr. James Dunphy died, pastor of Arklow for 57 years.
Elections-Polling Day	Wed	02	12	1914	J.T. Donovan elected M.P. for Wicklow West at the By-Election caused by the death Edward P. O'Kelly
Railways	Fri	04	12	1914	A train derailment took place at Avoca
Ships/Yachts	Fri	11	12	1914	The vessel "Rover" shipwrecked of the Wicklow Coast
Bank Building				1914	The AIB Bank Building, Main Street, Arklow, built
Glendalough				1914	A statue to St. Kevin erected near St. Kevins bed Glendalough.
Condren. Daniel				1914	Daniel Condren held the post of Chairman of Wicklow County Council 1914-1920
Post Office				1914	A sub Post Office of Bray established at Newtown Vevay, Bray
Post Office				1914	A sub Post Office of Bray established at Dargle Road, Bray
International Hotel				1914	The International Hotel was converted into The Princess Patricia Hospital for wounded soldiers
Holy Redeemer, Bray				1914	Organ gallery and organ installed in the Holy Redeemer Church Bray
Film				1914	The film "Ireland a Nation" filmed on locations in Baltinglass and Glendalough. The film had only one public showing in Dublin 1917.
Arklow				1914	Arklow Presbyterian Church built

Section One: Data by Date

Name	Year	Mth	Day	Day	Event
Blake. Samuel H.	1914				Samuel Hume Blake died
Campbell. Arthur	1914				Arthur Campbell (Photographer and Artist) lived in Arklow. Co. Wicklow 1914-1921
Road Labourers Wages	1914				Wicklow County Council, Road Labourers Wages. 60 hour week. 10/s to 15/s per week
Donovan. J.T.	1914				J.T. Donovan elected M.P. for Wicklow West 1914-1918
Woodburn. William	1915	01	15	Fri	William Woodburn died
Wicklow Ward	1915	02	08	Mon	The Wicklow Ward for wounded soldiers was opened in St. Patrick Dun's Hospital, Dublin by Lady Powerscourt
Cochrane. Stanley	1915	02	10	Wed	Sir Stanley Herbert Cochrane, of Woodbrook, Bray created a Baronet
Bestic. Albert A.	1915	05	07	Fri	Albert A Bestic junior 3rd Officer on the S.S. Lusitania when sunk of the Old Head of Kinsale, Co. Cork
Ashford Church	1915	06	15	Tue	The foundation stone laid for the Church at Ashford by Rev. Dr. Walsh Archbishop of Dublin
Hodson	1915	07	08	Thu	Richard Edmond Hodson of Coolfadda House, Bandon, Co. Cork died
Barrington. R.C	1915	09	15	Wed	Zoologist, Botanist, Climber Richard Manliffe Barrington of Fassaroe, Bray died
Arklow	1915	09	22	Wed	The official opening of Arklow Technical School
Synge	1915	10	21	Thu	Francis Patrick Hamilton Synge of Glanmore Castle, Ashford awarded the Military Cross
Ships/Yachts	1915	11	12	Fri	The vessel "Triflylea" shipwrecked of the Wicklow Coast
Parnell. H.T.	1915	11	24	Wed	Henry Tudor Parnell a brother of Charles S Parnell died
Kilcoole	1915				Sea erosion at Kilcoole and Ballygannon, Co. Wicklow
Bernard. John Henry	1915				John Henry Bernard became Archbishop of Dublin
Errity. Tom	1915				Private Tom Errity aged 20, of Newtownmountkennedy County Wicklow was killed at Gallipoli in World War I
Books	1915				A legend of Wicklow and other poems by Bruce Malaher
Arklow	1915				Arklow Presbyterian Church dedicated
Doran. Felix	1915				Feilx Doran (uilleann pipe player) born Rathnew, County Wicklow. A brother of Johnny Doran
Lifeboats	1915				A motor lifeboat arrived in Arklow
Butler. Eleanor	1915				Eleanor Butler born in Dublin
Le Fanu. Henry	1915				Henry Frewen Le Fanu appointed Coadjutor Bishop of Brisbane, Australia 1915 -1929
Cochrane	1915				W. B Cochrane sold Bailieborough Castle, Co. Cavan to the Marist Brothers Order
Pearce. Thomas	1915				Thomas Pearce died
Jackman. Joseph	1916	03	19	Sun	Joseph Jackman born in Dun Laoghaire and educated at St. Gerard's School, Bray
Casement. Roger	1916	04	21	Fri	Roger Casement hanged
Power. Jenny Wyse	1916	04	24	Mon	The Proclamation of the Republic read by P. Pearse outside the GPO, was signed in J.W.Power house in Henry Street. Dublin

The County Wicklow Database: 432 AD to 2006 AD

A–Z Reference	Day	Date	Month	Year	DATA
Ireland	Tue	25	04	1916	Easter Rising begins
Daly, Edward	Thu	04	05	1916	Edward Daly executed for his part in the 1916 Rebellion, Commandant of the Four Courts
Connolly, James	Fri	12	05	1916	James Connolly killed by firing squad at Kilmainham for his part in the Easter Rising
British Empire Day	Wed	24	05	1916	British Empire Day given official status in the United Kingdom, British Empire Day as 24th May, Queen Victoria's birthday
Royal Marine Hotel	Tue	22	08	1916	Royal Marine Hotel Bray (E. Bresilin Hotel) destroyed by fire
Ships/Yachts	Sat	28	10	1916	The vessel "Orphan Girl" shipwrecked of the Wicklow Coast
Le Brocquy. Louis	Fri	10	11	1916	Louis Le Brocquy (artist) born in Dublin and educated at St. Gerard's School, Bray
Books				1916	Portrait of the Artist by James Joyce published
Bray Harbour				1916	Three to Four colliers per week unloaded their cargo at Bray Harbour
Newspapers				1916	Wicklow Press Newspapers final edition
Baltinglass Hospital				1916	Baltinglass Hospital taken over by the Military as a barracks
Act				1916	Larceny Act
Byrne, Joseph				1916	Joseph Byrne aged 32 a native of Co. Wicklow, was killed fighting at Boland's Mill, 1916
Lifeboats				1916	Cahore Lifeboat Station closed
Yeats, Jack B.				1916	Jack B. Yeats elected a member of the Royal Hiberian Academy
Byrne, James				1916	James Byrne a native of County Wicklow Killed at Boland's Mill during the 1916 Rising
Parnell. Theodosia	Tue	30	01	1917	Theodosia Parnell husband Comm. Claude Paget died
Hamilton. Gladys Mary	Mon	12	03	1917	Gladys Mary Howard nee Hamilton died in Dublin
Wicklow. Earl of	Mon	12	03	1917	Lady Howard wife if the 7th Earl of Wicklow died
Arklow	Sun	25	03	1917	South Arklow Lightship sunk by a U-Boat
Barlow. Jane	Tue	17	04	1917	Jane Barlow (writer) died at Bray Co. Wicklow
Kinsella. Tommy			04	1917	Tommy Kinsella started serving as an alter boy in the Church Of the Holy Redeemer Bray
French. Robert	Tue	24	06	1917	Robert French died
Kynoch of Arklow	Fri	21	09	1917	Explosion took place at Kynocks Munitions Factory, Arklow. 27 killed and many more injured.
Film				1917	The film "Ireland a Nation" was banned by the British authorities but played to Packed houses in America
Airs/Music				1917	The man from Wicklow by Anna Nichols, lyrics by Fiske O'Hara and Bartley Costello. Music by Cass Freeborn
Kearney. Teresa				1917	Teresa Kearney awarded an MBE for her services to the British Army for aid given to sick and wounded soldiers

Section One: Data by Date

Keyword	Year	Month	Day	Weekday	Description
Railways	1917				Construction work completed at the Long Tunnel at Bray Head, designed by C.E. Moore
Campbell. F.George	1917				Frederick George Campbell (artist) was born in Arklow
Labourers Association	1917				County Wicklow Labourer's Association founded
Bray Head House	1917				Putland House (Bray Head House) sold to David Frame
M.P's	1918	02	06	Wed	Redistribution of Seats (Ireland) Act 1918, The limits of the number of M.P's for each county
Redmond.John E.	1918	03	06	Wed	John Edward Redmond died
Darley.J.C.	1918	03	31	Sun	Lt. Col. John Evelyn Carmichael Darley was killed in action, and is buried at Moreuil Communal Allied Cemetery
O'Dalaigh.Cearbhall	1918	04	15	Fri	Cearbhall O'Dalaigh first day at St.Cronans Boys National School Bray see President of Ireland
Parnell.Emily	1918	05	18	Sat	Emily Parnell a sister of Charles S. Parnell died in the South Dublin Union Infirmary
Hill.Arthur-6th	1918	05	29	Wed	Arthur Hill 6th Marquess of Downshire died
Garland.Donald Edward	1918	06	28	Fri	Donald Edward Garland (Flying Officer) born at Balancer, County Wicklow
Goulding.Valerie	1918	09			LadyValerie Goulding nee Monckton born in Kent, England
Ships/Yachts	1918	10	10	Thu	S.S. Leinster sunk when she was hit by torpedoes 4 miles east of the Kish Lighthouse
Ashford Church	1918	10	27	Sun	The Catholic Church Ashford which cost £3,000 was dedicated by Rev.John Staples P.P. of Wicklow
Wingfield.Emily	1918	11	03	Sun	Emily Wingfield nee Fitzpatrick died
Brabazon. Reginald	1918	11	04	Mon	Lady Mary Jane Brabazon nee Lauderdale the wife of the Reginald Brabazon the 12th Earl of Meath died
Ships/Yachts	1918	11	08	Fri	The vessel "Paragon" shipwrecked of the Wicklow Coast
Dunne. Sean	1918	12	18	Wed	Sean Dunne born
TD's for Wicklow	1918				1st Dail R.Barton (SF) The O'Mahony (N) J.R.Etchingham (SF)
Airs/Music	1918				A legend of Wicklow (song, words by F.P. Carrigan)
O'Kelly. Sean T	1918				Mr. Sean T O'Kelly former President of Ireland married Mary Ryan from Wexford
Elections-Polling Day	1918				General Election, Bray was part of the Wicklow/East Kildare Constituency
Newspapers	1918				Bray & South Dublin Herald newspaper cost 2d
Opera. Company Bray	1918				The Bray Opera Company founded
St. Gerard's School	1918				John James headmaster of St. Gerard's School. Bray. 1918-1934
Dublin Gas Company	1918				The Dublin Gas Company purchased the 'Braedale' ship from T.M.Collier coal importer and merchant in Bray.
St Patricks School	1918				The Governors of the Royal Drummond Institution, Dublin purchase the Meath Industrial School, Bray
Wicklow Corn Co.Ltd	1918				The Wicklow Corn Co.Ltd was established by William Clarke

A-Z Reference	Day	Date	Month	Year	DATA
Moorehead. Dr. Thomas G.				1918	During the First World War Dr Thomas Gillman Moorehead served in Cairo with the Royal Army Medical Corps
Bailieborough Castle				1918	Bailieborough Castle, Co.Cavan was accidentally destroyed by fire. Previous owners included Sir Stanley Cochrane and Mr W.B. Cochrane
Donovan. J.T.				1918	J.T. Donovan elected M.P. for Donegal South 1918
Hime. Sir Albert H.	Sat	25	01	1919	Sir Albert Henry Hime died
Drummond School			08	1919	The Royal Drummond school moved from Mulberry Hill, Chapelizod, Dublin to the Vevay Road, Bray (see 1944)
Act	Tue	23	12	1919	The British Government provided houses for ex-servicemen under the Irish Land (Provisions for Sailors and Soliders) Act 1919
Film				1919	The film "Rosaleen Dhu" mainly filmed in Bray , Arklow and Kilmacanogue. The film's premier was in a Bray cinema McDermott's
O'Tuairisc. Eoghan				1919	Eoghan O'Tuairisc (Eugene Waters) (poet and novelist) born in Ballinasloe, Co. Galway
Act				1919	The Local Goverment (Ireland) Act – Proportional Representation
St Patrick's School				1919	Prior to 1919 the Drummond Institute on the Vevay Road was known as the Meath Industrial School for Girls (see 1945)
Barton. Robert				1919	Robert Barton appointed Minister of Agriculture April 1919 – August 1921
War Memorial				1919	War Memorial erected on Qiunsborough Road, Bray
Ships/Yachts				1919	The vessel "Wicklow Head (1st) purchased from Palgrave Murphy & Co. Dublin and renamed "City of Munich"
Shanaganagh Castle				1919	Shanaganagh Castle bought by Harlod Nicolson
Hagan. John				1919	Rev John Hagan appointed rector of the Irish College in Rome
International Hotel				1919	Princess Patricia Hospital Quinsboro Road ceased as a hospital and resumed as the International Hotel
Boyle. Ina				1919	Ina Boyle Received a Carnegie Trust Award for her orchestral work "The Magic Harp"
Campbell. Flan				1919	Flan Campbell (educationist and historian) born in Glencree. Co. Wicklow
Wicklow GAA				1919	Seamus O Caomhanach Chairman of Wicklow GAA 1919
Guinness. R. W.				1919	Rev Robert Wyndham Guinness died
Police/Garda	Tue	24	01	1920	The RIC Barracks at Baltinglass attacked
Malynn. James Joseph	Tue	24	01	1920	Constable James Joseph Malynn shot during the attack on Baltinglass RIC Barracks
Plunket	Sat	24	01	1920	William Lee Plunket, 5th Baron Plunket of Old Connaught, Bray died and was succeeded by his son Terance Plunket 6th Baron
French. Percy	Tue	24	01	1920	Percy French died
Parnell. Theodosia	Wed	17	03	1920	Theodosia Parnell died in London

Electricity	Tue	02	04	1920	The Bray Electricity (Temporary Increase of Charges) Order, 1920
O'Dalaigh.Cearbhall	Sat	08	05	1920	Cearbhall O'Dalaigh last day at St. Cronans Boys National School Bray see President of Ireland
Plunkett. James	Fri	21	05	1920	The writer James Plunkett was born in Dublin, He wrote under the non-de-plume of James Plunkett Kelly
Elections–Polling Day	Fri	18	06	1920	Elections to county councils, rural district councils, and boards of guardians
Plunket	Fri	01	10	1920	Lady Victoria Plunket married Col. Frances Powell Braithwaite
Malynn. James Joseph	Wed	01	12	1920	Constable James Joseph Malynn died from the wounds received during the attack on Baltinglass RIC Barracks
Ballycorus Works			circa	1920	The lead mines ceased at Ballycorus near Bray
Boghall Brick			circa	1920	The Boghall Brick Company, Bray ceased production 1920's
Haughton's			circa	1920	Haughton's makers of Ink and Glues established in Bray
Rathdangan			's	1920	Harry Clarke Stained Glass windows placed in St. Mary's Church Rathdangan
Stuart. Francis				1920	Francis Stuart and Iseult lived at Barravore a cottage in Glenmalure
Barton. Robert				1920	Robert Childers Barton held the post of Chairman of Wicklow County Council 1920 - 1922
La Touche				1920	Bellevue the La Touche property at Delgany was sold for a sum in the region of £30,000
Act				1920	The Government of Ireland Act
Act				1920	Roads Act
Childers. R. E				1920	Robert Erskine Childers wrote Military Rule in Ireland
Tansey & Co				1920	Tansey & Co Drapers & Outfitters were established Quinsboro Road, Bray
Police/Garda				1920	County Wicklow RIC Const. Jeremiah O'Leary killed
Ravenswell. Bray				1920	An extension added to Ravenswell Primary School Little Bray
Harty.H.H				1920	Herbert Hamilton Harty appointed conductor of Halle Orchestra Manchester 1920-1933
Police/Garda				1920	County Wicklow RIC Const. Patrick MacKessy killed
Campbell. Joseph				1920	Joseph Campbell was acting Chairman of Wicklow Council 1920-1921 while Robert Barton was imprisoned
Stuart. Francis				1920	Francis Stuart married Iseult Gonne McBride
Police/Garda				1920	County Wicklow RIC Const. John Miller killed
Presentation Bray				1920	Bray Head House on the Putland Road, Bray bought by the Presentation Brothers
Police/Garda				1920	County Wicklow RIC Const. Charles Bustrock killed
Wicklow GAA				1920	An tAhair P. O Flannachain Chairman of Wicklow GAA 1920
Hodson	Mon	03	01	1921	Sir Robert Adair Hodson 4th Bart died and was succeeded by his nephew Edmond Adair Hodson 5th Bart,
O'Shea. Katherine	Sat	05	02	1921	Charles S. Parnell wife Katherine Wood the former wife of Capt. William O'Shea died

The County Wicklow Database: 432 AD to 2006 AD

A–Z Reference	Day	Date	Month	Year	DATA
Parnell. Kitty	Sat	05	02	1921	Kitty Parnell died
King. Cecil	Tue	22	02	1921	Cecil King (artist) was born near Rathdrum Co.Wicklow
Court House. Bray	Mon	18	04	1921	Two bombs were thrown through the door of the Court House, Bray
Arklow Hospital			04	1921	The Countess of Wicklow Memorial Cottage Hospital opened at the Sea Road, Arklow
Fitzgerald. John	Sun	03	07	1921	Two RIC Constables came under gunshot fire a half mile from Wicklow Town. Constable John Fitzgerald was shot
Fitzgerald. John	Mon	04	07	1921	Constable John Fitzgerald from Co. Westmeath died from his wounds
Police/Garda	Fri	08	07	1921	Three RIC Constables attacked at the Fair Green, Rathdrum including Constable Frederick J. Cromer
Cormer. Frederick J.	Fri	08	07	1921	Constable Frederick J. Cromer shot at the RIC Barracks, Rathdrum. He died from his wounds
Glenart Castle			07	1921	Glenart Castle near Arklow was destroyed by fire
TD's for Wicklow	Tue	16	08	1921	2nd Dail A.O'Connor (SF) D.O'Buchalla (SF) E.Childers (SF) R.Barton (SF) C.M.Byrne (CnanG)
Presentation	Mon	05	09	1921	The Archbishop of Dublin Dr.Byrne blessed and opened Presentation College, Putalnd Road, Bray
Tyrrell. Kate	Tue	04	10	1921	Kate Tyrrell who held a ships master certificate and a director of Tyrrell Shipping died
O'Byrne. John				1921	John O'Byrne legal adviser to Irish delegation at Anglo-Irish Treaty negotiations
Police/Garda				1921	County Wicklow RIC Const. Frederick J Cormer killed
Christan Brothers				1921	Colaiste Ciaran (Seminary) founded by the Christen Brothers in Old Connaught House, near Bray
Allen. Francis				1921	Constable Francis Allen (DMP 11502) awarded the King's Police Medal.
Wicklow GAA				1921	An tAhair E O Fearail Chairman of Wicklow GAA 1921 - 1926
Cochrane. Stanley				1921	Sir Stanley Cochrane established a nine hole golf course at Woodbrook, Bray
Healy. John				1921	Constable John Healy (DMP 10909) awarded the King's Police Medal
Health	Thu	12	01	1922	St Colemans Hospital Rathdrum Established
Books	Thu	02	02	1922	Ulysses by James Joyce published
Glen of Imaal			02	1922	The British War Office handed over to the National Army the lands and buildings in the Glen of Imaal
Colahan. Richard	Fri	17	03	1922	Rev Richard Colahan Parish Priest of the Holy Redeemer Parish Bray died and was buried in St. Peter's Graveyard, Bray
TD's for Wicklow	Fri	16	06	1922	3rd Dail R.Barton (SF) J. Everett (L) R. Wilson (Farmers) C.M. Byrne (CnanG)
Powerscourt			06	1922	Lord Powerscourt wrote to the Minister of Home Affairs about robbing and looting and intimidation on his estate in Enniskerry
Kane. Daniel	Wed	16	08	1922	Daniel Kane .Vol "A" Company IRA killed in action at Sally Gap County Wicklow
National Archives	Tue	19	09	1922	Dept. of Taoiseach Report S1984 The S.S. 'Wicklow Head' detention and compensation claim for period 19/09/1922 to 03/02/1923

Name	Day	Date	Month	Year	Event
Railways	Mon	16	10	1922	The signal Cabin at Newcastle Railway Station destroyed
Railways	Tue	17	10	1922	The signal Cabin at Glenealy Railway Station destroyed fire
Glen of Imaal			10	1922	The Department of Defence (Irish) took over control of the military lands and buildings in the Glen of Imaal
Childers.R.E	Fri	24	11	1922	Robert Erskine Childers court-martialled and shot in Beggars Bush barracks, Dublin
Childers.R.E			11	1922	Robert Erskine Childers arrested at Robert Bartons house, Annamoe, Co. Wicklow
Plunket	Mon	04	12	1922	Terrance Coyngham Plunket 6th Baron Plunket of Old Connaught married Dorothe Lewis
Power.Jenny Wyse		06	12	1922	Jenny Wyse Power a member of Seanad Eireann 6th December 1922 – 20th May 1936
O'Sandair.Cathal				1922	Cathal O'Sandair (writer) born Charles Saunders in Weston-Super-Mare, was educated at Colaiste Chiarain, Bray
Baltinglass Hospital				1922	The Military left Baltinglass Barracks and the building reverted to its original function as a hospital
La Touche				1922	John David Digues La Touche of Kiltymon, Newtown Co. Wicklow. Left the Imperial Maritime Customs Service, China 1882
Byrne. Christopher M.				1922	Christopher M. Byrne held the post of Chairman of Wicklow County Council 1922-1925
Sport				1922	Bray Wanderer's football club originally established
Bowden. Richard				1922	Very Rev Richard Bowden, Parish Priest of Bray, Little Bray and Greystones 1922 – 1939
Film				1922	The film "Wicklow Gold" released. Location scenes in Avoca
Greystones				1922	Greystones Swimming Club founded
Bower. Robert				1922	Robert Bower married Henrietta daughter of 1st Baron Strickland.
Railways	Thu	01	02	1923	The signal Cabin at Timahely Railway Station destroyed fire
Baltinglass Workhouse	Mon	05	02	1923	Baltinglass workhouse destroyed by fire
Railways	Sat	24	02	1923	The 7.40 am up Wexford train ran into a rock fall at Bray Head
Parnell.J.H.	Thu	03	05	1923	John Howard Parnell a brother of Charles S Parnell died
TD's for Wicklow	Mon	27	08	1923	Polling Day for 4th Dail J. Everett (L) C.M.Byrne (CnanG) R. Wilson (Farmers)
Plunket	Sat	08	09	1923	Patrick Terrance Plunket of Old Connaught, Bray born
Boyle. Ina				1923	Ina Boyle composed an orchestral work "Gaelic Hymns"
Rathdangan				1923	The Parish hall built at Rathdangan
Blessington				1923	The bells in the Church of Ireland were re-hung as a tribute and memorial to the servicemen of the parish who died during the Great War
Kearney.Teresa				1923	Teresa Kearney was one of the founders of the Little Sisters for St. Francis working in Uganda, Kenya,and Tanzania.
Saunders Grove				1923	Saunders Grove, Baltinglass was damaged by fire
Roundwood School				1923	Roundwood National School

A–Z Reference	Day	Date	Month	Year	DATA
Arklow				1923	Arklow Military Barracks closed
Waters.T				1923	Very Rev T. Waters became Parish Priest of R.C. Church Enniskerry
Boyle. Ina				1923	Ina Boyle composed an orchestral work "Sleep Song"
O'Halloran. P.J.	Mon	28	01	1924	Garda Patrick J. O'Halloran from Co. Galway was shot and wounded trying to arrest 2 bank raiders at Baltinglass. Co. Wicklow
O'Halloran. P.J.	Tue	29	01	1924	Garda Patrick Joseph O'Halloran (651) died following the Bank raid at Baltinglass, Co. Wicklow on 28/01/1924
Beit. Otto John	Mon	25	02	1924	Otto John Beit given the title 1st Baron Beit
St.John Whitty,Sophia	Tue	26	02	1924	Sophia St. John Whitty died
Mecredy. Richard J.	Sat	26	04	1924	Richard James Mecredy of Valambrosa, Bray died at Dumfries, Scotland
Wicklow Hills Bus Co	Thu	01	05	1924	The Wicklow Hills Bus Company was established it was based in the yard behind the Powerscourt Arms Hotel, Enniskerry
Railways			08	1924	Railway Act–The G W R & Dublin + South Eastern and 23 other railway companies formed Great Southern Railway
Newspapers	Fri	19	12	1924	Freeman's Journal Newspaper final edition
Act	Sat	27	12	1924	Railways Act, enacted by Dail Eireann
Wicklow Gaol				1924	Wicklow Gaol ceased to function as a Gaol
Stuart. Francis				1924	Francis Stuart rented a cottage in Glencree,
Film				1924	The film "Land of the Fathers" filmed in Enniskerry and Killarney, Co. Kerry
Griffin.Victor				1924	Victor Griffin (Church of Ireland Dean) born at Carnew Co. Wicklow
Cullen. Augustus				1924	Augustus Cullen acquired the legal firm established in 1887
Act				1924	The Old Age Pension Act, Pensions cut by 1/-s
O'Byrne.John				1924	John O'Byrne Appointed Attorney General of Ireland 07/061924– 09/01/1926
Books				1924	Dan Breen published his book "My Fight for Irish Freedom" (see 1894.1969)
Books				1924	The Flaming Wheel. Nature studies in the counties of Dublin and Wicklow by John St. Whitty
VEC. Bray				1924	Technical Instruction was transferred from Dept. of Agriculture to the Dept. Education
Presentation Bray				1924	The Presentation Brothers build a school behind Bray Head House, Putland Road, Bray
Cochrane. Stanley				1924	Sir Stanley Cochrane extended the nine hole golf course at Woodbrook, Bray to 18 holes course
Bray Wanderers				1924	Bray Wanderers won the Metropolitan Cup
Railways	Thu	01	01	1925	Great Southern Railway comes into effect following the Railway Act of 1924
Oranmore. Lord	Thu	05	02	1925	Baron Dominick Geoffrey Edward Browne married Mildred Helen Egerton

Regulations	Tue	07	04	1925	Séamus De Búrca Minster for Local Government and Public Health signed Electoral (County) Areas Order: Wicklow
Elections-Polling Day			06	1925	Local elections are held
Dunlavin Town Hall	Sun	02	08	1925	The Bell at the Dunlavin Town Hall given to the Black Abbey, Kilkenny to mark 700 anniversary of the Abbey
Plunket	Thu	03	12	1925	Robin Plunket born
Ships/Yachts	Sat	26	12	1925	The vessel "John Morrison" carrying Pit Props shipwrecked of the Wicklow Coast
DUTC				1925	The Dublin United Tramways (Omnibus Service) Act regulated the Bus service in Dublin
Enniskerry Dam				1925	The Glencree river was dammed near Enniskerry and a pumping station provided electricity for the village
Saunders Grove				1925	The house at Saunders Grove, Baltinglass rebuilt following the fire in 1923
BUDC				1925	The Bray Urban District Council vote to drop the name Bri Cualann and revert to that of Bray
La Touche				1925	Philip K. Love bought Marley Park and House, Rathfarnham once the home of the La Touche family
Bus				1925	The Dublin United Tramway (Omnibus Service) Act passed
St. Paul's. Bray				1925	Mr James M Moore a school master in Bray for forty years retired see 1957
Medical officer				1925	The Local Government Act, required every County Council to appoint a County Medical Officer
Harty.H.H				1925	Herbert Hamilton Harty knighted
Frame. David				1925	David Frame held the post of Chairman of Wicklow County Council 1925-1928
Condren. Daniel				1925	Daniel Condren died
Kiernan. Kitty				1925	Kitty Kiernan married Felix Cronin, Quartermaster General of the National Army
Enniskerry				1925	Street Lighting installed in Enniskerry Village
Bray Golf Club				1925	Bray Golf Club won the Barton Cup
Booth. Denton				1925	Denton Booth died
Weather	Sat	30	01	1926	Bray Seafront lashed by strong gale force winds some minor damage caused
Ships/Yachts	Sun	31	01	1926	The ketch "Marie Celine" was wrecked near Bray Harbour
Fitzgerald. Garret	Tue	09	02	1926	Garret Fitzgerald born in Dublin and educated in Bray at St.Brigid's School
Act	Thu	18	03	1926	Statistics Act-Census confidentiality guaranteed, enacted by Dail Eireann
Population Wicklow (t)	Sun	18	04	1926	Population of Wicklow Town 3,025 or 5.25% of County Population
Population Greystones	Sun	18	04	1926	Population of Greystones & Delgany 1,817 or 3.15 % pf County Population
Population Bray	Sun	18	04	1926	Population of Bray 8,637 or 14.99% of County Population
Population Arklow	Sun	18	04	1926	Population of Arklow Urban 4,535 or 7.87% of County Population
Population Enniskerry	Sun	18	04	1926	Population of Enniskerry urban 214 or 0.37% of County Population

A–Z Reference	Day	Date	Month	Year	DATA
Population Bray	Sun	18	04	1926	The Church of Ireland Population of Bray 1,470
Population County	Sun	18	04	1926	Population of County Wicklow 57,591 persons. 28,911 Males 28,680 Females
Act	Thu	27	05	1926	The School Attendance Act, enacted by Dail Eireann
Moorhead. Dr. Thomas G.			07	1926	Thomas G Moorhead while stepping down from a train at Euston Stn. London slipped and fell, he was conscious and blind
Woodbrook Golf Club				1926	Woodbrook Golf Club, Bray registered with the Golfing Union of Ireland
Allgood. Molly				1926	Molly Allgood married Arthur Sinclair
VEC. Bray				1926	Mr F.F.McCarthy became CEO of Bray Vocational Committee
Dun Loghaire				1926	Dun Laoghaire replaced the name Kingstown
Power. John Wyse				1926	John Wyse Power of Co. Waterford died. 1884 - 1887 General Secretary of the GAA
Film				1926	The film "Irish Destiny" exterior filming at Glendalough and Greystones. The film was banned in the U.K.
Newspapers				1926	Wicklow Newsletter and County Advertiser Newspaper final edition
Sheep Breeders				1926	The Wicklow Mountain Sheep Breeders Society was established
Boyle. Ina				1926	Ina Boyle composed an orchestral work "A Mountain Woman"
McAnally. Ray				1926	Ray McAnally born Co. Donegal
Bus				1926	The 45 Bus Route commenced by DUTC Dublin to Blackrock
Armstrong. Reg				1926	Reg Armstrong (motorcycle racer) born in Liverpool
Police/Garda				1926	Work began on reconstruction of the former RIC barracks at Hollywood, Co. Wicklow into a Garda Station
Green. Christy				1926	Christy Green (Golfer) born Co. Wicklow
Kennedy. Rev				1926	Rev. Kennedy became Parish priest of R.C. Church Enniskerry
Le Fanu. Margery				1926	Margery Le Fanu the wife of Henry Frewen Le Fanu died
Railways			04	1927	The South bound platform was added at Bray Railway Station at a cost of £35,000
Farrell. Margaret			05	1927	Margaret Farrell of Carriglineen, Co. Wicklow murdered
TD's for Wicklow	Thu	09	06	1927	Polling Day for 5th Dail J.Everett (L) S.Moore (FF) The O'Mahony (CnanG)
Pipe Band	Mon	18	07	1927	The Bray Pipers Band the only non Dublin band in the procession of Count Markiewiz funeral
Cochrane. Stanley	Fri	29	07	1927	Stanley Cochrane sold his Mercedes Registration Number IK183 to Mr Ernest Martin of Windsor
Monck	Thu	18	08	1927	Henry Power Charles Monck, 5th Viscount Monck died and was succeeded by his grandson Henry Wyndham Stanley Monck
Bernard. John Henry	Mon	29	08	1927	John Henry Bernard (Church of Ireland Archbishop and academic) died

Category	Day			Year	Event
TD's for Wicklow	Thu	15	09	1927	Polling Day for 6th Dail J.Everett (L) S.Moore (FF) The O'Mahony (CnanG)
Railways	Fri	30	09	1927	The Blessington & Poulaphouca Tramway ceased
Wayman. P.A	Sat	08	10	1927	Patrick Arthur Wayman (Astronomer) born in England
O'Neill William	Fri	02	12	1927	William O'Neill convicted of the murder of Margaret Farrell
O'Neill William	Thu	29	12	1927	William O'Neill was hanged in Dublin
Lugnaquilla Walk				1927	J.J. Cronin of Dublin completed Hart's High Level Route to Lugnaquilla in 20 hours 32 min
National Archives				1927	Business Records Survey Wicklow No. 32 Photocopies of Sports Club Account Book, Roundwood 1927-1933 and 1952-1961
Troy. Dermot				1927	Dermot Troy (tenor) born in Co.Wicklow
Higgins. Adian				1927	Adian Charles Higgins (writer) born Celbridge Co.Kildare. Live in Dalkey, Greystones, Dun Laoghaire
Library. County				1927	The County Councils transferred the library from the charge of the Board of Health to County Library Committee
Books				1927	Arklow, Co. Wicklow by J.W. Barrett published in Cheltenham
Arklow Golf Club				1927	Arklow Golf Club established
Bus				1927	The 45 Bus route extended to Bray
O'Neill. John				1927	Mr John O'Neill of Greystones was appointed the 1st Chief Scout of the Catholic Boys Scouts of Ireland -1927 -1930
Newspapers				1927	Bray Herald Newspaper final edition
Bus				1927	St. Kevins Bus Service (Doyle's) commenced trading
Electricity				1927	The Electricity Supply Board (ESB) established
Books				1927	The Official Handbook Wicklow, County Wicklow by E.J. Burrows. published in Cheltenham
Kilcroney				1927	The contents of Kilcroney House, Bray was auctioned
Barrett. Daniel				1927	The artist Daniel Barrett born in County Wicklow
Wicklow GAA				1927	Micheal O' Cealliagh Chairman of Wicklow GAA 1927 - 1928
Ball. FE	Sat	07	01	1928	Francis Elrington Ball, historian died
Bray Seafront	Fri	13	01	1928	Bray Town Commissioner seeks a grant of £5,000 from the Dept. of Local Government to build a Pavilion on Bray Seafront
Glanmore Castle			01	1928	Fire caused major damage at Glanmore Castle, Ashford
Kearney.Teresa	Thu	02	02	1928	Teresa Kearney established a novitiate convent at Holme Hall, Yorkshire
O'Faolain. Sean	Tue	03	06	1928	Sean O'Faolain married Eileen Gould in Boston, U.S.A.
BUDC	Tue	19	06	1928	Bray Urban District Council dissolved 19/06/1928 to 05/06/1934 Commissioner P.J. Meghan appointed
Elections-Polling Day			06	1928	Local elections are held

154 The County Wicklow Database: 432 AD to 2006 AD

A-Z Reference	Day	Date	Month	Year	DATA
Hodson	Sat	28	07	1928	Sir Edmond Adair Hodson 5th Bart. married Anne Elizabeth Ardderley, Sherbone, England and had two son's Michael and Patrick
D'olier. Bertrand	Fri	17	08	1928	Bertrand Guy D'Olier of Wingfield, Bray killed in a flying accident at Digby Aerodrome, Lincolnshire
Mc Mahon. Ella				1928	Her novel "Irish Vignettes" (working class seduction and betrayal with critical events taking place on a Easter Monday in Bray)
Bray Golf Club				1928	Bray Golf Club won The Irish Golf Clubs Junior Challenge Cup Tournament
Power. Richard				1928	Richard Power (writer) born in Kildare
Roads				1928	The Lower Dargle Road was connected from Bray Bridge to the Dargle Tavern
Town Hall. Bray				1928	A Weigh bridge installed at Bray Town Hall
Biggs. Michael				1928	The sculptor Michael Biggs was born in Stockport, Cheshire, England
Song				1928	"The Oaks of Glencree" a song by John Millington Synge
Sport				1928	J. Byrne of Bray Unknowns played for the Republic of Ireland Soccer team
Mount Kennedy House				1928	The Cunningham family sold Mount Kennedy House, Newtown Mount Kennedy
Wicklow Harbour				1928	Wicklow Harbour (Temporary Increase of Charges) Order 1928
Baltinglass Golf Club				1928	Baltinglass Golf Club established
Whitshed. E.A.F.H.				1928	Elizabeth (Hawkins–Whitshed, Burnaby, Main) Le Bond publishes her autobiography "Day in, Day Out"
Swimming Club				1928	Wicklow Swimming Club founded
Darley. Cecil W.				1928	Cecil West Darley died
Bayly. Lancelot				1928	Lancelot Bayly (artist) lived at Killarney Hill, Bray. Co. Wicklow
Monck	Thu	01	08	1929	Edith Monck nee Scott died
Brabazon. Reginald	Fri	11	10	1929	Reginald Brabazon the 12th Earl of Meath died and was succeeded by his son Reginald Le Normand Brabazon 13th Earl of Meath
Bus				1929	Paragon an independent omnibus ran a bus service from Dublin City to Ballymore Eustace.
O'Toole. Luke				1929	Luke O'Toole of Co. Wicklow died. 1901–1929 General Secretary of the GAA
Walsh. Mary				1929	Mary Walsh born Tinhely, Co. Wicklow
Douglas. James				1929	James Douglas born in Bray. He devised the RTE TV series The Riordans.
Arklow				1929	St. Josephs Church Templerainey near Arklow built
Wicklow GAA				1929	An tAhair O Haton Chairman of Wicklow GAA 1929 – 1930
Police/Garda	Wed	01	01	1930	The Garda Station opens on Convent Avenue, Bray
Beckett. Dr.G.P.G	Mon	20	01	1930	Dr. G.P.G. Beckett appointed first County Medical Officer of Health for County Wicklow

Beckett. Dr.G.P.G	Sat	01	02	1930	Dr. G.P.G. Beckett took up duty as County Medical Officer of Health for County Wicklow
Act	Wed	26	02	1930	The National Monuments Act, enacted by Dail Eireann
Armstrong-Jones. A	Fri	07	03	1930	Anthony Charles Armstrong-Jones born
Dunne. Seamus	Sun	13	04	1930	Seamus Dunne born in Co.Wicklow
Saul.Capt. P	Tue	24	06	1930	Captain Patrick Saul was navigator on the historic East–West trans Atlantic flight from Portmarnock to Newfoundland
Act	Mon	21	07	1930	The Vocational Education Act, enacted by Dail Eireann
Enniskerry	Wed	10	09	1930	Lord Powerscourt laid the foundation stone for the Parish Hall formerly British Legion Hall, Bray Road, Enniskerry
School Medical Service	Fri	19	09	1930	School Medical Service came into operation in County Wicklow
Air Crashes	Fri	21	11	1930	Air Corp Training Aircraft crashed landed on Bray Head, Crew taken to Bray Garda Station and then to hospital in Dublin
Beit. Otto John	Sun	07	12	1930	Sir Otto John Beit died and succeeded by his son Sir Alfred Beit 2nd Baron Beit
Mining			circa	1930	State Mining & Exploration Company developed the Avoca Mines
O'Faolain. Sean			's	1930	The O'Faolain family lived in a cottage in the Glencree Valley, Enniskerry
Hagan.John				1930	Rev John Hagan died
National Archives				1930	Business Records Survey Wicklow No. 06. Ships Arrivals and Departures 1930– 1966 at Arklow
National Archives				1930	Business Records Survey Wicklow No. 08. Brennan's Dressmakers, Carnew. Account Books 1930-1953
Handball				1930	Martin O'Nell and Luke Sherry won the All Ireland Handball Championships
La Touche				1930	Forest Service bought 250 acres at Bellevue Woods Glen of the Downes
Dublin Gas Company				1930	The Gas Showrooms, Main Street, Bray
Bray Head				1930	The Bray Urban District Council acquired the upper slopes around Bray Head
Roads				1930	O'Byrne Road, Bray built
de Buitlear. Eamon				1930	Eamon de Buitlear (naturalist and film-maker) born in Dublin the family moved to Bray in 1930
Kilcoole				1930	C.I.E. bring boulders from Portarlington to protect the railway line at Kilcoole from the sea
Stuart. Francis				1930	Francis Stuart purchased Laragh Castle near Glendalough
Kilcoole				1930	C.I.E placed rocks along the beach at Kilcoole to prevent Costal Erosion (some of the rocks contained fossil remains)
Mount Kennedy House				1930	The Gun Cunningham family sold the NewtownMountKennedy estate
Ploughing	Mon	16	02	1931	The first National Ploughing Championships held at Athy, Co Kildare. The Intercounty Horse Ploughing event Wicklow came 2nd
Ships/Yachts	Thu	19	02	1931	The vessel "Julia" shipwrecked of the Wicklow Coast
Bray Technical School	Sat	14	03	1931	Bray Technical School the first new school approved under the 1930 Vocational Education Act

A–Z Reference	Day	Date	Month	Year	DATA
Massy. Anne L.	Thu	16	04	1931	Anne L. Massy (Marine Scientist and Conservationist) died in Dublin
An Oige	Thu	07	05	1931	An Oige (Irish Youth Hostel Association) founded
Power. George	Tue	30	06	1931	Rev George Beresford Power, died
Powerscourt	Fri	07	08	1931	Lady Julia Coke wife of 7th Viscount Powerscourt died
Old Conna	Thu	12	11	1931	Article in the Irish Times about a weeping stone in Old Conna, Bray
Railways	Wed	02	12	1931	The official trial of the Drumm Battery Railcars from Westland Row Station at 11.00 am to Bray Railway Station and return
Mackintosh. C. Herbert	Tue	22	12	1931	Charles Herbert Mackintosh died at Ottawa, Canada
Dargle River				1931	The River Dargle broke its banks and flooded, Little Bray
Handball				1931	Martin O'Nell and Luke Sherry won the All Ireland Handball Championships
Beit. Alfred				1931	Sir Alfred Beit elected as a Conservative M.P. to the House of Commons, London
Boylan. Dom Eugene				1931	Dom Eugene Boylan entered Mount St. Josephs Abbey, Roscrea as a novice
Blessington				1931	Russborough House near Blessington was sold by Capt... Denis Daly
Powerscourt				1931	Julia Memorial Garden established in the grounds of Powerscourt in honour of the wife of the 7th Viscount
Bower. Robert				1931	Robert Bower elected MP in the House Commons for Cleveland (Yorkshire) 1931-1945
Wicklow GAA				1931	C. M. O'Broin Chairman of Wicklow GAA 1931 – 1946
Act	Tue	28	01	1932	Road Transport Act, enacted by Dail Eireann
TD's for Wicklow	Tue	16	02	1932	Polling Day for 7th Dail J.Everett (L) S.Moore (FF) The O'Mahony (CnanG)
Ploughing	Fri	19	02	1932	The National Ploughing Championships held at Gorey, Co Wexford, The Intercounty Horse Ploughing event Wicklow came 3rd
Hodson	Sat	05	03	1932	Michael Robin Adderley Hodson born
Kiltegan	Thu	17	03	1932	The St. Patrick's Missionary Society was founded a monastery at High Park House, Kiltegan, Co. Wicklow
Powerscourt	Sun	16	05	1932	Powerscourt Estate put up for sale, due to high cost of maintenance
Eucharistic Congress	Wed	22	06	1932	June 22–26 Eucharistic Congress held in Dublin
Ships/Yachts	Mon	25	07	1932	The vessel "Pacific" shipwrecked of the Wicklow Coast
Lawrence. William	Tue	09	08	1932	William Mervin Lawrence died
Bewley. Ernest	Sun	14	08	1932	Ernest Bewley died and is buried in the Friend's Burial Ground, Temple Hill, Blackrock. Co. Dublin
St. Cronan's BNS Bray	Sat	19	09	1932	St Cronan's Boys National School opened on the Vevay Road, Bray
Powerscourt	Fri	16	12	1932	Mervyn Patrick Wingfield 9th Viscount Powerscourt married Shelia Beddington

Section One: Data by Date

Topic	Weekday	Day	Mo	Year	Description
Railways	Sat	31	12	1932	The Dublin & Blessington Tramway Company ceased when the last tram car ran from Blessington to Terenure.
Housing				1932	Development of St. Bridget's Ter., St. Patrick's Sq.. St. Cronan's Rd, St.Columcills Ter., and St Lawrences Ter, Bray
Cliffwalk, Bray				1932	The Bray Urban District Council acquired part of the coastal path (railway path) around Bray Head, called the cliffwalk
O'Faolain. Sean				1932	Sean O'Faolain published his first collection of Short Stories "Midsummer Madness and other stories"
O'Higgins. Brigid				1932	Brigid O'Higgins nee Hogan born in Dublin and educated at the Dominican Convent Wicklow
TD's for Wicklow	Tue	24	01	1933	Polling Day for 8th Dail J.Everett (L) S.Moore (FF) The O'Mahony (CnanG)
Ploughing	Wed	15	02	1933	The National Ploughing Championships held at Clondalkin, Co. Dublin. The Intercounty Horse Ploughing event Wicklow came 1st
Cochrane. Ernest	Thu	23	02	1933	Sir Ernest C. Cochrane 2nd Bart., of Woodbrook, Bray married 3rd Flora Sandstrom
Weather	Fri	24	02	1933	A severe snow storms. Road and rail services suspended for a couple of days.
Glen of Imaal Terrier	Fri	17	03	1933	The Glen of Imaal Terrier was exhibited for the first time as a native terrier dog breed at the Dublin Dog Show
Fitzwilliam. 8th Earl	Wed	19	04	1933	William Fitzwilliam 8th Earl Fitzwilliam married Olive Plunkett
Moore.James	Mon	08	05	1933	James Edward Moore born, the son of Rev. Edward Francis Butler Moore of Bray
McDermott.J.E.	Fri	26	05	1933	The owner of Picture House (Mac's) Quinsborough Road J.E.(Jack) Mc Dermott died and is buried in St. Peter's Cemetery, Bray
Bray Technical School	Mon	18	09	1933	The Vocational School was constructed on the Florence Road at a cost of £5,783 and opened by T.Derrig Minister of Education
Bray Head	Sat	11	11	1933	An Obelisk on Bray Head to Queen Victoria was blown up.
Newcastle Hospital				1933	Newcastle Hospital near Newtown Mount Kennedy ceased to be a national TB sanatorium
Moorhead. Dr.Thomas G.				1933	Thomas Gillman Moorhead appointed President of the British and Irish Medical Associations
Kilmacoo N.S.				1933	Work began on Building Kilmacoo National School, at Kilmacoo in the Vale of Avoca, Co. Wicklow
National Archives	Tue	17	01	1934	Dept. of Justice Report A6/2/34- Jus 8/56 Intimidation of Wicklow man Thomas P.Keogh of Baltinglass at Dublin Cattle Market
Hodson	Tue	30	01	1934	Cecil George Hodson married Betty North of North Cray, Kent, England.
National Archives	Tue	15	05	1934	Dept. of Justice Report A/26/3/34 - Jus 8/184 Unlawful assembly at Bray on 15/05/1934
National Archives	Tue	19	06	1934	Dept. of Justice Report A26/5/34- Jus 8/185 Raid for Blue shirt on house of John Hanbidge, Feddan, Kitegan
Elections-Polling Day			06	1934	Local elections are held
O'Kelly. Sean T	Wed	18	07	1934	Mary Ryan the wife Mr. Sean T.O'Kelly former President of Ireland died
Whitshed. E.A.F.H.	Fri	27	07	1934	Elizabeth (Hawkins-Whitshed, Burnaby, Main) Le Bond died
Ships/Yachts	Sat	18	08	1934	The vessel "Pulteny" shipwrecked of the Wicklow Coast
Scharff. Robert F.	Thu	13	09	1934	Robert Francis Scharff (Naturalist) Died at his home in Sussex, England

A-Z Reference	Day	Date	Month	Year	DATA
Hodson	Tue	27	11	1934	Patrick Richard Hodson born
Delgany	Sat	08	12	1934	Two men Patrick & Charles O'Leary got trapped in a well at Birchville, near Delgany
St. Gerard's School				1934	Stuart Dodson Collingwood headmaster of St. Gerard's School. Bray. 1934-1937
Arklow Pottery				1934	Arklow Pottery established
National Archives				1934	Dept. of Justice Report C26/34 – Jus 8/315 Irish Republican Army Activities in Co. Wicklow
National Archives				1934	Dept. of Justice Report E26/3/34– Jus 8/570 No Rent, No Rates campaign in Co. Wicklow
Elliott. Shay				1934	Shay Elliott (cyclist) born in Dublin
St. Kevin's N.S.				1934	Work began on building St. Kevin's National School, Glendalough.
Ships/Yachts				1934	The vessel "The City of Munich" sold to Saortat & Continental SS Co., Dublin and renamed "City of Ghent"
Glenmalure				1934	A Major landslide took place in Glenmalure valley near the Youth Hostel
Books				1934	1st Edition of The Botanist in Ireland by Robert Lloyd Praeger, 2nd edition 1974 reprinted 1977 Co Wicklow pages 259 –269
Rathcoran				1934	Excavations took place at an Iron Age Hill fort at Rathcoran near Baltinglass
Bradshaw. Harry				1934	Harry Bradshaw became a professional golfer
Glen of Imaal Terrier				1934	The Glen of Imaal Terrier was recognized as a dog breed by the Irish Kennel Club
Davidson. Lillian				1934	Low Tide, Wicklow a painting in the Ulster Museum, Belfast by Lillian Lucy Davidson
Grey Fort				1934	Grey Fort House on the Sea Road, Kilcoole became a Knitting factory(men's socks)
Liverpool Cathedral				1934	Granite from Financially Quarry near Aughrim was sent to Liverpool for the building of Liverpool Cathedral.
Tracey. Liam				1934	Liam Tracey (artist) born Avoca, Co. Wicklow.
Books				1934	The Ages of Stone & Bronze in Co. Wicklow by Liam Price
Books				1934	The Botanist in Ireland by Robert L. Praeger first published
VEC. Bray				1934	Mr.J.Meagher became CEO of Bray Vocational Education Committee 1934-1964
Wicklow GAA				1934	Bray Emmetts GAA Club won the Wicklow Senior Football Championships
Electricity				1934	Bray Electricity Light Company was taken over by the ESB
Fitzwilliam. 8th Earl	Thu	24	01	1935	Lady Anne Juliet Dorothea Maud Fitzwilliam daughter of the 8th Earl Fitzwilliam born
Ships/Yachts	Fri	01	02	1935	The vessel "Fleck" shipwrecked of the Wicklow Coast
Ploughing	Wed	13	02	1935	The National Ploughing Championships held at Mallow, Co. Cork. The Intercounty Horse Ploughing event Wicklow came 2nd
Delany. Ronnie	Wed	06	03	1935	Ronnie Delany born at 4 Ferrybank, Arklow, Co. Wicklow

Section One: Data by Date

Subject	Day	Date	Month	Event	Year
Solus Teo	Mon	18	03	Solus Teo (light bulbs) commenced Trading at Corke Abbey, Bray	1935
La Touche	Mon	06	05	John David Digues La Touche of Kiltymon, Newtown Co. Wicklow. Died at sea returning from Majorca	1935
DeValois. N	Fri	05	07	Dame Ninette DeValois (Edris Stannus) married Arthur O'Connell	1935
Arklow Pottery	Mon	29	07	Arklow Pottery was officially opened by Sean Lemass	1935
Power. George	Sat	24	08	Constance Beresford Power 2nd dau of Charles Putland of Bray Head Co. Wicklow died	1935
Powerscourt	Tue	03	09	Mervyn Niall Wingfield 10th Viscount Powerscourt born	1935
Cinema. Bray	Thu	26	12	Royal Cinema opened in Bray	1935
Woods. Michael			12	Michael J. Woods Government Minster and TD for Dublin was born in Bray, Co. Wicklow	1935
Aughrim			circa	The Granite Quarries at Tinakilly near Aughrim ceased production	1935
Glendalough Hostel				The old schoolhouse Glendalough bought and rebuilt for An Oige with the aid of a grant from the Carnegie Trust	1935
Newspapers				Wicklow Post (Wicklow) first edition	1935
Courthouses				The Courthouses (Provision and Maintance) Act requires local authorities to provide and maintain courthouses.	1935
Housing				Bray Clearance Order – Housing allocation of new housing at Wolfe Tone Square and O'Byrne Road	1935
Housing				Cill Maintain Park, Bray built	1935
BUDC				SI No 408/1935; Street Trading (Bray Urban District) Regulations	1935
Comerford. Marie				Marie Comerford joined the Irish Press Newspapers	1935
Kearney. Teresa				Teresa Kearney established a novitiate convent at Mount Oliver, Dundalk, Co. Louth	1935
Kiosks				Building of Kiosks on Bray Seafront	1935
O'Brien. John				John Thomond O'Brien remains repatriated to Argentina	1935
Bray Rowing Club				Bray Rowing Club established	1935
National Archives				Dept. of Justice Report E26/35 – Jus 8/616 Execution of decrees for non-payment of land annuities, general file Co. Wicklow	1935
BUDC				Mr Edward Byrne Chairman Bray Urban District Council	1935
Moorhead. Dr. Thomas G.				Mai Quinn the wife of Dr. Thomas G. Moorhead died	1935
Avondale House				Some repairs carried out to Avondale House, Rathdrum	1935
Health				Mr John Duffy Chairman of Bray's Public Health Committee	1935
Arklow				Arklow Fever Hospital demolished	1935
Le Fanu. Henry				Henry Frewen Le Fanu appointed Primate of the Anglican Church of Australia 1935 - 1946	1935
Population Greystones	Sun	26	04	Population of Greystones & Delgany 2,000 or 3.41% of County Population	1936
Population Wicklow (t)	Sun	26	04	Population of Wicklow Town 3,183 or 5.43% of County Population	1936

The County Wicklow Database: 432 AD to 2006 AD

A–Z Reference	Day	Date	Month	Year	DATA
Population Enniskerry	Sun	26	04	1936	Population of Enniskerry urban 145 or 0.24% of County Population
Population Bray	Sun	26	04	1936	Population of Bray, 10,111 or 17.26% of County Population
Population County	Sun	26	04	1936	Population of County Wicklow 58,569 persons. 29,686 Males 28,701 Females
Population Arklow	Sun	26	04	1936	Population of Arklow Urban 4,680 or 7.99% of County Population
Guinness	Wed	29	04	1936	Oonagh Guinness married 4th Baron Oranmore and Browne
Wicklow Hills Bus Co			04	1936	The Wicklow Hills Bus Company owned by the Fitzpatrick family was taken over by the Dublin United Tramway Company
Wicklow GAA	Sun	02	08	1936	Leinster Junior Football Championship Final GAA. Wicklow 5-5 Kildare 0-3 played in Carlow
Green. Harry Plunket	Wed	19	08	1936	Harry Plunket Green (baritone singer and author) died in London
Wicklow GAA	Sun	13	09	1936	All Ireland Junior Football Championship Final GAA Wicklow 3-3 Mayo 2-5 played in Croke Park, Dublin
Carnew	Mon	14	09	1936	Carnew Vocational school built (Colaiste Bhride)
Ships/Yachts	Sat	17	10	1936	"Erne" a sloop was driven ashore at Bray
Bill				1936	Liffey Reservoir Bill introduced into Dail Eireann proposed to build Hydro-electric works at Poulaphouca and flood 6,500 acres
National Archives				1936	Dept. of Justice Report D46/36 – Jus 8/455 Steamers anchored in Wicklow Bay as reported in Irish Independent 09/11/1936
O'Kelly. Sean T				1936	Mr. Sean T. O'Kelly former President of Ireland married Phyllis Ryan a sister of Mary Ryan from Wexford
Books				1936	The Kynoch era in Arklow by Hilary Murphy
Newspapers				1936	Bray Tribune Newspaper first edition
Newspapers				1936	East Coast Express first edition
Christ Church, Bray				1936	The side chapel in Christ Church Bray was dedicated by Archbishop of Dublin Dr. Gregg
Harmon				1936	Count Louis Le Warner Harmon died in the USA (see 1866)
Greystones				1936	Carrig Eden Hotel Greystones sold
Bailieborough Castle				1936	Bailieborough Castle, Co. Cavan was demolished
Kelly. Alan				1936	Alan Kelly born
Bailieborough Castle				1936	The Marist Order of Brothers sold Bailieborough Castle, Co. Cavan to The Forestry Division of The department of Lands
Ploughing	Tue	09	02	1937	The National Ploughing Championships held at Greystones Co. Wicklow. The Intercounty Horse Ploughing event Wicklow came 2nd
Lifeboats	Fri	28	05	1937	A new lifeboat The Lady Kylsant, a Watson class lifeboat stationed at Wicklow
O'Rourke. Mary	Mon	31	05	1937	Mary O'Rourke (Politician) born Athlone, Co. Westmeath and educated at Loreto Convent, Bray
Elections-Polling Day	Thu	01	07	1937	Polling Day for Constitutional Referenda – endorse new constitution

Section One: Data by Date

	Day	Date	Month	Year	
TD's for Wicklow	Thu	01	07	1937	Polling Day for 9th Dail J.Everett (L) S.Moore (FF) The O'Mahony (CnanG)
Traffic Lights			08	1937	Ireland's earliest traffic lights installed at Merrion Sq – Clare Street Junction, Dublin
ESB			10	1937	The order was placed by the ESB for the main construction work on the Liffey Scheme at Pollaphouca and Golden Falls
Bus	Mon	20	12	1937	First Double Deck Buses to run in Dublin introduced by the Dublin United Tramway Company
Constitution	Wed	29	12	1937	The Irish Constitution came into operation
Kelleher, John				1937	Rev. John Kelleher of Bray ordained a priest. Appointed to Dublin parishes 1937-1989
Books				1937	17(98) in Wicklow by Rev. Bro. Luke Cullen
Luggala				1937	Lord Powerscourt sold Luggala, Roundwood to Ernest Guinness. Ernest Guinness gave it to his daughter Oonagh.
National Archives				1937	Dept. of Justice Report E26/37 – Jus 8/662 Execution of decrees for non-payment of land annuities, Co. Wicklow
Film				1937	The film "Parnell" released
Greystones Rugby Club				1937	Greystones Rugby Club founded
St. Gerard's School				1937	Desmond J. Murphy headmaster of St. Gerard's School. Bray. 1937-1963
Boylan. Dom Eugene				1937	Dom Eugene Boylan ordained a priest
Conacher. Lionel				1937	Lionel Conacher elected to the Ontario Legislature
Lifeboats	Wed	01	06	1938	The first service for the Lady Kylsant lifeboat of Wicklow was to a yacht called The Cygnet
TD's for Wicklow	Fri	17	06	1938	Polling Day for 10th Dail J.Everett (L) S.Moore (FF) Patrick Cogan (Ind)
Bus			06	1938	The 85 bus route from Bray Railway Station to Enniskerry was acquired by he GSR from The Shamrock Bus Company
Forsyth, Frederick	Mon	15	08	1938	Fredrick Forsyth (author) born
Lawlor. Hugh Jackson	Mon	26	12	1938	Hugh Jackson Lawlor died
Books				1938	Wicklow Heather by Annie M. P. Smithson, published by Talbot Press
Dwyer. Michael				1938	Restoration project was begun on Michael Dwyer's cottage at Derrynamuck, Co. Wicklow
Bray. Castle				1938	The Castle in Castle Street, Bray was removed
Moorhead. Dr. Thomas G.				1938	Thomas Gillman Moorhead married Shelia Gwynn in London. Shelia was the daughter of the author Stephen Gwynn
Lifeboats				1938	A new lifeboat arrived in Arklow
Plunket				1938	Terrance Coygnham Plunket 6th Baron and his wife Dorothy Lewis died in a plane crash in the U.S.A.
Lifeboats				1938	The lifeboat house at Arklow was modified for a new lifeboat
Publications				1938	The 1st Edition of Insurgent Wicklow was published under the title '98 in Wicklow by The People Newspapers, Wexford
Mount Kennedy House				1938	Mount Kennedy House, Newtown Mount Kennedy was bought by Mr Ernest Hull

A–Z Reference	Day	Date	Month	Year	DATA
Enniskerry				1938	An Archaeology find was found in a sandpit near Enniskerry
National Archives				1938	Dept. of Justice Report E26/38 – Jus 8/674 Execution of decrees for non-payment of land annuities, Co. Wicklow
Mucklagh N.S.				1938	Work began on building Mucklagh National School, at Mucklagh near Aughrim
Connolly, James				1938	Mrs James Connolly (nee Reynolds) died
Ploughing	Wed	08	02	1939	The National Ploughing Championships held at Killarney Co. Kerry. The Intercounty Horse Ploughing event Wicklow came 2nd
Heaney, Seamus			04	1939	Seamus Heaney born in Co. Derry
Bowden, Richard	Mon	12	06	1939	Rev Richard Bowden Parish Priest of Bray parish died and was buried in St. Peter's Graveyard, Bray
Browne, Garech	Sun	25	06	1939	Garech Brun grandson of Ernest Guinness and son of Baron Oranmore and Browne born in Dublin
Roads			10	1939	Road widening scheme at Loughlinstown, Co Dublin
Hussey, Gemma			11	1939	Gemma Hussey nee Moran born Bray, Co Wicklow. elected to Dail Eireann for Wicklow
Ships/Yachts	Mon	11	12	1939	The vessel "Eumaeus" shipwrecked of the Wicklow Coast
Nowlan, James				1939	Rev James Nowlan appointed Parish Priest of the Holy Redeemer Parish, Bray
Housing				1939	Wolfe Tone Square, Bray built
Wicklow Town F.C.				1939	Wicklow Town Football Club formed
O'Kelly, Sean T				1939	Mr. Sean T O'Kelly former President of Ireland came to live at Roundwood Park, Roundwood
Burgage Bridge				1939	The Burgage Bridge, Blessington removed before the flooding of Blessington lakes
Road Labourers Wages				1939	Wicklow County Council, Road Labourers Wages. 48 hour week. 30/s to 37s:6d per week
Nowlan, James				1939	Very Rev. James Nowlan Parish Priest of Bray 1939–1941
Books				1939	Finnegan's Wake by James Joyce
Holy Redeemer, Bray				1939	The mortuary chapel at the Holy Redeemer Church, Bray built
O'Toole				1939	The O'Tools Brothers establish the Harbour Bar, Bray
Dillion, J.M.				1939	John Myles Dillion (Regis Professor of Greek at Trinity College, Dublin) born 1939. educated at St. Gerard's School Bray
Twomey, John				1939	Fr. John Twomey appointed to Bray Parish
Newspapers				1939	East Coast Express final edition (continued in Dublin under various titles until 1952)
Monck Family				1939	The Monck family sold Charleville House, Enniskerry
Banotti, Mary				1939	Mary Banotti (Member of the European Parliament) born 1939, educated Dominican Convent Wicklow.
Costello, Seamus				1939	Seamus Costello born in Bray County Wicklow

Section One: Data by Date

Name	Day	Date	Month	Year	Event
Wicklow GAA	Tue	26	03	1940	The Arklow Geraldines GAA Club founded in Arklow
Blessington Lakes			03	1940	Some 6500 acres around Blessington were flooded to facilitate the Hydro-electric scheme at Pollaphouca
Garland. Donald Edward	Sun	12	05	1940	Flying Officer Donald Edward Garland from Co. Wicklow. Killed in action at Maastricht, Holland. Awarded Victoria Cross
Moore. Seamus			06	1940	Seamus Moore T.D. for Wicklow since 1927 died.
Ships/Yachts	Tue	02	07	1940	Arandora Star sunk by German U-Boat of Tory Island. The crew were buried in Glencree.
Tinahely	Sun	21	07	1940	'98 Memorial unveiled at Balyrahan, Tinahely. Co. Wicklow
Brabazon. Anthony	Tue	30	07	1940	Anthony Brabazon the 14th Earl of Meath married Elizabeth Bowbly
Carnew	Sun	08	09	1940	'98 Memorial unveiled at Carnew
Rathdrum	Fri	25	10	1940	An Unidentified aeroplane dropped bombs on the town lands of Ballyhad and Coppse, Rathdrum
Act	Thu	14	11	1940	Minerals Development Act, enacted by Dail Eireann
Ships/Yachts	Wed	18	12	1940	The vessel "Osage" shipwrecked of the Wicklow Coast
Short. Patrick	Thu	19	12	1940	Patrick Short of Bray was killed when the lighthouse tender ship Isolda was bombed off the Wexford Coast near Kilmore Quay
Bestic. Albert A.	Thu	19	12	1940	Albert A. Bestic was Master of the Isolda, a lighthouse tender ship when it was bombed off the Wexford Coast near Kilmore Quay
O'Faolain. Sean			's	1940	The O'Faolain moved from Enniskerry to Killiney, Co. Dublin
Delgany			's	1940	The Delgany Horticultural Society Founded
Greystones			's	1940	Extension added to Carrig Eden House, Greystones
St. Michael's N.S.				1940	Work began on building St. Michael's Convent National School, Rathdrum
Garland. Donald Edward				1940	Flying Officer Donald Edward Garland (reg no 443) 12 Squadron RAF; Memorial at Heverlee War Cemetery, Louvain, Belgium
St Mary's Enniskerry				1940	Rev. Dr Wall opens a New National School at Enniskerry; Cost £3,900 built of Irish made materials construction and furnishings
Children's Home				1940	West Bank Children's home established in Greystones on the La Touche Road.
Hewat. Richard				1940	Richard Hewat (Chief Executive of Heiton Holdings Plc) born 1940, educated at Aravon School, Bray.
BUDC				1940	Bray Urban District Council accepts a tender of £1,400 from Toft & Sons to provide Amusements on Seafront – Summer Season
Fatima Hall				1940	Fatima Hall, near Bray Railway Station built
National Archives				1940	Dept. of Justice Report S443/40 -Jus 8/825 Fr. Gleeson of Bray sermon 16/6/1940 relating to evictions at suit of BUDC
World War II	Thu	02	01	1941	Bomb dropped at Glencormick, (Stylebawn) ,Bray
Power. Jenny Wyse	Sun	05	01	1941	Jenny Wyse Power died in Dublin and is buried at Glasnevin Cemetery, Dublin
Joyce. James	Mon	13	01	1941	James Joyce writer died

A-Z Reference	Day	Date	Month	Year	DATA
Ploughing	Tue	18	02	1941	The National Ploughing Championships held at Navan Co. Meath. The Intercounty Horse Ploughing event Wicklow came 3rd
Harry.H.H	Wed	19	02	1941	Sir Herbert Hamilton Harry died at Brighton
Air Crashes	Fri	18	04	1941	An RAF plane crashed at Ballyknockan the crew of 4 killed and buried in Blessington
Brabazon_John	Mon	11	05	1941	John Anthony Brabazon the 15th Earl of Meath born
Glen of Imaal	Tue	16	09	1941	Sixteen soldiers killed by explosion while conducting a training exercise with anti-tank mines at Glen of Imaal, Co.Wicklow
Act	Tue	23	09	1941	Local Government Act, enacted by Dail Eireann
Jackman.Joseph	Tue	25	11	1941	Joseph Jackman led an assault on Ed Duda, Libya during the North African Campaign of World War II
Bray. Seafront				1941	Part of the Sea Wall at Bray collapsed
Bray Technical School				1941	An extension to the Vocational School, Florence Road, Bray at cost of £4,000
LDF/FCA				1941	Local Defence Force established. (see 1946)
Ships/Yachts				1941	The vessel "Wicklow Head" (2nd) built (2,873 Tons)
Ireland				1941	Tea rationing introduced
Bradshaw. Harry				1941	Harry Bradshaw became the Professional Golfer at the "Country Club" Killcroney House, Enniskerry
Bray Rovers Hockey				1941	Bray Rovers Hockey Club won the Railway Cup
Charleville House				1941	Charleville House bought by Donal Davis
Arklow Pipe Band				1941	St. Colmcilles Pipe Band, Arklow founded
Moriarity.Andrew				1941	Rev. Andrew Moriarity appointed Parish Priest of the Holy Redeemer Parish, Bray
Ploughing	Thu	12	02	1942	The National Ploughing Championships held at Cloghran Co.Dublin. The Intercounty Horse Ploughing event Wicklow came 1st
Act	Tue	24	02	1942	The Water Supply Act, enacted by Dail Eireann
Jackman.Joseph	Tue	31	03	1942	Joseph Jackman awarded posthumously the Victoria Cross for bravery in action at Ed Duda, Libya
Pim.Joshua	Wed	15	04	1942	Joshua Pim Wimbledon Tennis Champion 1893 and 1894 died and is buried in Deansgrange Cemetery
Air Crashes	Fri	24	04	1942	An RAF Training Aircraft Curtis's Tomahawh I serial no AH920 crash landed at Lecarrow Co. Wicklow
Elections-Polling Day			08	1942	Local elections are held
Jackman.Joseph	Wed	26	11	1942	Joseph Jackman died at Tobruk, Libya and was buried at Tobruk War Cemetery
Sport				1942	Bray Wanderes football club founded
Healy.P.T				1942	P.T.Healy appointed County Manager for Wicklow (Local Government). 1942-45
Boyle. Ina				1942	Ina Boyle composed an orchestral work "Wildgeese"

BUDC				1942	The number of seats on Bray Urban District Council reduced from 15 to 12 elected representives
Bus				1942	The 45A bus route was shortened to operate between Dun Loaghaire and Bray via Ballybrack and Shankill
Quigley. D.B				1942	Dermot B. Quigley born in Bray
St. Andrew's School				1942	St Andrew's School Bray destroyed by fire
Ploughing	Fri	12	02	1943	The National Ploughing Championships held at Portlaois Co.Laois. The Intercounty Horse Ploughing event Wicklow came 3rd
Fitzwilliam. 7th Earl	Mon	15	02	1943	William Fitzwilliam 7th Earl Fitzwilliam died and was succeeded by his son William Henry Fitzwilliam 8th Earl Fitzwilliam
Bewley. Thomas Arthur	Wed	31	03	1943	Emmeline Marion Bewley the widow of Thomas Arthur Bewley of Greystones died
Powerscourt			05	1943	The film Henry IV staring Sir L Oliver shot at Powerscourt Estate, Enniskerry
TD's for Wicklow	Tue	22	06	1943	Polling Day for 11th Dail J. Everett (L) Patrick Cogan (Ind) Christopher Byrne (FF)
Connolly. Roderick	Tue	22	06	1943	Roderick Connolly elected T.D. for Louth 1943-1944
Scott. G.D			10	1943	Rev. G.D.Scott retired after 50 years service as a rector and curate of Bray, He came to Bray in 1893
ESB			12	1943	The Golden Falls station was brought into commission by the ESB
Royal Hotel,Bray				1943	The Cavey family bought the Royal Hotel
Synge				1943	Glanmore Castle, Ashford sold following the death of its owner Robert Synge
Bray Harbour				1943	Bray Harbour the last commercial consignment landed
Woodbrook Golf Club				1943	Woodbrook Golf Club won the Barton Cup
Byrne. Edward				1943	Edward Byrne held the post of Chairman of Wicklow County Council 1943-1944
Police/Garda				1943	The Grada Station at Aughrim built
Photo Collection				1943	Lawrence photographic collection purchased by National Library on behalf of the State
St. Andrew's School				1943	St. Andrew's School, Bray destroyed by fire
Bridge				1943	A bridge near Hunters Hotel on the Newcastle/Rathnew Road built
Books				1943	Difficulties with Mental prayer by Dom Eugene Boylan
St. Andrew's School				1943	St Andrew's School Bray enlarged and reopened after the fire of 1942
Ploughing	Wed	09	02	1944	The National Ploughing Championships held at Ballinasloe Co. Galway. The Intercounty Horse Ploughing event Wicklow came 2nd
Railways	Mon	24	04	1944	Woodenbridge-Shillelagh Railway branch line closed
TD's for Wicklow	Tue	30	05	1944	Polling Day for 12th Dail J. Everett (L) Patrick Cogan (Ind) T.Brennan (FF)
D'Ombrain. Ernest A.	Fri	23	06	1944	Ernest Arthur D'Ombrain died at Killara, Sydney. Australia
Campbell. Joseph			06	1944	Joseph Campbell died in Glencree. Co.Wicklow

A-Z Reference	Day	Date	Month	Year	DATA
Act	Fri	08	12	1944	Transport Act, enacted by Dail Eireann
Smithson. Annie				1944	Annie Smithson autobiography "Myself and Others" published
Rohan. K. C.				1944	Kenneth C. Rohan (Property Developer) born 1944, educated at St. Gerard's School, Bray.
McCrea. John J.				1944	John J. McCrea held the post of Chairman of Wicklow County Council 1944-1950
St Patrick's School				1944	The Loreto Nuns buy Drummond Institute Vevay Road, Bray for £9,000
Kilmacurragh House				1944	Kilmacurragh House, Rathdrum sold to the Department of Lands
Beit. Alfred				1944	Sir Alfred Beit was Secretary for the Colonies in the UK Government 1944-195
Cogan. Denis J.				1944	Denis J. Cogan died at Laragh, Co. Wicklow and buried at Glendalough
Greystones Rugby Club				1944	Greystones Rugby Club won the Metropolitan Cup
Queen of Peace, Bray	Fri	05	01	1945	A public meeting called to fund the building of a new church in the Vevay area of Bray. Canon Moriarity chaired the meeting
Ploughing	Wed	21	02	1945	The National Ploughing Championships held at Tipperary Co. Tipperary. The Intercounty Horse Ploughing event Wicklow came 3rd
Act	Tue	20	03	1945	Minerals Company Act, enacted by Dail Eireann
VEC. Congress	Wed	06	06	1945	The 41st Congress of the Irish Vocational Education Association held in Bray on 6th, 7th and 8th June 1945
O'Kelly. Sean T	Mon	25	06	1945	Mr. Sean T O'Kelly succeeded Douglas Hyde as 2nd President of Ireland
Elections-Polling Day			06	1945	Presidential Election held
Elections-Polling Day			06	1945	Local elections are held
Owen. Nora			06	1945	Nora Owen nee O'Mahony (Politician) born 1945, educated at Dominican Convent, Wicklow
Kiernan. Kitty	Wed	25	07	1945	Kitty Kiernan died and was buried in Glasnevin, Dublin
Library. Bray	Sun	30	09	1945	Mr. William Burke Librarian Bray Library retired (1911-1945)
Troy. Aidan	Tue	09	10	1945	Fr Aidan Troy born at Bray. Co. Wicklow
Coastwatching	Mon	19	11	1945	The Coastwatching service disbanded
O'Nolan. Shaun			12	1945	Shaun O'Nolan (song writer) died in New York
Garvin. John				1945	John Garvin appointed (Acting) County Manager of Wicklow (Local Government)
Flannery. Michael				1945	Michael Flannery appointed County Manager of Wicklow (Local Government) 1945-1973
Altidore House				1945	The Emmet family acquired Altidore Castle, Kilpedder
St Patrick's School				1945	Loreto Nuns establish St.Patrick's National School in the old Meath Industrial School on the Vevay Road, Bray
Sport				1945	Bertie Smyllie was Captain of Delgany Golf Club 1945-46

Section One: Data by Date

Category	Day	Date	Month	Year	Event
Books				1945	The Barony of Ballinacor North. Vol 1, The Place Names of County Wicklow by Liam Price
Operation Shamrock				1945	Between 1945 and 1950 The Irish Red Cross and French Sisters Of Charity looked after Glencree Refugee Centre
Cullen. Gary				1945	Gary Cullen born 1945, educated at Presentation College, Bray. Former Chief Executive of Aer Lingus
St Patrick's School				1945	An extension was added to St. Patrick's School, Bray
Ships/Yachts				1945	The vessel "Wicklow Head" (2nd) purchased from the Ministry of War and Transport and renamed "Empire Wolfe"
O'Sullivan. Morgan				1945	Morgan O'Sullivan (Film Producer) born 1945, educated at Presentation College, Bray.
Kavanagh. Mark				1945	Mark Kavanagh (Property Developer) born 1945, educated at St. Gerard's School, Bray
Trade				1945	Mr. Hans Hautz founded Beverly Bags Ltd. Bray
Glencree				1945	Glencree Reformatory was used as a temporary refugee centre by the Red Cross
Brennan. Thomas				1945	Thomas Brennan elected to Wicklow County Council
LDF/FCA	Wed	06	02	1946	Foras Costanta Aitiuil (FCA) established, replacing the LDF
Ploughing	Thu	07	02	1946	The National Ploughing Championships held at Ballbriggan Co.Dublin. The Senior Individual Class, 1st John Halpin of Wicklow
Ploughing	Thu	07	02	1946	The National Ploughing Championships held at Ballbriggan Co.Dublin. The International Individual Class, 1st J Halpin of Wicklow
Ploughing	Thu	07	02	1946	The National Ploughing Championships held at Balbriggan Co.Dublin. The Senior Ploughing Championships Wicklow came 1st
Burke. William	Tue	19	03	1946	Mr. William Burke died
O'Dalaigh.Cearbhall	Tue	30	04	1946	Cearbhall O'Dalaigh appointed Attorney General of Ireland 30/04/1946-18/02/1948
Population Enniskerry	Sun	12	05	1946	Population of Enniskerry urban 145 or 0.23% of County Population
Population County	Sun	12	05	1946	Population of County Wicklow 60,451 persons. 30,152 Males 30,299 Females
Population Arklow	Sun	12	05	1946	Population of Arklow Urban 4,915 or 8.13% of County Population
Population	Sun	12	05	1946	36% of the Population of Ireland lives in an Urban Area
Population Greystones	Sun	12	05	1946	Population of Greystones & Delgany 2,857 or 4.72% of County Population
Population Wicklow (t)	Sun	12	05	1946	Population of Wicklow Town 3,183 or 5.26% of County Population
Population Bray	Sun	12	05	1946	The population of Bray 11,085 or 18.33% of County Population
Avondale House	Sun	03	06	1946	President Eamon de Valera unveiled a plaque in honour Charles S. Parnell at Avondale House, Rathdrum
Act	Wed	12	06	1946	The Forestry Act, enacted by Dail Eireann
Act	Wed	07	08	1946	Local Governments Act, enacted by Dail Eireann
Turkish Baths	Fri	09	08	1946	Fire destroys McDermott's Picture House (Turkish baths) Quinsboro Rd Bray.
Air Crashes	Mon	12	08	1946	Plane carrying French Girl Guides crashed on Djouce Mountain Co. Wicklow

A–Z Reference	Day	Date	Month	Year	DATA
Bus	Mon	02	09	1946	Wolfe Tone Square (Bray) Bus Terminus first used.
Twomey. John	Sat	14	09	1946	Fr. John Twomey of Bray Parish died and was buried in St. Peter's Graveyard, Bray
Wicklow. Earl of	Fri	11	10	1946	Ralph Francis Howard 7th Earl of Wicklow died and was succeeded by his son William
Queen of Peace, Bray	Sun	15	12	1946	Our Lady Queen of Peace church, Putland Rd built at cost of £11,850 is dedicated by the Archbishop of Dublin Charles McQuaid
Act	Tue	17	12	1946	Statistics (Amendment) Act, enacted by Dail Eireann
Glen of Imaal				1946	The Department of Defence purchased an additional 177 acres in the Glen of Imaal
Ward.J.J				1946	James J. Ward (Vice President of National University of Ireland, Galway) born 1946, educated De La Salle College, Wicklow
Rooney. Philip				1946	Philip Rooney published his best known novel Captain Boycott
Dwyer. Michael				1946	Michael Dwyer's cottage at Derrynamuck, Co. Wicklow opened to the public
Road Labourers Wages				1946	Wicklow County Council, Road Labourers Wages. 48 hour week. 47s: 6d to 54/s per week
Campbell. Flan				1946	Flan Campbell edited the Irish Democrat from 1946-1947
Chamber of Commerce				1946	Wicklow & District Chamber of Commerce established
Woodstock House				1946	Woodstock House bought by Mr. G Van den Bergh
Film				1946	The film "I See a dark Stranger" filmed on locations in Wicklow. The film was released under the title "The Adventuress"
Carnew Castle				1946	Carnew Castle and lands were sold to Mrs Constance Mary Spicer
Books				1946	The Barony of Ballincor South. Vol 2, The Place Names of County Wicklow by Liam Price
Breen. William				1946	Rev. William Breen appointed to the Holy Redeemer Parish (1946-1970)
Christ Church, Bray				1946	A porch was added to Christ Church Bray in memory of dead of the Second World War.
Parnell Bridge				1946	The Parnell Bridge (reconstructed) at the Mall Wicklow Town by Messer's Lee of Arklow
Newspapers				1946	Bray Tribune Newspaper final edition (continued in Dublin under various titles until 1952)
Road Tax Wicklow				1946	Road Tax raised from Agricultural Tractors in County Wicklow £323-10s-0d
Road Tax Wicklow				1946	Road Tax raised from Commercial Van and lorries in County Wicklow £8,407-2-0d
Tractors				1946	4,457 Agriculture Tractors registered in Ireland
Other Vehicles				1946	12,890 Other Vehicles registered in Ireland
Cars				1946	44,489 Private Cars registered in Ireland
Flusk. Michael				1946	Michael Flusk an able seaman on the S.S. Ocean Voyager died in Liverpool. He was a native of Arklow Co. Wicklow
Road Tax Wicklow				1946	Road Tax raised from Private cars in County Wicklow £10,562-16-0d

Vans & Lorries				1946	14,716 Commercial Van & Lorries registered in Ireland
Road Tax Wicklow				1946	Road Tax raised from Other Vehicles in County Wicklow £2,204-2s-4d
Weather	Sun	26	01	1947	Snow Blizzards sweep Ireland in January, February, March starting on 26/01/1947
Ploughing	Tue	11	02	1947	The National Ploughing Championships held at Maynooth Co.Kildare. The Senior Ploughing Championships Wicklow came 1st
Ships/Yachts	Tue	04	03	1947	M.S. Bolivar Norwegian ship sunk near Kish Lighthouse
Powerscourt	Fri	21	03	1947	Mervyn Richard Wingfield 8th Viscount Powerscourt died
Arklow Pottery			06	1947	Arklow Pottery converted from fuel burning equipment to fuel oil equipment in modernising the plant
Glenart Castle				1947	Glenart Castle bought by the Vincentian Fathers who renovated the building it is now called St. Kevin's, Glenart, Retreat-House
Greystones				1947	Ormonde Cinema Greystones built
Goulet. Yann Renard				1947	Yann Renard Goulet (sculptor and artist) and his family settled in Bray
Bradshaw. Harry				1947	Harry Bradshaw (broadcaster) born Bray. Co. Wicklow
Scannell. Brendan J.				1947	East of Ireland Amateur (Golf) Open Championship, winner B.J. Scannell of Woodbrook, Bray
Film				1947	The film Captain Boycott filmed in counties Wicklow, Westmeath and Mayo
Shelton Abbey				1947	Shelton Abbey was opened as a Hotel
McCormack. William				1947	The writer Hugh Maxton (pseud. of W.J. McCormack) born near Aughrim, Co. Wicklow
Bray Traffic				1947	Bray Traffic (Parking and Waiting) Bye-Laws 1947
Ships/Yachts				1947	The vessel "Empire Wolfe" was stranded of Nova Scotia and broke up
Bray Traffic				1947	Bray Traffic Bye-Laws 1947
McManus Liz				1947	Liz McManus born in Canada
Bradshaw. Harry				1947	Harry Bradshaw (The Brad) golfer Won the Irish Open
Police/Garda				1947	The Garda station at Barnaderg near Redcross built
McCormack. William				1947	William John McCormack a poet who used pseudonym Hugh Maxton born near Aughrim Co. Wicklow
Dargle River				1947	Flood waters destroy property in Little Bray when the River Dargle broke its banks
Road Tax Wicklow				1947	Road Tax raised from Other Vehicles in County Wicklow £3,144-1s-0d
Road Tax Wicklow				1947	Road Tax raised from Commercial Van and lorries in County Wicklow £14,785-12-0d
Road Tax Wicklow				1947	Road Tax raised from Private cars in County Wicklow £21,984-11s-0d
Wicklow GAA				1947	A. M. O' Broin Chairman of Wicklow GAA 1947 - 1946
Other Vehicles				1947	14,115 Other Vehicles registered in Ireland

A-Z Reference	Day	Date	Month	Year	DATA
Cars				1947	52,187 Private Cars registered in Ireland
Vans & Lorries				1947	18,838 Commercial Van & Lorries registered in Ireland
Road Tax Wicklow				1947	Road Tax raised from Agricultural Tractors in County Wicklow £951-10s-0d
Tractors				1947	5,234 Agriculture Tractors registered in Ireland
Act	Wed	14	01	1948	The Local Government Sanitary Services Act, enacted by Dail Eireann
Connolly. Roderick	Wed	04	02	1948	Roderick Connolly elected T.D. for Louth 1948-1951
TD's for Wicklow	Wed	04	02	1948	Polling Day for 13th Dail J.Everett (L) Patrick Cogan (Farmers) T.Brennan (FF)
Ploughing	Thu	19	02	1948	The National Ploughing Championships held at Limerick Co.Limerick. The Senior Ploughing Championships Wicklow came 1st
Smithson. Annie	Sat	21	02	1948	Annie Smithson died in Dublin
Jordan. Eddie	Tue	30	03	1948	Eddie Jordan the owner of the Jordan motor racing team . Was born in Bray. Co. Wicklow
Butler. Eleanor	Wed	14	04	1948	Eleanor Butler appointed to Seanad Eireann 14th April 1948 -31st July 1951
Fitzwilliam. 8th Earl	Wed	12	05	1948	William Fitzwilliam 8th Earl Fitzwilliam died succeeded by his cousin Eric Spencer
Fitzpatrick. Sean P.	Mon	21	06	1948	Sean P. Fitzpatrick born 1948, Chief Executive of Anglo Irish Bank Corporation, Educated at Presentation College, Bray
Brabazon. David	Sat	09	10	1948	Hon. David Brabazon the 2nd son of the 14th Earl of Meath born
Act	Tue	21	12	1948	The Republic of Ireland Act, enacted by Dail Eireann
Allen. Darina				1948	Darina Allen born 1948, Educated Dominican Convent Wicklow, Cookery School owner and TV Presenter
Wicklow Gas				1948	Wicklow Gas (Charges) Order 1948
Arklow Town Juniors				1948	Arklow Town Juniors Football Club formed
Bus				1948	CIE took delivery of four "Bolton" type double decked buses at North Wall, Dublin. One of the buses had Bray-45
Trade				1948	Patrick McAliden establishes the Record Press Printing Company Bray.
Housing				1948	New housing developments included St.Peters Road, Dwyer Park, Fr.Colohan Terrace and Fatima Terrace Bray
Police/Garda				1948	The Garda station at Avoca built
Bray Urban District				1948	Bray Urban District Council (Transfer of Institution) Order 1948
Road Tax Wicklow				1948	Road Tax raised from Other Vehicles in County Wicklow £4,311-4s-8d
Road Tax Wicklow				1948	Road Tax raised from Agricultural Tractors in County Wicklow £1,814-15s-0d
Kelly. John				1948	Rev. John Kelly Parish Priest of Tomacork, Carnew 1948 -1968
Tractors				1948	7,952 Agriculture Tractors registered in Ireland

Road Tax Wicklow					1948	Road Tax raised from Private cars in County Wicklow £26,673-14s-0d
Vans & Lorries					1948	22,806 Commercial Van & Lorries registered in Ireland
Old Connaught					1948	Old Connaught Graveyard, Bray closed by Ministerial Order
Guinness. P.W					1948	Rev Percy Wyndham Guinness died
Cars					1948	60,453 Private Cars registered in Ireland
Other Vehicles					1948	16,791 Other Vehicles registered in Ireland
Road Tax Wicklow					1948	Road Tax raised from Commercial Van and lorries in County Wicklow £15,651-0s-0d
Brabazon. Reginald	Thu	10	03		1949	Reginald Brabazon the 13th Earl of Meath died and was succeeded by Anthony Windham Normand Brabazon 14th Earl of Meath
Stamps	Mon	04	04		1949	A stamp with the value 1/-s and featuring Glendalough Co. Wicklow was issued as part of the Air Mail Series
Trams	Sun	10	07		1949	The last tram in Dublin City
Wicklow GAA			07		1949	Leinster Junior Football Championship Final GAA. Wicklow 5-2 Meath 2-10 played in Croke Park, Dublin
Railways			07		1949	C.I.E. withdraws the Drumm battery railcars and replaces them with diesel locomotives.
Cochrane. Stanley	Sun	23	10		1949	Sir Stanley Herbert Cochrane died. The 4th son of Sir Henry Cochrane 1st Bart, of Woodbrook, Bray
Greystones School					1949	Greystones Boys National School, Rathdowne Road Greystones built.
Tinakilly House					1949	Tinakilly House, Rathnew purchased by Augustus Cullen
Wicklow Harbour					1949	SI No. 172/1949 Harbour Rates (Wicklow Harbour) Order, 1949
Arklow Harbour					1949	Arklow Harbour Works Order 1949
Stuart. Francis					1949	Francis Stuart moved to Paris
White. J F de vere					1949	John Frederick de Vere White (Auctioneer) born 1949, educated at St. Gerard's School, Bray .
Bradshaw. Harry					1949	Harry Bradshaw (The Brad) golfer Won the Irish Open
Bray Wheelers					1949	Bray Wheelers Cycle Club formed.
Orange Lodge					1949	The Dublin and Wicklow District, King William III Prince of Orange LOL 1313 was founded
Books					1949	The Barony of Talbotstown Upper. Vol 3, The Place Names of County Wicklow by Liam Price
Kilcroney					1949	Kilcroney House Golf Club ceased and Kilcroney House, Bray became a Hotel
Tractors					1949	9,132 Agriculture Tractors registered in Ireland
Other Vehicles					1949	17,795 Other Vehicles registered in Ireland
Road Tax Wicklow					1949	Road Tax raised from Commercial Van and lorries in County Wicklow £16,463-6s-0d
Cars					1949	71,911 Private Cars registered in Ireland
Conacher. Lionel					1949	Lionel Conacher elected to the Canadian Parliament (1949-1954)

The County Wicklow Database: 432 AD to 2006 AD

A-Z Reference	Day	Date	Month	Year	DATA
Road Tax Wicklow				1949	Road Tax raised from Agricultural Tractors in County Wicklow £1,568-15s-0d
Vans & Lorries				1949	23,698 Commercial Van & Lorries registered in Ireland
Road Tax Wicklow				1949	Road Tax raised from Other Vehicles in County Wicklow £4,211-16s-0d
Road Tax Wicklow				1949	Road Tax raised from Private cars in County Wicklow £27,181-12s-0d
Doran, Johnny	Mon	09	01	1950	Johnny Doran died in St.Vincent's Hospital, Athy. County Kildare and he is buried in Rathnew Cemetery
Wicklow Town	Mon	17	04	1950	The Holy Rosary National School Wicklow town officially opened
Road Tax Wicklow	Wed	03	05	1950	Details of Road Tax raised in Wicklow of years 1946,1947,1948,1949 part of a debate in Dail Eireann
WTDA	Sat	06	05	1950	The Wicklow Tourist Development Association, International Races (Motor Bike) Wicklow Circuit
Trade			05	1950	The IDA (Industrial Development Authority) established
Kinch. Michael	Tue	13	06	1950	Mary Kinch of Bray, Co Wicklow gave birth Michael Anthony Kinch. Weighing 17lb 3oz the heaviest baby recorded in Ireland
Allgood. Sara	Wed	13	09	1950	Sara Allgood (actress) died
Lifeboats	Wed	13	09	1950	The Wicklow lifeboat was called to the vessel Cameo stranded of the Wicklow Coast
Scott. G.D	Thu	14	09	1950	Canon George Digby Scott died
Bray Head	Sun	23	09	1950	Holy Year Cross erected on Bray Head. dedicated
Elections-Polling Day			09	1950	Local elections are held
Printing Works	Tue	24	10	1950	Fire destroyed Bray Printing Works, Main Street, Bray
Baltinglass			12	1950	Michael Farrell resigned as sub-postmaster of Baltinglass and Miss Helen Cooke appointed as sub-postmaster
Greystones			's	1950	The Grand Hotel Greystones changed its name to the La Touche Hotel.
Glass Factory			's	1950	Glass factory on the Boghall Road opened.
Trade			's	1950	The Glass bottle factory at Boghall commenced trading
Bellevue House			's	1950	Bellevue House, Delgany demolished
Flora-Fauna			's	1950	Bray Head colonised by Fulmars (Fulmarus glacialis) sea-bird.
Town Hall. Bray			's	1950	Town Hall Bray major renovations
Royal Hotel, Bray			's	1950	The Royal Hotel, Bray was modernised
Kilmacanogue				1950	Glencormac House, Kilmacanogue became a hotel when the Jameson family sold it.
Booth. Evelyn Mary			s'	1950	Evelyn Mary Booth recorded the botanical plants of south-east Ireland
Books				1950	The Open Road by J.B.Malone lists some walk routes in Co. Wicklow
Christ Church, Bray				1950	The bells re-hung in Christ Church, Bray after repairs were carried out to the bells

Ships/Yachts					1950	The vessel "Mountain Ash" shipwrecked of the Wicklow Coast
Mining Company					1950	The Mining Company of Wicklow was established
Books					1950	Flora of County Wicklow by James Ponsonby Brunker
National Archives					1950	Business Records Survey Wicklow No. 31 Account Books of Frank Donnelly Draper of Bray 1950- 1965
Ledwidge. Peter					1950	Peter Ledwidge held the post of Chairman of Wicklow County Council 1950-1953
Lifeboats					1950	The Coxswain of the Wicklow Lifeboat Edward Kavanagh was awarded a Bronze Medal by the RNLI for the rescue of 13/09/1950
Baltinglass					1950	Mr. Michael Farrell appointed sub-postmaster of Baltinglass, prompted a boycott of postal services in the town
Bray Traffic					1950	Bray Special Speed Limit Regulations 1950
Bus					1950	CIE introduced its touring coach bus service
Luggala					1950	Garden temple erected in the grounds of Luggala. It originally stood in Templeogue House, Dublin
Baltinglass					1950	Dispute over the Minister of P&T appointment of Sub-postmaster in Baltinglass
Henderson. Brian					1950	The sculptor Brian Henderson born in Co. Wicklow
Ploughing	Thu	01	02		1951	The National Ploughing Championships held at Wexford Co. Wexford. The Senior Ploughing Championships Wicklow came 2nd
Population Enniskerry	Sun	08	04		1951	Population of Enniskerry urban 166 or 0.26% of County Population
Population Greystones	Sun	08	04		1951	Population of Greystones & Delgany 2,984 or 4.76% of County Population
Population Arklow	Sun	08	04		1951	Population of Arklow Urban 5,203 or 8.31% of County Population
Population Wicklow (t)	Sun	08	04		1951	Population of Wicklow Town 3,326 or 5.31% of County Population
Population County	Sun	08	04		1951	Population of County Wicklow 62,590 persons. 31,587 Males 31,003 Females
Population Bray	Sun	08	04		1951	Population of Bray 12,062 or 19.27% of County Population
TD's for Wicklow	Wed	30	05		1951	Polling Day for 14th Dail J. Everett (L) Patrick Coogan (Farmers) T. Brennan (FF)
O'Dalaigh. Cearbhall	Thu	14	06		1951	Cearbhall O'Dalaigh appointed Attorney General of Ireland 14/06/1951-11/07/1953
Devlin. Anne	Sun	16	09		1951	Mrs Sean T O'Kelly wife of President O'Kelly unveiled a plaque to Anne Devlin on the bridge in Aughrim
ICA	Tue	02	10		1951	The first meeting of the Wicklow Federation of the ICA took place
Dunne. Seamus	Wed	26	12		1951	Seamus Dunne played his debut match for Luton Town Football Club
Maguire. Brian					1951	Brian Maguire (painter) born Co. Wicklow
Plunket					1951	Robin Plunket married Jennifer Southwell
Scott. Charlotte					1951	Charlotte Jessy Scott nee Barington died
Monck					1951	Henry Wyndham Stanley Monck married Brenda Adkins
Esplanade Hotel					1951	The Lavelle family took over the running of the Hotel Esplanade, Bray.

A-Z Reference	Day	Date	Month	Year	DATA
Shelton Abbey				1951	Shelton Abbey was sold to the Department of Lands for use as State Forestry College
Stuart. Francis				1951	Francis Stuart moved to London
Wicklow Sailing Club				1951	Wicklow Sailing Club founded
Goulding Valerie				1951	Lady Valarie Goulding and Kathleen O'Rourke founded the Central Remedial Clinic, Dublin for children suffering with polio
Dunne. Seamus				1951	Seamus Dunne played for Shelbourne Football Club
Dunne. Seamus				1951	Seamus Dunne joined Luton Town Football Club (1951-1966)
Ploughing	Thu	07	02	1952	The National Ploughing Championships held at Athenry Co.Galway. The Senior Ploughing Championships Wicklow came 2nd
Ploughing	Thu	07	02	1952	The National Ploughing Championships held at Athenry Co.Galway. The Overall Tractor Champion W. Woodroofe of Wicklow
Bray Urban District	Wed	19	02	1952	Bray Urban District (Alteration of Boundary) Order 1952 (S.I. 42/1952)
Moriarty. Andrew	Sun	20	04	1952	Rev Andrew Moriarty of the Holy Redeemer Parish Bray died and was buried in St. Peter's Graveyard, Bray
Loughlinstown Hospital	Mon	09	06	1952	St. Columcilles Hospital at Loughlinstown was opened by Dr. Ryan the Minister for Health
Kearney. Teresa	Mon	09	06	1952	Teresa Kearney founded The Franciscan Missionary Sisters for Africa
O'Kelly. Sean T	Wed	25	06	1952	Mr. Sean T O'Kelly began his 2nd term as President of Ireland
Darcy. Eamonn	Thu	07	08	1952	Eamonn Darcy (golfer) born Delgany Co.Wicklow
Ships/Yachts			08	1952	The vessel "Agnes Craig" shipwrecked of the Wicklow Coast
Allgood. Molly	Sun	02	11	1952	Molly Allgood (actress) died
Troy. Dermot				1952	Dermot Troy won the Irish Independent Caruso competition for singers
Railways				1952	Fire destroys part of the roof of Bray Railway Station.
Brabazon. Anthony				1952	The Earl of Meath carries out major repairs to Killruddery House due to dry rot
Russborough House				1952	Sir Alfred Beit buys Russborough House, Blessington from Captain Daly
Bray Musical Society				1952	Bray Musical Society Founded
Fitzwilliam. 9th Earl				1952	Eric Spencer the 9th Earl of Fitzwilliam died
Police/Garda				1952	The Garda station at Roundwood built
Arklow Harbour				1952	Arklow Harbour Works Order 1952
Wicklow Gas				1952	Wicklow Gas (Charges) Order 1948 amended 1952
Bray Head Chairlift.				1952	Work begins on putting a Chairlift on Bray Head – Irish Holidays Ltd
Lough Dan				1952	The ESB proposed to build a dam at the southern of Lough Dan, Roundwood. An English firm carry out bore tests.

Section One: Data by Date

	Day	Date	Month	Year	Event
Bray Musical Society				1952	Bray Musical Society stages "Concert"
Bayly. Lancelot				1952	Lancelot Bayly (artist) died in Berkshire, England
Ploughing	Wed	11	02	1953	The National Ploughing Championships held at Mullingar Co. Westmeath. The Senior Ploughing Championships Wicklow came 1st
Monck	Thu	02	04	1953	Charles Stanley Monck born, later 7th Viscount Monck
National Archives			06	1953	Dept. of Taoiseach Report RA40/53 – 97/9/1269 Wicklow By-Election 1953 Taoiseach speeches
O'Dalaigh.Cearbhall	Mon	13	07	1953	Cearbhall O'Dalaigh appointed High Court Judge
Bus	Wed	22	07	1953	The CIE touring coach "The Dargle" featured in a publicity photographs for CIE taken in the Vale of Clara
Hill.Arthur-7th	Thu	23	07	1953	Arthur Hill 7th Marquis of Downshire married Noreen Gray Miller
Henry.Grace	Tue	11	08	1953	Grace Henry (artist) died
Library.Bray	Sat	17	11	1953	The Children's Section of Bray Library opened by Minister of Education Mr Sean Moylan (£180 from the Parnell monument fund)
Ships/Yachts	Fri	04	12	1953	The schooner ME Johnson ran a ground at the south pier Arklow and broke up under the force of the gale
Henry.Paul				1953	Paul Henry married Mable Florence Young
Byrne.Henry J.				1953	Henry J. Byrne held the post of Chairman of Wicklow County Council 1953-1960
Scannell.Brendan J.				1953	East of Ireland Amateur (Golf) Open Championship, runner-up B.J. Scannell of Woodbrook, Bray
Woolworths.WF				1953	W.F. Woolworths opened a store at 10-11 Main Street Bray.
Bradshaw.Harry				1953	Harry Bradshaw (The Brad) (golfer) Played on the Ryder Cup teams of 1953, 1955 and 1957
TD's for Wicklow				1953	14th Dail By-Election held following the death of Thomas Brennan, By-Election won by M.Deering (FG)
Books				1953	The new Invasion [An account of the author's experiences farming in Co. Wicklow from 1946 onward] by Winefride Nolan
Books				1953	Official Guide to Wicklow-Wexford
Bradshaw.Harry				1953	Harry Bradshaw won the Dunlop Masters Golf Championship
Wicklow GAA				1953	The Arklow Rock Parnells GAA Club founded in Arklow
Daly.Capt				1953	The owner of Russborough House, Blessington. Capt. Daly died
Stuart.Francis				1953	Iseult Gonne Stuart nee McBride died
Bray Musical Society				1953	Bray Musical Society stages "Where the Lark Sings"
Laragh				1953	The road bridge at Laragh Co. Wicklow was reinforced
Bus				1953	One of CIE touring coaches was named "The Dargle"
Books				1953	The Barony of Talbotstown Lower Vol 4, The Place Names of County Wicklow by Liam Price
Brennan.Thomas				1953	Thomas Brennan died
Nolan.Winifride				1953	Winifride Nolan of Aughrim, Co Wicklow wrote "The New Invasion"

A–Z Reference	Day	Date	Month	Year	DATA
Dunne. Seamus				1953	Seamus Dunne won his first cap for the Republic of Ireland football team , where he won 15 full caps (1953–1959)
O'Byrne. John	Thu	14	01	1954	John O'Byrne (Lawyer) died
TD's for Wicklow	Tue	18	05	1954	Polling Day for 15th Dail J. Everett (L) M.Deering (FG) P. Brennan (FF)
Conacher. Lionel	Wed	26	05	1954	Lionel Conacher died
Everett. James	Sat	12	06	1954	James Everett T.D. for Wicklow appointed Minister of Justice
Wicklow GAA	Sun	01	08	1954	Leinster Junior Hurling Championship Final GAA. Wicklow 4–15 Westmeath 1–3 played in Naas, Co. Kildare
Connolly Square	Sun	15	08	1954	Grotto in James Connolly Square Bray was blessed by Rev. John Fitzpatrick, Bray
Ward. Tony	Fri	08	10	1954	Tony Ward born in Dublin
Wolfe Tone Sq	Sun	05	12	1954	Grotto dedicated to Our lady was blessed by Rev Fr. Mitchell PP at Wolfe Tone Square, Bray.
Books				1954	[Pour l'heure Sainte mensuelle] The Holy Hour translated from French by the Earl of Wicklow
Byrne. Pat				1954	Pat Byrne born 1954, educated at Presentation College, Bray. Chief Executive of Cityjet (Dublin)
Arklow Harbour				1954	Arklow Harbour Works Order 1952 (Amendment) Order 1954
Bray Musical Society				1954	Bray Musical Society stages "Maritana"
Fitzpatrick. John				1954	Rev John Fitzpatrick appointed Parish Priest of the Holy Redeemer Parish Bray
Carnew				1954	The Church of the "Most Holy Rosary" constructed and opened in Carnew
Davidson. Lillian				1954	Lillian Lucy Davidson (artist) died.
Airs/Music				1954	To the Wicklow Hills (Song) words by R. G. Leigh, Lloyd Webber, William Southcombe
Scannell. Brendan J.				1954	East of Ireland Amateur (Golf) Open Championship, winner B.J. Scannell of Woodbrook, Bray
Dock Terrace				1954	Some cottages at Dock Terrace demolished
Kearney. Teresa				1954	Teresa Kearney established a novitiate convent at Boston. U.S.A.
Beatty. Sir A. C.				1954	Sir Alfred Chester Beatty was knighted by the Queen of England
Windgates School				1954	The school at Windgates, Greystones Co. Wicklow closed
Books				1954	The Passion of Our Lord Jesus Christ translated from French by the Earl of Wicklow
Books				1954	A Priest in Russia and the Baltic by Charles Bourgeois, translated from French by the Earl of Wicklow
Kish Lighthouse				1954	The "Gannet" lightship was placed on the Kish Bank, the colour of the lightship was changed from Black to Red
Ploughing	Fri	11	02	1955	The National Ploughing Championships held at Athy Co. Kildare. The Senior Horse Plough Champion John Halpin of Wicklow
Act	Tue	10	05	1955	Local Government Act, enacted by Dail Eireann

Elections-Polling Day			06	1955	Local elections are held
Wicklow GAA			10	1955	Leinster O'Byrne Cup Senior Football Final GAA. Wicklow 1-6 Westmeath 0-7 played in Newbridge, Co. Kildare
Robbie. John	Thur	17	11	1955	John Robbie was born in Dublin
Scannell. Brendan J.				1955	East of Ireland Amateur (Golf) Open Championship, winner B.J. Scannell of Woodbrook, Bray
Glen of Imaal				1955	The Department of Defence purchased an additional 142 acres in the Glen of Imaal
Kilcroney				1955	Kilcroney House was bought by the St. John of God Brothers
Glenmalure Hostel				1955	A small house at Barravoe Ford, Glenmalure was bequeathed to An Oige by Dr Kathleen Lynn
Cars				1955	Total Population of Ireland (estimated) 2,910,700 Cars Registered 127,511 Cars per 1000 persons 44
Delany. Ronnie				1955	Ronnie Delaney won the Irish title for the 880 yards in 1:50:0
Bray Musical Society				1955	Bray Musical Society stages "Countess Maritza"
Nolan. John				1955	Rev John Nolan appointed Parish Priest of the St. Mary's Church. Enniskerry
BUDC				1955	Mr Denis McCarthy appointed Town Clerk of Bray Urban District Council.
Hollywood N.S.				1955	Work began on building Hollywood National School.
Kelly. Alan				1955	Alan Kelly played for Bray Wanderers 1955-1956
Ploughing	Thu	02	02	1956	The National Ploughing Championships held at Nenagh Co. Tipperary. The Senior Horse Ploughing event Wicklow came 2nd
Act	Tue	14	02	1956	The Gaming and Lotteries Act, enacted by Dail Eireann
Act	Mon	27	02	1956	The Forestry Act, enacted by Dail Eireann
Population Arklow	Sun	08	04	1956	Population of Arklow Urban 5,292 or 8.83% of County Population
Population Greystones	Sun	08	04	1956	Population of Greystones & Delgany 3,565 or 5.95% of County Population
Population Enniskerry	Sun	08	04	1956	Population of Enniskerry urban 530 or 0.88% of County Population
Population Wicklow (t)	Sun	08	04	1956	Population of Wicklow Town 3,070 or 5.12% of County Population
Population County	Sun	08	04	1956	Population of County Wicklow 59,906 persons. 29,933 Males 29,973 Females
Population Bray	Sun	08	04	1956	Population of Bray Urban District 10,856 or 17.3% of County Population
Wingfield. Maurice	Sat	14	04	1956	Maurice Wingfield of Enniskerry died
Goulet. Yann Renard	Sun	20	05	1956	A memorial in the grounds of the Customs House costing £2815.11s.1d was sculptured by Yan Renard Goulet
Lifeboats	Thu	07	06	1956	The lifeboat William J Archer was stationed at Wicklow Harbour
Redmond. John E.	Mon	11	06	1956	The Department of Post and Telegraphs issued a stamp in honour of John Redmond
Lifeboats	Thu	14	06	1956	The naming ceremony of the Wicklow Lifeboat, William J Archer was performed by Mrs Sean T O'Kelly

A–Z Reference	Day	Date	Month	Year	DATA
Moore. James	Sun	24	06	1956	James Edward Moore became a Deacon in the Parish of Knock. Co. Down
Chamber of Commerce	Fri	02	11	1956	Bray Chamber of Commerce incorporated
Kelly. Alan	Sun	25	11	1956	Alan Kelly won his first cap for the Republic of Ireland Football team
Delany. Ronnie	Sat	01	12	1956	Ronnie Delany from Arklow won the 1,500m Gold medal at the 1956 Olympic Games held in Melbourne in a time of 3min:41:2
Avoca				1956	St. Patrick's Mining Company a subsidiary of a Canadian Company starts mining at Avoca
Wicklow Harbour				1956	Wicklow Harbour Works Order 1956
Wicklow GAA				1956	St.Mary's GAA Club Enniskerry established.
Bray Musical Society				1956	Bray Musical Society stages "Waltzes from Vienna"
Mining				1956	The Finance Act allowed new mining enterprise exemption from all tax for first 4 years and taxation on half profits for next 4 years
BUDC				1956	Bray Urban District Council carried out some repairs to the seafront and promenade
Luggala				1956	Luggala House a home of the Guinness family was burnt but rebuilt immediately
St. Brendans College				1956	Christian Brothers buy the Walcot Hotel at Old Conna, Bray and establish St. Brendans College
COI. Carnew				1956	The organ in the Parish Church of Tourmakeady was sold when the church closed and it was installed in Carnew, Parish Church
Loreto Convent Bray				1956	Loreto Convent School Vevay Road Bray extended
Books				1956	[Sainte Bernadette vous parle] Saint Bernadette speaks translated from French by the Earl of Wicklow
Kilcroney				1956	Kilcroney House became St. Joseph's Convalescent Home run by the St. John of God Brothers
Delgany Golf Club				1956	Delgany Golf Club won the Barton Cup
Laragh				1956	A new bridge opened in Laragh, replacing the old bridge. Engineer J.J.Rowan and County Engineer J.T. O'Byrne
Kelly. Alan				1956	Alan Kelly played goalkeeper for the Republic of Ireland football team, winning 47 caps 1956 –1973
Lifeboats	Fri	01	02	1957	The first service of the William J Archer Lifeboat of Wicklow was to remove an injured man from the Codling Lightship
Ploughing	Fri	08	02	1957	The National Ploughing Championships held at Boyle Co.Roscommon. "Queen of the Plough" Muriel Sutton of Wicklow
Act	Wed	13	02	1957	The Wicklow County (Extension of Boundary) Provisional Order, 1957 with effect from 01/07/1957
TD's for Wicklow	Tue	05	03	1957	Polling Day for 16th Dail J. Everett (L) J.O'Toole (FF) P.Brennan (FF)
O'Higgins. Brigid	Tue	05	03	1957	Brigid Hogan elected to Dail Eireann for South Galway
Yeats. Jack B.	Thu	28	03	1957	Jack B.Yeats died in Dublin
Moore. James	Sun	16	06	1957	James Edward Moore ordained a priest

					Section One: Data by Date
Act	Wed	26	06	1957	Small Dwellings Act, enacted by Dail Eireann
Bray Harbour	Thu	05	09	1957	The Lighthouse at Bray Harbour fell into the sea at 14:10 hrs following a storm
Wicklow GAA	Sun	06	10	1957	Leinster O'Byrne Cup Senior Football Final GAA. Wicklow 2-9 Kildare 1-10 played in Blessington, Co. Wicklow
O'Kelly. Sean T	Tue	07	10	1957	Roundwood Park the private residence of the former President of Ireland Sean T O'Kelly was destroyed by fire
Kearney. Teresa	Wed	16	10	1957	Teresa Kearney died at the convent in Boston and she was buried at Nkokonjeru, Uganda
O'Connor. Peter J.	Sat	09	11	1957	Peter J.O'Connor (athletics) died in Waterford
Books				1957	The Barony of Rathdown Vol 5, The Place Names of County Wicklow by Liam Price
Arklow Harbour				1957	Arklow Harbour Works Order 1957
BUDC				1957	Bray Urban District Council extended the town boundary
County Wicklow				1957	Wicklow County (District Electoral Divisions) Order 1957
Glendalough				1957	The Rock Climbers Guide to Glendalough compiled by the Irish Mountaineering Club
County Wicklow				1957	Wicklow County (Extension of Boundary) Provisional Order 1957 (Commencement) Order 1957
County Wicklow				1957	Wicklow County and Rathdown Public Assistant District (Dispensary Districts) Order 1957
Ardmore Studio				1957	Mr. Louis Elliman, Director of Ranks Cinemas in Ireland bought Ardmore House, Bray
Landscape Painting				1957	The Irish School of Landscape Painting founded at Ashford, Co. Wicklow
Old Conna House				1957	Old Conna House was purchased for £35,000 by James Stuart Roberston
Beatty. Sir A. C.				1957	Sir Alfred Chester Beatty became the first honorary citizen of Ireland
St. Pauls. Bray				1957	Due to wood worm the timbers of St. Pauls Church Bray were treated with chemicals.
Bray Musical Society				1957	Bray Musical Society stages "White Horse Inn"
Film				1957	The film "Professor Tim" outdoor scenes filmed near Enniskerry
Delany. Ronnie				1957	Ronnie Delaney won the Irish title for the 880 yards in 1:47:8
Film				1957	The film Boyds Shop - outdoor scenes filmed near Enniskerry
St. Paul's. Bray				1957	Mr James M Moore headmaster of St. Paul's School Bray died aged 96 years
Books				1957	[Ce petit moine dangereux] A dangerous little Friar, Father Titus Brandsma translated from French by the Earl of Wicklow
Costello. Seamus				1957	Seamus Costello was arrested in Glencree Co. Wicklow
Barrett. Daniel				1957	Artist Daniel Barrett receives International Jewirey Award
Kelly. Alan				1957	Alan Kelly played for Drumcondra Football Club - Won FAI Cup Medal 1957
Ships/Yachts	Tue	21	01	1958	The vessel "Anna Toop " shipwrecked of the Wicklow Coast

180 | The County Wicklow Database: 432 AD to 2006 AD

A-Z Reference	Day	Date	Month	Year	DATA
British Empire Day	Wed	12	03	1958	British Empire Day renamed British Commonwealth Day
Byrne. C.M.	Sat	12	04	1958	The former chairman of Wicklow County Council died
Ardmore Studio	Mon	12	05	1958	Minster of Industry & Commerce Sean Lemass opens Ardmore Film Studio, Bray
Henry. Paul	Sun	24	08	1958	Paul Henry RHA died at his home in Bray and was buried in St.Patricks Graveyard Enniskerry
Group Water Scheme			08	1958	The first ever group water scheme in Ireland near Manor Kilbride, Co. Wicklow
Regan.T	Fri	03	10	1958	Irish Angling Record for Sea Trout 12lb 0oz was set by T.Regan at River Dargle, Bray (Guinness Book of Records)
Bradshaw. Harry				1958	Harry Bradshaw won the Canada Cup (now the World Cup) Golf Championship
Wicklow GAA				1958	Aodh o'Broin of Wicklow held the post of President of the GAA 1958-1961
Books				1958	The Barony of Shillelagh Vol 6, The Place Names of County Wicklow by Liam Price
O'Higgins. Brigid				1958	Brigid Hogan married Michael O'Higgins the T.D. for Wicklow
Books				1958	"A Tale of Two Churches" by E.H.F.Campbell, The history of St. Paul's and Christ Church, Bray
Ravenswell. Bray				1958	An extension was added to Ravenswell National School, Bray at a cost of £50,000
Mr What				1958	Bray businessman Mr D.J. Coughlan owner of the race horse "Mr What" won the English Grand National at Aintree
Bray Musical Society				1958	Bray Musical Society stages "Maritanna" and "Countess Maritza"
Ardmore Studio				1958	Shooting commenced on "Home is the Hero" the first feature film at Ardmore Studio, Bray
Chamber of Commerce				1958	Mr H Hautz elected President of Bray Chamber of Commerce
Tidy Towns				1958	First Year of the Bord Failte Tidy Town Competition
Avoca				1958	Over 500 men employed by the mining companies at the Avoca Mines
Industrial Yarns				1958	Industrial Yarns Ltd Dublin Road, Bray commenced trading
Carnew				1958	Carnew Primary School built
Books				1958	[Nos enfants et nous] Our Children and ourselves translated from French by the Earl of Wicklow
Sea Park House				1958	Sea Park, Wicklow sold in 1958
Newspapers				1958	Weekly Gazette (Arklow) first edition published
Kelly.Alan				1958	Alan Kelly made 447 league appearances for Preston North End Football Club 1958-1973
Ploughing	Thu	29	01	1959	The National Ploughing Championships held at Bunchurch Co.Kilkenny.The Senior Horse Ploughing event Wicklow came 2nd
Ploughing	Thu	29	01	1959	The National Ploughing Championships held in Co.Kilkenny.The Snr. Indv. Horse Plough Champion 1st John Halpin of Wicklow

Ploughing	Thu	29	01	1959	The National Ploughing Championships held at Bunchurch Co.Kilkenny. "Queen of the Plough" Muriel Sutton of Wicklow
Bus	Fri	01	05	1959	The first double decked bus ran Dublin to Bray seafront terminus. Prior to 1959 double decked buses used a terminus on Meath Road, Bray
Elections-Polling Day	Wed	17	06	1959	Presidential Election held
Elections-Polling Day	Wed	17	06	1959	Polling Day for Constitutional Referenda– Introduction of plurality system
O'Kelly, Sean T	Wed	24	06	1959	Mr. Sean T O'Kelly President of Ireland retired
Kippure	Mon	28	09	1959	Lord Powerscourt sold 2 acres 1 rood and 28 perches in the town land of Powerscourt Mt. to the Broadcasting Commissioners
Kippure	Mon	28	09	1959	Lord Powerscourt sold 15 acres 2 roods and 12 perches in the town land of Kippure to the Broadcasting Commissioners
Chamber of Commerce				1959	Mr H.B. Hipwell elected President of Bray Chamber of Commerce 1959–1961
Wicklow Harbour				1959	Wicklow Harbour Works Order 1956 (Amendment) Order 1959
Tinakilly House				1959	Tinakilly House, Rathnew purchased by Mr Gunther Smith
Butler, Eleanor				1959	Eleanor Butler married William Cecil 8th Earl of Wicklow
Delgany				1959	The Delgany Horticultural Society renamed Delgany & District Horticultural Society
Books				1959	Margherita Sarto, mother of St Pius X translated from French by the Earl of Wicklow
Glencree				1959	The German War Graves Commission opened a cemetery at Glencree, Co. Wicklow.
Goulet, Yann Renard				1959	A monument at Ballyseedy, Tralee Co. Kerry dedicated to the Kerry No. 1 Brigade was sculpterd by Yann Renard Goulet
Somerville–Large. P.				1959	Philip Townsend Somerville–Large (engineer with C.I.E.) opposed the closure of Harcourt Street Railway line
Bray Musical Society				1959	Bray Musical Society stages "The Bohemian Girl"
Railways				1959	The Harcourt Street to Bray Railway Line closed
Books				1959	[Le Miracle irlandais] The Miracle of Ireland translated from French by the Earl of Wicklow
Woodbrook				1959	From 1959 to 1962 the Hospital Trust Tournaments were held at Woodbrook Golf Club
Armstrong-Jones. A	Wed	06	05	1960	Anthony Charles Armstrong-Jones 1st married H.R.H. Princess Margaret
Broadcasting Authority	Wed	01	06	1960	The Broadcasting Authority established
Elections-Polling Day	Wed	29	06	1960	Local elections are held
Gypsy Moth III	Thu	21	07	1960	Francis Chichester won the first solo transatlantic race with his boat Gypsy Moth III from Plymouth to New York in 40 days
Moorehead. Dr. Thomas G.	Wed	03	08	1960	Dr Thomas Gillman Moorehead died
Moorehead. Dr. Thomas G	Wed	03	08	1960	Prof. Thomas Gillman Moorehead died
Weather			09	1960	Major flooding at Glenmalure

A-Z Reference	Day	Date	Month	Year	DATA
Ploughing	Thu	10	11	1960	The National Ploughing Championships held at New Ross Co. Wexford. The Senior Horse Ploughing event Wicklow came 1st
Act	Wed	21	12	1960	Local Government (No. 2) Act, enacted by Dail Eireann
Mountain Rescue			circa	1960	The Dublin & Wicklow Mountain Rescue Team had its origins in the An Oige Mountain Rescue Team
Woodstock House			's	1960	Woodstock House and Estate bought by Mr & Mrs William Forwood
French School Bray			's	1960	The French School at Sidmonton Place Bray closed
Derralossary Church			's	1960	Derralossary Church near Roundwood closed
Showbands			's	1960	Bray based show bands included The Beavers Showband, The Mexicans Show band, The Tonics Show band
Showbands			's	1960	Arklow based show bands included The Echoes
Showbands			's	1960	Wicklow based show bands included The Columbia Show band
Cunningham. Larry			's	1960	Larry Cunningham and the show band The Mighty Avons recorded the song "Among the Wicklow Hills"
McCrea. John J.				1960	John J. McCrea held the post of Chairman of Wicklow County Council 1960-1968
Crinion. Peter				1960	Peter Crinion of Bray represented Ireland in cycling at the 1960 Olympic Games held in Rome
Messitt. Bertie				1960	Bertie Messitt of Bray represented Ireland in the marathon at the 1960 Olympic Games held in Rome
Film				1960	The film "The Night Fighters" filmed in Rathdrum, County Wicklow
Bray Sea Anglers				1960	Bray Sea Anglers Club at Bray Harbour established
Film				1960	The film "Webster Boy" filmed in part in Bray
Post Office				1960	The sub Post Office at Brennan's Parade, Bray ceased
Post Office				1960	A new Post Office built in Wicklow Town
Kilcoole				1960	A new national school opened near Kilcoole Village
Cars				1960	Total Population of Ireland (estimated) 2,834,300 Cars Registered 169,681 Cars per 1000 persons 60
Arklow Youth Club				1960	Arklow Youth Club founded
Police/Garda				1960	The Garda Station at Baltinglass built
Bray Musical Society				1960	Bray Musical Society stages "The Bells of Cornville"
Presentation Bray				1960	An extension was added to Presentation College, Putland Road, Bray
Tyrrell Shipping				1960	The yacht Gypsy Moth III built at Tyrrells boat yard Arklow
Maguire. Peter				1960	Rev Peter Maguire became Parish Priest of Enniskerry
Railways				1960	Steam Locomotives ceased to be used on suburban rail service
Cheshire Home				1960	At Ardeen near Shillelagh. Group Captain Leonard Cheshire opened a Cheshire home

Section One: Data by Date

Key	Weekday	Day	Month	Year	Description
Blessington S C				1960	Blessington Sailing Club founded
Bush School				1960	The Bush School at Knockroe, Kilcoole closed
Curtlestown				1960	St Patrick's National School, Curtlestown built
Brunker, James P.				1960	James P. Brunker died
Murphy, William				1960	Rev William Murphy appointed Parish Priest of Queen of Peace Parish, Bray
Population Enniskerry	Sun	09	04	1961	Population of Enniskerry urban 652 or 1.11% of County Population
Population Bray	Sun	09	04	1961	Population of Bray Urban District 11,856 or 19.8% of County Population
Population Greystones	Sun	09	04	1961	Population of Greystones & Delgany 3,551 or 6.07% of County Population
Population Wicklow (t)	Sun	09	04	1961	Population of Wicklow Town 3,125 or 5.34% of County Population
Population Arklow	Sun	09	04	1961	Population of Arklow Urban 5,390 or 9.21% of County Population
Population County	Sun	09	04	1961	Population of County Wicklow 58,473 persons. 29,150 Males 29,323 Females
Population	Sun	09	04	1961	The Counties of Dublin, Meath & Wicklow accounted for 32.2% of the Republic population
Act	Sat	29	07	1961	Road Traffic Act, enacted by Dail Eireann
Arklow Hospital	Sat	07	07	1961	The Countess of Wicklow Memorial Cottage Hospital at the Sea Road, Arklow was closed
Kippure	Sat	08	09	1961	The first live TV test in Ireland was carried out using the Kippure TV Transmitter
Crosby, Bing	Sun	17	09	1961	Bing Crosby played a game of golf at Woodbrook, in aid of The Irish Society for the Prevention Cruelty to Children
TD's for Wicklow	Wed	04	10	1961	Polling Day for 17th Dail J. Everett (L) M.J. O'Higgins (FG) P.Brennan (FF)
Ploughing	Thu	09	11	1961	The National Ploughing Championships held at Killarney Co.Kerry. Under 21 Champion Patrick Brennan of Wicklow
Ploughing	Thu	09	11	1961	The National Ploughing Championships held at Killarney Co.Kerry."Queen of the Plough" Eileen Brennan of Wicklow
Kippure	Fri	01	12	1961	The Kippure TV transmitter came into operation
O'Dalaigh, Cearbhall				1961	Cearbhall O'Dalaigh appointed Chief Justice
Armstrong-Jones, A				1961	Anthony Charles Armstrong-Jones given the title 1st Earl of Snowdon
Arklow CBS				1961	The first boys enrolled in St Kevin's CBS Arklow
Books				1961	[Aze'lie Martin, me're de Sainte, se de l'enfant Jesus] Azelie Martain, Mother of the little Flower translated from French by the Earl of Wicklow
Cliffwalk, Bray				1961	Legal Case Miss Celcilia Healy took legal action against Bray UDC for injuries she sustained while walking on cliffwalk
Film				1961	The film "Johnny Noobdy" was filmed at Enniskerry, Carrickmines, Mountjoy jail and Wicklow Mountains
Books				1961	[Une Flamme d'amour. L'humble Pere Bonnard] The Humble Pere Bonnard translated from French by the Earl of Wicklow
Holy Redeemer, Bray				1961	Work on the re-design of the Holy Redeemer Church, Bray began

A-Z Reference	Day	Date	Month	Year	DATA
Powerscourt				1961	Mr & Mrs Ralph Slazenger purchased Powerscourt House & Estate from the 9th Viscount Powerscourt
Solus Teo				1961	Solus changed its light bulb wrapper
Bray Musical Society				1961	Bray Musical Society stages "Grand Concert"
St. Peters School				1961	St. Peters Boys National School move from the grounds of St.Peters Church, Little Bray to a new school at Hawthorn Crescent
Railways				1961	Bray Railway Station new booking office and general maintance carried out
Kippure				1961	Television Mast erected on Kippure Mountain
Sport				1961	Andy McEvoy (footballer) got his first Republic of Ireland cap against Scotland.
County Wicklow				1961	County Wicklow (Dispensary Districts) Order 1961
Mortell. Mark				1961	Mark Mortell (Director of Advertising Company and Chairman of Bord Failte) born 1961, educated at Presentation College, Bray
Rooney. Philip			03	1962	Philip Rooney died at his home in Bray
Boylan. Dom Eugene			07	1962	Dom Eugene Boylan elected Abbot of Mount St. Josephs Abbey, Roscrea
Eisenhower. Gen	Thu	23	08	1962	Gen. Eisenhower former President of USA paid a visit to the former President of Ireland Sean T.O'Kelly at his Roundwood home
Troy. Dermot	Thu	06	09	1962	Dermot troy died
Arcadia Ballroom	Wed	24	10	1962	Arcadia Ballroom, Bray was destroyed by fire
Bestic. Albert A.	Thu	20	12	1962	Capt. Albert A. Bestic, died. He lived at Prince of Wales Terrace Bray. Junior 3rd Officer on the Lusitania and Master of the Isolda
Roads				1962	Road Traffic (Signs) Regulations
Books				1962	The Shell Guide to Ireland (First Edition) by Killanin and Duignan
Powerscourt				1962	Mervyn Niall Wingfield married Wendy Slazenger
Coolattin Golf Club				1962	Coolattin Golf Club, Shillelagh, Co. Wicklow established
Avoca				1962	Avoca mines ceased production
Housing				1962	The island (Dargan Cottages) on the seafront near the railway gates removed
Bray Musical Society				1962	Bray Musical Society stages "Pink Champagne"
Film				1962	The film "The Quare Fellow" filmed at Ardmore Studio and Kilmainham jail
Film				1962	The film " Running Man" Interiors filmed at Ardmore and some exteriors shots in Bray
Books				1962	Dublin and Wicklow in Colour by J.B.Vesey
Tinakilly House				1962	Mr. Gunther Smith nephew Mr Heinrich Rolfe inherited Tinakilly House, Rathnew
Booth. Evelyn Mary				1962	The Atlas of Flora of Great Britain and Ireland published. Evelyn Mary Booth wrote the section on South-east Ireland

Section One: Data by Date

Hatton, Jimmy				1962	Jimmy Hatton of Wicklow. Refereed The All Ireland Minor GAA Football Final
Kish Lighthouse			07	1963	Construction of the base of the Kish Lighthouse commenced in Dun Laoghaire Harbour
Act	Wed	07	08	1963	Local Government (Planning and Development) Act, enacted by Dail Eireann
Powerscourt	Wed	21	08	1963	Mervyn Anthony Wingfield son of the 10th Viscount Powerscourt born
Ploughing	Thu	07	11	1963	The National Ploughing Championships held at Athenry Co.Galway."Queen of the Plough" Eileen Brennan of Wicklow
Ploughing	Thu	07	11	1963	The National Ploughing Championships held at Athenry Co.Galway.The Senior Horse Plough Champion Wicklow came 1st
Elliott.Shay				1963	Shay Elliott became the first Irishman to wear the Yellow Jersey in the Tour de France
Film				1963	The film "Dementia 13" Filmed at Ardmore Studios and in the village of NewtownMountKennedy
Wicklow Rugby Club				1963	Wicklow Rugby Club established
Wicklow Golf Club				1963	Wicklow Golf Club won the Barton Cup
Arklow CBS				1963	St. Kevin's CBS, Arklow officially opened
Bus				1963	The CIE touring coach HZD 580 featured in a publicity photographs for CIE taken in Powerscourt Gardens
Bray Musical Society				1963	Bray Musical Society stages "The Gypsy Baron"
McGuckian.Mary				1963	Mary McGuckian (Film Maker) born 1963, educated at St. Gerard's School Bray.
Douglas.MJ				1963	Mark Douglas born 1963, Businessman founded Ireland's first Pizza delivery Service, Educated at St. Gerard's Bray.
St. Gerard's School				1963	Joseph C. Maher headmaster of St. Gerard's School. Bray. 1963-1966
Old Conna				1963	Old Conna House Hotel, Bray closed
Hatton.Jimmy				1963	Jimmy Hatton of Wicklow. Refereed The All Ireland Senior GAA Hurling Final
Woodbrook				1963	Carrolls International Golf Tournament held at Woodbrook Golf Club, Bray. Winner B. J. Hunt
Boylan.Dom Eugene	Sun	05	01	1964	Dom Eugene Boylan died in Roscommon County Hospital, following a car accident in Mid December 1963
Murphy.William	Tue	25	02	1964	Rev. William Murphy P.P. of Our Lady Queen of Peace Parish, Putland Road died and is buried in St. Peter's Graveyard, Bray
Railways	Mon	30	03	1964	Woodenbridge Railway Station closed
Kay.Dorothy	Wed	13	05	1964	The artist Dorothy Kay died
Wicklow GAA	Sun	14	06	1964	Leinster Junior Hurling Championship Final GAA. Wicklow 4-8 Kildare 2-6 played in Enniscorthy, Co. Wexford
Chichester. Sir. F	Mon	22	06	1964	Francis Chichester sets a new record for crossing the Atlantic in under 30 days
French School Bray	Sat	18	07	1964	French School at Sidmonton Road, Bray put up for sale.
Keegan. Charlie	Fri	25	09	1964	Charlie Keegan from Enniskerry won the World Ploughing Championship in Austria
Credit Union				1964	Bray Credit Union established.

A-Z Reference	Day	Date	Month	Year	DATA
Bray Musical Society				1964	Bray Musical Society stages "The Merry Widow"
Film				1964	The film "Girl with Green Eyes" Filmed on locations in Dublin and Wicklow
Books				1964	Walking in Wicklow. A guide for travellers, afoot & awheel, thorugh the Wicklow Mountains by J.B. Malone
Tourism				1964	Regional Tourism Boards established
Woodbrook				1964	Carrolls International Golf Tournament held at Woodbrook Golf Club, Bray. Winner Christy.O'Connor (Royal Dublin)
Bray Head				1964	Bray Head Fishing and Social Club founded
Books				1964	Partnership with Christ by Dom Eugene Boylan
Greystones				1964	Greystones Operatic and Dramatic Society founded
Post Office				1964	A sub Post Office of Bray established at Albert Avenue, Bray
Railways				1964	Kilcoole Railway Station closed
Pigott, John				1964	Rev.John Pigott appointed Parish Priest of the Holy Redeemer Parish Bray
Wicklow Harbour				1964	Wicklow Harbour Works Order 1964
Film				1964	The film The Spy Who Came in from the Cold was filmed at Ardmore and locations around Ireland including Co.Wicklow
Power, Richard				1964	Richard Power wrote The Land of Youth
Newcastle Hospital				1964	Newcastle Hospital near Newtown Mount Kennedy became a psychiatric Unit
Nitrigin Eireann Teo.				1964	Nitrigin Eireann Teoranta (NET) open a factory near Arklow for the manufacture of fertiliser
Bewley, Victor				1964	Victor Bewley along with Fr. Tom Fehily, Lady Wicklow founded the Dublin Committee for Travelling People
Hatton, Jimmy				1964	Jimmy Hatton of Wicklow. Refereed The All Ireland Senior GAA Football Final
Lamb, Charles Vincent				1964	Charles Vincent Lamb died
O'Dea, Jimmy	Thu	07	01	1965	Jimmy O'Dea (comedian) died in Dublin
TD's for Wicklow	Wed	07	04	1965	Polling Day for 18th Dail J. Everett (L) M.J.O'Higgins (FG) P.Brennan (FF)
Kish Lighthouse	Tue	29	06	1965	The constructed section of the Kish Lighthouse was towed from Dun Laoghaire to the Kish Bank
Newspapers	Fri	02	07	1965	Newspaper Strike in Ireland between 2nd July and 12th September
Wicklow GAA	Sun	25	07	1965	Leinster Junior Hurling Championship Final GAA. Wicklow 4-8 Kildare 1-8 played in Croke Park, Dublin
Kish Lighthouse	Tue	27	07	1965	The Kish Lighthouse was completed
Scouting	Wed	29	09	1965	The 5th Wicklow (Bray Sea Scout) Group formed
Kish Lighthouse	Tue	09	11	1965	The Kish Light vessel was withdrawn

Keyword	Weekday	Day	Month	Year	Description
Ploughing	Wed	17	11	1965	The All Ireland Ploughing Championships held at Enniskerry on 17th and 18th November 1965
Bray Traffic				1965	Bray Traffic and Parking Bye-Laws 1965
Cars				1965	Total Population of Ireland (estimated) 2,870,900 Cars Registered 281,448 Cars per 1000 persons 98
County Wicklow				1965	Wicklow County and Dublin Health Authority Area (Registrars' Districts) Order 1965
Police/Garda				1965	The Garda Station at Rathdrum built
Film				1965	The film Blue Max was filmed at Ardmore and locations around Ireland including Co. Wicklow
Valuation				1965	Bray Valuation stood at £62,008 and rateable valuation at 51/-s
Dargle River				1965	Flooding took place in Little Bray when the River Dargle burst its banks
Books				1965	Walking in Wicklow by J. B. Malone published
Delaney. John				1965	Rev John Delaney became Parish Priest of St. Mary's Church Enniskerry
Bray Musical Society				1965	Bray Musical Society stages "The Gypsy Princess"
Failte Park				1965	Failte Park on Adelaide Road opened by Erskine H. Childers Minister for Transport and Power
St. Cronan's. Bray				1965	St. Cronan's House Main Street Bray (former home of the Parish Priest of Holy Redeemer Parish) used a Vocational School
Ballinacor House				1965	Capt. W.D.O. Kemmis bequeathed Ballinacor House, Rathdrum to his maternal cousin Major Richard Lomer
Glendalough				1965	The last boat to St. Kevin's bed was rowed by Larry Bolger
Coles. Neil				1965	Carrolls International Golf Tournament held at Woodbrook Golf Club, Bray. Winner Neil Coles (England)
Hatton. Jimmy				1965	Jimmy Hatton of Wicklow. Refereed The All Ireland Minor GAA Football Final
Nelsons Pillar	Tue	08	03	1966	The upper half of Nelson Pillar in O'Connell Street, Dublin was shattered by an explosion
Nelsons Pillar	Wed	09	03	1966	The remainder of Nelson's Pillar, Dublin was blown up by Army engineers
Population Greystones	Sun	17	04	1966	Population of Greystones & Delgany 3,952 or 6.54% of County Population
Population Enniskerry	Sun	17	04	1966	Population of Enniskerry urban 707 or 1.2% of County Population
Population Wicklow (t)	Sun	17	04	1966	Population of Wicklow Town 3,340 or 5.52% of County Population
Population Bray	Sun	17	04	1966	Population of Bray Urban District 11,688 or 20.0% of County Population
Population Arklow	Sun	17	04	1966	Population of Arklow Urban 6,083 or 10.06% of County Population
Population County	Sun	22	04	1966	Population of County Wicklow 60,428 persons. 30,231 Males 30,197 Females
Wicklow GAA	Sun	22	05	1966	Leinster Special Minor Hurling Championship GAA Wicklow 3-4 Kildare 2-5 played in Ashford, Co. Wicklow
Arklow Shipping			05	1966	Arklow Shipping Ltd founded
Act	Tue	12	07	1966	Housing Act, enacted by Dail Eireann
Nitrigin Eireann Teo.	Wed	27	07	1966	Taoiseach Sean Lemass officially opened Nitrigin Eireann Teo., plant at Arklow

The County Wicklow Database: 432 AD to 2006 AD

A-Z Reference	Day	Date	Month	Year	DATA
Kilcoole	Sun	07	08	1966	A plaque unveiled at the on the shore at Kilcoole to mark the Kilcoole Gun Running of 1914
O'Kelly. Sean T	Wed	23	11	1966	Mr. Sean T O'Kelly former President of Ireland died
Railways				1966	Bray Railway Station re-named Daly station in honour of Edward Daly who took part in the 1916 Rebellion
Bray Musical Society				1966	Bray Musical Society stages "White Horse Inn"
Hanlon. Andrew				1966	Andrew Hanlon (TV presenter and producer with TV3) of Bray born 1966, Educated at Presentation College, Bray.
Carlisle Grounds				1966	Bray Urban District Council purchase the Carlisle Grounds, Bray with the aid of a grant of £8,920 from Bord Failte
Road Safety				1966	Bray Area Road Safety Committee established.
Tourism				1966	Guest houses and Hotels in Bray had 750 rooms listed and registered with the Eastern Regional Tourism Organisation (ERTO)
Roundwood				1966	Roundwood Caravan Park established
St. Gerard's School				1966	Colum O'Cleirigh headmaster of St. Gerard's School. Bray. 1966-1971
British Empire Day				1966	British Commonwealth Day renamed Commonwealth Day and the date moved from 24th May to June 11th
Campbell. F.George				1966	Frederick George Campbell (artist) won the President Hyde Gold Medal
St. Kevins Pipe Band				1966	St. Kevin's Pipe Band was reformed after a lapse of 26 years
Boyle. Ina				1966	Ina Boyle composed an orchestral work "Maudlin of Paplewick"
Newcastle Hospital				1966	Newcastle Hospital near Newtown Mount Kennedy became a psychiatric hospital
Elections-Polling Day				1966	Presidential Election held
Biggs. Michael				1966	Michael Biggs was commissioned to erect the Garda Memorial at the Gadra Headquarters Phoenix Park, Dublin
Hatton. Jimmy				1966	Jimmy Hatton of Wicklow. Refereed The All Ireland Senior GAA Hurling Final
Hatton. Jimmy				1966	Jimmy Hatton of Wicklow. Refereed The All Ireland Minor GAA Hurling Final (Replay)
Woodbrook				1966	Carrolls International Golf Tournament held at Woodbrook Golf Club, Bray. Winner Christy O'Connor (Royal Dublin)
Nolan. Winifride				1966	Winifride Nolan of Aughrim, Co. Wicklow wrote "Seven Fat Kine" published in Dublin
Costello. Seamus				1966	Seamus Costello founded a Tenants Association in Bray
Hatton. Jimmy				1966	Jimmy Hatton of Wicklow. Refereed The All Ireland Senior GAA Football Final
Chichester. Sir. F	Fri	27	01	1967	Sir Francis Chichester was knighted after finishing round the world voyage in his yacht Gypsy Moth III
Boyle. Ina	Fri	10	03	1967	Ina Boyle died
Kilmacanogue	Sat	11	03	1967	Glencormac House, Kilmacanogue destroyed by fire.

Baltinglass	Mon	26	05	1967	Baltinglass Cattle Market opened
Elections–Polling Day	Wed	28	06	1967	Local elections are held
Kennedy. Mrs. J.F.	Sun	02	07	1967	Mrs John F. Kennedy planted a tree on a visit to Powerscourt Estate
Wicklow GAA	Sun	30	07	1967	Leinster Junior Hurling Championship Final GAA. Wicklow 4-13 Meath 0-8 played in Croke Park, Dublin
Wicklow GAA	Sun	30	07	1967	Leinster Special Minor Hurling Championship GAA. Wicklow 3-15 Meath 1-7 played in Croke Park, Dublin
Wicklow GAA	Sun	15	10	1967	All Ireland Special Minor Hurling Championship GAA Wicklow 5-5 Down 3-4 played in Croke Park, Dublin
Wicklow GAA	Sun	22	10	1967	All Ireland Junior Hurling Championship Final GAA. Wicklow 3-14 London 4-7 played in Kilkenny
Avondale House			10	1967	Forestry School opened at Avondale House, Rathdrum by Minister of Lands Sean Flanagan
Everett. James	Mon	18	12	1967	James Everett died, was T.D. for Wicklow from 1922 to 1967 held Ministerial posts in Justice , Post and Telegraphs
Bray Urban District				1967	Bray Urban District Local Electoral Areas Order 1967
Bray Urban District				1967	Bray Urban District Local Electoral Areas Order 1967, (Revocation) Order 1974
Carnew Credit Union				1967	Carnew Credit Union established
Lifeboats				1967	Arklow harbour redeveloped, the Lifeboat house was demolished
Bray Musical Society				1967	Bray Musical Society stages "Sweethearts"
Books				1967	The Baronies of Newcastle and Arklow. Vol 7, The Place Names of County Wicklow by Liam Price
Arklow				1967	Arklow Parking Temporary Rules 1967
Books				1967	The Shell Guide to Ireland (2nd Edition) by Killanin and Duignan
Woodbrook				1967	Carrolls International Golf Tournament held at Woodbrook Golf Club, Bray. Winner Christy. O'Connor (Royal Dublin)
Dargle River				1967	River Dargle at Bray flooded
Police/Garda				1967	The Garda Station at Carnew built
Hatton. Jimmy				1967	Jimmy Hatton of Wicklow. Refereed The All Ireland Intermediate GAA Hurling Final
Carnew Musical Society				1967	Carnew Musical Society established
Costello. Seamus				1967	Seamus Costello elected to Bray Urban District Council and Wicklow County Council
Cars	Mon	01	01	1968	Car Reg LNI 671 issued by Wicklow Motor Tax Office
Beatty. Sir A. C.	Sun	20	01	1968	Sir Alfred Chester Beatty died in Monte Carlo. He spent his later years at the Clonmannon retirement village Ashford, Co. Wicklow
Bord Failte	Fri	29	03	1968	Bord Failte Report showed that a sum of £100,600:0s:0d was spent on projects in Bray in the previous twelve months
Cars			03	1968	Car Reg MNI 1 issued by Wicklow Motor Tax Office
Sheep	Fri	26	04	1968	Wicklow Cheviot Sheep owners Association established

A-Z Reference	Day	Date	Month	Year	DATA
Kilcoole			04	1968	The Catholic Church at Kilcoole was opened and dedicated by the Archbishop of Dublin Dr McQuaid
Saul. Capt. P	Sat	22	06	1968	Captain Patrick Saul died and is buried in St. Patrick's graveyard Enniskerry
Bray Festival	Sat	22	06	1968	Bray Festival 22nd to 30th June 1968
Elections–Polling Day	Wed	16	10	1968	Polling Day for Constitutional Referenda- Introduction plurality system
Elections–Polling Day	Wed	16	10	1968	Polling Day for Constitutional Referenda- T.D. -population ratio
Cars			10	1968	Car Reg NNI 1 issued by Wicklow Motor Tax Office
Bray for Holidays	Wed	13	11	1968	The Department of Post and Telegraphs gives approval for the slogan Bray for Holidays to appear on letters posted in Bray
Griffin. Victor			11	1968	Victor Griffin became Dean of St. Patrick's Cathedral, Dublin
Synge	Fri	06	12	1968	Trinity College Dublin pays £50,000 for the papers of John Millington Synge
Doyle. Peter				1968	Peter Doyle of Bray represented Ireland in cycling at the 1968 Olympic Games held in Mexico
Darcy. Eamonn				1968	Eamonn Darcy became a professional golfer
Price. Cecil				1968	Rev Cecil Price became rector of Delgany Parish
BUDC				1968	Bray Urban District Council dissolved and Commissioner appointed 1968-1973
TD's for Wicklow				1968	18th Dail By-election G. Timmins (FG)
Arklow Silver Band				1968	Arklow Silver Band founded
Bus				1968	C.I.E. had 720 Double Deck Buses, 80 Single deck buses. Total work-force of 3,000
O'Toole. Garry				1968	Garry O'Toole (swimmer) born 1968, Bray Co. Wicklow
Arklow				1968	Arklow Parking Temporary Rules 1968
Film				1968	The film "The Violent Enemy" interior scenes filmed at Ardmore Studio, Bray and exteriors filmed around Dublin
Glor na Gael				1968	Bray won the Glor na Gael prize for the use of Irish, in the large town category. Prize was presented by President E. De Valera
Wynne. Gladys				1968	Gladys Wynne (artist) daughter of the Archdeacon of Aghadoe died
Wicklow Harbour				1968	Wicklow Harbour Works Order 1968
O'Tuairisc. Eoghan				1968	Eoghan O'Tuairisc began teaching in Hacketstown Technical College
Mc Alinden				1968	The Mc Alinden family establish the Lithographic Universal Ltd in Bray. The family also ran the Record Press Ltd.
Bray Musical Society				1968	Bray Musical Society stages "New Moon"
Electricity				1968	Work started on the electricity generating station at Turlough hill near Glendalough
Byrne. Henry J.				1968	Henry J. Byrne held the post of Chairman of Wicklow County Council 1968-1969

Section One: Data by Date

Keyword	Description	Year			
Weston. Galen	Roundwood Park was bought by Mr Galen Weston who rebuilt Roundwood Park House. (see 1983)	1968			
Woodbrook	Carrolls International Golf Tournament held at Woodbrook Golf Club, Bray. Winner Jimmy Martin (Edmonstown)	1968			
Speed Limits	The Road Traffic (Speed Limits) (County Wicklow) Regulations 1968 (S.I. No. 212 of 1968)	1968			
Wicklow GAA	Padraig O Murchu Chairman of Wicklow GAA 1968 – 1969	1968			
Doran. John	Rev. John Doran Parish Priest of Tomacork, Carnew 1968-1977	1968			
Cars	Car Reg NNI 270 issued by Wicklow Motor Tax Office	1969	01	Wed	
Roads	Roads reclassified into 4 groups, 1 National Primary, 2 National Secondary, 3 Regional and 4 County	1969	01	Wed	
Larkin. James	James Larkin, Putland Road, Bray died, General Secretary Workers Union of Ireland, son of James Larkin (Big Jim)	1969	02	Tue	18
Bray for Holidays	The slogan Bray for Holidays and Conferences first appeared on letters posted in Bray	1969	02		
Greystones	Greystones Credit Union was established	1969	05	Fri	09
Cars	Car Reg ONI 1 issued by Wicklow Motor Tax Office	1969	05		
BUDC	Bray Urban District Council failed to strike a rate for the town, disbanded by Minister of Local Government Kevin Boland	1969	06	Thu	05
TD's for Wicklow	Polling Day for 19th Dail L.Kavanagh (L) P.Brennan (FF) G.Timmons (FG)	1969	06	Wed	18
Dunne. Sean	Sean Dunne T.D. died, He lived at 46 Wolfe Tone Square North, Bray	1969	06	Wed	25
Wicklow GAA	Leinster Junior Football Championship Final GAA. Wicklow 2-5 Meath 0-5 played in Croke Park, Dublin	1969	07	Sun	06
Courage. Michael	Irish Angling Record for Greater Spotted Dogfish 19lb 12oz was set by Michael Courage at, Bray (Guinness Book of Records)	1969	07	Sun	06
Currency	Farthings and halfpennies no longer legal tender	1969	08	Fri	01
Currency	5p and 10p coins introduced as legal tender	1969	09	Mon	01
Wicklow GAA	All Ireland Junior Football Championship Final GAA Wicklow 0-12 Kerry 1-8 played in Croke Park, Dublin	1969	09	Sun	14
Avondale House	Extension added to the Forestry School at Avondale, Rathdrum Co. Wicklow	1969	10	Thu	09
Breen. Dan	Dan Breen died in a Nursing Home at Kilcroney, Bray	1969	12	Sat	27
Dargle River	Flood prevention scheme was put in place at the Dargle River costing £120,000	1969			
Film	The film McKenize Break stating Brian Keith, Ian Hendry and Helmut Greim was shot in Bray and other locations in Ireland	1969			
Walsh. Mary	Mary Walsh held the post of Chairperson of Wicklow County Council 1969-1970. The first woman to hold the position.	1969			
Campbell. F.George	Frederick George Campbell (artist) won the Oireachtas Prize for Landscape	1969			
Keegan. Claire	The writer Claire Keegan born in Wicklow	1969			
Books	The First Dail by Marie Comerford	1969			
Arklow	Arklow Parking Temporary Rules 1969	1969			

A-Z Reference	Day	Date	Month	Year	DATA
Bray Musical Society				1969	Bray Musical Society stages "Rose Marie"
O'Tuairisc. Eoghan				1969	Eoghan O'Tuairisc bought a house on the Wicklow/Carlow border near Hacketstown
Fitzgerald. Garret				1969	Garret Fitzgerald elected as a T.D. for Dublin South-East
Avoca				1969	Discovery Mines of Canada re-open some mines in the Avoca area
Power. Richard				1969	Richard Power wrote The Hungry Grass
Hollybrooke House				1969	Hollybrooke House, Bray damaged by fire. The family seat of Hodson Family
Bowe. Laura				1969	Laura Bowe (Set Dresser) born 1969, educated at St. Gerard's College, Bray
Plunkett. James				1969	James Plunkett best known novel Strumpet City was published
Woodbrook				1969	Carrolls International Golf Tournament held at Woodbrook Golf Club, Bray. Winner Ronnie Shade (Scotland)
Henderson. Brian				1969	Brian Henderson won the Carroll Award at the Irish Exhibition of Living Art
Cars	Thu	01	01	1970	Car Reg ONI 919 issued by Wicklow Motor Tax Office
Cars			01	1970	Car Reg PNI 1 issued by Wicklow Motor Tax Office
Power. Richard	Thu	12	02	1970	Richard Power (writer) died at Bray Co. Wicklow
Flood. Francis	Mon	30	03	1970	Francis Flood of Grangecon, Co. Wicklow trained Garoupe the winner of the Irish Grand National held at Fairyhouse Racecourse
Breman. Paudge	Fri	08	05	1970	Paudge Breman resigned as Parliamentary Secretary for Local Government
Railways	Fri	10	07	1970	The last C.I.E. horse drawn cart to leave Bray Railway Goods Yard on deliveries around the town
Cars			08	1970	Car Reg RNI 1 issued by Wicklow Motor Tax Office
Carnew Credit Union			's	1970	The Carnew Credit Union transferred its offices to the school building built in 1829
Glenbride Lodge			s'	1970	Glenbride Lodge, Valleymount was An Oige Hostel, the lodge was kindly given by the Marquis of Waterford
Cullen. Fr. John				1970	Fr. John Cullen died
Lifeboats				1970	A new lifeboat workshop and store was built close to the lifeboat moorings in Arklow Dock
Books				1970	The story of Baltinglass. A history of the parishes of Baltingals, Ballynure and Rathbran published in the Kilkenny Journal
Bray Development Co.				1970	Bray Development Company established.
Baltinglass Hospital				1970	Baltinglass Hospital administration changed from Wicklow County Council to the Eastern Health Board under the Health Act 1970
Arklow				1970	Arklow Parking Temporary Rules 1970
Whelan. J.				1970	James J. Whelan held the post of Chairman of Wicklow County Council 1970-1971
Bray Musical Society				1970	Bray Musical Society stages "Desert Song"

Biggs. Michael				1970	Michael Biggs did the lettering for the Central Bank tender notes from 1970
Cars				1970	Total Population of Ireland (estimated) 2,959,400 Cars Registered 389,338 Cars per 1000 persons 132
Breen. William				1970	Rev. William Breen appointed to the Parish of Arklow.
Bus				1970	86 Bus Route service was discontinued between Cabinteely and Bray. Except school buses serving St Ann's, Milltown etc
Books				1970	(1st edition) Guide to National Monuments of Ireland by Peter Harbinson
St. Brendans College				1970	St. Brendans College at Old Connaught closed and new College built at Woodbrook, Bray
Bill				1970	Film Bill presented to Dail Eireann
Pony Club				1970	Wicklow Pony Club founded
Hatton. Jimmy				1970	Jimmy Hatton of Wicklow. Refereed The All Ireland Intermediate GAA Hurling Final
Henderson. Brian				1970	Brian Henderson won the Carroll Award at the Irish Exhibition of Living Art
Hatton. Jimmy				1970	Jimmy Hatton of Wicklow. Refereed The All Ireland Senior GAA Hurling Final
Wicklow GAA				1970	Seamus O' Broin Chairman of Wicklow GAA 1970 - 1975
McCormack. William				1970	(Hugh Maxton) William John McCormack wrote "Stones"
Arklow Music Festival				1970	Arklow Music Festival established
Woodbrook				1970	Carrolls International Golf Tournament held at Woodbrook Golf Club, Bray. Winner Brian Huggett
Cars	Fri	01	01	1971	Car Reg RNI 689 issued by Wicklow Motor Tax Office
Cars			03	1971	Car Reg SNI 1 issued by Wicklow Motor Tax Office
Population County	Sun	18	04	1971	Population of County Wicklow 66,295 persons. 33,318 Males 32,977 Females
Population Wicklow (t)	Sun	18	04	1971	Population of Wicklow Town 3,786 or 5.71% of County Population
Population Greystones	Sun	18	04	1971	Population of Greystones & Delgany 4,496 or 7.4% of County Population
Population Enniskerry	Sun	18	04	1971	Population of Enniskerry urban 789 or 1.3% of County Population
Population Bray	Sun	18	04	1971	Population of Bray Urban District 15,537 or 25.7% of County Population
Population Arklow	Sun	18	04	1971	Population of Arklow Urban 6,948 or 10.48% of County Population
Elliott.Shay			05	1971	Shay Elliott (cyclist) died and is buried in Kilmacanogue Graveyard
Breen. Dan	Thu	08	07	1971	The Taoiseach, Jack Lynch inaugurates the Dan Breen Memorial Fund for Handicapped Youth
Wicklow GAA	Sun	18	07	1971	Leinster Intermediate Hurling Championship Final GAA. Wicklow 1-15 Dublin 2-9 played in Carlow
Byrne. Shane	Sun	18	07	1971	Shane Byrne (Irish rugby international) from Aughrim. County Wicklow, born in Dublin
Ploughing	Thu	28	10	1971	The National Ploughing Championships held at Finglas Co.Dublin. The Senior Tractor Ploughing 1st Charles Keegan of Wicklow
Cars			10	1971	Car Reg TNI 1 issued by Wicklow Motor Tax Office

A–Z Reference	Day	Date	Month	Year	DATA
Brennan. Paduge	Wed	17	11	1971	Paudge Brennan T.D. for Wicklow expelled from the Fianna Fail Party
Wicklow GAA	Sun	28	11	1971	All Ireland Junior Hurling Championship Final GAA. Wicklow 4-6 Herts 3-8 played in Croke Park, Dublin
Bray Musical Society				1971	Bray Musical Society stages "The Arcadians"
Loreto Convent Bray				1971	Extension added to the school at Loreto Convent Bray
Arklow				1971	Arklow Traffic and Parking Bye-Laws 1971
Woodbrook				1971	Carrolls International Golf Tournament held at Woodbrook Golf Club, Bray. Winner N. C Coles (England)
Trade				1971	1,419 persons engaged in IDA granted manufacturing firms in Bray
Wicklow GAA				1971	Leinster Junior Hurling Championship Final GAA. Wicklow 3-12 Kildare 0-7 played in Croke Park, Dublin
Mulcare. P				1971	East of Ireland Amateur (Golf) Open Championship winner P.Mulcare of Woodbrook, Bray
Fox.Mildred				1971	Mildred Fox (Politician) born 1971, educated at St. Kilian's Community School, Bray.
Hynes. Frank				1971	Frank Hynes held the post of Chairman of Wicklow County Council 1971-1972
Film				1971	The film "Act without Words" part filmed in Ardmore studio. The film never went on release
Mount Kennedy House				1971	Mount Kennedy House, Newtown Mount Kennedy was bought by Noel Griffin a director of Waterford Glass
Large. R.G				1971	Rev. R.G.Large appointed Rector of Bray Parish
La Touche				1971	An oil painting (Peter La Touche) was purchased by the National Gallery of Ireland (NGI 4034) from Appleby Bros. Ltd, London
Books				1971	West Wicklow by Kamac Publications
Camera Club				1971	Bray Camera Club established
St. Gerard's School				1971	Michael P. O'Horan headmaster of St. Gerard's School. Bray. 1971-1998
Bus				1971	The CIE touring coach "The Dargle" was withdrawn form service
St. Andrew's School				1971	St. Andrew's School Bray amalgamated with St Paul's School Bray
Cars	Mon	03	01	1972	Car Reg TNI 367 issued by Wicklow Motor Tax Office
St. Kiernan's Bray	Fri	18	01	1972	Archbishop of Dublin Dr. McQuaid blessed and opened St. Kiernan's School for itinerant children at Old Connaught, Bray
Cars			04	1972	Car Reg UNI 1 issued by Wicklow Motor Tax Office
Elections-Polling Day	Wed	10	05	1972	Polling Day for Constitutional Referenda- Allow E.E.C. membership
Scouting	Thu	18	05	1972	9th Wicklow Arklow Sea Scout Troop (S.A.I.) established
Campbell. Christopher	Thu	18	05	1972	Christopher Campbell (artist) buried at Glendalough
Goulet.Yann Renard	Thu	01	06	1972	A Yann Renard Goulet sculptured monument to the East Mayo Brigade was unveiled at Kilkelly. Co. Mayo

Section One: Data by Date

	Weekday	Day	Month	Year	Event
Chichester. Sir. F	Sat	26	08	1972	Sir Francis Chichester died
Scouting	Thu	31	08	1972	10th Wicklow Presentation College Scout Troop (S.A.I.) established
Rotary Club of Bray	Wed	20	09	1972	Rotary Club of Bray, chartered
Cars			10	1972	Car RegVNI 1 issued by Wicklow Motor Tax Office
Kelly. Alan			10	1972	Alan Kelly became the first goalkeeper to captain the Republic of Ireland Football Team, when Ireland played the Soviet Union
Elections–Polling Day	Thu	07	12	1972	Polling Day for Constitutional Referenda– Lower voting age to 18
Elections–Polling Day	Thu	07	12	1972	Polling Day for Constitutional Referenda– Abolish "special position" of the Catholic Church
Heaney. Seamus				1972	Seamus Heaney lived in Co. Wicklow and later in Dublin
Doran. Felix				1972	Felix Doran died in Manchester
Bray Musical Society				1972	Bray Musical Society stages "The Merry Widow"
Presentation Bray				1972	New school was added to Presentation College, Putland Road, Bray
Marley Park				1972	Dublin County Council bought Marley Park and House, Rathfarnham from Mr.P.K. Love. One the home of the LaTouche Family
Mulcare. P				1972	East of Ireland Amateur (Golf) Open Championship winner P.Mulcare of Woodbrook, Bray
St. Pauls. Bray				1972	St. Paul's School on Herbert Road Bray demolished.
O'Dalaigh.Cearbhall				1972	Cearbhall O'Dalaigh appointed the first Irish member of the Court of Justice in the European Community
Ravens well. Bray				1972	An Extension was added to Ravens well School, Bray
Woodbrook				1972	Carroll's International Golf Tournament held at Woodbrook Golf Club, Bray. Winner Christy. O'Connor (Royal Dublin)
Tate Gallery London				1972	Purchased a painting (Reference TO1815), by John Butts oil on canvas Poachers:View in the Dargle circa 1760
Traffic Lights				1972	The first set of Traffic lights in County Wicklow was at the junction of Herbert Road, Quinsborough Road and Main Street, Bray
Film				1972	The film "Images" Filmed at Ardmore Studio, and at Powerscourt and other locations in Wicklow.
Doyle. Peter				1972	Peter Doyle of Bray represented Ireland in cycling at the 1972 Olympic Games held in Munich
Deering. Mark				1972	Mark Deering held the post of Chairman of Wicklow County Council 1972-1973
Books				1972	Glendalough and St. Kevin by Lennox Barrow
Shelton Abbey				1972	Shelton Abbey was transferred to the Department of Justice for use as a detention centre for young offenders
Newcastle Hospital				1972	The Co. Wicklow Association for Mentally Handicapped established St Catherien's School in the grounds of Newcastle Hospital
Bray Bookshop				1972	The Bray Bookshop established by Mrs Clear on the Quinsborough Road, Bray
Servier (Ireland)				1972	Servvier (Ireland) Industries Limited , Arklow. Co. Wicklow established
Books				1972	(2nd Edition) Guide to National Monuments of Ireland by Peter Harbinson

A–Z Reference	Day	Date	Month	Year	DATA
Cars	Mon	01	01	1973	Car Reg VNI 331 issued by Wicklow Motor Tax Office
TD's for Wicklow	Wed	28	02	1973	Polling Day for 20th Dail L.Kavanagh (L) G.Timmins (FG) C.Murphy (FF)
Fitzgerald. Garret	Wed	14	03	1973	Garret Fitzgerald appointed Minister for Foreign Affairs
Powerscourt	Tue	03	04	1973	Mervyn Patrick Wingfield 9th Viscount Powerscourt died
Cars			04	1973	Car Reg WNI 1 issued by Wicklow Motor Tax Office
Walsh. Mary	Tue	01	05	1973	Mary Walsh appointed to Seanad Eireann 1st May 1973-August 1976
Elections–Polling Day	Wed	30	05	1973	Presidential Election held
Childers. E. H.	Mon	25	06	1973	Arsine Hamilton Childers became President of Ireland
Act	Thu	26	07	1973	Road Traffic (Amendment) Act, enacted by Dial Eire Ann
Cars			08	1973	Car Reg XNI 1 issued by Wicklow Motor Tax Office
Act	Mon	24	12	1973	Arts Act, enacted by Dail Eireann
Electricity				1973	Electricity generating station at Turlough hill near Glendalough was commissioned
Film				1973	The film Zeros staring Sean Connery, Charlotte Rumpling was filmed at Ardmore Studio and Hollybrooke House, Bray
Brook House School				1973	Brook House School established on the Herbert Road, Bray
Ardmore Studio				1973	Goverment buys Ardmore Studios, Bray for £390,000
Superquinn				1973	The site of the Record Press Printing Company was acquired to build a shopping centre in Castle Street, Bray
Bray Harbour				1973	Bray Harbour Development Association established to manage the affairs of Bray harbour.
Royal Hotel, Bray				1973	The One din Rooms were added to the Royal Starlight Hotel. based on The Onedin Line was a popular TV series in 1970's
Car Park, Bray				1973	The first public car-park was built on the site of St. Pails School, Herbert Road, Bray at a cost of £15,000
Bray Musical Society				1973	Bray Musical Society stages "Mariana"
Bray Traffic				1973	Bray Traffic and Parking Bye-Laws 1973
Books				1973	Wicklow Rock Climbs (Glendalough and Luggala) edited by Pat Redmond
Scannell. Brendan J.				1973	European Amateur Golf Team Championship held at Penina, Portugal. The captain of the Irish team was B.J.Scannell of Bray
Smurfit.Victoria				1973	Victoria "Vicky" Smurfit (Actress) born 1973, educated at Aravon School Bray
Woodbrook				1973	Carroll's International Golf Tournament held at Woodbrook Golf Club, Bray. Winner Paddy McGuire (Co. Louth)
Whelan. J.				1973	James J.Whelan held the post of Chairman of Wicklow County Council 1973-1974
Wolf Tone Youth Club				1973	Wolf Tone Youth Club formed

Section One: Data by Date

Keyword	Year	Month	Day	Weekday	Description
Nicol. Erskine	1973				The Erskine Nicol painting of Bray Seafront purchased by the National Gallery of Ireland
Books	1973				Brittas bay, a planning and conservation study by Foras Forbartha Project leader K.A. Mawhinney
Scouting	1973				A Sea Scout Group established in Arklow
O'Brien. FJ	1973	01			Francis J.O'Brien appointed County Manager of Wicklow (Local Government) 1973–1976
Cars	1974	01	01	Tue	Car Reg XNI 530 issued by Wicklow Motor Tax Office
Henry. Paul	1974	02	08	Fri	Mable Young the wife of Paul Henry died
Glencree Peace Centre	1974	03	10	Sun	Glencree Peace Centre opens in an old barracks and reformatory
Cars	1974	03			Car Reg YNI 1 issued by Wicklow Motor Tax Office
International Hotel	1974	06	14	Fri	International Hotel, Quinsborough Road, Bray destroyed by fire
Elections–Polling Day	1974	06			Local elections are held
Cinema. Bray	1974	07	01	Mon	The Odeon (Ireland) Ltd sold the Royal Cinema at Bray, Co. Wicklow to Mr. Michael Collins
Drumm. James	1974	07	18	Thu	James Drumm (Battery Train) died
Wicklow GAA	1974	07			Leinster Minor Football Championship Final GAA. Wicklow 5–6 Longford 1–9 played in Croke Park, Dublin
Wicklow GAA	1974	07			Leinster Special Minor Hurling Championship Final GAA. Wicklow 2–9 Westmeath 4–2 played in Newbridge, Co.Kildare
Wicklow GAA	1974	08			All Ireland Special Minor Hurling Championship Final GAA. Wicklow 2–7 Roscommon 2–6 played in Tullamore
Cars	1974	09			Car Reg ZNI 1 issued by Wicklow Motor Tax Office
Ploughing	1974	10	17	Thu	The National Ploughing Championships held in Co.Cork. The Snr. Indv. Horse Plough Champion 1st John Halpin of Wicklow
Powerscourt	1974	11	04	Mon	Powerscourt House, Enniskerry destroyed by fire
Childers. E.H	1974	11	17	Sun	The President Erskine H. Childers died. The First President of Ireland to die in office
Childers. E. H.	1974	11	21	Thu	The remains of President Erskine Childers are buried in Derralossary graveyard, Roundwood, Co. Wicklow
O'Dalaigh. Cearbhall	1974	12	19	Thu	Cearbhall O'Dalaigh installed as President of Ireland
Newspapers	1974				East Coast Newspaper final edition
County Wicklow	1974				Wicklow County Council (Amendment) Order 1974
Baltinglass Golf Club	1974				Baltinglass Golf Club won the Barton Cup
Police/Garda	1974				The Garda Station at Enniskerry was restored.
Powerscourt	1974				Mervyn Niall Wingfield marriage to Wendy Slazenger dissolved
Newspapers	1974				East Coast Newspaper first edition
Hynes. Frank	1974				Frank Hynes held the post of Chairman of Wicklow County Council 1974–1975
Brangan. Pamela	1974				Pamela Brangan (Model) educated at Our Lady's School, Claremont, Rathnew

A–Z Reference	Day	Date	Month	Year	DATA
Wicklow GAA				1974	Sean Doherty from Glenealy played on the Dublin Team that won the All Ireland Senior Football Championship GAA
Cars				1974	Total Population of Ireland (estimated) 3,085,300 Cars Registered 488,522 Cars per 1000 persons 158
Kilmacanogue				1974	Kilmacanogue Roman Catholic Parish was constituted into a separate parish from Enniskerry
Books				1974	The Botanist in Ireland by Robert L.Praeger republished (Co. Wicklow, pages 261-269)(Bray Head and River, pages 267-268)
Russborough House				1974	19 paintings stolen from Russborough House, Blessington
Bray Musical Society				1974	Bray Musical Society stages "Pink Champagne"
Woodbrook				1974	Carrolls International Golf Tournament held at Woodbrook Golf Club, Bray. Winner Bernard Gallagher (Scotland)
Speed Limits				1974	The Road Traffic (Speed Limits) (County Wicklow) (Amendment)Regulations 1974 (S.I. No. 263 of 1974)
Cars	Wed	01	01	1975	Car Reg ZNI 369 issued by Wicklow Motor Tax Office
Byrne. Andrew W.	Sun	28	03	1975	Andrew W. Byrne owner of the Rathdrum Tanning Company died
Cars			05	1975	Car Reg NI 1 issued by Wicklow Motor Tax Office
Ardmore Studio	Wed	04	06	1975	The Irish Film Board established to run Ardmore Studios and attract film companies to make films in Ireland (see 1973,1958)
Bower. Robert		05	07	1975	Robert Bower died
Miami Showband	Thu	31	07	1975	Fran O'Toole from Bray and two other members of the Miami Showband are killed in an ambush near Newry, County Down.
Barton. Robert	Sun	10	08	1975	Robert Barton the longest surviving signatory of the Treaty of 1921 died
O'Dalaigh.Cearbhall	Sun	21	09	1975	President Cearbhall O'Dalaigh visited his home town and a civic reception was held in his honour
Cars	Wed	31	12	1975	Car Reg NI 983 issued by Wicklow Motor Tax Office
Wicklow Rovers F.C.				1975	Wicklow Rovers Football Club formed
Woodbrook				1975	The Irish Open Championships at Woodbrook Golf Club winner C.o'Connor(Shannon)
Marley Park				1975	Dublin County Council opened Marley Park and part of the House to the public.
Timmins. Godfrey				1975	Godfrey Timmins held the post of Chairman of Wicklow County Council 1975-1976
St. Patrick's School				1975	Extension to St. Patrick's Primary school, Bray completed
Bray Musical Society				1975	Bray Musical Society stages "Summer Song"
Glen of Imaal Terrier				1975	The Glen of Imaal Terrier was recognized as a dog breed by the Kennel Club of England
Wicklow Rovers				1975	Wicklow Rovers Football Club in Wicklow Town established
Books				1975	(3rd edition) Guide to National Monuments of Ireland by Peter Harbinson

Category	Day	Date	Month	Year	Description
Arklow Harbour				1975	Arklow Harbour Works Order 1975
Ballorney House				1975	Ballyorney House bought by Mr. Peter Blake.
Plunket				1975	Patrick Terrance Plunket, 7th Baron Plunket died and was succeeded by his brother Robin Plunket 8th Baron
Chess Club				1975	Bray, Greystones Chess Club founded
Scannell. Brendan J.				1975	European Amateur GolfTeam Championship, held Killarney, Ireland. The captain of the Irish team. B.J.Scannell of Bray
Books				1975	Penrose family of Helston, Cornwall and Wheldrake, Yorkshire and County Wicklow by Charles Penrose
Books				1975	The birds of Dublin and Wicklow edited by Clive D Hutchinson
Cars	Thu	01	01	1976	Car Reg 984 NI issued by Wicklow Motor Tax Office
Robbie.John	Sat	17	01	1976	John Robbie of Greystones won his 1st cap on the Irish National Rugby team against Australia in Dublin
Railways	Fri	12	03	1976	Garda Siochana foil a raid on a train at Wicklow Town, carrying cash for Banks and Post Offices in the south-east
Lighthouse	Wed	31	03	1976	The Lighthouse on Wicklow Head was converted from incandescent paraffin to electric
St. Gerard's School	Wed	28	04	1976	The Minister of Education Richard Burke an extension to St. Gerard's School, Bray
St.Fergal's. Bray			05	1976	St.Fergal's Parish, Bray was constituted into a separate parish
Sport	Sun	06	06	1976	Eamon Darcy of Delgany won the under 25 world golf championships in France.
Walsh. Mary			08	1976	Mary Walsh died
Railways	Mon	06	09	1976	Wicklow, Murrough Railway Station closed for goods traffic
Ploughing	Thu	14	10	1976	The National Ploughing Championships held in Co.Wexford. The Snr. Indv. Horse Plough Champion 1st John Halpin of Wicklow
O'Dalaigh.Cearbhall	Fri	22	10	1976	Cearbhall O'Dalaigh 5th President of Ireland, resigned
Arklow				1976	Arklow Maritime Museum established
Cars	Fri	31	12	1976	Car Reg 3298 NI issued by Wicklow Motor Tax Office
WDSL				1976	The County Wicklow & District Schoolboys Football League formed
Wicklow Rugby Club				1976	Club house built at Wicklow Rugby Club
Lugnaquilla Walk				1976	The fastest time set for the Lugnaquilla walk was 17 hours 39 minutes Gaffney and Rice
Bray Musical Society				1976	Bray Musical Society stages "Waltzes from Vienna"
Newtown FC				1976	Newtown Football Club formed (NewtownMountKennedy)
St. Kiernan's Bray				1976	Fire destroyed some of the buildings at St. Kiernan's Craft Centre at Old Connaught (Old Walcot Hotel site)
Books				1976	The Kynoch era in Arklow by Hilary Murphy (2nd edition)
Town Hall. Bray				1976	An electric clock was installed in the Council Chamber of the Town Hall, Bray

A-Z Reference	Day	Date	Month	Year	DATA
St Mary's Enniskerry				1976	Work began on an extension to St. Mary's School Enniskerry. The work was completed in 1978
Miley. Jim				1976	Jim Miley held the post of Chairman of Wicklow County Council 1976-1977
Higgins. John				1976	John Higgins appointed (Acting) County Manager of Wicklow (Local Government) 1976-1777
Wicklow Traffic				1976	Wicklow Traffic and Parking Bye-Laws 1976
Bray Head Chairlift.				1976	The chairlift on Bray Head last ran commercially in 1976, the fittings were removed from 1977
Baltinglass Hospital				1976	Surgical Services ceased at Baltinglass Hospital
Cars				1976	Petrol ration coupons issued to all owners of registered vehicles in Ireland but rationing was not introduced
Bray Wanderers				1976	Bray Wanderers won the Metropolitan Cup, Paul McNaughton scored two goals
McCormack. William				1976	(Hugh Maxton) William John McCormack wrote "The noise in the Fields"
Gaffeney & Rice				1976	Walkers Gaffney & Rice completed the Lug Walk in 17hrs 30 minutes
Wicklow GAA				1976	Liam O Cuillinn Chairman of Wicklow GAA 1976 - 1977
Cars	Mon	03	01	1977	Car Reg 3299 NI issued by Wicklow Motor Tax Office
Heatley. Elizabeth	Tue	08	03	1977	Elizabeth Heatley former Headmistress of French School Bray died and buried at St. Patrick's Graveyard, Enniskerry
British Empire Day	Mon	14	03	1977	Since 1977 Commonwealth Day observed on the 2nd Monday in March
Scouting	Tue	29	03	1977	13th Wicklow Scout Troop (S.A.I.) Enniskerry, established
Glen of Imaal	Thu	26	05	1977	Five soldiers killed in training accident on the Military Range at Glen of Imaal, Co. Wicklow
TD's for Wicklow	Thu	16	06	1977	Polling Day for 21st Dail L.Kavanagh (L) G.Timmins (FG) C.Murphy (FF)
Stamps	Mon	27	06	1977	A stamp with a value of 12p with Lough Tay, Co. Wicklow was issued by the Irish Postal Service
Fitzgerald. Garret	Fri	01	07	1977	Garret Fitzgerald appointed leader of the Fine Gael party
Wicklow GAA			07	1977	Leinster Special Minor Hurling Championship Final GAA. Wicklow2-8 Meath 3-3 played in Aughrim, Co. Wicklow
Goulding. Valerie	Thu	25	08	1977	Lady Valerie Goulding appointed to Seanad Eireann 25th August 1977- 11th August 1981
Costelloe. Seamus	Wed	05	10	1977	Seamus Costelloe (Clr.and MCC) the founder and chairman of the Irish Republican Socialist Party, shot dead in Dublin.
Ploughing	Thu	20	10	1977	The National Ploughing Championships held at Cashel Co. Tipperary. "Queen of the Plough" Gretta O'Toole of Wicklow
Cars	Fri	30	12	1977	Car Reg 5868 NI issued by Wicklow Motor Tax Office
Kavanagh. Liam				1977	Liam Kavanagh held the post of Chairman of Wicklow County Council 1977-1978
Sumbeam House Services				1977	Sumbeam House Services founded, offering support to adults with learning disabilities in County Wicklow
Bray Musical Society				1977	Bray Musical Society stages "Lisa"

Books				1977	The Kynoch era in Arklow by Hilary Murphy (3rd edition)
Wicklow Harbour				1977	Wicklow Harbour Works Order 1977
Historical Society				1977	Cualann Historical Society founded, later became the Bray Cualann Historical Society
Police/Garda				1977	The Garda Station at Blessington built
Act				1977	Water Pollution Act
Scoil Chualann				1977	Scoil Chualann established on a site behind Queen of Peace Church, Putland Road, Bray.
Housing				1977	537 New Local Authority Houses completed in Wicklow
BUDC				1977	Bray Urban Extension Boundary Order 1977 with effect from 01/1/1979
VEC. Bray				1977	Mr. Ronan Rice became CEO of Bray VEC 1977-1978
Nixdorf				1977	Nixdorf Computers established a production plant on the Boghall Road, Bray
Economic Survey				1977	A Economic Survey showed Bray as the Best Value Town in Ireland
St. Anthony's F.C.				1977	St. Anthony's Football Club Kilcoole formed
Woods. Michael				1977	Dr. Michael Woods elected to Dail Eireann
Bray School Project				1977	Bray School Project Association established
Darcy. Eamonn				1977	Eamonn Darcy won the Greater Manchester Open Golf Classic
St. Pauls. Bray				1977	St. Paul's Church, Bray closed and sold to Kenneth Jones Ltd manufacturer of Organs
Film				1977	Newcastle Hospital was used in the making of the film Equus staring Richard Burton and Jenny Agutter
Tritschler. Robin				1977	Robin Tritschler (Tenor) born 1977, educated St. David's School, Greystones.
Hayes. Seamus				1977	Seamus Hayes appointed County Manager of Wicklow (Local Government) 1977-1984
Books				1977	Guide to National Monuments of Ireland by Peter Harbinson
Hussey. Gemma				1977	Gemma Hussey elected to Seanad Eireann
McCarthy. John				1977	Rev. John McCarthy Parish Priest of Tomacork, Carnew 1977-
Bewley. Victor				1977	Victor Bewley retired as Chairman of Bewley's Oriental Cafes Ltd.
Cars	Mon	02	01	1978	Car Reg 5869 NI issued by Wicklow Motor Tax Office
Ward. Tony	Sat	21	01	1978	Tony Ward won his international debut cap on the Irish Rugby Team against Scotland
Killruddery	Sat	11	02	1978	Killruddery was the feature gardening article by Ruth Isabel Ross in the Irish Times on 11/02/1978
O'Dalaigh. Cearbhall	Tue	21	03	1978	Cearbhall O'Dalaigh former President of Ireland died at Sneem, Co. Kerry
Royal Visit	Wed	26	04	1978	The Queen of Denmark paid an official visit to Bray and Powerscourt,
Act	Tue	16	05	1978	Road Transport Act, enacted by Dail Eireann

The County Wicklow Database: 432 AD to 2006 AD

A-Z Reference	Day	Date	Month	Year	DATA
Powerscourt	Tue	06	06	1978	Princess Grace of Monaco visited Powerscourt Gardens and planted a tree
Ploughing	Thu	12	10	1978	The National Ploughing Championships held at Knocktopher Co.Kilkenny."Queen of the Plough" Pauline O'Toole of Wicklow
Armstrong-Jones. A	Fri	15	12	1978	Anthony Charles Armstrong-Jones 2nd marriage Lucy Davies of Bushey Park, Enniskerry
Cars	Fri	29	12	1978	Car Reg 9147 NI issued by Wicklow Motor Tax Office
Rates				1978	Domestic rates abolished
Aravon School				1978	Aravon School Playing field between Sidmonton Road and Meath Road, Bray was sold for housing
Books				1978	Russborough, Blessington, Co Wicklow was presented to the state by Sir Alfred Beit
Tinakilly House				1978	Dermot and Anne Garland purchased Tinakilly House, Rathnew
Post Office				1978	Saturday Postal delivery service ceased in Bray.
Naylor's Cove				1978	The Diving board at Bray Cove Baths fell into the sea.
Esplanade Hotel				1978	The Esplanade Hotel sold to the Kiley Family
Armstrong-Jones. A				1978	Anthony Charles Armstrong-Jones marriage to H.R.H. Princess Margaret dissolved
Tidy Towns				1978	Bray earned 99 marks in the Bord Failte Tidy Towns Competition
Books				1978	A hundred years of Bray and its neighbourhood from 1770 to 1780 by an old inhabitant[Mrs Francis J Seymour]
Blainroe Golf Club				1978	Blainroe Golf Club (south of Wicklow town) established
Timmins. Godfrey				1978	Godfrey Timmins held the post of Chairman of Wicklow County Council 1978-1979
Wicklow. Earl of				1978	William Cecil 8th Earl of Wicklow died
St Fergal's FC				1978	St. Fergal's Football Club Bray formed
Newspapers				1978	Southside and Bray News first edition
Radio Station				1978	Southside radio station established in Bray
Bray Musical Society				1978	Bray Musical Society stages "Oklahoma"
Film				1978	The TV Series film "Bracken" 1978-1983 locations in County Wicklow, including Roundwood, NewtownMountKennedy,Kilcoole
Ward.Tony				1978	Tony Ward the Greystones rugby player scored a record 38 in his debut Five Nations season
Wicklow GAA				1978	Padraig O Murchu Chairman of Wicklow GAA 1978 - 1982
Bray Urban District				1978	The Urban District of Bray (Alteration of Boundary) Order, 1978 (S.I. No 370 of 1978)
Speed Limits				1978	The Road Traffic (Speed Limits) (County Wicklow) Regulations 1978 (S.I. No. 31 of 1978)
McNaughton. Paul				1978	Paul McNaughton of Greystones Rugby Club won 18 caps for Ireland between 1978 and 1981

BUDC	Mon	01	01		1979	Bray Urban Boundary Order came into effect
Cars	Mon	01	01		1979	Car Reg 9148 NI issued by Wicklow Motor Tax Office
Bray Urban District	Thu	15	02		1979	Bray Urban District Local Electoral Areas Order 1979
Deverell. Averill	Sat	17	02		1979	Averill Deverell died at her home in Greystones, Co. Wicklow
Cars			03		1979	Car Reg 1 ANI issued by Wicklow Motor Tax Office
Population Bray	Sun	01	04		1979	Population of Bray Urban District 21,773 or 25.9% of County Population
Population Wicklow (t)	Sun	01	04		1979	Population of Wicklow Town 4,981 or 5.93% of County Population
Population Arklow	Sun	01	04		1979	Population of Arklow Urban 8,451 or 10.06% of County Population
Population County	Sun	01	04		1979	Population of County Wicklow 83,950 persons. 41,969 Males 41,981 Females
Population Enniskerry	Sun	01	04		1979	Population of Enniskerry urban 1,185 or 1.4% of County Population
Population Greystones	Sun	01	04		1979	Population of Greystones & Delgany 6,921 or 8.24% of County Population
Glen of Imaal	Sun	15	04		1979	Three boys are killed in an explosion in the Glen of Imaal, Co. Wicklow
The Riordan's	Fri	11	05		1979	The cameras roll for the final TV episode of the R.T.E's The Riordans, Mrs. Riodran played by Moira Deedy from Greystones.
Campbell. F.George	Fri	18	05		1979	Frederick George Campbell (artist) of Arklow died in Dublin and buried at Laragh, Co. Wicklow
Elections–Polling Day	Thu	07	06		1979	Local elections are held
Elections–Polling Day	Thu	07	06		1979	The first direct elections of representives to the European Parliament
Cars			06		1979	Car Reg 1 BNI issued by Wicklow Motor Tax Office
Elections–Polling Day	Thu	05	07		1979	Polling Day for Constitutional Referenda– Protect adoption system
Elections–Polling Day	Thu	05	07		1979	Polling Day for Constitutional Referenda– Allow alteration of university representation in Seanad Eireann
Pope John Paul II	Sat	29	09		1979	Pope John Paul II pays a three day visit to Ireland
Pope John Paul II	Sat	29	09		1979	Pope John Paul II blessed the foundation stone for St. Fergals Church at Ballywaltrim, Bray
Arklow	Wed	03	10		1979	Thirty Two persons injured in a train crash near Arklow
Scouting	Mon	22	10		1979	15th Wicklow Caislean na SeanChuirte Scout Troop (S.A.I.) Bray established
Armstrong. Reg	Sat	24	11		1979	Reg Armstrong (motorcycle racer) died in an accident near Avoca. Co. Wicklow
Cars			11		1979	Car Reg 1 CNI issued by Wicklow Motor Tax Office
Act	Wed	12	12		1979	Local Government (Tolls Roads) Act, enacted by Dail Eireann
Woods. Michael			12		1979	Dr Michael Woods appointed Minister for Health & Social Welfare (December 1979 - June 1981)
Railways					1979	C.I.E. announces DART (Dublin Area Rapid Transit) a new railway service between Bray and Howth
Tidy Towns					1979	Bray earned 102 marks in the Bord Failte Tidy Towns Competition

A-Z Reference	Day	Date	Month	Year	DATA
Cinema. Bray				1979	The Royal Cinema was converted into two cinemas by the new owner Michael Collins
Film				1979	The film "The Outsiders" interiors shots filmed at Ardmore Studio
Wicklow Harbour				1979	Wicklow Harbour Works Order 1979
Newspapers				1979	Bray People Newspaper first edition
Browne. Maurice				1979	Fr. Maurice Browne died. Author of several novels and priest in Ballymore Eustace
Currency				1979	Ireland broke the link with Sterling where ir£=£stg (see 1826)
Scannell. Brendan J.				1979	Brendan J. Scannell of Bray. President of the Golfing Union of Ireland 1979-1980
Johnston. Jennifer				1979	The Jennifer Johnston novel "The Old Jest" is set in Co. Wicklow
Delgany Golf Club				1979	Leinster Youths Amateur Open Championship, held at Delgany Golf Club
Fitzwilliam. 10th Earl				1979	William Thomas George Fitzwilliam died. The title Earl of Fitzwilliam created in 1716 became extinct
Books				1979	Arklow & Wicklow County Guide and Directory
Greystones United F.C.				1979	Greystones United Football Club formed
Books				1979	The East. Dublin, Wicklow by David Herman
Murphy. Ciaran				1979	Ciaran Murphy held the post of Chairman of Wicklow County Council 1979-1980
Radio Station				1979	Bray Local Broadcasting (BLB) established
Bray Musical Society				1979	Bray Musical Society stages "The Arcadians"
Ardmore Rovers				1979	Ardmore Rovers football Club, Bray established
Books				1979	(reprinted) Guide to National Monuments of Ireland by Peter Harbinson
Books				1979	The soils of Avondale Forest Park, Rathdrum by J.F.Collins, E.P. Farell and P.O'Toole
Powerscourt				1979	Mervyn Niall Wingfield married Pauline Van
VEC. Bray				1979	Larry McCluskey became CEO of Bray VEC 1979-1980
Booth. Evelyn Mary				1979	Evelyn Mary Booth published the Flora of County Carlow
Cars	Tue	01	01	1980	Car Reg 111 CNI issued by Wicklow Motor Tax Office
Bray Harbour	Wed	23	01	1980	The road bridge at Bray Harbour collapsed
Turkish Baths	Mon	19	02	1980	Turkish Baths Quinsborough Road, Bray demolished
VEC. Bray	Tue	18	03	1980	St. Thoma's Community College, Novara Road was officially opened
Cars			03	1980	Car Reg 1 DNI issued by Wicklow Motor Tax Office
Kelly. Alan	Wed	30	04	1980	Alan Kelly was manager of a friendly match between the Republic of Ireland Football Team v Switzerland

Category	Day	Date	Month	Year	Description
Forsyth, Frederick	Sun	25	05	1980	Frederick Forsyth (author) sells his home Kilgarron House, Enniskerry
Railways	Mon	09	06	1980	Kilcoole Railway Station re-opened
Cars			07	1980	Car Reg 1 ENI issued by Wicklow Motor Tax Office
Mount Usher	Wed	13	08	1980	Mount Usher, Ashford sold by the Walpole family to Mrs Jay
Wicklow Way	Sun	17	08	1980	Stage 1 of the Wicklow Way was opened by Hugh Tunney T.D. in Marley Park, Rathfarnham.
Ploughing	Wed	08	10	1980	The National Ploughing Championships held in Co.Tipperary. The Snr. Indv. Horse Plough Champion 1st John Halpin of Wicklow
Connolly, Roderick	Tue	16	12	1980	Roderick Connolly of Bray died
Holy Redeemer, Bray	Sat	20	12	1980	Our Lady's Choral Society presented the "Messiah" in the Holy Redeemer Church, Bray to mark the new organ.
St.Fergal's. Bray	Sun	21	12	1980	St.Fergal's Church Ballywaltrim dedicated
Cars	Wed	31	12	1980	Car Reg 874 ENI issued by Wicklow Motor Tax Office
Loughlinstown Hospital			's	1980	An extension was added to Loughlinstown Hospital
Housing				1980	Building of houses started at Seapoint Court, in Doyle's field, Dock Hill, Bray
Books				1980	Dublin and North Wicklow by Christopher Moriarty
Books				1980	The Irish journals of Elizabeth Smith 1840 -1850
Books				1980	C.S.Parnell by Paul Brew
Old Conna Golf Club				1980	Old Conna Golf Club (Bray) established
Books				1980	Bray: architectural heritage by William Garner
Housing				1980	Housing Estate built at Corke Abbey, Bray
Camera Club				1980	Produced a slide show on Bray called "Under Your Nose"
West Wicklow His. Soc.				1980	The West Wicklow Historical Society founded
Baltinglass Hospital				1980	The Maternity Unit at Baltinglass Hospital closed
Baltinglass Hospital				1980	Baltinglass District Hospital became a Day Care Centre with 94 beds
Fitzgerald. Paul				1980	Paul Fitzgerald of Arklow represented Ireland in Boxing at the 1980 Olympic Games held in Moscow
Plunkett. James				1980	James Plunkett best known novel Strumpet City was adapted for television by RTÉ
Hynes. Frank				1980	Frank Hynes held the post of Chairman of Wicklow County Council 1980-1981
Delgany Golf Club				1980	Leinster Youths Amateur Open Championship, held at Delgany Golf Club
Golf Championship				1980	The All Ireland County Golf Championship, won by County Wicklow
Bray Musical Society				1980	Bray Musical Society stages "Frederica"
Tidy Towns				1980	Bray earned 107 marks in the Bord Failte Tidy Towns Competition

A–Z Reference	Day	Date	Month	Year	DATA
Rates				1980	The Rate Valuation of Bray was set at £11.46 per £1 of Valuation
Youth Group				1980	A youth group Alpha 80 established in Bray
Martin. Colbert				1980	Colbert Martin (local historian) published a book about Little Bray "A Drink from Broderick's Well"
Holy Redeemer, Bray				1980	A new organ installed in the Holy Redeemer Church, Bray by Kenneth Jones organ builder Bray.
Railways				1980	The turn-table at Bray Railway station removed.
VEC. Bray				1980	The VEC school on the Florence Road, Bray became the Adult Education Centre
Car Park, Bray				1980	2nd Public Car Park in Bray opened in Craig's Yard, Florence Road, Bray
Brien. Christy				1980	Christy Brien (local historian) published "Know your Parish"
Carnew AFC				1980	The Carnew AFC established
Cars	Thu	01	01	1981	Car Reg 875 ENI issued by Wicklow Motor Tax Office
Cars			01	1981	Car Reg 1 FNI issued by Wicklow Motor Tax Office
St. Thomas' College	Wed	18	03	1981	St. Thomas' Community College, Bray opened.
Robbie. John	Sat	21	03	1981	John Robbie won his 9th and last cap on the Irish National Rugby team in a game against Scotland in Murrayfield
Cars			03	1981	Car Reg 1 GNI issued by Wicklow Motor Tax Office
Population Arklow	Sun	05	04	1981	Population of Arklow Urban 8,646 or 9.90% of the County Population
Population County	Sun	05	04	1981	Population of County Wicklow 87,449 persons. 43,663 Males 43,768 Females
Population Wicklow (t)	Sun	05	04	1981	Population of Wicklow Town 5,178 or 5.9% of the County Population
Population Greystones	Sun	05	04	1981	Population of Greystones & Delgany 7,442 or 8.51% of County Population
Population	Sun	05	04	1981	According to the 1981 census 70% of the population of Ireland lives in an urban area .
Population	Sun	05	04	1981	Population of Glenealy 418 or 0.47% of the County Population
Population	Sun	05	04	1981	Population of Avoca 289 or 0.33% of the County population
Population	Sun	05	04	1981	Population of Blessington 988 or 1.12% of the County Population
Population Enniskerry	Sun	05	04	1981	Population of Enniskerry urban 1,228 or 1.4% of the County Population
Population Bray	Sun	05	04	1981	Population of Bray Urban District 22,853 or 26.1% of County Population
Brabazon. Reginald	Fri	08	05	1981	Andrew Marsh wrote a feature article about the 12th Earl of Meath in The Evening Press Newspaper on 08/05/1981
Owen. Nora	Thu	11	06	1981	Nora Owen elected to Dail Eireann
TD's for Wicklow	Thu	11	06	1981	Polling Day for 22nd Dail L.Kavanagh (L) G.Timmins (FG) C.Murphy (FF) P.Brennan (FF)

Delaney. John	Thu	25	06	1981	Rev John Delaney Parish Priest of Enniskerry died
Fitzgerald. Garret	Tue	30	06	1981	Garret Fitzgerald appointed Taoiseach and forms a coalition government with the Labour Party
Wicklow GAA	Sun	05	07	1981	St.Mary's GAA Club Enniskerry open Parc na Sillogue Enniskerry on land donated by Frederick Forsyth (author)
Cars			07	1981	Car Reg 1 HNI issued by Wicklow Motor Tax Office
Bray Gas Works			08	1981	The Gasometer at Dock Hill, Bray removed.
Bray School Project	Tue	01	09	1981	Bray School Project open a national school in Bray
Wicklow Way	Sun	27	09	1981	Stage 2 of the Wicklow Way opened near Laragh. Co. Wicklow
Powerscourt	Thu	19	11	1981	Powerscourt Town House Centre opens in Dublin
Bray Directory	Mon	30	11	1981	Bray Chamber of Commerce published "Bray Directory A-Z Guide"
Cars			11	1981	Car Reg 1 INI issued by Wicklow Motor Tax Office
Cars	Thu	31	12	1981	Car Reg 48 INI issued by Wicklow Motor Tax Office
Kenny. William			12	1981	Rev. William Kenny Parish Priest of Our Lady Queen of Peace Parish, Putland Road, Bray died
Failte Park				1981	Bray Urban District Council purchased Failte Park from Bray Enterprise Ltd
St. Brendans College				1981	25th Anniversary of St. Brendans College, Woodbrook, Bray
Ballywaltrim College				1981	Ballywaltrim Community College, Bray established
O'Rourke. Mary				1981	Mary O'Rourke elected to Seanad Eireann
Tidy Towns				1981	Bray earned 104 marks in the Bord Failte Tidy Towns Competition
McCabe. Peter				1981	Rev. Peter McCabe appointed Parish Priest of Enniskerry Parish
Timmins. Godfrey				1981	Godfrey Timmins held the post of Chairman of Wicklow County Council 1981-1982
Delgany Golf Club				1981	Leinster Youths Amateur Open Championship, held at Delgany Golf Club
Bray Musical Society				1981	Bray Musical Society stages "The Desert Song"
Delgany Golf Club				1981	Delgany Golf Club won the Barton Cup
Maps				1981	The Wicklow Way (Sli Cualann Nua) Map produced by the Ordnance Survey
Cullen. Augustus				1981	The legal E J H Hopkins acquired the legal firm of Augustus Cullen & Sons
Carnew Castle				1981	Carnew Castle was sold by Mrs Constance Mary Spicer
O'Connell. John				1981	Rev John O'Connell appointed Parish Priest of the Holy Redeemer Parish Bray
Blessington				1981	Our Lady of the Most Holy Sacrament, Main Street, Blessington built
Cars	Fri	01	01	1982	Car Reg 49 INI issued by Wicklow Motor Tax Office
Weather	Fri	08	01	1982	Snow drifts cut off many communities in Wicklow for over two weeks starting on 08/01/1982

A–Z Reference	Day	Date	Month	Year	DATA
Goulding. Basil Sir	Sat	16	01	1982	Sir Basil Goulding (industrialist and art connoisseur) of Kilcroney, Bray died
Weather			01	1982	Large falls of snow causes road an rail chaos in many parts of the country
Hussey. Gemma	Thu	18	02	1982	Gemma Hussey nee Moran the first woman elected Dail Eireann for Wicklow
TD's for Wicklow	Thu	18	02	1982	Polling Day for 23rd Dail L.Kavanagh (L) G.Timmins (FG) C.Murphy (FF) G.Hussey (FG)
Woods. Michael			03	1982	Dr Michael Woods appointed Minister for Health & Social Welfare (March 1982 – December 1982)
Cars			04	1982	Car Reg 1 JNI issued by Wicklow Motor Tax Office
Lough Dan	Sat	15	05	1982	The Scout National Camp Site at Lough Dan opened by Dr. Patrick Hillery President of Ireland
Arklow	Sat	21	08	1982	Arklow twinned with Chateaudun, France
O'Tuairisc. Eoghan	Tue	24	08	1982	Eoghan O'Tuairisc (Eugene Waters) (poet and novelist) died
Unemployment			08	1982	Unemployment figure for Bray 2,272
Harbour			08	1982	Tenders invited by Bray Urban District Council to build a road bridge at Bray Harbour, to replace a bridge that had collapsed.
Ardmore Studio			09	1982	Ardmore Film Studio bought by Vincent Donohoe for £1.1m
Killruddery	Wed	13	10	1982	Sean Eagan wrote a feature article about Killruddery in The Irish Independent Newspaper on 13/10/1982
Cars			10	1982	Car Reg 1 KNI issued by Wicklow Motor Tax Office
Royal Hotel,Bray	Sat	13	11	1982	Part of the Royal Hotel on the Quinsborough Road junction demolished to make way for shops and offices
Fitzgerald. Garret	Wed	24	11	1982	Garret Fitzgerald appointed taoiseach for the 2nd time and leads a coalition government with the Labour Party
TD's for Wicklow	Wed	24	11	1982	Polling Day for 24th Dail L.Kavanagh (L) G.Timmins (FG) P.Brennan (FF) G.Hussey (FG)
Avoca				1982	Avoca Mines Closed
Marino Clinic,Bray				1982	Extension added to the Marino Clinic, Church Road, Bray
Delgany Golf Club				1982	Leinster Youths Amateur Open Championship, held at Delgany Golf Club, won by P. Errity, Delgany
Royal Hotel,Bray				1982	Jim McGettigan bought the Royal Starlight Hotel, Bray
Tinakilly House				1982	William and Bee Power purchased Tinakilly House, Rathnew
Old Conna House				1982	Old Conna House sold for 0.75 Million Pounds
Goulet.Yann Renard				1982	Yann Renard Goulet made a member of Aosdana
Arklow Shipping				1982	Arklow Shipping vessel Arklow Day built
Hussey. Gemma				1982	Gemma Hussey appointed Minister for Education December 1982– February 1986
Monck				1982	Henry Wyndham Stanley Monck died, 6th Viscount Monck his son Charles Stanley Monck

Section One: Data by Date

				Year	Event
O'Rourke. Mary				1982	Mary O'Rourke elected to Dail Eireann for constituency of Longford – Roscommon
Phone Number				1982	7 digit phone number introduced for the 01 area
Miley. Jim				1982	Jim Miley held the post of Chairman of Wicklow County Council 1982–1983
Tidy Towns				1982	25th Anniversary of Tidy Towns Competition 797 towns and villages took part
Woodbrook Golf Club				1982	The Irish Amateur Close Championship, held at Woodbrook Golf Club, Bray
Comerford. Marie				1982	Marie Comerford died
Tidy Towns				1982	Bray earned 100 marks in the Bord Failte Tidy Towns Competition
Books				1982	The Journal of the Arklow Historical Society
Ryan. Tony				1982	Tony Ryan(businessman) purchased Dargle Glen, Kilcroney, Bray
Bray Musical Society				1982	Bray Musical Society stages "La Vie Parisenne"
Arklow Sports Centre				1982	Arklow Sports and Leisure Club completed at Seview Avenue, Arklow.
MacMahon. John				1982	Rev John MacMahon became Parish Priest of Our Lady Queen of Peace Parish, Putland Road, Bray
Unemployment				1982	The live register showed 2,307 out of work in Bray
McCormack. William				1982	(Hugh Maxton) William John McCormack wrote "Jubilee for Renegades"
Cars	Mon	03	01	1983	Car Reg 215 KNI issued by Wicklow Motor Tax Office
Cars	Sun	01	05	1983	Car Reg 1LNI issued by Wicklow Motor Tax Office
Scouting			05	1983	14th Wicklow Scout Troop (S.A.I.) Avoca, established
St Andrew's. Bray			05	1983	125th Anniversary of St.Andrew's Presbyterian Church, Bray
Greystones			06	1983	Greystones Town Commissioners established under the terms of the Town Improvements (Ireland) Act 1854
O'Dalaigh. Cearbhall	Mon	06	06	1983	President Hillery unveiled a sculpture to the late President Cearbhall O'Dalaigh at Sneem, Co. Kerry
Act	Wed	13	07	1983	Postal and Telecommunications Service Act, enacted by Dail Eireann
Weston. Galen	Sun	07	08	1983	An attempt made to kidnap supermarket owner Galen Weston from his Roundwood home. Kidnap attempt foiled by Garda
Elections–Polling Day	Wed	07	09	1983	Polling Day for Constitutional Referenda– Prohibit legalisation of abortion
Cars			09	1983	Car Reg 1 MNI issued by Wicklow Motor Tax Office
Glenroe	Fri	11	11	1983	The first episode of Glenroe broadcast on RTE 1
O'Kelly. Sean T	Sat	19	11	1983	Phyllis Ryan the wife Mr. Sean T.O'Kelly former President of Ireland died
Kavanagh. Liam	Tue	13	12	1983	Liam Kavanagh appointed Minister for the Environment
Jones. Kenneth				1983	Kenneth Jones, Organ builder from Bray installed an organ in Whitefriars Street Church, Dublin
Arklow Shipping				1983	Arklow Shipping vessel Arklow Dawn built

A–Z Reference	Day	Date	Month	Year	DATA
Jones. Kenneth				1983	Kenneth Jones, Organ builder from Bray installed an organ in the First Presbyterian Church, Hannibal, USA
Newspapers				1983	North Wicklow News (Wicklow) first edition
Darcy. Eamonn				1983	Eamonn Darcy won the Benson & Hedges Spanish Open Golf Classic
Newcastle N.S				1983	Work began on building Newcastle National School, Co. Wicklow
Books				1983	"If you seek Monuments" by Kathleen Turner
Dwyer. Michael				1983	The Bray Branch of the Irish National Foresters the Michael Dwyer branch was disbanded after 98 years
Wicklow Sub Aqua Club				1983	Wicklow Sub Aqua Club founded
Books				1983	Mount Usher Gardens, Ashford, County Wicklow by Madelaine Jay
Delgany Golf Club				1983	Leinster Youths Amateur Open Championship, held at Delgany Golf Club
Ryan. Kevin				1983	Kevin Ryan held the post of Chairman of Wicklow County Council 1983-1984
Bray Musical Society				1983	Bray Musical Society stages "The Great Waltz"
Murphy. Matt				1983	Matt Murphy appointed first Principal of St. Thomas's Community College, Bray
Kelly. Alan				1983	Alan Kelly was manager of Preston North End Football Club 1983 - 1985
Film				1983	The TV Series film "Gelnroe" 1983 -2001 location scenes in County Wicklow , main location Kilcoole.
Wicklow GAA				1983	Peadar Mac Eochaidh Chairman of Wicklow GAA 1983 - 1985
McCormack. William				1983	(Hugh Maxton) William John McCormack wrote "The Enlighted Cave and Inscriptions"
Cars	Mon	02	01	1984	Car Reg 321 MNI issued by Wicklow Motor Tax Office
Unemployment			01	1984	3,174 Unemployed in Bray
Cars			03	1984	Car Reg 1 NNI issued by Wicklow Motor Tax Office
Bray Harbour			04	1984	Dargan Road Bridge at Bray Harbour open to traffic
Davidson. Rosanna			04	1984	Rosanna Davidson born
Elections-Polling Day	Thu	14	06	1984	2nd election of representives to the European Parliament
Elections-Polling Day	Thu	14	06	1984	Polling Day for Constitutional Referenda- Extend voting rights to non-citizens
Earthquake	Thu	19	07	1984	An earthquake occurred in Ireland and West England it measured 5.5 on the Richter Scale
Railways	Mon	23	07	1984	The Dublin Area Rapid Transit (DART) rail system came into service.
Cars			09	1984	Car Reg 1 ONI issued by Wicklow Motor Tax Office
Court House. Bray			09	1984	Bray Court House on the Boghall Road opened
Roundwood			09	1984	A new school opened at Roundwood

Ploughing	Thu	04	10	1984	The National Ploughing Championships held in Co.Kilkenny.The 3 Furrow Tractor Champion 1st Edward Dowse of Wicklow
Woolworths. W.F	Sat	06	10	1984	W.F. Woolworths store at Main Street Bray closed.
Galtrim House			10	1984	Fire destroys Galtrim House. Galtrim Road, Bray
Roads			12	1984	Bray-Shankill By Pass sanctioned by European Commission cost estimated at £4m
Library. Bray			12	1984	Tenders invited for extension to Bray Library, Florence Road, Bray
Nitrigin Eireann Teo.				1984	Nitrigin Eireann Teoranta (NET) the state-owned fertiliser company begins merger talks with Imperial Chemical Industries (ICI)
Trade				1984	Made in Bray Exhibition- Industrial and Craft Fair
Books				1984	Stones of Bray by Canon Scott reprinted
Aravon School				1984	Aravon School bought Old Conn Hill (House) once the home of Count John Mc Cormack
Jones. Kenneth				1984	Kenneth Jones, Organ builder from Bray installed an organ in Christ Church, Dublin
Calary Church				1984	150th anniversary of Calary Church,Roundwood
Bray Musical Society				1984	Bray Musical Society stages "Bless the Bride"
Johnston. Brian				1984	Brian Johnston appointed (Acting) County Manager of Wicklow (Local Government) 1984-1985
Wicklow Harbour				1984	Wicklow Harbour Works Order 1984
Delgany Golf Club				1984	Leinster Youths Amateur Open Championship, held at Delgany Golf Club
Collis. J.S				1984	John Stewart Collis (writer and naturalist) died
Books				1984	In the Lands of Brien published by Christopher Brien
Aravon School				1984	Aravon School moved from Sidmonton Road, Bray to Old Conna Hill House, Bray
Jones. George				1984	George Jones held the post of Chairman of Wicklow County Council 1984-1985
Film				1984	The film "Cal" location scenes at Crone Wood, Enniskerry and a potato field in Delgany
Curtlestown				1984	Extension added to St. Patrick's National School, Curtlestown that was built in 1960.
Film				1984	The film "Anne Deviln" location scenes at Wicklow Town
Cars	Tue	01	01	1985	Car Reg 270 ONI issued by Wicklow Motor Tax Office
Act	Tue	12	02	1985	The Age of Majority Act reduces the age limit from 21 to 18, enacted by Dail Eireann
Wicklow. Earl of	Sat	23	03	1985	Lady Wicklow, one of the founders of Glencree Reconciliation Centre, is conferred with an Hon. Doctor of Laws degree at NUI
Cars			03	1985	Car Reg 1 PNI issued by Wicklow Motor Tax Office
Elections–Polling Day	Thu	20	06	1985	Electorate in the Bray Area 16,600 for County Council 6 seats L.McManus,J.Byrne,C.Murphy,M.Mortell,M. Lawlor,M.Ledwidge
Elections–Polling Day	Thu	20	06	1985	Local Elections, Urban District and County Council

A-Z Reference	Day	Date	Month	Year	DATA
Elections-Polling Day	Thu	20	06	1985	Local elections are held
Heritage Centre	Mon	08	07	1985	Dr. Garret Fitzgerald opens a Heritage Centre in Bray Town Hall
Housing	Mon	08	07	1985	Tenders invited for Housing development at Ballwaltrim/Irishtown Stage II (51 two storyed dwellings)
Cars			09	1985	Car Reg 1 RNI issued by Wicklow Motor Tax Office
Scouting	Wed	09	10	1985	6th Wicklow Scout Troop (S.A.I.) Aughrim, Co Wicklow established
Kilmacanogue	Sat	26	10	1985	Kilmacanogue Parish Church became a chapel of eves of Enniskerry Parish Church St. Mary's
Trade	Wed	30	10	1985	The 2nd Made in Bray Trade Fair took place 30-31 October & 1st November
Mountain Rescue			circa	1985	The An Oige Mountain Rescue was reformed as the Dublin & Wicklow Mountain Rescue Team
Greystones			circa	1985	Greystones Bowling Club established.
Wicklow Gaol				1985	Wicklow County Council established an advisory group to develop Wicklow Gaol as Heritage/Visitor's Centre
Carrig. Blessington				1985	Excavations at Carrig near Blessington an Stone Age burial chamber discovered
Bus				1985	The 145a Bus route, new route included a feeder service to Bray DART station from Ballywaltrim, Bray
Books				1985	The spatial pattern of state a forestation in County Wicklow by P.G. Clinch
Greystones Golf Club				1985	Greystones Golf Club won the Barton Cup
Bus				1985	The 45 Bus route service to the Seafront was reduced but extended on the Killarney Road Service
Bray Musical Society				1985	Bray Musical Society stages "Fiddler on the Roof"
Tracey. Blaise				1985	Blaise Tracey appointed County Manager of Wicklow (Local Government) 1985-2000
Bray Directory				1985	2nd Bray Directory by Bray Chamber of Commerce published
Large. R.G				1985	Rev. R.G.Large retires as Rector of Bray parish
Hospital				1985	Extension to St Colmcille's Hospital Loughlinstown
Books				1985	By the Banks of the Dargle, a history of Bray Emmets GAA Club 1885-1985 compiled by Jim Brophy
Books				1985	Arklow -last stronghold of gail.Arklow ships from 1850-1985 by Jim Rees and Liam Charlton
Keenan.Tom				1985	Tom Keenan held the post of Chairman of Wicklow County Council 1985-1986
Greenan Bottle Museum				1985	The Greenan Bottle Museum, Glenmalure established
Derralossary Church				1985	Derralossary Church near Roundwood deconsecrated
Arklow				1985	An extension added to Arklow Presbyterian Church
County Wicklow				1985	County of Wicklow Traffic and Parking Temporary Rules 1985

Section One: Data by Date

Subject	Weekday	Day	Month	Year	Description
Wicklow GAA				1985	Wicklow Referee locked in boot of his car after a Wicklow GAA match
Delgany Golf Club				1985	Leinster Youths Amateur Open Championship, held at Delgany Golf Club
Carnew				1985	Extension added to Carnew Primary School
McCormack. William				1985	(Hugh Maxton) William John McCormack wrote "Surviving Poems"
McCormack. William				1985	(Hugh Maxton) William John McCormack wrote "Snapdragons and Passage"
Historical Society				1985	Bray Cualann Historical Society published its 1st Historical Journal
Cars	Wed	01	01	1986	Car Reg 396 RNI issued by Wicklow Motor Tax Office
McShane. Paul	Mon	06	01	1986	Paul McShane born Kilpedder Co. Wicklow
Cars			03	1986	Car Reg 1SNI issued by Wicklow Motor Tax Office
King. Cecil	Mon	07	04	1986	Cecil King (artist) died at Dun Laoghaire Co. Dublin
Population Shillelagh	Sun	13	04	1986	Population of Shillelagh rural area 6,395 or 6.76% of the County Population
Population Rathdown	Sun	13	04	1986	Population of Rathdown No 2 rural area 13,613 or 14.39% of the County Population
Population Wicklow (t)	Sun	13	04	1986	Population of Wicklow Town 5,304 or 5.6% of County Population
Population	Sun	13	04	1986	Census of Population
Population	Sun	13	04	1986	The population of the counties Dublin, Kildare, Meath and Wicklow accounted for 37.7% of the Population of Ireland
Population Baltinglass	Sun	13	04	1986	Population of Baltinglass No1 rural area 11,902 or 12.58% of the County Population
Population Rathdrum	Sun	13	04	1986	Population of Rathdrum Rural area 24,254 or 25.65% of the County Population
Population County	Sun	13	04	1986	Population of County Wicklow 94,542 persons. 46,980 Males 47,562 Females
Population Arklow	Sun	13	04	1986	Population of Arklow Urban 8,388 or 8.90% of the County Population
Population Greystones	Sun	13	04	1986	Population of Greystones & Delgany 8,455 or 8.94% of County Population
Population Enniskerry	Sun	13	04	1986	Population of Enniskerry urban 1,229 or 1.3% of County Population
Population Bray	Sun	13	04	1986	Population of Bray Urban District 24,686 or 26.1% of County Population
Russborough House	Wed	21	05	1986	18 paintings stolen from Russborough House, Blessington
Elections-Polling Day	Thu	26	06	1986	Polling Day for Constitutional Referenda– Allow legalisation of divorce
Elections-Polling Day	Thu	26	06	1986	Polling Day for the 10th Amendment to the Constitution (Proposed the introduction of divorce in Ireland) Against 63% For 36%
Urban Renewal Scheme			06	1986	The Urban Renewal Act provides for the renewal of designated urban areas. Bray included 01/05/1990
Dargle River	Sun	24	08	1986	Over 1000 persons given shelter in Ravenswell, Little Flower Hall, and Parochial Hall Novara Road after floods in Little Bray
Avoca Bridge	Sun	24	08	1986	The bridge at Avoca washed away by flooding

A–Z Reference	Day	Date	Month	Year	DATA
Dargle River	Sun	24	08	1986	Flooding took place in Little Bray after a day of heavy rain. Over 1000 persons taken from their homes
Parnell. Charles S	Mon	01	09	1986	Liam Kavanagh Minister for Tourism, Fisheries and Forestry opens the Charles Stewart Parnell Museum in Avondale House
Cars			09	1986	Car Reg 1 TNI issued by Wicklow Motor Tax Office
Ploughing	Thu	09	10	1986	The National Ploughing Championships held in Co.Kilkenny. The 3 Furrow Tractor Champion 1st Peadar Shortt of Wicklow
Ploughing	Thu	09	10	1986	The National Ploughing Championships held in Co.Kilkenny. The Snr. Indv. Horse Plough Champion 1st John Halpin of Wicklow
Act	Tue	11	12	1986	Transport (Reorganisation of C.I.E) Act , enacted by Dail Eireann with effect 2/2/1987
Cars			12	1986	Car Reg 426 TNI issued by Wicklow Motor Tax Office
Books				1986	History of Bray by Arthur Flynn
Tidy Towns				1986	Greystones earned 136 marks in the Bord Failte Tidy Towns Competition
Tidy Towns				1986	Arklow earned 150 marks in the Bord Failte Tidy Towns Competition
Books				1986	The Parish of Powerscourt by Rev A.E. Stokes reprinted by the Old Bray Society
Tidy Towns				1986	Enniskerry earned 148 marks in the Bord Failte Tidy Towns Competition
Coins				1986	Coinage (Calling In) Order -removal of half penny from circulation with effect 01/01/1987
Tidy Towns				1986	Delgany earned 171 marks in the Bord Failte Tidy Towns Competition
Tidy Towns				1986	Kilcoole earned 143 marks in the Bord Failte Tidy Towns Competition
Tidy Towns				1986	Newcastle earned 138 marks in the Bord Failte Tidy Towns Competition
Tidy Towns				1986	Ashford earned 119 marks in the Bord Failte Tidy Towns Competition
Mulligan. Rev				1986	Fr. Mulligan of the Queen of Peace Parish, Putland Road, Bray died
Post Office				1986	Fergal Quinn Chairman of An Post opened a new sorting office at Bray Post Office
Books				1986	Water Quality Management Plan for the River Slaney Catchment in accordance with S.15 Local Government (Water Pollution) Act
Library. Bray				1986	Work began on the extension to Bray Library
Tidy Towns				1986	Wicklow Town earned 144 marks in the Bord Failte Tidy Towns Competition
Brien. Christy				1986	Christopher (Christy) Brien (local historian) died
Books				1986	A view from the DART by Vincent Caprani
Tidy Towns				1986	Bray earned 140 marks in the Bord Failte Tidy Towns Competition
Sport				1986	Bray Wanderes AFC 1st Division Champions of FAI
Hynes. Frank				1986	Frank Hynes held the post of Chairman of Wicklow County Council 1986-1987

Category	Day		Month	Year	Event
Tidy Towns				1986	Glendalough earned 147 marks in the Bord Failte Tidy Towns Competition
Hussey. Gemma				1986	Gemma Hussey appointed Minister for Social Welfare 1986-1987
Rathnew A.F.C.				1986	Rathnew Football Club formed
Film				1986	The film "Rawhead Rex" filmed in County Wicklow
Wicklow Golf Club				1986	Wicklow Golf Club won the Barton Cup
Wicklow GAA				1986	Leinster O'Byrne Cup Senior Football Final GAA. Wicklow 1-7 Westmeath 0-6
Water Scheme				1986	Work began on a new water and sewerage scheme . From Peoples Park, Bray to Bray Harbour
County Wicklow				1986	County of Wicklow Traffic and Parking Bye-Laws 1986
Tidy Towns				1986	Roundwood earned 136 marks in the Bord Failte Tidy Towns Competition
Lifeboats				1986	The lifeboat Ger Tigchlaar No 14-19 trent class stationed at Arklow Lifeboat station
Delgany Golf Club				1986	Leinster Youths Amateur Open Championship, held at Delgany Golf Club
Bray Musical Society				1986	Bray Musical Society stages "My Fair Lady"
Film				1986	The film "Eat the Peach" filmed on locations in Wicklow , County Meath, County Kildare and Dublin
Wicklow GAA				1986	Liam O Lochlain Chairman of Wicklow GAA 1986 - 1988
McCormack. William				1986	(Hugh Maxton) William John McCormack wrote "At the Protestant Museum"
Historical Society				1986	Bray Cualann Historical Society published its 2nd Historical Journal
Milne. Charles Ewart	Wed	14	01	1987	Charles Ewart Milne died
Cars			01	1987	Car Reg 87 WW 1 issued by Wicklow Motor Tax Office
CIE	Mon	02	02	1987	Transport (Reorganisation of C.I.E) Act came into effect
TD's for Wicklow	Tue	17	02	1987	Polling Day for 25th Dail J.Jacob (FF) L.Kavanagh (L) G.Hussey (FG) D.Roche (FF)
Fitzgerald. Garret	Wed	11	03	1987	Garret Fitzgerald announces his resignation from leadership of the Fine Gael party and succeeded by Alan Dukes
Ryan. Tony			03	1987	Tony Ryan buys Dargle Glen former home of Sir Basil and Lady Goulding
Elections-Polling Day	Tue	26	05	1987	Single European Amendment Act - Wicklow Voted Yes 69,4% No 30.60% Electorate 65,393 Turnout 45,95%
Elections-Polling Day	Tue	26	05	1987	Polling Day for Constitutional Referenda- Allow singing of Single European Act
Ward. Tony	Wed	03	06	1987	Tony Ward last game of the Irish National Rugby Team was against Tonga in Brisbrane
Kilterman			09	1987	Kilterman Dairy ceased trading
Eksund	Fri	30	10	1987	French Customs authorities seize Eksund ship carrying 150 tons of armaments. Two Wicklow men arrested
IFI			10	1987	Irish Fertiliser Industries begins trading a merger of the Irish operations of ICI and NET
Air Crashes	Sat	12	12	1987	Plane crashed near Ballybrew, Enniskerry , Three persons killed

A–Z Reference	Day	Date	Month	Year	DATA
VEC–Outdoor Centre				1987	Baltinglass Outdoor Education Centre established under the aegis of County Wicklow VEC
Books				1987	Greystones Presbyterian Church 1887–1987
Glen of Imaal Terrier				1987	The Glen of Imaal Terrier was recognized as a dog breed by the States Kennel Club of America
School, Wicklow Town				1987	The East Glendalough School, Station Road, Wicklow Town founded
Carnew				1987	Extension added to Carnew Vocational School
Jones. George				1987	George Jones held the post of Chairman of Wicklow County Council 1987–1988
Hussey. Gemma				1987	Gemma Hussey appointed Minister for Labour 1987
Books				1987	The Avonmore brown trout fishery at Rathdrum, Co. Wicklow by E. Fahy.
Darcy. Eamonn				1987	Eamonn Darcy played on the Ryder Cup Team. The first time a European Cup team won the match on US soil
Bray Musical Society				1987	Bray Musical Society stages "The Merry Widow"
Delgany Golf Club				1987	Leinster Youths Amateur Open Championship, held at Delgany Golf Club
Genealogy Service				1987	Wicklow County Council established genealogy service
Woods. Michael				1987	Dr Michael Woods appointed Minister of Social Welfare (1987 – 1991)
Jones. Kenneth				1987	Kenneth Jones, Organ builder from Bray installed an organ in the First United Methodist Church, Crestview, Florida, USA
Darcy. Eamonn				1987	Eamonn Darcy won the Volvo Belgian Open Golf Classic
Kilmacanogue				1987	Avoca Handweavers acquired the property of Glencormac House, Kilmacanogue
Cars			01	1988	Car Reg 88 WW 1 issued by Wicklow Motor Tax Office
Coilte			02	1988	Coilte Teoranta– The Irish Forestry Board was established under the Forestry Act of 1988
BL&FHS			04	1988	The Blessington Local and Family History Society founded.
Seaside Festival	Fri	01	07	1988	Bray Seaside Festival 1st July to 10th July 1988
Sweeney, John	Mon	11	07	1988	John Sweeney held the post of Chairman of Wicklow County Council from July 1988 until his death on 03/12/1988
Rotary Club of Wicklow	Sat	26	11	1988	Rotary Club of Wicklow, chartered and given registration number 116
Arklow Shipping				1988	Arklow Shipping vessel Arklow Mill built
Lifeboats				1988	A new assembly building and store was constructed on the quayside at Arklow adjacent to the lifeboat moorings
Arklow Shipping				1988	Arklow Shipping vessel Arklow Marsh built
Arklow Shipping				1988	Arklow Shipping vessel Arklow Bay built

Section One: Data by Date

Category	Event	Year	Month	Weekday	Day
Smith. Sir W.C.	An oil painting of Sir William-Cusack Smith presented to the National Gallery of Ireland (NGI 4554) by Mrs Davies, England	1988			
Film	Part of the film My Left Foot shot on location in County Wicklow.	1988			
Books	The Wicklow Way from Marley to Glenmalure. a walking guide by Michael Fewer	1988			
Water Treatment	Bray Sewerage Pump Station at Bray harbour and out fall pipe constructed at cost £1.6m	1988			
Melifont Hotel	Melifont Hotel Quinsborough Road, Bray sold and reopened as Westbourne Hotel.	1988			
Smith. Sir Michael	An oil painting of Sir Michael Smith presented to the National Gallery of Ireland (NGI 4555) by Mrs Davies, England	1988			
Books	Maritime Arklow by Frank Forde	1988			
Winston's	Winston's open at store in the old Lipton's Supermarket Main Street, Bray	1988			
Bray Bookshop	The Bray Bookshop moved to the Main Street, Bray	1988			
Bray Musical Society	Bray Musical Society stages "Die Fledermaus"	1988			
Film	The film "The Real Charlotte" filmed at Ardmore Studio	1988			
Delgany Golf Club	Leinster Youths Amateur Open Championship, held at Delgany Golf Club	1988			
Newspapers	North Wicklow Times (Bray) first edition	1988			
Lotto	An Post run Lotto system introduced	1988			
Keenan. Tom	Tom Keenan held the post of Chairman of Wicklow County Council 1988-1989	1988			
Film	The film "The Dawning" set in County Wicklow, filmed on locations in Wicklow and Cork	1988			
Glendalough	Glendalough Visitor Centre built.	1988			
Books	The Complete Wicklow Way by J.B. Malone.	1988			
Booth. Evelyn Mary	Evelyn Mary Booth died	1988			
Bread	Johnston Mooney and O'Brien. -Dublin oldest bakery-closed, including its outlets in Dun Laoghaire and Bray	1989	01	Fri	27
Cars	Car Reg 89 WW 1 issued by Wicklow Motor Tax Office	1989	01		
Elections-Polling Day	3rd election of representives to the European Parliament	1989	06	Thu	15
TD's for Wicklow	Polling Day for 26th Dail L.Kavanagh (L),J.Jacob (FF), G.Timmins (FG), D.Roche (FF)	1989	06	Thu	15
McAnally. Ray	Ray McAnally (Actor) died at his Co. Wicklow home, buried St. Fintans Cemetery, Sutton, Dublin	1989	06	Thu	15
Kelleher. John	Rev. John Kelleher died and was buried in St. Peter's Graveyard, Bray	1989	07	Mon	10
Pigott. John	Rev.John Pigott Parish Priest of Holy Redeemer Parish died and is buried in St. Peter's Graveyard, Bray	1989	08	Wed	23
Roads	The Government approves the Bray- Shankill By pass costing £25m	1989	08		
Newspapers	Bray may have been a Roman Settlement appeared in the Irish Times Newspaper	1989	09	Thu	21
Roads	Sean Walsh Chairman of Dublin City Council turned the first sod of the Bray-Shankill By Pass at Wilford near Bray	1989	09	Fri	29

A-Z Reference	Day	Date	Month	Year	DATA
Lifeboats	Sat	30	09	1989	The Lifeboat Annie Lydia Blaker was stationed at Wicklow Harbour
Radio	Wed	25	10	1989	Horizon Radio goes on air 94.9FM from 11 Quinsborough Rd, Bray
Ships/Yachts	Sat	28	10	1989	The vessel "Irwell" shipwrecked of the Wicklow Coast
Malone, J.B.			10	1989	J.B.Malone Hill walker and Author died
Trade			10	1989	Bray Chamber of commerce hosted Bray Industrial and Motor Fair
Books			11	1989	The Book of Bray compiled and edited by John O'Sullivan,Tony Dunne, Seamus Cannon
Weather			12	1989	Storm damages part of the North pier at Bray harbour and the Seawall
Books				1989	A History of Wicklow Lifeboat Station. From Dauntless to Annie by Ciaran Doyle
Delgany Golf Club				1989	Leinster Youths Amateur Open Championship, held at Delgany Golf Club
Arklow				1989	Servier (Ireland) Industries Ltd, a pharmaceutical company opened a plant on the Gorey Road, Arklow
Books				1989	Dublin South & Wicklow Regional Plan
Trade				1989	Lepatrick Dairies of Notheren Ireland bought Chieftain Foods based in Bray
Trade				1989	Shamrock Foods (IAWS) bought Braycot Biscuits Ltd.
Books				1989	The Shell Guide to Ireland (3rd Edition) by Killanin and Duignan (Revised and updated by Peter Harbison)
Housing				1989	20 Town houses built at Failte Park, Bray
Hynes. Frank				1989	Frank Hynes held the post of Chairman of Wicklow County Council 1989-1990
Sport				1989	John Ryan of Bray Wanderers was leading goal scorer of FAI 1st Division season 1989/90 with 16 goals
Housing				1989	Loreto Nuns sell part of their grounds at Vevay Road Bray,for housing Loreto Grange Built.
Tulfarris Golf Club				1989	Tulfarris Golf Club (Blessington) established
Books				1989	On foot in Dublin and Wicklow. exploring the wilderness by Christopher Moriarty
FCA				1989	30th Anniversary of the 21st Battalion FCA
Price. Cecil				1989	Rev. Cecil Price appointed Archdeacon of Glendalough
Bray Musical Society				1989	Bray Musical Society stages "The Boy Friend"
Film				1989	The film "My left Foot" Filmed on locations in Dublin and Wicklow. The first Irish-produced film to win an Oscar.
O'Toole. Garry				1989	Garry O'Toole (swimmer) won silver in the 200m breaststroke at European Championships
Wicklow GAA				1989	Roibeard O Duiginn Chairman of Wicklow GAA 1989 – 1991
Delgany	Sat	13	01	1990	Mr. Peter Sutherland former Attorney General and EU Commissioner turned the first sod for Delgany School

Trade	Tue	23	01		1990	Nixdorf Computers announced it was reducing its workforce by 5,000 including its plant at Boghall Road, Bray
Weather	Wed	24	01		1990	Snow showers cover most of the country
Cars			01		1990	Car Reg 90 WW 1 issued by Wicklow Motor Tax Office
Scouting	Mon	26	03		1990	15th Wicklow Scout Troop (S.A.I.) Little Bray established
Film			03		1990	The film "My Left Foot" wins 2 Oscars Daniel Day Lewis and Brenda Fricker
Local Government			03		1990	Government announces that a review of Local government functions are taking place and the elections June will not be held.
National Park			04		1990	The Wicklow Mountains National Park established about 20,000 Hectares or (49,421 acres).
Sport	Sun	13	05		1990	FAI Cup Final held at Landwdowne Road Result: Bray Wanderers 1 St Francis 0
Water – Vartry	Sun	21	10		1990	The Vartry Reservoir at Roundwood drooped to an all time low of 27.3 feet below high water mark
Bray Pumping Station	Fri	26	10		1990	Minister of Environment P. Flynn opened Bray Pumping Station at Dock Hill, Bray
Bradshaw. Harry	Sat	22	12		1990	Harry Bradshaw (The Brad) golfer died
Darcy. Eamonn					1990	Eamonn Darcy won the Emirates Airlines Desert Golf Classic
Scouting					1990	Work began on the extension to the 5th Wicklow (Bray Sea Scout) Group den at Bray harbour
International Hotel					1990	Work began on a new leisure centre on the old International Hotel site
Bray Musical Society					1990	Bray Musical Society stages "The Pyjama Game"
Bray Main Street					1990	New street furniture and pavements slabs on Main Street. Bray
Books					1990	The history of the Parish of St James Crinken, Bray Co. Dublin published by the Parish of St James.
Books					1990	The Wicklow way by Ken Boyle and Orla Bourke
Film					1990	The film "December Bride" Interior filming at MTM Ardmore Studio
McManus Liz					1990	Act of Subversion a novel by Liz McManus T.D. for Wicklow
Arklow Shipping					1990	Arklow Shipping vessel Forester built
Books					1990	Between the mountains and the sea. The Story of Delgany, 1789-1990. a parish history, by Judith Flannery
Arklow Shipping					1990	Arklow Shipping vessel Thruster built
Arklow Shipping					1990	Arklow Shipping vessel Arklow Moor built
Bray Cancer Group					1990	Bray Cancer Support Centre founded
Film					1990	The film "Fools of Fortune" Interior filming at MTM Ardmore Studio
Maxtor					1990	Maxtor Ltd replaces Nixdorf Ltd on the Boghall Road.
Greystones Golf Club					1990	Leinster Youths Amateur Open Championship, held at Greystones Golf Club
Jones. George					1990	George Jones held the post of Chairman of Wicklow County Council 1990-1991

A-Z Reference	Day	Date	Month	Year	DATA
Quigley. D.B				1990	Bray man Dermot B. Quigley appointed to the board of Revenue Commissioners
Elections–Polling Day				1990	Presidential Election held
Film				1990	The film "The Field" locations scenes at Ardmore studio
Film				1990	The film "The Lilac Bus" location scene at Ballyknockan, Powerscourt, Bray, Enniskerry
Historical Society				1990	Bray Cualann Historical Society published its 3rd Historical Journal
Film				1990	The film "The Commitments" locations scenes at Bray Head Hotel, Bray
Cars			01	1991	Car Reg 91 WW 1 issued by Wicklow Motor Tax Office
O'Faolain. Sean	Sat	20	04	1991	Sean O'Faolain died
Population Wicklow (t)	Sun	21	04	1991	Population of Wicklow Town 5,847 or 6.0% of County Population
Population Greystones	Sun	21	04	1991	Population of Greystones & Delgany 9,649 or 9.92% of County Population
Population	Sun	21	04	1991	Census of Population took place in Ireland
Population County	Sun	21	04	1991	Population of County Wicklow 97,256 persons, 48,076 Males 49,189 Females
Population Enniskerry	Sun	21	04	1991	Population of Enniskerry urban 1,238 or 1.3% of County Population
Population Bray	Sun	21	04	1991	Population of Bray Urban District 25,096 or 25,8% of County Population
Population Arklow	Sun	21	04	1991	Population of Arklow Urban 7,987 or 8.20% of the County Population
Population Shillelagh	Sun	24	04	1991	Population of Shillelagh rural area 6,410 or 6.59% of the County Population
Population Rathdrum	Sun	24	04	1991	Population of Rathdrum Rural area 24,865 or 25.56% of the County Population
Population Rathdown	Sun	24	04	1991	Population of Rathdown No 2 rural area 15,093 or 15.51% of the County Population
Population Baltinglass	Sun	24	04	1991	Population of Baltinglass No1 rural area 11,976 or 12.30% of the County Population
Somerville–Large. P.	Sun	19	05	1991	Philip Townsend Somerville–Large (engineer) of Bray died
Sport	Sun	21	07	1991	Bray Head Golf (Public Course) at Raheen Park opened by President Mary Robinson
Bus Crash			07	1991	A bus overturned at Jack Whites Inn on the N11 near Arklow
Roads	Thu	24	10	1991	Bray-Shankill By Pass opened by Minister of Environment P. Flynn
Air Crashes	Fri	27	12	1991	Private aircraft crashed at Blessington, Co.Wicklow
Books				1991	Holy Redeemer Church, 1792-1992. a Bray parish. edited by Brendan O'Cathaoir
Arklow Shipping				1991	Arklow Shipping vessel Arklow Dusk built
Arklow Shipping				1991	Arklow Shipping vessel Arklow View built
Delgany Golf Club				1991	Leinster Youths Amateur Open Championship, held at Delgany Golf Club

Books		1991	The Love Story of Parnell & Katharine O'Shea by Margery Brady published Mercier Press
Jones, Kenneth		1991	Kenneth Jones, Organ builder from Bray installed an organ in the River Road, Presbyterian Church, Richmond, USA
Jones, Kenneth		1991	Kenneth Jones, Organ builder from Bray installed an organ in the National Concert Hall, Dublin
Arklow Shipping		1991	Arklow Shipping vessel Wilster built
Woods, Michael		1991	Dr Michael Woods appointed Minister of Agriculture & Food (1991 – 1992)
Tinakilly House		1991	The Power family added an extension to Tinakilly House, Rathnew
Books		1991	Fanny & Anna Parnell by Jane McL. Cote published Gill and Macmillan
Books		1991	Guide to Co. Kildare and West Wicklow by Con Costello
O'Toole, Garry		1991	Garry O'Toole (swimmer) won gold in the 200m breast stroke at World Student Games
Books		1991	Ashford and District Historical Journal
Newspapers		1991	Wicklow Times (Bray) first edition
Newspapers		1991	South and West Wicklow Times (Bray) first edition
Film		1991	The film "The Miracle" set in Bray
Agriculture Census		1991	The Agricultural Census showed 2730 farmers engaged in Agriculture in County Wicklow
Fox, John		1991	John Fox held the post of Chairman of Wicklow County Council 1991–1992
Books		1991	Antiquities of Old Rathdown by Christian Corlett published Wordwell
Aughrim Rangers F.C.		1991	Aughrim Rangers Football Club formed
Delgany Golf Club		1991	Delgany Golf Club won the Barton Cup
Agriculture Census		1991	The average farm size in County Wicklow was 38.1 ha
Fire Station		1991	New Fire station for Bray built on the Boghall Road.
Moran, Joe		1991	Joe Moran of Greystones appointed Chief Executive Officer of the ESB (Electricity Supply Board) 1991 – 1996
Colaiste Raithin		1991	Colaiste Raithin, Bray founded
Tomcork		1991	The church at Tomacork, Carnew was remodelled
de Buitlear, Eamon		1991	Eamon de Buitlear (naturalist and film-maker) granted honurary Dsc at NUI
Homicide in Ireland		1991	Homicide in Ireland between 1972 and 1991. Total 587. The number of killings by men 545 and 42 by women
St. Andrew's School		1991	St. Andrew's School moved to the Newcourt Road, Bray
Cars	01	1992	Car Reg 92 WW 1 issued by Wicklow Motor Tax Office
Kish Lighthouse	03	1992	The Kish Lighthouse was converted to automatic operation and the Keepers were withdrawn from the Lighthouse

A–Z Reference	Day	Date	Month	Year	DATA
Nun's Cross, Ashford	Fri	05	06	1992	The Church of Ireland Primary School at Nun's Cross, Ashford opened by Archbishop of Dublin, Dr. Donal Caird
Elections–Polling Day	Thu	18	06	1992	Polling Day for Constitutional Referenda– Allow ratification of the Maastricht Treaty of European Union
Seaside Festival	Sun	05	07	1992	Bray Seaside Festival 5th July to 12th July 1992
Enniskerry	Sat	01	08	1992	A stolen bus crashed into the Clock Tower, Enniskerry
Seminole County	Mon	07	09	1992	Seminole County near Orlando. USA was twinned with County Wicklow
Flower Festival			09	1992	Flower Festival held in the Holy Redeemer Church, Bray to celebrate the bi- centenary of the of the Holy Redeemer Parish
TD's for Wicklow	Wed	25	11	1992	Polling Day for 27th Dail L.Kavanagh (L) J.Jacob (FF) G.Timmins (FG) L.McManus (DL) J.Fox (Ind)
Elections–Polling Day	Wed	25	11	1992	General Election. Wicklow 5 Seats Electorate 77,133
Elections–Polling Day	Wed	25	11	1992	Polling Day for Constitutional Referenda– Restrict availability of abortion
Elections–Polling Day	Wed	25	11	1992	Polling Day for Constitutional Referenda– Right to travel guarantee
Elections–Polling Day	Wed	25	11	1992	Polling Day for Constitutional Referenda– Right to Information guarantee
Books				1992	A Short History of Gleanealy and its Church of Ireland Parish bicentenary 1792–1992 by R.John.H.Corbett
Woods, Michael				1992	Dr Michael Woods appointed Minister of Marine
Wayman. P.A				1992	Patrick Arthur Wayman (Astronomer) 1992 – 1998 lived in Wicklow Town
Books				1992	The Life of Captain Robert Charles Halpin by Jim Rees published Dee-Jay Publications
Knocksink, Enniskerry				1992	The National Conservation Education Centre at Knocksink Wood, Enniskerry built.
Books				1992	A short history of Gleanealy and its Church of Ireland parish, bicentenary 1792–1992 by John H. Corbett
Wicklow GAA				1992	Wicklow won the All Ireland "B" Football Championship GAA.
Kilcoole Golf Club				1992	Kilcoole Golf Club established
Greystones Golf Club				1992	Leinster Youths Amateur Open Championship, held at Greystones Golf Club
Town Hall. Bray				1992	Under the Urban Renewal Scheme Bray Town Hall was renovated and the Pound and Fire Station closed
Humewood Castle				1992	Humewood Castle, Kiltegan, Co. Wicklow bought by Renata Coleman (Coleman's Mustard)
The European G C				1992	The European Golf Club (Brittas Bay) established
Charlesland G & C Club				1992	Charlesland Golf and Country Club (Greystones) established
Dwyer, Michael				1992	Michael Dwyer's cottage at Derrynamuck, Co. Wicklow re-roofed
Wicklow Film Com.				1992	The County Wicklow Film Commission established
O'Toole. Garry				1992	Gary O'Toole of Bray represented Ireland in swimming at the 1992 Olympic Games held in Barcelona

Film					1992	The film "Far and Away" filmed on locations in Wicklow (Killruddery House), County Kerry and Dublin
Byrne. John					1992	John Byrne held the post of Chairman of Wicklow County Council 1992-1993
General Election					1992	The Minister for Environment and Local Government makes County Wicklow and East Carlow constituency a five seater
Wicklow Rural					1992	Wicklow Rural Partnership evolved from Wicklow Rural Enterprise Ltd.
Arklow Shipping					1992	Arklow Shipping vessel Arklow Freedom built
Arklow Shipping					1992	Arklow Shipping vessel Arklow Fame built
Arklow Shipping					1992	Arklow Shipping vessel Arklow Faith built
Arklow Shipping					1992	Arklow Shipping vessel Arklow Valley built
Travellers Group					1992	Wicklow Travellers Group founded
Film					1992	The film "The Bargain Shop" interior scenes filmed at Ardmore Studio, Bray
Wicklow GAA					1992	Seamus O' Duinn Chairman of Wicklow GAA 1992 - 1994
Wingfield, Shelia					1992	Shelia Wingfield nee Beddington died, wife of 9th Lord Powerscourt
Cars				01	1993	Car Reg 93 WW 1 issued by Wicklow Motor Tax Office
Roads	Fri	12		02	1993	Fassaroe Road Bridge over the M11 near Bray was opened
Dublin California	Tue	02		03	1993	Bray twinned with Dublin, Califorina, U.S.A.
Flood. Francis	Mon	12		04	1993	Francis Flood of Grangecon, Co. Wicklow trained Ebony Jane the winner of the Irish Grand National held at Fairyhouse Racecourse
Air Crashes	Tue	04		05	1993	Cessna Light aircraft crashed landed on Bray Head, The occupants taken to Loughlinstown Hospital
Act	Sat	26		06	1993	Roads Act, enacted by Dail Eireann
Heritage Centre				06	1993	Bray Heritage Centre was opened in the Old Court House, Main Street, Bray
Baltinglass Golf Club					1993	Baltinglass Golf Club won the Barton Cup
Polo					1993	The first indoor arena Polo match in Ireland, was played near Wicklow Town
Woodstock House					1993	Woodstock House and Estate bought by a consortium of business persons
Delgany Golf Club					1993	Leinster Youths Amateur Open Championship, held at Delgany Golf Club, won by K. Nolan, Bray
Books					1993	Wicklow in the Ice Age. an introduction and guide to the glacial geology of the Wicklow district by William P. Warren
Honan. Thomas					1993	Thomas Honan held the post of Chairman of Wicklow County Council 1993-1994
Books					1993	A guide to the archaeology of County Wicklow by Eoin Grogan and Tom Hillery
Beit. Alfred					1993	Sir Alfred Beit and his wife Clemetine made honorary citizens of Ireland
Film					1993	The film" Into the West" filmed on locations in County Wicklow, Dublin, Offaly and Galway

A-Z Reference	Day	Date	Month	Year	DATA
Biggs. Michael				1993	Michael Biggs died and is buried in St Patrick's Graveyard, Enniskerry
Film				1993	The film "The Snapper" interior scenes filmed at Ardmore Studio, Bray
Castlekevin House				1993	The film actor Daniel Day Lewis purchased Castlekevin House
Woods. Michael				1993	Dr Michael Woods appointed Minister of Social Welfare (1993-1994)
Books				1993	Ancient Rathdown and St. Crispin's Cell edited by Chris Small
Jacob.Joe				1993	Joe Jacob TD for Wicklow was appointed Leas-Cheann Comhairle of Dail Eireann 1993-1997
McCormack.William				1993	(Hugh Maxton) William John McCormack wrote "Sheridan le Fanu and Victorian Ireland"
McCormack.William				1993	(Hugh Maxton) William John McCormack wrote "Dublin Paper war of 1786-1788"
Cars			01	1994	Car Reg 94 WW 1 issued by Wicklow Motor Tax Office
Campbell. Flan	Sun	06	03	1994	Flan Campbell died in Dublin
Lighthouse	Sun	31	03	1994	The lighthouse on Wicklow Head built in 1818 was automated
Sport	Sat	07	05	1994	Andy McEvoy (footballer) died at his home in Bray
Beit. Alfred	Thu	12	05	1994	Sir Alfred Beit died
Gillis. Alan	Thu	09	06	1994	Alan Gillis of Grange Con, Co. Wicklow elected as MEP representing Leinster
Elections–Polling Day	Thu	09	06	1994	Local Elections and 4th election of representives to the European Parliament
Ahern. Nuala	Thu	09	06	1994	Nuala Ahern of Greystones, Co. Wicklow elected as MEP representing Leinster
Bray Festival	Sun	03	07	1994	Bray Seaside Festival 3rd to 10th July 1994
Wicklow Rural			09	1994	Wicklow Rural Partnership Limited (WRP) was established for administering the LEADER II Program in Wicklow
Books				1994	The insider's guide to Dublin, Wicklow and the Boyne Valley by Paul Cullen and Ken Boyle
Bray Urban District				1994	Bray Urban District Local Electoral Order 1994
Books				1994	The ecology and management of uplands vegetation in the Wicklow Mountains by Mortimer C.P. Loftus
Wicklow GAA				1994	Jack Boothman of Blessington held the post of President of the GAA 1994-1997
Synge				1994	David M. Kiely published his book John Millington Synge, A Biography
Montigny				1994	Wicklow town twinned with Montigny le Bretonneux, France.-20 miles south west of Paris
Arklow				1994	The alter in the Catholic Church Arklow St. Mary & St. Patrick was rededicated
Glen of Imaal Terrier				1994	The Glen of Imaal Terrier was recognized as a dog breed by the United Kennel Club (U.K.C.)
Books				1994	Wicklow History and Society by Ken Hannigan and William Nolan

Section One: Data by Date

Category	Weekday	Day	Month	Year	Description
Film				1994	The film "Scarlett" filmed in part at Ardmore Studio, Bray and locations scenes at Old Connaught, Bray
McManus Liz				1994	Liz McManus Minister for Housing and Urban Renewal 1994-1997
Books				1994	Geology of Kildare–Wicklow by B.McConnell and M.E. Philcox
Books				1994	The higher lakes of Wicklow by John O. McCormick
Lawlor. Michael				1994	Michael Lawlor held the post of Chairman of Wicklow County Council 1994-1995
Books				1994	Insider's Guide to Dublin, Wicklow, and Boyne Valley by Paul Cullen and Ken Boyle
Books				1994	Emerging from the Shadow. The lives of S.A.Lawerson and L.O.Kingston based on personal diaries 1883-1969 edited D.Swanton
Woods. Michael				1994	Dr Michael Woods appointed Minister of Health (1994)
Books				1994	The Bray Diary 1797-1899 by Francis Loughrey
Owen. Nora				1994	Nora Owen appointed Minister for Justice 1994-1997
Books				1994	Geology of Kildare & Wicklow by B.McConnell and M. E. Philcox
Gaelscoil				1994	Gaelscoil Uí Cheadaigh, Bray founded
Wicklow Golf Club				1994	Wicklow Golf Club extended its 9 hole course to 18 hole course
Film				1994	The film "Braveheart" locations scenes at Ardmore studio, Glendalough, and the Coronation Plantation, Glen of Imaal
Film				1994	The film "Widow's Peak" location scenes at Ballyknockan and Blessington
McCormack. William				1994	(Hugh Maxton) William John McCormack wrote "From Burke to Beckett"
Cars			01	1995	Car Reg 95 WW 1 issued by Wicklow Motor Tax Office
Moore.James	Fri	31	03	1995	James Edward Moore appointed Bishop of Connor
Begles	Fri	05	05	1995	Bray twinned with Begles near Bordeaux, France (Bray Ceremony)
WCEB	Thu	08	06	1995	Wicklow County Enterprise Board was incorporated as a limited company under the Industrial Development Act 1995
TD's for Wicklow	Thu	29	06	1995	By-election M.Fox (Ind)
Wicklow GAA			06	1995	All Ireland Senior "B" Home Final – Hurling. GAA Wicklow 3-12 Kildare 1-8 played in Kilkenny
Trudder House	Thu	07	09	1995	Gardai begin investigating allegations of sexual abuse at Trudder House, a residential home for children near Roundwood
Film	Sun	24	09	1995	The Carlisle Grounds Bray used in the shooting of the film Michael Collins
Elections-Polling Day	Fri	24	11	1995	Polling Day for Constitutional Referenda– Right to divorce
Druids Glen Golf Club				1995	Druids Glen Golf Club established in the grounds of Woodstock Estate, Delgany
Books				1995	Ninety Years of Technical Education in an Irish Maritime Town. Arklow Community College 1905-1995 by N.O'Cleirigh
Rathsallagh Golf Club				1995	Rathsallagh Golf Club (Dunlavin) established

A–Z Reference	Day	Date	Month	Year	DATA
St. Colman's Hospital				1995	Trousers was introduced as part of the nurse's uniform at St. Colman's Hospital Rathdrum
Books				1995	Ninety years of technical education in an Irish maritime town. the story of Arklow Community College 1905-1995 by N O'Cleirigh
Books				1995	A survey of soil and vegetation in the area surrounding the Avoca Mines. Co. Wicklow by C. O'Neill
Lifeboats				1995	An inshore lifeboat D-518 was stationed at Wicklow Town
Greystones Golf Club				1995	Lenister Seniors Amateur Open Championship, held at Greystones Golf Club
Cullen. Thomas				1995	Thomas Cullen held the post of Chairman of Wicklow County Council 1995-1996
Arklow Shipping				1995	Arklow Shipping vessel Arklow Brook built
COI. Carnew				1995	R. E Mates & Son (Dublin) carried out repairs to the church organ in All Saints Church of Ireland, Carnew. Co. Wicklow.
Heaney. Seamus				1995	Seamus Heaney won the Nobel Prize for Literature
Wicklow GAA				1995	Paidraig O Laighleis Chairman of Wicklow GAA 1995 - 1997
Film				1995	The film "Moll Flanders" location scenes at Powerscourt, Brittas Bay and Wicklow Harbour, Old Conna, Bray, Glendalough
Barrett. Daniel				1995	Artist Daniel Barrett receives Schenectady 1995 Cultural Heritage Award
Film				1995	The film "The Van" location scenes at Ardmore studio
Film				1995	The film "The Old Curiosity Shop" location scenes at Ardmore Studio, Killruddery House, Luggala Estate, Wicklow Head
Film				1995	The film "Kidnapped" location scenes at Annamoe, Brittas Bay and Wicklow harbour
Cars		01		1996	Car Reg 96 WW 1 issued by Wicklow Motor Tax Office
St. Peters School		01		1996	St. Peter's School Little Bray damaged by fire
Tinahely		01		1996	Culture & Heritage Centre opened in the old Courthouse in Tinahely
St. Mary's. Enniskerry	Sun	04	02	1996	The Church of St. Mary's Enniskerry re-dedicated by Archbishop of Dublin. Renovations cost £170,000
O'Sandair. Cathal	Sun	18	02	1996	Cathal O'Sandair died in Dublin
Kish Lighthouse	Thu	29	02	1996	The signal from the Kish Lighthouse was changed 2 White Flashes every 30 seconds to 2 White Flashes every 20 seconds
Nevin. Tom	Tue	19	03	1996	Tom Nevin founded murder in his home at Jack's White Inn, Ballinapark, near Brittas Bay, Co. Wicklow
Population Greystones	Sun	28	04	1996	Population of Greystones & Delgany 11,236 or 10.9%. of County Population
Population Arklow	Sun	28	04	1996	Population of Arklow Urban 8,519 or 8.30% of the County Population
Population Roundwood	Sun	28	04	1996	Population of Roundwood 1,624 persons 1.58% of the County Population
Population County	Sun	28	04	1996	Population of County Wicklow 102,683 persons. 50,823 Males 51,860 Females
Population Enniskerry	Sun	28	04	1996	Population of Enniskerry urban 2,118 or 2.06% of County Population

Section One: Data by Date

Population Bray	Sun	28	04	1996	Population of Bray Urban District 25,252 or 24.6% of County Population
Population Rathdrum	Sun	28	04	1996	Population of Rathdrum Rural area 26,9326 or 26.22% of the County Population
Population Shillelagh	Sun	28	04	1996	Population of Shillelagh rural area 6,420 or 6.25% of the County Population
Population Rathdown	Sun	28	04	1996	Population of Rathdown No 2 rural area 16,359 or 15.96% of the County Population
Population Baltinglass	Sun	28	04	1996	Population of Baltinglass No1 rural area 12,749 or 12.41% of the County Population
Population Wicklow (t)	Sun	28	04	1996	Population of Wicklow Town 6,416 or 6.2% of the County Population
Carnew	Fri	10	05	1996	Carnew Enterprise Centre opened
Bray Festival	Sun	07	07	1996	Bray Seaside Festival 7th to 14th July 1996
School, Wicklow Town	Mon	02	09	1996	The Gaelscoil Cill Mhantain in Wicklow Town opened
Henry. Paul	Wed	25	09	1996	The Paul Henry painting the "Potato harvest" was sold in Dublin for £104,000
Parnell. Charles S			09	1996	The Central Bank of Ireland launches its £100 note featuring C.S. Parnell and Avondale House
Elections–Polling Day	Thu	28	11	1996	Polling Day for Constitutional Referenda– Restriction on right to bail
Books				1996	Radon in dwellings, the National Radon Survey Cavan, Dublin, Louth, Monaghan, and Wicklow by J. T. Duffy
Books				1996	The Wicklow world of Elizabeth Smith 1840-1850 edited by Dermot James and Seamus O'Maitiu
Railways				1996	The Government approves the extension of the DART Railway line to Greystones at a cost of £8.7m
Scouting				1996	7th Wicklow Scout Troop (S.A.I.) Blessington Co. Wicklow closed
Powerscourt Golf Club				1996	Powerscourt Golf Club (Enniskerry) established
Gaelscoil				1996	Gaelscoil Cill Mhantain, founded
Arklow Shipping				1996	Arklow Shipping vessel Arklow Bridge built
Greystones Golf Club				1996	Leinster Youths Amateur Open Championship, held at Greystones Golf Club
Roundwood Golf Club				1996	Roundwood Golf Club established
Glen Mill Golf Club				1996	The Glen Mill Golf Club (Newcastle) established
Glen of the Downes				1996	Eco Warriors encamp in the Glen of the Downes to prevent road widening scheme
Timmins. Godfrey				1996	Godfrey Timmins held the post of Chairman of Wicklow County Council 1996-1997
Djouce Mountain G. C.				1996	Djouce Mountain Golf Club (Roundwood) established
Arklow Shipping				1996	Arklow Shipping vessel Arklow Castle built
Druids Glen Golf Club				1996	The Irish Open Golf Championship held at Druid's Glen Golf Club, Delgany
Arklow Shipping				1996	Arklow Shipping vessel Arklow Spray built
Books				1996	A Pictorial History of Kilcoole, Newcastle, NewtownMountKennedy, Glen o'the Downes and Greystones by Derek Paine

The County Wicklow Database: 432 AD to 2006 AD

A–Z Reference	Day	Date	Month	Year	DATA
Wicklow Harbour				1996	Wicklow Harbour Works Order 1996
Books				1996	Wicklow Roots by Wicklow County Genealogical Society
Tate Gallery London				1996	The Tate gallery London purchased Francis Wheatley view of Enniskerry
McCann. W.J.				1996	William J. McCann of Bray appointed Chairman of the ESB (Electricity Supply Board) 1996 - 2001
O'Moore. Sean				1996	Sean O'Moore of Bray carried out a rescue in Bray Harbour. Sean was awarded Bronze Cross for gallantry
O'Moore. Sean				1996	Sean O'Moore of Bray was the first person in Ireland to be presented a Commendation from the Royal Life Saving Society
Film				1996	The film "September" location scenes at Ardmore studio
Film				1996	The BBC Film series "Ballykissangel" 1996–1998 location scenes Avoca, Luggla Estate, Brittas Bay,
Scott. Olive	Fri	17	01	1997	Mrs Olive Moore the wife of Rev F.B. Moore, and the last surviving daughter of Rev George Digby Scott of Bray died
Cars			01	1997	Car Reg 97 WW 1 issued by Wicklow Motor Tax Office
Parking	Mon	17	02	1997	Disc Parking introduced in Bray
VEC. Bray	Fri	21	02	1997	The Minister of Education signs an order to abolish all town Vocational Education Committee's with effect from 01/01/1998
Butler. Eleanor			02	1997	Eleanor Butler Countess of Wicklow died
O'Byrne. Feagh McHugh	Sun	11	05	1997	A monument to Feagh McHugh O'Byrne unveiled at Rathdrum by Brig. General P.D. Hogan
Powerscourt	Thu	22	05	1997	A painting by William Ashford of Powerscourt Demesne was sold at Sotherby's of London
TD's for Wicklow	Fri	06	06	1997	Polling Day for 28th Dail J.Jacob (FF) L.McManus(DL) B.Timmins (FG) M.Fox (Ind) D.Roche (FF)
Queen of Peace, Bray	Fri	06	06	1997	The Archbishop of Dublin Dr. Connell celebrated mass to mark 50 years of Queen of Peace as a Parish, Putland Rd, Bray
Bray Festival	Sun	06	07	1997	Bray Seaside Festival 6th to 13th July 1997
Elections–Polling Day	Thu	30	10	1997	Presidential Election held
Elections–Polling Day	Thu	30	10	1997	Polling Day for Constitutional Referenda- Cabinet Confidentiality
Cattle				1997	The total number of Heifers in calf in County Wicklow 6,700
Sheep				1997	The Total number of Sheep in County Wicklow 526,500 including 272,700 Ewes
Druids Glen Golf Club				1997	The Irish Open Golf Championship held at Druid's Glen Golf Club, Delgany
Books				1997	Baronies of Sheilelagh & Ballinacor South, 1837. by National Archives
Cattle				1997	The total number of beef cows in County Wicklow 25,400
Avoca				1997	Avoca, Co. Wicklow twinned with Bromham, Wiltshire, England
Books				1997	The Tellicherry V The transportation of Michael Dwyer & Wicklow Rebels by Kieran Sheedy

Section One: Data by Date

Category	Year	Event
Woods. Michael	1997	Dr Michael Woods appointed Minister of Marine and Natural Resources (1997–1999)
Cattle	1997	The total number of bulls in County Wicklow 1,000
Tillage Barley	1997	The total number of hectares in County Wicklow under Barley 6,300
La Touche	1997	The Bank of Ireland purchased in London the Amorino Marble statue for £520,000, commissioned by David La Touche in 1792
Books	1997	Ballyknockan a Wicklow Stonecutter's Village by Seamas O'Maitiu and Barry O'Reilly
Softball Club	1997	Bray Allsorts Softball Club founded
Tillage Wheat	1997	The total number of hectares in County Wicklow under Wheat 4,900
Cattle	1997	The total number of cattle 1–2 years in County Wicklow 31,600
Cattle	1997	The total number of cattle under 1 year in County Wicklow 31,700
Books	1997	Chemistry of precipitation, through fall and soil water, Cork, Wicklow and Galway regions by E.P. Farrell
Bray Softball Club	1997	The Bray Allsorts Softball Club founded
Books	1997	This way up, access routes into the Wicklow Mountains by David Herman
Books	1997	This Way Up access routes into the Wicklow Mountains by David Herman
Lifeboats	1997	An new access ramp to the moorings installed at Arklow Lifeboat Station.
St.Fergals Boxing Club	1997	St. Fergals Boxing Club Bray founded
Vance. Pat	1997	Pat Vance held the post of Chairman of Wicklow County Council 1997-1998
Books	1997	Wicklow Mountains National Park study, prepared for the Department of Arts Culture and the Gaeltacht by firm RPS Cairns
Green. Christy	1997	Christy Green (Golfer) died
Tinakilly House	1997	The Power family added an extension to the East wing of Tinakilly House, Rathnew
Cattle	1997	The total number of cattle over 2 years in County Wicklow 16,500
Housing	1997	Building of apartments at the Lithographic site on the Dargle Road
Mountain Rescue	1997	The Dublin & Wicklow Mountain Rescue Team responded to 47 callouts
Litographic	1997	Lithographic Ltd move to a new building on the Southern Cross Route, Bray
Books	1997	Baronies of Shillelagh & Ballinacor South, Co. Wicklow: a memorial, 1837 extracted (O.P.1837/133) National Archives of Ireland
Books	1997	Archaeological inventory of County Wicklow. compiled by Eoin Grogan and Annaba Kilfeather
Cattle	1997	The total number of dairy cows in County Wicklow 21,300
Film	1997	The film "Oliver Twist" location scenes at Ardmore Studio and Killruddery House
Film	1997	The film "Mystic Knights" location scenes at Ardmore Studio, Greystones, Belmont House, and Kilcoole

A–Z Reference	Day	Date	Month	Year	DATA
Film				1997	The film "The Boxer" location scenes at Ardmore studio
Film				1997	The film "The Butcher Boy" location scenes at Ardmore studio
VEC. Bray	Thu	01	01	1998	Bray Vocational Education Committee taken under control of the County Vocational Education Committee
Cars			01	1998	Car Reg 98 WW 1 issued by Wicklow Motor Tax Office
Glencree	Fri	06	02	1998	Dr Mo Mowlan and Liz O'Donnell opened the "Wicklow wing" of the Glencree Reconciliation Centre in honour of Lady Wicklow
Bray. Seafront	Thu	23	04	1998	Bray Sea life Centre opened by President Mary McAleese
Elections–Polling Day	Mon	22	06	1998	Polling Day for Constitutional Referenda- Northern Ireland Agreement
Elections–Polling Day	Mon	22	06	1998	Polling Day for Constitutional Referenda- Ratification of Amsterdam Treaty
Act	Wed	01	07	1998	Roads (Amendment) Act, enacted by Dail Eireann
Quigley. D.B	Fri	03	07	1998	Bray man Dermot B. Quigley appointed Chairman of the board of Revenue Commissioners
Bray Festival	Sun	05	07	1998	Bray Seaside Festival 5th to 12th July 1998
Bowling Championships	Mon	27	07	1998	The Bowling League of Ireland Championships held at Failte Park, Bray between 27/07/1998 and 01/08/1998
Arklow Pottery			08	1998	Arklow Pottery was in financial difficulties and liquidators appointed
Kinsella. Tommy			08	1998	Tommy Kinsella retired as an alter server in the Holy Redremmer Church, Bray
Bray. Seafront			09	1998	Coastal Erosion scheme at Bray Seafront commenced
La Touche	Wed	11	11	1998	The marble statue of Amorino went on display in the National Gallery of Ireland
Brabazon. Geoffery	Mon	23	11	1998	Geoffery Brabazon grandson of 14th Earl of Meath died while felling trees in Co. Meath
Brabazon. Anthony	Sat	19	12	1998	Anthony Brabazon the 14th Earl of Meath died and was succeeded by John Anthony Brabazon 15th Earl of Meath
Wayman. P.A	Mon	21	12	1998	Patrick Arthur Wayman (Astronomer) died in Dublin
Books				1998	County Wicklow, Arklow Town Family Roots by Noel Farrell
Roads				1998	Road widening scheme at Loughlinstown, Co Dublin
Books				1998	Victorian Bray by Liam Clare, Maynooth Studies in Local History
Tidy Towns				1998	Bray earned 208 marks in Bord Failte Tidy Towns Competition
Arklow Shipping				1998	Arklow Shipping vessel Arklow Sand built
Industrial Yarns				1998	Industrial Yarns Ltd Dublin Road, Bray ceased trading
Books				1998	Wicklow County arts directory edited by Jessica Fuller
Books				1998	Stream of gliding sun. a Wicklow anthology. edited by David Wheatley

Section One: Data by Date

Category	Year	Description
Books	1998	Rebellion in Wicklow. General Joseph Holt's personal account 1798. edited by Peter O'Shaughnessy
Arklow Shipping	1998	Arklow Shipping vessel Arklow Sea built
Books	1998	Dublin & South Eastern Railway by Ernie Shepherd and Gerry Beesley published Midland Press
Books	1998	Turn of the tide by Joan O'Neill
O'Toole. Garry	1998	Gary O'Toole of Bray represented Ireland in swimming at the 1988 Olympic Games held in Seoul
Books	1998	The rebellion in Wicklow 1798 by Ruan O'Donnell
Film	1998	The film "Glendalough – Mystical Journey" released
Gaelscoil	1998	Gaelscoil Inbhir Mhoir, founded
Maps	1998	Irish Historic Town Atlas Number 9 Bray by K.M. Davies published Royal Irish Academy
Books	1998	Stream and Gliding Sun a Wicklow Anthology edited by David Wheatley
St. Gerard's School	1998	Gerard Foley headmaster of St. Gerard's School. Bray. 1998 –
Wicklow Gaol	1998	Restoration work on Wicklow Gaol was completed and opened by President of Ireland Mary McAleese
Books	1998	Kilcoole, County Wicklow History and Folklore by Robert Jennings
Bray Urban District	1998	Bray Urban District Local Electoral Areas Order 1998
Books	1998	County Wicklow Arts Directory editor Jessica Fuller
Books	1998	I am the Crocus poems by children from County Wicklow edited by David Wheatly
Ecology Centre	1998	The Dominican Sisters established the Dominican Farm and Ecology Centre in Wicklow Town
Books	1998	Rebellion in Wicklow –General Holt's personal Account of 1798 edited by Peter O'Shaughnessy
Books	1998	Avoca– our mining heritage a brief history of metal mining in the Vale of Avoca, Co. Wicklow by A. Thomas and P. McArdle
Kavanagh. Liam	1998	Liam Kavanagh held the post of Chairman of Wicklow County Council 1998-1999
Glen of the Downes	1998	Glen of the Downes Golf Club, Coolnaskeagh, Delgany. Established
Boystown Golf Club	1998	Boystown Golf Club, Baltyboys, Blessington, Co. Wicklow established.
Druids Glen Golf Club	1998	The Irish Open Golf Championship held at Druid's Glen Golf Club, Delgany
County Wicklow	1998	County of Wicklow Local Electoral Areas Order 1998
Meath Hospital	1998	The Meath Hospital joined with a number of other Dublin hospitals and moved to a new hospital at Tallaght
Film	1998	The film "Durango" location scenes at Ardmore studio, Arklow, Glencree/Sally Gap, Glenmalure, Kilbride, Kippure, Redcross, Rathdrum, Hollywood
Film	1998	The film "Night Train" location scenes at Ardmore Studio
Wicklow GAA	1998	Michael O hAgain Chairman of Wicklow GAA 1998 - 2000
Film	1998	The film "The Nephew" locations scenes used included Enniskerry, Altidore castle Kilpedder, Luggala Estate Roundwood and Wicklow Town

A–Z Reference	Day	Date	Month	Year	DATA
Film				1998	The film "Sweeney Todd" location scenes at Ardmore studio
Arklow By-Pass	Fri	29	01	1999	Arklow By-Pass opened
Cars			01	1999	Car Reg 99 WW 1 issued by Wicklow Motor Tax Office
Post Office	Tue	09	03	1999	A new Post Office opened at Church Road, Greystones by Joe Jacob, Minister of State at Dept. of Public Enterprise
Kinsella. Tommy	Thu	01	04	1999	Tommy Kinsella died
Arklow Pottery			04	1999	Arklow Pottery ceased production
Sport	Sun	09	05	1999	FAI Cup Final at Tolka Park –Bray Wanderers 0 Finn Harps 0
Sport	Sat	15	05	1999	FAI Cup Final Replay at Tolka Park. Bray Wanderers 2 Finn Harps 2 after extra time
Bewley. Victor	Wed	19	05	1999	Victor Bewley died
Sport	Thu	20	05	1999	FAI CUP Final 2nd Replay Bray Wanderers 2 Finn Harps 1
Elections-Polling Day	Fri	11	06	1999	Polling Day for Constitutional Referenda- Local Government
Youth Hostel	Sat	19	06	1999	Glendalough An Oige Hostel opened by Mark Mortell of Bord Failte
Loughman. Joe	Sat	03	07	1999	Joe Loughman (cyclist and historian) died
British Navy	Mon	12	07	1999	Four British Navy Patrol Vessels visited Wicklow Harbour the first since 1920's
McCabe. Peter			07	1999	Rev. Peter McCabe Parish Priest of Enniskerry Parish retired
Ballywaltrim Sports	Wed	04	08	1999	The official opening of the Ballywaltrim Sport Complex, Bray
Goulet. Yann Renard	Sun	22	08	1999	Yann Renard Goulet died.
Goulet. Yann Renard	Wed	25	08	1999	Goulet. Yann Renard obituarity appeared in The Irish Times Newspaper
City of Wurtzburg	Tue	02	11	1999	Bray and County Wicklow twinned with the City of Wurzburg, Germany (Bray Ceremony)
Tinnehinch House			11	1999	Tinnehinch House, Enniskerry (once the home of H. Grattan) put up for sale
Glen of the Downes	Tue	07	12	1999	Wicklow County Officials begin felling of trees in the Glen of the Downes for road widening scheme
Tinnehinch House			12	1999	Tinnehinch House, Enniskerry (once the home of H. Grattan) sold for £1.9m
Ships/Yachts			12	1999	The barge Skerchi working on Bray Coastal Protection Scheme broke its moorings
Bray Tennis Club				1999	New Club house erected at Bray Tennis Club, Vevay Road Bray
Police/Garda				1999	Work began on the extension of Bray Garda Station at Convent Avenue, Bray
Books				1999	Wicklow Gold by Ray Cranley
Books				1999	Through the eyes of Emerald- a short history of Wicklow Town by Class 4 Dominican College Wicklow

Section One: Data by Date

Arklow Shipping				1999	Arklow Shipping vessel Arklow Star built
Books				1999	The Buildings of Clara Vale by Pat Dargan
Druids Glen Golf Club				1999	The Irish Open Golf Championship held at Druid's Glen Golf Club, Delgany
St.Mary Convent. Arklow				1999	St. Mary's Convent Arklow used as one of the locations for the film Angles Ashes
St. Cronan's BNS Bray				1999	St. Cronan's Boys National School move to a new school on the Vevay Road, Bray
Sport				1999	Bray Tennis Club building restored
Woods. Michael				1999	Dr Michael Woods appointed Minister of Education and Science (1999 - 2002)
Mountain Rescue				1999	The Dublin & Wicklow Mountain Rescue Team responded to 37 callouts
Roads				1999	Arklow Road By Pass on the N11 completed
Glencormac United F.C.				1999	Glencormac United Football Club Kilmacanogue formed
Books				1999	Through the eyes of Emerald. a short history of Wicklow Town, by class 4 Emerald (1998-99) Dominican College Wicklow.
Greystones Rugby Club				1999	Greystones Rugby Club won the Metropolitan Cup
Film				1999	The film "Animal Farm" location scenes at Ardmore studio and Roundwood
Film				1999	The film "The Unexpected Mrs Pollifax" location scenes at Ardmore studio , Enniskerry and Roundwood
Cars			01	2000	Car Reg 00 WW 1 issued by Wicklow Motor Tax Office
Stuart. Francis	Wed	02	02	2000	Francis Stuart died
Ships/Yachts	Thu	03	02	2000	The cargo ship Asian Parade ran aground on the codling bank six miles east of Greystones
Bus Crash	Mon	14	02	2000	A double deck bus crashed into a bridge near Bray Railway Station
Nevin. Catherine	Mon	14	02	2000	Catherine Nevin goes on trial at the Central Criminal Court for the murder of her husband Tom in March 1996
St. Cronan's BNS Bray			03	2000	The premises occupied by St Cronan's Boys National School from 1932-1999 put up for sale
Ships/Yachts	Mon	03	04	2000	A barge (Ascon Skerchi) working on Bray Coastal Protection Scheme, broke its moorings in a gale and drifted onto the shore
Railways	Mon	10	04	2000	Greystones commuters provided with a limited DART Service
Nevin. Catherine	Tue	11	04	2000	Catherine Nevin found guilty of murder of her husband Tom
St. Cronan's BNS Bray			04	2000	The Department of Education and Science purchase the Old ST. Cronan's BNS for Gaelscoil Ui Cheadaigh, Bray
Old Connaught House			04	2000	Old Connaught House put up for sale
Le Brocquy. Louis			05	2000	The painting "Travelling Woman with Newspaper" by Louis Le Brocquy fetched £1.15 million sterling at auction in London
Blue Flag			06	2000	Blue Flags were awarded to the following beach's in Co. Wicklow, Brittas Bay North & South, Greystones South, Bray Prom
Agriculture Census			06	2000	The Agricultural Census showed 2410 farmers engaged in Agriculture in County Wicklow

A-Z Reference	Day	Date	Month	Year	DATA
Agriculture Census			06	2000	The average farm size in County Wicklow was 42.2 ha
Library. County	Wed	05	07	2000	County Wicklow Library Head quarters on the Boghall Road, Bray opened by the Minister of The Environment Noel Dempsy
Wicklow County Show	Mon	07	08	2000	The 65th Annual Wicklow County Show held at Tinahely
St Patricks School	Thu	10	08	2000	Part of St Patrick's School Bray destroyed by fire
Roads	Mon	28	08	2000	Wicklow County Council Compulsory Purchase (Newtownmountkennedy to Ballynabarny Road Improvement Scheme) No. 2 Order
Post Office	Fri	29	09	2000	A new Postal Delivery Office was opened at the Murrough, Wicklow by Joe Jacob, Minister of State at Dept. of Public Enterprise
Wicklow GAA			09	2000	Bray Emmets GAA Club hold the inaugural Kick Fada competition in Emmet Park, Bray. Winner Mark Herbert
Flower Festival			09	2000	Flower Festival held in the Holy Redeemer Church, Bray to celebrate the Millennium
Powerscourt			10	2000	The war medals of Mervyn Patrick Wingfield 9th Viscount Powerscourt sold at auction in London
Weather	Sun	05	11	2000	Bray Seafront and Arklow flooded. Photo of Bray Seafront on front cover of Evening Herald 06/11/2000
Brabazon. John	Thu	07	12	2000	Ballinacor House, Greenan, Rathdrum was put up for sale by the Earl of Meath (Picture and Details Irish Times, Property Section)
Railways	Fri	08	12	2000	Landslide at Killiney all Dart and Rail Services between Dalkey and Bray cancelled
Railways	Fri	15	12	2000	Rail services south of Killiney resumed following the landslide of 08/12/2000
Library. Bray	Fri	29	12	2000	A Branch Library of Bray Library opened on Boghall Road, Bray
Fitzpatrick. Hubert				2000	Hubert Fitzpatrick appointed (Acting) County Manager of Wicklow (Local Government) December 2000
Books				2000	Images of Ireland, South Dublin from the Liffey to Greystones compiled by Derek Stanley
Maps				2000	County Wicklow in 1861 by K.M. Davies published Wordwell
Maps				2000	Heffernan's 1876 illustrated plan of Bray by K.M. Davies published Wordwell
Woodbrook Golf Club				2000	Two pedestrian underpasses constructed under the railway line at Woodbrook Golf Club
Jones. George				2000	George Jones held the post of Chairman of Wicklow County Council 2000-2001
Books				2000	Surplus people. the Fitzwilliam clearances 1847-1956 by Jim Rees
Baltinglass Hospital				2000	Baltinglass Hospital administration changed from Eastern Health Board to the South Western Area Health Board
St. Peter's F.C.				2000	St. Peter's Football Club Bray formed
Arklow Celtic F.C.				2000	Arklow Celtic Football Club formed
Loreto Convent Bray				2000	Loreto Convent, Bray won the All Ireland Schools' Hockey Championship (Leinster Senior Cup)
Mountain Rescue				2000	The Dublin & Wicklow Mountain Rescue Team responded to 20 callouts

Keyword	Year	Month	Weekday	Day	Event
Crampton Collection	2000				The National Library of Ireland purchased 21 drawings by John Crampton and 15 drawings by Selina Crampton
Bray Musical Society	2000				Bray Musical Society stages "Hello Dolly"
Wicklow Town	2000				Parking Disc system introduced in Wicklow Town
Books	2000				Canon Frederick Donovan's Dunlavin, 1884–1896; a west Wicklow village in nineteenth century by Chris Lawlor
Cars	2001	01			Car Reg 01 WW 1 issued by Wicklow Motor Tax Office
Young Scientist	2001	01			S.Browne, P.Taylor, M.O'Toole won the Young Scientist of the Year project Investigating symmetrical shapes formed by polygons
Foot & Mouth Scare	2001	02			Due to a Foot and Mouth scare many sport fixtures in County Wicklow called off, and tourist attractions closed
De Valois. N	2001	03	Thu	08	Dame Ninette De Valois (Edris Stannus) died in London
Bray Harbour	2001	03			The Goverment announces a Grant of £625,000 for repair work to Bray Harbour
St. Therese of Lisieux	2001	04	Sat	07	The reliquary of St. Therese of Lisieux, arrived at the Carmelite Convent, Delgany, where it remained for 22 hours
St. Therese of Lisieux	2001	04	Sun	08	The reliquary of St. Therese of Lisieux, departed at the Carmelite Convent, Delgany, where it had remained for 22 hours
Timmins. Godfrey	2001	04	Wed	11	Godfrey Timmins died
Books	2001	05	Mon	14	The Ordnance Survey Letters – Wicklow published
Avoca	2001	05	Tue	22	Fire destroys the Vale View Hotel, Avoca
Sunnybank, Bray	2001	05			Fire destroys the former Sunnybank Inn Bray.
Honner.Thomas	2001	05			Thomas Honner of Kiltegan elected the 29th President of Macra na Feirme
Byrne. Shane	2001	06	Sat	02	Shane Byrne of Aughrim Co. Wicklow got his Irish International Rugby Debut against Romania
Elections–Polling Day	2001	06	Thu	07	Voting on 24th Amendment of the Constitution Bill, 2001–The Treaty of Nice
Elections–Polling Day	2001	06	Thu	07	Voting on 23rd Amendment of the Constitution Bill, 2001–Acceptanance of the Jurisdiction of the International Criminal Court
Elections–Polling Day	2001	06	Thu	07	Voting on 21st Amendment of the Constitution (No. 2) Bill, 2001 Abolition of Death Penalty
Elections–Polling Day	2001	06	Fri	08	Voting on 2001–The Treaty of Nice, Electorate Wicklow 85,067. Total Poll 32,587, Yes 14,839 (46.2%) No 17,274(53.7%)
O'Connor.Joyce	2001	06	Mon	11	Joyce O'Connor nee Fitzpatrick of Bray appointed chairperson of FETAC by Minister of Education
Wicklow 200 Km	2001	06	Sun	17	The 19th Wicklow 200 km – Wicklow Gap Challenge Cycling Event
St. Cronan's BNS Bray	2001	06	Mon	18	Minister of Education Dr. Michael Woods opens the new St. Cronan's BNS on the Vevay Road, Bray
Historical Society	2001	06	Mon	25	Bray Cualann Historical Society published its 4th Historical Journal
Russborough House	2001	06	Tue	26	2 paintings stolen from Russborough House, Blessington
Bray Festival	2001	07	Sun	01	Bray Seaside Festival 1st to 8th July 2001

A–Z Reference	Day	Date	Month	Year	DATA
Compulsory Purchase	Thu	05	07	2001	Wicklow County Council Compulsory Purchase (Kilcoole) No. 1 Order, 2001
Greystones	Fri	06	07	2001	The refurbished Railway Station at Greystones opened
Carlisle Grounds	Thu	26	07	2001	The Minister for Sport Dr McDaid announced £200,000 Sport Capital Grant for improvements at the Carlisle Grounds, Bray
O'Shaughnessy. Jimmy			07	2001	Jimmy O'Shaughnessy held the post of Chairman of Wicklow County Council 2001-2002
Carnew Playschool	Mon	24	09	2001	The Little Acorns Community Playschool opened in Carnew
Bray Civic Centre	Thu	27	09	2001	The foundation stone of Bray Civic Centre unveiled by Taoiseach Bertie Ahern
Wicklow GAA			09	2001	Bray Emmets GAA Club hold Kick Fada competition in St Thomas's College, Bray. Winner Mark Herbert
Dunlavin	Mon	22	10	2001	Illegally dumped hospital waste found near Dunlavin, Co. Wicklow
Loreto Convent Bray			10	2001	An Astroturf Pitch opened at Loreto Convent, Bray
Lamb. Charles Vincent			10	2001	Charles Vincent Lamb oil on canvas "The Farmstead, Wicklow Hills" sold for 4316
Railways	Thu	08	11	2001	A runaway train at Arklow, Halted 3 miles north of Arklow.
Presentation College	Mon	19	11	2001	Minister of Education Dr. Michael Woods announced £5m school building programme for Presentation College, Bray
Donard	Wed	21	11	2001	Illegally dumped hospital waste found near Donard, Co. Wicklow
Euro Coins	Fri	14	12	2001	Euro Coins starter packs go on sale in Banks and Post Offices. The Euro becomes legal tender in 12 countries from 01/01/2002
Rathnew	Sun	16	12	2001	GAA Lenister Club Championship Final held in Newbridge, Co. Kildare Na Finna(Dublin) 1-6 Rathnew(Wicklow) 0-9 a draw
BUDC	Tue	18	12	2001	S.I.591/2001 of 18/12/1001 gave effect with 1/01/2002 the change Bray Urban District Council to Bray Town Council
Arklow Town Council	Tue	18	12	2001	S.I.591/2001 of 18/12/1001 gave effect with 1/01/2002 the change Arklow Urban District Council to Arklow Town Council
Wicklow Town Council	Tue	18	12	2001	S.I.591/2001 of 18/12/1001 gave effect with 1/01/2002 the change Wicklow Urban District Council to Wicklow Town Council
Rathnew	Sun	23	12	2001	GAA Lenister Club Championship Final (replay) held in Newbridge, Co. Kildare Na Finna(Dublin) 1-10 Rathnew(Wicklow) 2-16
Books				2001	National Childcare Census report. County Wicklow by Department of Justice, Equality and Law reform
Books				2001	Old Ironsides (a book about the Stewart and Parnell Families) by Colin Stewart and Jean Costelloe
Sheehy. Eddie				2001	Eddie Sheehy appointed County Manager of Wicklow (Local Government)
Avonmore F.C.				2001	Avonmore Football Club Rathdrum formed
BBK United				2001	BBK United Football Club Brittas Bay formed
Tidy Towns				2001	Aughrim earned 258 marks in the Tidy Towns Competition
Tidy Towns				2001	Stratford on Slaney earned 228 marks in the Tidy Towns Competition

Tidy Towns				2001	Enniskerry earned 224 marks in the Tidy Towns Competition
Bray Musical Society				2001	Bray Musical Society stages "Chess"
Loreto Convent Bray				2001	Loreto Convent, Bray won the All Ireland Schools' Hockey Championship (Leinster Senior Cup)
Railways				2001	New footbridge at Bray Railway station
Putland Road				2001	New housing scheme called Headlands built in the grounds of Presentation College, Putland Road, Bray
Kinsella. Tommy				2001	Page 49 of the 2001 Guinness Book of Records. Tommy Kinsella is shown as the longest serving alter boy in the world
Wicklow GAA				2001	Donal Mac Giolla Chuda Chairman of Wicklow GAA 2001 - 2003
Tree Survey				2001	The tallest tree in Ireland Pseudotsuga menziesii (Douglas Fir) on Powerscourt Estate, Enniskerry 56 meters Ref: Tree Council of Ireland
Books				2001	Wire Ropes Ltd, Wicklow 1951-2001 author Andrew O'Brien
Currency	Tue	01	01	2002	The Euro currency notes and coins becomes legal tender in 12 countries
Cars			01	2002	Car Reg 02 WW 1 issued by Wicklow Motor Tax Office
Greystones			01	2002	Greystones granted Town Council status
Roads	Thu	07	02	2002	Wicklow County Council sign contracts with John Sisks Ltd and S.M. Morris to build Ashford-Rathnew By Pass, Cost 94m Euro
Caprani	Sat	09	02	2002	Caprani Pork Butchers, Main Street, Bray ceased trading after 70 years
Royal Visit	Fri	15	02	2002	Prince Charles and Brian Cowen Minister for Foreign Affairs jointly opened the new Bridge Building at Glencree Centre
Elections-Polling Day	Wed	06	03	2002	Wicklow Electorate 86,763 Total Poll 41,041 Yes 16,788 No.24,032
Elections-Polling Day	Wed	06	03	2002	Polling Day for Referendum 25th Amendment of the Constitution (Protection of Human Life in Pregnancy) Bill, 2001
Quigley. D.B	Wed	06	03	2002	Dermot Quigley retired as Chairman of the Revenue Commissioners
Troy. Aidan	Fri	12	04	2002	Fr. Aidan Troy a past pupil of St. Brendan's College, Bray. was Honoured at a function in Bray.
Population Shillelagh	Sun	28	04	2002	Population of Shillelagh rural area 6,708 or 5.84% of the County Population
Population Bray	Sun	28	04	2002	Population of Bray Urban District 26,215 or 22.8% of the County Population
Population Greystones	Sun	28	04	2002	Population of Greystones & Delgany 11,871 or 10.3%.of the County Population
Population Arklow	Sun	28	04	2002	Population of Arklow Urban 9,963 or 8.68% of the County Population
Population Enniskerry	Sun	28	04	2002	Population of Enniskerry urban 2,804 or 1.84% of the County Population
Population County	Sun	28	04	2002	Population of County Wicklow 114,676 persons. 56,800 Males 57,876 Females
Population Wicklow (t)	Sun	28	04	2002	Population of Wicklow Town 7,007 or 6.10% of County Population
Population Baltinglass	Sun	28	04	2002	Population of Baltinglass No1 rural area 14,715 or 12.82% of the County Population
Population	Sun	28	04	2002	Census of Population in Ireland

A-Z Reference	Day	Date	Month	Year	DATA
Population Rathdown	Sun	28	04	2002	Population of Rathdown No 2 rural area 19,025 or 16.58% of the County Population
Population Rathdrum	Sun	28	04	2002	Population of Rathdrum Rural area 31,086 or 27.09% of the County Population
Population County	Sun	28	04	2002	Number of private households County Wicklow with a personal computer and internet access 36,138
Druids Glen Hotel			04	2002	The Druid's Glen Marriott Hotel and Country Club opened
Books			04	2002	"Blessington Now and Then" compiled by the Members of The Blessington Local and Family History Society
Henry. Paul	Wed	08	05	2002	The 1931 painting by Paul Henry of "Trees, Co. Wicklow" went on sale in Dublin on 08/05/2002
Elections-Polling Day	Fri	17	05	2002	Polling Day for 29th Dail D Roche(FF) L. McManus(Lab) B.Timmins(FG) J.Jacob(FF) M. Fox (Ind)
Elections-Polling Day	Fri	17	05	2002	General Election for 29th Dail
Elections-Polling Day	Sat	18	05	2002	Counting of the Votes of General Election 17/05/2002, Electorate 86,763, Total Poll 55,283, Turnout 62.72%
Elections-Polling Day	Sun	19	05	2002	1st Recount of votes cast on 17/05/2002
Elections-Polling Day	Thu	23	05	2002	2nd Recount of votes cast on 17/05/2002 completed 25th May 2002
Roche. Dick	Thu	06	06	2002	Dick Roche TD for Wicklow & East Carlow appointed Minister of State at the Department of the Taoiseach
Bray Traffic Plan	Fri	14	06	2002	Proposed Traffic Management Plan for Bray Town Centre announced
Wicklow 200 Km	Sun	16	06	2002	The 20th Wicklow 200 km -Wicklow Gap Challenge Cycling Event
Bray Arts Centre	Thu	27	06	2002	The Mermaid Arts Centre, Bray officially opened
Blue Flag			06	2002	Blue Flags were awarded to the following beach's in Co. Wicklow, Brittas Bay North & South, Greystones South
Delgany			06	2002	The Archbishop of Dublin and Glendalough opened an extension to Delgany National School
Bray Festival	Sun	07	07	2002	Bray Seaside Festival 7th July to 14th July 2002
McShane. Paul	Mon	08	07	2002	Paul McShane signed for the Manchester United Football Club (academy)
Arklow	Thu	18	07	2002	Arklow Seabreeze Festival 18/07/2002- 21/07/2002
Post Office	Mon	29	07	2002	A new sub-Post Office opened at 97 Main Street, Bray
Byrne. John			07	2002	Cllr. John Byrne appointed Catharoirleach of Bray Town Council
Blake. Vincent			07	2002	Vincent Blake held the post of Chairman of Wicklow County Council 2002-2003
Greystones	Fri	02	08	2002	Greystones Arts Festival 2nd-5th August 2002
County Show	Mon	05	08	2002	The 67th Annual Wicklow County Show held in Tinahely
Oranmore. Lord	Wed	07	08	2002	Dominick Geoffrey Edward Browne, Lord Oranmore died
Bray Arts Centre	Sat	31	08	2002	The 242 seater Mermaid Arts Centre, Bray opened to the public

Section One: Data by Date

Name	Day		Month	Year	Description
Blessington Fire Stn.			08	2002	Wicklow County Council invite tenders to build a fire station in Blessington
Order of Malta, Bray			08	2002	Bray Order of Malta take delivery of a new Ambulance and minibus
Wicklow GAA	Sat	14	09	2002	Bray Emmets GAA Club hold Kick Fada competition in St Thomas's College, Bray. Winner Mark Herbert
Russborough House	Sun	29	09	2002	5 paintings stolen from Russborough House, Blessington
Bray Head			09	2002	The Eagles Nest property on Bray Head put up for sale with a price tag of 2.5m Euro
Baltinglass Fire Stn			09	2002	The Department Environment and Local Government approved a grant of 46,000 Euro to build a drill tower at Baltinglass Fire Stn.
Bray Fire Stn.			09	2002	The Department Environment and Local Government approved a grant of 20,000 Euro for upgrading facilities at Bray Fire Station
Forestry	Tue	08	10	2002	Forestry planting of Other Conifers, 741 (net area ha.) in County Wicklow *stats provided by Coilte
Forestry	Tue	08	10	2002	County Wicklow has 26250 (Net area ha.) of Forestry. 1920-1929 (Net area ha) 69 *Stats provided by Coilte
Forestry	Tue	08	10	2002	County Wicklow has 26250 (Net area ha.) of Forestry. Pre 1920 (Net area ha.) 379 *Stats provided by Coilte
Forestry	Tue	08	10	2002	Forestry planting of Douglas Fir, 1921 (net area ha.) in County Wicklow *stats provided by Coilte
Forestry	Tue	08	10	2002	Forestry planting of Scots Pine, 1131 (net area ha.) in County Wicklow *stats provided by Coilte
Forestry	Tue	08	10	2002	Forestry planting of Larches, 1295 (net area ha.) in County Wicklow *stats provided by Coilte
Forestry	Tue	08	10	2002	County Wicklow has 26250 (Net area ha.) of Forestry *Stats provided by Coilte
Forestry	Tue	08	10	2002	Forestry planting of Stika Spruce, 18343 (net area ha.) in County Wicklow *stats provided by Coilte
Forestry	Tue	08	10	2002	Forestry planting of Norway Spruce, 981 (net area ha.) in County Wicklow *stats provided by Coilte
Forestry	Tue	08	10	2002	Forestry planting of Lodgepole Pine, 522(net area ha.) in County Wicklow *stats provided by Coilte
Forestry	Tue	08	10	2002	Forestry planting of Broadleaf , 1314(net area ha.) in County Wicklow *stats provided by Coilte
Forestry	Tue	08	10	2002	County Wicklow has 26250 (Net area ha.) of Forestry. 1970-1979 (Net area ha) 4359 *Stats provided by Coilte
Forestry	Tue	08	10	2002	County Wicklow has 26250 (Net area ha.) of Forestry. 1980-1989 (Net area ha) 4892 *Stats provided by Coilte
Forestry	Tue	08	10	2002	County Wicklow has 26250 (Net area ha.) of Forestry. 1960-1969 (Net area ha) 4626 *Stats provided by Coilte
Forestry	Tue	08	10	2002	County Wicklow has 26250 (Net area ha.) of Forestry. 1990-1999 (Net area ha) 6569 *Stats provided by Coilte
Forestry	Tue	08	10	2002	County Wicklow has 26250 (Net area ha.) of Forestry. 2000-2002 (Net area ha) 614 *Stats provided by Coilte
Forestry	Tue	08	10	2002	County Wicklow has 26250 (Net area ha.) of Forestry. 1950-1959 (Net area ha) 3608 *Stats provided by Coilte
Forestry	Tue	08	10	2002	County Wicklow has 26250 (Net area ha.) of Forestry. 1940-1949 (Net area ha) 662 *Stats provided by Coilte
Forestry	Tue	08	10	2002	County Wicklow has 26250 (Net area ha.) of Forestry. 1930-1939 (Net area ha) 472 *Stats provided by Coilte
IFI	Wed	16	10	2002	IFI announces the closure of its Fertiliser plants in Cork, Belfast and Arklow Co. Wicklow with the loss of 620 jobs

A–Z Reference	Day	Date	Month	Year	DATA
Elections–Polling Day	Sat	19	10	2002	Voting on 26th Amendment of the Constitution Bill, 2002–The Treaty of Nice
Elections–Polling Day	Sun	20	10	2002	Voting on 2002–The Treaty of Nice, Electorate Wicklow 86,763. Total Poll 46,789, Yes 29,710 (63.8%) No 16,832(36.1%)
Driving	Thu	31	10	2002	Penalty points for careless driving introduced by Minister of Transport
McManus Liz			10	2002	Liz McManus of Bray appointed deputy leader of the Labour Party
Arklow Fire Station			11	2002	Arklow Fire Station opened by the Minister for the Environment and Local Government Pat the Cope Gallagher T.D.
East Coast Radio			11	2002	East Coast Radio Headquarters on the Killarney Road Bray officially opened
Carnew College				2002	4.4m Euro extension approved to Carnew Community College by Dept. Of Education
Cattle				2002	Number of Cattle in County Wicklow 128,459
Marriages				2002	Marriages in County Wicklow. 717
Deaths				2002	Deaths in County Wicklow. 774
Births				2002	Births in County Wicklow. 1,864
East Coast Radio				2002	East Coast Radio opened a new studio on the Killarney Road, Bray
Wicklow GAA				2002	Wicklow won the All Ireland Junior Football Championship GAA
Greystones				2002	New building for Greystones Credit Union opened on Church Road, Greystones
Bray Musical Society				2002	Bray Musical Society stages "Hot Mikado"
Arklow Shipping				2002	Arklow Shipping vessel Arklow Rose built
St. L. O'Toole F.C.				2002	St. Laurance O'Toole Football Club Roundwood formed
Roundwood F.C.				2002	Roundwood Football Club formed
Mountain Rescue				2002	The Dublin & Wicklow Mountain Rescue Team responded to 7 callouts
Taylor. Katie				2002	Katie Taylor of Bray the first Irish girl to Box in the National Boxing Stadium, Dublin.
Farmed land				2002	Area farmed in County Wicklow 101,707 hectares
Books				2002	Rathdrum: a pictorial history editor Joan Kavanagh, Rathdrum Historical Society
White. Larry				2002	Rev Larry White appointed Parish Priest of Queen of Peace Parish, Bray
Stats				2002	The number of Marriages in Wicklow for 2002 was 717
Stats				2002	The number of Births in Wicklow for year 2002 was 1,864
Area Farmed				2002	Area farmed in Co. Wicklow in 2002 was 101,707 hectares
Stats				2002	The number of Deaths in Wicklow for 2002 was 774

	Weekday	Day	Month	Year	
Wicklow Golf Club				2002	New Club house built at Wicklow Golf Club
Cars			01	2003	Car Reg 03 WW 1 issued by Wicklow Motor Tax Office
Scannell. Brendan J.	Sat	15	03	2003	Brendan J. Scannell of Bray died
Driving	Mon	28	04	2003	A report for the first 6 months of Penalty Points System 505 Drivers in Wicklow had 2 penalty points, 12 drivers had 4 penalty points
Holy Redeemer, Bray			04	2003	A new centre piece added to the Rose Window at the Holy Redeemer Church, Bray
McHugh. Eugene	Sun	11	05	2003	Eugene McHugh of Greystones appointed Chief Commissioner of Scouting Ireland SAI
Chamber of Commerce	Fri	14	05	2003	Bray a& District Chamber of commerce, Endeavour Awards
Stamps	Tue	20	05	2003	The 41 cent stamp issued for the Special Olympic World Games featured Shauna Bradley of Baltinglass
Murder	Thu	22	05	2003	Georgina Eager of NewtownMountKennedy found murdered in Dublin
Plunkett. James	Wed	28	05	2003	James Plunkett who lived near Bray, died in a Dublin Nursing Home
Bandstand			05	2003	A copper roof placed on the Bandstand at Bray Esplanade
Wicklow 200 Km	Sun	08	06	2003	The 21st Wicklow 200 km – Wicklow Gap Challenge Cycling Event
People's Park Bray	Mon	23	06	2003	A club house and changing rooms opened at the Peoples' Park, Bray
Croatia			06	2003	Greystones Co. Wicklow played host to the delegation from Croatia taking part in the Special Olympic World Games 2003
Blue Flag			06	2003	Blue Flags were awarded to the following beach in Co. Wicklow, Greystones South
Singapore			06	2003	Arklow Co. Wicklow played host to the delegation from Singapore taking part in the Special Olympic World Games 2003
American Samoa			06	2003	Dunlavin Co. Wicklow played host to the delegation from American Samoa taking part in the Special Olympic World Games 2003
Bahrain			06	2003	Rathdrum Co. Wicklow played host to the delegation from Bahrain taking part in the Special Olympic World Games 2003
China			06	2003	Bray Co. Wicklow played host to the delegation from China taking part in the Special Olympic World Games 2003
Seychelles			06	2003	Baltinglass Co. Wicklow played host to the delegation from Seychelles taking part in the Special Olympic World Games 2003
Syria			06	2003	Wicklow Town Co. Wicklow played host to the delegation from Syria taking part in the Special Olympic World Games 2003
Bray Summer Fest	Sat	02	07	2003	Bray Summer fest 2nd July to 13th July 2003
CCTV	Sat	26	07	2003	The proposed locations for Close Circuit TV (CCTV) cameras in Bray. Public Notice in National Papers by Dept of Justice
Goulding. Valerie	Mon	28	07	2003	LadyValerie Goulding nee Monckton died
Carlisle Grounds	Wed	06	08	2003	Andy McEvoy Challenge Match Bray Wanderers AFC versus Blackburn Rovers FC. Result: Bray Wanderers 2 Blackburn Rovers 3
Bray Seafront	Thu	25	09	2003	The new lighting on Bray Seafront officially switched on
Halpin. Robert	Tue	30	09	2003	Captain Robert Halpin of Wicklow commerated in a 57 cent stamp issued by An Post

A-Z Reference	Day	Date	Month	Year	DATA
Wicklow GAA	Sun	05	10	2003	County Wicklow senior Football Final Bray Emmets 1-5 Rathnew 0-8 (draw)
Wicklow GAA	Sun	12	10	2003	County Wicklow senior Football Final (replay) Bray Emmets 0-6 Rathnew 0-11
Books	Thu	16	10	2003	The official launch of "A History Of County Wicklow" by Arthur Flynn at County Buildings
Keegan. Charlie	Mon	29	12	2003	Charlie Keegan of Enniskerry died
Davidson. Rosanna				2003	Rosanna Davidson from County Wicklow crowned Miss World
Wicklow GAA				2003	Bray Emmets GAA Club hold Kick Fada competition in St Thomas's College, Bray. Winner Mark Herbert
St. Brendans College				2003	Tony Bellew of Bray appointed Principle of St Brendans College, Woodbrook, Bray
Potato				2003	Potato census 2003 Wicklow - 23 Registered Growers 289 Hectares of potato's
Wind Farm				2003	Arklow Bank Wind Park in the Irish Sea , construction commenced late summer 2003
Cars			01	2004	The number of (new Private cars) vehicles registered for the first time in County Wicklow was 445 (Source CSO)
Cars			03	2004	The number of (new Private cars) vehicles registered for the first time in County Wicklow was 530
Greystones	Sun	25	04	2004	The sod was turned on a new community centre attached to St. Patrick's Church, Greystones. Cost of new centre 1.7m
Cars			04	2004	The number of (new Private cars) vehicles registered for the first time in County Wicklow was 476
Roads			05	2004	Bord Pleanala the approves development of the N11 between Ballinclare Co. Wexford and Cooadanagan Co. Wicklow
Cavendish. Andrew			05	2004	The Duke of Devonshire Andrew Cavendish died at Chatsworth house, England in his 84 year
Cars			05	2004	The number of (new Private cars) vehicles registered for the first time in County Wicklow was 374
St Patrick's School	Wed	02	06	2004	The official opening of 7 new classrooms, quite room and library at St. Patrick's School, Vevay Road, Bray
Elections-Polling Day	Fri	11	06	2004	County Council Elections
Elections-Polling Day	Fri	11	06	2004	European Elections
Elections-Polling Day	Fri	11	06	2004	27th Amendment of the Constitution Bill 2004
Elections-Polling Day	Fri	11	06	2004	Local Elections
Elections-Polling Day	Sat	12	06	2004	Bray Area Electorate 26,906 Seats 7, Total Poll 14,635 Turnout 54.39% Spoiled Votes 328, Total Valid poll 14,3075 Quota 1,789
Elections-Polling Day	Sat	12	06	2004	Baltinglass Area. Electorate 12,204 Seats 3, Total Poll 8,098 Turnout 66.36% Spoiled Votes 103, Total Valid poll 7,995 Quota 1,999
Elections-Polling Day	Sat	12	06	2004	Wicklow Area Electorate 19,250 Seats 5, Total Poll 11,3111 Turnout 58.76% Spoiled Votes 275, Total Valid poll 11,036 Quota 1,840
Gaffney & Rice	Sat	31	07	2004	The Gaffney and Rice record for the Lug Walk was broken in 16 hours and 21 minutes by Bob Lawlor
Royal Visits	Fri	10	09	2004	H.R.H. Princess Anne visited the Festina Lente Foundation Old Connaught, Bray

Section One: Data by Date

Category	Event	Year	Month	Day	Weekday
Railways	The Minister of Transport unveils a plaque at Bray railway station to mark 150 years of Railways at Bray	2004	09	19	Sun
Railways	Iarnrod Eireann, RPSI, Bray Tourism, Bray UDC and Bray Chamber of Commerce mark 150 years of Railway in Bray	2004	09	19	Sun
Railways	Three steams trains ran between Bray and Wicklow Town.	2004	09	19	Sun
Rathnew	Rathnew By Pass opened by the Minister of Transport Seamus Brennan	2004	09	27	Mon
Roche. Dick	Dick Roche T.D. appointed Minister of the Environment, Local Government and Heritage	2004	09	29	Wed
Railways	Bray station refurbished	2004	09		
Wicklow GAA	Micheal O hAgain Chairman of Wicklow GAA 2004 -	2004			
Books	Enclosing the commons Dalkey, the Sugar Loaves and Bray, 1820-1870 by Liam Clare (Maynooth Series)	2004			
Housing	Bray Town Council Compulsory Purchase (Bray)	2004			
Historical Society	Bray Cualann Historical Society published its 5th Historical Journal	2004			
Walking Routes	Dispute over walking routes in the Glencree valley	2004			
Speed Limits	Speed Limits go Metric	2005	01	20	Thu
Knocksink Wood	Minister for Environment, Local Government, Heritage Mr Dick Roche opened two new footbridges at Knocksink Wood, Enniskerry	2005	01	25	Tue
Moore. James	Bishop Edward James Moore died in Bangor Hospital, Co Down	2005	03	16	Wed
A.O.Smith	A.O.Smith Corporation announced the closure of its Bray plant	2005	04	15	Fri
National Park	Mr Dick Roche opened Wicklow Mountains National Park Headquarters at Kilafin, Laragh Co. Wicklow	2005	04	29	Fri
Byrne. Shane	Shane Byrne selected for the British Lions Rugby team	2005	04		
Glencree	Wicklow Circuit Court beings to hear case regarding Walking access routes in the Glencree valley	2005	05	10	Tue
Blessington	Blessington Fire Station opened by Minister for Environment, Local Government, Heritage Mr Dick Roche	2005	05	23	Mon
Roundwood	Roundwood Caravan Park put up for sale	2005	05	25	Wed
Glencree	Judge Bryan McMahon delivered his judgement in favour of the Hill walkers in their case re access rights at Lambs Lane, Glencree	2005	06	08	Wed
Roads	The Minister of Transport Martin Cullen opened the final section of the M50 between Sandyford and Loughlinstown	2005	06	30	Thu
Little Bray	2m scheme announced to develop the site of the Bray Golf Club in Little Bray	2005	06		
Cliffwalk, Bray	CliffWalk between Bray and Greystones Officially re-opened after closure for repair	2005	07	09	Sat
Murder	A man shot dead in his home in Bray	2005	08	10	Wed
Arklow	The first round the town bus service introduced in Arklow	2005	08	20	Sat
Air Show	Bray International Air Show	2005	08	21	Sun
Powerscourt	120m project announced for Powerscourt Estate with the building of Ritz-Carlton Hotel	2005	08		

A–Z Reference	Day	Date	Month	Year	DATA
Enniskerry			08	2005	Fr. John Sinnott (a native of Bray) appointed Parish Priest of Enniskerry, Curtlestown and Glencree.
Arklow			08	2005	Tenders sought by Wicklow County Council to drill for boreholes– reference Arklow Water Supply Scheme
Enniskerry			08	2005	Fr. Pat Farnan retired as Parish Priest of Enniskerry, Curtlestown and Glencree
Delany. Ronnie	Mon	05	09	2005	Dublin City Council agree to give Sir Bob Geldof and Ronnie Delany the Freedom of the City of Dublin
Murder	Tue	06	09	2005	Christopher Newman found guilty in London Court for the murder of Georgina Eager in 2003
Wicklow Town	Mon	12	09	2005	Wicklow Town Council introduce Pay & Display Parking in Wicklow Town. It replaced Parking Disc
Railways	Sat	24	09	2005	Full weekend DART services resumed on the full DART line between Howth/Malahide and Greystones.
Blessington	Fri	14	10	2005	Minister of Environment formally announced approval for a new library for Blessington. Co. Wicklow
Railways			10	2005	Repair work began on the canopy on the southbound platform at Bray Railway Station
Powerscourt Arms Hotel	Wed	30	11	2005	Irish Independent Property Supplement . Sale of the Powerscort Arms Hotel on 12/12/2005
Books	Wed	07	12	2005	A Pictorial History of Bray Co. Wicklow, Volume Three, The Town and its People – Part Two, published
Weather	Wed	14	12	2005	A minor earthquake measuring 2.6 on the Richter Scale centred 30 miles off Bray Head at 3.20 am
Population County	Sun	23	04	2006	Census of Population in Ireland

Section Two:
Data in Alphabetical Order

A-Z Reference	Day	Date	Month	Year	DATA
A.O. Smith	Fri	15	04	2005	A.O. Smith Corporation announced the closure of its Bray plant
Act				1902	Licensing (Ireland) Act
Act	Fri	14	08	1903	Motor Car Act, required motor vehicles to be registered and licensed
Act				1906	The Trade Disputes Act
Act				1906	The Dogs Act
Act	Fri	21	12	1906	Town Tenant's Act
Act				1908	The Children's Act
Act				1908	The Old Age Pensions Act
Act				1916	Larceny Act
Act				1919	The Local Government (Ireland) Act – Proportional Representation
Act	Tue	23	12	1919	The British Government provided houses for ex-servicemen under the Irish Land (Provisions for Sailors and Soliders) Act 1919
Act				1920	Roads Act
Act				1920	The Government of Ireland Act
Act				1924	The Old Age Pension Act, Pensions cut by 1/-s
Act	Sat	27	12	1924	Railways Act, enacted by Dail Eireann
Act	Thu	18	03	1926	Statistics Act–Census confidentiality guaranteed, enacted by Dail Eireann
Act	Thu	27	05	1926	The School Attendance Act, enacted by Dail Eireann
Act	Wed	26	02	1930	The National Monuments Act, enacted by Dail Eireann
Act	Mon	21	07	1930	The Vocational Education Act, enacted by Dail Eireann
Act	Tue	28	01	1932	Road Transport Act, enacted by Dail Eireann
Act	Thu	14	11	1940	Minerals Development Act, enacted by Dail Eireann
Act	Tue	23	09	1941	Local Government Act, enacted by Dail Eireann
Act	Tue	24	02	1942	The Water Supply Act, enacted by Dail Eireann
Act	Fri	08	12	1944	Transport Act, enacted by Dail Eireann
Act	Tue	20	03	1945	Minerals Company Act, enacted by Dail Eireann
Act	Wed	12	06	1946	The Forestry Act, enacted by Dail Eireann
Act	Tue	17	12	1946	Statistics (Amendment) Act, enacted by Dail Eireann

Act	Wed	07	08	1946	Local Governments Act, enacted by Dail Eireann
Act	Wed	14	01	1948	The Local Government Sanitary Services Act, enacted by Dail Eireann
Act	Tue	21	12	1948	The Republic of Ireland Act, enacted by Dail Eireann
Act	Tue	10	05	1955	Local Government Act, enacted by Dail Eireann
Act	Mon	27	02	1956	The Forestry Act, enacted by Dail Eireann
Act	Tue	14	02	1956	The Gaming and Lotteries Act, enacted by Dail Eireann
Act	Wed	13	02	1957	The Wicklow County (Extension of Boundary) Provisional Order, 1957 with effect from 01/07/1957
Act	Wed	26	06	1957	Small Dwellings Act, enacted by Dail Eireann
Act	Wed	21	12	1960	Local Government (No. 2) Act, enacted by Dail Eireann
Act	Sat	29	07	1961	Road Traffic Act, enacted by Dail Eireann
Act	Wed	07	08	1963	Local Government (Planning and Development) Act, enacted by Dail Eireann
Act	Tue	12	07	1966	Housing Act, enacted by Dail Eireann
Act	Mon	24	12	1973	Arts Act, enacted by Dail Eireann
Act	Thu	26	07	1973	Road Traffic (Amendment) Act, enacted by Dial Eire Ann
Act				1977	Water Pollution Act
Act	Tue	16	05	1978	Road Transport Act, enacted by Dail Eireann
Act	Wed	12	12	1979	Local Government (Tolls Roads) Act, enacted by Dail Eireann
Act	Wed	13	07	1983	Postal and Telecommunications Service Act, enacted by Dail Eireann
Act	Tue	12	02	1985	The Age of Majority Act reduces the age limit from 21 to 18, enacted by Dail Eireann
Act	Tue	11	12	1986	Transport (Reorganisation of C.I.E) Act , enacted by Dail Eireann with effect 2/2/1987
Act	Sat	26	06	1993	Roads Act, enacted by Dail Eireann
Act	Wed	01	07	1998	Roads (Amendment) Act, enacted by Dail Eireann
Agriculture Census				1991	The average farm size in County Wicklow was 38.1 ha
Agriculture Census				1991	The Agricultural Census showed 2730 farmers engaged in Agriculture in County Wicklow
Agriculture Census			06	2000	The Agricultural Census showed 2410 farmers engaged in Agriculture in County Wicklow
Agriculture Census			06	2000	The average farm size in County Wicklow was 42.2 ha
Ahern. Nuala	Thu	09	06	1994	Nuala Ahern of Greystones, Co.Wicklow elected as MEP representing Leinster
Air Crashes	Fri	21	11	1930	Air Corp Training Aircraft crashed landed on Bray Head, Crew taken to Bray Garda Station and then to hospital in Dublin

A-Z Reference	Day	Date	Month	Year	DATA
Air Crashes	Fri	18	04	1941	An RAF plane crashed at Ballyknockan the crew of 4 killed and buried in Blessington
Air Crashes	Fri	24	04	1942	An RAF Training Aircraft Curtis's Tomahawh I serial no AH920 crash landed at Lecarrow Co. Wicklow
Air Crashes	Mon	12	08	1946	Plane carrying French Girl Guides crashed on Djouce Mountain Co. Wicklow
Air Crashes	Sat	12	12	1987	Plane crashed near Ballybrew, Enniskerry , Three persons killed
Air Crashes	Fri	27	12	1991	Private aircraft crashed at Blessington, Co. Wicklow
Air Crashes	Tue	04	05	1993	Cessna Light aircraft crashed landed on Bray Head, The occupants taken to Loughlinstown Hospital
Air Show	Sun	21	08	2005	Bray International Air Show
Airs/Music				1917	The man from Wicklow by Anna Nichols, lyrics by Fiske O'Hara and Bartley Costello. Music by Cass Freeborn
Airs/Music				1918	A legend of Wicklow (song, words by F.P. Carrigan)
Airs/Music				1954	To the Wicklow Hills (Song) words by R.G.Leigh, Lloyd Webber, William Southcombe
Alcock. Dr. N.	Mon	04	04	1904	A plaque on an outcrop at Ballyman, Enniskerry in memory to Dr. Nathaniel Alcock who died on April 4 1904
Alexander. William				1911	William Alexander died in Torquay
Allen. Darina				1948	Darina Allen born 1948, Educated Dominican Convent Wicklow, Cookery School owner and TV Presenter
Allen. Francis				1921	Constable Francis Allen (DMP 11502) awarded the King's Police Medal.
Allgood. Molly				1907	Sara Allgood (actress) and her sister Molly Allgood (actress) lived in Glencree, Co. Wicklow
Allgood. Molly				1911	Molly Allgood married George Herbert Mair
Allgood. Molly				1926	Molly Allgood married Arthur Sinclair
Allgood. Molly	Sun	02	11	1952	Molly Allgood (actress) died
Allgood. Sara	Wed	13	09	1950	Sara Allgood (actress) died
Altidore House				1945	The Emmet family acquired Altidore Castle, Kilpedder
American Samoa			06	2003	Dunlavin Co. Wicklow played host to the delegation from American Samoa taking part in the Special Olympic World Games 2003
An Oige	Thu	07	05	1931	An Oige (Irish Youth Hostel Association) founded
Aravon School				1978	Aravon School Playing field between Sidmonton Road and Meath Road, Bray was sold for housing
Aravon School				1984	Aravon School moved from Sidmonton Road, Bray to Old Conna Hill House, Bray
Aravon School				1984	Aravon School bought Old Conn Hill (House) once the home of Count John Mc Cormack
Arcadia Ballroom	Wed	24	10	1962	Arcadia Ballroom, Bray was destroyed by fire

Name	Event	Year	Month	Day	Day
Ardmore Rovers	Ardmore Rovers football Club, Bray established	1979			
Ardmore Studio	Mr. Louis Elliman, Director of Ranks Cinemas in Ireland bought Ardmore House, Bray	1957			
Ardmore Studio	Minster of Industry & Commerce Sean Lemass opens Ardmore Film Studio, Bray	1958	05	12	Mon
Ardmore Studio	Shooting commenced on "Home is the Hero" the first feature film at Ardmore Studio, Bray	1958			
Ardmore Studio	Goverment buys Ardmore Studios, Bray for £390,000	1973			
Ardmore Studio	The Irish Film Board established to run Ardmore Studios and attract film companies to make films in Ireland (see 1973,1958)	1975	06	04	Wed
Ardmore Studio	Ardmore Film Studio bought by Vincent Donohoe for £1.1m	1982	09		
Area Farmed	Area farmed in Co. Wicklow in 2002 was 101,707 hectares	2002			
Arklow	(17)'98 Memorial unveiled at Arklow	1993			
Arklow	Arklow Vocational School established	1995			
Arklow	Arklow Presbyterian Church built	1914			
Arklow	The official opening of Arklow Technical School	1915	09	22	Wed
Arklow	Arklow Presbyterian Church dedicated	1915			
Arklow	South Arklow Lightship sunk by a U–Boat	1917	03	25	Sun
Arklow	Arklow Military Barracks closed	1923			
Arklow	St. Josephs Church Templerainey near Arklow built	1929			
Arklow	Arklow Fever Hospital demolished	1935			
Arklow	Arklow Parking Temporary Rules 1967	1967			
Arklow	Arklow Parking Temporary Rules 1968	1968			
Arklow	Arklow Parking Temporary Rules 1969	1969			
Arklow	Arklow Parking Temporary Rules 1970	1970			
Arklow	Arklow Traffic and Parking Bye-Laws 1971	1971			
Arklow	Arklow Maritime Museum established	1976	10		
Arklow	Thirty Two persons injured in a train crash near Arklow	1979	10	03	Wed
Arklow	Arklow twinned with Chateaudun, France	1982	08	21	Sat
Arklow	An extension added to Arklow Presbyterian Church	1985			
Arklow	Servier (Ireland) Industries Ltd, a pharmaceutical company opened a plant on the Gorey Road, Arklow	1989			
Arklow	The alter in the Catholic Church Arklow St. Mary & St. Patrick was rededicated	1994			
Arklow	Arklow Seabreeze Festival 18/07/2002– 21/07/2002	2002	07	18	Thu
Arklow	The first round the town bus service introduced in Arklow	2005	08	20	Sat

A–Z Reference	Day	Date	Month	Year	DATA
Arklow			08	2005	Tenders sought by Wicklow County Council to drill for boreholes– reference Arklow Water Supply Scheme
Arklow By–Pass	Fri	29	01	1999	Arklow By–Pass opened
Arklow CBS				1961	The first boys enrolled in St Kevin's CBS Arklow
Arklow CBS				1963	St. Kevin's CBS, Arklow officially opened
Arklow Celtic F.C.				2000	Arklow Celtic Football Club formed
Arklow Cinema	Mon	17	11	1913	The Cosy Picture House (Cinema) opened on the South Quay, Arklow
Arklow District Council	Sat	01	10	1910	Arklow Urban District Council established
Arklow Fire Station			11	2002	Arklow Fire Station opened by the Minister for the Environment and Local Government Pat the Cope Gallagher T.D.
Arklow Golf Club				1927	Arklow Golf Club established
Arklow Harbour				1949	Arklow Harbour Works Order 1949
Arklow Harbour				1952	Arklow Harbour Works Order 1952
Arklow Harbour				1954	Arklow Harbour Works Order 1952 (Amendment) Order 1954
Arklow Harbour				1957	Arklow Harbour Works Order 1957
Arklow Harbour				1975	Arklow Harbour Works Order 1975
Arklow Hospital			04	1921	The Countess of Wicklow Memorial Cottage Hospital opened at the Sea Road, Arklow
Arklow Hospital			07	1961	The Countess of Wicklow Memorial Cottage Hospital at the Sea Road, Arklow was closed
Arklow Music Festival				1970	Arklow Music Festival established
Arklow Pipe Band				1941	St. Colmcilles Pipe Band, Arklow founded
Arklow Pottery				1934	Arklow Pottery established
Arklow Pottery	Mon	29	07	1935	Arklow Pottery was officially opened by Sean Lemass
Arklow Pottery			06	1947	Arklow Pottery converted from fuel burning equipment to fuel oil equipment in modernising the plant
Arklow Pottery			08	1998	Arklow Pottery was in financial difficulties and liquidators appointed
Arklow Pottery			04	1999	Arklow Pottery ceased production
Arklow Shipping			05	1966	Arklow Shipping Ltd founded
Arklow Shipping				1982	Arklow Shipping vessel Arklow Day built
Arklow Shipping				1983	Arklow Shipping vessel Arklow Dawn built
Arklow Shipping				1988	Arklow Shipping vessel Arklow Mill built
Arklow Shipping				1988	Arklow Shipping vessel Arklow Marsh built

Name	Day	Date	Month	Year	Event
Arklow Shipping				1988	Arklow Shipping vessel Arklow Bay built
Arklow Shipping				1990	Arklow Shipping vessel Arklow Moor built
Arklow Shipping				1990	Arklow Shipping vessel Thruster built
Arklow Shipping				1990	Arklow Shipping vessel Forester built
Arklow Shipping				1991	Arklow Shipping vessel Wilster built
Arklow Shipping				1991	Arklow Shipping vessel Arklow Dusk built
Arklow Shipping				1991	Arklow Shipping vessel Arklow View built
Arklow Shipping				1992	Arklow Shipping vessel Arklow Valley built
Arklow Shipping				1992	Arklow Shipping vessel Arklow Freedom built
Arklow Shipping				1992	Arklow Shipping vessel Arklow Faith built
Arklow Shipping				1992	Arklow Shipping vessel Arklow Fame built
Arklow Shipping				1995	Arklow Shipping vessel Arklow Brook built
Arklow Shipping				1996	Arklow Shipping vessel Arklow Spray built
Arklow Shipping				1996	Arklow Shipping vessel Arklow Bridge built
Arklow Shipping				1996	Arklow Shipping vessel Arklow Castle built
Arklow Shipping				1998	Arklow Shipping vessel Arklow Sand built
Arklow Shipping				1998	Arklow Shipping vessel Arklow Sea built
Arklow Shipping				1999	Arklow Shipping vessel Arklow Star built
Arklow Shipping				2002	Arklow Shipping vessel Arklow Rose built
Arklow Silver Band				1968	Arklow Silver Band founded
Arklow Sports Centre				1982	Arklow Sports and Leisure Club completed at Seview Avenue, Arklow.
Arklow Town Council	Tue	18	12	2001	S.I.591/2001 of 18/12/1001 gave effect with 1/01/2002 the change Arklow Urban District Council to Arklow Town Council
Arklow Town Juniors				1948	Arklow Town Juniors Football Club formed
Arklow Youth Club				1960	Arklow Youth Club founded
Armstrong, G.F.S				1906	George F.S.Armstrong died in County Down
Armstrong, Reg				1926	Reg Armstrong (motorcycle racer) born in Liverpool
Armstrong, Reg	Sat	24	11	1979	Reg Armstrong (motorcycle racer) died in an accident near Avoca. Co.Wicklow
Armstrong-Jones.A	Fri	07	03	1930	Anthony Charles Armstrong-Jones born
Armstrong-Jones.A		06	05	1960	Anthony Charles Armstrong-Jones 1st married H.R.H. Princess Margaret

A-Z Reference	Day	Date	Month	Year	DATA
Armstrong-Jones. A				1961	Anthony Charles Armstrong-Jones given the title 1st Earl of Snowdon
Armstrong-Jones. A	Fri	15	12	1978	Anthony Charles Armstrong-Jones 2nd marriage Lucy Davies of Bushey Park, Enniskerry
Armstrong-Jones. A				1978	Anthony Charles Armstrong-Jones marriage to H.R.H. Princess Margaret dissolved
Ashford Church	Tue	15	06	1915	The foundation stone laid for the Church at Ashford by Rev. Dr. Walsh Archbishop of Dublin
Ashford Church	Sun	27	10	1918	The Catholic Church Ashford which cost £3,000 was dedicated by Rev. John Staples P.P. of Wicklow
Aughrim				1912	Aughrim Community Hall built
Aughrim			circa	1935	The Granite Quarries at Tinakilly near Aughrim ceased production
Aughrim Rangers F.C.				1991	Aughrim Rangers Football Club formed
Avoca				1956	St. Patrick's Mining Company a subsidiary of a Canadian Company starts mining at Avoca
Avoca				1958	Over 500 men employed by the mining companies at the Avoca Mines
Avoca				1962	Avoca mines ceased production
Avoca				1969	Discovery Mines of Canada re-open some mines in the Avoca area
Avoca				1982	Avoca Mines Closed
Avoca	Tue	22	05	1997	Avoca, Co. Wicklow twinned with Bromham, Wiltshire, England
Avoca	Sun	24	08	2001	Fire destroys the Vale View Hotel, Avoca
Avoca Bridge				1986	The bridge at Avoca washed away by flooding
Avondale House				1904	The Department of Agriculture and Technical Instruction bought Avondale House, Rathdrum once the home of C.S. Parnell
Avondale House				1904	The State buys Avondale estate from William Boylan of Phisboro, Dublin
Avondale House				1935	Some repairs carried out to Avondale House, Rathdrum
Avondale House	Sun	03	06	1946	President Eamon de Valera unveiled a plaque in honour Charles S. Parnell at Avondale House, Rathdrum
Avondale House			10	1967	Forestry School opened at Avondale House, Rathdrum by Minister of Lands Sean Flanagan
Avondale House	Thu	09	10	1969	Extension added to the Forestry School at Avondale, Rathdrum Co. Wicklow
Avonmore F.C.				2001	Avonmore Football Club Rathdrum formed
Bahrain			06	2003	Rathdrum Co. Wicklow played host to the delegation from Bahrain taking part in the Special Olympic World Games 2003
Bailieborough Castle				1918	Bailieborough Castle, Co.Cavan was accidentally destroyed by fire. Previous owners included Sir Stanley Cochrane and Mr W.B. Cochrane
Bailieborough Castle				1936	Bailieborough Castle, Co. Cavan was demolished

Bailieborough Castle				1936	The Marist Order of Brothers sold Bailieborough Castle, Co. Cavan to The Forestry Division of The department of Lands
Ball. F.E	Sat	07	01	1928	Francis Elrington Ball, historian died
Ballinacor House				1965	Capt. W.D.O. Kemmis bequeathed Ballinacor House, Rathdrum to his maternal cousin Major Richard Lomer
Ballorney House				1975	Ballyorney House bought by Mr. Peter Blake.
Ballycorus Works			circa	1920	The lead mines ceased at Ballycorus near Bray
Ballywaltrim College				1981	Ballywaltrim Community College, Bray established
Ballywaltrim Sports	Wed	04	08	1999	The official opening of the Ballywaltrim Sport Complex, Bray
Baltinglass				1950	Mr. Michael Farrell appointed sub-postmaster of Baltinglass, prompted a boycott of postal services in the town
Baltinglass				1950	Dispute over the Minister of P&T appointment of Sub-postmaster in Baltinglass
Baltinglass			12	1950	Michael Farrell resigned as sub-postmaster of Baltinglass and Miss Helen Cooke appointed as sub-postmaster
Baltinglass	Mon	26	05	1967	Baltinglass Cattle Market opened
Baltinglass Fire Stn			09	2002	The Department Environment and Local Government approved a grant of 46,000 Euro to build a drill tower at Baltinglass Fire Stn.
Baltinglass Golf Club				1928	Baltinglass Golf Club established
Baltinglass Golf Club				1974	Baltinglass Golf Club won the Barton Cup
Baltinglass Golf Club				1993	Baltinglass Golf Club won the Barton Cup
Baltinglass Hospital				1916	Baltinglass Hospital taken over by the Military as a barracks
Baltinglass Hospital				1922	The Military left Baltinglass Barracks and the building reverted to its original function as a hospital
Baltinglass Hospital				1970	Baltinglass Hospital administration changed from Wicklow County Council to the Eastern Health Board under the Health Act 1970
Baltinglass Hospital				1976	Surgical Services ceased at Baltinglass Hospital
Baltinglass Hospital				1980	The Maternity Unit at Baltinglass Hospital closed
Baltinglass Hospital				1980	Baltinglass District Hospital became a Day Care Centre with 94 beds
Baltinglass Hospital				2000	Baltinglass Hospital administration changed from Eastern Health Board to the South Western Area Health Board
Baltinglass Workhouse	Mon	05	02	1923	Baltinglass workhouse destroyed by fire
Bandstand			05	2003	A copper roof placed on the Bandstand at Bray Esplanade
Bank Building				1914	The AIB Bank Building, Main Street, Arklow, built
Banotti. Mary				1939	Mary Banotti (Member of the European Parliament) born 1939, educated Dominican Convent Wicklow.
Barlow. Jane	Tue	17	04	1917	Jane Barlow (writer) died at Bray Co. Wicklow
Barn Owls				1907	The National Museum of Ireland has a Barn Owl donated S. Cregan location Co. Wicklow

A–Z Reference	Day	Date	Month	Year	DATA
Barn Owls				1910	The National Museum of Ireland has 2 Barn Owls donated by Williams. Location of find Co. Wicklow
Barrett. Daniel				1927	The artist Daniel Barrett born in County Wicklow
Barrett. Daniel				1957	Artist Daniel Barrett receives International Jewirey Award
Barrett. Daniel				1995	Artist Daniel Barrett receives Schenectady 1995 Cultural Heritage Award
Barrington. Elizabeth			05	1907	Elizabeth Barrington nee Darley died
Barrington. R.C	Wed	15	09	1915	Zoologist, Botanist, Climber Richard Manliffe Barrington of Fassaroe, Bray died
Barton. Robert				1919	Robert Barton appointed Minister of Agriculture April 1919 - August 1921
Barton. Robert				1920	Robert Childers Barton held the post of Chairman of Wicklow County Council 1920 - 1922
Barton. Robert	Sun	10	08	1975	Robert Barton the longest surviving signatory of the Treaty of 1921 died
Bayly. Catherine				1908	Catherine Bayly died
Bayly. Lancelot				1928	Lancelot Bayly (artist) lived at Killarney Hill, Bray. Co. Wicklow
Bayly. Lancelot				1952	Lancelot Bayly (artist) died in Berkshire, England
Bayly. Richard	Fri	11	10	1907	Lt-Col Richard Bayly died
BBK United				2001	BBK United Football Club Brittas Bay formed
Beatty.Sir A. C.				1954	Sir Alfred Chester Beatty was knighted by the Queen of England
Beatty.Sir A. C.				1957	Sir Alfred Chester Beatty became the first honorary citizen of Ireland
Beatty.Sir A. C.	Sun	20	01	1968	Sir Alfred Chester Beatty died in Monte Carlo. He spent his later years at the Clonmannon retirement village Ashford, Co. Wicklow
Beckett. Dr.G.P.G	Sat	01	02	1930	Dr. G.P.G. Beckett took up duty as County Medical Officer of Health for County Wicklow
Beckett. Dr.G.P.G	Mon	20	01	1930	Dr. G.P.G. Beckett appointed first County Medical Officer of Health for County Wicklow
Begles	Fri	05	05	1995	Bray twinned with Begles near Bordeaux, France (Bray Ceremony)
Beit. Alfred	Mon	19	01	1903	Sir Alfred Beit born
Beit. Alfred				1931	Sir Alfred Beit elected as a Conservative M.P. to the House of Commons, London
Beit. Alfred				1944	Sir Alfred Beit was Secretary for the Colonies in the UK Government 1944-195
Beit. Alfred				1993	Sir Alfred Beit and his wife Clemetine made honorary citizens of Ireland
Beit. Alfred	Thu	12	05	1994	Sir Alfred Beit died
Beit. Otto John	Mon	25	02	1924	Otto John Beit given the title 1st Baron Beit
Beit. Otto John	Sun	07	12	1930	Sir Otto John Beit died and succeeded by his son Sir Alfred Beit 2nd Baron Beit

Bellevue House			's	1950	Bellevue House, Delgany demolished
Bernard. John Henry				1915	John Henry Bernard became Archbishop of Dublin
Bernard. John Henry	Mon	29	08	1927	John Henry Bernard (Church of Ireland Archbishop and academic) died
Bestic. Albert A.	Fri	07	05	1915	Albert A Bestic junior 3rd Officer on the S.S. Lusitania when sunk of the Old Head of Kinsale, Co. Cork
Bestic. Albert A.	Thu	19	12	1940	Albert A. Bestic was Master of the Isolda, a lighthouse tender ship when it was bombed off the Wexford Coast near Kilmore Quay
Bestic. Albert A.	Thu	20	12	1962	Capt. Albert A. Bestic, died. He lived at Prince of Wales Terrace Bray. Junior 3rd Officer on the Lusitania and Master of the Isolda
Bewley. Ernest				1903	The first Jersey Cows were imported into Ireland from Jersey Island by Ernest Bewley in 1903.
Bewley. Ernest	Sun	14	08	1932	Ernest Bewley died and is buried in the Friend's Burial Ground, Temple Hill, Blackrock. Co. Dublin
Bewley. Joshua	Tue	27	11	1906	Margaret H Bewley the wife of Joshua Bewley died.
Bewley. Thomas Arthur	Wed	31	03	1943	Emmeline Marion Bewley the widow of Thomas Arthur Bewley of Greystones died
Bewley. Victor				1912	Victor Bewley the son of Ernest Bewley was born in Dublin
Bewley. Victor				1964	Victor Bewley along with Fr. Tom Fehily, Lady Wicklow founded the Dublin Committee for Travelling People
Bewley. Victor				1977	Victor Bewley retired as Chairman of Bewley's Oriental Cafes Ltd.
Bewley. Victor	Wed	19	05	1999	Victor Bewley died
Biggs. Michael				1928	The sculptor Michael Biggs was born in Stockport, Cheshire, England
Biggs. Michael				1966	Michael Biggs was commissioned to erect the Garda Memorial at the Gadra Headquarters Phoenix Park, Dublin
Biggs. Michael				1970	Michael Biggs did the lettering for the Central Bank tender notes from 1970
Biggs. Michael				1993	Michael Biggs died and is buried in St Patrick's Graveyard, Enniskerry
Bill				1912	Home Rule Bill
Bill				1936	Liffey Reservoir Bill introduced into Dail Eireann proposed to build Hydro-electric works at Poulaphouca and flood 6,500 acres
Bill				1970	Film Bill presented to Dail Eireann
Births				1907	The Notification of Births Act, Local medical officers had to be notified of any birth within 36 hours
Births				2002	Births in County Wicklow. 1,864
BL&FHS			04	1988	The Blessington Local and Family History Society founded.
Blainroe Golf Club				1978	Blainroe Golf Club (south of Wicklow town) established
Blake. Edward				1912	Edward Blake died, M.P. for South Longford in the House of Commons
Blake. Samuel H.				1914	Samuel Hume Blake died

A–Z Reference	Day	Date	Month	Year	DATA
Blake.Vincent			07	2002	Vincent Blake held the post of Chairman of Wicklow County Council 2002-2003
Blessington				1923	The bells in the Church of Ireland were re-hung as a tribute and memorial to the servicemen of the parish who died during the Great War
Blessington				1931	Russborough House near Blessington was sold by Capt... Denis Daly
Blessington				1981	Our Lady of the Most Holy Sacrament, Main Street, Blessington built
Blessington	Mon	23	05	2005	Blessington Fire Station opened by Minister for Environment, Local Government, Heritage Mr Dick Roche
Blessington	Fri	14	10	2005	Minister of Environment formally announced approval for a new library for Blessington. Co. Wicklow
Blessington Fire Stn.			08	2002	Wicklow County Council invite tenders to build a fire station in Blessington
Blessington Lakes			03	1940	Some 6500 acres around Blessington were flooded to facilitate the Hydro-electric scheme at Polluphouca
Blessington S C				1960	Blessington Sailing Club founded
Blue Flag			06	2000	Blue Flags were awarded to the following beach's in Co. Wicklow, Brittas Bay North & South, Greystones South, Bray Prom
Blue Flag			06	2002	Blue Flags were awarded to the following beach's in Co. Wicklow, Brittas Bay North & South, Greystones South
Blue Flag			06	2003	Blue Flags were awarded to the following beach in Co. Wicklow, Greystones South
Boghall Brick			circa	1920	The Boghall Brick Company, Bray ceased production 1920's
Books	Mon	06	07	1902	History of the County of Dublin by Francis E. Ball 1st vol...... published 1902. Completed 4 vols in 1906
Books				1903	Bray & Environs by A. L. Doran Price 1/-s
Books				1903	A Description and History of Powerscourt by M. Wingfield
Books				1905	Wildfoot, the Wanderer of Wicklow by Edwin J. Brett
Books				1907	Black's Guide to Dublin and the Wicklow Mountains published by Charles Black of Edinburgh
Books				1907	Rambles in Eirinn by William Bulfin
Books				1911	In Wicklow, West Kerry and Connemara by John Millington Synge
Books				1912	[updated] In Wicklow, West Kerry and Connemara by John Millington Synge
Books				1912	Black's Guide to Dublin and the Wicklow Mountains published by Charles Black of Edinburgh
Books				1913	The Stones of Bray by Canon George Digby Scott
Books				1915	A legend of Wicklow and other poems by Bruce Malaher
Books				1916	Portrait of the Artist by James Joyce published
Books	Thu	02	02	1922	Ulysses by James Joyce published

Books					1924	The Flaming Wheel. Nature studies in the counties of Dublin and Wicklow by John St. Whitty
Books					1924	Dan Breen published his book "My Fight for Irish Freedom" (see 1894,1969)
Books					1927	Arklow, Co. Wicklow by J. W. Barrett published in Cheltenham
Books					1927	The Official Handbook Wicklow, County Wicklow by E. J. Burrows. published in Cheltenham
Books					1934	The Botanist in Ireland by Robert L. Praeger first published
Books					1934	1st Edition of The Botanist in Ireland by Robert LLoyd Praeger, 2nd edition 1974 reprinted 1977 Co Wicklow pages 259 -269
Books					1934	The Ages of Stone & Bronze in Co. Wicklow by Liam Price
Books					1936	The Kynoch era in Arklow by Hilary Murphy
Books					1937	17(98) in Wicklow by Rev. Bro. Luke Cullen
Books					1938	Wicklow Heather by Annie M. P. Smithson, published by Talbot Press
Books					1939	Finnegan's Wake by James Joyce
Books					1943	Difficulties with Mental prayer by Dom Eugene Boylan
Books					1945	The Barony of Ballinacor North. Vol 1, The Place Names of County Wicklow by Liam Price
Books					1946	The Barony of Ballincor South. Vol 2, The Place Names of County Wicklow by Liam Price
Books					1949	The Barony of Talbotstown Upper. Vol 3, The Place Names of County Wicklow by Liam Price
Books					1950	Flora of County Wicklow by James Ponsonby Brunker
Books					1950	The Open Road by J.B. Malone lists some walk routes in Co. Wicklow
Books					1953	Official Guide to Wicklow-Wexford
Books					1953	The new Invasion [An account of the author's experiences farming in Co. Wicklow from 1946 onward] by Winefride Nolan
Books					1953	The Barony of Talbotstown Lower Vol 4, The Place Names of County Wicklow by Liam Price
Books					1954	[Pour l'heure Sainte mensuelle] The Holy Hour translated from French by the Earl of Wicklow
Books					1954	A Priest in Russia and the Baltic by Charles Bourgeois, translated from French by the Earl of Wicklow
Books					1954	The Passion of Our Lord Jesus Christ translated from French by the Earl of Wicklow
Books					1956	[Sainte Bernadette vous parle] Saint Bernadette speaks translated from French by the Earl of Wicklow
Books					1957	The Barony of Rathdown Vol 5, The Place Names of County Wicklow by Liam Price
Books					1957	[Ce petit moine dangereux] A dangerous little Friar, Father Titus Brandsma translated from French by the Earl of Wicklow
Books					1958	[Nos enfants et nous] Our Children and ourselves translated from French by the Earl of Wicklow

A–Z Reference	Day	Date	Month	Year	DATA
Books				1958	"A Tale of Two Churches" by E.H.F.Campbell, The history of St. Paul's and Christ Church, Bray
Books				1958	The Barony of Shillelagh Vol 6, The Place Names of County Wicklow by Liam Price
Books				1959	[Le Miracle irlandais] The Miracle of Ireland translated from French by the Earl of Wicklow
Books				1959	Margherita Sarto, mother of St Pius X translated from French by the Earl of Wicklow
Books				1961	[Une Flamme d'amour. L'humble Pere Bonnard] The Humble Pere Bonnard translated from French by the Earl of Wicklow
Books				1961	[Aze'lie Martin, me're de Sainte, se de l'enfant Jesus] Azelie Martain, Mother of the little Flower translated from French by the Earl of Wicklow
Books				1962	Dublin and Wicklow in Colour by J.B.Vesey
Books				1962	The Shell Guide to Ireland (First Edition) by Killanin and Duignan
Books				1964	Partnership with Christ by Dom Eugene Boylan
Books				1964	Walking in Wicklow. A guide for travellers, afoot & awheel, thorugh the Wicklow Mountains by J.B. Malone
Books				1965	Walking in Wicklow by J. B. Malone published
Books				1967	The Shell Guide to Ireland (2nd Edition) by Killanin and Duignan
Books				1967	The Baronies of Newcastle and Arklow. Vol 7, The Place Names of County Wicklow by Liam Price
Books				1969	The First Dail by Marie Comerford
Books				1970	The story of Baltinglass. A history of the parishes of Baltingalss, Ballynure and Rathbran published in the Kilkenny Journal
Books				1970	(1st edition) Guide to National Monuments of Ireland by Peter Harbinson
Books				1971	West Wicklow by Kamac Publications
Books				1972	Glendalough and St. Kevin by Lennox Barrow
Books				1972	(2nd Edition) Guide to National Monuments of Ireland by Peter Harbinson
Books				1973	Wicklow Rock Climbs (Glendalough and Luggala) edited by Pat Redmond
Books				1973	Brittas bay. a planning and conservation study by Foras Forbartha Project leader K.A. Mawhinney
Books				1974	The Botanist in Ireland by Robert L.Praeger republished (Co. Wicklow, pages 261–269)(Bray Head and River, pages 267–268)
Books				1975	The birds of Dublin and Wicklow edited by Clive D Hutchinson
Books				1975	(3rd edition) Guide to National Monuments of Ireland by Peter Harbinson
Books				1975	Penrose family of Helston, Cornwall and Wheldrake, Yorkshire and County Wicklow by Charles Penrose
Books				1976	The Kynoch era in Arklow by Hilary Murphy (2nd edition)

Section Two: Data in Alphabetical Order

Category	Year	Title
Books	1977	Guide to National Monuments of Ireland by Peter Harbinson
Books	1977	The Kynoch era in Arklow by Hilary Murphy (3rd edition)
Books	1978	Russborough, Blessington, Co Wicklow was presented to the state by Sir Alfred Beit
Books	1978	A hundred years of Bray and its neighbourhood from 1770 to 1780 by an old inhabitant[Mrs Francis J Seymour]
Books	1979	The East. Dublin, Wicklow by David Herman
Books	1979	The soils of Avondale Forest Park, Rathdrum by J.F.Collins, E.P. Farell and P.O'Toole
Books	1979	Arklow & Wicklow County Guide and Directory
Books	1979	(reprinted) Guide to National Monuments of Ireland by Peter Harbinson
Books	1980	Bray: architectural heritage by William Garner
Books	1980	Dublin and North Wicklow by Christopher Moriarty
Books	1980	C.S.Parnell by Paul Brew
Books	1980	The Irish journals of Elizabeth Smith 1840 -1850
Books	1982	The Journal of the Arklow Historical Society
Books	1983	"If you seek Monuments"by Kathleen Turner
Books	1983	Mount Usher Gardens, Ashford, County Wicklow by Madelaine Jay
Books	1984	In the Lands of Brien published by Christopher Brien
Books	1984	Stones of Bray by Canon Scott reprinted
Books	1985	The spatial pattern of state a forestation in County Wicklow by P.G. Clinch
Books	1985	By the Banks of the Dargle, a history of Bray Emmets GAA Club 1885-1985 compiled by Jim Brophy
Books	1985	Arklow -last stronghold of gail. Arklow ships from 1850-1985 by Jim Rees and Liam Charlton
Books	1986	The Parish of Powerscourt by Rev A.E. Stokes reprinted by the Old Bray Society
Books	1986	A view from the DART by Vincent Caprani
Books	1986	Water Quality Management Plan for the River Slaney Catchment in accordance with S.15 Local Government (Water Pollution) Act
Books	1986	History of Bray by Arthur Flynn
Books	1987	Greystones Presbyterian Church 1887-1987
Books	1987	The Avonmore brown trout fishery at Rathdrum, Co.Wicklow by E. Fahy.
Books	1988	The Wicklow Way from Marley to Glenmalure. a walking guide by Michael Fewer
Books	1988	Maritime Arklow by Frank Forde

A-Z Reference	Day	Date	Month	Year	DATA
Books				1988	The Complete Wicklow Way by J.B. Malone.
Books				1989	A History of Wicklow Lifeboat Station. From Dauntless to Annie by Ciaran Doyle
Books				1989	Dublin South & Wicklow Regional Plan
Books				1989	The Shell Guide to Ireland (3rd Edition) by Killanin and Duignan (Revised and updated by Peter Harbison)
Books				1989	On foot in Dublin and Wicklow. exploring the wilderness by Christopher Moriarty
Books			11	1989	The Book of Bray compiled and edited by John O'Sullivan, Tony Dunne, Seamus Cannon
Books				1990	Between the mountains and the sea. The Story of Delgany, 1789-1990. a parish history, by Judith Flannery
Books				1990	The Wicklow way by Ken Boyle and Orla Bourke
Books				1990	The history of the Parish of St James Crinken, Bray Co. Dublin published by the Parish of St James.
Books				1991	Holy Redeemer Church, 1792-1992. a Bray parish. edited by Brendan O'Cathaoir
Books				1991	Ashford and District Historical Journal
Books				1991	Guide to Co. Kildare and West Wicklow by Con Costello
Books				1991	Antiquities of Old Rathdown by Christian Corlett published Wordwell
Books				1991	Fanny & Anna Parnell by Jane McL. Cote published Gill and Macmillan
Books				1991	The Love Story of Parnell & Katharine O'Shea by Margery Brady published Mercier Press
Books				1992	A Short History of Gleanealy and its Church of Ireland Parish bicentenary 1792-1992 by R.John.H.Corbett
Books				1992	A short history of Glenealy and its Church of Ireland parish, bicentenary 1792-1992 by John H. Corbett
Books				1992	The Life of Captain Robert Charles Halpin by Jim Rees published Dee-Jay Publications
Books				1993	Ancient Rathdown and St. Crispin's Cell edited by Chris Small
Books				1993	A guide to the archaeology of County Wicklow by Eoin Grogan and Tom Hillery
Books				1993	Wicklow in the Ice Age. an introduction and guide to the glacial geology of the Wicklow district by William P. Warren
Books				1994	The ecology and management of uplands vegetation in the Wicklow Mountains by Mortimer C.P.Loftus
Books				1994	Wicklow History and Society by Ken Hannigan and William Nolan
Books				1994	Insider's Guide to Dublin, Wicklow, and Boyne Valley by Paul Cullen and Ken Boyle
Books				1994	The Bray Diary 1797-1899 by Francis Loughrey
Books				1994	Geology of Kildare–Wicklow by B.McConnell and M.E.Philcox
Books				1994	The insider's guide to Dublin, Wicklow and the Boyne Valley by Paul Cullen and Ken Boyle

Books					1994	The higher lakes of Wicklow by John O. McCormick
Books					1994	Emerging from the Shadow. The lives of S.A.Lawerson and L.O.Kingston based on personal diaries 1883-1969 edited D. Swanton
Books					1994	Geology of Kildare & Wicklow by B.McConnell and M. E. Philcox
Books					1995	A survey of soil and vegetation in the area surrounding the Avoca Mines. Co. Wicklow by C. O'Neill
Books					1995	Ninety Years of Technical Education in an Irish Maritime Town. Arklow Community College 1905-1995 by N.O'Cleirigh
Books					1995	Ninety years of technical education in an Irish maritime town. the story of Arklow Community College 1905-1995 by N O'Cleirigh
Books					1996	Radon in dwellings, the National Radon Survey Cavan, Dublin, Louth, Monaghan, and Wicklow by J.T. Duffy
Books					1996	A Pictorial History of Kilcoole, Newcastle, NewtownMountKennedy, Glen o'the Downes and Greystones by Derek Paine
Books					1996	Wicklow Roots by Wicklow County Genealogical Society
Books					1996	The Wicklow world of Elizabeth Smith 1840-1850 edited by Dermot James and Seamus O'Maitiu
Books					1997	Baronies of Shillelagh & Ballinacor South, Co. Wicklow: a memorial, 1837 extracted (O.P. 1837/133) National Archives of Ireland
Books					1997	This way up, access routes into the Wicklow Mountains by David Herman
Books					1997	Wicklow Mountains National Park study. prepared for the Department of Arts Culture and the Gaeltacht by firm RPS Cairns
Books					1997	Baronies of Sheilelagh & Ballinacor South, 1837. by National Archives
Books					1997	The Tellicherrry V The transportation of Michael Dwyer & Wicklow Rebels by Kieran Sheedy
Books					1997	This Way Up access routes into the Wicklow Mountains by David Herman
Books					1997	Archaeological inventory of County Wicklow. compiled by Eoin Grogan and Annaba Kilfeather
Books					1997	Ballyknockan a Wicklow Stonecutter's Village by Seamas O'Maitiu and Barry O'Reilly
Books					1997	Chemistry of precipitation, through fall and soil water, Cork, Wicklow and Galway regions by E.P. Farrell
Books					1998	Victorian Bray by Liam Clare, Maynooth Studies in Local History
Books					1998	The rebellion in Wicklow 1798 by Ruan O'Donnell
Books					1998	Dublin & South Eastern Railway by Ernie Shepherd and Gerry Beesley published Midland Press
Books					1998	Avoca- our mining heritage a brief history of metal mining in the Vale of Avoca, Co. Wicklow by A. Thomas and P. McArdle
Books					1998	I am the Crocus poems by children from County Wicklow edited by David Wheatly
Books					1998	County Wicklow Arts Directory editor Jessica Fuller
Books					1998	Wicklow County arts directory edited by Jessica Fuller

A–Z Reference	Day	Date	Month	Year	DATA
Books				1998	Turn of the tide by Joan O'Neill
Books				1998	Rebellion in Wicklow. General Joseph Holt's personal account 1798. edited by Peter O'Shaughnessy
Books				1998	Stream of gliding sun. a Wicklow anthology. edited by David Wheatley
Books				1998	Kilcoole, County Wicklow History and Folklore by Robert Jennings
Books				1998	Stream and Gliding Sun a Wicklow Anthology edited by David Wheatley
Books				1998	County Wicklow, Arklow Town Family Roots by Noel Farrell
Books				1998	Rebellion in Wicklow –General Holt's personal Account of 1798 edited by Peter O'Shaughnessy
Books				1999	Wicklow Gold by Ray Cranley
Books				1999	The Buildings of Clara Vale by Pat Dargan
Books				1999	Through the eyes of Emerald- a short history of Wicklow Town by Class 4 Dominican College Wicklow
Books				1999	Through the eyes of Emerald. a short history of Wicklow Town, by class 4 Emerald (1998-99) Dominican College Wicklow.
Books				2000	Canon Frederick Donovan's Dunlavin, 1884-1896; a west Wicklow village in nineteenth century by Chris Lawlor
Books				2000	Surplus people. the Fitzwilliam clearances 1847-1956 by Jim Rees
Books				2000	Images of Ireland, South Dublin from the Liffey to Greystones compiled by Derek Stanley
Books				2001	National Childcare Census report. County Wicklow by Department of Justice, Equality and Law reform
Books				2001	Old Ironsides (a book about the Stewart and Parnell Families) by Colin Stewart and Jean Costelloe
Books	Mon	14	05	2001	The Ordnance Survey Letters - Wicklow published
Books				2001	Wire Ropes Ltd, Wicklow 1951-2001 author Andrew O'Brien
Books			04	2002	"Blessington Now and Then" compiled by the Members of The Blessington Local and Family History Society
Books				2002	Rathdrum: a pictorial history editor Joan Kavanagh, Rathdrum Historical Society
Books	Thu	16	10	2003	The official launch of "A History Of County Wicklow" by Arthur Flynn at County Buildings
Books				2004	Enclosing the commons Dalkey, the Sugar Loaves and Bray, 1820-1870 by Liam Clare (Maynooth Series)
Books	Wed	07	12	2005	A Pictorial History of Bray Co. Wicklow, Volume Three, The Town and its People - Part Two, published
Booth. Denton				1925	Denton Booth died
Booth. Evelyn Mary			s'	1950	Evelyn Mary Booth recorded the botanical plants of south-east Ireland
Booth. Evelyn Mary				1962	The Atlas of Flora of Great Britain and Ireland published. Evelyn Mary Booth wrote the section on South-east Ireland
Booth. Evelyn Mary				1979	Evelyn Mary Booth published the Flora of County Carlow

Booth. Evelyn Mary				1988	Evelyn Mary Booth died
Bord Failte	Fri	29	03	1968	Bord Failte Report showed that a sum of £100,600:0s:0d was spent on projects in Bray in the previous twelve months
Bowden. Richard				1922	Very Rev Richard Bowden, Parish Priest of Bray, Little Bray and Greystones 1922 – 1939
Bowden. Richard	Mon	12	06	1939	Rev Richard Bowden Parish Priest of Bray parish died and was buried in St. Peter's Graveyard, Bray
Bowe. Laura				1969	Laura Bowe (Set Dresser) born 1969, educated at St. Gerard's College, Bray
Bower. Robert				1922	Robert Bower married Henrietta daughter of 1st Baron Strickland.
Bower. Robert				1931	Robert Bower elected MP in the House Commons for Cleveland (Yorkshire) 1931-1945
Bower. Robert		05	07	1975	Robert Bower died
Bowling Championships	Mon	27	07	1998	The Bowling League of Ireland Championships held at Failte Park, Bray between 27/07/1998 and 01/08/1998
Boylan. Dom Eugene				1904	Dom Eugene Boylan (Atomic Physicists, Monk, Writer) born in Bray
Boylan. Dom Eugene				1931	Dom Eugene Boylan entered Mount St. Josephs Abbey, Roscrea as a novice
Boylan. Dom Eugene				1937	Dom Eugene Boylan ordained a priest
Boylan. Dom Eugene			07	1962	Dom Eugene Boylan elected Abbot of Mount St. Josephs Abbey, Roscrea
Boylan. Dom Eugene	Sun	05	01	1964	Dom Eugene Boylan died in Roscommon County Hospital, following a car accident in Mid December 1963
Boyle. Ina				1919	Ina Boyle Received a Carnegie Trust Award for her orchestral work "The Magic Harp"
Boyle. Ina				1923	Ina Boyle composed an orchestral work "Gaelic Hymns"
Boyle. Ina				1923	Ina Boyle composed an orchestral work "Sleep Song"
Boyle. Ina				1926	Ina Boyle composed an orchestral work "A Mountain Woman"
Boyle. Ina				1942	Ina Boyle composed an orchestral work "Wildgeese"
Boyle. Ina				1966	Ina Boyle composed an orchestral work "Maudlin of Paplewick"
Boyle. Ina	Fri	10	03	1967	Ina Boyle died
Boystown Golf Club				1998	Boystown Golf Club, Baltyboys, Blessington, Co. Wicklow established.
Brabazon. Anthony	Thu	03	11	1910	Anthony Brabazon the 14th Earl of Meath born
Brabazon. Anthony	Tue	30	07	1940	Anthony Brabazon the 14th Earl of Meath married Elizabeth Bowbly
Brabazon. Anthony				1952	The Earl of Meath carries out major repairs to Killruddery House due to dry rot
Brabazon. Anthony	Sat	19	12	1998	Anthony Brabazon the 14th Earl of Meath died and was succeeded by John Anthony Brabazon 15th Earl of Meath
Brabazon. David	Sat	09	10	1948	Hon. David Brabazon the 2nd son of the 14th Earl of Meath born
Brabazon. Geoffery	Mon	23	11	1998	Geoffery Brabazon grandson of 14th Earl of Meath died while felling trees in Co. Meath

A–Z Reference	Day	Date	Month	Year	DATA
Brabazon.John	Mon	11	05	1941	John Anthony Brabazon the 15th Earl of Meath born
Brabazon.John	Thu	07	12	2000	Ballinacor House, Greenan, Rathdrum was put up for sale by the Earl of Meath (Picture and Details Irish Times, Property Section)
Brabazon. Reginald	Thu	13	04	1905	Reginald Brabazon the 12th Earl of Meath, Killruddery, Bray invested into the Order of St...... Patrick at Dublin Castle
Brabazon. Reginald				1906	The water clock in the front courtyard at Killruddery built by the Reginald Brabazon the 13th Earl of Meath
Brabazon. Reginald				1906	Above the entrance to the stable yard at Killruddery there is a clock built 1906-1909
Brabazon. Reginald	Wed	12	02	1908	Reginald Brabazon 13th Earl of Meath married Lady Aileen Wyndham Quin
Brabazon. Reginald	Mon	04	11	1918	Lady Mary Jane Brabazon nee Lauderdale the wife of the Reginald Brabazon the 12th Earl of Meath died
Brabazon. Reginald	Fri	11	10	1929	Reginald Brabazon the 12th Earl of Meath died and was succeeded by his son Reginald Le Normand Brabazon 13th Earl of Meath
Brabazon. Reginald	Thu	10	03	1949	Reginald Brabazon the 13th Earl of Meath died and was succeeded by Anthony Windham Normand Brabazon 14th Earl of Meath
Brabazon. Reginald	Fri	08	05	1981	Andrew Marsh wrote a feature article about the 12th Earl of Meath in The Evening Press Newspaper on 08/05/1981
Bradshaw. Harry	Thu	09	10	1913	Harry Bradshaw (The Brad) golfer born Delgany Co. Wicklow
Bradshaw. Harry				1934	Harry Bradshaw became a professional golfer
Bradshaw. Harry				1941	Harry Bradshaw became the Professional Golfer at the "Country Club" Killcroney House, Enniskerry
Bradshaw. Harry				1947	Harry Bradshaw (broadcaster) born Bray. Co. Wicklow
Bradshaw. Harry				1947	Harry Bradshaw (The Brad) golfer Won the Irish Open
Bradshaw. Harry				1949	Harry Bradshaw (The Brad) golfer Won the Irish Open
Bradshaw. Harry				1953	Harry Bradshaw won the Dunlop Masters Golf Championship
Bradshaw. Harry				1953	Harry Bradshaw (The Brad) (golfer) Played on the Ryder Cup teams of 1953, 1955 and 1957
Bradshaw. Harry				1958	Harry Bradshaw won the Canada Cup (now the World Cup) Golf Championship
Bradshaw. Harry	Sat	22	12	1990	Harry Bradshaw (The Brad) golfer died
Brangan. Pamela				1974	Pamela Brangan (Model) educated at Our Lady's School, Claremont, Rathnew
Bray Arts Centre	Sat	31	08	2002	The 242 seater Mermaid Arts Centre, Bray opened to the public
Bray Arts Centre	Thu	27	06	2002	The Mermaid Arts Centre, Bray officially opened
Bray Ball				1995	Bray Commercial Ball held in Town Hall, Bray
Bray Bookshop				1972	The Bray Bookshop established by Mrs Clear on the Quinsborough Road, Bray
Bray Bookshop				1988	The Bray Bookshop moved to the Main Street, Bray

Bray Cancer Group				1990	Bray Cancer Support Centre founded
Bray Civic Centre	Thu	27	09	2001	The foundation stone of Bray Civic Centre unveiled by Taoiseach Bertie Ahern
Bray Development Co.				1970	Bray Development Company established.
Bray Directory	Mon	30	11	1981	Bray Chamber of Commerce published "Bray Directory A-Z Guide"
Bray Directory				1985	2nd Bray Directory by Bray Chamber of Commerce published
Bray Electric Works	Wed	10	07	1912	Accident at Bray Electric Light Works, Christopher Coates was killed and 1 man injured
Bray Festival	Sat	22	06	1968	Bray Festival 22nd to 30th June 1968
Bray Festival	Sun	03	07	1994	Bray Seaside Festival 3rd to 10th July 1994
Bray Festival	Sun	07	07	1996	Bray Seaside Festival 7th to 14th July 1996
Bray Festival	Sun	06	07	1997	Bray Seaside Festival 6th to 13th July 1997
Bray Festival	Sun	05	07	1998	Bray Seaside Festival 5th to 12th July 1998
Bray Festival	Sun	01	07	2001	Bray Seaside Festival 1st to 8th July 2001
Bray Festival	Sun	07	07	2002	Bray Seaside Festival 7th July to 14th July 2002
Bray Fire Stn.			09	2002	The Department Environment and Local Government approved a grant of 20,000 Euro for upgrading facilities at Bray Fire Station
Bray for Holidays	Wed	13	11	1968	The Department of Post and Telegraphs gives approval for the slogan Bray for Holidays to appear on letters posted in Bray
Bray for Holidays			02	1969	The slogan Bray for Holidays and Conferences first appeared on letters posted in Bray
Bray Furniture				1905	Bray Art Furniture Industry established
Bray Furniture				1905	Celtic Alter Cross by John Burke of Bray was exhibited in Dublin
Bray Furniture				1907	Bray Art Furniture Industry opened a shop at 81 Main Street, Bray.
Bray Gas Works			08	1981	The Gasometer at Dock Hill, Bray removed.
Bray Golf Club				1905	Bray Golf Club won the Barton Cup
Bray Golf Club				1907	Bray Golf Club won the Barton Cup
Bray Golf Club				1925	Bray Golf Club won the Barton Cup
Bray Golf Club				1928	Bray Golf Club won The Irish Golf Clubs Junior Challenge Cup Tournament
Bray Harbour				1916	Three to Four colliers per week unloaded their cargo at Bray Harbour
Bray Harbour				1943	Bray Harbour the last commercial consignment landed
Bray Harbour	Thu	05	09	1957	The Lighthouse at Bray Harbour fell into the sea at 14:10 hrs following a storm
Bray Harbour				1973	Bray Harbour Development Association established to manage the affairs of Bray harbour.

A–Z Reference	Day	Date	Month	Year	DATA
Bray Harbour	Wed	23	01	1980	The road bridge at Bray Harbour collapsed
Bray Harbour			04	1984	Dargan Road Bridge at Bray Harbour open to traffic
Bray Harbour			03	2001	The Goverment announces a Grant of £625,000 for repair work to Bray Harbour
Bray Head				1930	The Bray Urban District Council acquired the upper slopes around Bray Head
Bray Head	Sat	11	11	1933	An Obelisk on Bray Head to Queen Victoria was blown up.
Bray Head	Sun	23	09	1950	Holy Year Cross erected on Bray Head. dedicated
Bray Head				1964	Bray Head Fishing and Social Club founded
Bray Head			09	2002	The Eagles Nest property on Bray Head put up for sale with a price tag of 2.5m Euro
Bray Head Chairlift.				1952	Work begins on putting a Chairlift on Bray Head – Irish Holidays Ltd
Bray Head Chairlift.				1976	The chairlift on Bray Head last ran commercially in 1976, the fittings were removed from 1977
Bray Head House				1917	Putland House (Bray Head House) sold to David Frame
Bray Laundry				1905	Bray Laundry opened at the Dargle Road, Bray
Bray Main Street				1990	New street furniture and pavements slabs on Main Street. Bray
Bray Musical Society				1952	Bray Musical Society Founded
Bray Musical Society				1952	Bray Musical Society stages "Concert"
Bray Musical Society				1953	Bray Musical Society stages "Where the Lark Sings"
Bray Musical Society				1954	Bray Musical Society stages "Maritana"
Bray Musical Society				1955	Bray Musical Society stages "Countess Maritza"
Bray Musical Society				1956	Bray Musical Society stages "Waltzes from Vienna"
Bray Musical Society				1957	Bray Musical Society stages "White Horse Inn"
Bray Musical Society				1958	Bray Musical Society stages "Maritanna" and "Countess Maritza"
Bray Musical Society				1959	Bray Musical Society stages "The Bohemian Girl"
Bray Musical Society				1960	Bray Musical Society stages "The Bells of Cornville"
Bray Musical Society				1961	Bray Musical Society stages "Grand Concert"
Bray Musical Society				1962	Bray Musical Society stages "Pink Champagne"
Bray Musical Society				1963	Bray Musical Society stages "The Gypsy Baron"
Bray Musical Society				1964	Bray Musical Society stages "The Merry Widow"
Bray Musical Society				1965	Bray Musical Society stages "The Gypsy Princess"

Bray Musical Society				1966	Bray Musical Society stages "White Horse Inn"
Bray Musical Society				1967	Bray Musical Society stages "Sweethearts"
Bray Musical Society				1968	Bray Musical Society stages "New Moon"
Bray Musical Society				1969	Bray Musical Society stages "Rose Marie"
Bray Musical Society				1970	Bray Musical Society stages "Desert Song"
Bray Musical Society				1971	Bray Musical Society stages "The Arcadians"
Bray Musical Society				1972	Bray Musical Society stages "The Merry Widow"
Bray Musical Society				1973	Bray Musical Society stages "Mariana"
Bray Musical Society				1974	Bray Musical Society stages "Pink Champagne"
Bray Musical Society				1975	Bray Musical Society stages "Summer Song"
Bray Musical Society				1976	Bray Musical Society stages "Waltzes from Vienna"
Bray Musical Society				1977	Bray Musical Society stages "Lisa"
Bray Musical Society				1978	Bray Musical Society stages "Oklahoma"
Bray Musical Society				1979	Bray Musical Society stages "The Arcadians"
Bray Musical Society				1980	Bray Musical Society stages "Frederica"
Bray Musical Society				1981	Bray Musical Society stages "The Desert Song"
Bray Musical Society				1982	Bray Musical Society stages "La Vie Parisenne"
Bray Musical Society				1983	Bray Musical Society stages "The Great Waltz"
Bray Musical Society				1984	Bray Musical Society stages "Bless the Bride"
Bray Musical Society				1985	Bray Musical Society stages "Fiddler on the Roof"
Bray Musical Society				1986	Bray Musical Society stages "My Fair Lady"
Bray Musical Society				1987	Bray Musical Society stages "The Merry Widow"
Bray Musical Society				1988	Bray Musical Society stages "Die Fledermaus"
Bray Musical Society				1989	Bray Musical Society stages "The Boy Friend"
Bray Musical Society				1990	Bray Musical Society stages "The Pyjama Game"
Bray Musical Society				2000	Bray Musical Society stages "Hello Dolly"
Bray Musical Society				2001	Bray Musical Society stages "Chess"
Bray Musical Society				2002	Bray Musical Society stages "Hot Mikado"
Bray Pumping Station	Fri	26	10	1990	Minister of Environment P. Flynn opened Bray Pumping Station at Dock Hill, Bray

A–Z Reference	Day	Date	Month	Year	DATA
Bray Rovers Hockey				1941	Bray Rovers Hockey Club won the Railway Cup
Bray Rowing Club				1935	Bray Rowing Club established
Bray School				1907	The Bray School in Castle Street closed and transferred to the Herbert Rd (Headmaster Mr. Moore)
Bray School Project				1977	Bray School Project Association established
Bray School Project	Tue	01	09	1981	Bray School Project open a national school in Bray
Bray Sea Anglers				1960	Bray Sea Anglers Club at Bray Harbour established
Bray Seafront	Fri	13	01	1928	Bray Town Commissioner seeks a grant of £5,000 from the Dept. of Local Government to build a Pavilion on Bray Seafront
Bray Seafront	Thu	25	09	2003	The new lighting on Bray Seafront officially switched on
Bray Softball Club				1997	The Bray Allsorts Softball Club founded
Bray Summer Fest	Sat	02	07	2003	Bray Summer fest 2nd July to 13th July 2003
Bray Technical School	Sat	14	03	1931	Bray Technical School the first new school approved under the 1930 Vocational Education Act
Bray Technical School	Mon	18	09	1933	The Vocational School was constructed on the Florence Road at a cost of £5,783 and opened by T.Derrig Minister of Education
Bray Technical School				1941	An extension to the Vocational School, Florence Road, Bray at cost of £4,000
Bray Tennis Club				1999	New Club house erected at Bray Tennis Club, Vevay Road Bray
Bray Traffic				1947	Bray Traffic (Parking and Waiting) Bye-Laws 1947
Bray Traffic				1947	Bray Traffic Bye-Laws 1947
Bray Traffic				1950	Bray Special Speed Limit Regulations 1950
Bray Traffic				1965	Bray Traffic and Parking Bye-Laws 1965
Bray Traffic				1973	Bray Traffic and Parking Bye-Laws 1973
Bray Traffic Plan	Fri	14	06	2002	Proposed Traffic Management Plan for Bray Town Centre announced
Bray Urban District				1948	Bray Urban District Council (Transfer of Institution) Order 1948
Bray Urban District	Wed	19	02	1952	Bray Urban District (Alteration of Boundary) Order 1952 (S.I. 42/1952)
Bray Urban District				1967	Bray Urban District Local Electoral Areas Order 1967
Bray Urban District				1967	Bray Urban District Local Electoral Areas Order 1967, (Revocation) Order 1974
Bray Urban District				1978	The Urban District of Bray (Alteration of Boundary) Order, 1978 (S.I. No 370 of 1978)
Bray Urban District	Thu	15	02	1979	Bray Urban District Local Electoral Areas Order 1979

Keyword	Weekday	Day	Month	Year	Description
Bray Urban District				1994	Bray Urban District Local Electoral Order 1994
Bray Urban District				1998	Bray Urban District Local Electoral Areas Order 1998
Bray Wanderers				1924	Bray Wanderers won the Metropolitan Cup
Bray Wanderers				1976	Bray Wanderers won the Metropolitan Cup, Paul McNaughton scored two goals
Bray Wheelers				1949	Bray Wheelers Cycle Club formed.
Bray.Castle				1938	The Castle in Castle Street, Bray was removed
Bray.Seafront				1941	Part of the Sea Wall at Bray collapsed
Bray.Seafront	Thu	23	04	1998	Bray Sea life Centre opened by President Mary McAleese
Bray.Seafront			09	1998	Coastal Erosion scheme at Bray Seafront commenced
Bread	Fri	27	01	1989	Johnston Mooney and O'Brien.-Dublin oldest bakery-closed, including its outlets in Dun Laoghaire and Bray
Breen.Dan	Sat	27	12	1969	Dan Breen died in a Nursing Home at Kilcroney, Bray
Breen.Dan	Thu	08	07	1971	The Taoiseach,Jack Lynch inaugurates the Dan Breen Memorial Fund for HandicappedYouth
Breen.William				1946	Rev. William Breen appointed to the Holy Redeemer Parish (1946-1970)
Breen.William				1970	Rev. William Breen appointed to the Parish of Arklow.
Brennan.Paduge	Wed	17	11	1971	Paudge Brennan T.D. for Wicklow expelled from the Fianna Fail Party
Brennan.Paudge	Fri	08	05	1970	Paudge Brennan resigned as Parliamentary Secretary for Local Government
Brennan.Thomas				1945	Thomas Brennan elected to Wicklow County Council
Brennan.Thomas				1953	Thomas Brennan died
Bridge				1943	A bridge near Hunters Hotel on the Newcastle/Rathnew Road built
Brien.Christy				1980	Christy Brien (local historian) published "Know your Parish"
Brien.Christy				1986	Christopher (Christy) Brien (local historian) died
British Empire Day	Mon	21	07	1902	British Empire Day instituted by Reginald Brabazon 12th Earl of Meath, to encourage schoolchildren to become good citizens
British Empire Day	Wed	24	05	1916	British Empire Day given official status in the United Kingdom, British Empire Day as 24th May, Queen Victoria's birthday
British Empire Day	Wed	12	03	1958	British Empire Day renamed British Commonwealth Day
British Empire Day				1966	British Commonwealth Day renamed Commonwealth Day and the date moved from 24th May to June 11th
British Empire Day	Mon	14	03	1977	Since 1977 Commonwealth Day observed on the 2nd Monday in March
British Navy	Mon	12	07	1999	Four British Navy Patrol Vessels visited Wicklow Harbour the first since 1920's
Broadcasting Authority	Wed	01	06	1960	The Broadcasting Authority established

A–Z Reference	Day	Date	Month	Year	DATA
Brook House School				1973	Brook House School established on the Herbert Road, Bray
Browne, Garech	Sun	25	06	1939	Garech Brun grandson of Ernest Guinness and son of Baron Oranmore and Browne born in Dublin
Browne. Maurice				1979	Fr. Maurice Browne died. Author of several novels and priest in Ballymore Eustace
Brunker, James P.				1960	James P. Brunker died
BUDC				1909	Patrick Bateman appointed Rate Collector by the Bray Urban District Council
BUDC			04	1914	Patrick McDonnell Town Clerk of Bray Urban District Council died. He lived at Beechfield, Bray
BUDC				1925	The Bray Urban District Council vote to drop the name Bri Cualann and revert to that of Bray
BUDC	Tue	19	06	1928	Bray Urban District Council dissolved 19/06/1928 to 05/06/1934 Commissioner P.J. Meghan appointed
BUDC				1935	SI No 408/1935; Street Trading (Bray Urban District) Regulations
BUDC				1935	Mr Edward Byrne Chairman Bray Urban District Council
BUDC				1940	Bray Urban District Council accepts a tender of £1,400 from Toft & Sons to provide Amusements on Seafront – Summer Season
BUDC				1942	The number of seats on Bray Urban District Council reduced from 15 to 12 elected representives
BUDC				1955	Mr Denis McCarthy appointed Town Clerk of Bray Urban District Council.
BUDC				1956	Bray Urban District Council carried out some repairs to the seafront and promenade
BUDC				1957	Bray Urban District Council extended the town boundary
BUDC				1968	Bray Urban District Council dissolved and Commissioner appointed 1968-1973
BUDC	Thu	05	06	1969	Bray Urban District Council failed to strike a rate for the town, disbanded by Minister of Local Government Kevin Boland
BUDC				1977	Bray Urban Extension Boundary Order 1977 with effect from 01/1/1979
BUDC	Mon	01	01	1979	Bray Urban Boundary Order came into effect
BUDC	Tue	18	12	2001	S.I.591/2001 of 18/12/1001 gave effect with 1/01/2002 the change Bray Urban District Council to Bray Town Council
Burgage Bridge				1939	The Burgage Bridge, Blessington removed before the flooding of Blessington lakes
Burke. William	Tue	19	03	1946	Mr. William Burke died
Bus				1906	The first public bus service commenced in Dublin
Bus				1925	The Dublin United Tramway (Omnibus Service) Act passed
Bus				1926	The 45 Bus Route commenced by DUTC Dublin to Blackrock
Bus				1927	The 45 Bus route extended to Bray

Bus				1927	St. Kevins Bus Service (Doyle's) commenced trading
Bus				1929	Paragon an independent omnibus ran a bus service from Dublin City to Ballymore Eustace.
Bus	Mon	20	12	1937	First Double Deck Buses to run in Dublin introduced by the Dublin United Tramway Company
Bus			06	1938	The 85 bus route from Bray Railway Station to Enniskerry was acquired by he GSR from The Shamrock Bus Company
Bus				1942	The 45A bus route was shortened to operate between Dun Loaghaire and Bray via Ballybrack and Shankill
Bus	Mon	02	09	1946	Wolfe Tone Square (Bray) Bus Terminus first used.
Bus				1948	CIE took delivery of four "Bolton" type double decked buses at North Wall, Dublin. One of the buses had Bray-45
Bus				1950	CIE introduced its touring coach bus service
Bus	Wed	22	07	1953	The CIE touring coach "The Dargle" featured in a publicity photographs for CIE taken in the Vale of Clara
Bus				1953	One of CIE touring coaches was named "The Dargle"
Bus	Fri	01	05	1959	The first double decked bus ran Dublin to Bray seafront terminus. Prior to 1959 double decked buses used a terminus on Meath Road, Bray
Bus				1963	The CIE touring coach HZD 580 featured in a publicity photographs for CIE taken in Powerscourt Gardens
Bus				1968	C.I.E. had 720 Double Deck Buses, 80 Single deck buses. Total work-force of 3,000
Bus				1970	86 Bus Route service was discontinued between Cabinteely and Bray. Except school buses serving St Ann's, Milltown etc
Bus				1971	The CIE touring coach "The Dargle" was withdrawn form service
Bus				1985	The 45 Bus route service to the Seafront was reduced but extended on the Killarney Road Service
Bus				1985	The 145a Bus route, new route included a feeder service to Bray DART station from Ballywaltrim, Bray
Bus Crash			07	1991	A bus overturned at Jack Whites Inn on the N11 near Arklow
Bus Crash	Mon	14	02	2000	A double deck bus crashed into a bridge near Bray Railway Station
Bush School				1960	The Bush School at Knockroe, Kilcoole closed
Butler. Eleanor				1915	Eleanor Butler born in Dublin
Butler. Eleanor	Wed	14	04	1948	Eleanor Butler appointed to Seanad Eireann 14th April 1948 -31st July 1951
Butler. Eleanor				1959	Eleanor Butler married William Cecil 8th Earl of Wicklow
Butler. Eleanor			02	1997	Eleanor Butler Countess of Wicklow died
Byrne. Andrew W.	Sun	28	03	1975	Andrew W. Byrne owner of the Rathdrum Tanning Company died
Byrne. C.M.	Sat	12	04	1958	The former chairman of Wicklow County Council died
Byrne. Christopher M.				1922	Christopher M. Byrne held the post of Chairman of Wicklow County Council 1922-1925
Byrne. Edward				1943	Edward Byrne held the post of Chairman of Wicklow County Council 1943-1944

A-Z Reference	Day	Date	Month	Year	DATA
Byrne. Henry J.				1953	Henry J. Byrne held the post of Chairman of Wicklow County Council 1953-1960
Byrne. Henry J.				1968	Henry J. Byrne held the post of Chairman of Wicklow County Council 1968-1969
Byrne. James				1916	James Byrne a native of County Wicklow Killed at Boland's Mill during the 1916 Rising
Byrne. John				1992	John Byrne held the post of Chairman of Wicklow County Council 1992-1993
Byrne. John			07	2002	Cllr. John Byrne appointed Catharoirleach of Bray Town Council
Byrne. Joseph				1916	Joseph Byrne aged 32 a native of Co. Wicklow, was killed fighting at Boland's Mill, 1916
Byrne. Pat				1954	Pat Byrne born 1954, educated at Presentation College, Bray. Chief Executive of Cityjet (Dublin)
Byrne. Shane	Sun	18	07	1971	Shane Byrne (Irish rugby international) from Aughrim. County Wicklow, born in Dublin
Byrne. Shane	Sat	02	06	2001	Shane Byrne of Aughrim Co. Wicklow got his Irish International Rugby Debut against Romania
Byrne. Shane			04	2005	Shane Byrne selected for the British Lions Rugby team
Calary Church				1984	150th anniversary of Calary Church, Roundwood
Camera Club				1971	Bray Camera Club established
Camera Club				1980	Produced a slide show on Bray called "Under Your Nose"
Campbell. Arthur	Tue	09	11	1909	Arthur Campbell (Photographer and Artist) born in Belfast, brother of Frederick George Campbell
Campbell. Arthur				1914	Arthur Campbell (Photographer and Artist) lived in Arklow. Co. Wicklow 1914-1921
Campbell. Christopher				1908	Christopher Campbell (artist) born in Dublin
Campbell. Christopher	Thu	18	05	1972	Christopher Campbell (artist) buried at Glendalough
Campbell. F. George				1917	Frederick George Campbell (artist) was born in Arklow
Campbell. F. George				1966	Frederick George Campbell (artist) won the President Hyde Gold Medal
Campbell. F. George				1969	Frederick George Campbell (artist) won the Oireachtas Prize for Landscape
Campbell. F. George	Fri	18	05	1979	Frederick George Campbell (artist) of Arklow died in Dublin and buried at Laragh, Co. Wicklow
Campbell. Flan				1919	Flan Campbell (educationist and historian) born in Glencree. Co. Wicklow
Campbell. Flan				1946	Flan Campbell edited the Irish Democrat from 1946-1947
Campbell. Flan	Sun	06	03	1994	Flan Campbell died in Dublin
Campbell. Joseph	Sun	23	10	1910	Joseph Campbell married Nancy Maude and both lived at Lackendarragh, Glencree. Co. Wicklow.
Campbell. Joseph				1920	Joseph Campbell was acting Chairman of Wicklow Council 1920-1921 while Robert Barton was imprisoned
Campbell. Joseph			06	1944	Joseph Campbell died in Glencree. Co. Wicklow
Caprani	Sat	09	02	2002	Caprani Pork Butchers, Main Street, Bray ceased trading after 70 years

Section Two: Data in Alphabetical Order

Keyword	Day	Date	Mth	Year	Event
Car Park, Bray				1973	The first public car-park was built on the site of St. Pails School, Herbert Road, Bray at a cost of £15,000
Car Park, Bray				1980	2nd Public Car Park in Bray opened in Craigh's Yard, Florence Road, Bray
Carlisle Grounds				1966	Bray Urban District Council purchase the Carlisle Grounds, Bray with the aid of a grant of £8,920 from Bord Failte
Carlisle Grounds	Thu	26	07	2001	The Minister for Sport Dr McDaid announced £200,000 Sport Capital Grant for improvements at the Carlisle Grounds, Bray
Carlisle Grounds	Wed	06	08	2003	Andy McEvoy Challenge Match Bray Wanderers AFC versus Blackburn Rovers FC. Result: Bray Wanderers 2 Blackburn Rovers 3
Carnew	Mon	14	09	1936	Carnew Vocational school built (Colaiste Bhride)
Carnew	Sun	08	09	1940	'98 Memorial unveiled at Carnew
Carnew				1954	The Church of the "Most Holy Rosary" constructed and opened in Carnew
Carnew				1958	Carnew Primary School built
Carnew				1985	Extension added to Carnew Primary School
Carnew				1987	Extension added to Carnew Vocational School
Carnew	Fri	10	05	1996	Carnew Enterprise Centre opened
Carnew AFC				1980	The Carnew AFC established
Carnew Castle			09	1901	Fire destroys Carnew Castle Co. Wicklow the home of Lord and Lady Milton
Carnew Castle				1946	Carnew Castle and lands were sold to Mrs Constance Mary Spicer
Carnew Castle				1981	Carnew Castle was sold by Mrs Constance Mary Spicer
Carnew College				2002	4.4m Euro extension approved to Carnew Community College by Dept. Of Education
Carnew Credit Union				1967	Carnew Credit Union established
Carnew Credit Union			's	1970	The Carnew Credit Union transferred its offices to the school building built in 1829
Carnew Musical Society				1967	Carnew Musical Society established
Carnew Playschool	Mon	24	09	2001	The Little Acorns Community Playschool opened in Carnew
Carrig, Blessington				1985	Excavations at Carrig near Blessington an Stone Age burial chamber discovered
Cars	Fri	01	01	1904	The Motor Car Act came into operation
Cars				1904	Muriel E. Bland the first woman granted a car licence by Wicklow County Council
Cars				1904	Michael J. Rahilly of Wilford Cottage, Bray held the first Motor Vehicle licensed by Wicklow County Council
Cars				1904	The death of the first Irish Car passenger occurred at Marlton Hill, Wicklow
Cars				1905	The first multiple death in a road traffic accident occurred at Balgrad Beg. Co. Wicklow when the chauffer and passenger were killed
Cars				1911	The Public Road (Ireland) Act set the Maximum speed for motor cars at 20 MPH

A-Z Reference	Day	Date	Month	Year	DATA
Cars				1946	44,489 Private Cars registered in Ireland
Cars				1947	52,187 Private Cars registered in Ireland
Cars				1948	60,453 Private Cars registered in Ireland
Cars				1949	71,911 Private Cars registered in Ireland
Cars				1955	Total Population of Ireland (estimated) 2,910,700 Cars Registered 127,511 Cars per 1000 persons 44
Cars				1960	Total Population of Ireland (estimated) 2,834,300 Cars Registered 169,681 Cars per 1000 persons 60
Cars				1965	Total Population of Ireland (estimated) 2,870,900 Cars Registered 281,448 Cars per 1000 persons 98
Cars			10	1968	Car Reg NNI 1 issued by Wicklow Motor Tax Office
Cars	Mon	01	01	1968	Car Reg LNI 671 issued by Wicklow Motor Tax Office
Cars			03	1968	Car Reg MNI 1 issued by Wicklow Motor Tax Office
Cars			05	1969	Car Reg ONI 1 issued by Wicklow Motor Tax Office
Cars	Wed	01	01	1969	Car Reg NNI 270 issued by Wicklow Motor Tax Office
Cars			08	1970	Car Reg RNI 1 issued by Wicklow Motor Tax Office
Cars			01	1970	Car Reg PNI 1 issued by Wicklow Motor Tax Office
Cars	Thu	01	01	1970	Car Reg ONI 919 issued by Wicklow Motor Tax Office
Cars				1970	Total Population of Ireland (estimated) 2,959,400 Cars Registered 389,338 Cars per 1000 persons 132
Cars	Fri	01	01	1971	Car Reg RNI 689 issued by Wicklow Motor Tax Office
Cars			03	1971	Car Reg SNI 1 issued by Wicklow Motor Tax Office
Cars			10	1971	Car Reg TNI 1 issued by Wicklow Motor Tax Office
Cars			04	1972	Car Reg UNI 1 issued by Wicklow Motor Tax Office
Cars			10	1972	Car Reg VNI 1 issued by Wicklow Motor Tax Office
Cars	Mon	03	01	1972	Car Reg TNI 367 issued by Wicklow Motor Tax Office
Cars	Mon	01	01	1973	Car Reg VNI 331 issued by Wicklow Motor Tax Office
Cars			04	1973	Car Reg WNI 1 issued by Wicklow Motor Tax Office
Cars			08	1973	Car Reg XNI 1 issued by Wicklow Motor Tax Office
Cars				1974	Total Population of Ireland (estimated) 3,085,300 Cars Registered 488,522 Cars per 1000 persons 158
Cars	Tue	01	01	1974	Car Reg XNI 530 issued by Wicklow Motor Tax Office
Cars			03	1974	Car Reg YNI 1 issued by Wicklow Motor Tax Office

Section Two: Data in Alphabetical Order

Cars	Car Reg ZNI 1 issued by Wicklow Motor Tax Office	1974	09			
Cars	Car Reg ZNI 369 issued by Wicklow Motor Tax Office	1975	01	01	Wed	
Cars	Car Reg NI 1 issued by Wicklow Motor Tax Office	1975	05			
Cars	Car Reg NI 983 issued by Wicklow Motor Tax Office	1975	12	31	Wed	
Cars	Car Reg 3298 NI issued by Wicklow Motor Tax Office	1976	12	31	Fri	
Cars	Petrol ration coupons issued to all owners of registered vehicles in Ireland but rationing was not introduced	1976				
Cars	Car Reg 984 NI issued by Wicklow Motor Tax Office	1976	01	01	Thu	
Cars	Car Reg 3299 NI issued by Wicklow Motor Tax Office	1977	01	03	Mon	
Cars	Car Reg 5868 NI issued by Wicklow Motor Tax Office	1977	12	30	Fri	
Cars	Car Reg 9147 NI issued by Wicklow Motor Tax Office	1978	12	29	Fri	
Cars	Car Reg 5869 NI issued by Wicklow Motor Tax Office	1978	01	02	Mon	
Cars	Car Reg 1 ANI issued by Wicklow Motor Tax Office	1979	03			
Cars	Car Reg 1 CNI issued by Wicklow Motor Tax Office	1979	11			
Cars	Car Reg 1 BNI issued by Wicklow Motor Tax Office	1979	06			
Cars	Car Reg 9148 NI issued by Wicklow Motor Tax Office	1979	01	01	Mon	
Cars	Car Reg 1 ENI issued by Wicklow Motor Tax Office	1980	07			
Cars	Car Reg 874 ENI issued by Wicklow Motor Tax Office	1980	12	31	Wed	
Cars	Car Reg 111 CNI issued by Wicklow Motor Tax Office	1980	01	01	Tue	
Cars	Car Reg 1 DNI issued by Wicklow Motor Tax Office	1980	03			
Cars	Car Reg 1 HNI issued by Wicklow Motor Tax Office	1981	07			
Cars	Car Reg 1 INI issued by Wicklow Motor Tax Office	1981	11			
Cars	Car Reg 1 GNI issued by Wicklow Motor Tax Office	1981	03			
Cars	Car Reg 1 FNI issued by Wicklow Motor Tax Office	1981	01			
Cars	Car Reg 875 ENI issued by Wicklow Motor Tax Office	1981	01	01	Thu	
Cars	Car Reg 48 INI issued by Wicklow Motor Tax Office	1981	12	31	Thu	
Cars	Car Reg 49 INI issued by Wicklow Motor Tax Office	1982	01	01	Fri	
Cars	Car Reg 1 JNI issued by Wicklow Motor Tax Office	1982	04			
Cars	Car Reg 1 KNI issued by Wicklow Motor Tax Office	1982	10			
Cars	Car Reg 215 KNI issued by Wicklow Motor Tax Office	1983	01	03	Mon	
Cars	Car Reg 1 MNI issued by Wicklow Motor Tax Office	1983	09			

A–Z Reference	Day	Date	Month	Year	DATA
Cars			03	1983	Car Reg 1LNI issued by Wicklow Motor Tax Office
Cars			03	1984	Car Reg 1 NNI issued by Wicklow Motor Tax Office
Cars			09	1984	Car Reg 1 ONI issued by Wicklow Motor Tax Office
Cars	Mon	02	01	1984	Car Reg 321 MNI issued by Wicklow Motor Tax Office
Cars			03	1985	Car Reg 1 PNI issued by Wicklow Motor Tax Office
Cars			09	1985	Car Reg 1 RNI issued by Wicklow Motor Tax Office
Cars			01	1985	Car Reg 270 ONI issued by Wicklow Motor Tax Office
Cars	Tue	01	03	1986	Car Reg 1SNI issued by Wicklow Motor Tax Office
Cars			01	1986	Car Reg 396 RNI issued by Wicklow Motor Tax Office
Cars	Wed	01	09	1986	Car Reg 1 TNI issued by Wicklow Motor Tax Office
Cars			12	1986	Car Reg 426 TNI issued by Wicklow Motor Tax Office
Cars			01	1987	Car Reg 87 WW 1 issued by Wicklow Motor Tax Office
Cars			01	1988	Car Reg 88 WW 1 issued by Wicklow Motor Tax Office
Cars			01	1989	Car Reg 89 WW 1 issued by Wicklow Motor Tax Office
Cars			01	1990	Car Reg 90 WW 1 issued by Wicklow Motor Tax Office
Cars			01	1991	Car Reg 91 WW 1 issued by Wicklow Motor Tax Office
Cars			01	1992	Car Reg 92 WW 1 issued by Wicklow Motor Tax Office
Cars			01	1993	Car Reg 93 WW 1 issued by Wicklow Motor Tax Office
Cars			01	1994	Car Reg 94 WW 1 issued by Wicklow Motor Tax Office
Cars			01	1995	Car Reg 95 WW 1 issued by Wicklow Motor Tax Office
Cars			01	1996	Car Reg 96 WW 1 issued by Wicklow Motor Tax Office
Cars			01	1997	Car Reg 97 WW 1 issued by Wicklow Motor Tax Office
Cars			01	1998	Car Reg 98 WW 1 issued by Wicklow Motor Tax Office
Cars			01	1999	Car Reg 99 WW 1 issued by Wicklow Motor Tax Office
Cars			01	2000	Car Reg 00 WW 1 issued by Wicklow Motor Tax Office
Cars			01	2001	Car Reg 01 WW 1 issued by Wicklow Motor Tax Office
Cars			01	2002	Car Reg 02 WW 1 issued by Wicklow Motor Tax Office
Cars			01	2003	Car Reg 03 WW 1 issued by Wicklow Motor Tax Office

Cars			04	2004	The number of (new Private cars) vehicles registered for the first time in County Wicklow was 476
Cars			01	2004	The number of (new Private cars) vehicles registered for the first time in County Wicklow was 445 (Source CSO)
Cars			05	2004	The number of (new Private cars) vehicles registered for the first time in County Wicklow was 374
Cars			03	2004	The number of (new Private cars) vehicles registered for the first time in County Wicklow was 530
Casement. Roger	Fri	21	04	1916	Roger Casement hanged
Castlekevin House				1993	The film actor Daniel Day Lewis purchased Castlekevin House
Cattle				1997	The total number of cattle over 2 years in County Wicklow 16,500
Cattle				1997	The total number of cattle under 1 year in County Wicklow 31,700
Cattle				1997	The total number of bulls in County Wicklow 1,000
Cattle				1997	The total number of Heifers in calf in County Wicklow 6,700
Cattle				1997	The total number of cattle 1-2 years in County Wicklow 31,600
Cattle				1997	The total number of beef cows in County Wicklow 25,400
Cattle				1997	The total number of dairy cows in County Wicklow 21,300
Cattle				2002	Number of Cattle in County Wicklow 128,459
Cavendish. Andrew			05	2004	The Duke of Devonshire Andrew Cavendish died at Chatsworth house, England in his 84 year
CCTV	Sat	26	07	2003	The proposed locations for Close Circuit TV (CCTV) cameras in Bray. Public Notice in National Papers by Dept of Justice
Chamber of Commerce				1946	Wicklow & District Chamber of Commerce established
Chamber of Commerce	Fri	02	11	1956	Bray Chamber of Commerce incorporated
Chamber of Commerce				1958	Mr H Hautz elected President of Bray Chamber of Commerce
Chamber of Commerce				1959	Mr H.B. Hipwell elected President of Bray Chamber of Commerce 1959-1961
Chamber of Commerce	Fri	14	05	2003	Bray a& District Chamber of commerce, Endeavour Awards
Charlesland G & C Club				1992	Charlesland Golf and Country Club (Greystones) established
Charleville House				1941	Charleville House bought by Donal Davis
Cheshire Home				1960	At Ardeen near Shillelagh. Group Captain Leonard Cheshire opened a Cheshire home
Chess Club				1975	Bray, Greystones Chess Club founded
Chichester. Sir. F	Tue	17	09	1901	Francis Chichester born at Barnstaple, Devon
Chichester. Sir. F	Mon	22	06	1964	Francis Chichester sets a new record for crossing the Atlantic in under 30 days
Chichester. Sir. F	Fri	27	01	1967	Sir Francis Chichester was knighted after finishing round the world voyage in his yacht Gypsy Moth III

A–Z Reference	Day	Date	Month	Year	DATA
Chichester. Sir. F	Sat	26	08	1972	Sir Francis Chichester died
Childers. E. H.	Mon	25	06	1973	Erskine Hamilton Childers became President of Ireland
Childers. E. H.	Thu	21	11	1974	The remains of President Erskine Childers are buried in Derralossary graveyard, Roundwood, Co. Wicklow
Childers. E.H	Mon	11	12	1905	Erskine Hamilton Childers born in London
Childers. E.H	Sun	17	11	1974	The President Erskine H. Childers died. The First President of Ireland to die in office
Childers. R. E				1903	Robert Erskine Childers wrote The Riddle of the Sands
Childers. R. E				1904	Robert Erskine Childers married Mary Ellen Osgood
Childers. R. E				1910	Robert Erskine Childers wrote War and the Arme Blanche
Childers. R. E				1911	Robert Erskine Childers wrote The Framework of Home Rule
Childers. R. E				1920	Robert Erskine Childers wrote Military Rule in Ireland
Childers. R. E	Fri	24	11	1922	Robert Erskine Childers court-martialled and shot in Beggars Bush barracks, Dublin
Childers. R. E			11	1922	Robert Erskine Childers arrested at Robert Bartons house, Annamoe, Co. Wicklow
Children's Home				1940	West Bank Children's home established in Greystones on the La Touche Road.
China			06	2003	Bray Co. Wicklow played host to the delegation from China taking part in the Special Olympic World Games 2003
Christ Church, Bray				1911	New organ for Christ Church Bray built by Conachar of Huddersfield
Christ Church, Bray				1912	Celtic Cross erected in memory of Canon Scott in Front of Christ Church Bray
Christ Church, Bray				1936	The side chapel in Christ Church Bray was dedicated by Archbishop of Dublin Dr. Gregg
Christ Church, Bray				1946	A porch was added to Christ Church Bray in memory of dead of the Second World War.
Christ Church, Bray				1950	The bells re-hung in Christ Church, Bray after repairs were carried out to the bells
Christan Brothers				1921	Colaiste Ciaran (Seminary) founded by the Christen Brothers in Old Connaught House, near Bray
CIE	Mon	02	02	1987	Transport (Reorganisation of C.I.E) Act came into effect
Cinema. Bray	Thu	26	12	1935	Royal Cinema opened in Bray
Cinema. Bray	Mon	01	07	1974	The Odeon (Ireland) Ltd sold the Royal Cinema at Bray, Co. Wicklow to Mr. Michael Collins
Cinema. Bray				1979	The Royal Cinema was converted into two cinemas by the new owner Michael Collins
City of Wurtzburg	Tue	02	11	1999	Bray and County Wicklow twinned with the City of Wurzburg, Germany (Bray Ceremony)
Cliffwalk, Bray				1932	The Bray Urban District Council acquired part of the coastal path (railway path) around Bray Head, called the cliffwalk

Name	Weekday	Day	Month	Year	Event
Cliffwalk, Bray				1961	Legal Case Miss Celcilia Healy took legal action against Bray UDC for injuries she sustained while walking on cliffwalk
Cliffwalk, Bray	Sat	09	07	2005	CliffWalk between Bray and Greystones Officially re-opened after closure for repair
Coastwatching	Mon	19	11	1945	The Coastwatching service disbanded
Cochrane				1915	W. B Cochrane sold Bailieborough Castle, Co. Cavan to the Marist Brothers Order
Cochrane. Ernest	Tue	12	09	1911	Sir Ernest C. Cochrane 2nd Bart., of Woodbrook, Bray married 2nd Elsa Schumacher
Cochrane. Ernest	Thu	23	02	1933	Sir Ernest C. Cochrane 2nd Bart., of Woodbrook, Bray married 3rd Flora Sandstrom
Cochrane. Henry	Thu	08	10	1903	Sir Henry Cochrane, of Woodbrook, Bray created 1st Baronet Cochrane
Cochrane. Henry	Sun	11	09	1904	Sir Henry Cochrane died and was succeeded by his son Ernest 2nd Bart., of Woodbrook, Bray
Cochrane. Margaret	Sat	07	12	1901	Margaret Cochrane, of Woodbrook, Bray died
Cochrane. Stanley				1905	Stanley Cochrane purchased the Mercedes that won the Gordon Bennett Race of 1903, Car given Road Registration IK 183
Cochrane. Stanley				1910	Sir Stanley Cochrane sold Bailieborough Castle, Co. Cavan to his cousin W. B. Cochrane a solicitor from Bailieborough
Cochrane. Stanley	Wed	10	02	1915	Sir Stanley Herbert Cochrane, of Woodbrook, Bray created a Baronet
Cochrane. Stanley				1921	Sir Stanley Cochrane established a nine hole golf course at Woodbrook, Bray
Cochrane. Stanley				1924	Sir Stanley Cochrane extended the nine hole golf course at Woodbrook, Bray to 18 holes course
Cochrane. Stanley	Fri	29	07	1927	Stanley Cochrane sold his Mercedes Registration Number IK183 to Mr Ernest Martin of Windsor
Cochrane. Stanley	Sun	23	10	1949	Sir Stanley Herbert Cochrane died. The 4th son of Sir Henry Cochrane 1st Bart, of Woodbrook, Bray
Cogan. Denis J.				1944	Denis J. Cogan died at Laragh, Co. Wicklow and buried at Glendalough
COI. Carnew				1912	Messers Geroge Benson of Manchester build an organ for the Parish Church at Tourmakeady, Co Mayo
COI. Carnew				1956	The organ in the Parish Church of Tourmakeady was sold when the church closed and it was installed in Carnew, Parish Church
COI. Carnew				1995	R. E Mates & Son (Dublin) carried out repairs to the church organ in All Saints Church of Ireland, Carnew. Co.Wicklow.
Coilte			02	1988	Coilte Teoranta– The Irish Forestry Board was established under the Forestry Act of 1988
Coins				1986	Coinage (Calling In) Order –removal of half penny from circulation with effect 01/01/1987
Colahan. Richard				1912	Rev Richard Colahan appointed Parish Priest of Bray, Little Bray and Greystones.
Colahan. Richard	Fri	17	03	1922	Rev Richard Colahan Parish Priest of the Holy Redeemer Parish Bray died and was buried in St. Peter's Graveyard, Bray
Colaiste Raithin				1991	Colaiste Raithin, Bray founded
Coles. Neil				1965	Carrolls International Golf Tournament held at Woodbrook Golf Club, Bray. Winner Neil Coles (England)
Collis. J.S				1984	John Stewart Collis (writer and naturalist) died

A-Z Reference	Day	Date	Month	Year	DATA
Comerford. Marie				1935	Marie Comerford joined the Irish Press Newspapers
Comerford. Marie				1982	Marie Comerford died
Compulsory Purchase	Thu	05	07	2001	Wicklow County Council Compulsory Purchase (Kilcoole) No. 1 Order, 2001
Conacher. Lionel	Fri	24	05	1901	Lionel Conacher (Ice Hockey player) was born in Toronto Canada. His grandmother Elizabeth Black came from County Wicklow
Conacher. Lionel				1937	Lionel Conacher elected to the Ontario Legislature
Conacher. Lionel				1949	Lionel Conacher elected to the Canadian Parliament (1949-1954)
Conacher. Lionel	Wed	26	05	1954	Lionel Conacher died
Condren. Daniel				1914	Daniel Condren held the post of Chairman of Wicklow County Council 1914-1920
Condren. Daniel				1925	Daniel Condren died
Connolly Square	Sun	15	08	1954	Grotto in James Connolly Square Bray was blessed by Rev. John Fitzpatrick, Bray
Connolly. James				1903	Mona Connolly the eldest child of James Connolly and Lillie Reynolds killed in an accident
Connolly. James	Fri	12	05	1916	James Connolly killed by firing squad at Kilmainham for his part in the Easter Rising
Connolly. James				1938	Mrs James Connolly (nee Reynolds) died
Connolly. Roderick	Fri	11	01	1901	Roderick Connolly the son of James and Lillie Connolly born
Connolly. Roderick	Tue	22	06	1943	Roderick Connolly elected T.D. for Louth 1943-1944
Connolly. Roderick	Wed	04	02	1948	Roderick Connolly elected T.D. for Louth 1948-1951
Connolly. Roderick	Tue	16	12	1980	Roderick Connolly of Bray died
Constitution	Wed	29	12	1937	The Irish Constitution came into operation
Convent, Greystones				1906	The Holy Faith Convent established in Greystones
Coolattin Golf Club				1962	Coolattin Golf Club, Shillelagh, Co. Wicklow established
Corbett. W.J.	Mon	01	12	1909	W.J. Corbett M.P. for Wicklow died
Corke Lodge	Sat	06		1906	Sir Stanley Cochrane acquired Corke Lodge, Shankill Road, Bray
Cormer. Frederick J.			07	1901	Frederick J. Cromer born in Middlesex, England
Cormer. Frederick J.	Fri	08	07	1921	Constable Frederick J. Cromer shot at the RIC Barracks, Rathdrum. He died from his wounds
Costal Erosion				1908	A Royal Commission on Coast Erosion held a meeting in Bray
Costello. Seamus				1939	Seamus Costello born in Bray County Wicklow
Costello. Seamus				1957	Seamus Costello was arrested in Glencree Co. Wicklow

Keyword	Event	Year			
Costello. Seamus	Seamus Costello founded a Tenants Association in Bray	1966			
Costello. Seamus	Seamus Costello elected to Bray Urban District Council and Wicklow County Council	1967			
Costelloe. Seamus	Seamus Costelloe (Clr.and MCC) the founder and chairman of the Irish Republican Socialist Party, shot dead in Dublin.	1977	10	05	Wed
County Show	The 67th Annual Wicklow County Show held in Tinahely	2002	08	05	Mon
County Wicklow	Wicklow County and Rathdown Public Assistant District (Dispensary Districts) Order 1957	1957			
County Wicklow	Wicklow County (District Electoral Divisions) Order 1957	1957			
County Wicklow	Wicklow County (Extension of Boundary) Provisional Order 1957 (Commencement) Order 1957	1957			
County Wicklow	County Wicklow (Dispensary Districts) Order 1961	1961			
County Wicklow	Wicklow County and Dublin Health Authority Area (Registrars' Districts) Order 1965	1965			
County Wicklow	Wicklow County Council (Amendment) Order 1974	1974			
County Wicklow	County of Wicklow Traffic and Parking Temporary Rules 1985	1985			
County Wicklow	County of Wicklow Traffic and Parking Bye-Laws 1986	1986			
County Wicklow	County of Wicklow Local Electoral Areas Order 1998	1998			
Courage. Michael	Irish Angling Record for Greater Spotted Dogfish 19lb 12oz was set by Michael Courage at, Bray (Guinness Book of Records)	1969	07	06	Sun
Court House. Bray	Two bombs were thrown through the door of the Court House, Bray	1921	04	18	Mon
Court House. Bray	Bray Court House on the Boghall Road opened	1984	09		
Courthouses	The Courthouses (Provision and Maintance) Act requires local authorities to provide and maintain court-houses.	1935			
Crampton Collection	The National Library of Ireland purchased 21 drawings by John Crampton and 15 drawings by Selina Crampton	2000			
Credit Union	Bray Credit Union established.	1964			
Cricket	All Ireland Cricket Team played Yorkshire Cricket Team at Woodbrook, Bray	1907	05	02	Thu
Cricket	South African Cricket Touring Team played Sir Stanley Cochrane's X1 Cricket team at Woodbrook	1907	08	12	Mon
Cricket	First Class Cricket match Sir Stanley Cochrane XI v Australians at Woobrook, Bray	1909	09	17	Fri
Cricket	First Class Cricket match C.B. Fry's XI v Australians held at Woodbrook, Bray.	1912	09	12	Thu
Cricket	First Class Cricket match Ireland v South Africans held at Woodbrook, Bray.	1912	07	25	Thu
Cricket	First Class Cricket match Woodbrook Cricket Club and Ground v South Africans held at Woodbrook, Bray.	1912	07	22	Mon
Crimmins. PJ	Very Rev P.J. Crimmins became Parish Priest of Enniskerry	1910			
Crinion. Peter	Peter Crinion of Bray represented Ireland in cycling at the 1960 Olympic Games held in Rome	1960			

A–Z Reference	Day	Date	Month	Year	DATA
Croatia			06	2003	Greystones Co. Wicklow played host to the delegation from Croatia taking part in the Special Olympic World Games 2003
Crosby. Bing	Sun	17	09	1961	Bing Crosby played a game of golf at Woodbrook, in aid of The Irish Society for the Prevention Cruelty to Children
Cullen. Augustus				1924	Augustus Cullen acquired the legal firm established in 1887
Cullen. Augustus				1981	The legal E J H Hopkins acquired the legal firm of Augustus Cullen & Sons
Cullen. Fr. John				1970	Fr. John Cullen died
Cullen. Gary				1945	Gary Cullen born 1945, educated at Presentation College, Bray. Former Chief Executive of Aer Lingus
Cullen. Thomas				1995	Thomas Cullen held the post of Chairman of Wicklow County Council 1995–1996
Cunningham. Larry			's	1960	Larry Cunningham and the show band The Mighty Avons recorded the song "Among the Wicklow Hills"
Currency	Fri	01	08	1969	Farthings and halfpennies no longer legal tender
Currency	Mon	01	09	1969	5p and 10p coins introduced as legal tender
Currency				1979	Ireland broke the link with Sterling where ir$£ = £$stg (see 1826)
Currency	Tue	01	01	2002	The Euro currency notes and coins becomes legal tender in 12 countries
Curtlestown				1960	St Patrick's National School, Curtlestown built
Curtlestown				1984	Extension added to St. Patrick's National School, Curtlestown that was built in 1960.
Cycle Polo	Sat	28	09	1901	The first international cycle polo match between Ireland and England took place at Crystal Palace London (Irl. 10, G.B. 5)
Cycle Polo			07	1908	Cycle Polo competition in the Olympic games. Ireland beat Germany in the final (3–1) held at Shepard's Bush Stadium London
Daly. Capt				1953	The owner of Russborough House, Blessington. Capt. Daly died
Daly. Edward	Thu	04	05	1916	Edward Daly executed for his part in the 1916 Rebellion, Commandant of the Four Courts
Darcy. Eamonn	Thu	07	08	1952	Eamonn Darcy (golfer) born Delgany Co. Wicklow
Darcy. Eamonn				1968	Eamonn Darcy became a professional golfer
Darcy. Eamonn				1977	Eamonn Darcy won the Greater Manchester Open Golf Classic
Darcy. Eamonn				1983	Eamonn Darcy won the Benson & Hedges Spanish Open Golf Classic
Darcy. Eamonn				1987	Eamonn Darcy played on the Ryder Cup Team. The first time a European Cup team won the match on US soil
Darcy. Eamonn				1987	Eamonn Darcy won the Volvo Belgian Open Golf Classic
Darcy. Eamonn				1990	Eamonn Darcy won the Emirates Airlines Desert Golf Classic
Dargle River	Thu	24	08	1905	The River Dargle broke its banks and flooded, Little Bray

Section Two: Data in Alphabetical Order

Name	Day	Date	Month	Year	Event
Dargle River	Thu	03	09	1931	The River Dargle broke its banks and flooded, Little Bray
Dargle River				1947	Flood waters destroy property in Little Bray when the River Dargle broke its banks
Dargle River				1965	Flooding took place in Little Bray when the River Dargle burst its banks
Dargle River				1967	River Dargle at Bray flooded
Dargle River				1969	Flood prevention scheme was put in place at the Dargle River costing £120,000
Dargle River	Sun	24	08	1986	Over 1000 persons given shelter in Ravenswell, Little Flower Hall, and Parochial Hall Novara Road after floods in Little Bray
Dargle River	Sun	24	08	1986	Flooding took place in Little Bray after a day of heavy rain. Over 1000 persons taken from their homes
Darley, Cecil W.				1928	Cecil West Darley died
Darley, F.M				1910	Sir Frederick Matthew Darley, Australian Statesman, died
Darley, J. C.	Sun	31	03	1918	Lt. Col. John Evelyn Carmichael Darley was killed in action, and is buried at Moreuil Communal Allied Cemetery
Darley, Sir F.M				1901	Sir Frederick Matthew Darley was created G.C.M.G
Darley, Sir F.M	Tue	04	01	1910	Sir Frederick Matthew Darley died in London
Davidson, Lillian				1934	Low Tide, Wicklow a painting in the Ulster Museum, Belfast by Lillian Lucy Davidson
Davidson, Lillian				1954	Lillian Lucy Davidson (artist) died.
Davidson, Rosanna			04	1984	Rosanna Davidson born
Davidson, Rosanna				2003	Rosanna Davidson from County Wicklow crowned Miss World
de Buitlear, Eamon				1930	Eamon de Buitlear (naturalist and film-maker) born in Dublin the family moved to Bray in 1930
de Buitlear, Eamon				1991	Eamon de Buitlear (naturalist and film-maker) granted honuary Dsc at NUI
De la Salle		01		1912	The De la Salle community establish a school in Wicklow Town
De Valois, N	Fri	05	07	1935	Dame Ninette De Valois (Edris Stannus) married Arthur O'Connell
De Valois, N	Thu	08	03	2001	Dame Ninette De Valois (Edris Stannus) died in London
Deaths				2002	Deaths in County Wicklow. 774
Deering, Mark				1972	Mark Deering held the post of Chairman of Wicklow County Council 1972-1973
Delaney, John				1965	Rev John Delaney became Parish Priest of St. Mary's Church Enniskerry
Delaney, John	Thu	25	06	1981	Rev John Delaney Parish Priest of Enniskerry died
Delany, Ronnie	Wed	06	03	1935	Ronnie Delany born at 4 Ferrybank. Arklow, Co. Wicklow
Delany, Ronnie				1955	Ronnie Delaney won the Irish title for the 880 yards in 1:50.0
Delany, Ronnie	Sat	01	12	1956	Ronnie Delany from Arklow won the 1,500m Gold medal at the 1956 Olympic Games held in Melbourne in a time of 3min:41:2

A–Z Reference	Day	Date	Month	Year	DATA
Delany. Ronnie				1957	Ronnie Delaney won the Irish title for the 880 yards in 1:47:8
Delany. Ronnie	Mon	05	09	2005	Dublin City Council agree to give Sir Bob Geldof and Ronnie Delany the Freedom of the City of Dublin
Delgany	Sat	08	12	1934	Two men Patrick & Charles O'Leary got trapped in a well at Birchville, near Delgany
Delgany			's	1940	The Delgany Horticultural Society Founded
Delgany				1959	The Delgany Horticultural Society renamed Delgany & District Horticultural Society
Delgany	Sat	13	01	1990	Mr. Peter Sutherland former Attorney General and EU Commissioner turned the first sod for Delgany School
Delgany			06	2002	The Archbishop of Dublin and Glendalough opened an extension to Delgany National School
Delgany Golf Club				1956	Delgany Golf Club won the Barton Cup
Delgany Golf Club				1979	Leinster Youths Amateur Open Championship, held at Delgany Golf Club
Delgany Golf Club				1980	Leinster Youths Amateur Open Championship, held at Delgany Golf Club
Delgany Golf Club				1981	Delgany Golf Club won the Barton Cup
Delgany Golf Club				1981	Leinster Youths Amateur Open Championship, held at Delgany Golf Club
Delgany Golf Club				1982	Leinster Youths Amateur Open Championship, held at Delgany Golf Club, won by P. Errity, Delgany
Delgany Golf Club				1983	Leinster Youths Amateur Open Championship, held at Delgany Golf Club
Delgany Golf Club				1984	Leinster Youths Amateur Open Championship, held at Delgany Golf Club
Delgany Golf Club				1985	Leinster Youths Amateur Open Championship, held at Delgany Golf Club
Delgany Golf Club				1986	Leinster Youths Amateur Open Championship, held at Delgany Golf Club
Delgany Golf Club				1987	Leinster Youths Amateur Open Championship, held at Delgany Golf Club
Delgany Golf Club				1988	Leinster Youths Amateur Open Championship, held at Delgany Golf Club
Delgany Golf Club				1989	Leinster Youths Amateur Open Championship, held at Delgany Golf Club
Delgany Golf Club				1991	Leinster Youths Amateur Open Championship, held at Delgany Golf Club
Delgany Golf Club				1991	Delgany Golf Club won the Barton Cup
Delgany Golf Club				1993	Leinster Youths Amateur Open Championship, held at Delgany Golf Club, won by K. Nolan, Bray
Derralossary Church			's	1960	Derralossary Church near Roundwood closed
Derralossary Church				1985	Derralossary Church near Roundwood deconsecrated
Deverell. Averill	Sat	17	02	1979	Averill Deverell died at her home in Greystones, Co. Wicklow
Devlin. Anne	Sun	16	09	1951	Mrs Sean T O'Kelly wife of President O'Kelly unveiled a plaque to Anne Devlin on the bridge in Aughrim

Dillion. J.M.				1939	John Myles Dillion (Regis Professor of Greek at Trinity College, Dublin) born 1939. educated at St. Gerard's School Bray
Djouce Mountain G. C.				1996	Djouce Mountain Golf Club (Roundwood) established
Dock Terrace				1954	Some cottages at Dock Terrace demolished
D'olier. Bertrand	Fri	17	08	1928	Bertrand Guy D'Olier of Wingfield, Bray killed in a flying accident at Digby Aerodrome, Lincolnshire
D'Ombrain. Ernest A.	Fri	23	06	1944	Ernest Arthur D'Ombrain died at Killara, Sydney. Australia
Donard	Wed	21	11	2001	Illegally dumped hospital waste found near Donard, Co. Wicklow
Donovan. J.T.				1914	J.T. Donovan elected M.P. for Wicklow West 1914 -1918
Donovan. J.T.				1918	J.T. Donovan elected M.P. for Donegal South 1918
Doran. Felix				1915	Feilx Doran (uilleann pipe player) born Rathnew, County Wicklow. A brother of Johnny Doran
Doran. Felix				1972	Felix Doran died in Manchester
Doran. John				1968	Rev. John Doran Parish Priest of Tomacork, Carnew 1968–1977
Doran. Johnny				1907	Johnny Doran (uilleann pipe player) born in Rathnew. County Wicklow
Doran. Johnny	Mon	09	01	1950	Johnny Doran died in St. Vincent's Hospital, Athy. County Kildare and he is buried in Rathnew Cemetery
Douglas. James				1929	James Douglas born in Bray. He devised the RTE TV series The Riordans.
Douglas. M.J				1963	Mark Douglas born 1963, Businessman founded Ireland's first Pizza delivery Service, Educated at St. Gerard's Bray.
Doyle. Peter				1968	Peter Doyle of Bray represented Ireland in cycling at the 1968 Olympic Games held in Mexico
Doyle. Peter				1972	Peter Doyle of Bray represented Ireland in cycling at the 1972 Olympic Games held in Munich
Driving	Thu	31	10	2002	Penalty points for careless driving introduced by Minister of Transport
Driving	Mon	28	04	2003	A report for the first 6 months of Penalty Points System 505 Drivers in Wicklow had 2 penalty points, 12 drivers had 4 penalty points
Druids Glen Golf Club				1995	Druids Glen Golf Club established in the grounds of Woodstock Estate, Delgany
Druids Glen Golf Club				1996	The Irish Open Golf Championship held at Druid's Glen Golf Club, Delgany
Druids Glen Golf Club				1997	The Irish Open Golf Championship held at Druid's Glen Golf Club, Delgany
Druids Glen Golf Club				1998	The Irish Open Golf Championship held at Druid's Glen Golf Club, Delgany
Druids Glen Golf Club				1999	The Irish Open Golf Championship held at Druid's Glen Golf Club, Delgany
Druids Glen Hotel			04	2002	The Druid's Glen Marriott Hotel and Country Club opened
Drumm. James	Thu	18	07	1974	James Drumm (Battery Train) died
Drummond School			08	1919	The Royal Drummond school moved from Mulberry Hill, Chapelizod, Dublin to the Vevay Road, Bray (see 1944)
Dublin California	Tue	02	03	1993	Bray twinned with Dublin, Califorina, U.S.A.

A-Z Reference	Day	Date	Month	Year	DATA
Dublin Gas Company				1918	The Dublin Gas Company purchased the 'Braedale' ship from T.M.Collier coal importer and merchant in Bray.
Dublin Gas Company				1930	The Gas Showrooms, Main Street, Bray
Dublin Lock Out	Fri	17	10	1913	Dockers clash with the police at Bray Harbour, when a coal boat for Heitons is off loaded, during the Dublin lock out of 1913
Dun Loghaire				1926	Dun Laoghaire replaced the name Kingstown
Dunlavin	Mon	22	10	2001	Illegally dumped hospital waste found near Dunlavin, Co. Wicklow
Dunlavin Town Hall	Sun	02	08	1925	The Bell at the Dunlavin Town Hall given to the Black Abbey, Kilkenny to mark 700 anniversary of the Abbey
Dunne. Seamus	Sun	13	04	1930	Seamus Dunne born in Co. Wicklow
Dunne. Seamus				1951	Seamus Dunne played for Shelbourne Football Club
Dunne. Seamus	Wed	26	12	1951	Seamus Dunne played his debut match for Luton Town Football Club
Dunne. Seamus				1951	Seamus Dunne joined Luton Town Football Club (1951-1966)
Dunne. Seamus				1953	Seamus Dunne won his first cap for the Republic of Ireland football team ,where he won 15 full caps (1953-1959)
Dunne. Sean	Wed	18	12	1918	Sean Dunne born
Dunne. Sean	Wed	25	06	1969	Sean Dunne T.D. died, He lived at 46 Wolfe Tone Square North, Bray
Dunphy. Fr. James			11	1914	Fr. James Dunphy died, pastor of Arklow for 57 years.
DUTC				1925	The Dublin United Tramways (Omnibus Service) Act regulated the Bus service in Dublin
Dwyer. Michael	Sun	15	06	1902	The foundation stone laid for the memorial to Michael Dwyer and Sam McAllister at Baltinglass
Dwyer. Michael	Sun	08	05	1904	Memorial to Michael Dwyer and Sam McAllister unveiled at Baltinglass
Dwyer. Michael				1938	Restoration project was begun on Michael Dwyer's cottage at Derrynamuck, Co. Wicklow
Dwyer. Michael				1946	Michael Dwyer's cottage at Derrynamuck, Co. Wicklow opened to the public
Dwyer. Michael				1983	The Bray Branch of the Irish National Foresters the Michael Dwyer branch was disbanded after 98 years
Dwyer. Michael				1992	Michael Dwyer's cottage at Derrynamuck, Co. Wicklow re-roofed
Earthquake	Thu	19	07	1984	An earthquake occurred in Ireland and West England it measured 5.5 on the Richter Scale
East Coast Radio				2002	East Coast Radio opened a new studio on the Killarney Road, Bray
East Coast Radio			11	2002	East Coast Radio Headquarters on the Killarney Road Bray officially opened
Ecology Centre				1998	The Dominican Sisters established the Dominican Farm and Ecology Centre in Wicklow Town
Economic Survey				1977	A Economic Survey showed Bray as the Best Value Town in Ireland

Section Two: Data in Alphabetical Order

Subject	Event	Year	Mth	Day	Day
Eisenhower. Gen	Gen. Eisenhower former President of USA paid a visit to the former President of Ireland Sean T.O'Kelly at his Roundwood home	1962	08	23	Thu
Eksund	French Customs authorities seize Eskund ship carrying 150 tons of armaments. Two Wicklow men arrested	1987	10	30	Fri
Elections–Polling Day	Elections to Bray Urban District Council took place	1905	01	16	Mon
Elections–Polling Day	Denis Joseph Cogan elected M.P. for Wicklow East at the General Election, Number of electors 4954	1906	01	15	Mon
Elections–Polling Day	James O'Connor elected M.P. for Wicklow West at the General Election, Number of electors 4406	1906	01	16	Tue
Elections–Polling Day	John Muldoon elected M.P. for Wicklow East at the By-Election caused when Denis J Cogan resigned	1907	07	29	Mon
Elections–Polling Day	John Muldoon elected M.P. for Wicklow East at the General Election, Number of electors 4710	1910	12	12	Mon
Elections–Polling Day	John Muldoon elected M.P. for Wicklow East at the General Election, Number of electors 4710	1910	01	17	Mon
Elections–Polling Day	Edward P. O'Kelly elected M.P. for Wicklow West at the General Election, Number of electors 4417	1910	12	06	Tue
Elections–Polling Day	Edward P. O'Kelly elected M.P. for Wicklow West at the By-Election caused by the death James O'Connor	1910	03	29	Tue
Elections–Polling Day	James O'Connor elected M.P. for Wicklow West at the General Election, Number of electors 4417	1910	01	18	Tue
Elections–Polling Day	Capt. Anthony J. C. Donelan elected M.P. for Wicklow East at the By-Election caused by John Muldoon resigned	1911	07	13	Thu
Elections–Polling Day	J.T. Donovan elected M.P. for Wicklow West at the By-Election caused by the death Edward P. O'Kelly	1914	12	02	Wed
Elections–Polling Day	Elections to Bray Urban District Council took place	1914	01	15	Thu
Elections–Polling Day	General Election, Bray was part of the Wicklow/East Kildare Constituency	1918			
Elections–Polling Day	Elections to county councils, rural district councils, and boards of guardians	1920	06	18	Fri
Elections–Polling Day	Local elections are held	1925	06		
Elections–Polling Day	Local elections are held	1928	06		
Elections–Polling Day	Local elections are held	1934	06		
Elections–Polling Day	Polling Day for Constitutional Referenda – endorse new constitution	1937	07	01	Thu
Elections–Polling Day	Local elections are held	1942	08		
Elections–Polling Day	Presidential Election held	1945	06		
Elections–Polling Day	Local elections are held	1945	06		
Elections–Polling Day	Local elections are held	1950	09		
Elections–Polling Day	Local elections are held	1955	06		
Elections–Polling Day	Presidential Election held	1959	06	17	Wed
Elections–Polling Day	Polling Day for Constitutional Referenda– Introduction of plurality system	1959	06	17	Wed
Elections–Polling Day	Local elections are held	1960	06	29	Wed

A–Z Reference	Day	Date	Month	Year	DATA
Elections–Polling Day				1966	Presidential Election held
Elections–Polling Day	Wed	28	06	1967	Local elections are held
Elections–Polling Day	Wed	16	10	1968	Polling Day for Constitutional Referenda– T.D.-population ratio
Elections–Polling Day	Wed	16	10	1968	Polling Day for Constitutional Referenda– Introduction plurality system
Elections–Polling Day	Thu	07	12	1972	Polling Day for Constitutional Referenda– Abolish "special position" of the Catholic Church
Elections–Polling Day	Wed	10	05	1972	Polling Day for Constitutional Referenda– Allow E.E.C. membership
Elections–Polling Day	Thu	07	12	1972	Polling Day for Constitutional Referenda– Lower voting age to 18
Elections–Polling Day	Wed	30	05	1973	Presidential Election held
Elections–Polling Day			06	1974	Local elections are held
Elections–Polling Day	Thu	05	07	1979	Polling Day for Constitutional Referenda– Allow alteration of university representation in Seanad Eireann
Elections–Polling Day	Thu	07	06	1979	The first direct elections of representives to the European Parliament
Elections–Polling Day	Thu	07	06	1979	Local elections are held
Elections–Polling Day	Thu	05	07	1979	Polling Day for Constitutional Referenda– Protect adoption system
Elections–Polling Day	Wed	07	09	1983	Polling Day for Constitutional Referenda– Prohibit legalisation of abortion
Elections–Polling Day	Thu	14	06	1984	2nd election of representives to the European Parliament
Elections–Polling Day	Thu	14	06	1984	Electorate in the Bray Area 16,600 for County Council 6 seats L.McManus,J.Byrne,C.Murphy,M.Mortell,M.Lawlor,M.Ledwidge
Elections–Polling Day	Thu	20	06	1985	Local Elections, Urban District and County Council
Elections–Polling Day	Thu	20	06	1985	Local elections are held
Elections–Polling Day	Thu	26	06	1986	Polling Day for Constitutional Referenda– Allow legalisation of divorce
Elections–Polling Day	Thu	26	06	1986	Polling Day for the 10th Amendment to the Constitution (Proposed the introduction of divorce in Ireland) Against 63% For 36%
Elections–Polling Day	Tue	26	05	1987	Polling Day for Constitutional Referenda– Allow singing of Single European Act
Elections–Polling Day	Tue	26	05	1987	Single European Amendment Act – Wicklow Voted Yes 69,4% No 30.60% Electorate 65,393 Turnout 45.95%
Elections–Polling Day	Thu	15	06	1989	3rd election of representives to the European Parliament
Elections–Polling Day				1990	Presidential Election held
Elections–Polling Day	Wed	25	11	1992	General Election. Wicklow 5 Seats Electorate 77,133
Elections–Polling Day	Wed	25	11	1992	Polling Day for Constitutional Referenda– Restrict availability of abortion

Section Two: Data in Alphabetical Order

	Day	Date	Month	Year	Description
Elections–Polling Day	Wed	25	11	1992	Polling Day for Constitutional Referenda– Right to Information guarantee
Elections–Polling Day	Wed	25	11	1992	Polling Day for Constitutional Referenda– Right to travel guarantee
Elections–Polling Day	Thu	18	06	1992	Polling Day for Constitutional Referenda– Allow ratification of the Maastricht Treaty of European Union
Elections–Polling Day	Thu	09	06	1994	Local Elections and 4th election of representives to the European Parliament
Elections–Polling Day	Fri	24	11	1995	Polling Day for Constitutional Referenda– Right to divorce
Elections–Polling Day	Thu	28	11	1996	Polling Day for Constitutional Referenda– Restriction on right to bail
Elections–Polling Day	Thu	30	10	1997	Presidential Election held
Elections–Polling Day	Thu	30	10	1997	Polling Day for Constitutional Referenda– Cabinet Confidentiality
Elections–Polling Day	Mon	22	06	1998	Polling Day for Constitutional Referenda– Northern Ireland Agreement
Elections–Polling Day	Mon	22	06	1998	Polling Day for Constitutional Referenda– Ratification of Amsterdam Treaty
Elections–Polling Day	Fri	11	06	1999	Polling Day for Constitutional Referenda– Local Government
Elections–Polling Day	Thu	07	06	2001	Voting on 23rd Amendment of the Constitution Bill, 2001–Acceptance of the Jurisdiction of the International Criminal Court
Elections–Polling Day	Thu	07	06	2001	Voting on 24th Amendment of the Constitution Bill, 2001–The Treaty of Nice
Elections–Polling Day	Thu	07	06	2001	Voting on 21st Amendment of the Constitution (No. 2) Bill, 2001 Abolition of Death Penalty
Elections–Polling Day	Fri	08	06	2001	Voting on 2001–The Treaty of Nice, Electorate Wicklow 85,067. Total Poll 32,587,Yes 14,839 (46.2%) No 17,274(53.7%)
Elections–Polling Day	Wed	06	03	2002	Polling Day for Referendum 25th Amendment of the Constitution (Protection of Human Life in Pregnancy) Bill, 2001
Elections–Polling Day	Fri	17	05	2002	General Election for 29th Dail
Elections–Polling Day	Sat	18	05	2002	Counting of the Votes of General Election 17/05/2002, Electorate 86,763, Total Poll 55,283, Turnout 62.72%
Elections–Polling Day	Fri	17	05	2002	Polling Day for 29th Dail D Roche(FF) L. McManus(Lab) B.Timmins(FG) J.Jacob(FF) M. Fox (Ind)
Elections–Polling Day	Sat	19	10	2002	Voting on 26th Amendment of the Constitution Bill, 2002–The Treaty of Nice
Elections–Polling Day	Sun	20	10	2002	Voting on 2002–The Treaty of Nice, Electorate Wicklow 86,763. Total Poll 46,789,Yes 29,710 (63.8%) No 16,832(36.1%)
Elections–Polling Day	Thu	23	05	2002	2nd Recount of votes cast on 17/05/2002 completed 25th May 2002
Elections–Polling Day	Sun	19	05	2002	1st Recount of votes cast on 17/05/2002
Elections–Polling Day	Wed	06	03	2002	Wicklow Electorate 86,763 Total Poll 41,041 Yes 16,788 No.24,032
Elections–Polling Day	Fri	11	06	2004	27th Amendment of the Constitution Bill 2004
Elections–Polling Day	Fri	11	06	2004	County Council Elections
Elections–Polling Day	Sat	12	06	2004	Wicklow Area Electorate 19,250 Seats 5, Total Poll 11,3111 Turnout 58.76% Spoiled Votes 275, Total Valid poll 11,036 Quota 1,840

A-Z Reference	Day	Date	Month	Year	DATA
Elections–Polling Day	Fri	11	06	2004	European Elections
Elections–Polling Day	Sat	12	06	2004	Baltinglass Area. Electorate 12,204 Seats 3, Total Poll 8,098 Turnout 66.36% Spoiled Votes 103, Total Valid poll 7,995 Quota 1,999
Elections–Polling Day	Sat	12	06	2004	Bray Area Electorate 26,906 Seats 7, Total Poll 14,635 Turnout 54.39% Spoiled Votes 328, Total Valid poll 14,3075 Quota 1,789
Elections–Polling Day	Fri	11	06	2004	Local Elections
Electricity	Tue	02	04	1920	The Bray Electricity (Temporary Increase of Charges) Order, 1920
Electricity				1927	The Electricity Supply Board (ESB) established
Electricity				1934	Bray Electricity Light Company was taken over by the ESB
Electricity				1968	Work started on the electricity generating station at Turlough hill near Glendalough
Electricity				1973	Electricity generating station at Turlough hill near Glendalough was commissioned
Elliott. Shay				1934	Shay Elliott (cyclist) born in Dublin
Elliott.Shay				1963	Shay Elliott became the first Irishman to wear the Yellow Jersey in the Tour de France
Elliott.Shay			05	1971	Shay Elliott (cyclist) died and is buried in Kilmacanogue Graveyard
Elliston. Henry	Sat	29	05	1909	Henry Elliston died
Enniskerry				1925	Street Lighting installed in Enniskerry Village
Enniskerry	Wed	10	09	1930	Lord Powerscourt laid the foundation stone for the Parish Hall formerly British Legion Hall, Bray Road, Enniskerry
Enniskerry				1938	An Archaeology find was found in a sandpit near Enniskerry
Enniskerry	Sat	01	08	1992	A stolen bus crashed into the Clock Tower, Enniskerry
Enniskerry			08	2005	Fr. John Simnott (a native of Bray) appointed Parish Priest of Enniskerry, Curtlestown and Glencree.
Enniskerry			08	2005	Fr. Pat Farnan retired as Parish Priest of Enniskerry, Curtlestown and Glencree
Enniskerry Dam				1925	The Glencree river was dammed near Enniskerry and a pumping station provided electricity for the village
Enniskerry Library				1911	Enniskerry Public Library built at Church Road, Enniskerry
Errity.Tom				1915	Private Tom Errity aged 20, of Newtownmountkennedy County Wicklow was killed at Gallipoli in World War I
ESB			10	1937	The order was placed by the ESB for the main construction work on the Liffey Scheme at Pollaphouca and Golden Falls
ESB			12	1943	The Golden Falls station was brought into commission by the ESB
Esplanade Hotel				1951	The Lavelle family took over the running of the Hotel Esplanade, Bray.
Esplanade Hotel				1978	The Esplanade Hotel sold to the Kiley Family

Section Two: Data in Alphabetical Order

Term	Day	Date	Month	Year	Event
Eucharistic Congress	Wed	22	06	1932	June 22-26 Eucharistic Congress held in Dublin
Euro Coins	Fri	14	12	2001	Euro Coins starter packs go on sale in Banks and Post Offices. The Euro becomes legal tender in 12 countries from 01/01/2002
Everett, James	Sat	12	06	1954	James Everett T.D. for Wicklow appointed Minister of Justice
Everett, James	Mon	18	12	1967	James Everett died, was T.D. for Wicklow from 1922 to 1967 held Ministerial posts in Justice, Post and Telegraphs
Failte Park				1965	Failte Park on Adelaide Road opened by Erskine H. Childers Minister for Transport and Power
Failte Park				1981	Bray Urban District Council purchased Failte Park from Bray Enterprise Ltd
Farmed land				2002	Area farmed in County Wicklow 101,707 hectares
Farrell, Margaret			05	1927	Margaret Farrell of Carrigbeen, Co. Wicklow murdered
Fatima Hall				1940	Fatima Hall, near Bray Railway Station built
FCA				1989	30th Anniversary of the 21st Battalion FCA
Feis	Thu	21	05	1903	The first Wicklow County Feis started on 21/05/1903 and was held in Rathdrum, Co. Wicklow
Film				1914	The film "Ireland a Nation" filmed on locations in Baltinglass and Glendalough. The film had only one public showing in Dublin in 1917.
Film				1917	The film "Ireland a Nation" was banned by the British authorities but played to Packed houses in America
Film				1919	The film "Rosaleen Dhu" mainly filmed in Bray, Arklow and Kilmacanogue. The film's premier was in a Bray cinema McDermott's
Film				1922	The film "Wicklow Gold" released. Location scenes in Avoca
Film				1924	The film "Land of the Fathers" filmed in Enniskerry and Killarney, Co. Kerry
Film				1926	The film "Irish Destiny" exterior filming at Glendalough and Greystones. The film was banned in the U.K.
Film				1937	The film "Parnell" released
Film				1946	The film "I See a dark Stranger" filmed on locations in Wicklow. The film was released under the title "The Adventuress"
Film				1947	The film Captain Boycott filmed in counties Wicklow, Westmeath and Mayo
Film				1957	The film Boyds Shop – outdoor scenes filmed near Enniskerry
Film				1957	The film "Professor Tim" outdoor scenes filmed near Enniskerry
Film				1960	The film "The Night Fighters" filmed in Rathdrum, County Wicklow
Film				1960	The film "Webster Boy" filmed in part in Bray
Film				1961	The film "Johnny Noobdy" was filmed at Enniskerry, Carrickmines, Mountjoy jail and Wicklow Mountains
Film				1962	The film "Running Man" Interiors filmed at Ardmore and some exteriors shots in Bray
Film				1962	The film "The Quare Fellow" filmed at Ardmore Studio and Kilmainham jail

A–Z Reference	Day	Date	Month	Year	DATA
Film				1963	The film "Dementia 13" Filmed at Ardmore Studios and in the village of NewtownMountKennedy
Film				1964	The film The Spy Who Came in from the Cold was filmed at Ardmore and locations around Ireland including Co. Wicklow
Film				1964	The film "Girl with Green Eyes" Filmed on locations in Dublin and Wicklow
Film				1965	The film Blue Max was filmed at Ardmore and locations around Ireland including Co. Wicklow
Film				1968	The film "The Violent Enemy" interior scenes filmed at Ardmore Studio, Bray and exteriors filmed around Dublin
Film				1969	The film McKenize Break stating Brian Keith, Ian Hendry and Helmut Greim was shot in Bray and other locations in Ireland
Film				1971	The film "Act without Words" part filmed in Ardmore studio. The film never went on release
Film				1972	The film "Images" Filmed at Ardmore Studio, and at Powerscourt and other locations in Wicklow.
Film				1973	The film Zeros staring Sean Connery, Charlotte Rumpling was filmed at Ardmore Studio and Hollybrooke House, Bray
Film				1977	Newcastle Hospital was used in the making of the film Equus staring Richard Burton and Jenny Agutter
Film				1978	The TV Series film "Bracken" 1978–1983 locations in County Wicklow, including Roundwood, NewtownMountKennedy, Kilcoole
Film				1979	The film "The Outsiders" interiors shots filmed at Ardmore Studio
Film				1983	The TV Series film "Gelnroe" 1983 –2001 location scenes in County Wicklow , main location Kilcoole.
Film				1984	The film "Cal" location scenes at Crone Wood, Enniskerry and a potato field in Delgany
Film				1984	The film "Anne Deviln" location scenes at Wicklow Town
Film				1986	The film "Rawhead Rex" filmed in County Wicklow
Film				1986	The film "Eat the Peach" filmed on locations in Wicklow ,County Meath, County Kildare and Dublin
Film				1988	Part of the film My Left Foot shot on location in County Wicklow.
Film				1988	The film "The Dawning" set in County Wicklow, filmed on locations in Wicklow and Cork
Film				1988	The film "The Real Charlotte" filmed at Ardmore Studio
Film				1989	The film "My left Foot" Filmed on locations in Dublin and Wicklow. The first Irish-produced film to win an Oscar.
Film				1990	The film "The Commitments" locations scenes at Bray Head Hotel, Bray
Film				1990	The film "The Lilac Bus" location scene at Balltknockan, Powerscourt, Bray, Enniskerry
Film				1990	The film "The Field" locations scenes at Ardmore studio
Film			03	1990	The film "My Left Foot" wins 2 Oscars Daniel Day Lewis and Brenda Fricker

Type	Day			Year	
Film				1990	The film "December Bride" Interior filming at MTM Ardmore Studio
Film				1990	The film "Fools of Fortune" Interior filming at MTM Ardmore Studio
Film				1991	The film "The Miracle" set in Bray
Film				1992	The film "Far and Away" filmed on locations in Wicklow (Killruddery House), County Kerry and Dublin
Film				1992	The film "The Bargain Shop" interior scenes filmed at Ardmore Studio, Bray
Film				1993	The film "Into the West" filmed on locations in County Wicklow, Dublin, Offaly and Galway
Film				1993	The film "The Snapper" interior scenes filmed at Ardmore Studio, Bray
Film				1994	The film "Widow's Peak" location scenes at Ballyknockan and Blessington
Film				1994	The film "Braveheart" locations scenes at Ardmore studio, Glendalough, and the Coronation Plantation, Glen of Imaal
Film				1994	The film "Scarlett" filmed in part at Ardmore Studio, Bray and locations scenes at Old Connaught, Bray
Film				1995	The film "The Van" location scenes at Ardmore studio
Film				1995	The film "The Old Curiosity Shop" location scenes at Ardmore Studio, Killruddery House, Luggala Estate, Wicklow Head
Film	Sun	24	09	1995	The Carlisle Grounds Bray used in the shooting of the film Michael Collins
Film				1995	The film "Kidnapped" location scenes at Annamoe, Brittas Bay and Wicklow harbour
Film				1995	The film "Moll Flanders" location scenes at Powerscourt, Brittas Bay and Wicklow Harbour, Old Conna, Bray, Glendalough
Film				1996	The BBC Film series "Ballykissangel" 1996–1998 location scenes Avoca, Luggla Estate, Brittas Bay,
Film				1996	The film "September" location scenes at Ardmore studio
Film				1997	The film "Oliver Twist" location scenes at Ardmore Studio and Killruddery House
Film				1997	The film "Mystic Knights" location scenes at Ardmore Studio, Greystones, Belmont House, and Kilcoole
Film				1997	The film "The Butcher Boy" location scenes at Ardmore studio
Film				1997	The film "The Boxer" location scenes at Ardmore studio
Film				1998	The film "Durango" location scenes at Ardmore studio, Arklow, Glencree/Sally Gap, Glenmalure, Kilbride, Kippure, Redcross, Rathdrum, Hollywood
Film				1998	The film "The Nephew" locations scenes used included Enniskerry, Altidore castle Kilpedder, Luggala Estate Roundwood and Wicklow Town
Film				1998	The film "Glendalough – Mystical Journey" released
Film				1998	The film "Night Train" location scenes at Ardmore Studio
Film				1998	The film "Sweeney Todd" location scenes at Ardmore studio

A–Z Reference	Day	Date	Month	Year	DATA
Film				1999	The film "Animal Farm" location scenes at Ardmore studio and Roundwood
Film				1999	The film "The Unexpected Mrs Pollifax" location scenes at Ardmore studio , Enniskerry and Roundwood
Findlater. Alex				1901	Alex Findlater & Co, wine and spirit merchants and grocers opened at shop in Bray
Fire Station				1991	New Fire station for Bray built on the Boghall Road.
Fitzgerald. Garret	Tue	09	02	1926	Garret Fitzgerald born in Dublin and educated in Bray at St.Brigid's School
Fitzgerald. Garret				1969	Garret Fitzgerald elected as a T.D. for Dublin South-East
Fitzgerald. Garret	Wed	14	03	1973	Garret Fitzgerald appointed Minister for Foreign Affairs
Fitzgerald. Garret	Fri	01	07	1977	Garret Fitzgerald appointed leader of the Fine Gael party
Fitzgerald. Garret	Tue	30	06	1981	Garret Fitzgerald appointed Taoiseach and forms a coalition government with the Labour Party
Fitzgerald. Garret	Wed	24	11	1982	Garret Fitzgerald appointed taoiseach for the 2nd time and leads a coalition government with the Labour Party
Fitzgerald. Garret	Wed	11	03	1987	Garret Fitzgerald announces his resignation from leadership of the Fine Gael party and succeeded by Alan Dukes
Fitzgerald. John	Thu	31	07	1902	John Fitzgerald born Co. Westmeath
Fitzgerald. John	Mon	04	07	1921	Constable John Fitzgerald from Co. Westmeath died from his wounds
Fitzgerald. John	Sun	03	07	1921	Two RIC Constables came under gunshot fire a half mile from Wicklow Town. Constable John Fitzgerald was shot
Fitzgerald. Paul				1980	Paul Fitzgerald of Arklow represented Ireland in Boxing at the 1980 Olympic Games held in Moscow
Fitzpatrick. Hubert				2000	Hubert Fitzpatrick appointed (Acting) County Manager of Wicklow (Local Government) December 2000
Fitzpatrick. John				1954	Rev John Fitzpatrick appointed Parish Priest of the Holy Redeemer Parish Bray
Fitzpatrick. Sean P.	Mon	21	06	1948	Sean P. Fitzpatrick born 1948, Chief Executive of Anglo Irish Bank Corporation, Educated at Presentation College, Bray
Fitzwilliam. 10th Earl				1904	William Thomas George Fitzwilliam born
Fitzwilliam. 10th Earl				1979	William Thomas George Fitzwilliam died. The title Earl of Fitzwilliam created in 1716 became extinct
Fitzwilliam. 6th Earl	Thu	20	02	1902	William Fitzwilliam 6th Earl Fitzwilliam died and was succeeded by his grandson William Fitzwilliam 7th Earl Fitzwilliam
Fitzwilliam. 7th Earl	Mon	15	02	1943	William Fitzwilliam 7th Earl Fitzwilliam died and was succeeded by his son William Henry Fitzwilliam 8th Earl Fitzwilliam
Fitzwilliam. 8th Earl	Sat	31	12	1910	William Fitzwilliam 8th Earl Fitzwilliam born
Fitzwilliam. 8th Earl	Wed	19	04	1933	William Fitzwilliam 8th Earl Fitzwilliam married Olive Plunkett
Fitzwilliam. 8th Earl	Thu	24	01	1935	Lady Anne Juliet Dorothea Maud Fitzwilliam daughter of the 8th Earl Fitzwilliam born

Fitzwilliam. 8th Earl	Wed	12	05	1948	William Fitzwilliam 8th Earl Fitzwilliam died succeeded by his cousin Eric Spencer
Fitzwilliam. 9th Earl				1952	Eric Spencer the 9th Earl of Fitzwilliam died
Flannery. Michael				1945	Michael Flannery appointed County Manager of Wicklow (Local Government) 1945-1973
Flood. Francis	Mon	30	03	1970	Francis Flood of Grangecon, Co. Wicklow trained Garoupe the winner of the Irish Grand National held at Fairyhouse Racecourse
Flood. Francis	Mon	12	04	1993	Francis Flood of Grangecon, Co. Wicklow trained Ebony Jane the winner of the Irish Grand National held at Fairyhouse Racecourse
Flora-Fauna			's	1950	Bray Head colonised by Fulmars (Fulmarus glacialis) sea-bird.
Flower Festival			09	1992	Flower Festival held in the Holy Redeemer Church, Bray to celebrate the bi- centenary of the of the Holy Redeemer Parish
Flower Festival			09	2000	Flower Festival held in the Holy Redeemer Church, Bray to celebrate the Millennium
Flusk. Michael				1946	Michael Flusk an able seaman on the S.S. Ocean Voyager died in Liverpool. He was a native of Arklow Co. Wicklow
Foot & Mouth	Mon	01	07	1912	A serious outbreak of foot & mouth disease effects Dublin, Wicklow, Meath and Kildare. Strict movement of Cattle
Foot & Mouth Scare			02	2001	Due to a Foot and Mouth scare many sport fixtures in County Wicklow called off, and tourist attractions closed
Forestry	Tue	08	10	2002	County Wicklow has 26250 (Net area ha.) of Forestry. 2000-2002 (Net area ha) 614 *Stats provided by Coilte
Forestry	Tue	08	10	2002	County Wicklow has 26250 (Net area ha.) of Forestry. 1990-1999 (Net area ha) 6569 *Stats provided by Coilte
Forestry	Tue	08	10	2002	Forestry planting of Scots Pine, 1131 (net area ha.) in County Wicklow *stats provided by Coilte
Forestry	Tue	08	10	2002	County Wicklow has 26250 (Net area ha.) of Forestry *Stats provided by Coilte
Forestry	Tue	08	10	2002	Forestry planting of Stika Spruce, 18343 (net area ha.) in County Wicklow *stats provided by Coilte
Forestry	Tue	08	10	2002	Forestry planting of Norway Spruce, 981 (net area ha.) in County Wicklow *stats provided by Coilte
Forestry	Tue	08	10	2002	Forestry planting of Lodgepole Pine, 522 (net area ha.) in County Wicklow *stats provided by Coilte
Forestry	Tue	08	10	2002	Forestry planting of Douglas Fir, 1921 (net area ha.) in County Wicklow *stats provided by Coilte
Forestry	Tue	08	10	2002	County Wicklow has 26250 (Net area ha.) of Forestry. 1930-1939 (Net area ha) 472 *Stats provided by Coilte
Forestry	Tue	08	10	2002	Forestry planting of Larches, 1295 (net area ha.) in County Wicklow *stats provided by Coilte
Forestry	Tue	08	10	2002	County Wicklow has 26250 (Net area ha.) of Forestry. 1980-1989 (Net area ha) 4892 *Stats provided by Coilte
Forestry	Tue	08	10	2002	Forestry planting of Other Confiers, 741 (net area ha.) in County Wicklow *stats provided by Coilte
Forestry	Tue	08	10	2002	County Wicklow has 26250 (Net area ha.) of Forestry. 1950-1959 (Net area ha) 3608 *Stats provided by Coilte
Forestry	Tue	08	10	2002	Forestry planting of Broadleaf , 1314 (net area ha.) in County Wicklow *stats provided by Coilte
Forestry	Tue	08	10	2002	County Wicklow has 26250 (Net area ha.) of Forestry. Pre 1920 (Net area ha) 379 *Stats provided by Coilte

A-Z Reference	Day	Date	Month	Year	DATA
Forestry	Tue	08	10	2002	County Wicklow has 26250 (Net area ha.) of Forestry. 1920-1929 (Net area ha) 69 ★Stats provided by Coilte
Forestry	Tue	08	10	2002	County Wicklow has 26250 (Net area ha.) of Forestry. 1940-1949 (Net area ha) 662 ★Stats provided by Coilte
Forestry	Tue	08	10	2002	County Wicklow has 26250 (Net area ha.) of Forestry. 1970-1979 (Net area ha) 4359 ★Stats provided by Coilte
Forestry	Tue	08	10	2002	County Wicklow has 26250 (Net area ha.) of Forestry. 1960-1969 (Net area ha) 4626 ★Stats provided by Coilte
Forsyth, Frederick	Mon	15	08	1938	Fredrick Forsyth (author) born
Forsyth, Frederick	Sun	25	05	1980	Frederick Forsyth (author) sells his home Kilgarron House, Enniskerry
Fox. John				1991	John Fox held the post of Chairman of Wicklow County Council 1991-1992
Fox.Mildred				1971	Mildred Fox (Politician) born 1971, educated at St. Kilian's Community School, Bray.
Frame. David				1925	David Frame held the post of Chairman of Wicklow County Council 1925-1928
Free Mason's Hall				1903	The Free Mason's Hall at Ferrybank, Arklow built
French School Bray			's	1960	The French School at Sidmonton Place Bray closed
French School Bray	Sat	18	07	1964	French School at Sidmonton Road, Bray put up for sale.
French. Percy	Tue	24	01	1920	Percy French died
French. Robert	Tue	24	06	1917	Robert French died
Gaelscoil				1994	Gaelscoil Ui Cheadaigh, Bray founded
Gaelscoil				1996	Gaelscoil Cill Mhantain, founded
Gaelscoil				1998	Gaelscoil Inbhir Mhoir, founded
Gaffeney & Rice				1976	Walkers Gaffney &Rice completed the Lug Walk in 17hrs 30 minutes
Gaffnet & Rice	Sat	31	07	2004	The Gaffney and Rice record for the Lug Walk was broken in 16 hours and 21 minutes by Bob Lawlor
Galtrim House			10	1984	Fire destroys Galtrim House. Galtrim Road, Bray
Garland. Donald Edward	Fri	28	06	1918	Donald Edward Garland (Flying Officer) born at Balancer, County Wicklow
Garland. Donald Edward				1940	Flying Officer Donald Edward Garland (reg no 443) 12 Squadron RAF, Memorial at Heverlee War Cemetery, Louvain, Belgium
Garland. Donald Edward	Sun	12	05	1940	Flying Officer Donald Edward Garland from Co. Wicklow. Killed in action at Maastricht, Holland. Awarded Victoria Cross
Garvin. John				1945	John Garvin appointed (Acting) County Manager of Wicklow (Local Government)
Genealogy Service				1987	Wicklow County Council established genealogy service
General Election				1992	The Minister for Environment and Local Government makes County Wicklow and East Carlow constituency a five seater

Name	Weekday	Day	Month	Year	Event
Gillis, Alan	Thu	09	06	1994	Alan Gillis of Grange Con, Co.Wicklow elected as MEP representing Leinster
Glanmore Castle			01	1928	Fire caused major damage at Glanmore Castle, Ashford
Glass Factory			's	1950	Glass factory on the Boghall Road opened.
Glen Mill Golf Club				1996	The Glen Mill Golf Club (Newcastle) established
Glen of Imaal			05	1905	The British War Office acquired an additional 1,262 acres at the Glen of Imaal
Glen of Imaal				1909	The British War Office purchased the additional 1,262 acres it acquired in 1905 at the Glen of Imaal
Glen of Imaal			03	1912	The British War Office bought Coolmoney House in the Glen of Imaal from Adelaide Margaret Tighe
Glen of Imaal			02	1922	The British War Office handed over to the National Army the lands and buildings in the Glen of Imaal
Glen of Imaal			10	1922	The Department of Defence (Irish) took over control of the military lands and buildings in the Glen of Imaal
Glen of Imaal	Tue	16	09	1941	Sixteen soldiers killed by explosion while conducting a training exercise with anti-tank mines at Glen of Imaal, Co.Wicklow
Glen of Imaal				1946	The Department of Defence purchased an additional 177 acres in the Glen of Imaal
Glen of Imaal				1955	The Department of Defence purchased an additional 142 acres in the Glen of Imaal
Glen of Imaal	Thu	26	05	1977	Five soldiers killed in training accident on the Military Range at Glen of Imaal, Co.Wicklow
Glen of Imaal	Sun	15	04	1979	Three boys are killed in an explosion in the Glen of Imaal, Co. Wicklow
Glen of Imaal Terrier	Fri	17	03	1933	The Glen of Imaal Terrier was exhibited for the first time as a native terrier dog breed at the Dublin Dog Show
Glen of Imaal Terrier				1934	The Glen of Imaal Terrier was recognized as a dog breed by the Irish Kennel Club
Glen of Imaal Terrier				1975	The Glen of Imaal Terrier was recognized as a dog breed by the Kennel Club of England
Glen of Imaal Terrier				1987	The Glen of Imaal Terrier was recognized as a dog breed by the States Kennel Club of America
Glen of Imaal Terrier				1994	The Glen of Imaal Terrier was recognized as a dog breed by the United Kennel Club (U.K.C.)
Glen of the Downes				1995	National School at Downs, Fairgreen
Glen of the Downes				1906	The Office of Public Works carried out repairs to St.Mary's Abbey, Glen of the Downes.
Glen of the Downes				1996	Eco Warriors encamp in the Glen of the Downes to prevent road widening scheme
Glen of the Downes				1998	Glen of the Downes Golf Club, Coolnaskeagh, Delgany. Established
Glen of the Downes	Tue	07	12	1999	Wicklow County Officials begin felling of trees in the Glen of the Downes for road widening scheme
Glenart Castle			07	1921	Glenart Castle near Arklow was destroyed by fire
Glenart Castle				1947	Glenart Castle bought by the Vincentian Fathers who renovated the building it is now called St. Kevin's, Glenart, Retreat-House
Glenbride Lodge			s'	1970	Glenbride Lodge, Valleymount was An Oige Hostel, the lodge was kindly given by the Marquis of Waterford
Glencormac United F.C.				1999	Glencormac United Football Club Kilmacanogue formed

A–Z Reference	Day	Date	Month	Year	DATA
Glencree				1945	Glencree Reformatory was used as a temporary refugee centre by the Red Cross
Glencree				1959	The German War Graves Commission opened a cemetery at Glencree, Co. Wicklow.
Glencree	Fri	06	02	1998	Dr Mo Mowlan and Liz O'Donnell opened the "Wicklow wing" of the Glencree Reconciliation Centre in honour of Lady Wicklow
Glencree	Wed	08	06	2005	Judge Bryan McMahon delivered his judgement in favour of the Hill walkers in their case re access rights at Lambs Lane, Glencree
Glencree	Tue	10	05	2005	Wicklow Circuit Court beings to hear case regarding Walking access routes in the Glencree valley
Glencree Peace Centre	Sun	10	03	1974	Glencree Peace Centre opens in an old barracks and reformatory
Glendalough				1914	A statue to St. Kevin erected near St. Kevins bed Glendalough.
Glendalough				1957	The Rock Climbers Guide to Glendalough compiled by the Irish Mountaineering Club
Glendalough				1965	The last boat to St. Kevin's bed was rowed by Larry Bolger
Glendalough				1988	Glendalough Visitor Centre built.
Glendalough Hostel				1935	The old schoolhouse Glendalough bought and rebuilt for An Oige with the aid of a grant from the Carnegie Trust
Glenmalure				1934	A Major landslide took place in Glenmalure valley near the Youth Hostel
Glenmalure Hostel				1955	A small house at Barravoe Ford, Glenmalure was bequeathed to An Oige by Dr Kathleen Lynn
Glenroe	Fri	11	11	1983	The first episode of Glenroe broadcast on RTE 1
Glor na Gael				1968	Bray won the Glor na Gael prize for the use of Irish, in the large town category. Prize was presented by President E. De Valera
Golf Championship				1980	The All Ireland County Golf Championship, won by County Wicklow
Gordon Bennett Race	Thu	02	07	1903	Camille Jenatzy won the Gordon Bennett Road race in a Mercedes Registration No GY 5145
Goulding, Basil Sir	Thu	04	11	1909	Sir Basil Goulding born
Goulding, Basil Sir	Sat	16	01	1982	Sir Basil Goulding (industrialist and art connoisseur) of Kilcroney, Bray died
Goulding, Valerie			09	1918	Lady Valerie Goulding nee Monckton born in Kent, England
Goulding, Valerie				1951	Lady Valarie Goulding and Kathleen O'Rourke founded the Central Remedial Clinic, Dublin for children suffering with polio
Goulding, Valerie	Thu	25	08	1977	Lady Valerie Goulding appointed to Seanad Eireann 25th August 1977– 11th August 1981
Goulding, Valerie	Mon	28	07	2003	Lady Valerie Goulding nee Monckton died
Goulet, Yann Renard	Thu	20	08	1914	Yann Renard Goulet (sculptor and artist) born St. Nazaire, Brittany, France
Goulet, Yann Renard				1947	Yann Renard Goulet (sculptor and artist) and his family settled in Bray

Goulet. Yann Renard	Sun	20	05	1956	A memorial in the grounds of the Customs House costing £2815.11s.1d was sculptured by Yan Renard Goulet
Goulet. Yann Renard				1959	A monument at Ballyseedy, Tralee Co. Kerry dedicated to the Kerry No. 1 Brigade was sculpterd by Yann Renard Goulet
Goulet. Yann Renard	Thu	01	06	1972	A Yann Renard Goulet sculptured monument to the East Mayo Brigade was unveiled at Kilkelly. Co. Mayo
Goulet. Yann Renard				1982	Yann Renard Goulet made a member of Aosdana
Goulet. Yann Renard	Wed	25	08	1999	Goulet. Yann Renard obituarity appeared in The Irish Times Newspaper
Goulet. Yann Renard	Sun	22	08	1999	Yann Renard Goulet died.
Green. Christy				1926	Christy Green (Golfer) born Co. Wicklow
Green. Christy				1997	Christy Green (Golfer) died
Green. Harry Plunket	Wed	19	08	1936	Harry Plunket Green (baritone singer and author) died in London
Greenan Bottle Museum				1985	The Greenan Bottle Museum, Glenmalure established
Grey Fort				1934	Grey Fort House on the Sea Road, Kilcoole became a Knitting factory(men's socks)
Greystones				1901	Building started on the Burnbay Estate, Greystones
Greystones	Thu	26	02	1903	The roof is blown off the temporary R.C. Church Greystones during a storm
Greystones				1908	Work began on the building of the Holy Rosary Church, Greystones
Greystones				1909	Dr. Walsh Archbishop of Dublin solemnly opened the Catholic Church, The Holy Rosary, Greystones
Greystones				1910	Greystones Electric Light and Power Co, formed taken over by the ESB in 1927.
Greystones				1922	Greystones Swimming Club founded
Greystones				1936	Carrig Eden Hotel Greystones sold
Greystones			's	1940	Extension added to Carrig Eden House, Greystones
Greystones				1947	Ormonde Cinema Greystones built
Greystones			's	1950	The Grand Hotel Greystones changed its name to the La Touche Hotel.
Greystones				1964	Greystones Operatic and Dramatic Society founded
Greystones	Fri	09	05	1969	Greystones Credit Union was established
Greystones			05	1983	Greystones Town Commissioner's established under the terms of the Town Improvements (Ireland) Act 1854
Greystones			circa	1985	Greystones Bowling Club established.
Greystones	Fri	06	07	2001	The refurbished Railway Station at Greystones opened
Greystones			01	2002	Greystones granted Town Council status
Greystones	Fri	02	08	2002	Greystones Arts Festival 2nd-5th August 2002

A–Z Reference	Day	Date	Month	Year	DATA
Greystones				2002	New building for Greystones Credit Union opened on Church Road, Greystones
Greystones	Sun	25	04	2004	The sod was turned on a new community centre attached to St. Patrick's Church, Greystones. Cost of new centre 1.7m
Greystones Golf Club				1985	Greystones Golf Club won the Barton Cup
Greystones Golf Club				1990	Leinster Youths Amateur Open Championship, held at Greystones Golf Club
Greystones Golf Club				1992	Leinster Youths Amateur Open Championship, held at Greystones Golf Club
Greystones Golf Club				1995	Leinster Seniors Amateur Open Championship, held at Greystones Golf Club
Greystones Golf Club				1996	Leinster Youths Amateur Open Championship, held at Greystones Golf Club
Greystones Rugby Club				1937	Greystones Rugby Club founded
Greystones Rugby Club				1944	Greystones Rugby Club won the Metropolitan Cup
Greystones Rugby Club				1999	Greystones Rugby Club won the Metropolitan Cup
Greystones School				1949	Greystones Boys National School, Rathhdowne Road Greystones built.
Greystones United F.C.				1979	Greystones United Football Club formed
Griffin. Victor				1924	Victor Griffin (Church of Ireland Dean) born at Carnew Co. Wicklow
Griffin. Victor			11	1968	Victor Griffin became Dean of St. Patrick's Cathedral, Dublin
Group Water Scheme			08	1958	The first ever group water scheme in Ireland near Manor Kilbride, Co. Wicklow
Guinness	Tue	22	02	1910	Oonagh Guinness daughter of Ernest Guinness born
Guinness	Wed	29	04	1936	Oonagh Guinness married 4th Baron Oranmore and Browne
Guinness. P.W				1948	Rev Percy Wyndham Guinness died
Guinness. R. W.				1919	Rev Robert Wyndham Guinness died
Gypsy Moth III	Thu	21	07	1960	Francis Chichester won the first solo transatlantic race with his boat Gypsy Moth III from Plymouth to New York in 40 days
Hagan. John				1904	Rev John Hagan appointed vice-rector of the Irish College in Rome
Hagan. John				1919	Rev John Hagan appointed rector of the Irish College in Rome
Hagan. John				1930	Rev John Hagan died
Halpin. Robert	Tue	30	09	2003	Captain Robert Halpin of Wicklow commerated in a 57 cent stamp issued by An Post
Hamilton. Gladys Mary	Tue	14	01	1902	Gladys Mary Hamilton the daughter of the Earl of Abercorn married Ralph Francis Howard 7th Earl of Wicklow in London
Hamilton. Gladys Mary	Mon	12	03	1917	Gladys Mary Howard nee Hamilton died in Dublin
Handball				1930	Martin O'Nell and Luke Sherry won the All Ireland Handball Championships

Handball				1931	Martin O'Nell and Luke Sherry won the All Ireland Handball Championships
Hanlon. Andrew				1966	Andrew Hanlon (TV presenter and producer with TV3) of Bray born 1966, Educated at Presentation College, Bray.
Harbour			08	1982	Tenders invited by Bray Urban District Council to build a road bridge at Bray Harbour, to replace a bridge that had collapsed.
Harmon				1936	Count Louis Le Warner Harmon died in the USA (see 1866)
Hart, Henry C.	Fri	07	08	1908	Henry Chichester Hart died, Carrablagh, Co. Donegal
Harty.H.H				1901	Herbert Hamilton Harty organist at Christ Church, Bray left for London.
Harty.H.H	Fri	15	07	1904	Herbert Hamilton Harty married Agnes Helen Nicholls an operatic soprano and concert singer
Harty.H.H				1920	Herbert Hamilton Harty appointed conductor of Halle Orchestra Manchester 1920-1933
Harty.H.H				1925	Herbert Hamilton Harty knighted
Harty.H.H	Wed	19	02	1941	Sir Herbert Hamilton Harty died at Brighton
Hatton. Jimmy				1962	Jimmy Hatton of Wicklow. Refereed The All Ireland Minor GAA Football Final
Hatton. Jimmy				1963	Jimmy Hatton of Wicklow. Refereed The All Ireland Senior GAA Hurling Final
Hatton. Jimmy				1964	Jimmy Hatton of Wicklow. Refereed The All Ireland Senior GAA Football Final
Hatton. Jimmy				1965	Jimmy Hatton of Wicklow. Refereed The All Ireland Minor GAA Football Final
Hatton. Jimmy				1966	Jimmy Hatton of Wicklow. Refereed The All Ireland Minor GAA Hurling Final (Replay)
Hatton. Jimmy				1966	Jimmy Hatton of Wicklow. Refereed The All Ireland Senior GAA Football Final
Hatton. Jimmy				1966	Jimmy Hatton of Wicklow. Refereed The All Ireland Senior GAA Hurling Final
Hatton. Jimmy				1967	Jimmy Hatton of Wicklow. Refereed The All Ireland Intermediate GAA Hurling Final
Hatton. Jimmy				1970	Jimmy Hatton of Wicklow. Refereed The All Ireland Intermediate GAA Hurling Final
Hatton. Jimmy				1970	Jimmy Hatton of Wicklow. Refereed The All Ireland Senior GAA Hurling Final
Haughton's			circa	1920	Haughton's makers of Ink and Glues established in Bray
Hayes. Seamus				1977	Seamus Hayes appointed County Manager of Wicklow (Local Government) 1977-1984
Health				1903	Henry Raverty was Medical Officer for Bray
Health	Thu	12	01	1922	St Colemans Hospital Rathdrum Established
Health				1935	Mr John Duffy Chairman of Bray's Public Health Committee
Health Association				1907	Women's National Health Association founded by Lady Aberdeen, with branches in Co. Wicklow
Healy. John				1921	Constable John Healy (DMP 10909) awarded the King's Police Medal
Healy. P.T				1942	P.T.Healy appointed County Manager for Wicklow (Local Government). 1942-45
Heaney. Seamus			04	1939	Seamus Heaney born in Co. Derry

A-Z Reference	Day	Date	Month	Year	DATA
Heaney, Seamus				1972	Seamus Heaney lived in Co. Wicklow and later in Dublin
Heaney, Seamus				1995	Seamus Heaney won the Nobel Prize for Literature
Heatley. Elizabeth	Tue	08	03	1977	Elizabeth Heatley former Headmistress of French School Bray died and buried at St. Patrick's Graveyard, Enniskerry
Henderson. Brian				1950	The sculptor Brian Henderson born in Co. Wicklow
Henderson. Brian				1969	Brian Henderson won the Carroll Award at the Irish Exhibition of Living Art
Henderson. Brian				1970	Brian Henderson won the Carroll Award at the Irish Exhibition of Living Art
Hennessy. Henry	Fri	08	03	1901	Henry Hennessy (Physicist and Mathematician) died at Bray. Co. Wicklow
Henry. Grace	Thu	17	09	1903	Grace Mitchell married Paul Henry (artist)
Henry. Grace	Tue	11	08	1953	Grace Henry (artist) died
Henry. Paul				1953	Paul Henry married Mable Florence Young
Henry. Paul	Sun	24	08	1958	Paul Henry RHA died at his home in Bray and was buried in St.Patricks Graveyard Enniskerry
Henry. Paul	Fri	08	02	1974	Mable Young the wife of Paul Henry died
Henry. Paul	Wed	25	09	1996	The Paul Henry painting the "Potato harvest" was sold in Dublin for £104,000
Henry. Paul	Wed	08	05	2002	The 1931 painting by Paul Henry of "Trees, Co. Wicklow" went on sale in Dublin on 08/05/2002
Heritage Centre	Mon	08	07	1985	Dr. Garret Fitzgerald opens a Heritage Centre in Bray Town Hall
Heritage Centre			06	1993	Bray Heritage Centre was opened in the Old Court House, Main Street, Bray
Hewat. Richard				1940	Richard Hewat (Chief Executive of Heiton Holdings Plc) born 1940, educated at Aravon School, Bray.
Higgins.Adian				1927	Adian Charles Higgins (writer) born Celbridge Co.Kildare. Live in Dalkey, Greystones, Dun Laoghaire
Higgins.John				1976	John Higgins appointed (Acting) County Manager of Wicklow (Local Government) 1976-1777
Hill.Arthur-6th	Wed	29	05	1918	Arthur Hill 6th Marquess of Downshire died
Hill.Arthur-7th	Thu	23	07	1953	Arthur Hill 7th Marquis of Downshire married Noreen Gray Miller
Hime. Sir Albert H.				1902	Sir Albert Henry Hime was made a Privy Councillor
Hime. Sir Albert H.	Sat	26	07	1902	Wicklow man Sir Albert Henry Hime given the Freedom of the City of Edinburgh
Hime. Sir Albert H.	Sat	25	01	1919	Sir Albert Henry Hime died
Historical Society				1977	Cualann Historical Society founded, later became the Bray Cualann Historical Society
Historical Society				1985	Bray Cualann Historical Society published its 1st Historical Journal
Historical Society				1986	Bray Cualann Historical Society published its 2nd Historical Journal

Section Two: Data in Alphabetical Order

Subject	Day	Date	Month	Year	Event
Historical Society				1990	Bray Cualann Historical Society published its 3rd Historical Journal
Historical Society	Mon	25	06	2001	Bray Cualann Historical Society published its 4th Historical Journal
Historical Society				2004	Bray Cualann Historical Society published its 5th Historical Journal
Hodson	Sat	17	03	1906	Meriel Hodson nee Neville died
Hodson	Thu	20	04	1911	Sir Robert Adair Hodson 4th Bart. married Emily Beresford of Waterford
Hodson	Thu	08	07	1915	Richard Edmond Hodson of Coolfadda House, Bandon, Co. Cork died
Hodson	Mon	03	01	1921	Sir Robert Adair Hodson 4th Bart died and was succeeded by his nephew Edmond Adair Hodson 5th Bart,
Hodson	Sat	28	07	1928	Sir Edmond Adair Hodson 5th Bart. married Anne Elizabeth Ardderley, Sherbone, England and had two son's Michael and Patrick
Hodson	Sat	05	03	1932	Michael Robin Adderley Hodson born
Hodson	Tue	30	01	1934	Cecil George Hodson married Betty North of North Cray, Kent, England.
Hodson	Tue	27	11	1934	Patrick Richard Hodson born
Hollybrooke House				1969	Hollybrooke House, Bray damaged by fire. The family seat of Hodson Family
Hollywood N.S.				1955	Work began on building Hollywood National School.
Holy Redeemer, Bray				1914	Organ gallery and organ installed in the Holy Redeemer Church Bray
Holy Redeemer, Bray				1939	The mortuary chapel at the Holy Redeemer Church, Bray built
Holy Redeemer, Bray				1961	Work on the re-design of the Holy Redeemer Church, Bray began
Holy Redeemer, Bray				1980	A new organ installed in the Holy Redeemer Church, Bray by Kenneth Jones organ builder Bray.
Holy Redeemer, Bray	Sat	20	12	1980	Our Lady's Choral Society presented the "Messiah" in the Holy Redeemer Church, Bray to mark the new organ.
Holy Redeemer, Bray			04	2003	A new centre piece added to the Rose Window at the Holy Redeemer Church, Bray
Homicide in Ireland				1991	Homicide in Ireland between 1972 and 1991. Total 587. The number of killings by men 545 and 42 by women
Honan. Thomas				1993	Thomas Honan held the post of Chairman of Wicklow County Council 1993-1994
Honner. Thomas			05	2001	Thomas Honner of Kiltegan elected the 29th President of Macra na Feirme
Hopper. Nora				1901	Nora Hopper married Wilfrid Hugh Chesson
Hopper. Nora	Sat	14	04	1906	Nora Hopper died
Hospital				1985	Extension to St Colmcille's Hospital Loughlinstown
Housing				1909	Building of Connolly and St.Kevins Square (Purcells fields) Bray
Housing				1932	Development of St. Bridget's Ter., St. Patrick's Sq., St. Cronan's Rd., St.Columcills Ter., and St Lawrences Ter., Bray
Housing				1935	Bray Clearance Order – Housing allocation of new housing at Wolfe Tone Square and O'Byrne Road

A-Z Reference	Day	Date	Month	Year	DATA
Housing				1935	Cill Maintain Park, Bray built
Housing				1939	Wolfe Tone Square, Bray built
Housing				1948	New housing developments included St.Peters Road, Dwyer Park, Fr.Colohan Terrace and Fatima Terrace Bray
Housing				1962	The island (Dargan Cottages) on the seafront near the railway gates removed
Housing				1977	537 New Local Authority Houses completed in Wicklow
Housing				1980	Building of houses started at Seapoint Court, in Doyle's field, Dock Hill, Bray
Housing				1980	Housing Estate built at Corke Abbey, Bray
Housing	Mon	08	07	1985	Tenders invited for Housing development at Ballwaltrim/Irishtown Stage 11 (51 two storyed dwellings)
Housing				1989	Loreto Nuns sell part of their grounds at Vevay Road Bray,for housing Loreto Grange Built.
Housing				1989	20 Town houses built at Failte Park, Bray
Housing				1997	Building of apartments at the Lithographic site on the Dargle Road
Housing				2004	Bray Town Council Compulsory Purchase (Bray) No.2 Order 2004 - In the town lands of Old Connaught and Bray Commons
Humewood Castle				1992	Humewood Castle, Kiltegan, Co.Wicklow bought by Renata Coleman (Coleman's Mustard)
Hussey. Gemma		11		1939	Gemma Hussey nee Moran born Bray, Co Wicklow. elected to Dail Eireann for Wicklow
Hussey. Gemma				1977	Gemma Hussey elected to Seanad Eireann
Hussey. Gemma	Thu	18	02	1982	Gemma Hussey nee Moran the first woman elected Dail Eireann for Wicklow
Hussey. Gemma				1982	Gemma Hussey appointed Minister for Education December 1982- February 1986
Hussey. Gemma				1986	Gemma Hussey appointed Minister for Social Welfare 1986-1987
Hussey. Gemma				1987	Gemma Hussey appointed Minister for Labour 1987
Hynes. Frank				1971	Frank Hynes held the post of Chairman of Wicklow County Council 1971-1972
Hynes. Frank				1974	Frank Hynes held the post of Chairman of Wicklow County Council 1974-1975
Hynes. Frank				1980	Frank Hynes held the post of Chairman of Wicklow County Council 1980-1981
Hynes. Frank				1986	Frank Hynes held the post of Chairman of Wicklow County Council 1986-1987
Hynes. Frank				1989	Frank Hynes held the post of Chairman of Wicklow County Council 1989-1990
ICA	Tue	02	10	1951	The first meeting of the Wicklow Federation of the ICA took place
IFI			10	1987	Irish Fertiliser Industries begins trading a merger of the Irish operations of ICI and NET
IFI	Wed	16	10	2002	IFI announces the closure of its Fertiliser plants in Cork, Belfast and Arklow Co.Wicklow with the loss of 620 jobs

Section Two: Data in Alphabetical Order

Name	Day	Date	Month	Year	Event
Industrial School	Wed	03	12	1902	91 names were on the roll of The Meath Protestant Industrial School (for Girls)
Industrial Yarns				1958	Industrial Yarns Ltd Dublin Road, Bray commenced trading
Industrial Yarns				1998	Industrial Yarns Ltd Dublin Road, Bray ceased trading
International Hotel				1914	The International Hotel was converted into The Princess Patricia Hospital for wounded soldiers
International Hotel				1919	Princess Patricia Hospital Quinsboro Road ceased as a hospital and resumed as the International Hotel
International Hotel	Fri	14	06	1974	International Hotel, Quinsborough Road, Bray destroyed by fire
International Hotel				1990	Work began on a new leisure centre on the old International Hotel site
Ireland	Tue	25	04	1916	Easter Rising begins
Ireland				1941	Tea rationing introduced
Ivers. M				1909	Very Rev M.Ivers became Parish Priest of Enniskerry
Jackman, Joseph	Sun	19	03	1916	Joseph Jackman born in Dun Laoghaire and educated at St. Gerard's School, Bray
Jackman, Joseph	Tue	25	11	1941	Joseph Jackman led an assault on Ed Duda, Libya during the North African Campaign of World War II
Jackman, Joseph	Wed	26	11	1942	Joseph Jackman died at Tobruk, Libya and was buried at Tobruk War Cemetery
Jackman, Joseph	Tue	31	03	1942	Joseph Jackman awarded posthumously the Victoria Cross for bravery in action at Ed Duda, Libya
Jacob. Joe				1993	Joe Jacob TD for Wicklow was appointed Leas-Cheann Comhairle of Dail Eireann 1993-1997
Johnston. Brian				1984	Brian Johnston appointed (Acting) County Manager of Wicklow (Local Government) 1984-1985
Johnston. Jennifer				1979	The Jennifer Johnston novel "The Old Jest" is set in Co. Wicklow
Jones. George				1984	George Jones held the post of Chairman of Wicklow County Council 1984-1985
Jones. George				1987	George Jones held the post of Chairman of Wicklow County Council 1987-1988
Jones. George				1990	George Jones held the post of Chairman of Wicklow County Council 1990-1991
Jones. George				2000	George Jones held the post of Chairman of Wicklow County Council 2000-2001
Jones. Kenneth				1983	Kenneth Jones, Organ builder from Bray installed an organ in the First Presbyterian Church, Hannibal, USA
Jones. Kenneth				1983	Kenneth Jones, Organ builder from Bray installed an organ in Whitefriars Street Church, Dublin
Jones. Kenneth				1984	Kenneth Jones, Organ builder from Bray installed an organ in Christ Church, Dublin
Jones. Kenneth				1987	Kenneth Jones, Organ builder from Bray installed an organ in the First United Methodist Church, Crestview, Florida, USA
Jones. Kenneth				1991	Kenneth Jones, Organ builder from Bray installed an organ in the River Road, Presbyterian Church, Richmond, USA
Jones. Kenneth				1991	Kenneth Jones, Organ builder from Bray installed an organ in the National Concert Hall, Dublin
Jordan. Eddie	Tue	30	03	1948	Eddie Jordan the owner of the Jordan motor racing team . Was born in Bray. Co. Wicklow

306 — The County Wicklow Database: 432 AD to 2006 AD

A–Z Reference	Day	Date	Month	Year	DATA
Joyce, James	Mon	20	12	1909	Volta Cinema, Dublin first custom built cinema in Ireland. Manager James Joyce
Joyce, James	Mon	13	01	1941	James Joyce writer died
Kane, Daniel	Wed	16	08	1922	Daniel Kane. Vol "A" Company IRA killed in action at Sally Gap County Wicklow
Kavanagh, Liam				1977	Liam Kavanagh held the post of Chairman of Wicklow County Council 1977-1978
Kavanagh, Liam	Tue	13	12	1983	Liam Kavanagh appointed Minister for the Environment
Kavanagh, Liam				1998	Liam Kavanagh held the post of Chairman of Wicklow County Council 1998-1999
Kavanagh, Mark				1945	Mark Kavanagh (Property Developer) born 1945, educated at St. Gerard's School, Bray
Kay, Dorothy	Wed	13	05	1964	The artist Dorothy Kay died
Kearney, Teresa				1917	Teresa Kearney awarded an MBE for her services to the British Army for aid given to sick and wounded soldiers
Kearney, Teresa				1923	Teresa Kearney was one of the founders of the Little Sisters for St. Francis working in Uganda, Kenya, and Tanzania.
Kearney, Teresa	Thu	02	02	1928	Teresa Kearney established a novitiate convent at Holme Hall, Yorkshire
Kearney, Teresa				1935	Teresa Kearney established a novitiate convent at Mount Oliver, Dundalk, Co. Louth
Kearney, Teresa	Mon	09	06	1952	Teresa Kearney founded The Franciscan Missionary Sisters for Africa
Kearney, Teresa				1954	Teresa Kearney established a novitiate convent at Boston. U.S.A.
Kearney, Teresa	Wed	16	10	1957	Teresa Kearney died at the convent in Boston and she was buried at Nkokonjeru, Uganda
Keegan, Charlie	Fri	25	09	1964	Charlie Keegan from Enniskerry won the World Ploughing Championship in Austria
Keegan, Charlie	Mon	29	12	2003	Charlie Keegan of Enniskerry died
Keegan, Claire				1969	The writer Claire Keegan born in Wicklow
Keenan, Tom				1985	Tom Keenan held the post of Chairman of Wicklow County Council 1985-1986
Keenan, Tom				1988	Tom Keenan held the post of Chairman of Wicklow County Council 1988-1989
Kelleher, John				1912	Rev. John Kelleher born in Bray
Kelleher, John				1937	Rev. John Kelleher of Bray ordained a priest. Appointed to Dublin parishes 1937-1989
Kelleher, John	Mon	10	07	1989	Rev. John Kelleher died and was buried in St. Peter's Graveyard, Bray
Kelly, Alan				1936	Alan Kelly born
Kelly, Alan				1955	Alan Kelly played for Bray Wanderers 1955-1956
Kelly, Alan	Sun	25	11	1956	Alan Kelly won his first cap for the Republic of Ireland Football team
Kelly, Alan				1956	Alan Kelly played goalkeeper for the Republic of Ireland football team, winning 47 caps 1956-1973

Section Two: Data in Alphabetical Order

Name				Year	Event
Kelly. Alan				1957	Alan Kelly played for Drumcondra Football Club – Won FAI Cup Medal 1957
Kelly. Alan				1958	Alan Kelly made 447 league appearances for Preston North End Football Club 1958–1973
Kelly. Alan			10	1972	Alan Kelly became the first goalkeeper to captain the Republic of Ireland Football Team, when Ireland played the Soviet Union
Kelly. Alan	Wed	30	04	1980	Alan Kelly was manager of a friendly match between the Republic of Ireland Football Team v Switzerland
Kelly. Alan				1983	Alan Kelly was manager of Preston North End Football Club 1983 – 1985
Kelly. John				1948	Rev. John Kelly Parish Priest of Tomacork, Carnew 1948 -1968
Kennedy: Mrs. J.F.	Sun	02	07	1967	Mrs John F. Kennedy planted a tree on a visit to Powerscourt Estate
Kennedy: Rev				1926	Rev. Kennedy became Parish priest of R.C. Church Enniskerry
Kenny. William			12	1981	Rev. William Kenny Parish Priest of Our Lady Queen of Peace Parish, Putland Road, Bray died
Kiernan. Kitty				1925	Kitty Kiernan married Felix Cronin, Quartermaster General of the National Army
Kiernan. Kitty	Wed	25	07	1945	Kitty Kiernan died and was buried in Glasnevin, Dublin
Kilcoole				1913	The Forresters Hall in Kilcoole built
Kilcoole	Sat	01	08	1914	The Irish National Volunteers land 5,000 rifles at Kilcoole, Co. Wicklow
Kilcoole				1915	Sea erosion at Kilcoole and Ballygannon, Co. Wicklow
Kilcoole				1930	C.I.E placed rocks along the beach at Kilcoole to prevent Costal Erosion (some of the rocks contained fossil remains)
Kilcoole				1930	C.I.E. bring boulders from Portarlington to protect the railway line at Kilcoole from the sea
Kilcoole				1960	A new national school opened near Kilcoole Village
Kilcoole	Sun	07	08	1966	A plaque unveiled at the on the shore at Kilcoole to mark the Kilcoole Gun Running of 1914
Kilcoole			04	1968	The Catholic Church at Kilcoole was opened and dedicated by the Archbishop of Dublin Dr McQuaid
Kilcoole Golf Club				1992	Kilcoole Golf Club established
Kilcroney				1927	The contents of Kilcroney House, Bray was auctioned
Kilcroney				1949	Kilcroney House Golf Club ceased and Kilcroney House, Bray became a Hotel
Kilcroney				1955	Kilcroney House was bought by the St. John of God Brothers
Kilcroney				1956	Kilcroney House became St.Joseph's Convalescent Home run by the St.John of God Brothers
Killruddery	Sat	11	02	1978	Killruddery was the feature gardening article by Ruth Isabel Ross in the Irish Times on 11/02/1978
Killruddery	Wed	13	10	1982	Sean Eagan wrote a feature article about Killruddery in The Irish Independent Newspaper on 13/10/1982
Kilmacanogue			's	1950	Glencormac House, Kilmacanogue became a hotel when the Jameson family sold it.
Kilmacanogue	Sat	11	03	1967	Glencormac House, Kilmacanogue destroyed by fire.

The County Wicklow Database: 432 AD to 2006 AD

A–Z Reference	Day	Date	Month	Year	DATA
Kilmacanogue				1974	Kilmacanogue Roman Catholic Parish was constituted into a separate parish from Enniskerry
Kilmacanogue	Sat	26	10	1985	Kilmacanogue Parish Church became a chapel of eves of Enniskerry Parish Church St. Mary's
Kilmacanogue				1987	Avoca Handweavers acquired the property of Glencormac House, Kilmacanogue
Kilmacoo N.S.				1933	Work began on Building Kilmacoo National School, at Kilmacoo in the Vale of Avoca, Co. Wicklow
Kilmacurragh House				1944	Kilmacurragh House, Rathdrum sold to the Department of Lands
Kiltegan	Thu	17	03	1932	The St. Patrick's Missionary Society was founded a monastery at High Park House, Kiltegan, Co. Wicklow
Kilternan				1904	Kilternan Dairies established by the Verney family in 1904
Kilternan			09	1987	Kilternan Dairy ceased trading
Kinch. Michael	Tue	13	06	1950	Mary Kinch of Bray, Co Wicklow gave birth Michael Anthony Kinch. Weighing 17lb 3oz the heaviest baby recorded in Ireland
King. Cecil	Tue	22	02	1921	Cecil King (artist) was born near Rathdrum Co. Wicklow
King. Cecil	Mon	07	04	1986	Cecil King (artist) died at Dun Laoghaire Co. Dublin
Kinsella. Tommy				1906	Tommy Kinsella Born
Kinsella. Tommy			04	1917	Tommy Kinsella started serving as an alter boy in the Church Of the Holy Redeemer Bray
Kinsella. Tommy			08	1998	Tommy Kinsella retired as an alter server in the Holy Redremmer Church, Bray
Kinsella. Tommy	Thu	01	04	1999	Tommy Kinsella died
Kinsella. Tommy				2001	Page 49 of the 2001 Guinness Book of Records. Tommy Kinsella is shown as the longest serving alter boy in the world
Kiosks				1935	Building of Kiosks on Bray Seafront
Kippure	Mon	28	09	1959	Lord Powerscourt sold 15 acres 2 roods and 12 perches in the town land of Kippure to the Broadcasting Commissioners
Kippure	Mon	28	09	1959	Lord Powerscourt sold 2 acres 1 rood and 28 perches in the town land of Powerscourt Mt. to the Broadcasting Commissioners
Kippure	Sat	08	09	1961	The first live TV test in Ireland was carried out using the Kippure TV Transmitter
Kippure				1961	Television Mast erected on Kippure Mountain
Kippure	Fri	01	12	1961	The Kippure TV transmitter came into operation
Kish Lighthouse				1954	The "Gannet" lightship was placed on the Kish Bank, the colour of the lightship was changed from Black to Red
Kish Lighthouse			07	1963	Construction of the base of the Kish Lighthouse commenced in Dun Laoghaire Harbour
Kish Lighthouse	Tue	27	07	1965	The Kish Lighthouse was completed
Kish Lighthouse	Tue	29	06	1965	The constructed section of the Kish Lighthouse was towed from Dun Laoghaire to the Kish Bank

Kish Lighthouse	Tue	09	11	1965	The Kish Light vessel was withdrawn
Kish Lighthouse			03	1992	The Kish Lighthouse was converted to automatic operation and the Keepers were withdrawn from the Lighthouse
Kish Lighthouse	Thu	29	02	1996	The signal from the Kish Lighthouse was changed 2 White Flashes every 30 seconds to 2 White Flashes every 20 seconds
Knocksink Wood	Tue	25	01	2005	Minister for Environment, Local Government, Heritage Mr Dick Roche opened two new footbridges at Knocksink Wood, Enniskerry
Knocksink, Enniskerry				1992	The National Conservation Education Centre at Knocksink Wood, Enniskerry built.
Kynoch of Arklow	Fri	21	09	1917	Explosion took place at Kynocks Munitions Factory, Arklow. 27 killed and many more injured.
La Touche	Tue	01	04	1902	Major Peter la Touche of Bellevue, Delgany married Sophia Dora Elizabeth Tottenham
La Touche				1904	When Major Peter La Touche died, sister Frances Cecilia and her husband Dr Archer moved into Bellevue, Delgany
La Touche	Wed	13	04	1904	Major Peter La Touche died.
La Touche	Wed	09	05	1906	An Executors sale took place at Bellevue, Delgany following the death of Major Peter La Touche
La Touche				1908	Dr Archer became first President of the Golf club established at Bellevue Estate
La Touche				1913	The Archers left Bellevue estate and moved into a smaller house in Delgany Village
La Touche				1920	Bellevue the La Touche property at Delgany was sold for a sum in the region of £30,000
La Touche				1922	John David Digues La Touche of Kiltymon, Newtown Co. Wicklow. Left the Imperial Maritime Customs Service, China 1882
La Touche				1925	Philip K. Love bought Marley Park and House, Rathfarnham once the home of the La Touche family
La Touche				1930	Forest Service bought 250 acres at Bellevue Woods Glen of the Downes
La Touche	Mon	06	05	1935	John David Digues La Touche of Kiltymon, Newtown Co. Wicklow. Died at sea returning from Majorca
La Touche				1971	An oil painting (Peter La Touche) was purchased by the National Gallery of Ireland (NGI 4034) from Appleby Bros. Ltd, London
La Touche				1997	The Bank of Ireland purchased in London the Amorino Marble statue for £520,000, commissioned by David La Touche in 1792
La Touche	Wed	11	11	1998	The marble statue of Amorino went on display in the National Gallery of Ireland
Labourers Association				1917	County Wicklow Labourer's Association founded
Lamb. Charles Vincent				1964	Charles Vincent Lamb died
Lamb. Charles Vincent			10	2001	Charles Vincent Lamb oil on canvas "The Farmstead, Wicklow Hills" sold for 4316
Landscape Painting				1957	The Irish School of Landscape Painting founded at Ashford, Co. Wicklow
Laragh				1953	The road bridge at Laragh Co. Wicklow was reinforced
Laragh				1956	A new bridge opened in Laragh, replacing the old bridge. Engineer J.J. Rowan and County Engineer J.T. O'Byrne
Large. R.G				1971	Rev. R.G. Large appointed Rector of Bray Parish

A–Z Reference	Day	Date	Month	Year	DATA
Large. R.G				1985	Rev. R.G.Large retires as Rector of Bray parish
Larkin. James	Tue	18	02	1969	James Larkin, Putland Road, Bray died, General Secretary Workers Union of Ireland, son of James Larkin (Big Jim)
Lawlor. Hugh Jackson	Mon	26	12	1938	Hugh Jackson Lawlor died
Lawlor. Michael				1994	Michael Lawlor held the post of Chairman of Wicklow County Council 1994-1995
Lawrence. William	Tue	09	08	1932	William Mervin Lawrence died
LDF/FCA				1941	Local Defence Force established. (see 1946)
LDF/FCA	Wed	06	02	1946	Foras Costanta Aitiuil (FCA) established, replacing the LDF
Le Brocquy. Louis	Fri	10	11	1916	Louis Le Brocquy (artist) born in Dublin and educated at St. Gerard's School, Bray
Le Brocquy. Louis			05	2000	The painting "Travelling Woman with Newspaper" by Louis Le Brocquy fetched £1.15 million sterling at auction in London
Le Fanu. Henry				1905	Henry Frewen Le Fanu appointed Canon of St. John's Cathedral, Brisbane, Australia 1905-1915
Le Fanu. Henry				1915	Henry Frewen Le Fanu appointed Coadjutor Bishop of Brisbane, Australia 1915 -1929
Le Fanu. Henry				1935	Henry Frewen Le Fanu appointed Primate of the Anglican Church of Australia 1935 - 1946
Le Fanu. Margery				1926	Margery Le Fanu the wife of Henry Frewen Le Fanu died
Le Faun. Henry				1904	Henry Frewen Le Fanu married Margery Ingle
Ledwidge. Peter				1950	Peter Ledwidge held the post of Chairman of Wicklow County Council 1950-1953
Leland. Dr. Thomas				1913	An oil painting of Dr. Thomas Leland acquired by the National Gallery of Ireland (NGI 655)
Library. Bray				1911	William Burke appointed as head of Bray Library service.
Library. Bray				1911	Bray Public library built on Florence Road at a cost of £2,000
Library. Bray	Sun	30	09	1945	Mr. William Burke Librarian Bray Library retired (1911-1945)
Library. Bray	Sat	17	11	1953	The Children's Section of Bray Library opened by Minister of Education Mr Sean Moylan (£180 from the Parnell monument fund)
Library. Bray			12	1984	Tenders invited for extension to Bray Library, Florence Road, Bray
Library. Bray				1986	Work began on the extension to Bray Library
Library. Bray	Fri	29	12	2000	A Branch Library of Bray Library opened on Boghall Road, Bray
Library. County				1927	The County Councils transferred the library from the charge of the Board of Health to County Library Committee
Library. County	Wed	05	07	2000	County Wicklow Library Head quarters on the Boghall Road, Bray opened by the Minister of The Environment Noel Dempsy
Library. Greystones				1910	Greystones Library established and opened 17/06/1912.

Life Saving	Fri	25	08	1905	J. W. Reigh was given Bronze Royal Humane Society Medal. With the help of others he conveyed persons to safety in Bray Flood
Lifeboats	Fri	03	03	1911	The Lifeboat Robert Theophilus Garden IV stationed at Wicklow was the first motor lifeboat in Ireland
Lifeboats	Fri	03	03	1911	A new 40ft Motor Lifeboat Robert Theophilus Garden IV arrived at Wicklow Lifeboat Station
Lifeboats				1912	The slipway at the Arklow Lifeboat station was adapted for a motor lifeboat.
Lifeboats				1915	A motor lifeboat arrived in Arklow
Lifeboats				1916	Cahore Lifeboat Station closed
Lifeboats	Fri	28	05	1937	A new lifeboat The Lady Kylsant, a Watson class lifeboat stationed at Wicklow
Lifeboats				1938	The lifeboat house at Arklow was modified for a new lifeboat
Lifeboats	Wed	01	06	1938	The first service for the Lady Kylsant lifeboat of Wicklow was to a yacht called The Cygnet
Lifeboats				1938	A new lifeboat arrived in Arklow
Lifeboats	Wed	13	09	1950	The Wicklow lifeboat was called to the vessel Cameo stranded of the Wicklow Coast
Lifeboats				1950	The Coxswain of the Wicklow Lifeboat Edward Kavanagh was awarded a Bronze Medal by the RNLI for the rescue of 13/09/1950
Lifeboats	Thu	14	06	1956	The naming ceremony of the Wicklow Lifeboat, William J Archer was performed by Mrs Sean T O'Kelly
Lifeboats	Thu	07	06	1956	The lifeboat William J Archer was stationed at Wicklow Harbour
Lifeboats	Fri	01	02	1957	The first service of the William J Archer Lifeboat of Wicklow was to remove an injured man from the Codling Lightship
Lifeboats				1967	Arklow harbour redeveloped, the Lifeboat house was demolished
Lifeboats				1970	A new lifeboat workshop and store was built close to the lifeboat moorings in Arklow Dock
Lifeboats				1986	The lifeboat Ger Tigchlaar No 14-19 trent class stationed at Arklow Lifeboat station
Lifeboats				1988	A new assembly building and store was constructed on the quayside at Arklow adjacent to the lifeboat moorings
Lifeboats	Sat	30	09	1989	The Lifeboat Annie Lydia Blaker was stationed at Wicklow Harbour
Lifeboats				1995	An inshore lifeboat D-518 was stationed at Wicklow Town
Lifeboats				1997	An new access ramp to the moorings installed at Arklow Lifeboat Station.
Lighthouse	Tue	21	08	1906	The Lighthouse on Wicklow Head was converted from gas to incandescent paraffin
Lighthouse	Wed	31	03	1976	The Lighthouse on Wicklow Head was converted from incandescent paraffin to electric
Lighthouse	Sun	31	03	1994	The lighthouse on Wicklow Head built in 1818 was automated
Litographic				1997	Lithographic Ltd move to a new building on the Southern Cross Route, Bray
Little Bray			06	2005	2m scheme announced to develop the site of the Bray Golf Club in Little Bray
Liverpool Cathedral				1934	Granite from Financially Quarry near Aughrim was sent to Liverpool for the building of Liverpool Cathedral.

A-Z Reference	Day	Date	Month	Year	DATA
Local Government			03	1990	Government announces that a review of Local government functions are taking place and the elections June will not be held.
Loreto Convent Bray				1956	Loreto Convent School Vevay Road Bray extended
Loreto Convent Bray				1971	Extension added to the school at Loreto Convent Bray
Loreto Convent Bray				2000	Loreto Convent, Bray won the All Ireland Schools' Hockey Championship (Leinster Senior Cup)
Loreto Convent Bray			10	2001	An Astroturf Pitch opened at Loreto Convent, Bray
Loreto Convent Bray				2001	Loreto Convent, Bray won the All Ireland Schools' Hockey Championship (Leinster Senior Cup)
Lotto				1988	An Post run Lotto system introduced
Lough Dan				1952	The ESB proposed to build a dam at the southern of Lough Dan, Roundwood. An English firm carry out bore tests.
Lough Dan	Sat	15	05	1982	The Scout National Camp Site at Lough Dan opened by Dr. Patrick Hillery President of Ireland
Loughlinstown Hospital	Mon	09	06	1952	St. Columcilles Hospital at Loughlinstown was opened by Dr. Ryan the Minister for Health
Loughlinstown Hospital			's	1980	An extension was added to Loughlinstown Hospital
Loughman.Joe	Sat	03	07	1999	Joe Loughman (cyclist and historian) died
Luggala				1937	Lord Powerscourt sold Luggala, Roundwood to Ernest Guinness. Ernest Guinness gave it to his daughter Oonagh.
Luggala				1950	Garden temple erected in the grounds of Luggala. It originally stood in Templeogue House, Dublin
Luggala				1956	Luggala House a home of the Guinness family was burnt but rebuilt immediately
Lugnaquilla Walk				1927	J.J. Cronin of Dublin completed Hart's High Level Route to Lugnaquilla in 20 hours 32 min
Lugnaquilla Walk				1976	The fastest time set for the Lugnaquilla walk was 17 hours 39 minutes Gaffney and Rice
M.P's	Wed	06	02	1918	Redistribution of Seats (Ireland) Act 1918, The limits of the number of M.P's for each county
Mackintosh. C. Herbert				1908	Charles Herbert mackintosh wrote "Potential Resources of British Columbia
Mackintosh. C. Herbert	Tue	22	12	1931	Charles Herbert Mackintosh died at Ottawa, Canada
MacMahon.John				1982	Rev John MacMahon became Parish Priest of Our Lady Queen of Peace Parish, Putland Road, Bray
Maguire. Brian				1951	Brian Maguire (painter) born Co.Wicklow
Maguire. Peter				1960	Rev Peter Maguire became Parish Priest of Enniskerry
Maguire. Thomas	Sat	14	12	1912	Police Sergeant Thomas Maguire was stabbed by William Burke at Aughrim, Co.Wicklow
Malone. J.B.			10	1989	J.B.Malone Hill walker and Author died
Malynn.James Joseph	Tue	24	01	1920	Constable James Joseph Malynn shot during the attack on Baltinglass RIC Barracks
Malynn.James Joseph	Wed	01	12	1920	Constable James Joseph Malynn died from the wounds received during the attack on Baltinglass RIC Barracks

Section Two: Data in Alphabetical Order

Subject	Weekday	Day	Month	Year	Detail
Maps				1901	Wicklow Sheet Map 121 engraved 1853, published 1855, republished 1901
Maps				1908	Bray Head, Greystones and Kilcoole, NewtownMount Kennedy surveyed by Ordnance Survey 6inches to Mile Map
Maps				1981	The Wicklow Way (Sli Cualann Nua) Map produced by the Ordnance Survey
Maps				1998	Irish Historic Town Atlas Number 9 Bray by K.M. Davies published Royal Irish Academy
Maps				2000	Heffernan's 1876 illustrated plan of Bray by K.M. Davies published Wordwell
Maps				2000	County Wicklow in 1861 by K.M. Davies published Wordwell
Marino Clinic, Bray				1982	Extension added to the Marino Clinic, Church Road, Bray
Marley Park				1972	Dublin County Council bought Marley Park and House, Rathfarnham from Mr.P.K. Love. One the home of the La Touche Family
Marley Park				1975	Dublin County Council opened Marley Park and part of the House to the public.
Marriage Rate				1911	In the period 1851 – 1911 County Wicklow was the only east coast county to show an increase in the Marriage rate
Marriages				2002	Marriages in County Wicklow. 717
Martin. Colbert				1980	Colbert Martin (local historian) published a book about Little Bray "A Drink from Broderick's Well"
Masonic Lodge				1910	The Tynte 236 Masonic Lodge, Baltinglass was established in 1910
Massy. Anne L.	Thu	16	04	1931	Anne L. Massy (Marine Scientist and Conservationist) died in Dublin
Maxtor				1990	Maxtor Ltd replaces Nixdorf Ltd on the Boghall Road.
Mc Alinden				1968	The Mc Alinden family establish the Lithographic Universal Ltd in Bray. The family also ran the Record Press Ltd.
Mc Mahon. Ella				1928	Her novel "Irish Vignettes" (working class seduction and betrayal with critical events taking place on a Easter Monday in Bray)
McAnally. Ray				1926	Ray McAnally born Co. Donegal
McAnally. Ray	Thu	15	06	1989	Ray McAnally (Actor) died at his Co. Wicklow home, buried St. Fintans Cemetery, Sutton, Dublin
McCabe. Peter				1981	Rev. Peter McCabe appointed Parish Priest of Enniskerry Parish
McCabe. Peter			07	1999	Rev. Peter McCabe Parish Priest of Enniskerry Parish retired
McCann. W.J.				1996	William J. McCann of Bray appointed Chairman of the ESB (Electricity Supply Board) 1996 – 2001
McCarthy. John				1977	Rev. John McCarthy Parish Priest of Tomacork, Carnew 1977–
McCormack. William				1947	The writer Hugh Maxton (pseud. of W.J. McCormack) born near Aughrim, Co. Wicklow
McCormack. William				1947	William John McCormack a poet who used pseudonym Hugh Maxton born near Aughrim Co. Wicklow
McCormack. William				1970	(Hugh Maxton) William John McCormack wrote "Stones"
McCormack. William				1976	(Hugh Maxton) William John McCormack wrote "The noise in the Fields"
McCormack. William				1982	(Hugh Maxton) William John McCormack wrote "Jubilee for Renegades"

A–Z Reference	Day	Date	Month	Year	DATA
McCormack. William				1983	(Hugh Maxton) William John McCormack wrote "The Enlighted Cave and Inscriptions"
McCormack. William				1985	(Hugh Maxton) William John McCormack wrote "Snapdragons and Passage"
McCormack. William				1985	(Hugh Maxton) William John McCormack wrote "Surviving Poems"
McCormack. William				1986	(Hugh Maxton) William John McCormack wrote "At the Protestant Museum"
McCormack. William				1993	(Hugh Maxton) William John McCormack wrote "Sheridan le Fanu and Victorian Ireland"
McCormack. William				1993	(Hugh Maxton) William John McCormack wrote "Dublin Paper war of 1786–1788"
McCormack. William				1994	(Hugh Maxton) William John McCormack wrote "From Burke to Beckett"
McCrea. John J.				1944	John J. McCrea held the post of Chairman of Wicklow County Council 1944–1950
McCrea. John J.				1960	John J. McCrea held the post of Chairman of Wicklow County Council 1960–1968
McDermott. J.E.	Fri	26	05	1933	The owner of Picture House (Mac's) Quinsborough Road J.E. (Jack) Mc Dermott died and is buried in St. Peter's Cemetery, Bray
McGuckian. Mary				1963	Mary McGuckian (Film Maker) born 1963, educated at St. Gerard's School Bray.
McHugh. Eugene	Sun	11	05	2003	Eugene McHugh of Greystones appointed Chief Commissioner of Scouting Ireland SAI
McManus Liz				1947	Liz McManus born in Canada
McManus Liz				1990	Act of Subversion a novel by Liz McManus T.D. for Wicklow
McManus Liz				1994	Liz McManus Minister for Housing and Urban Renewal 1994–1997
McManus Liz			10	2002	Liz McManus of Bray appointed deputy leader of the Labour Party
McNaughton. Paul				1978	Paul McNaughton of Greystones Rugby Club won 18 caps for Ireland between 1978 and 1981
McShane. Paul	Mon	06	01	1986	Paul McShane born Kilpedder Co. Wicklow
McShane. Paul	Mon	08	07	2002	Paul McShane signed for the Manchester United Football Club (academy)
Meath Hospital				1998	The Meath Hospital joined with a number of other Dublin hospitals and moved to a new hospital at Tallaght
Meceedy. Ralph				1912	Ralph Mecredy of Bray represented Ireland in cycling at the 1912 Olympic Games held in Stockholm
Mecredy. Richard J.	Sat	26	04	1924	Richard James Mecredy of Valambrosa, Bray died at Dumfries, Scotland
Medical officer				1925	The Local Government Act, required every County Council to appoint a County Medical Officer
Melifont Hotel				1988	Melifont Hotel Quinsborough Road, Bray sold and reopened as Westbourne Hotel.
Messitt. Bertie				1960	Bertie Messitt of Bray represented Ireland in the marathon at the 1960 Olympic Games held in Rome
Miami Showband	Thu	31	07	1975	Fran O'Toole from Bray and two other members of the Miami Showband are killed in an ambush near Newry, County Down.
Miley. Jim				1976	Jim Miley held the post of Chairman of Wicklow County Council 1976–1977

Name	Day	DD	MM	Year	Event
Miley. Jim				1982	Jim Miley held the post of Chairman of Wicklow County Council 1982-1983
Milne. Charles Ewart	Mon	25	05	1903	Charles Ewart Milne (poet, sailor) born in Dublin, educated at Nun's Cross school, Ashford.
Milne. Charles Ewart	Wed	14	01	1987	Charles Ewart Milne died
Mining			circa	1930	State Mining & Exploration Company developed the Avoca Mines
Mining				1956	The Finance Act allowed new mining enterprise exemption from all tax for first 4 years and taxation on half profits for next 4 years
Mining Company				1950	The Mining Company of Wicklow was established
Monck	Mon	11	12	1905	Henry Wyndham Stanley Monck, later 6th Viscount Monck born
Monck	Thu	18	08	1927	Henry Power Charles Monck, 5th Viscount Monck died and was succeeded by his grandson Henry Wyndham Stanley Monck
Monck	Thu	01	08	1929	Edith Monck nee Scott died
Monck				1951	Henry Wyndham Stanley Monck married Brenda Adkins
Monck	Thu	02	04	1953	Charles Stanley Monck born, later 7th Viscount Monck
Monck				1982	Henry Wyndham Stanley Monck died, 6th Viscount Monck his son Charles Stanley Monck
Monck Family				1939	The Monck family sold Charleville House, Enniskerry
Monck Family Estates				1903	The remainder of the Monck Family Estates in County Wicklow, excluding Charleville House sold to the Land Commission
Montague. Daniel	Sun	04	02	1912	Daniel Montague died and is buried at Annapolis, Virginia, USA
Montigny				1994	Wicklow town twinned with Montigny le Bretonneux, France.-20 miles south west of Paris
Moore. James	Mon	08	05	1933	James Edward Moore born, the son of Rev. Edward Francis Butler Moore of Bray
Moore. James	Sun	24	06	1956	James Edward Moore became a Deacon in the Parish of Knock. Co. Down
Moore. James	Sun	16	06	1957	James Edward Moore ordained a priest
Moore. James	Fri	31	03	1995	James Edward Moore appointed Bishop of Connor
Moore. James	Wed	16	03	2005	Bishop Edward James Moore died in Bangor Hospital, Co Down
Moore. Seamus			06	1940	Seamus Moore T.D. for Wicklow since 1927 died.
Moorhead. Dr. Thomas G	Wed	03	08	1960	Prof. Thomas Gillman Moorhead died
Moorhead. Dr. Thomas G.				1905	Thomas Gillman Moorhead appointed a member of the Royal College of Physicians of Ireland
Moorhead. Dr. Thomas G.				1906	Thomas Gillman Moorhead appointed a fellow of the Royal College of Physicians of Ireland
Moorhead. Dr. Thomas G.				1907	Thomas Gillman Moorhead married Mai Quinn.
Moorhead. Dr. Thomas G.				1910	Thomas Gillman Moorhead appointed President of the Royal College of Physicians of Ireland
Moorhead. Dr. Thomas G.				1918	During the First World War Dr Thomas Gillman Moorehead served in Cairo with the Royal Army Medical Corps

A-Z Reference	Day	Date	Month	Year	DATA
Moorhead. Dr. Thomas G.			07	1926	Thomas G Moorhead while stepping down from a train at Euston Stn. London slipped and fell, he was conscious and blind
Moorhead. Dr. Thomas G.				1933	Thomas Gillman Moorhead appointed President of the British and Irish Medical Associations
Moorhead. Dr. Thomas G.				1935	Mai Quinn the wife of Dr. Thomas G. Moorhead died
Moorhead. Dr. Thomas G.				1938	Thomas Gillman Moorhead married Shelia Gwynn in London. Shelia was the daughter of the author Stephen Gwynn
Moorhead. Dr. Thomas G.	Wed	03	08	1960	Dr Thomas Gillman Moorehead died
Moran. Joe				1991	Joe Moran of Greystones appointed Chief Executive Officer of the ESB (Electricity Supply Board) 1991 - 1996
Moriarity. Andrew				1941	Rev. Andrew Moriarity appointed Parish Priest of the Holy Redeemer Parish, Bray
Moriarty. Andrew	Sun	20	04	1952	Rev Andrew Moriarty of the Holy Redeemer Parish Bray died and was buried in St. Peter's Graveyard, Bray
Mortell. Mark				1961	Mark Mortell (Director of Advertising Company and Chairman of Bord Failte) born 1961, educated at Presentation College, Bray
Mount Kennedy House				1928	The Cunningham family sold Mount Kennedy House, Newtown Mount Kennedy
Mount Kennedy House				1930	The Gun Cunningham family sold the NewtownMountKennedy estate
Mount Kennedy House				1938	Mount Kennedy House, Newtown Mount Kennedy was bought by Mr Ernest Hull
Mount Kennedy House				1971	Mount Kennedy House, Newtown Mount Kennedy was bought by Noel Griffin a director of Waterford Glass
Mount Usher	Wed	13	08	1980	Mount Usher, Ashford sold by the Walpole family to Mrs Jay
Mountain Rescue			circa	1960	The Dublin & Wicklow Mountain Rescue Team had its origins in the An Oige Mountain Rescue Team
Mountain Rescue			circa	1985	The An Oige Mountain Rescue was reformed as the Dublin & Wicklow Mountain Rescue Team
Mountain Rescue				1997	The Dublin & Wicklow Mountain Rescue Team responded to 47 callouts
Mountain Rescue				1999	The Dublin & Wicklow Mountain Rescue Team responded to 37 callouts
Mountain Rescue				2000	The Dublin & Wicklow Mountain Rescue Team responded to 20 callouts
Mountain Rescue				2002	The Dublin & Wicklow Mountain Rescue Team responded to 7 callouts
Mr What				1958	Bray businessman Mr D.J. Coughlan owner of the race horse "Mr What" won the English Grand National at Aintree
Mucklagh N.S.				1938	Work began on building Mucklagh National School, at Mucklagh near Aughrim
Mulcare. P				1971	East of Ireland Amateur (Golf) Open Championship winner P.Mulcare of Woodbrook, Bray
Mulcare. P				1972	East of Ireland Amateur (Golf) Open Championship winner P.Mulcare of Woodbrook, Bray
Muldoon. John				1905	John Muldoon elected M.P. for Donegal North 1095-1906
Muldoon. John				1907	John Muldoon elected M.P. for Wicklow East 1907-1911

Muldoon.John	1911				John Muldoon elected M.P. for Cork East 1911–1918
Mulligan. Rev	1986	05	Thu	22	Fr. Mulligan of the Queen of Peace Parish, Putland Road, Bray died
Murder	2003	08	Wed	10	Georgina Eager of NewtownMountKennedy found murdered in Dublin
Murder	2005	09	Tue	06	A man shot dead in his home in Bray
Murder	2005				Christopher Newman found guilty in London Court for the murder of Georgina Eager in 2003
Murphy. Ciaran	1979				Ciaran Murphy held the post of Chairman of Wicklow County Council 1979–1980
Murphy.James	1913				James Murphy died at Dun Laoghaire Co. Dublin
Murphy. Matt	1983				Matt Murphy appointed first Principal of St. Thomas's Community College, Bray
Murphy.William	1960				Rev William Murphy appointed Parish Priest of Queen of Peace Parish, Bray
Murphy.William	1964	02	Tue	25	Rev. William Murphy P.P. of Our Lady Queen of Peace Parish, Putland Road died and is buried in St. Peter's Graveyard, Bray
National Archives	1922	09		19	Dept. of Taoiseach Report S1984 The S.S. 'Wicklow Head' detention and compensation claim for period 19/09/1922 to 03/02/1923
National Archives	1927				Business Records Survey Wicklow No. 32 Photocopies of Sports Club Account Book, Roundwood 1927–1933 and 1952–1961
National Archives	1930				Business Records Survey Wicklow No. 06. Ships Arrivals and Departures 1930– 1966 at Arklow
National Archives	1930				Business Records Survey Wicklow No. 08. Brennan's Dressmakers, Carnew. Account Books 1930–1953
National Archives	1934	01	Tue	17	Dept. of Justice Report A6/2/34– Jus 8/56 Intimidation of Wicklow man Thomas P.Keogh of Baltinglass at Dublin Cattle Market
National Archives	1934	06	Tue	19	Dept. of Justice Report A26/5/34 – Jus 8/185 Raid for Blue shirt on house of John Hanbidge, Feddan, Kiltegan
National Archives	1934				Dept. of Justice Report C26/34 – Jus 8/315 Irish Republican Army Activities in Co. Wicklow
National Archives	1934				Dept. of Justice Report E26/3/34 – Jus 8/570 No Rent, No Rates campaign in Co. Wicklow
National Archives	1934	05	Tue	15	Dept. of Justice Report A/26/3/34 – Jus 8/184 Unlawful assembly at Bray on 15/05/1934
National Archives	1935				Dept. of Justice Report E26/35 – Jus 8/616 Execution of decrees for non-payment of land annuities, general file Co. Wicklow
National Archives	1936				Dept. of Justice Report D46/36 – Jus 8/455 Steamers anchored in Wicklow Bay as reported in Irish Independent 09/11/1936
National Archives	1937				Dept. of Justice Report E26/37 – Jus 8/662 Execution of decrees for non-payment of land annuities, Co. Wicklow
National Archives	1938				Dept. of Justice Report E26/38 – Jus 8/674 Execution of decrees for non-payment of land annuities, Co. Wicklow
National Archives	1940				Dept. of Justice Report S443/40 –Jus 8/825 Fr. Gleeson of Bray sermon 16/6/1940 relating to evictions at suit of BUDC
National Archives	1950				Business Records Survey Wicklow No. 31 Account Books of Frank Donnelly Draper of Bray 1950– 1965
National Archives	1953	06			Dept. of Taoiseach Report RA40/53 – 97/9/1269 Wicklow By-Election 1953 Taoiseach speeches
National Park	1990	04			The Wicklow Mountains National Park established about 20,000 Hectares or (49,421 acres).

A–Z Reference	Day	Date	Month	Year	DATA
National Park	Fri	29	04	2005	Mr Dick Roche opened Wicklow Mountains National Park Headquarters at Kilafin, Laragh Co. Wicklow
Naylor's Cove				1978	The Diving board at Bray Cove Baths fell into the sea.
Needham. Mary	Thu	07	11	1907	Mary P Needham (writer) died, Mary was born at Ballynure, Co. Wicklow where her father was rector.
Nelsons Pillar	Tue	08	03	1966	The upper half of Nelson Pillar in O'Connell Street, Dublin was shattered by an explosion
Nelsons Pillar	Wed	09	03	1966	The remainder of Nelson's Pillar, Dublin was blown up by Army engineers
Nevin. Catherine	Mon	14	02	2000	Catherine Nevin goes on trial at the Central Criminal Court for the murder of her husband Tom in March 1996
Nevin. Catherine	Tue	11	04	2000	Catherine Nevin found guilty of murder of her husband Tom
Nevin. Tom	Tue	19	03	1996	Tom Nevin founded murder in his home at Jack's White Inn, Ballinapark, near Brittas Bay, Co. Wicklow
Newcastle Hospital				1933	Newcastle Hospital near Newtown Mount Kennedy ceased to be a national TB sanatorium
Newcastle Hospital				1964	Newcastle Hospital near Newtown Mount Kennedy became a psychiatric Unit
Newcastle Hospital				1966	Newcastle Hospital near Newtown Mount Kennedy became a psychiatric hospital
Newcastle Hospital				1972	The Co. Wicklow Association for Mentally Handicapped established St Catherien's School in the grounds of Newcastle Hospital
Newcastle N.S				1983	Work began on building Newcastle National School, Co. Wicklow
Newspapers				1905	Wicklow Press Newspaper first edition
Newspapers				1916	Wicklow Press Newspapers final edition
Newspapers				1918	Bray & South Dublin Herald newspaper cost 2d
Newspapers	Fri	19	12	1924	Freeman's Journal Newspaper final edition
Newspapers				1926	Wicklow Newsletter and County Advertiser Newspaper final edition
Newspapers				1927	Bray Herald Newspaper final edition
Newspapers				1935	Wicklow Post (Wicklow) first edition
Newspapers				1936	Bray Tribune Newspaper first edition
Newspapers				1936	East Coast Express first edition
Newspapers				1939	East Coast Express final edition (continued in Dublin under various titles until 1952)
Newspapers				1946	Bray Tribune Newspaper final edition (continued in Dublin under various titles until 1952)
Newspapers				1958	Weekly Gazette (Arklow) first edition published
Newspapers	Fri	02	07	1965	Newspaper Strike in Ireland between 2nd July and 12th September

Section Two: Data in Alphabetical Order

Name	Description	Year	Day	Weekday
Newspapers	East Coast Newspaper first edition	1974		
Newspapers	East Coast Newspaper final edition	1974		
Newspapers	Southside and Bray News first edition	1978		
Newspapers	Bray People Newspaper first edition	1979		
Newspapers	North Wicklow News (Wicklow) first edition	1983		
Newspapers	North Wicklow Times (Bray) first edition	1988		
Newspapers	Bray may have been a Roman Settlement appeared in the Irish Times Newspaper	1989	21	Thu
Newspapers	South and West Wicklow Times (Bray) first edition	1991		
Newspapers	Wicklow Times (Bray) first edition	1991		
Newtown FC	Newtown Football Club formed (NewtownMountKennedy)	1976		
Nicol.Erskine	Erskine Nicol died	1904		
Nicol.Erskine	The Erskine Nicol painting of Bray Seafront purchased by the National Gallery of Ireland	1973		
Nitrigin Eireann Teo.	Nitrigin Eireann Teoranta (NET) open a factory near Arklow for the manufacture of fertiliser	1964		
Nitrigin Eireann Teo.	Taoiseach Sean Lemass officially opened Nitrigin Eireann Teo.,plant at Arklow	1966	27	Wed
Nitrigin Eireann Teo.	Nitrigin Eireann Teoranta (NET) the state-owned fertiliser company begins merger talks with Imperial Chemical Industries (ICI)	1984		
Nixdorf	Nixdorf Computers established a production plant on the Boghall Road, Bray	1977		
Nolan.John	Rev John Nolan appointed Parish Priest of the St. Mary's Church. Enniskerry	1955		
Nolan.Winifride	Winifride Nolan born in Wales, lived on a farm near Aughrim, Co. Wicklow	1913		
Nolan.Winifride	Winifride Nolan of Aughrim, Co Wicklow wrote "The New Invasion"	1953		
Nolan.Winifride	Winifride Nolan of Aughrim, Co. Wicklow wrote "Seven Fat Kine" published in Dublin	1966		
Nowlan.James	Rev James Nowlan appointed Parish Priest of the Holy Redeemer Parish, Bray	1939		
Nowlan.James	Very Rev. James Nowlan Parish Priest of Bray 1939-1941	1939		
Nun's Cross, Ashford	The Church of Ireland Primary School at Nun's Cross, Ashford opened by Archbishop of Dublin, Dr. Donal Caird	1992	06	Fri
O'Brien.FJ	Francis J.O'Brien appointed County Manager of Wicklow (Local Government) 1973-1976	1973		
O'Brien.John	John Thomond O'Brien remains repatriated to Argentina	1935		
O'Byrne.Feagh McHugh	A monument to Feagh McHugh O'Byrne unveiled at Rathdrum by Brig. General P.D. Hogan	1997	11	Sun
O'Byrne.John	John O'Byrne legal adviser to Irish delegation at Anglo-Irish Treaty negotiations	1921		
O'Byrne.John	John O'Byrne Appointed Attorney General of Ireland 07/061924- 09/01/1926	1924		
O'Byrne.John	John O'Byrne (Lawyer) died	1954	14	Thu

A-Z Reference	Day	Date	Month	Year	DATA
O'Connell. John				1981	Rev John O'Connell appointed Parish Priest of the Holy Redeemer Parish Bray
O'Connor. Joyce	Mon	11	06	2001	Joyce O'Connor nee Fitzpatrick of Bray appointed chairperson of FETAC by Minister of Education
O'Connor. Peter J.	Mon	05	08	1901	Peter J.O'Connor (athletics) set a long jump record at Ballsbridge Dublin of 24ft 11"
O'Connor. Peter J.	Mon	05	08	1901	Peter O'Connor set a World and Irish Long Jump record in the RDS, Dublin with a jump of 24ft 11 and three quarters inches
O'Connor. Peter J.	Sun	28	07	1901	Peter O'Connor jumped 24ft 11 and half inches in the long jump at Annacurra. Co Wicklow
O'Connor. Peter J.				1906	Peter J.O'Connor (athletics) won the Silver Medal at the Intercalated Games held in Athens for the long jump
O'Connor. Peter J.				1906	Peter J.O'Connor (athletics) won the Gold Medal at the Intercalated Games held in Athens for the triple jump
O'Connor. Peter J.	Sat	09	11	1957	Peter J.O'Connor (athletics) died in Waterford
O'Dalaigh. Cearbhall	Sun	12	02	1911	Cearbhall O'Dalaigh born at 85 Main Street, Bray. 1974 became President of Ireland
O'Dalaigh. Cearbhall	Fri	15	04	1918	Cearbhall O'Dalaigh first day at St.Cronans Boys National School Bray see President of Ireland
O'Dalaigh. Cearbhall	Sat	08	05	1920	Cearbhall O'Dalaigh last day at St. Cronans Boys National School Bray see President of Ireland
O'Dalaigh. Cearbhall	Tue	30	04	1946	Cearbhall O'Dalaigh appointed Attorney General of Ireland 30/04/1946-18/02/1948
O'Dalaigh. Cearbhall	Thu	14	06	1951	Cearbhall O'Dalaigh appointed Attorney General of Ireland 14/06/1951-11/07/1953
O'Dalaigh. Cearbhall	Mon	13	07	1953	Cearbhall O'Dalaigh appointed High Court Judge
O'Dalaigh. Cearbhall				1961	Cearbhall O'Dalaigh appointed Chief Justice
O'Dalaigh. Cearbhall				1972	Cearbhall O'Dalaigh appointed the first Irish member of the Court of Justice in the European Community
O'Dalaigh. Cearbhall	Thu	19	12	1974	Cearbhall O'Dalaigh installed as President of Ireland
O'Dalaigh. Cearbhall	Sun	21	09	1975	President Cearbhall O'Dalaigh visited his home town and a civic reception was held in his honour
O'Dalaigh. Cearbhall	Fri	22	10	1976	Cearbhall O'Dalaigh 5th President of Ireland, resigned
O'Dalaigh. Cearbhall	Tue	21	03	1978	Cearbhall O'Dalaigh former President of Ireland died at Sneem, Co. Kerry
O'Dalaigh. Cearbhall	Mon	06	06	1983	President Hillery unveiled a sculpture to the late President Cearbhall O'Dalaigh at Sneem, Co. Kerry
O'Dea. Jimmy	Thu	07	01	1965	Jimmy O'Dea (comedian) died in Dublin
O'Faolain. Sean	Tue	03	06	1928	Sean O'Faolain married Eileen Gould in Boston, U.S.A.
O'Faolain. Sean			's	1930	The O'Faolain family lived in a cottage in the Glencree Valley, Enniskerry
O'Faolain. Sean				1932	Sean O'Faolain published his first collection of Short Stories "Midsummer Madness and other stories"
O'Faolain. Sean			's	1940	The O'Faolain moved from Enniskerry to Killiney, Co. Dublin
O'Faolain. Sean	Sat	20	04	1991	Sean O'Faolain died

Name	Day	Date	Month	Year	Details
O'Gorman. Tiomthy				1904	The Very Rev. Tiomthy O'Gorman appointed Parish Priest of Bray, Little Bray and Greystones 1904-1912
O'Halloran. P.J.	Tue	29	01	1924	Garda Patrick Joseph O'Halloran (651) died following the Bank raid at Baltinglass, Co. Wicklow on 28/01/1924
O'Halloran. P.J.	Mon	28	01	1924	Garda Patrick J. O'Halloran from Co. Galway was shot and wounded trying to arrest 2 bank raiders at Baltinglass. Co. Wicklow
O'Higgins. Brigid				1932	Brigid O'Higgins nee Hogan born in Dublin and educated at the Dominican Convent Wicklow
O'Higgins. Brigid	Tue	05	03	1957	Brigid Hogan elected to Dail Eireann for South Galway
O'Higgins. Brigid				1958	Brigid Hogan married Michael O'Higgins the T.D. for Wicklow
O'Kelly Edward Peter			07	1914	Edward P. O'Kelly M.P. for West Wicklow died in London
O'Kelly. Sean T				1918	Mr. Sean T O'Kelly former President of Ireland married Mary Ryan from Wexford
O'Kelly. Sean T	Wed	18	07	1934	Mary Ryan the wife Mr. Sean T.O'Kelly former President of Ireland died
O'Kelly. Sean T				1936	Mr. Sean T. O'Kelly former President of Ireland married Phyllis Ryan a sister of Mary Ryan from Wexford
O'Kelly. Sean T				1939	Mr. Sean T O'Kelly former President of Ireland came to live at Roundwood Park, Roundwood
O'Kelly. Sean T	Mon	25	06	1945	Mr. Sean T O'Kelly succeeded Douglas Hyde as 2nd President of Ireland
O'Kelly. Sean T	Wed	25	06	1952	Mr. Sean T O'Kelly began his 2nd term as President of Ireland
O'Kelly. Sean T	Tue	07	10	1957	Roundwood Park the private residence of the former President of Ireland Sean T O'Kelly was destroyed by fire
O'Kelly. Sean T	Wed	24	06	1959	Mr. Sean T O'Kelly President of Ireland retired
O'Kelly. Sean T	Wed	23	11	1966	Mr. Sean T O'Kelly former President of Ireland died
O'Kelly. Sean T	Sat	19	11	1983	Phyllis Ryan the wife Mr. Sean T.O'Kelly former President of Ireland died
Old Conna	Thu	12	11	1931	Article in the Irish Times about a weeping stone in Old Conna, Bray
Old Conna				1963	Old Conna House Hotel, Bray closed
Old Conna Golf Club				1980	Old Conna Golf Club (Bray) established
Old Conna House				1957	Old Conna House was purchased for £35,000 by James Stuart Roberston
Old Conna House				1982	Old Conna House sold for 0.75 Million Pounds
Old Connaught				1948	Old Connaught Graveyard, Bray closed by Ministerial Order
Old Connaught House			04	2000	Old Connaught House put up for sale
O'Moore. Sean				1996	Sean O'Moore of Bray was the first person in Ireland to be presented a Commendation from the Royal Life Saving Society
O'Moore. Sean				1996	Sean O'Moore of Bray carried out a rescue in Bray Harbour. Sean was awarded Bronze Cross for gallantry
O'Neill William	Fri	02	12	1927	William O'Neill convicted of the murder of Margaret Farrell
O'Neill William	Thu	29	12	1927	William O'Neill was hanged in Dublin

The County Wicklow Database: 432 AD to 2006 AD

A-Z Reference	Day	Date	Month	Year	DATA
O'Neill, John				1927	Mr John O'Neill of Greystones was appointed the 1st Chief Scout of the Catholic Boys Scouts of Ireland –1927–1930
O'Nolan. Shaun			12	1945	Shaun O'Nolan (song writer) died in New York
Opera. Company Bray				1918	The Bray Opera Company founded
Operation Shamrock				1945	Between 1945 and 1950 The Irish Red Cross and French Sisters Of Charity looked after Glencree Refugee Centre
Orange Lodge				1949	The Dublin and Wicklow District, King William III Prince of Orange LOL 1313 was founded
Oranmore. Lord	Mon	21	10	1901	Baron Dominick Geoffrey Edward Browne born
Oranmore. Lord	Thu	05	02	1925	Baron Dominick Geoffrey Edward Browne married Mildred Helen Egerton
Oranmore. Lord	Wed	07	08	2002	Dominick Geoffrey Edward Browne, Lord Oranmore died
Order of Malta, Bray			08	2002	Bray Order of Malta take delivery of a new Ambulance and minibus
O'Rourke. Mary	Mon	31	05	1937	Mary O'Rourke (Politician) born Athlone, Co. Westmeath and educated at Loreto Convent, Bray
O'Rourke. Mary				1981	Mary O'Rourke elected to Seanad Eireann
O'Rourke. Mary				1982	Mary O'Rourke elected to Dail Eireann for constituency of Longford – Roscommon
O'Sandair. Cathal				1922	Cathal O'Sandair (writer) born Charles Saunders in Weston-Super-Mare, was educated at Colaiste Chiarain, Bray
O'Sandair. Cathal	Sun	18	02	1996	Cathal O'Sandair died in Dublin
O'Shaughnessy, Jimmy			07	2001	Jimmy O'Shaughnessy held the post of Chairman of Wicklow County Council 2001-2002
O'Shea. Katherine	Sat	05	02	1921	Charles S. Parnell wife Katherine Wood the former wife of Capt. William O'Shea died
O'Sullivan. Morgan				1945	Morgan O'Sullivan (Film Producer) born 1945, educated at Presentation College, Bray.
Other Vehicles				1946	12,890 Other Vehicles registered in Ireland
Other Vehicles				1947	14,115 Other Vehicles registered in Ireland
Other Vehicles				1948	16,791 Other Vehicles registered in Ireland
Other Vehicles				1949	17,795 Other Vehicles registered in Ireland
O'Toole				1939	The O'Tools Brothers establish the Harbour Bar, Bray
O'Toole. Garry				1968	Garry O'Toole (swimmer) born 1968, Bray Co. Wicklow
O'Toole. Garry				1989	Garry O'Toole (swimmer) won silver in the 200m breaststroke at European Championships
O'Toole. Garry				1991	Garry O'Toole (swimmer) won gold in the 200m breast stroke at World Student Games
O'Toole. Garry				1992	Garry O'Toole of Bray represented Ireland in swimming at the 1992 Olympic Games held in Barcelona
O'Toole. Garry				1998	Garry O'Toole of Bray represented Ireland in swimming at the 1988 Olympic Games held in Seoul

Section Two: Data in Alphabetical Order

Name	Event	Year			
O'Toole. Luke	Luke O'Toole. 1901–1929 General Secretary of the GAA and played a major role in the purchase of the Croke Park site	1913			
O'Toole. Luke	Luke O'Toole of Co.Wicklow died. 1901–1929 General Secretary of the GAA	1929			
O'Tuairisc. Eoghan	Eoghan O'Tuairisc (Eugene Waters) (poet and novelist) born in Ballinasloe, Co. Galway	1919			
O'Tuairisc. Eoghan	Eoghan O'Tuairisc began teaching in Hacketstown Technical College	1968			
O'Tuairisc. Eoghan	Eoghan O'Tuairisc bought a house on the Wicklow/Carlow border near Hacketstown	1969			
O'Tuairisc. Eoghan	Eoghan O'Tuairisc (Eugene Waters) (poet and novelist) died	1982	Tue	24	08
Owen. Nora	Nora Owen nee O'Mahony (Politician) born 1945, educated at Dominican Convent, Wicklow	1945			
Owen. Nora	Nora Owen elected to Dail Eireann	1981	Thu	11	06
Owen. Nora	Nora Owen appointed Minister for Justice 1994-1997	1994			06
Parking	Disc Parking introduced in Bray	1997	Mon	17	02
Parnell Bridge	The Parnell Bridge (reconstructed) at the Mall Wicklow Town by Messer's Lee of Arklow	1946			
Parnell. Anna	Anna Parnell published "The Tale of a Great Sham" in Dublin in 1905	1905			
Parnell. Anna	Catherine Anna Parnell (Cerisa Palmer) drowned off Ilfracombe, Devon, England	1911	Wed	20	09
Parnell. Charles S	A statue to Charles S. Parnell was unveiled by Mr. John Redmond M.P. at Upper Sackville Street now O'Connell Street	1911	Sun	01	10
Parnell. Charles S	Liam Kavanagh Minister for Tourism, Fisheries and Forestry opens the Charles Stewart Parnell Museum in Avondale House	1986	Mon	01	09
Parnell. Charles S	The Central Bank of Ireland launches its £100 note featuring C.S. Parnell and Avondale House	1996			09
Parnell. Emily	Emily Parnell a sister of Charles S. Parnell died in the South Dublin Union Infirmary	1918	Sat	18	05
Parnell. H.T.	Henry Tudor Parnell a brother of Charles S Parnell died	1915	Wed	24	11
Parnell. J.H.	John Howard Parnell a brother of Charles S Parnell died in London	1923	Thu	03	05
Parnell. J.H.	J. H. Parnell elected M.P. for Meath South 1903	1903			
Parnell. Kitty	Kitty Parnell died	1921	Sat	05	02
Parnell. Street	Great Britain Street, Dublin renamed Parnell Street.	1911	Mon	02	10
Parnell. Theodosia	Theodosia Parnell husband Comm. Claude Paget died	1917	Tue	30	01
Parnell. Theodosia	Theodosia Parnell died in London	1920	Wed	17	03
Pearce. Thomas	Thomas Pearce died	1915			
People's Park Bray	A club house and changing rooms opened at the Peoples' Park, Bray	2003	Mon	23	06
Phone Number	7 digit phone number introduced for the 01 area	1982			
Photo Collection	Valentine Collection held in National Library (Photos 1903 –1950) Photo JV 84198 Glendalough	1903			

A-Z Reference	Day	Date	Month	Year	DATA
Photo Collection				1906	Pictures in colour of Counties Dublin and Wicklow by W. Lawrence
Photo Collection				1910	The Eason collection of photographic negatives 1910 to 1930 held in the National Library
Photo Collection				1943	Lawrence photographic collection purchased by National Library on behalf of the State
Pigott.John				1964	Rev.John Pigott appointed Parish Priest of the Holy Redeemer Parish Bray
Pigott.John	Wed	23	08	1989	Rev.John Pigott Parish Priest of Holy Redeemer Parish died and is buried in St. Peter's Graveyard, Bray
Pim.Joshua				1902	Joshua Pim played on the Davis Cup Tennis team
Pim.Joshua	Wed	15	04	1942	Joshua Pim Wimbledon Tennis Champion 1893 and 1894 died and is buried in Deansgrange Cemetery
Pipe Band				1912	St Kevins Pipe Band, Bray founded
Pipe Band	Mon	18	07	1927	The Bray Pipers Band the only non Dublin band in the procession of Count Markiewiz funeral
Ploughing	Mon	16	02	1931	The first National Ploughing Championships held at Athy, Co Kildare. The Intercounty Horse Ploughing event Wicklow came 2nd
Ploughing	Fri	19	02	1932	The National Ploughing Championships held at Gorey, Co Wexford, The Intercounty Horse Ploughing event Wicklow came 3rd
Ploughing	Wed	15	02	1933	The National Ploughing Championships held at Clondalkin, Co. Dublin. The Intercounty Horse Ploughing event Wicklow came 1st
Ploughing	Wed	13	02	1935	The National Ploughing Championships held at Mallow, Co. Cork. The Intercounty Horse Ploughing event Wicklow came 2nd
Ploughing	Tue	09	02	1937	The National Ploughing Championships held at Greystones Co.Wicklow. The Intercounty Horse Ploughing event Wicklow came 2nd
Ploughing	Wed	08	02	1939	The National Ploughing Championships held at Killarney Co. Kerry. The Intercounty Horse Ploughing event Wicklow came 2nd
Ploughing	Tue	18	02	1941	The National Ploughing Championships held at Navan Co. Meath. The Intercounty Horse Ploughing event Wicklow came 3rd
Ploughing	Thu	12	02	1942	The National Ploughing Championships held at Cloghran Co.Dublin. The Intercounty Horse Ploughing event Wicklow came 1st
Ploughing	Fri	12	02	1943	The National Ploughing Championships held at Portlaois Co.Laois. The Intercounty Horse Ploughing event Wicklow came 3rd
Ploughing	Wed	09	02	1944	The National Ploughing Championships held at Ballinasloe Co. Galway. The Intercounty Horse Ploughing event Wicklow came 2nd
Ploughing	Wed	21	02	1945	The National Ploughing Championships held at Tipperary Co.Tipperary. The Intercounty Horse Ploughing event Wicklow came 3rd
Ploughing	Thu	07	02	1946	The National Ploughing Championships held at Ballbriggan Co.Dublin. The International Individual Class,1st J Halpin of Wicklow
Ploughing	Thu	07	02	1946	The National Ploughing Championships held at Ballbriggan Co.Dublin. The Senior Individual Class,1st John Halpin of Wicklow

Section Two: Data in Alphabetical Order

Category	Day			Year	Description
Ploughing	Thu	07	02	1946	The National Ploughing Championships held at Balbriggan Co.Dublin. The Senior Ploughing Championships Wicklow came 1st
Ploughing	Tue	11	02	1947	The National Ploughing Championships held at Maynooth Co.Kildare. The Senior Ploughing Championships Wicklow came 1st
Ploughing	Thu	19	02	1948	The National Ploughing Championships held at Limerick Co.Limerick. The Senior Ploughing Championships Wicklow came 1st
Ploughing	Thu	01	02	1951	The National Ploughing Championships held at Wexford Co.Wexford. The Senior Ploughing Championships Wicklow came 2nd
Ploughing	Thu	07	02	1952	The National Ploughing Championships held at Athenry Co.Galway. The Overall Tractor Champion W. Woodroofe of Wicklow
Ploughing	Thu	07	02	1952	The National Ploughing Championships held at Athenry Co.Galway. The Senior Ploughing Championships Wicklow came 2nd
Ploughing	Wed	11	02	1953	The National Ploughing Championships held at Mullingar Co.Westmeath. The Senior Ploughing Championships Wicklow came 1st
Ploughing	Fri	11	02	1955	The National Ploughing Championships held at Athy Co.Kildare. The Senior Horse Plough Champion John Halpin of Wicklow
Ploughing	Thu	02	02	1956	The National Ploughing Championships held at Nenagh Co.Tipperary. The Senior Horse Ploughing event Wicklow came 2nd
Ploughing	Fri	08	02	1957	The National Ploughing Championships held at Boyle Co.Roscommon. "Queen of the Plough" Muriel Sutton of Wicklow
Ploughing	Thu	29	01	1959	The National Ploughing Championships held at Bunchurch Co.Kilkenny. "Queen of the Plough" Muriel Sutton of Wicklow
Ploughing	Thu	29	01	1959	The National Ploughing Championships held at Bunchurch Co.Kilkenny. The Senior Horse Ploughing event Wicklow came 2nd
Ploughing	Thu	29	01	1959	The National Ploughing Championships held in Co.Kilkenny. The Snr. Indv. Horse Plough Champion 1st John Halpin of Wicklow
Ploughing	Thu	10	11	1960	The National Ploughing Championships held at New Ross Co.Wexford. The Senior Horse Ploughing event Wicklow came 1st
Ploughing	Thu	09	11	1961	The National Ploughing Championships held at Killarney Co.Kerry. Under 21 Champion Patrick Brennan of Wicklow
Ploughing	Thu	09	11	1961	The National Ploughing Championships held at Killarney Co.Kerry. "Queen of the Plough" Eileen Brennan of Wicklow
Ploughing	Thu	07	11	1963	The National Ploughing Championships held at Athenry Co.Galway. The Senior Horse Plough Champion Wicklow came 1st
Ploughing	Thu	07	11	1963	The National Ploughing Championships held at Athenry Co.Galway. "Queen of the Plough" Eileen Brennan of Wicklow
Ploughing	Wed	17	11	1965	The All Ireland Ploughing Championships held at Enniskerry on 17th and 18th November 1965
Ploughing	Thu	28	10	1971	The National Ploughing Championships held at Finglas Co.Dublin. The Senior Tractor Ploughing 1st Charles Keegan of Wicklow
Ploughing	Thu	17	10	1974	The National Ploughing Championships held in Co.Cork. The Snr. Indv. Horse Plough Champion 1st John Halpin of Wicklow

A–Z Reference	Day	Date	Month	Year	DATA
Ploughing	Thu	14	10	1976	The National Ploughing Championships held in Co. Wexford. The Snr. Indv. Horse Plough Champion 1st John Halpin of Wicklow
Ploughing	Thu	20	10	1977	The National Ploughing Championships held at Cashel Co. Tipperary. "Queen of the Plough" Gretta O'Toole of Wicklow
Ploughing	Thu	12	10	1978	The National Ploughing Championships held at Knocktopher Co. Kilkenny. "Queen of the Plough" Pauline O'Toole of Wicklow
Ploughing	Wed	08	10	1980	The National Ploughing Championships held in Co. Tipperary. The Snr. Indv. Horse Plough Champion 1st John Halpin of Wicklow
Ploughing	Thu	04	10	1984	The National Ploughing Championships held in Co. Kilkenny. The 3 Furrow Tractor Champion 1st Edward Dowse of Wicklow
Ploughing	Thu	09	10	1986	The National Ploughing Championships held in Co. Kilkenny. The 3 Furrow Tractor Champion 1st Peadar Shortt of Wicklow
Ploughing	Thu	09	10	1986	The National Ploughing Championships held in Co. Kilkenny. The Snr. Indv. Horse Plough Champion 1st John Halpin of Wicklow
Plunket				1904	1904-1910 William Lee Plunket, 5th Baron Plunket held the post of Governor and Com. in Chief of the Dominion of New Zealand
Plunket	Fri	01	10	1920	Lady Victoria Plunket married Col. Frances Powell Braithwaite
Plunket	Sat	24	01	1920	William Lee Plunket, 5th Baron Plunket of Old Connaught, Bray died and was succeeded by his son Terance Plunket 6th Baron
Plunket	Mon	04	12	1922	Terrance Coyngham Plunket 6th Baron Plunket of Old Connaught married Dorothe Lewis
Plunket	Sat	08	09	1923	Patrick Terrance Plunket of Old Connaught, Bray born
Plunket	Thu	03	12	1925	Robin Plunket born
Plunket				1938	Terrance Coygnham Plunket 6th Baron and his wife Dorothy Lewis died in a plane crash in the U.S.A.
Plunket				1951	Robin Plunket married Jennifer Southwell
Plunket				1975	Patrick Terrance Plunket, 7th Baron Plunket died and was succeeded by his brother Robin Plunket 8th Baron
Plunkett. James	Fri	21	05	1920	The writer James Plunkett was born in Dublin, He wrote under the non-de-plume of James Plunkett Kelly
Plunkett. James				1969	James Plunkett best known novel Strumpet City was published
Plunkett. James				1980	James Plunkett best known novel Strumpet City was adapted for television by RTÉ
Plunkett. James	Wed	28	05	2003	James Plunkett who lived near Bray, died in a Dublin Nursing Home
Pobje. Bessie				1905	Bessie Pobje died in Dublin
Police/Garda				1920	County Wicklow RIC Const. Charles Bustrock killed
Police/Garda				1920	County Wicklow RIC Const. John Miller killed
Police/Garda				1920	County Wicklow RIC Const. Patrick MacKessy killed

Section Two: Data in Alphabetical Order

Police/Garda	Tue	24	01	1920	The RIC Barracks at Baltinglass attacked
Police/Garda				1920	County Wicklow RIC Const. Jeremiah O'Leary killed
Police/Garda	Fri	08	07	1921	Three RIC Constables attacked at the Fair Green, Rathdrum including Constable Frederick J. Cromer
Police/Garda				1921	County Wicklow RIC Const. Frederick J Cormer killed
Police/Garda				1926	Work began on reconstruction of the former RIC barracks at Hollywood, Co. Wicklow into a Garda Station
Police/Garda	Wed	01	01	1930	The Garda Station opens on Convent Avenue, Bray
Police/Garda				1943	The Grada Station at Aughrim built
Police/Garda				1947	The Garda station at Barnaderg near Redcross built
Police/Garda				1948	The Garda station at Avoca built
Police/Garda				1952	The Garda station at Roundwood built
Police/Garda				1960	The Garda Station at Baltinglass built
Police/Garda				1965	The Garda Station at Rathdrum built
Police/Garda				1967	The Garda Station at Carnew built
Police/Garda				1974	The Garda Station at Enniskerry was restored.
Police/Garda				1977	The Garda Station at Blessington built
Police/Garda				1999	Work began on the extension of Bray Garda Station at Convent Avenue, Bray
Polo				1993	The first indoor arena Polo match in Ireland, was played near Wicklow Town
Pony Club				1970	Wicklow Pony Club founded
Pope John Paul II	Sat	29	09	1979	Pope John Paul II pays a three day visit to Ireland
Pope John Paul II	Sat	29	09	1979	Pope John Paul II blessed the foundation stone for St. Fergals Church at Ballywaltrim, Bray
Population	Sun	31	03	1901	According to the Census of population 28% of the population of Ireland lived in an Urban area
Population	Sun	12	05	1946	36% of the Population of Ireland lives in an Urban Area
Population	Sun	09	04	1961	The Counties of Dublin, Meath & Wicklow accounted for 32.2% of the Republic population
Population	Sun	05	04	1981	Population of Glenealy 418 or 0.47% of the County Population
Population	Sun	05	04	1981	According to the 1981 census 70% of the population of Ireland lives in an urban area.
Population	Sun	05	04	1981	Population of Blessington 988 or 1.12% of the County Population
Population	Sun	05	04	1981	Population of Avoca 289 or 0.33% of the County population
Population	Sun	13	04	1986	Census of Population

A-Z Reference	Day	Date	Month	Year	DATA
Population	Sun	13	04	1986	The population of the counties Dublin, Kildare, Meath and Wicklow accounted for 37.7% of the Population of Ireland
Population	Sun	21	04	1991	Census of Population took place in Ireland
Population	Sun	28	04	2002	Census of Population in Ireland
Population Arklow	Sun	31	03	1901	Population of Arklow Urban 4,944 or 8.12% of County Population
Population Arklow	Sun	02	04	1911	Population of Arklow Urban 5,042 or 8.30% of County Population
Population Arklow	Sun	18	04	1926	Population of Arklow Urban 4,535 or 7.87% of County Population
Population Arklow	Sun	26	04	1936	Population of Arklow Urban 4,680 or 7.99% of County Population
Population Arklow	Sun	12	05	1946	Population of Arklow Urban 4,915 or 8.13% of County Population
Population Arklow	Sun	08	04	1951	Population of Arklow Urban 5,203 or 8.31% of County Population
Population Arklow	Sun	08	04	1956	Population of Arklow Urban 5,292 or 8.83% of County Population
Population Arklow	Sun	09	04	1961	Population of Arklow Urban 5,390 or 9.21% of County Population
Population Arklow	Sun	17	04	1966	Population of Arklow Urban 6,083 or 10.06% of County Population
Population Arklow	Sun	18	04	1971	Population of Arklow Urban 6,948 or 10.48% of County Population
Population Arklow	Sun	01	04	1979	Population of Arklow Urban 8,451 or 10.06% of County Population
Population Arklow	Sun	05	04	1981	Population of Arklow Urban 8,646 or 9.90% of the County Population
Population Arklow	Sun	13	04	1986	Population of Arklow Urban 8,388 or 8.90% of the County Population
Population Arklow	Sun	21	04	1991	Population of Arklow Urban 7,987 or 8.20% of the County Population
Population Arklow	Sun	28	04	1996	Population of Arklow Urban 8,519 or 8.30% of the County Population
Population Arklow	Sun	28	04	2002	Population of Arklow Urban 9,963 or 8.68% of the County Population
Population Baltinglass	Sun	13	04	1986	Population of Baltinglass No1 rural area 11,902 or 12.58% of the County Population
Population Baltinglass	Sun	24	04	1991	Population of Baltinglass No1 rural area 11,976 or 12.30% of the County Population
Population Baltinglass	Sun	28	04	1996	Population of Baltinglass No1 rural area 12,749 or 12.41% of the County Population
Population Baltinglass	Sun	28	04	2002	Population of Baltinglass No1 rural area 14,715 or 12.82% of the County Population
Population Bray	Sun	31	03	1901	Population of Bray 7,424 or 12.20% of County Population
Population Bray				1903	Population of Bray 7,424 ★not a census year★
Population Bray	Sun	02	04	1911	Population of Bray 7,691 or 12.66% of County Population
Population Bray	Sun	18	04	1926	The Church of Ireland Population of Bray 1,470

Section Two: Data in Alphabetical Order

Population Bray	Sun	18	04	1926	Population of Bray 8,637 or 14.99% of County Population
Population Bray	Sun	26	04	1936	Population of Bray .10,111 or 17.26% of County Population
Population Bray	Sun	12	05	1946	The population of Bray 11,085 or 18.33% of County Population
Population Bray	Sun	08	04	1951	Population of Bray 12,062 or 19.27% of County Population
Population Bray	Sun	08	04	1956	Population of Bray Urban District 10,856 or 17.3% of County Population
Population Bray	Sun	09	04	1961	Population of Bray Urban District 11,856 or 19.8% of County Population
Population Bray	Sun	17	04	1966	Population of Bray Urban District 11,688 or 20.0% of County Population
Population Bray	Sun	18	04	1971	Population of Bray Urban District 15,537 or 25.7% of County Population
Population Bray	Sun	01	04	1979	Population of Bray Urban District 21,773 or 25.9% of County Population
Population Bray	Sun	05	04	1981	Population of Bray Urban District 22,853 or 26.1% of County Population
Population Bray	Sun	13	04	1986	Population of Bray Urban District 24,686 or 26.1% of County Population
Population Bray	Sun	21	04	1991	Population of Bray Urban District 25,096 or 25.8% of County Population
Population Bray	Sun	28	04	1996	Population of Bray Urban District 25,252 or 24.6% of County Population
Population Bray	Sun	28	04	2002	Population of Bray Urban District 26,215 or 22.8% of the County Population
Population County	Sun	31	03	1901	Population of County Wicklow 60,824 persons. 30,584 Males 30,240 Females
Population County	Sun	02	04	1911	Population of County Wicklow 60,711 persons. 31,113 Males 29,598 Females
Population County	Sun	18	04	1926	Population of County Wicklow 57,591 persons. 28,911 Males 28,680 Females
Population County	Sun	26	04	1936	Population of County Wicklow 58,569 persons. 29,686 Males 28,701 Females
Population County	Sun	12	05	1946	Population of County Wicklow 60,451 persons. 30,152 Males 30,299 Females
Population County	Sun	08	04	1951	Population of County Wicklow 62,590 persons. 31,587 Males 31,003 Females
Population County	Sun	08	04	1956	Population of County Wicklow 59,906 persons. 29,933 Males 29,973 Females
Population County	Sun	09	04	1961	Population of County Wicklow 58,473 persons. 29,150 Males 29,323 Females
Population County	Sun	17	04	1966	Population of County Wicklow 60,428 persons. 30,231 Males 30,197 Females
Population County	Sun	18	04	1971	Population of County Wicklow 66,295 persons. 33,318 Males 32,977 Females
Population County	Sun	01	04	1979	Population of County Wicklow 83,950 persons. 41,969 Males 41,981 Females
Population County	Sun	05	04	1981	Population of County Wicklow 87,449 persons. 43,663 Males 43,768 Females
Population County	Sun	13	04	1986	Population of County Wicklow 94,542 persons. 46,980 Males 47,562 Females
Population County	Sun	21	04	1991	Population of County Wicklow 97,256 persons. 48,076 Males 49,189 Females
Population County	Sun	28	04	1996	Population of County Wicklow 102,683 persons. 50,823 Males 51,860 Females

A-Z Reference	Day	Date	Month	Year	DATA
Population County	Sun	28	04	2002	Population of County Wicklow 114,676 persons, 56,800 Males 57,876 Females
Population County	Sun	28	04	2002	Number of private households County Wicklow with a personal computer and internet access 36,138
Population County	Sun	23	04	2006	Census of Population in Ireland
Population Enniskerry	Sun	31	03	1901	Population of Enniskerry urban 235 or 0.38% of County Population
Population Enniskerry	Sun	02	04	1911	Population of Enniskerry urban 221 or 0.36% of County Population
Population Enniskerry	Sun	18	04	1926	Population of Enniskerry urban 214 or 0.37% of County Population
Population Enniskerry	Sun	26	04	1936	Population of Enniskerry urban 145 or 0.24% of County Population
Population Enniskerry	Sun	12	05	1946	Population of Enniskerry urban 145 or 0.23% of County Population
Population Enniskerry	Sun	08	04	1951	Population of Enniskerry urban 166 or 0.26% of County Population
Population Enniskerry	Sun	08	04	1956	Population of Enniskerry urban 530 or 0.88% of County Population
Population Enniskerry	Sun	09	04	1961	Population of Enniskerry urban 652 or 1.11% of County Population
Population Enniskerry	Sun	17	04	1966	Population of Enniskerry urban 707 or 1.2% of County Population
Population Enniskerry	Sun	18	04	1971	Population of Enniskerry urban 789 or 1.3% of County Population
Population Enniskerry	Sun	01	04	1979	Population of Enniskerry urban 1,185 or 1.4% of County Population
Population Enniskerry	Sun	05	04	1981	Population of Enniskerry urban 1,228 or 1.4% of the County Population
Population Enniskerry	Sun	13	04	1986	Population of Enniskerry urban 1,229 or 1.3% of County Population
Population Enniskerry	Sun	21	04	1991	Population of Enniskerry urban 1,238 or 1.3% of County Population
Population Enniskerry	Sun	28	04	1996	Population of Enniskerry urban 2,118 or 2.06% of County Population
Population Enniskerry	Sun	28	04	2002	Population of Enniskerry urban 2,804 or 1.84% of the County Population
Population Greystones	Sun	31	03	1901	Population of Greystones & Delgany 1,063 or 1.74% of County Population
Population Greystones	Sun	02	04	1911	Population of Greystones & Delgany 1,449 or 2.38% of County Population
Population Greystones	Sun	18	04	1926	Population of Greystones & Delgany 1,817 or 3.15 % pf County Population
Population Greystones	Sun	26	04	1936	Population of Greystones & Delgany 2,000 or 3.41% of County Population
Population Greystones	Sun	12	05	1946	Population of Greystones & Delgany 2,857 or 4.72% of County Population
Population Greystones	Sun	08	04	1951	Population of Greystones & Delgany 2,984 or 4.76% of County Population
Population Greystones	Sun	08	04	1956	Population of Greystones & Delgany 3,565 or 5.95% of County Population
Population Greystones	Sun	09	04	1961	Population of Greystones & Delgany 3,551 or 6.07% of County Population
Population Greystones	Sun	17	04	1966	Population of Greystones & Delgany 3,952 or 6.54% of County Population

Section Two: Data in Alphabetical Order

Population Greystones	Sun	18	04	1971	Population of Greystones & Delgany 4,496 or 7.4% of County Population
Population Greystones	Sun	01	04	1979	Population of Greystones & Delgany 6,921 or 8.24% of County Population
Population Greystones	Sun	05	04	1981	Population of Greystones & Delgany 7,442 or 8.51% of County Population
Population Greystones	Sun	13	04	1986	Population of Greystones & Delgany 8,455 or 8.94% of County Population
Population Greystones	Sun	21	04	1991	Population of Greystones & Delgany 9,649 or 9.92% of County Population
Population Greystones	Sun	28	04	1996	Population of Greystones & Delgany 11,236 or 10.9% of County Population
Population Greystones	Sun	28	04	2002	Population of Greystones & Delgany 11,871 or 10.3% of the County Population
Population of Brockagh	Sun	31	03	1901	The estimated population of the Electoral District of Brockagh in 1901 was 500 persons
Population Rathdown	Sun	13	04	1986	Population of Rathdown No 2 rural area 13,613 or 14.39% of the County Population
Population Rathdown	Sun	24	04	1991	Population of Rathdown No 2 rural area 15,093 or 15.51% of the County Population
Population Rathdown	Sun	28	04	1996	Population of Rathdown No 2 rural area 16,359 or 15.96% of the County Population
Population Rathdown	Sun	28	04	2002	Population of Rathdown No 2 rural area 19,025 or 16.58% of the County Population
Population Rathdrum	Sun	13	04	1986	Population of Rathdrum Rural area 24,254 or 25.65% of the County Population
Population Rathdrum	Sun	24	04	1991	Population of Rathdrum Rural area 24,865 or 25.56% of the County Population
Population Rathdrum	Sun	28	04	1996	Population of Rathdrum Rural area 26,9326 or 26.22% of the County Population
Population Rathdrum	Sun	28	04	2002	Population of Rathdrum Rural area 31,086 or 27.09% of the County Population
Population Roundwood	Sun	28	04	1996	Population of Roundwood 1,624 persons 1.58% of the County Population
Population Shillelagh	Sun	13	04	1986	Population of Shillelagh rural area 6,395 or 6.76% of the County Population
Population Shillelagh	Sun	24	04	1991	Population of Shillelagh rural area 6,410 or 6.59% of the County Population
Population Shillelagh	Sun	28	04	1996	Population of Shillelagh rural area 6,420 or 6.25% of the County Population
Population Shillelagh	Sun	28	04	2002	Population of Shillelagh rural area 6,708 or 5.84% of the County Population
Population Wicklow (t)	Sun	31	03	1901	Population of Wicklow Town 3,288 or 5.40% of County Population
Population Wicklow (t)	Sun	02	04	1911	Population of Wicklow Town 3,243 or 5.34% of County Population
Population Wicklow (t)	Sun	18	04	1926	Population of Wicklow Town 3,025 or 5.25% of County Population
Population Wicklow (t)	Sun	26	04	1936	Population of Wicklow Town 3,183 or 5.43% of County Population
Population Wicklow (t)	Sun	12	05	1946	Population of Wicklow Town 3,183 or 5.26% of County Population
Population Wicklow (t)	Sun	08	04	1951	Population of Wicklow Town 3,326 or 5.31% of County Population
Population Wicklow (t)	Sun	08	04	1956	Population of Wicklow Town 3,070 or 5.12% of County Population
Population Wicklow (t)	Sun	09	04	1961	Population of Wicklow Town 3,125 or 5.34% of County Population

A-Z Reference	Day	Date	Month	Year	DATA
Population Wicklow (t)	Sun	17	04	1966	Population of Wicklow Town 3,340 or 5.52% of County Population
Population Wicklow (t)	Sun	18	04	1971	Population of Wicklow Town 3,786 or 5.71% of County Population
Population Wicklow (t)	Sun	01	04	1979	Population of Wicklow Town 4,981 or 5.93% of County Population
Population Wicklow (t)	Sun	05	04	1981	Population of Wicklow Town 5,178 or 5.9% of the County Population
Population Wicklow (t)	Sun	13	04	1986	Population of Wicklow Town 5,304 or 5.6% of County Population
Population Wicklow (t)	Sun	21	04	1991	Population of Wicklow Town 5,847 or 6.0% of County Population
Population Wicklow (t)	Sun	28	04	1996	Population of Wicklow Town 6,416 or 6.2% of the County Population
Population Wicklow (t)	Sun	28	04	2002	Population of Wicklow Town 7,007 or 6.10% of County Population
Post Office				1904	The Post Office on the Quinsboro Road, Bray built.
Post Office				1914	A sub Post Office of Bray established at Dargle Road, Bray
Post Office				1914	A sub Post Office of Bray established at Newtown Vevay, Bray
Post Office				1960	The sub Post Office at Brennan's Parade, Bray ceased
Post Office				1960	A new Post Office built in Wicklow Town
Post Office				1964	A sub Post Office of Bray established at Albert Avenue, Bray
Post Office				1978	Saturday Postal delivery service ceased in Bray.
Post Office				1986	Fergal Quinn Chairman of An Post opened a new sorting office at Bray Post Office
Post Office	Tue	09	03	1999	A new Post Office opened at Church Road, Greystones by Joe Jacob, Minister of State at Dept. of Public Enterprise
Post Office	Fri	29	09	2000	A new Postal Delivery Office was opened at the Murrough, Wicklow by Joe Jacob, Minister of State at Dept. of Public Enterprise
Post Office	Mon	29	07	2002	A new sub-Post Office opened at 97 Main Street, Bray
Potato				2003	Potato census 2003 Wicklow – 23 Registered Growers 289 Hectares of potato's
Power. George	Tue	30	06	1931	Rev George Beresford Power, died
Power. George	Sat	24	08	1935	Constance Beresford Power 2nd dau of Charles Putland of Bray Head Co. Wicklow died
Power. Jenny Wyse	Mon	24	04	1916	The Proclamation of the Republic read by P. Pearse outside the GPO, was signed in J.W.Power house in Henry Street. Dublin
Power. Jenny Wyse		06	12	1922	Jenny Wyse Power a member of Seanad Eireann 6th December 1922 – 20th May 1936
Power. Jenny Wyse	Sun	05	01	1941	Jenny Wyse Power died in Dublin and is buried at Glasnevin Cemetery, Dublin
Power. John Wyse				1926	John Wyse Power of Co. Waterford died. 1884 – 1887 General Secretary of the GAA

Section Two: Data in Alphabetical Order

Name	Event	Year	Month	Day	Weekday
Power, Richard	Richard Power (writer) born in Kildare	1928			
Power, Richard	Richard Power wrote The Land of Youth	1964			
Power, Richard	Richard Power wrote The Hungry Grass	1969			
Power, Richard	Richard Power (writer) died at Bray Co. Wicklow	1970	02	12	Thu
Powerscort Arms Hotel	Irish Independent Property Supplement . Sale of the Powerscort Arms Hotel on 12/12/2005	2005	11	30	Wed
Powerscourt	Mervyn Richard Wingfield 8th Viscount Powerscourt married Sybil Bouverie	1903	06	09	Tue
Powerscourt	Mervyn Wingfield 7th Viscount Powerscourt died	1904	06	05	Sun
Powerscourt	Mervyn Patrick Wingfield 9th Viscount Powerscourt born	1905	08	22	Tue
Powerscourt	The Japanese Gardens at Powerscourt designed by the 8th Viscount and his wife Sybil	1908			
Powerscourt	Lord Powerscourt wrote to the Minister of Home Affairs about robbing and looting and intimidation on his estate in Enniskerry	1922	06		
Powerscourt	Julia Memorial Garden established in the grounds of Powerscourt in honour of the wife of the 7th Viscount	1931			
Powerscourt	Lady Julia Coke wife of 7th Viscount Powerscourt died	1931	08	07	Fri
Powerscourt	Mervyn Patrick Wingfield 9th Viscount Powerscourt married Shelia Beddington	1932	12	16	Fri
Powerscourt	Powerscourt Estate put up for sale, due to high cost of maintenance	1932	05	16	Sun
Powerscourt	Mervyn Niall Wingfield 10th Viscount Powerscourt born	1935	09	03	Tue
Powerscourt	The film Henry IV staring Sir L Oliver shot at Powerscourt Estate, Enniskerry	1943	05		
Powerscourt	Mervyn Richard Wingfield 8th Viscount Powerscourt died	1947	03	21	Fri
Powerscourt	Mr & Mrs Ralph Slazenger purchased Powerscourt House & Estate from the 9th Viscount Powerscourt	1961			
Powerscourt	Mervyn Niall Wingfield married Wendy Slazenger	1962			
Powerscourt	Mervyn Anthony Wingfield son of the 10th Viscount Powerscourt born	1963	08	21	Wed
Powerscourt	Mervyn Patrick Wingfield 9th Viscount Powerscourt died	1973	04	03	Tue
Powerscourt	Mervyn Niall Wingfield marriage to Wendy Slazenger dissolved	1974			
Powerscourt	Powerscourt House, Enniskerry destroyed by fire	1974	11	04	Mon
Powerscourt	Princess Grace of Monaco visited Powerscourt Gardens and planted a tree	1978	06	06	Tue
Powerscourt	Mervyn Niall Wingfield married Pauline Van	1979			
Powerscourt	Powerscourt Town House Centre opens in Dublin	1981	11	19	Thu
Powerscourt	A painting by William Ashford of Powerscourt Demesne was sold at Sotherby's of London	1997	05	22	Thu
Powerscourt	The war medals of Mervyn Patrick Wingfield 9th Viscount Powerscourt sold at auction in London	2000	10		
Powerscourt	120m project announced for Powerscourt Estate with the building of Ritz-Carlton Hotel	2005	08		

A–Z Reference	Day	Date	Month	Year	DATA
Powerscourt Golf Club				1996	Powerscourt Golf Club (Enniskerry) established
Prandy. James				1911	Rev. James Prandy Parish Priest of Tomacork, Carnew 1911–1948
Presentation	Mon	05	09	1921	The Archbishop of Dublin Dr.Byrne blessed and opened Presentation College, Putalnd Road, Bray
Presentation Bray				1920	Bray Head House on the Putland Road, Bray bought by the Presentation Brothers
Presentation Bray				1924	The Presentation Brothers build a school behind Bray Head House, Putland Road, Bray
Presentation Bray				1960	An extension was added to Presentation College, Putland Road, Bray
Presentation Bray				1972	New school was added to Presentation College, Putland Road, Bray
Presentation College	Mon	19	11	2001	Minister of Education Dr. Michael Woods announced £5m school building programme for Presentation College, Bray
Price. Cecil				1968	Rev Cecil Price became rector of Delgany Parish
Price. Cecil				1989	Rev. Cecil Price appointed Archdeacon of Glendalough
Printing Works	Tue	24	10	1950	Fire destroyed Bray Printing Works, Main Street, Bray
Proby. Hon. William	Sat	04	09	1909	William Proby 5th Earl of Carysfort died, as the Earl had no children the Earldom ceased.
Publications				1938	The 1st Edition of Insurgent Wicklow was published under the title '98 in Wicklow by The People Newspapers, Wexford
Putland				1902	Rev John West Neligan died
Putland Road				2001	New housing scheme called Headlands built in the grounds of Presentation College, Putland Road, Bray
Queen of Peace, Bray	Fri	05	01	1945	A public meeting called to fund the building of a new church in the Vevay area of Bray. Canon Moriarity chaired the meeting
Queen of Peace, Bray	Sun	15	12	1946	Our Lady Queen of Peace church, Putland Rd built at cost of £11,850 is dedicated by the Archbishop of Dublin Charles McQuaid
Queen of Peace, Bray	Fri	06	06	1997	The Archbishop of Dublin Dr. Connell celebrated mass to mark 50 years of Queen of Peace as a Parish, Putland Rd, Bray
Quigley. D.B				1942	Dermot B. Quigley born in Bray
Quigley. D.B				1990	Bray man Dermot B. Quigley appointed to the board of Revenue Commissioners
Quigley. D.B	Fri	03	07	1998	Bray man Dermot B. Quigley appointed Chairman of the board of Revenue Commissioners
Quigley. D.B	Wed	06	03	2002	Dermot Quigley retired as Chairman of the Revenue Commissioners
Radio	Wed	25	10	1989	Horizon Radio goes on air 94.9FM from 11 Quinsborough Rd, Bray
Radio Station				1978	Southside radio station established in Bray
Radio Station				1979	Bray Local Broadcasting (BLB) established
Railways				1903	The affairs of the Bray & Enniskerry Light Railway Co. wound up by the Courts

Railways				1903	Dublin, Wicklow and Wexford Railway Act
Railways				1905	Railway Locomotive Number 21 built and named Kilcoole, Withdrawn from service 1925
Railways				1906	Dublin and Wicklow and Wexford Act changed of title to Dublin & South Eastern Railway Co with effect 1/1/1907
Railways	Tue	01	01	1907	The Dublin, Wicklow & Wexford Railway changed its name to the Dublin & South Eastern Railway
Railways				1907	Railway Locomotive Number 31 built and named Glen of the Downes, Withdrawn from service 1923
Railways				1908	The Railway and Canal Commission established
Railways				1913	Work on the Long Tunnel, Bray Head to a design by C.E. Moore, the work was done by Naylor's of Huddersfield
Railways	Fri	04	12	1914	A train derailment took place at Avoca
Railways				1917	Construction work completed at the Long Tunnel at Bray Head, designed by C.E. Moore
Railways	Tue	17	10	1922	The signal Cabin at Glenealy Railway Station destroyed fire
Railways	Mon	16	10	1922	The signal Cabin at Newcastle Railway Station destroyed
Railways	Thu	01	02	1923	The signal Cabin at Tinahely Railway Station destroyed fire
Railways	Sat	24	02	1923	The 7.40 am up Wexford train ran into a rock fall at Bray Head
Railways			08	1924	Railway Act-The G W R & Dublin + South Eastern and 23 other railway companies formed Great Southern Railway
Railways	Thu	01	01	1925	Great Southern Railway comes into effect following the Railway Act of 1924
Railways			04	1927	The South bound platform was added at Bray Railway Station at a cost of £35,000
Railways	Fri	30	09	1927	The Blessington & Poulaphouca Tramway ceased
Railways	Wed	02	12	1931	The official trial of the Drumm Battery Railcars from Westland Row Station at 11.00 am to Bray Railway Station and return
Railways	Sat	31	12	1932	The Dublin & Blessington Tramway Company ceased when the last tram car ran from Blessington to Terenure.
Railways	Mon	24	04	1944	Woodenbridge-Shillelagh Railway branch line closed
Railways			07	1949	C.I.E. withdraws the Drumm battery railcars and replaces them with diesel locomotives.
Railways				1952	Fire destroys part of the roof of Bray Railway Station.
Railways				1959	The Harcourt Street to Bray Railway Line closed
Railways				1960	Steam Locomotives ceased to be used on suburban rail service
Railways				1961	Bray Railway Station new booking office and general maintance carried out
Railways				1964	Kilcoole Railway Station closed
Railways	Mon	30	03	1964	Woodenbridge Railway Station closed

A-Z Reference	Day	Date	Month	Year	DATA
Railways				1966	Bray Railway Station re-named Daly station in honour of Edward Daly who took part in the 1916 Rebellion
Railways	Fri	10	07	1970	The last C.I.E. horse drawn cart to leave Bray Railway Goods Yard on deliveries around the town
Railways	Fri	12	03	1976	Garda Siochana foil a raid on a train at Wicklow Town, carrying cash for Banks and Post Offices in the south-east
Railways	Mon	06	09	1976	Wicklow, Murrough Railway Station closed for goods traffic
Railways				1979	C.I.E. announces DART (Dublin Area Rapid Transit) a new railway service between Bray and Howth
Railways	Mon	09	06	1980	Kilcoole Railway Station re-opened
Railways				1980	The turn-table at Bray Railway station removed.
Railways	Mon	23	07	1984	The Dublin Area Rapid Transit (DART) rail system came into service.
Railways				1996	The Government approves the extension of the DART Railway line to Greystones at a cost of £8.7m
Railways	Fri	08	12	2000	Landslide at Killiney all Dart and Rail Services between Dalkey and Bray cancelled
Railways	Mon	10	04	2000	Greystones commuters provided with a limited DART Service
Railways	Fri	15	12	2000	Rail services south of Killiney resumed following the landslide of 08/12/2000
Railways				2001	New footbridge at Bray Railway station
Railways	Thu	08	11	2001	A runaway train at Arklow, Halted 3 miles north of Arklow.
Railways			09	2004	Bray station refurbished
Railways	Sun	19	09	2004	The Minister of Transport unveils a plaque at Bray railway station to mark 150 years of Railways at Bray
Railways	Sun	19	09	2004	Three steams trains ran between Bray and Wicklow Town.
Railways	Sun	19	09	2004	Iarnrod Eireann, RPSI, Bray Tourism , Bray UDC and Bray Chamber of Commerce mark 150 years of Railway in Bray
Railways			10	2005	Repair work began on the canopy on the southbound platform at Bray Railway Station
Railways	Sat	24	09	2005	Full weekend DART services resumed on the full DART line between Howth/Malahide and Greystones.
Rates				1978	Domestic rates abolished
Rates				1980	The Rate Valuation of Bray was set at £11.46 per £1 of Valuation
Rathcoran				1934	Excavations took place at an Iron Age Hill fort at Rathcoran near Baltinglass
Rathdangan			'5	1920	Harry Clarke Stained Glass windows placed in St. Mary's Church Rathdangan
Rathdangan				1923	The Parish hall built at Rathdangan
Rathdrum	Fri	25	10	1940	An Unidentified aeroplane dropped bombs on the town lands of Ballyhad and Coppse, Rathdrum

Section Two: Data in Alphabetical Order

	Day			Year	Event
Rathnew	Sun	23	12	2001	GAA Lenister Club Championship Final (replay) held in Newbridge, Co. Kildare Na Finna(Dublin) 1-10 Rathnew(Wicklow) 2-16
Rathnew	Sun	16	12	2001	GAA Lenister Club Championship Final held in Newbridge, Co. Kildare Na Finna(Dublin) 1-6 Rathnew(Wicklow) 0-9 a draw
Rathnew	Mon	27	09	2004	Rathnew By Pass opened by the Minister of Transport Seamus Brennan
Rathnew A.F.C.				1986	Rathnew Football Club formed
Rathsallagh Golf Club				1995	Rathsallagh Golf Club (Dunlavin) established
Ravens well. Bray				1972	An Extension was added to Ravens well School, Bray
Ravenswell. Bray				1901	The Sisters of Charity establish Ravenswell School, Little Bray
Ravenswell. Bray				1920	An extension added to Ravenswell Primary School Little Bray
Ravenswell. Bray				1958	An extension was added to Ravenswell National School, Bray at a cost of £50,000
Redmond. John E.	Sun	20	09	1914	John E. Redmond M.P. at Woodenbridge near Arklow calls on the Irish Volunteers to fight for England in the Great War 1914-18
Redmond. John E.	Wed	06	03	1918	John Edward Redmond died
Redmond. John E.	Mon	11	06	1956	The Department of Post and Telegraphs issued a stamp in honour of John Redmond
Reform Association				1901	The international conference of the Philanthropic Reform Association was held at Killruddery, Bray
Regan. T	Fri	03	10	1958	Irish Angling Record for Sea Trout 12lb 0oz was set by T.Regan at River Dargle, Bray (Guinness Book of Records)
Regulations	Tue	07	04	1925	Séamus De Búrca Minster for Local Government and Public Health signed Electoral (County) Areas Order: Wicklow
Reynolds. B				1907	The Very Rev. B. Reynolds became Parish Priest of Enniskerry
Road Labourers Wages				1914	Wicklow County Council, Road Labourers Wages. 60 hour week. 10/s to 15/s per week
Road Labourers Wages				1939	Wicklow County Council, Road Labourers Wages. 48 hour week. 30/s to 37s: 6d per week
Road Labourers Wages				1946	Wicklow County Council, Road Labourers Wages. 48 hour week. 47s: 6d to 54/s per week
Road Safety				1966	Bray Area Road Safety Committee established.
Road Tax Wicklow				1946	Road Tax raised from Commercial Van and lorries in County Wicklow £8,407-2-0d
Road Tax Wicklow				1946	Road Tax raised from Agricultural Tractors in County Wicklow £323-10s-0d
Road Tax Wicklow				1946	Road Tax raised from Other Vehicles in County Wicklow £2,204-2s-4d
Road Tax Wicklow				1946	Road Tax raised from Private cars in County Wicklow £10,562-16-0d
Road Tax Wicklow				1947	Road Tax raised from Agricultural Tractors in County Wicklow £951-10s-0d
Road Tax Wicklow				1947	Road Tax raised from Commercial Van and lorries in County Wicklow £14,785-12-0d
Road Tax Wicklow				1947	Road Tax raised from Other Vehicles in County Wicklow £3,144-1s-0d

A-Z Reference	Day	Date	Month	Year	DATA
Road Tax Wicklow				1947	Road Tax raised from Private cars in County Wicklow £21,984-11s-0d
Road Tax Wicklow				1948	Road Tax raised from Other Vehicles in County Wicklow £4,311-4s-8d
Road Tax Wicklow				1948	Road Tax raised from Agricultural Tractors in County Wicklow £1,814-15s-0d
Road Tax Wicklow				1948	Road Tax raised from Commercial Van and lorries in County Wicklow £15,651-0s-0d
Road Tax Wicklow				1948	Road Tax raised from Private cars in County Wicklow £26,673-14s-0d
Road Tax Wicklow				1949	Road Tax raised from Private cars in County Wicklow £27,181-12s-0d
Road Tax Wicklow				1949	Road Tax raised from Commercial Van and lorries in County Wicklow £16,463-6s-0d
Road Tax Wicklow				1949	Road Tax raised from Other Vehicles in County Wicklow £4,211-16s-0d
Road Tax Wicklow				1949	Road Tax raised from Agricultural Tractors in County Wicklow £1,568-15s-0d
Road Tax Wicklow	Wed	03	05	1950	Details of Road Tax raised in Wicklow of years 1946,1947,1948,1949 part of a debate in Dail Eireann
Roads				1909	The Galtrim Road extended to join the Adelaide Road, Bray
Roads				1928	The Lower Dargle Road was connected from Bray Bridge to the Dargle Tavern
Roads				1930	O'Byrne Road, Bray built
Roads			10	1939	Road widening scheme at Loughlinstown, Co Dublin
Roads				1962	Road Traffic (Signs) Regulations
Roads	Wed	01	01	1969	Roads reclassified into 4 groups, 1 National Primary, 2 National Secondary, 3 Regional and 4 County
Roads			12	1984	Bray-Shankill By Pass sanctioned by European Commission cost estimated at £4m
Roads			08	1989	The Government approves the Bray- Shankill By pass costing £25m
Roads	Fri	29	09	1989	Sean Walsh Chairman of Dublin City Council turned the first sod of the Bray-Shankill By Pass at Wilford near Bray
Roads	Thu	24	10	1991	Bray-Shankill By Pass opened by Minister of Environment P. Flynn
Roads	Fri	12	02	1993	Fassaroe Road Bridge over the M11 near Bray was opened
Roads				1998	Road widening scheme at Loughlinstown, Co Dublin
Roads				1999	Arklow Road By Pass on the N11 completed
Roads	Mon	28	08	2000	Wicklow County Council Compulsory Purchase (Newtownmountkennedy to Ballynabarny Road Improvement Scheme) No. 2 Order
Roads	Thu	07	02	2002	Wicklow County Council sign contracts with John Sisks Ltd and S.M. Morris to build Ashford-Rathnew By Pass, Cost 94m Euro

Roads			05	2004	Bord Pleanala the approves development of the N11 between Ballinclare Co. Wexford and Cooadanagan Co. Wicklow
Roads	Thu	30	06	2005	The Minister of Transport Martin Cullen opened the final section of the M50 between Sandyford and Loughlinstown
Robbie. John	Thur	17	11	1955	John Robbie was born in Dublin
Robbie. John	Sat	17	01	1976	John Robbie of Greystones won his 1st cap on the Irish National Rugby team against Australia in Dublin
Robbie. John	Sat	21	03	1981	John Robbie won his 9th and last cap on the Irish National Rugby team in a game against Scotland in Murrayfield
Roche. Dick	Thu	06	06	2002	Dick Roche TD for Wicklow & East Carlow appointed Minister of State at the Department of the Taoiseach
Roche. Dick	Wed	29	09	2004	Dick Roche T.D. appointed Minister of the Environment , Local Government and Heritage
Rohan. K. C.				1944	Kenneth C. Rohan (Property Developer) born 1944, educated at St. Gerard's School, Bray.
Rooney. Philip				1907	Philip Rooney born Colooney, Co. Sligo
Rooney. Philip				1946	Philip Rooney published his best known novel Captain Boycott
Rooney. Philip			03	1962	Philip Rooney died at his home in Bray
Rotary Club of Bray	Wed	20	09	1972	Rotary Club of Bray, chartered
Rotary Club of Wicklow	Sat	26	11	1988	Rotary Club of Wicklow, chartered and given registration number 116
Roundwood				1966	Roundwood Caravan Park established
Roundwood			09	1984	A new school opened at Roundwood
Roundwood	Wed	25	05	2005	Roundwood Caravan Park put up for sale
Roundwood F.C.				2002	Roundwood Football Club formed
Roundwood Golf Club				1996	Roundwood Golf Club established
Roundwood School				1923	Roundwood National School
Royal Hotel, Bray			's	1950	The Royal Hotel, Bray was modernised
Royal Hotel, Bray				1973	The One din Rooms were added to the Royal Starlight Hotel. based on The Onedin Line was a popular TV series in 1970's
Royal Hotel, Bray				1943	The Cavey family bought the Royal Hotel
Royal Hotel, Bray	Sat	13	11	1982	Part of the Royal Hotel on the Quinsborough Road junction demolished to make way for shops and offices
Royal Hotel, Bray				1982	Jim McGettigan bought the Royal Starlight Hotel, Bray
Royal Inn Glendalough			02	1902	Royal Hotel Glendalough destroyed by fire
Royal Marine Hotel	Tue	22	08	1916	Royal Marine Hotel Bray (E. Bresilin Hotel) destroyed by fire
Royal Visit	Mon	10	07	1911	The Prince of Wales and Princess Mary visited Lord and Lady Meath at Killruddery

A–Z Reference	Day	Date	Month	Year	DATA
Royal Visit	Wed	26	04	1978	The Queen of Denmark paid an official visit to Bray and Powerscourt,
Royal Visit	Fri	15	02	2002	Prince Charles and Brian Cowen Minister for Foreign Affairs jointly opened the new Bridge Building at Glencree Centre
Royal Visits	Fri	10	09	2004	H.R.H. Princess Anne visited the Festina Lente Foundation Old Connaught, Bray
Russborough House				1952	Sir Alfred Beit buys Russborough House, Blessington from Captain Daly
Russborough House				1974	19 paintings stolen from Russborough House, Blessington
Russborough House	Wed	21	05	1986	18 paintings stolen from Russborough House, Blessington
Russborough House	Tue	26	06	2001	2 paintings stolen from Russborough House, Blessington
Russborough House	Sun	29	09	2002	5 paintings stolen from Russborough House, Blessington
Ryan, Tony				1982	Tony Ryan(businessman) purchased Dargle Glen, Kilcroney, Bray
Ryan, Kevin				1983	Kevin Ryan held the post of Chairman of Wicklow County Council 1983–1984
Ryan, Tony			03	1987	Tony Ryan buys Dargle Glen former home of Sir Basil and Lady Goulding
Saul. Capt. P	Sat	22	06	1968	Captain Patrick Saul died and is buried in St. Patrick's graveyard Enniskerry
Saul.Capt. P	Tue	24	06	1930	Captain Patrick Saul was navigator on the historic East–West trans Atlantic flight from Portmarnock to Newfoundland
Saunders Grove				1923	Saunders Grove, Baltinglass was damaged by fire
Saunders Grove				1925	The house at Saunders Grove, Baltinglass rebuilt following the fire in 1923
Saunders. Robert				1908	Robert Joseph Pratt Saunders died, former High Sheriff of Wicklow
Scannell. Brendan J.				1947	East of Ireland Amateur (Golf) Open Championship, winner B.J. Scannell of Woodbrook, Bray
Scannell. Brendan J.				1953	East of Ireland Amateur (Golf) Open Championship, runner-up B.J. Scannell of Woodbrook, Bray
Scannell. Brendan J.				1954	East of Ireland Amateur (Golf) Open Championship, winner B.J. Scannell of Woodbrook, Bray
Scannell. Brendan J.				1955	East of Ireland Amateur (Golf) Open Championship, winner B.J. Scannell of Woodbrook, Bray
Scannell. Brendan J.				1973	European Amateur Golf Team Championship held at Penina, Portugal. The captain of the Irish team was B.J.Scannell of Bray
Scannell. Brendan J.				1975	European Amateur Golf Team Championship, held Killarney, Ireland. The captain of the Irish team. B.J.Scannell of Bray
Scannell. Brendan J.				1979	Brendan J. Scannell of Bray. President of the Golfing Union of Ireland 1979–1980
Scannell. Brendan J.	Sat	15	03	2003	Brendan J. Scannell of Bray died
Scharff. Robert F.	Thu	13	09	1934	Robert Francis Scharff (Naturalist) Died at his home in Sussex, England
School Medical Service	Fri	19	09	1930	School Medical Service came into operation in County Wicklow

Name	Day			Year	Description
School, Wicklow Town				1987	The East Glendalough School, Station Road, Wicklow Town founded
School, Wicklow Town	Mon	02	09	1996	The Gaelscoil Cill Mhantain in Wicklow Town opened
Scoil Chualann				1977	Scoil Chualann established on a site behind Queen of Peace Church, Putland Road, Bray.
Scott. Charlotte				1951	Charlotte Jessy Scott nee Barington died
Scott. G.D	Tue	04	06	1901	Rev. George Digby Scott Rector of Bray married Charlotte Jessy Barrington
Scott. G.D			10	1910	Rev. G.D.Scott elected Canon of Christ Church Dublin
Scott. G.D			10	1943	Rev. G.D.Scott retired after 50 years service as a rector and curate of Bray, He came to Bray in 1893
Scott. G.D	Thu	14	09	1950	Canon George Digby Scott died
Scott.J.G.	Fri	12	01	1912	Canon James George Scott died, father of Canon George Digby Scott
Scott. Olive	Fri	17	01	1997	Mrs Olive Moore the wife of Rev F.B. Moore, and the last surviving daughter of Rev George Digby Scott of Bray died
Scouting				1908	1st Wicklow Scout Troop Greystones Founded.The Greystones troop and one in Dundalk were the first formed in Ireland.
Scouting			02	1910	1st Bray Scout Troop established
Scouting				1912	1st Bray Sea Scouts Troop established in Bray
Scouting	Wed	29	09	1965	The 5th Wicklow (Bray Sea Scout) Group formed
Scouting	Thu	18	05	1972	9th Wicklow Arklow Sea Scout Troop (S.A.I.) established
Scouting	Thu	31	08	1972	10th Wicklow Presentation College Scout Troop (S.A.I.) established
Scouting				1973	A Sea Scout Group established in Arklow
Scouting	Tue	29	03	1977	13th Wicklow Scout Troop (S.A.I.) Enniskerry, established
Scouting	Mon	22	10	1979	15th Wicklow Caislean na SeanChuirte Scout Troop (S.A.I.) Bray established
Scouting	Sun	01	05	1983	14th Wicklow Scout Troop (S.A.I.) Avoca, established
Scouting	Wed	09	10	1985	6th Wicklow Scout Troop (S.A.I.) Aughrim, Co Wicklow established
Scouting	Mon	26	03	1990	15th Wicklow Scout Troop (S.A.I.) Little Bray established
Scouting				1990	Work began on the extension to the 5th Wicklow (Bray Sea Scout) Group den at Bray harbour
Scouting				1996	7th Wicklow Scout Troop (S.A.I.) Blessington Co. Wicklow closed
Sea Park House				1958	Sea Park, Wicklow sold in 1958
Seaside Festival	Fri	01	07	1988	Bray Seaside Festival 1st July to 10th July 1988
Seaside Festival	Sun	05	07	1992	Bray Seaside Festival 5th July to 12th July 1992
Seminole County	Mon	07	09	1992	Seminole County near Orlando. USA was twinned with County Wicklow

A–Z Reference	Day	Date	Month	Year	DATA
Servier (Ireland)				1972	Servier (Ireland) Industries Limited , Arklow. Co. Wicklow established
Seychelles			06	2003	Baltinglass Co. Wicklow played host to the delegation from Seychelles taking part in the Special Olympic World Games 2003
Shanaganagh Castle				1919	Shanaganagh Castle bought by Harlod Nicolson
Sheehy.Eddie				2001	Eddie Sheehy appointed County Manager of Wicklow (Local Government)
Sheep				1907	The Sheep Dipping (Ireland) Order required each local authority to set up sheep dips between 15th June and 31st Aug each year
Sheep				1907	102,206 Sheep dipped in County Wicklow
Sheep	Fri	26	04	1968	Wicklow Cheviot Sheep owners Association established
Sheep				1997	The Total number of Sheep in County Wicklow 526,500 including 272,700 Ewes
Sheep Breeders				1926	The Wicklow Mountain Sheep Breeders Society was established
Shelton Abbey				1947	Shelton Abbey was opened as a Hotel
Shelton Abbey				1951	Shelton Abbey was sold to the Department of Lands for use as State Forestry College
Shelton Abbey				1972	Shelton Abbey was transferred to the Department of Justice for use as a detention centre for young offenders
Ships/Yachts	Sat	12	11	1901	The vessel "Forest Deer" shipwrecked of the Wicklow Coast
Ships/Yachts	Mon	02	06	1902	The vessel "Hematite" shipwrecked of the Wicklow Coast
Ships/Yachts	Fri	27	02	1903	The vessel "1902 Brackley" shipwrecked of the Wicklow Coast
Ships/Yachts	Wed	03	01	1906	The vessel "Speranza" carrying coal shipwrecked of the Wicklow Coast
Ships/Yachts	Tue	20	03	1906	The coal vessel the Velenheli ran aground near Bray Harbour. Captain Hollingsworth
Ships/Yachts	Fri	09	08	1907	The Arklow Schooner Celtic ran aground and broke up in Skaill Bay, Orkney Islands.
Ships/Yachts	Tue	06	10	1908	The steamer "Amethyst" shipwrecked of the Wicklow Coast
Ships/Yachts			04	1909	The schooner ME Johnson bought by Captain Frank Tyrrell and Thomas Price of Arklow
Ships/Yachts	Sat	21	10	1911	The vessel "Champion of the Seas" shipwrecked of the Wicklow Coast
Ships/Yachts	Fri	11	12	1914	The vessel "Rover" shipwrecked of the Wicklow Coast
Ships/Yachts	Fri	12	11	1915	The vessel "Triftylea" shipwrecked of the Wicklow Coast
Ships/Yachts	Sat	28	10	1916	The vessel "Orphan Girl" shipwrecked of the Wicklow Coast
Ships/Yachts	Fri	08	11	1918	The vessel "Paragon" shipwrecked of the Wicklow Coast
Ships/Yachts	Thu	10	10	1918	S.S. Leinster sunk when she was hit by torpedoes 4 miles east of the Kish Lighthouse
Ships/Yachts				1919	The vessel "Wicklow Head (1st) purchased from Palgrave Murphy & Co. Dublin and renamed "City of Munich"

Ships/Yachts	Sat	26	12		1925	The vessel "John Morrison" carrying Pit Props shipwrecked of the Wicklow Coast
Ships/Yachts	Sun	31	01		1926	The ketch "Marie Celine" was wrecked near Bray Harbour
Ships/Yachts	Thu	19	02		1931	The vessel "Julia" shipwrecked of the Wicklow Coast
Ships/Yachts	Mon	25	07		1932	The vessel "Pacific" shipwrecked of the Wicklow Coast
Ships/Yachts	Sat	18	08		1934	The vessel "Pulteny" shipwrecked of the Wicklow Coast
Ships/Yachts					1934	The vessel "The City of Munich" sold to Saortat & Continental SS Co., Dublin and renamed "City of Ghent"
Ships/Yachts	Fri	01	02		1935	The vessel "Fleck" shipwrecked of the Wicklow Coast
Ships/Yachts	Sat	17	10		1936	"Erne" a sloop was driven ashore at Bray
Ships/Yachts	Mon	11	12		1939	The vessel "Eumaeus" shipwrecked of the Wicklow Coast
Ships/Yachts	Tue	02	07		1940	Arandora Star sunk by German U-Boat of Tory Island. The crew were buried in Glencree.
Ships/Yachts	Wed	18	12		1940	The vessel "Osage" shipwrecked of the Wicklow Coast
Ships/Yachts					1941	The vessel "Wicklow Head" (2nd) built (2,873 Tons)
Ships/Yachts					1945	The vessel "Wicklow Head" (2nd) purchased from the Ministry of War and Transport and renamed "Empire Wolfe"
Ships/Yachts	Tue	04	03		1947	M.S. Bolivar Norwegian ship sunk near Kish Lighthouse
Ships/Yachts					1947	The vessel "Empire Wolfe" was stranded of Nova Scotia and broke up
Ships/Yachts					1950	The vessel "Mountain Ash" shipwrecked of the Wicklow Coast
Ships/Yachts			08		1952	The vessel "Agnes Craig" shipwrecked of the Wicklow Coast
Ships/Yachts	Fri	04	12		1953	The schooner ME Johnson ran a ground at the south pier Arklow and broke up under the force of the gale
Ships/Yachts	Tue	21	01		1958	The vessel "Anna Toop " shipwrecked of the Wicklow Coast
Ships/Yachts	Sat	28	10		1989	The vessel "Irwell" shipwrecked of the Wicklow Coast
Ships/Yachts			12		1999	The barge Skerchi working on Bray Coastal Protection Scheme broke its moorings
Ships/Yachts	Mon	03	04		2000	A barge (Ascon Skerchi) working on Bray Coastal Protection Scheme, broke its moorings in a gale and drifted onto the shore
Ships/Yachts	Thu	03	02		2000	The cargo ship Asian Parade ran aground on the codling bank six miles east of Greystones
Short. Patrick	Thu	19	12		1940	Patrick Short of Bray was killed when the lighthouse tender ship Isolda was bombed off the Wexford Coast near Kilmore Quay
Showbands			's		1960	Wicklow based show bands included The Columbia Show band
Showbands			's		1960	Arklow based show bands included The Echoes
Showbands			's		1960	Bray based show bands included The Beavers Showband, The Mexicans Show band, The Tonics Show band
Singapore			06		2003	Arklow Co. Wicklow played host to the delegation from Singapore taking part in the Special Olympic World Games 2003

A–Z Reference	Day	Date	Month	Year	DATA
Smith. Sir Michael				1988	An oil painting of Sir Michael Smith presented to the National Gallery of Ireland (NGI 4555) by Mrs Davies, England
Smith. Sir W.C.				1988	An oil painting of Sir William-Cusack Smith presented to the National Gallery of Ireland (NGI 4554) by Mrs Davies, England
Smithson. Annie				1944	Annie Smithson autobiography "Myself and Others" published
Smithson. Annie	Sat	21	02	1948	Annie Smithson died in Dublin
Smurfit. Victoria				1973	Victoria "Vicky" Smurfit (Actress) born 1973, educated at Aravon School Bray
Smyth. Algernon	Sun	15	11	1914	Capt. Algernon Bersford Smyth of Bray Head House, Bray was killed in the Battle of Ypres
Softball Club				1997	Bray Allsorts Softball Club founded
Solus Teo	Mon	18	03	1935	Solus Teo (light bulbs) commenced Trading at Corke Abbey, Bray
Solus Teo				1961	Solus changed its light bulb wrapper
Somerville-Large. P.				1901	Philip Townsend Somerville-Large (engineer) born in Bray
Somerville-Large. P.				1959	Philip Townsend Somerville-Large (engineer with C.I.E.) opposed the closure of Harcourt Street Railway line
Somerville-Large. P.	Sun	19	05	1991	Philip Townsend Somerville-Large (engineer) of Bray died
Song				1928	"The Oaks of Glencree" a song by John Millington Synge
Speed limit				1903	The national speed limit for cars was set at 20 mph
Speed Limits				1968	The Road Traffic (Speed Limits) (County Wicklow) Regulations 1968 (S.I. No. 212 of 1968)
Speed Limits				1974	The Road Traffic (Speed Limits) (County Wicklow) (Amendment)Regulations 1974 (S.I. No. 263 of 1974)
Speed Limits				1978	The Road Traffic (Speed Limits) (County Wicklow) Regulations 1978 (S.I. No. 31 of 1978)
Speed Limits	Thu	20	01	2005	Speed Limits go Metric
Sport	Fri	17	04	1908	Delgany Golf Club founded. The course was opened on Good Friday 1908
Sport	Sat	26	12	1908	Clem Robertson scored a round of 77 of a handicap of 15 at the new Delgany Golf Course
Sport				1922	Bray Wanderer's football club originally established
Sport				1928	J. Byrne of Bray Unknowns played for the Republic of Ireland Soccer team
Sport				1942	Bray Wanderes football club founded
Sport				1945	Bertie Smyllie was Captain of Delgany Golf Club 1945-46
Sport				1961	Andy McEvoy (footballer) got his first Republic of Ireland cap against Scotland.
Sport	Sun	06	06	1976	Eamon Darcy of Delgany won the under 25 world golf championships in France.
Sport				1986	Bray Wanderes AFC 1st Division Champions of FAI

Sport				1989	John Ryan of Bray Wanderers was leading goal scorer of FAI 1st Division season 1989/90 with 16 goals
Sport	Sun	13	05	1990	FAI Cup Final held at Landwdowne Road Result: Bray Wanderers 1 St Francis 0
Sport	Sun	21	07	1991	Bray Head Golf (Public Course) at Raheen Park opened by President Mary Robinson
Sport	Sat	07	05	1994	Andy McEvoy (footballer) died at his home in Bray
Sport	Sat	15	05	1999	FAI Cup Final Replay at Tolka Park. Bray Wanderers 2 Finn Harps 2 after extra time
Sport	Thu	20	05	1999	FAI CUP Final 2nd Replay Bray Wanderers 2 Finn Harps 1
Sport	Sun	09	05	1999	FAI Cup Final at Tolka Park –Bray Wanderers 0 Finn Harps 0
Sport				1999	Bray Tennis Club building restored
St Andrew's. Bray			05	1983	125th Anniversary of St. Andrew's Presbyterian Church, Bray
St Fergal's F.C				1978	St. Fergal's Football Club Bray formed
St Mary's Enniskerry				1940	Rev. Dr Wall opens a New National School at Enniskerry, Cost £3,900 built of Irish made materials construction and furnishings
St Mary's Enniskerry				1976	Work began on an extension to St. Mary's School Enniskerry. The work was completed in 1978
St Patricks School				1918	The Governors of the Royal Drummond Institution, Dublin purchase the Meath Industrial School, Bray
St Patricks School	Thu	10	08	2000	Part of St Patrick's School Bray destroyed by fire
St Patrick's School				1902	An extension was added to the Meath Industrial School, Bray.
St Patrick's School				1919	Prior to 1919 the Drummond Institute on the Vevay Road was known as the Meath Industrial School for Girls (see 1945)
St Patrick's School				1944	The Loreto Nuns buy Drummond Institute Vevay Road, Bray for £9,000
St Patrick's School				1945	Loreto Nuns establish St. Partick's National School in the old Meath Industrial School on the Vevay Road, Bray
St Patrick's School				1945	An extension was added to St. Patrick's School, Bray
St Patrick's School	Wed	02	06	2004	The official opening of 7 new classrooms, quite room and library at St. Partick's School, Vevay Road, Bray
St. Andrew's School				1942	St Andrew's School Bray destroyed by fire
St. Andrew's School				1943	St Andrew's School Bray enlarged and reopened after the fire of 1942
St. Andrew's School				1943	St. Andrew's School, Bray destroyed by fire
St. Andrew's School				1971	St. Andrew's School Bray amalgamated with St Paul's School Bray
St. Andrew's School				1991	St. Andrew's School moved to the Newcourt Road, Bray
St. Anthony's F.C.				1977	St. Anthony's Football Club Kilcoole formed
St. Brendans College				1956	Christian Brothers buy the Walcot Hotel at Old Conna, Bray and establish St. Brendans College
St. Brendans College				1970	St. Brendans College at Old Connaught closed and new College built at Woodbrook, Bray

A-Z Reference	Day	Date	Month	Year	DATA
St. Brendans College				1981	25th Anniversary of St. Brendans College, Woodbrook, Bray
St. Brendans College				2003	Tony Bellew of Bray appointed Principle of St Brendans College, Woodbrook, Bray
St. Colman's Hospital				1995	Trousers was introduced as part of the nurse's uniform at St. Colman's Hospital Rathdrum
St. Cronan's BNS Bray	Sat	19	09	1932	St Cronan's Boys National School opened on the Vevay Road, Bray
St. Cronan's BNS Bray				1999	St. Cronan's Boys National School move to a new school on the Vevay Road, Bray
St. Cronan's BNS Bray			03	2000	The premises occupied by St Cronan's Boys National School from 1932-1999 put up for sale
St. Cronan's BNS Bray			04	2000	The Department of Education and Science purchase the Old ST. Cronan's BNS for Gaelscoil Ui Cheadaigh, Bray
St. Cronan's BNS Bray	Mon	18	06	2001	Minister of Education Dr. Michael Woods opens the new St. Cronan's BNS on the Vevay Road, Bray
St. Cronan's. Bray				1965	St. Cronan's House Main Street Bray (former home of the Parish Priest of Holy Redeemer Parish) used a Vocational School
St. David's School	Mon	03	09	1906	The Holy Faith Sisters opened a junior school in Greystones (St. David's)
St. Gerard's School				1918	John James headmaster of St. Gerard's School. Bray. 1918-1934
St. Gerard's School				1934	Stuart Dodson Collingwood headmaster of St. Gerard's School. Bray. 1934-1937
St. Gerard's School				1937	Desmond J. Murphy headmaster of St. Gerard's School. Bray. 1937-1963
St. Gerard's School				1963	Joseph C. Maher headmaster of St. Gerard's School. Bray. 1963-1966
St. Gerard's School				1966	Colum O'Cleirigh headmaster of St. Gerard's School. Bray. 1966-1971
St. Gerard's School				1971	Michael P. O'Horan headmaster of St. Gerard's School. Bray. 1971-1998
St. Gerard's School	Wed	28	04	1976	The Minister of Education Richard Burke an extension to St. Gerard's School, Bray
St. Gerard's School				1998	Gerard Foley headmaster of St. Gerard's School. Bray. 1998 –
St. Kevins Pipe Band				1966	St. Kevin's Pipe Band was reformed after a lapse of 26 years
St. Kiernan's Bray	Fri	18	01	1972	Archbishop of Dublin Dr. McQuaid blessed and opened St. Kiernan's School for itinerant children at Old Connaught, Bray
St. Kiernan's Bray				1976	Fire destroyed some of the buildings at St. Kiernan's Craft Centre at Old Connaught (Old Walcot Hotel site)
St. L. O'Toole F.C.				2002	St. Laurance O'Toole Football Club Roundwood formed
St. Mary's. Enniskerry	Sun	04	02	1996	The Church of St. Mary's. Enniskerry re-dedicated by Archbishop of Dublin. Renovations cost £170,000
St. Michael's N.S.				1940	Work began on building St. Michael's Convent National School, Rathdrum
St. Patrick's School				1975	Extension to St. Patrick's Primary school, Bray completed
St. Pauls. Bray				1910	Repairs carried out at St.Pauls Church Bray.

St. Pauls. Bray	Sat	17	02	1912	St.Pauls Church reopens after repairs
St. Pauls. Bray				1957	Due to wood worm the timbers of St.Pauls Church Bray were treated with chemicals.
St. Pauls. Bray				1972	St. Paul's School on Herbert Road Bray demolished.
St. Pauls. Bray				1977	St. Paul's Church, Bray closed and sold to Kenneth Jones Ltd manufacturer of Organs
St. Paul's. Bray				1911	Repairs carried out on St.Pauls Church Bray
St. Paul's. Bray				1925	Mr James M Moore a school master in Bray for forty years retired see 1957
St. Paul's. Bray				1957	Mr James M Moore headmaster of St. Paul's School Bray died aged 96 years
St. Peter's F.C.				2000	St. Peter's Football Club Bray formed
St. Peters School				1961	St. Peters Boys National School move from the grounds of St.Peters Church, Little Bray to a new school at Hawthorn Crescent
St. Peters School			01	1996	St. Peter's School Little Bray damaged by fire
St. Therese of Lisieux	Sat	07	04	2001	The reliquary of St. Therese of Lisieux, arrived at the Carmelite Convent, Delgany, where it remained for 22 hours
St. Therese of Lisieux	Sun	08	04	2001	The reliquary of St. Therese of Lisieux, departed at the Carmelite Convent, Delgany, where it had remained for 22 hours
St. Thomas' College	Wed	18	03	1981	St. Thomas' Community College, Bray opened.
St.Fergals Boxing Club				1997	St. Fergals Boxing Club Bray founded
St.Fergal's. Bray			05	1976	St.Fergal's Parish, Bray was constituted into a separate parish
St.Fergal's. Bray	Sun	21	12	1980	St.Fergal's Church Ballywaltrim dedicated
St.John Whitty,Sophia				1902	Sophia St. John Whitty was employed, as a teacher of woodwork, at Bray Technical School & Bray Furniture
St.John Whitty,Sophia	Tue	26	02	1924	Sophia St. John Whitty died
St.Joseph's Wicklow				1912	St.Josephs College Wicklow Town established
St.Kevin's N.S.				1934	Work began on building St. Kevin's National School, Glendalough.
St.Mary Convent.Arklow				1999	St. Mary's Convent Arklow used as one of the locations for the film Angles Ashes
St.Pauls N.S.				1904	Work began on St Pauls National School, Herbert Road Bray
Stamps	Mon	04	04	1949	A stamp with the value 1/-s and featuring Glendalough Co. Wicklow was issued as part of the Air Mail Series
Stamps	Mon	27	06	1977	A stamp with a value of 12p with Lough Tay, Co. Wicklow was issued by the Irish Postal Service
Stamps	Tue	20	05	2003	The 41cent stamp issued for the Special Olympic World Games featured Shauna Bradley of Baltinglass
Stats				2002	The number of Deaths in Wicklow for 2002 was 774
Stats				2002	The number of Marriages in Wicklow for 2002 was 717
Stats				2002	The number of Births in Wicklow for year 2002 was 1,864

348 The County Wicklow Database: 432 AD to 2006 AD

A–Z Reference	Day	Date	Month	Year	DATA
Stuart, Francis	Tue	29	04	1902	Henry Francis Stuart (writer) born Townsville, Australia
Stuart, Francis				1920	Francis Stuart and Iseult lived at Barravore a cottage in Glenmalure
Stuart, Francis				1920	Francis Stuart married Iseult Gonne McBride
Stuart, Francis				1924	Francis Stuart rented a cottage in Glencree,
Stuart, Francis				1930	Francis Stuart purchased Laragh Castle near Glendalough
Stuart, Francis				1949	Francis Stuart moved to Paris
Stuart, Francis				1951	Francis Stuart moved to London
Stuart, Francis				1953	Iseult Gonne Stuart nee McBride died
Stuart, Francis	Wed	02	02	2000	Francis Stuart died
Sunbeam House Services				1977	Sunbeam House Services founded, offering support to adults with learning disabilities in County Wicklow
Sunnybank, Bray			05	2001	Fire destroys the former Sunnybank Inn Bray.
Superquinn				1973	The site of the Record Press Printing Company was acquired to build a shopping centre in Castle Street, Bray
Sweeney, John	Mon	11	07	1988	John Sweeney held the post of Chairman of Wicklow County Council from July 1988 until his death on 03/12/1988
Swimming Club				1928	Wicklow Swimming Club founded
Synge				1903	In the Shadow of the Glen, a one act play by John Millington Synge set in Co. Wicklow
Synge				1905	The Well of the Saints a play by J.M. Synge set in Co. Wicklow
Synge				1906	John Millington Synge published "The Vagrants of Wicklow"
Synge				1907	John Millington Synge published "At a Wicklow Fair" in the Manchester Guardian
Synge	Mon	26	10	1908	John Millington Synge mother Kathleen Synge nee Traill died
Synge				1908	John Millington Synge published "In Wicklow. On the Road" in the Manchester Guardian
Synge	Wed	24	03	1909	John Millington Synge died at Elpis Nursing Home, Dublin and was buried in Mount Jerome Cemetery, Dublin
Synge				1909	The Tinkers Wedding a play by J.M. Synge set in Co. Wicklow
Synge				1910	In Wicklow and West Kerry, a travel book by John Millington Synge
Synge	Thu	21	10	1915	Francis Patrick Hamilton Synge of Glanmore Castle, Ashford awarded the Military Cross
Synge				1943	Glanmore Castle, Ashford sold following the death of its owner Robert Synge
Synge	Fri	06	12	1968	Trinity College Dublin pays £50,000 for the papers of John Millington Synge
Synge				1994	David M. Kiely published his book John Millington Synge, A Biography

Section Two: Data in Alphabetical Order

Subject	Event	Year			
Syria	Wicklow Town Co. Wicklow played host to the delegation from Syria taking part in the Special Olympic World Games 2003	2003	06		
Tansey & Co	Tansey & Co Drapers & Outfitters were established Quinsboro Road, Bray	1920			
Tate Gallery London	Purchased a painting (Reference TO1815), by John Butts oil on canvas Poachers:View in the Dargle circa 1760	1972			
Tate Gallery London	The Tate gallery London purchased Francis Wheatley view of Enniskerry	1996			
Taylor. Katie	Katie Taylor of Bray the first Irish girl to Box in the National Boxing Stadium, Dublin.	2002			
TD's for Wicklow	1st Dail R.Barton (SF) The O'Mahony (N) J.R.Etchingham (SF)	1918	08	16	Tue
TD's for Wicklow	2nd Dail A.O'Connor (SF) D.O'Buchalla (SF) E.Childers (SF) R.Barton (SF) C.M.Byrne (CnanG)	1921	06	16	Fri
TD's for Wicklow	3rd Dail R.Barton (SF) J.Everett (L) R. Wilson (Farmers) C.M. Byrne (CnanG)	1922	08	27	Mon
TD's for Wicklow	Polling Day for 4th Dail J. Everett (L) C.M.Byrne (CnanG) R. Wilson (Farmers)	1923	09	15	Thu
TD's for Wicklow	Polling Day for 6th Dail J.Everett (L) S.Moore (FF) The O'Mahony (CnanG)	1927	06	09	Thu
TD's for Wicklow	Polling Day for 5th Dail J.Everett (L) S.Moore (FF) The O'Mahony (CnanG)	1927	02	16	Tue
TD's for Wicklow	Polling Day for 7th Dail J.Everett (L) S.Moore (FF) The O'Mahony (CnanG)	1932	01	24	Tue
TD's for Wicklow	Polling Day for 8th Dail J.Everett (L) S.Moore (FF) The O'Mahony (CnanG)	1933	07	01	Thu
TD's for Wicklow	Polling Day for 9th Dail J.Everett (L) S.Moore (FF) The O'Mahony (CnanG)	1937	06	17	Fri
TD's for Wicklow	Polling Day for 10th Dail J. Everett (L) S.Moore (FF) Patrick Cogan (Ind)	1938	06	22	Tue
TD's for Wicklow	Polling Day for 11th Dail J. Everett (L) Patrick Cogan (Ind) Christopher Byrne (FF)	1943	05	30	Tue
TD's for Wicklow	Polling Day for 12th Dail J. Everett (L) Patrick Cogan (Ind) T.Brennan (FF)	1944	02	04	Wed
TD's for Wicklow	Polling Day for 13th Dail J.Everett (L) Patrick Cogan (Farmers) T.Brennan (FF)	1948	05	30	Wed
TD's for Wicklow	Polling Day for 14th Dail J.Everett (L) Patrick Coogan (Farmers) T. Brennan (FF)	1951	05		Wed
TD's for Wicklow	14th Dail By-Election held following the death of Thomas Brennan, By-Election won by M.Deering (FG)	1953			
TD's for Wicklow	Polling Day for 15th Dail J. Everett (L) M.Deering (FG) P. Brennan (FF)	1954	05	18	Tue
TD's for Wicklow	Polling Day for 16th Dail J. Everett (L) J.O'Toole (FF) P.Brennan (FF)	1957	03	05	Tue
TD's for Wicklow	Polling Day for 17th Dail J. Everett (L) M.J. O'Higgins (FG) P.Brennan (FF)	1961	10	04	Wed
TD's for Wicklow	Polling Day for 18th Dail J. Everett (L) M.J. O'Higgins (FG) P.Brennan (FF)	1965	04	07	Wed
TD's for Wicklow	18th Dail By-election G.Timmins (FG)	1968			
TD's for Wicklow	Polling Day for 19th Dail L.Kavanagh (L) P.Brennan (FF) G.Timmons (FG)	1969	06	18	Wed
TD's for Wicklow	Polling Day for 20th Dail L.Kavanagh (L) G.Timmins (FG) C.Murphy (FF)	1973	02	28	Wed
TD's for Wicklow	Polling Day for 21st Dail L.Kavanagh (L) G.Timmins (FG) C.Murphy (FF)	1977	06	16	Thu
TD's for Wicklow	Polling Day for 22nd Dail L.Kavanagh (L) G.Timmins (FG) C.Murphy (FF) P.Brennan (FF)	1981	06	11	Thu

A-Z Reference	Day	Date	Month	Year	DATA
TD's for Wicklow	Thu	18	02	1982	Polling Day for 23rd Dail L.Kavanagh (L) G.Timmins (FG) C.Murphy (FF) G.Hussey (FG)
TD's for Wicklow	Wed	24	11	1982	Polling Day for 24th Dail L.Kavanagh (L) G.Timmins (FG) P. Brennan (FF) G.Hussey (FG)
TD's for Wicklow	Tue	17	02	1987	Polling Day for 25th Dail J.Jacob (FF) L.Kavanagh (L) G.Hussey (FG) D.Roche (FF)
TD's for Wicklow	Thu	15	06	1989	Polling Day for 26th Dail L.Kavanagh (L), J.Jacob (FF), G.Timmins (FG), D.Roche (FF)
TD's for Wicklow	Wed	25	11	1992	Polling Day for 27th Dail L.Kavanagh (L) J.Jacob (FF) G.Timmins (FG) L.McManus (DL) J.Fox (Ind)
TD's for Wicklow	Thu	29	06	1995	By-election M.Fox (Ind)
TD's for Wicklow	Fri	06	06	1997	Polling Day for 28th Dail J.Jacob (FF) L.McManus(DL) B.Timmins (FG) M.Fox (Ind) D.Roche (FF)
The European G C				1992	The European Golf Club (Brittas Bay) established
The Riordan's	Fri	11	05	1979	The cameras roll for the final TV episode of the R.T.E's The Riordans, Mrs. Riodran played by Moira Deedy from Greystones.
Tidy Towns				1958	First Year of the Bord Failte Tidy Town Competition
Tidy Towns				1978	Bray earned 99 marks in the Bord Failte Tidy Towns Competition
Tidy Towns				1979	Bray earned 102 marks in the Bord Failte Tidy Towns Competition
Tidy Towns				1980	Bray earned 107 marks in the Bord Failte Tidy Towns Competition
Tidy Towns				1981	Bray earned 104 marks in the Bord Failte Tidy Towns Competition
Tidy Towns				1982	25th Anniversary of Tidy Towns Competition 797 towns and villages took part
Tidy Towns				1982	Bray earned 100 marks in the Bord Failte Tidy Towns Competition
Tidy Towns				1986	Roundwood earned 136 marks in the Bord Failte Tidy Towns Competition
Tidy Towns				1986	Glendalough earned 147 marks in the Bord Failte Tidy Towns Competition
Tidy Towns				1986	Bray earned 140 marks in the Bord Failte Tidy Towns Competition
Tidy Towns				1986	Newcastle earned 138 marks in the Bord Failte Tidy Towns Competition
Tidy Towns				1986	Delgany earned 171 marks in the Bord Failte Tidy Towns Competition
Tidy Towns				1986	Arklow earned 150 marks in the Bord Failte Tidy Towns Competition
Tidy Towns				1986	Greystones earned 136 marks in the Bord Failte Tidy Towns Competition
Tidy Towns				1986	Wicklow Town earned 144 marks in the Bord Failte Tidy Towns Competition
Tidy Towns				1986	Enniskerry earned 148 marks in the Bord Failte Tidy Towns Competition
Tidy Towns				1986	Ashford earned 119 marks in the Bord Failte Tidy Towns Competition
Tidy Towns				1986	Kilcoole earned 143 marks in the Bord Failte Tidy Towns Competition

Section Two: Data in Alphabetical Order

Keyword	Day	Date	Month	Year	Event
Tidy Towns				1998	Bray earned 208 marks in Bord Faite Tidy Towns Competition
Tidy Towns				2001	Aughrim earned 258 marks in the Tidy Towns Competition
Tidy Towns				2001	Stratford on Slaney earned 228 marks in the Tidy Towns Competition
Tidy Towns				2001	Enniskerry earned 224 marks in the Tidy Towns Competition
Tillage Barley				1997	The total number of hectares in County Wicklow under Barley 6,300
Tillage Wheat				1997	The total number of hectares in County Wicklow under Wheat 4,900
Timmins. Godfrey				1975	Godfrey Timmins held the post of Chairman of Wicklow County Council 1975-1976
Timmins. Godfrey				1978	Godfrey Timmins held the post of Chairman of Wicklow County Council 1978-1979
Timmins. Godfrey				1981	Godfrey Timmins held the post of Chairman of Wicklow County Council 1981-1982
Timmins. Godfrey				1996	Godfrey Timmins held the post of Chairman of Wicklow County Council 1996-1997
Timmins. Godfrey	Wed	11	04	2001	Godfrey Timmins died
Tinahely	Sun	21	07	1940	'98 Memorial unveiled at Balyrahan, Tinahely, Co. Wicklow
Tinahely			01	1996	Culture & Heritage Centre opened in the old Courthouse in Tinahely
Tinakilly House				1949	Tinakilly House, Rathnew purchased by Augustus Cullen
Tinakilly House				1959	Tinakilly House, Rathnew purchased by Mr Gunther Smith
Tinakilly House				1962	Mr. Gunther Smith nephew Mr Heinrich Rolfe inherited Tinakilly House, Rathnew
Tinakilly House				1978	Dermot and Anne Garland purchased Tinakilly House, Rathnew
Tinakilly House				1982	William and Bee Power purchased Tinakilly House, Rathnew
Tinakilly House				1991	The Power family added an extension to Tinakilly House, Rathnew
Tinakilly House				1997	The Power family added an extension to the East wing of Tinakilly House, Rathnew
Tinnehinch House			12	1999	Tinnehinch House, Enniskerry (once the home of H. Grattan) sold for £1.9m
Tinnehinch House			11	1999	Tinnehinch House, Enniskerry (once the home of H. Grattan) put up for sale
Tomcork				1991	The church at Tomacork, Carnew was remodelled
Tottenham. C.R.W	Thu	08	01	1903	Charles Robert Worsley Tottenham of Woodstock House, Kilcoole died
Tourism				1964	Regional Tourism Boards established
Tourism				1966	Guest houses and Hotels in Bray had 750 rooms listed and registered with the Eastern Regional Tourism Organisation (ERTO)
Town Hall. Bray				1928	A Weigh bridge installed at Bray Town Hall
Town Hall. Bray			's	1950	Town Hall Bray major renovations
Town Hall. Bray				1976	An electric clock was installed in the Council Chamber of the Town Hall, Bray

A–Z Reference	Day	Date	Month	Year	DATA
Town Hall. Bray				1992	Under the Urban Renewal Scheme Bray Town Hall was renovated and the Pound and Fire Station closed
Tracey, Blaise				1985	Blaise Tracey appointed County Manager of Wicklow (Local Government) 1985–2000
Tracey, Liam				1934	Liam Tracey (artist) born Avoca, Co. Wicklow.
Tractors				1946	4,457 Agriculture Tractors registered in Ireland
Tractors				1947	5,234 Agriculture Tractors registered in Ireland
Tractors				1948	7,952 Agriculture Tractors registered in Ireland
Tractors				1949	9,132 Agriculture Tractors registered in Ireland
Trade				1945	Mr. Hans Hautz founded Beverly Bags Ltd. Bray
Trade				1948	Patrick McAliden establishes the Record Press Printing Company Bray.
Trade			's	1950	The Glass bottle factory at Boghall commenced trading
Trade			05	1950	The IDA (Industrial Development Authority) established
Trade				1971	1,419 persons engaged in IDA granted manufacturing firms in Bray
Trade				1984	Made in Bray Exhibition– Industrial and Craft Fair
Trade	Wed	30	10	1985	The 2nd Made in Bray Trade Fair took place 30–31 October & 1st November
Trade			10	1989	Bray Chamber of commerce hosted Bray Industrial and Motor Fair
Trade				1989	Lepatrick Dairies of Notheren Ireland bought Chieftain Foods based in Bray
Trade				1989	Shamrock Foods (IAWS) bought Braycot Biscuits Ltd.
Trade	Tue	23	01	1990	Nixdorf Computers announced it was reducing its workforce by 5,000 including its plant at Boghall Road, Bray
Trade Union				1911	The Bray branch of the I.T.W.U. (Irish Transport Workers Union) formed
Traffic Lights			08	1937	Ireland's earliest traffic lights installed at Merrion Sq – Clare Street Junction, Dublin
Traffic Lights				1972	The first set of Traffic lights in County Wicklow was at the junction of Herbert Road, Quinsborough Road and Main Street, Bray
Trams	Sun	10	07	1949	The last tram in Dublin City
Travellers Group				1992	Wicklow Travellers Group founded
Tree Survey				2001	The tallest tree in Ireland Pseudotsuga menziesii (Douglas Fir) on Powerscourt Estate, Enniskerry 56 meters Ref:Tree Council of Ireland
Tritschler. Robin				1977	Robin Tritschler (Tenor) born 1977, educated St. David's School, Greystones.
Troy. Aidan	Tue	09	10	1945	Fr Aidan Troy born at Bray. Co. Wicklow
Troy. Aidan	Fri	12	04	2002	Fr. Aidan Troy a past pupil of St. Brendan's College, Bray. was Honoured at a function in Bray.

Troy. Dermot				1927	Dermot Troy (tenor) born in Co. Wicklow
Troy. Dermot				1952	Dermot Troy won the Irish Independent Caruso competition for singers
Troy. Dermot	Thu	06	09	1962	Dermot troy died
Trudder House	Thu	07	09	1995	Gardai begin investigating allegations of sexual abuse at Trudder House, a residential home for children near Roundwood
Tuberculosis				1913	Tuberculosis (Ireland) Order
Tulfarris Golf Club				1989	Tulfarris Golf Club (Blessington) established
Turkish Baths	Fri	09	08	1946	Fire destroys McDermott's Picture House (Turkish baths) Quinsboro Rd Bray.
Turkish Baths	Mon	19	02	1980	Turkish Baths Quinsborough Road, Bray demolished
Twomey. John				1939	Fr. John Twomey appointed to Bray Parish
Twomey. John	Sat	14	09	1946	Fr. John Twomey of Bray Parish died and was buried in St. Peter's Graveyard, Bray
Tyrrell Shipping				1960	The yacht Gypsy Moth III built at Tyrrells boat yard Arklow
Tyrrell. Kate	Tue	04	10	1921	Kate Tyrrell who held a ships master certificate and a director of Tyrrell Shipping died
Unemployment			08	1982	Unemployment figure for Bray 2,272
Unemployment				1982	The live register showed 2,307 out of work in Bray
Unemployment			01	1984	3,174 Unemployed in Bray
Urban Renewal Scheme			06	1986	The Urban Renewal Act provides for the renewal of designated urban areas. Bray included 01/05/1990
Valuation				1965	Bray Valuation stood at £62,008 and rateable valuation at 51/-s
Vance. Pat				1997	Pat Vance held the post of Chairman of Wicklow County Council 1997-1998
Vans & Lorries				1946	14,716 Commercial Van & Lorries registered in Ireland
Vans & Lorries				1947	18,838 Commercial Van & Lorries registered in Ireland
Vans & Lorries				1948	22,806 Commercial Van & Lorries registered in Ireland
Vans & Lorries				1949	23,698 Commercial Van & Lorries registered in Ireland
VEC. Bray				1901	Vocational School at Brighton Terrace, Bray
VEC. Bray				1924	Technical Instruction was transferred from Dept.. of Agriculture to the Dept. Education
VEC. Bray				1926	Mr F.F.McCarthy became CEO of Bray Vocational Committee
VEC. Bray				1934	Mr.J.Meagher became CEO of Bray Vocational Education Committee 1934-1964
VEC. Bray				1977	Mr. Ronan Rice became CEO of Bray VEC 1977-1978
VEC. Bray				1979	Larry McCluskey became CEO of Bray VEC. 1979-1980
VEC. Bray	Tue	18	03	1980	St. Thoma's Community College, Novara Road was officially opened

A–Z Reference	Day	Date	Month	Year	DATA
VEC. Bray				1980	The VEC school on the Florence Road, Bray became the Adult Education Centre
VEC. Bray	Fri	21	02	1997	The Minister of Education signs an order to abolish all town Vocational Education Committee's with effect from 01/01/`1998
VEC. Bray	Thu	01	01	1998	Bray Vocational Education Committee taken under control of the County Vocational Education Committee
VEC. Congress	Wed	06	06	1945	The 41st Congress of the Irish Vocational Education Association held in Bray on 6th, 7th and 8th June 1945
VEC-Outdoor Centre				1987	Baltinglass Outdoor Education Centre established under the aegis of County Wicklow VEC
Walking Routes				2004	Dispute over walking routes in the Glencree valley
Walsh. Mary				1929	Mary Walsh born Tinhely, Co. Wicklow
Walsh. Mary				1969	Mary Walsh held the post of Chairperson of Wicklow County Council 1969-1970. The first woman to hold the position.
Walsh. Mary	Tue	01	05	1973	Mary Walsh appointed to Seanad Eireann 1st May 1973-August 1976
Walsh. Mary			08	1976	Mary Walsh died
War Memorial				1919	War Memorial erected on Qiunsborough Road, Bray
Ward. Tony	Fri	08	10	1954	Tony Ward born in Dublin
Ward. Tony	Sat	21	01	1978	Tony Ward won his international debut cap on the Irish Rugby Team against Scotland
Ward. Tony				1978	Tony Ward the Greystones rugby player scored a record 38 in his debut Five Nations season
Ward. Tony	Wed	03	06	1987	Tony Ward last game of the Irish National Rugby Team was against Tonga in Brisbane
Ward. J.J				1946	James J. Ward (Vice President of National University of Ireland, Galway) born 1946, educated De La Salle College, Wicklow
Water - Vartry				1908	Work began on the North Reservoir of the Vartry Water Supply at Roundwood. The work took place between 1908-1925
Water - Vartry	Sun	21	10	1990	The Vartry Reservoir at Roundwood drooped to an all time low of 27.3 feet below high water mark
Water Scheme				1986	Work began on a new water and sewerage scheme . From Peoples Park, Bray to Bray Harbour
Water Treatment				1988	Bray Sewerage Pump Station at Bray harbour and out fall pipe constructed at cost £1.6m
Waters. T				1923	Very Rev T. Waters became Parish Priest of R.C. Church Enniskerry
Wayman. P.A	Sat	08	10	1927	Patrick Arthur Wayman (Astronomer) born in England
Wayman. P.A				1992	Patrick Arthur Wayman (Astronomer) 1992 - 1998 lived in Wicklow Town
Wayman. P.A	Mon	21	12	1998	Patrick Arthur Wayman (Astronomer) died in Dublin
WCEB	Thu	08	06	1995	Wicklow County Enterprise Board was incorporated as a limited company under the Industrial Development Act 1995

Section Two: Data in Alphabetical Order

	Day	Date	Month	Year	Event
WDSL				1976	The County Wicklow & District Schoolboys Football League formed
Weather	Fri	25	08	1905	In a 24 hour period 5.5 inches of rain fell in the Rocky Valley, near Bray
Weather	Sat	30	01	1926	Bray Seafront lashed by strong gale force winds some minor damage caused
Weather	Fri	24	02	1933	A severe snow storms. Road and rail services suspended for a couple of days.
Weather	Sun	26	01	1947	Snow Blizzards sweep Ireland in January, February, March starting on 26/01/1947
Weather			09	1960	Major flooding at Glenmalure
Weather			01	1982	Large falls of snow causes road an rail chaos in many parts of the country
Weather	Fri	08	01	1982	Snow drifts cut off many communities in Wicklow for over two weeks starting on 08/01/1982
Weather			12	1989	Storm damages part of the North pier at Bray harbour and the Seawall
Weather	Wed	24	01	1990	Snow showers cover most of the country
Weather	Sun	05	11	2000	Bray Seafront and Arklow flooded. Photo of Bray Seafront on front cover of Evening Herald 06/11/2000
Weather	Wed	14	12	2005	A minor earthquake measuring 2.6 on the Richter Scale centred 30 miles off Bray Head at 3.20 am
Wednesday	Tue	03	06	1913	Wednesday is fixed as early closing day under the Shops Act of 1913
West Wicklow His. Soc.				1980	The West Wicklow Historical Society founded
Weston. Galen				1968	Roundwood Park was bought by Mr Galen Weston who rebuilt Roundwood Park House. (see 1983)
Weston. Galen	Sun	07	08	1983	An attempt made to kidnap supermarket owner Galen Weston from his Roundwood home. Kidnap attempt foiled by Garda
Whelan.J.				1970	James J. Whelan held the post of Chairman of Wicklow County Council 1970-1971
Whelan.J.				1973	James J. Whelan held the post of Chairman of Wicklow County Council 1973-1974
White. J F de vere				1949	John Frederick de Vere White (Auctioneer) born 1949, educated at St. Gerard's School, Bray .
White. Larry				2002	Rev Larry White appointed Parish Priest of Queen of Peace Parish, Bray
Whitshed. E.A.F.H.				1907	Elizabeth (Hawkins-Whtshed, Burnaby, Main) Le Bond founder of the Ladies Alpine Club, President 1907-1934
Whitshed. E.A.F.H.				1928	Elizabeth (Hawkins-Whtshed, Burnaby, Main) Le Bond publishes her autobiography "Day in, Day Out"
Whitshed. E.A.F.H.	Fri	27	07	1934	Elizabeth (Hawkins-Whtshed, Burnaby, Main) Le Bond died
Wicklow 200 Km	Sun	17	06	2001	The 19th Wicklow 200 km - Wicklow Gap Challenge Cycling Event
Wicklow 200 Km	Sun	16	06	2002	The 20th Wicklow 200 km - Wicklow Gap Challenge Cycling Event
Wicklow 200 Km	Sun	08	06	2003	The 21st Wicklow 200 km - Wicklow Gap Challenge Cycling Event
Wicklow Corn Co. Ltd				1918	The Wicklow Corn Co. Ltd was established by William Clarke
Wicklow County Show	Mon	07	08	2000	The 65th Annual Wicklow County Show held at Tinahely

A–Z Reference	Day	Date	Month	Year	DATA
Wicklow Film Com.				1992	The County Wicklow Film Commission established
Wicklow GAA				1901	Luke O'Toole of Wicklow appointed the first full time Secretary of the GAA 1901-1929
Wicklow GAA				1902	Mait Mac Muireartaih Chairman of Wicklow GAA 1902- 1905
Wicklow GAA				1904	Bray Emmets (Dublin Selection) won the all Ireland Football (GAA) title (referred to 1902)title
Wicklow GAA	Wed	15	11	1905	The Arklow Gaelic Pastimes Club founded
Wicklow GAA				1906	Labhras O Pleimeann Chairman of Wicklow GAA 1906 - 1909
Wicklow GAA	Sun	28	07	1907	Leinster 2nd Division Football Final GAA. Wicklow 1-11 Westmeath 0-0
Wicklow GAA				1910	C. M. O Broin Chairman of Wicklow GAA 1910 - 1918
Wicklow GAA	Sun	23	01	1910	Leinster Junior Football Championship Final GAA Wicklow 1-10 Westmeath 1-3
Wicklow GAA				1919	Seamus O Caomhanach Chairman of Wicklow GAA 1919
Wicklow GAA				1920	An tAhair P. O Flannachain Chairman of Wicklow GAA 1920
Wicklow GAA				1921	An tAhair E O Fearail Chairman of Wicklow GAA 1921 - 1926
Wicklow GAA				1927	Micheal O' Ceallaigh Chairman of Wicklow GAA 1927 - 1928
Wicklow GAA				1929	An tAhair O Haton Chairman of Wicklow GAA 1929 - 1930
Wicklow GAA				1931	C. M. O' Broin Chairman of Wicklow GAA 1931 - 1946
Wicklow GAA				1934	Bray Emmetts GAA Club won the Wicklow Senior Football Championships
Wicklow GAA	Sun	02	08	1936	Leinster Junior Football Championship Final GAA. Wicklow 5-5 Kildare 0-3 played in Carlow
Wicklow GAA	Sun	13	09	1936	All Ireland Junior Football Championship Final GAA Wicklow 3-3 Mayo 2-5 played in Croke Park, Dublin
Wicklow GAA	Tue	26	03	1940	The Arklow Geraldines GAA Club founded in Arklow
Wicklow GAA				1947	A. M. O' Broin Chairman of Wicklow GAA 1947 - 1946
Wicklow GAA			07	1949	Leinster Junior Football Championship Final GAA. Wicklow 5-2 Meath 2-10 played in Croke Park, Dublin
Wicklow GAA				1953	The Arklow Rock Parnells GAA Club founded in Arklow
Wicklow GAA	Sun	01	08	1954	Leinster Junior Hurling Championship Final GAA. Wicklow 4-15 Westmeath 1-3 played in Naas, Co. Kildare
Wicklow GAA			10	1955	Leinster O'Byrne Cup Senior Football Final GAA. Wicklow 1-6 Westmeath 0-7 played in Newbridge, Co. Kildare
Wicklow GAA				1956	St.Mary's GAA Club Enniskerry established.
Wicklow GAA	Sun	06	10	1957	Leinster O'Byrne Cup Senior Football Final GAA. Wicklow 2-9 Kildare 1-10 played in Blessington, Co. Wicklow
Wicklow GAA				1958	Aodh o'Broin of Wicklow held the post of President of the GAA 1958-1961

Section Two: Data in Alphabetical Order

Category	Day			Year	Description
Wicklow GAA	Sun	14	06	1964	Leinster Junior Hurling Championship Final GAA. Wicklow 4-8 Kildare 2-6 played in Enniscorthy, Co. Wexford
Wicklow GAA	Sun	25	07	1965	Leinster Junior Hurling Championship Final GAA. Wicklow 4-8 Kildare 1-8 played in Croke Park, Dublin
Wicklow GAA	Sun	22	05	1966	Leinster Special Minor Hurling Championship GAA Wicklow 3-4 Kildare 2-5 played in Ashford, Co.Wicklow
Wicklow GAA	Sun	30	07	1967	Leinster Special Minor Hurling Championship GAA. Wicklow 3-15 Meath 1-7 played in Croke Park,Dublin
Wicklow GAA	Sun	22	10	1967	All Ireland Junior Hurling Championship Final GAA. Wicklow 3-14 London 4-7 played in Kilkenny
Wicklow GAA	Sun	15	10	1967	All Ireland Special Minor Hurling Championship GAA Wicklow 5-5 Down 3-4 played in Croke Park, Dublin
Wicklow GAA	Sun	30	07	1967	Leinster Junior Hurling Championship Final GAA. Wicklow 4-13 Meath 0-8 played in Croke Park, Dublin
Wicklow GAA				1968	Padraig O Murchu Chairman of Wicklow GAA 1968 - 1969
Wicklow GAA	Sun	14	09	1969	All Ireland Junior Football Championship Final GAA Wicklow 0-12 Kerry 1-8 played in Croke Park, Dublin
Wicklow GAA	Sun	06	07	1969	Leinster Junior Football Championship Final GAA. Wicklow 2-5 Meath 0-5 played in Croke Park, Dublin
Wicklow GAA				1970	Seamus O' Broin Chairman of Wicklow GAA 1970 - 1975
Wicklow GAA	Sun	28	11	1971	All Ireland Junior Hurling Championship Final GAA. Wicklow 4-6 Herts 3-8 played in Croke Park,Dublin
Wicklow GAA				1971	Leinster Junior Hurling Championship Final GAA. Wicklow 3-12 Kildare 0-7 played in Croke Park, Dublin
Wicklow GAA	Sun	18	07	1971	Leinster Intermediate Hurling Championship Final GAA. Wicklow 1-15 Dublin 2-9 played in Carlow
Wicklow GAA			07	1974	Leinster Minor Football Championship Final GAA. Wicklow 5-6 Longford 1-9 played in Croke Park, Dublin
Wicklow GAA			07	1974	Leinster Special Minor Hurling Championship Final GAA. Wicklow 2-9 Westmeath 4-2 played in Newbridge, Co. Kildare
Wicklow GAA			08	1974	All Ireland Special Minor Hurling Championship Final GAA. Wicklow 2-7 Roscommon 2-6 played in Tullamore
Wicklow GAA				1974	Sean Doherty from Glenealy played on the Dublin Team that won the All Ireland Senior Football Championship GAA
Wicklow GAA				1976	Liam O Cuillinn Chairman of Wicklow GAA 1976 - 1977
Wicklow GAA			07	1977	Leinster Special Minor Hurling Championship Final GAA. Wicklow 2-8 Meath 3-3 played in Aughrim, Co. Wicklow
Wicklow GAA				1978	Padraig O Murchu Chairman of Wicklow GAA 1978 - 1982
Wicklow GAA	Sun	05	07	1981	St.Mary's GAA Club Enniskerry open Parc na Sillogue Enniskerry on land donated by Frederick Forsyth (author)
Wicklow GAA				1983	Peadar Mac Eochaidh Chairman of Wicklow GAA 1983 - 1985
Wicklow GAA				1985	Wicklow Referee locked in boot of his car after a Wicklow GAA match
Wicklow GAA				1986	Leinster O'Byrne Cup Senior Football Final GAA. Wicklow 1-7 Westmeath 0-6
Wicklow GAA				1986	Liam O Lochlain Chairman of Wicklow GAA 1986 - 1988
Wicklow GAA				1989	Roibeard O Duiginn Chairman of Wicklow GAA 1989 - 1991

A-Z Reference	Day	Date	Month	Year	DATA
Wicklow GAA				1992	Wicklow won the All Ireland "B" Football Championship GAA.
Wicklow GAA				1992	Seamus O' Duinn Chairman of Wicklow GAA 1992 – 1994
Wicklow GAA				1994	Jack Boothman of Blessington held the post of President of the GAA 1994-1997
Wicklow GAA			06	1995	All Ireland Senior "B" Home Final – Hurling. GAA Wicklow 3-12 Kildare 1-8 played in Kilkenny
Wicklow GAA				1995	Paidraig O Laighleis Chairman of Wicklow GAA 1995 - 1997
Wicklow GAA				1998	Michael O hAgain Chairman of Wicklow GAA 1998 – 2000
Wicklow GAA			09	2000	Bray Emmets GAA Club hold the inaugural Kick Fada competition in Emmet Park, Bray. Winner Mark Herbert
Wicklow GAA				2001	Donal Mac Giolla Chuda Chairman of Wicklow GAA 2001 – 2003
Wicklow GAA			09	2001	Bray Emmets GAA Club hold Kick Fada competition in St Thomas's College, Bray. Winner Mark Herbert
Wicklow GAA	Sat	14	09	2002	Bray Emmets GAA Club hold Kick Fada competition in St Thomas's College, Bray. Winner Mark Herbert
Wicklow GAA				2002	Wicklow won the All Ireland Junior Football Championship GAA
Wicklow GAA	Sun	12	10	2003	County Wicklow senior Football Final (replay) Bray Emmets 0-6 Rathnew 0-11
Wicklow GAA				2003	Bray Emmets GAA Club hold Kick Fada competition in St Thomas's College, Bray. Winner Mark Herbert
Wicklow GAA	Sun	05	10	2003	County Wicklow senior Football Final Bray Emmets 1-5 Rathnew 0-8 (draw)
Wicklow GAA				2004	Micheal O hAgain Chairman of Wicklow GAA 2004 -
Wicklow Gaol				1924	Wicklow Gaol ceased to function as a Gaol
Wicklow Gaol				1985	Wicklow County Council established an advisory group to develop Wicklow Gaol as Heritage/Visitor's Centre
Wicklow Gaol				1998	Restoration work on Wicklow Gaol was completed and opened by President of Ireland Mary McAleese
Wicklow Gas				1948	Wicklow Gas (Charges) Order 1948
Wicklow Gas				1952	Wicklow Gas (Charges) Order 1948 amended 1952
Wicklow Golf Club	Fri	14	10	1904	Wicklow Golf Club established
Wicklow Golf Club				1963	Wicklow Golf Club won the Barton Cup
Wicklow Golf Club				1986	Wicklow Golf Club won the Barton Cup
Wicklow Golf Club				1994	Wicklow Golf Club extended its 9 hole course to 18 hole course
Wicklow Golf Club				2002	New Club house built at Wicklow Golf Club
Wicklow Harbour				1907	Building work began on the new pier at Wicklow Harbour, total cost of the harbour £93,000
Wicklow Harbour				1928	Wicklow Harbour (Temporary Increase of Charges) Order 1928

Wicklow Harbour				1949	SI No. 172/1949 Harbour Rates (Wicklow Harbour) Order, 1949
Wicklow Harbour				1956	Wicklow Harbour Works Order 1956
Wicklow Harbour				1959	Wicklow Harbour Works Order 1956 (Amendment) Order 1959
Wicklow Harbour				1964	Wicklow Harbour Works Order 1964
Wicklow Harbour				1968	Wicklow Harbour Works Order 1968
Wicklow Harbour				1977	Wicklow Harbour Works Order 1977
Wicklow Harbour				1979	Wicklow Harbour Works Order 1979
Wicklow Harbour				1984	Wicklow Harbour Works Order 1984
Wicklow Harbour				1996	Wicklow Harbour Works Order 1996
Wicklow Hills Bus Co	Thu	01	05	1924	The Wicklow Hills Bus Company was established it was based in the yard behind the Powerscourt Arms Hotel, Enniskerry
Wicklow Hills Bus Co			04	1936	The Wicklow Hills Bus Company owned by the Fitzpatrick family was taken over by the Dublin United Tramway Company
Wicklow Regiment				1909	The Wicklow Artillery Regiment disbanded
Wicklow Rovers				1975	Wicklow Rovers Football Club in Wicklow Town established
Wicklow Rovers F.C.				1975	Wicklow Rovers Football Club formed
Wicklow Rugby Club				1963	Wicklow Rugby Club established
Wicklow Rugby Club				1976	Club house built at Wicklow Rugby Club
Wicklow Rural				1992	Wicklow Rural Partnership evolved from Wicklow Rural Enterprise Ltd.
Wicklow Rural			09	1994	Wicklow Rural Partnership Limited (WRP) was established for administering the LEADER II Program in Wicklow
Wicklow Sailing Club				1951	Wicklow Sailing Club founded
Wicklow Sub Aqua Club				1983	Wicklow Sub Aqua Club founded
Wicklow Town	Mon	17	04	1950	The Holy Rosary National School Wicklow town officially opened
Wicklow Town				2000	Parking Disc system introduced in Wiclow Town
Wicklow Town	Mon	12	09	2005	Wicklow Town Council introduce Pay & Display Parking in Wicklow Town. It replaced Parking Disc
Wicklow Town Council	Tue	18	12	2001	S.I.591/2001 of 18/12/1001 gave effect with 1/01/2002 the change Wicklow Urban District Council to Wicklow Town Council
Wicklow Town F.C.				1939	Wicklow Town Football Club formed
Wicklow Traffic				1976	Wicklow Traffic and Parking Bye-Laws 1976
Wicklow Ward	Mon	08	02	1915	The Wicklow Ward for wounded soldiers was opened in St. Patrick Dun's Hospital, Dublin by Lady Powerscourt

A–Z Reference	Day	Date	Month	Year	DATA
Wicklow Way	Sun	17	08	1980	Stage 1 of the Wicklow Way was opened by Hugh Tunney T.D. in Marley Park, Rathfarnham.
Wicklow Way	Sun	27	09	1981	Stage 2 of the Wicklow Way opened near Laragh. Co. Wicklow
Wicklow. Earl of	Tue	14	01	1902	Ralph Howard 7th Earl of Wicklow married Lady Gladys Mary Hamilton dau of James 2nd Duke of Abercorn
Wicklow. Earl of	Thu	30	10	1902	William Cecil 8th Earl of Wicklow born
Wicklow. Earl of	Mon	12	03	1917	Lady Howard wife if the 7th Earl of Wicklow died
Wicklow. Earl of	Fri	11	10	1946	Ralph Francis Howard 7th Earl of Wicklow died and was succeeded by his son William
Wicklow. Earl of				1978	William Cecil 8th Earl of Wicklow died
Wicklow. Earl of	Sat	23	03	1985	Lady Wicklow, one of the founders of Glencree Reconciliation Centre, is conferred with an Hon. Doctor of Laws degree at NUI
Wind Farm				2003	Arklow Bank Wind Park in the Irish Sea , construction commenced late summer 2003
Windgates School				1954	The school at Windgates, Greystones Co. Wicklow closed
Wingfield, Shelia				1992	Shelia Wingfield nee Beddington died, wife of 9th Lord Powerscourt
Wingfield. Emily	Sun	03	11	1918	Emily Wingfield nee Fitzpatrick died
Wingfield. Maurice	Sat	14	04	1956	Maurice Wingfield of Enniskerry died
Winston's				1988	Winston's open at store in the old Lipton's Supermarket Main Street, Bray
Wolf Tone Youth Club				1973	Wolf Tone Youth Club formed
Wolfe Tone Sq	Sun	05	12	1954	Grotto dedicated to Our lady was blessed by Rev Fr. Mitchell PP at Wolfe Tone Square, Bray.
Woodbrook				1959	From 1959 to 1962 the Hospital Trust Tournaments were held at Woodbrook Golf Club
Woodbrook				1963	Carrolls International Golf Tournament held at Woodbrook Golf Club, Bray. Winner B. J. Hunt
Woodbrook				1964	Carrolls International Golf Tournament held at Woodbrook Golf Club, Bray. Winner Christy. O'Connor (Royal Dublin)
Woodbrook				1966	Carrolls International Golf Tournament held at Woodbrook Golf Club, Bray. Winner Christy. O'Connor (Royal Dublin)
Woodbrook				1967	Carrolls International Golf Tournament held at Woodbrook Golf Club, Bray. Winner Christy. O'Connor (Royal Dublin)
Woodbrook				1968	Carrolls International Golf Tournament held at Woodbrook Golf Club, Bray. Winner Jimmy Martin (Edmonstown)
Woodbrook				1969	Carrolls International Golf Tournament held at Woodbrook Golf Club, Bray. Winner Ronnie Shade (Scotland)
Woodbrook				1970	Carrolls International Golf Tournament held at Woodbrook Golf Club, Bray. Winner Brian Huggett
Woodbrook				1971	Carrolls International Golf Tournament held at Woodbrook Golf Club, Bray. Winner N. C Coles (England)

Section Two: Data in Alphabetical Order

Name	Day			Year	Event
Woodbrook				1972	Carroll's International Golf Tournament held at Woodbrook Golf Club, Bray. Winner Christy. O'Connor (Royal Dublin)
Woodbrook				1973	Carroll's International Golf Tournament held at Woodbrook Golf Club, Bray. Winner Paddy McGuire (Co. Louth)
Woodbrook				1974	Carrolls International Golf Tournament held at Woodbrook Golf Club, Bray. Winner Bernard Gallagher (Scotland)
Woodbrook				1975	The Irish Open Championships at Woodbrook Golf Club winner C.o'Connor(Shannon)
Woodbrook Golf Club				1926	Woodbrook Golf Club, Bray registered with the Golfing Union of Ireland
Woodbrook Golf Club				1943	Woodbrook Golf Club won the Barton Cup
Woodbrook Golf Club				1982	The Irish Amateur Close Championship, held at Woodbrook Golf Club, Bray
Woodbrook Golf Club				2000	Two pedestrian underpasses constructed under the railway line at Woodbrook Golf Club
Woodburn. William	Fri	15	01	1915	William Woodburn died
Woodenbridge	Thu	02	02	1911	A great storm sweeps Ireland. Tom Moore's tree at Woodenbridge up rooted.
Woods. Michael			12	1935	Michael J. Woods Government Minster and TD for Dublin was born in Bray, Co. Wicklow
Woods. Michael				1977	Dr. Michael Woods elected to Dail Eireann
Woods. Michael			12	1979	Dr Michael Woods appointed Minister for Health & Social Welfare (December 1979 – June 1981)
Woods. Michael			03	1982	Dr Michael Woods appointed Minister for Health & Social Welfare (March 1982 – December 1982)
Woods. Michael				1987	Dr Michael Woods appointed Minister of Social Welfare (1987 - 1991)
Woods. Michael				1991	Dr Michael Woods appointed Minister of Agriculture & Food (1991 - 1992)
Woods. Michael				1992	Dr Michael Woods appointed Minister of Marine
Woods. Michael				1993	Dr Michael Woods appointed Minister of Social Welfare (1993 -1994)
Woods. Michael				1994	Dr Michael Woods appointed Minister of Health (1994)
Woods. Michael				1997	Dr Michael Woods appointed Minister of Marine and Natural Resources (1997 -1999)
Woods. Michael				1999	Dr Michael Woods appointed Minister of Education and Science (1999 - 2002)
Woodstock House				1946	Woodstock House bought by Mr. G Van den Bergh
Woodstock House			's	1960	Woodstock House and Estate bought by Mr & Mrs William Forwood
Woodstock House				1993	Woodstock House and Estate bought by a consortium of business persons
Woolworths. W.F				1953	W.F Woolworths opened a store at 10-11 Main Street Bray.
Woolworths. W.F	Sat	06	10	1984	W.F Woolworths store at Main Street Bray closed.
World War II	Thu	02	01	1941	Bomb dropped at Glencormick, (Stylebawn) ,Bray
WTDA	Sat	06	05	1950	The Wicklow Tourist Development Association, International Races (Motor Bike) Wicklow Circuit

A–Z Reference	Day	Date	Month	Year	DATA
Wynne. Gladys				1907	Gladys Wynne (artist) daughter of the Archdeacon of Aghadoe (Kerry) lived at the Lake Cottage, Glendalough
Wynne. Gladys				1968	Gladys Wynne (artist) daughter of the Archdeacon of Aghadoe died
Yeats. Jack B.				1910	Jack B. Yeats lived between 1910–1917 at Redford House, Greystones
Yeats. Jack B.				1916	Jack B. Yeats elected a member of the Royal Hiberian Academy
Yeats. Jack B.	Thu	28	03	1957	Jack B. Yeats died in Dublin
Young Scientist			01	2001	S. Browne, P. Taylor, M. O'Toole won the Young Scientist of the Year project Investigating symmetrical shapes formed by polygons
Youth Group				1980	A youth group Alpha 80 established in Bray
Youth Hostel	Sat	19	06	1999	Glendalough An Oige Hostel opened by Mark Mortell of Bord Failte

Section Three:
Index

The County Wicklow Database: 432 AD to 2006 AD

A-Z Reference	Year	A-Z Reference	Year	A-Z Reference	Year
A.O.Smith	2005	Act	1881	Act	1948
Abdey. Humphrey	1665	Act	1883	Act	1948
Act	1420	Act	1885	Act	1955
Act	1660	Act	1885	Act	1956
Act	1738	Act	1886	Act	1956
Act	1765	Act	1887	Act	1957
Act	1793	Act	1887	Act	1957
Act	1800	Act	1888	Act	1960
Act	1801	Act	1888	Act	1961
Act	1804	Act	1890	Act	1963
Act	1830	Act	1890	Act	1966
Act	1835	Act	1890	Act	1973
Act	1836	Act	1891	Act	1973
Act	1838	Act	1891	Act	1977
Act	1838	Act	1892	Act	1978
Act	1840	Act	1895	Act	1979
Act	1846	Act	1896	Act	1983
Act	1847	Act	1898	Act	1985
Act	1847	Act	1898	Act	1986
Act	1847	Act	1900	Act	1993
Act	1849	Act	1902	Act	1998
Act	1849	Act	1903	Acton. Caroline	1879
Act	1851	Act	1906	Acton. Charles	1830
Act	1852	Act	1906	Acton. Henry	1745
Act	1854	Act	1906	Acton.Thomas	1711
Act	1854	Act	1908	Acton.Thomas	1716
Act	1858	Act	1908	Acton.Thomas	1716
Act	1858	Act	1916	Acton.Thomas	1750
Act	1859	Act	1919	Acton.Thomas	1780
Act	1861	Act	1919	Acton.Thomas	1826
Act	1863	Act	1920	Acton.Thomas	1857
Act	1863	Act	1920	Acton. William	1711
Act	1866	Act	1924	Acton. William	1736
Act	1866	Act	1924	Acton. William	1779
Act	1869	Act	1926	Acton. William	1789
Act	1869	Act	1926	Acton. William	1818
Act	1870	Act	1930	Acton. William	1820
Act	1870	Act	1930	Adair. Foster	1750
Act	1870	Act	1932	Aghavanagh Barracks	1803
Act	1871	Act	1940	Aghold	1716
Act	1871	Act	1941	Aghold	1814
Act	1872	Act	1942	Aghold	1814
Act	1875	Act	1944	Agriculture Census	1991
Act	1878	Act	1945	Agriculture Census	1991
Act	1878	Act	1946	Agriculture Census	2000
Act	1881	Act	1946	Agriculture Census	2000
Act	1881	Act	1946	Ahern. Nuala	1994

Section Three: Index

A–Z Reference	Year
Air Crashes	1930
Air Crashes	1941
Air Crashes	1942
Air Crashes	1946
Air Crashes	1987
Air Crashes	1991
Air Crashes	1993
Air Show	2005
Airs/Music	1796
Airs/Music	1808
Airs/Music	1810
Airs/Music	1892
Airs/Music	1893
Airs/Music	1917
Airs/Music	1918
Airs/Music	1954
Alcock. Dr. N.	1904
Alexander. William	1824
Alexander. William	1850
Alexander. William	1896
Alexander. William	1911
Alexandra Bridge	1864
Allen. Darina	1948
Allen. Elizabeth	1750
Allen. Francis	1894
Allen. Francis	1921
Allen. John	1745
Allen. John	1745
Allen. Joshua	1709
Allgood. Molly	1887
Allgood. Molly	1907
Allgood. Molly	1911
Allgood. Molly	1926
Allgood. Molly	1952
Allgood. Sara	1883
Allgood. Sara	1950
Altidore House	1945
American Samoa	2003
An Oige	1931
Anderson. James Arthur	1843
Anderson. James Arthur	1899
Annacharter School	1737
Annacurra	1825
Annacurra	1862
Annamoe	1801
Antler Hotel	1855
Antrim Militia	1797

A–Z Reference	Year
Aravon School	1862
Aravon School	1871
Aravon School	1876
Aravon School	1978
Aravon School	1984
Aravon School	1984
Arcadia Ballroom	1962
Archer. Anthony	1699
Archer. Richard	1732
Archer. Thomas	1799
Archer. Thomas	1800
Archer. William	1813
Ardmore Rovers	1979
Ardmore Studio	1957
Ardmore Studio	1958
Ardmore Studio	1958
Ardmore Studio	1973
Ardmore Studio	1975
Ardmore Studio	1982
Area Farmed	2002
Arklow	1172
Arklow	1599
Arklow	1759
Arklow	1799
Arklow	1803
Arklow	1806
Arklow	1847
Arklow	1854
Arklow	1855
Arklow	1858
Arklow	1861
Arklow	1869
Arklow	1869
Arklow	1879
Arklow	1897
Arklow	1897
Arklow	1899
Arklow	1903
Arklow	1905
Arklow	1914
Arklow	1915
Arklow	1915
Arklow	1917
Arklow	1923
Arklow	1929
Arklow	1935
Arklow	1967

A–Z Reference	Year
Arklow	1968
Arklow	1969
Arklow	1970
Arklow	1971
Arklow	1976
Arklow	1979
Arklow	1982
Arklow	1985
Arklow	1989
Arklow	1994
Arklow	2002
Arklow	2005
Arklow	2005
Arklow Barony	1841
Arklow Barony	1851
Arklow Barony	1861
Arklow Barony	1871
Arklow Barony	1891
Arklow Barracks	1715
Arklow By-Pass	1999
Arklow CBS	1961
Arklow CBS	1963
Arklow Celtic F.C.	2000
Arklow Cinema	1913
Arklow Convent	1879
Arklow Convent	1881
Arklow District Council	1910
Arklow Fire Station	2002
Arklow Golf Club	1927
Arklow Harbour	1949
Arklow Harbour	1952
Arklow Harbour	1954
Arklow Harbour	1957
Arklow Harbour	1975
Arklow Harbour Act	1882
Arklow Hospital	1921
Arklow Hospital	1961
Arklow Music Festival	1970
Arklow Pipe Band	1941
Arklow Pottery	1934
Arklow Pottery	1935
Arklow Pottery	1947
Arklow Pottery	1998
Arklow Pottery	1999
Arklow School	1839
Arklow School	1878
Arklow Shipping	1966

A-Z Reference	Year	A-Z Reference	Year	A-Z Reference	Year
Arklow Shipping	1982	Ashford Church	1918	Ballinacor Nth. Barony	1851
Arklow Shipping	1983	Assembly Hall	1890	Ballinacor Nth. Barony	1861
Arklow Shipping	1988	Aughrim	1782	Ballinacor Nth. Barony	1871
Arklow Shipping	1988	Aughrim	1887	Ballinacor Nth. Barony	1891
Arklow Shipping	1988	Aughrim	1890	Ballinacor Sth. Barony	1841
Arklow Shipping	1990	Aughrim	1912	Ballinacor Sth. Barony	1851
Arklow Shipping	1990	Aughrim	1935	Ballinacor Sth. Barony	1861
Arklow Shipping	1990	Aughrim Rangers F.C.	1991	Ballinacor Sth. Barony	1871
Arklow Shipping	1991	Avoca	1837	Ballinacor Sth. Barony	1891
Arklow Shipping	1991	Avoca	1839	Ballorney House	1975
Arklow Shipping	1991	Avoca	1840	Ballyarthur House	1680
Arklow Shipping	1992	Avoca	1862	Ballyboy House	1798
Arklow Shipping	1992	Avoca	1956	Ballycoog	1780
Arklow Shipping	1992	Avoca	1958	Ballycorus Works	1920
Arklow Shipping	1992	Avoca	1962	Ballycurry House	1808
Arklow Shipping	1995	Avoca	1969	Ballygahan Mine	1833
Arklow Shipping	1996	Avoca	1982	Ballygannon Hse.	1896
Arklow Shipping	1996	Avoca	1997	Ballyman	1172
Arklow Shipping	1996	Avoca	2001	Ballymore Eustace	1373
Arklow Shipping	1998	Avoca Bridge	1868	Ballymore Eustace	1814
Arklow Shipping	1998	Avoca Bridge	1869	Ballymurrin House	1675
Arklow Shipping	1999	Avoca Bridge	1986	Ballynaclash	1753
Arklow Shipping	2002	Avoca Handeweavers	1723	Ballynockan	1888
Arklow Silver Band	1968	Avondale House	1779	Ballywaltrim College	1981
Arklow Sports Centre	1982	Avondale House	1795	Ballywaltrim Sports	1999
Arklow Town Council	2001	Avondale House	1891	Baltinglass	1148
Arklow Town Juniors	1948	Avondale House	1904	Baltinglass	1228
Arklow Youth Club	1960	Avondale House	1904	Baltinglass	1541
Arklow. Battle of	1798	Avondale House	1935	Baltinglass	1556
Armstrong. G.F.S	1845	Avondale House	1946	Baltinglass	1585
Armstrong. G.F.S	1886	Avondale House	1967	Baltinglass	1627
Armstrong. G.F.S	1906	Avondale House	1969	Baltinglass	1672
Armstrong. G.F.S.	1891	Avonmore F.C.	2001	Baltinglass	1759
Armstrong. G.F.S.	1892	Bahrain	2003	Baltinglass	1780
Armstrong. Reg	1926	Bailieborough Castle	1918	Baltinglass	1839
Armstrong. Reg	1979	Bailieborough Castle	1936	Baltinglass	1860
Armstrong-Jones. A	1930	Bailieborough Castle	1936	Baltinglass	1880
Armstrong-Jones. A	1960	Baldwin. Arthur	1725	Baltinglass	1950
Armstrong-Jones. A	1961	Baldwin. Richard	1756	Baltinglass	1950
Armstrong-Jones. A	1978	Baldwin. Robert	1744	Baltinglass	1950
Armstrong-Jones. A	1978	Ball. F.E	1928	Baltinglass	1967
Armstrong's Hotel	1798	Ball. Teresa	1794	Baltinglass Fire Stn	2002
Ashford	1799	Ball. Teresa	1861	Baltinglass Golf Club	1928
Ashford	1819	Ball. Teresa	1850	Baltinglass Golf Club	1974
Ashford	1864	Ballinacor House	1780	Baltinglass Golf Club	1993
Ashford	1895	Ballinacor House	1965	Baltinglass Hospital	1916
Ashford Church	1915	Ballinacor Nth. Barony	1841	Baltinglass Hospital	1922

Section Three: Index

A-Z Reference	Year	A-Z Reference	Year	A-Z Reference	Year
Baltinglass Hospital	1970	Bayly. Edward S	1835	Bewley. Ernest	1932
Baltinglass Hospital	1976	Bayly. Edward S	1837	Bewley. Joshua	1819
Baltinglass Hospital	1980	Bayly. Edward S	1884	Bewley. Joshua	1869
Baltinglass Hospital	1980	Bayly. Henry	1774	Bewley. Joshua	1900
Baltinglass Hospital	2000	Bayly. Henry	1816	Bewley. Joshua	1906
Baltinglass Workhouse	1837	Bayly. Henry	1827	Bewley. Thomas Arthur	1889
Baltinglass Workhouse	1841	Bayly. Lancelot	1869	Bewley. Thomas Arthur	1943
Baltinglass Workhouse	1923	Bayly. Lancelot	1928	Bewley. Victor	1912
Baltinglass, Convent	1879	Bayly. Lancelot	1952	Bewley. Victor	1964
Bandstand	2003	Bayly. Richard	1845	Bewley. Victor	1977
Bank Building	1914	Bayly. Richard	1907	Bewley. Victor	1999
Banotti. Mary	1939	Bayview	1866	Biggs. Michael	1928
Barlow. Jane	1857	BBK United	2001	Biggs. Michael	1966
Barlow. Jane	1917	Beatty. Sir A. C.	1875	Biggs. Michael	1970
Barn Owls	1893	Beatty. Sir A. C.	1954	Biggs. Michael	1993
Barn Owls	1907	Beatty. Sir A. C.	1957	Bill	1852
Barn Owls	1910	Beatty. Sir A. C.	1968	Bill	1912
Barnes. E	1861	Beckett. Dr.G.P.G	1930	Bill	1936
Barony of Talbotstown	1797	Beckett. Dr.G.P.G	1930	Bill	1970
Barre. W.J.	1867	Begles	1995	Births	1907
Barret. George	1732	Beit. Alfred	1903	Births	2002
Barrett. Daniel	1927	Beit. Alfred	1931	BL&FHS	1988
Barrett. Daniel	1957	Beit. Alfred	1944	Blachford. John	1808
Barrett. Daniel	1995	Beit. Alfred	1993	Blacklion	1860
Barrington. Charlotte	1862	Beit. Alfred	1994	Blainroe Golf Club	1978
Barrington. Elizabeth	1907	Beit. Otto John	1865	Blake. Edward	1833
Barrington. R.C	1849	Beit. Otto John	1924	Blake. Edward	1912
Barrington. R.C	1915	Beit. Otto John	1930	Blake. Samuel H.	1835
Barrington. R.M.	1886	Bell	800	Blake. Samuel H.	1914
Barrington. R.M.	1896	Bellevue House	1754	Blake. Vincent	2002
Barrington. R.M.	1896	Bellevue House	1950	Blake. William H.	1809
Barrington. R.M.	1900	Belyng. Sir Henry	1614	Blake. William H.	1870
Barrington. Sir William	1815	Beresford. William	1764	Blessington	1547
Barrington. Sir William	1859	Beresford. William	1835	Blessington	1669
Barrington. Sir William	1872	Bernard. John Henry	1860	Blessington	1740
Barter. Dr. Richard	1803	Bernard. John Henry	1915	Blessington	1849
Barter. Dr. Richard	1870	Bernard. John Henry	1927	Blessington	1923
Barton. Hugh	1881	Bernard. Rev W.H.	1767	Blessington	1931
Barton. Robert	1881	Bernard. Rev W.H.	1795	Blessington	1981
Barton. Robert	1919	Bernard. Rev W.H.	1818	Blessington	2005
Barton. Robert	1920	Bernard. W.H.	1791	Blessington	2005
Barton. Robert	1975	Bestic. Albert A.	1890	Blessington Fire Stn.	2002
Barton. T.J.	1838	Bestic. Albert A.	1915	Blessington Fountain	1865
Barton. T.J.	1840	Bestic. Albert A.	1940	Blessington House	1673
Battley. Col. D'Oyly	1889	Bestic. Albert A.	1962	Blessington Lakes	1940
Bayly. Catherine	1908	Bewley. Ernest	1860	Blessington S C	1960
Bayly. Edward S	1807	Bewley. Ernest	1903	Blessington. Countess	1789

The County Wicklow Database: 432 AD to 2006 AD

A-Z Reference	Year	A-Z Reference	Year	A-Z Reference	Year
Blessington. Countess	1836	Books	1868	Books	1936
Blessington. Countess	1849	Books	1870	Books	1937
Blue Flag	2000	Books	1871	Books	1938
Blue Flag	2002	Books	1871	Books	1939
Blue Flag	2003	Books	1872	Books	1943
Boewn. Edward	1836	Books	1874	Books	1945
Boghall Brick	1870	Books	1875	Books	1946
Boghall Brick	1920	Books	1875	Books	1949
Bond. Henry	1751	Books	1876	Books	1950
Book	1815	Books	1878	Books	1950
Books	1639	Books	1878	Books	1953
Books	1678	Books	1879	Books	1953
Books	1741	Books	1879	Books	1953
Books	1798	Books	1881	Books	1954
Books	1801	Books	1881	Books	1954
Books	1814	Books	1884	Books	1954
Books	1821	Books	1885	Books	1956
Books	1822	Books	1886	Books	1957
Books	1823	Books	1886	Books	1957
Books	1823	Books	1891	Books	1958
Books	1824	Books	1892	Books	1958
Books	1832	Books	1894	Books	1958
Books	1832	Books	1895	Books	1959
Books	1835	Books	1897	Books	1959
Books	1835	Books	1899	Books	1961
Books	1835	Books	1900	Books	1961
Books	1841	Books	1900	Books	1962
Books	1841	Books	1902	Books	1962
Books	1842	Books	1903	Books	1964
Books	1842	Books	1903	Books	1964
Books	1842	Books	1905	Books	1965
Books	1844	Books	1907	Books	1967
Books	1844	Books	1907	Books	1967
Books	1848	Books	1911	Books	1969
Books	1849	Books	1912	Books	1970
Books	1849	Books	1912	Books	1970
Books	1851	Books	1913	Books	1971
Books	1853	Books	1915	Books	1972
Books	1853	Books	1916	Books	1972
Books	1853	Books	1922	Books	1973
Books	1854	Books	1924	Books	1973
Books	1856	Books	1924	Books	1974
Books	1856	Books	1927	Books	1975
Books	1856	Books	1927	Books	1975
Books	1860	Books	1934	Books	1975
Books	1867	Books	1934	Books	1976
Books	1867	Books	1934	Books	1977

Section Three: Index

A–Z Reference	Year
Books	1977
Books	1978
Books	1978
Books	1979
Books	1979
Books	1979
Books	1979
Books	1980
Books	1980
Books	1980
Books	1980
Books	1982
Books	1983
Books	1983
Books	1984
Books	1984
Books	1985
Books	1985
Books	1985
Books	1986
Books	1986
Books	1986
Books	1986
Books	1987
Books	1987
Books	1988
Books	1988
Books	1988
Books	1989
Books	1989
Books	1989
Books	1989
Books	1989
Books	1990
Books	1990
Books	1990
Books	1991
Books	1991
Books	1991
Books	1991
Books	1991
Books	1991
Books	1992
Books	1992
Books	1992
Books	1993
Books	1993

A–Z Reference	Year
Books	1993
Books	1994
Books	1994
Books	1994
Books	1994
Books	1994
Books	1994
Books	1994
Books	1994
Books	1994
Books	1995
Books	1995
Books	1995
Books	1996
Books	1996
Books	1996
Books	1996
Books	1997
Books	1997
Books	1997
Books	1997
Books	1997
Books	1997
Books	1997
Books	1997
Books	1998
Books	1998
Books	1998
Books	1998
Books	1998
Books	1998
Books	1998
Books	1998
Books	1998
Books	1998
Books	1998
Books	1998
Books	1998
Books	1999
Books	1999
Books	1999
Books	1999
Books	2000
Books	2000
Books	2000

A–Z Reference	Year
Books	2001
Books	2001
Books	2001
Books	2001
Books	2002
Books	2002
Books	2003
Books	2004
Books	2005
Booth. Denton	1852
Booth. Denton	1893
Booth. Denton	1925
Booth. Evelyn Mary	1897
Booth. Evelyn Mary	1950
Booth. Evelyn Mary	1962
Booth. Evelyn Mary	1979
Booth. Evelyn Mary	1988
Booth. George	1885
Bord Failte	1968
Borough of Carysfort	1628
Borough of Wicklow	1613
Boswell. John	1670
Boswell. John	1671
Boswell. John	1715
Boucicault. Dion	1820
Boucicault. Dion	1864
Boucicault. Dion	1890
Bowden. Richard	1922
Bowden. Richard	1939
Bowe. Laura	1969
Bower. Robert	1894
Bower. Robert	1922
Bower. Robert	1931
Bower. Robert	1975
Bowling Championships	1998
Boyd. Patrick	1774
Boylan. Dom Eugene	1904
Boylan. Dom Eugene	1931
Boylan. Dom Eugene	1937
Boylan. Dom Eugene	1962
Boylan. Dom Eugene	1964
Boyle. Ina	1889
Boyle. Ina	1919
Boyle. Ina	1923
Boyle. Ina	1923
Boyle. Ina	1926
Boyle. Ina	1942

A-Z Reference	Year	A-Z Reference	Year	A-Z Reference	Year
Boyle. Ina	1966	Brabazon. John	1866	Bradshaw. Harry	1913
Boyle. Ina	1967	Brabazon. John	1941	Bradshaw. Harry	1934
Boyle. Michael	1661	Brabazon. John	2000	Bradshaw. Harry	1941
Boyle. Michael	1663	Brabazon. Killruddery	1616	Bradshaw. Harry	1947
Boyle. Michael	1669	Brabazon. Killruddery	1682	Bradshaw. Harry	1947
Boyle. Michael	1678	Brabazon. Mary	1625	Bradshaw. Harry	1949
Boyle. Michael	1702	Brabazon. Reginald	1841	Bradshaw. Harry	1953
Boystown Golf Club	1998	Brabazon. Reginald	1868	Bradshaw. Harry	1953
Brabazon Family	1834	Brabazon. Reginald	1869	Bradshaw. Harry	1958
Brabazon. Anthony	1721	Brabazon. Reginald	1872	Bradshaw. Harry	1990
Brabazon. Anthony	1758	Brabazon. Reginald	1873	Brangan. Pamela	1974
Brabazon. Anthony	1790	Brabazon. Reginald	1875	Bray & Kilternan	1824
Brabazon. Anthony	1812	Brabazon. Reginald	1883	Bray Arts Centre	2002
Brabazon. Anthony	1910	Brabazon. Reginald	1887	Bray Arts Centre	2002
Brabazon. Anthony	1940	Brabazon. Reginald	1892	Bray Ball	1905
Brabazon. Anthony	1952	Brabazon. Reginald	1897	Bray Bookshop	1972
Brabazon. Anthony	1998	Brabazon. Reginald	1905	Bray Bookshop	1988
Brabazon. Chambre	1682	Brabazon. Reginald	1906	Bray Bye Laws	1869
Brabazon. Chambre	1692	Brabazon. Reginald	1906	Bray Bye Laws	1875
Brabazon. Chaworth	1686	Brabazon. Reginald	1908	Bray Bye Laws	1899
Brabazon. Chaworth	1731	Brabazon. Reginald	1918	Bray Cancer Group	1990
Brabazon. Chaworth	1753	Brabazon. Reginald	1929	Bray Civic Centre	2001
Brabazon. Chaworth	1758	Brabazon. Reginald	1949	Bray Coastguard	1876
Brabazon. Chaworth	1763	Brabazon. Reginald	1981	Bray Development Co.	1970
Brabazon. David	1948	Brabazon. Sir Edward	1585	Bray Directory	1981
Brabazon. Edward	1627	Brabazon. Sir Edward	1616	Bray Directory	1985
Brabazon. Edward	1628	Brabazon. Sir Edward	1625	Bray Electric Works	1912
Brabazon. Edward	1632	Brabazon. Sir William	1534	Bray Festival	1968
Brabazon. Edward	1634	Brabazon. Sir William	1535	Bray Festival	1994
Brabazon. Edward	1651	Brabazon. Sir William	1550	Bray Festival	1996
Brabazon. Edward	1691	Brabazon. Sir William	1552	Bray Festival	1997
Brabazon. Edward	1702	Brabazon. Sir William	1607	Bray Festival	1998
Brabazon. Edward	1704	Brabazon. Sir William	1618	Bray Festival	2001
Brabazon. Edward	1704	Brabazon. William	1671	Bray Festival	2002
Brabazon. Edward	1707	Brabazon. William	1675	Bray Fire Stn.	2002
Brabazon. Edward	1720	Brabazon. William	1685	Bray for Holidays	1968
Brabazon. Edward	1762	Brabazon. William	1769	Bray for Holidays	1969
Brabazon. Edward	1772	Brabazon. William	1797	Bray Furniture	1887
Brabazon. Geoffery	1998	Brabazon. William	1797	Bray Furniture	1905
Brabazon. Jane	1644	Brabazon. William	1797	Bray Furniture	1905
Brabazon. John	1772	Brabazon. William	1803	Bray Furniture	1907
Brabazon. John	1801	Brabazon. William	1837	Bray Gas Works	1858
Brabazon. John	1821	Brabazon. William	1856	Bray Gas Works	1859
Brabazon. John	1824	Brabazon. William	1861	Bray Gas Works	1981
Brabazon. John	1824	Brabazon. William	1887	Bray Golf Club	1897
Brabazon. John	1831	Brabazon. Chambre	1715	Bray Golf Club	1905
Brabazon. John	1851	Brabazon. Killruddery	1820	Bray Golf Club	1907

Section Three: Index

A–Z Reference	Year
Bray Golf Club	1925
Bray Golf Club	1928
Bray Harbour	1861
Bray Harbour	1880
Bray Harbour	1891
Bray Harbour	1897
Bray Harbour	1897
Bray Harbour	1897
Bray Harbour	1916
Bray Harbour	1943
Bray Harbour	1957
Bray Harbour	1973
Bray Harbour	1980
Bray Harbour	1984
Bray Harbour	2001
Bray Head	1824
Bray Head	1861
Bray Head	1887
Bray Head	1930
Bray Head	1933
Bray Head	1950
Bray Head	1964
Bray Head	2002
Bray Head Chairlift.	1952
Bray Head Chairlift.	1976
Bray Head Hotel	1862
Bray Head House	1917
Bray Hunt	1837
Bray Hunt	1850
Bray Hunt Club	1872
Bray Laundry	1905
Bray Main Street	1990
Bray Musical Society	1952
Bray Musical Society	1952
Bray Musical Society	1953
Bray Musical Society	1954
Bray Musical Society	1955
Bray Musical Society	1956
Bray Musical Society	1957
Bray Musical Society	1958
Bray Musical Society	1959
Bray Musical Society	1960
Bray Musical Society	1961
Bray Musical Society	1962
Bray Musical Society	1963
Bray Musical Society	1964
Bray Musical Society	1965

A–Z Reference	Year
Bray Musical Society	1966
Bray Musical Society	1967
Bray Musical Society	1968
Bray Musical Society	1969
Bray Musical Society	1970
Bray Musical Society	1971
Bray Musical Society	1972
Bray Musical Society	1973
Bray Musical Society	1974
Bray Musical Society	1975
Bray Musical Society	1976
Bray Musical Society	1977
Bray Musical Society	1978
Bray Musical Society	1979
Bray Musical Society	1980
Bray Musical Society	1981
Bray Musical Society	1982
Bray Musical Society	1983
Bray Musical Society	1984
Bray Musical Society	1985
Bray Musical Society	1986
Bray Musical Society	1987
Bray Musical Society	1988
Bray Musical Society	1989
Bray Musical Society	1990
Bray Musical Society	2000
Bray Musical Society	2001
Bray Musical Society	2002
Bray Pumping Station	1990
Bray River	1787
Bray River	1787
Bray Rovers Hockey	1941
Bray Rowing Club	1935
Bray Sailing Club	1896
Bray School	1820
Bray School	1829
Bray School	1878
Bray School	1878
Bray School	1880
Bray School	1880
Bray School	1887
Bray School	1907
Bray School Project	1977
Bray School Project	1981
Bray Sea Anglers	1960
Bray Seafront	1883
Bray Seafront	1885

A–Z Reference	Year
Bray Seafront	1928
Bray Seafront	2003
Bray Softball Club	1997
Bray Summer Fest	2003
Bray Technical School	1931
Bray Technical School	1933
Bray Technical School	1941
Bray Tennis Club	1999
Bray Town Hall	1884
Bray Traffic	1947
Bray Traffic	1947
Bray Traffic	1950
Bray Traffic	1965
Bray Traffic	1973
Bray Traffic Plan	2002
Bray Urban District	1948
Bray Urban District	1952
Bray Urban District	1967
Bray Urban District	1967
Bray Urban District	1978
Bray Urban District	1979
Bray Urban District	1994
Bray Urban District	1998
Bray Wanderers	1924
Bray Wanderers	1976
Bray Wheelers	1949
Bray. Barracks	1692
Bray. Barracks	1811
Bray. Castle	1310
Bray. Castle	1440
Bray. Castle	1898
Bray. Castle	1938
Bray. Seafront	1875
Bray. Seafront	1878
Bray. Seafront	1941
Bray. Seafront	1998
Bray. Seafront	1998
Bray. Town Hall	1879
Bread	1989
Breen. Dan	1894
Breen. Dan	1969
Breen. Dan	1971
Breen. William	1946
Breen. William	1970
Brennan. John	1854
Brennan. Paduge	1971
Brennan. Paudge	1970

A-Z Reference	Year	A-Z Reference	Year	A-Z Reference	Year
Brennan. Thomas	1886	BUDC	1968	Butler. Eleanor	1915
Brennan. Thomas	1945	BUDC	1969	Butler. Eleanor	1948
Brennan. Thomas	1953	BUDC	1977	Butler. Eleanor	1959
Bridge	1943	BUDC	1979	Butler. Eleanor	1997
Bridge House Inn	1702	BUDC	2001	Byrne. A. W	1856
Brien. Christy	1980	Bull. George P.	1810	Byrne. Andrew W.	1975
Brien. Christy	1986	Burgage Bridge	1767	Byrne. Billy	1775
British Empire Day	1902	Burgage Bridge	1939	Byrne. Billy	1799
British Empire Day	1916	Burial Society	1880	Byrne. Billy	1899
British Empire Day	1958	Burke. William	1946	Byrne. C.M.	1958
British Empire Day	1966	Burnaby. F.G.	1842	Byrne. Christopher M.	1922
British Empire Day	1977	Burnaby. F.G.	1870	Byrne. Dr	1777
British Navy	1999	Burnaby. F.G.	1879	Byrne. Edward	1943
British Parliamentary Reports	1828	Burnaby. F.G.	1885	Byrne. Gerald	1612
British Parliamentary Reports	1830	Burnaby. H.S.V.G.	1880	Byrne. H.J.	1857
British Parliamentary Reports	1831	Burne. Moris	1610	Byrne. Henry J.	1953
British Parliamentary Reports	1850	Burrows. Thomas	1696	Byrne. Henry J.	1968
Broadcasting Authority	1960	Burton. John	1666	Byrne. Hugh	1567
Brocas. Samuel	1821	Bus	1906	Byrne. James	1916
Brook House School	1973	Bus	1925	Byrne. James (Pt.)	1822
Brooke. R.H	1850	Bus	1926	Byrne. James (Pt.)	1858
Brooke. R.H	1880	Bus	1927	Byrne. James (Pt.)	1859
Brookey's Bridge	1838	Bus	1927	Byrne. James (Pt.)	1872
Brookey's Bridge	1838	Bus	1929	Byrne. John	1675
Browne, Garech	1939	Bus	1937	Byrne. John	1992
Browne. Maurice	1891	Bus	1938	Byrne. John	2002
Browne. Maurice	1979	Bus	1942	Byrne. Joseph	1916
Brownrigg. Henry	1763	Bus	1946	Byrne. Pat	1954
Brunker. James P.	1855	Bus	1948	Byrne. Shane	1971
Brunker. James P.	1960	Bus	1950	Byrne. Shane	2001
BTIC	1899	Bus	1953	Byrne. Shane	2005
Buckley. Richard	1666	Bus	1953	Byrne. Thady	1688
BUDC	1909	Bus	1959	Byrne. Thady	1689
BUDC	1914	Bus	1963	Byrne. W. M.	1798
BUDC	1925	Bus	1968	Calary Church	1834
BUDC	1928	Bus	1970	Calary Church	1984
BUDC	1935	Bus	1971	Calendar	1752
BUDC	1935	Bus	1985	Callaghan. Christopher	1760
BUDC	1940	Bus	1985	Callaghan. Christopher	1785
BUDC	1942	Bus Crash	1991	Callaghan. Christopher	1794
BUDC	1955	Bus Crash	2000	Callow Hill	1863
BUDC	1956	Bush School	1960	Callow Hill	1866
BUDC	1957	Bushe. John	1730	Camera Club	1971
		Bushe. John	1746	Camera Club	1980
		Bushe. Letitia	1710	Campbell. Arthur	1909
		Bushe. Letitia	1736	Campbell. Arthur	1914
		Bushe. Letitia	1757	Campbell. Christopher	1908

Section Three: Index

A-Z Reference	Year	A-Z Reference	Year	A-Z Reference	Year
Campbell. Christopher	1972	Carnew Castle	1815	Cars	1973
Campbell. F.George	1917	Carnew Castle	1901	Cars	1973
Campbell. F.George	1966	Carnew Castle	1946	Cars	1973
Campbell. F.George	1969	Carnew Castle	1981	Cars	1974
Campbell. F.George	1979	Carnew College	2002	Cars	1974
Campbell. Flan	1919	Carnew Credit Union	1967	Cars	1974
Campbell. Flan	1946	Carnew Credit Union	1970	Cars	1974
Campbell. Flan	1994	Carnew Forge	1635	Cars	1975
Campbell. John Henry	1757	Carnew Musical Society	1967	Cars	1975
Campbell. John Henry	1800	Carnew Playschool	2001	Cars	1975
Campbell. John Henry	1828	Carnew School	1829	Cars	1976
Campbell. Joseph	1879	Carrig. Blessington	1985	Cars	1976
Campbell. Joseph	1910	Carroll. Alexander	1821	Cars	1976
Campbell. Joseph	1920	Carroll. C.A	1862	Cars	1977
Campbell. Joseph	1944	Carroll. Grorge	1772	Cars	1977
Candler. William	1728	Carroll. Henry	1826	Cars	1978
Canon Robinson	1888	Carroll. James	1739	Cars	1978
Caprani	2002	Carroll. James	1760	Cars	1979
Car Park, Bray	1973	Carroll. Walter	1798	Cars	1979
Car Park, Bray	1980	Cars	1904	Cars	1979
Carleton	1204	Cars	1904	Cars	1979
Carlisle Grounds	1862	Cars	1904	Cars	1980
Carlisle Grounds	1966	Cars	1904	Cars	1980
Carlisle Grounds	2001	Cars	1905	Cars	1980
Carlisle Grounds	2003	Cars	1911	Cars	1980
Carlow	1210	Cars	1946	Cars	1981
Carmelite Convent	1844	Cars	1947	Cars	1981
Carnew	1794	Cars	1948	Cars	1981
Carnew	1798	Cars	1949	Cars	1981
Carnew	1813	Cars	1955	Cars	1981
Carnew	1831	Cars	1960	Cars	1981
Carnew	1834	Cars	1965	Cars	1981
Carnew	1841	Cars	1968	Cars	1982
Carnew	1860	Cars	1968	Cars	1982
Carnew	1936	Cars	1968	Cars	1982
Carnew	1940	Cars	1969	Cars	1983
Carnew	1954	Cars	1969	Cars	1983
Carnew	1958	Cars	1970	Cars	1983
Carnew	1985	Cars	1970	Cars	1984
Carnew	1987	Cars	1970	Cars	1984
Carnew	1996	Cars	1970	Cars	1984
Carnew AFC	1980	Cars	1971	Cars	1985
Carnew Castle	1578	Cars	1971	Cars	1985
Carnew Castle	1610	Cars	1971	Cars	1985
Carnew Castle	1619	Cars	1972	Cars	1986
Carnew Castle	1638	Cars	1972	Cars	1986
Carnew castle	1782	Cars	1972	Cars	1986

A-Z Reference	Year	A-Z Reference	Year	A-Z Reference	Year
Cars	1987	Cemetery St. Peter's	1842	Christ Church, Bray	1912
Cars	1988	Chamber of Commerce	1946	Christ Church, Bray	1936
Cars	1989	Chamber of Commerce	1956	Christ Church, Bray	1946
Cars	1990	Chamber of Commerce	1958	Christ Church, Bray	1950
Cars	1991	Chamber of Commerce	1959	Christan Brothers	1921
Cars	1992	Chamber of Commerce	2003	Christian.Jonathan W.	1856
Cars	1993	Chambre. Calcot	1618	CIE	1987
Cars	1994	Chammey. Edward	1743	Cinema. Bray	1935
Cars	1995	Chammey. John	1650	Cinema. Bray	1974
Cars	1996	Chammey. Joseph	1738	Cinema. Bray	1979
Cars	1997	Chapel. Richard	1727	City of Wurtzburg	1999
Cars	1998	Chapman. Robert	1200	Clanwilliam. Earl	1776
Cars	1999	Charlesland G & C Club	1992	Clanwilliam.Viscount	1766
Cars	2000	Charleville House	1705	Clara	1730
Cars	2001	Charleville House	1792	Clara	1733
Cars	2002	Charleville House	1797	Clara	1799
Cars	2003	Charleville House	1810	Clara	1879
Cars	2004	Charleville House	1820	Clelland. Hugh	1799
Cars	2004	Charleville House	1873	Clermont House	1730
Cars	2004	Charleville House	1941	Cliffwalk, Bray	1932
Cars	2004	Cheshire Home	1960	Cliffwalk, Bray	1961
Carysfort Arms	1861	Chess Club	1975	Cliffwalk, Bray	2005
Casement. Julius	1877	Chichester. Sir. F	1901	Clonegal	1625
Casement. Julius	1890	Chichester. Sir. F	1964	Co. Wicklow Tennis	1894
Casement. Roger	1864	Chichester. Sir. F	1967	Coach House. Roundwood	1820
Casement. Roger	1916	Chichester. Sir. F	1972		
Cassidy. Peter	1810	Childers. E. H.	1973	Coastwatching	1945
Castle Howard	1812	Childers. E. H.	1974	Cochrane	1915
Castlekevin	1216	Childers. E.H	1905	Cochrane. Ernest	1873
Castlekevin	1225	Childers. E.H	1974	Cochrane. Ernest	1898
Castlekevin	1308	Childers. R. E	1870	Cochrane. Ernest	1911
Castlekevin	1636	Childers. R. E	1903	Cochrane. Ernest	1933
Castlekevin House	1993	Childers. R. E	1904	Cochrane. H.J.	1871
Castlemacadam	1819	Childers. R. E	1910	Cochrane. H.J.	1892
Castlemacadam	1870	Childers. R. E	1911	Cochrane. Henry	1836
Cattle	1997	Childers. R. E	1920	Cochrane. Henry	1865
Cattle	1997	Childers. R. E	1922	Cochrane. Henry	1903
Cattle	1997	Childers. R. E	1922	Cochrane. Henry	1904
Cattle	1997	Children's Home	1940	Cochrane. Margaret	1901
Cattle	1997	China	2003	Cochrane. Richard	1868
Cattle	1997	Christ Church, Bray	1861	Cochrane. Richard	1871
Cattle	1997	Christ Church, Bray	1863	Cochrane. Sir Henry	1897
Cattle	2002	Christ Church, Bray	1866	Cochrane. Stanley	1877
Cavan Militia	1798	Christ Church, Bray	1870	Cochrane. Stanley	1895
Cavanagh, Bryan	1625	Christ Church, Bray	1881	Cochrane. Stanley	1905
Cavendish. Andrew	2004	Christ Church, Bray	1889	Cochrane. Stanley	1910
CCTV	2003	Christ Church, Bray	1911	Cochrane. Stanley	1915

Section Three: Index

A–Z Reference	Year
Cochrane. Stanley	1921
Cochrane. Stanley	1924
Cochrane. Stanley	1927
Cochrane. Stanley	1949
Coddington. William	1656
Cogan. Denis	1900
Cogan. Denis J.	1859
Cogan. Denis J.	1944
Cogan. W.H.F	1863
COI. Carnew	1912
COI. Carnew	1956
COI. Carnew	1995
Coilte	1988
Coins	1789
Coins	1986
Colahan. Richard	1912
Colahan. Richard	1922
Colaiste Raithin	1991
Coles. Neil	1965
Collins. William	1720
Collins. William	1788
Collins. William	1847
Collins. William W.	1824
Collins. William W.	1889
Collis. J.S	1900
Collis. J.S	1984
Comerford. Marie	1893
Comerford. Marie	1935
Comerford. Marie	1982
Compulsory Purchase	2001
Comyn. John	1185
Comyn. John	1212
Conacher. Lionel	1901
Conacher. Lionel	1937
Conacher. Lionel	1949
Conacher. Lionel	1954
Condren. Daniel	1914
Condren. Daniel	1925
Connolly Square	1954
Connolly. James	1868
Connolly. James	1890
Connolly. James	1903
Connolly. James	1916
Connolly. James	1938
Connolly. Roderick	1901
Connolly. Roderick	1943
Connolly. Roderick	1948

A–Z Reference	Year
Connolly. Roderick	1980
Conran. John	1819
Conran. John	1859
Conran. John	1893
Conran. John	1893
Conran. John	1893
Conran. John	1894
Conran. John	1897
Conran. Margaret	1829
Conran. Margaret	1893
Constitution	1937
Convent, Greystones	1906
Convent. Kilcoole	1897
Cookson. Catherine	1832
Cookson. Catherine	1835
Cookson. Geroge James	1805
Cookson. Geroge James	1838
Coolattin Golf Club	1962
Coollatin House	1801
Coollattin Hunt	1850
Coolross House	1637
Coote. Charles	1641
Coote. Charles	1641
Coote. Chidley	1658
Corbett. W. J.	1909
Corke Lodge	1815
Corke Lodge	1906
Cormer. Frederick J.	1901
Cormer. Frederick J.	1921
Coronation Plantation	1831
Costal Erosion	1908
Costello. Seamus	1939
Costello. Seamus	1957
Costello. Seamus	1966
Costello. Seamus	1967
Costelloe. Seamus	1977
County Councils	1899
County Show	2002
County Wicklow	1957
County Wicklow	1957
County Wicklow	1957
County Wicklow	1961
County Wicklow	1965
County Wicklow	1974
County Wicklow	1985
County Wicklow	1986
County Wicklow	1998

A–Z Reference	Year
Courage. Michael	1969
Court Case	1879
Court House. Bray	1841
Court House. Bray	1921
Court House. Bray	1984
Courthouses	1824
Courthouses	1935
Cradock. Philip	1683
Cradock. Thomas	1774
Cramp. Geoffery	1335
Crampton Collection	2000
Crampton. Selina	1806
Crampton. Selina	1849
Crampton. Selina	1893
Crampton. Sir J.F.T.	1805
Crampton. Sir Philip	1777
Crampton. Sir Philip	1839
Crampton. Sir Philip	1858
Crampton. Sir J.F.T.	1826
Crampton. Sir J.F.T.	1830
Crampton. Sir J.F.T.	1834
Crampton. Sir J.F.T.	1839
Crampton. Sir J.F.T.	1839
Crampton. Sir J.F.T.	1844
Crampton. Sir J.F.T.	1845
Crampton. Sir J.F.T.	1858
Crampton. Sir J.F.T.	1858
Crampton. Sir J.F.T.	1860
Crampton. Sir J.F.T.	1886
Credit Union	1964
Cricken Church	1840
Cricket	1863
Cricket	1907
Cricket	1907
Cricket	1909
Cricket	1912
Cricket	1912
Cricket	1912
Cricket Club, Bray	1861
Crimmins. P.J	1910
Crinion. Peter	1960
Cripples Home, Bray	1874
Critchley. James	1802
Croatia	2003
Cromwell. William	1649
Cronebane Lodge	1810
Crosbie. Alexander	1596

The County Wicklow Database: 432 AD to 2006 AD

A-Z Reference	Year	A-Z Reference	Year	A-Z Reference	Year
Crosbie. Francis	1510	D&BST	1889	Darley. J. C.	1870
Crosbie. Francis	1580	D&BST	1895	Darley. J. C.	1918
Crosbie. Richard	1755	Daly. Capt	1953	Darley. Sir F.M	1830
Crosbie. Richard	1785	Daly. Edward	1891	Darley. Sir F.M	1860
Crosbie. Sir Edward	1798	Daly. Edward	1916	Darley. Sir F.M	1878
Crosbie. Sir Paul	1789	Daniel. Thomas	1624	Darley. Sir F.M	1886
Crosbie. Sir Paul	1793	Danyell. Laurence	1355	Darley. Sir F.M	1887
Crosbie. Sir Warren	1759	Darby. John Nelson	1800	Darley. Sir F.M	1897
Crosbie. Sir William	1794	Darby. John Nelson	1825	Darley. Sir F.M	1901
Crosbie. Sir William	1830	Darby. John Nelson	1826	Darley. Sir F.M	1910
Crosbie. Sir William	1860	Darcy. Eamonn	1952	Davidson. Lillian	1879
Crosby. Bing	1961	Darcy. Eamonn	1968	Davidson. Lillian	1934
Cuddihy. C	1890	Darcy. Eamonn	1977	Davidson. Lillian	1954
Cullen. Augustus	1887	Darcy. Eamonn	1983	Davidson. Rosanna	1984
Cullen. Augustus	1924	Darcy. Eamonn	1987	Davidson. Rosanna	2003
Cullen. Augustus	1981	Darcy. Eamonn	1987	Dawson. Joshua	1710
Cullen. Fr. John	1883	Darcy. Eamonn	1990	Dawson. Joshua	1727
Cullen. Fr. John	1970	Dargan. William	1799	de Buitlear. Eamon	1930
Cullen. Gary	1945	Dargan. William	1860	de Buitlear. Eamon	1991
Cullen. Luke	1793	Dargan. William	1867	De la Salle	1912
Cullen. Luke	1838	Dargle River	1657	de Mareys. Adam	1352
Cullen. Luke	1859	Dargle River	1666	de Riddelsford. Walter	1173
Cullen. Thomas	1995	Dargle River	1741	de Riddelsford. Walter	1174
Cunningham. Agnes E.	1877	Dargle River	1760	de Riddelsford. Walter	1181
Cunningham. George E.	1858	Dargle River	1849	de Riddelsford. Walter	1213
Cunningham. George E.	1859	Dargle River	1856	de Riddelsford. Walter	1220
Cunningham. Larry	1960	Dargle River	1867	de Riddelsford. Walter	1244
Cunningham. R.A.G	1792	Dargle River	1873	de Riddelsford. Walter	1276
Cunningham. R.A.G	1849	Dargle River	1882	de Robeck. Baron	1884
Cunningham. R.A.G	1877	Dargle River	1887	de Robeck. Bart. J.M.H	1839
Cunningham. Capt. C.	1886	Dargle River	1905	De Valois. N	1898
Currency	1826	Dargle River	1931	De Valois. N	1935
Currency	1969	Dargle River	1947	De Valois. N	2001
Currency	1969	Dargle River	1965	Deaths	2002
Currency	1979	Dargle River	1967	Deering. Mark	1972
Currency	2002	Dargle River	1969	Delahunt. S.V.	1870
Curry, Eugene	1838	Dargle River	1986	Delaney. John	1965
Curtlestown	1826	Dargle River	1986	Delaney. John	1981
Curtlestown	1834	Darley. Cecil W.	1842	Delany. Ronnie	1935
Curtlestown	1891	Darley. Cecil W.	1867	Delany. Ronnie	1955
Curtlestown	1960	Darley. Cecil W.	1881	Delany. Ronnie	1956
Curtlestown	1984	Darley. Cecil W.	1896	Delany. Ronnie	1957
Cycle Polo	1891	Darley. Cecil W.	1928	Delany. Ronnie	2005
Cycle Polo	1901	Darley. F.M	1830	Delgany	1022
Cycle Polo	1908	Darley. F.M	1910	Delgany	1172
Cycle Routes	1899	Darley. George	1795	Delgany	1225
D&BST	1887	Darley. George	1846	Delgany	1241

Section Three: Index

A-Z Reference	Year
Delgany	1301
Delgany	1725
Delgany	1789
Delgany	1790
Delgany	1856
Delgany	1934
Delgany	1940
Delgany	1959
Delgany	1990
Delgany	2002
Delgany Golf Club	1956
Delgany Golf Club	1979
Delgany Golf Club	1980
Delgany Golf Club	1981
Delgany Golf Club	1981
Delgany Golf Club	1982
Delgany Golf Club	1983
Delgany Golf Club	1984
Delgany Golf Club	1985
Delgany Golf Club	1986
Delgany Golf Club	1987
Delgany Golf Club	1988
Delgany Golf Club	1989
Delgany Golf Club	1991
Delgany Golf Club	1991
Delgany Golf Club	1993
Delgany, School	1839
Delgany, School	1845
Delgany, School	1846
Dempsey. Denis (Pt.)	1826
Dempsey. Denis (Pt.)	1857
Dempsey. Denis (Pt.)	1858
Dempsey. Denis (Pt.)	1860
Dempsey. Denis (Pt.)	1896
Dennis. M.C	1873
Dennis. T.S.	1810
Deputies Pass	1594
Dermot	1225
Derralossary Church	1834
Derralossary Church	1960
Derralossary Church	1985
Derrybawn Bridge	1779
Deverell. Averill	1890
Deverell. Averill	1890
Deverell. Averill	1979
Devil's Glen	1835
Devlin. Anne	1780

A-Z Reference	Year
Devlin. Anne	1851
Devlin. Anne	1951
Dick. Capt. Q	1898
Dillion. J.M.	1939
Dillon. John Talbot	1740
Dillon. John Talbot	1771
Dillon. John Talbot	1805
Dillon. Sir. James	1639
Dillon. Sir. James	1641
Dillon. Sir. James	1669
Dioceses of Dublin	1137
Dispensary. Bray	1811
Djouce Mountain G. C.	1996
Dock Terrace	1846
Dock Terrace	1954
Dolan. Bridget	1777
D'olier. Bertrand	1928
D'Ombrain. Ernest A.	1867
D'Ombrain. Ernest A.	1898
D'Ombrain. Ernest A.	1944
Dominican Convent	1870
Domvile. William	1641
Domville. Benjamin	1773
Donard	2001
Donard House	1813
Donegal Militia	1796
Donnellan. Michael	1799
Donnelly. James	1867
Donnelly. N	1894
Donovan. J.T.	1914
Donovan. J.T.	1918
Doran. Felix	1915
Doran. Felix	1972
Doran. John	1968
Doran. Johnny	1907
Doran. Johnny	1950
Douglas. James	1929
Douglas. M.J	1963
Downshire House	1798
Downshire. Marquis of	1801
Doyle. James	1779
Doyle. James	1808
Doyle. James	1823
Doyle. James	1826
Doyle. Peter	1968
Doyle. Peter	1972
Driving	2002

A-Z Reference	Year
Driving	2003
Dromin House	1900
Drought. G.M.J	1810
Druhan. Loughlin	1872
Druids Glen Golf Club	1995
Druids Glen Golf Club	1996
Druids Glen Golf Club	1997
Druids Glen Golf Club	1998
Druids Glen Golf Club	1999
Druids Glen Hotel	2002
Drumgoff Barracks	1803
Drumm. James	1896
Drumm. James	1974
Drummond School	1919
Dublin	1210
Dublin	1355
Dublin	1402
Dublin	1729
Dublin Archdiocese	1028
Dublin California	1993
Dublin City Militia	1800
Dublin Gas Company	1846
Dublin Gas Company	1877
Dublin Gas Company	1918
Dublin Gas Company	1930
Dublin Lock Out	1913
Duel	1787
Dun Laoghaire	1821
Dun Loghaire	1926
Duncairn Terrace. Bray	1859
Dunganstown Castle	1597
Dunlavin	1798
Dunlavin	1816
Dunlavin	1818
Dunlavin	1835
Dunlavin	2001
Dunlavin Town Hall	1925
Dunne. Seamus	1930
Dunne. Seamus	1951
Dunne. Seamus	1951
Dunne. Seamus	1951
Dunne. Seamus	1953
Dunne. Sean	1918
Dunne. Sean	1969
Dunphy. Fr. James	1914
Dunstone Hall	1844
DUTC	1896

A-Z Reference	Year	A-Z Reference	Year	A-Z Reference	Year
DUTC	1925	Elections–Polling Day	1817	Elections–Polling Day	1928
Dwyer. John	1784	Elections–Polling Day	1818	Elections–Polling Day	1934
Dwyer. Mary	1780	Elections–Polling Day	1820	Elections–Polling Day	1937
Dwyer. Mary	1861	Elections–Polling Day	1826	Elections–Polling Day	1942
Dwyer. Michael	1772	Elections–Polling Day	1830	Elections–Polling Day	1945
Dwyer. Michael	1798	Elections–Polling Day	1831	Elections–Polling Day	1945
Dwyer. Michael	1799	Elections–Polling Day	1832	Elections–Polling Day	1950
Dwyer. Michael	1800	Elections–Polling Day	1835	Elections–Polling Day	1955
Dwyer. Michael	1803	Elections–Polling Day	1837	Elections–Polling Day	1959
Dwyer. Michael	1806	Elections–Polling Day	1841	Elections–Polling Day	1959
Dwyer. Michael	1825	Elections–Polling Day	1847	Elections–Polling Day	1960
Dwyer. Michael	1885	Elections–Polling Day	1852	Elections–Polling Day	1966
Dwyer. Michael	1902	Elections–Polling Day	1857	Elections–Polling Day	1967
Dwyer. Michael	1904	Elections–Polling Day	1857	Elections–Polling Day	1968
Dwyer. Michael	1938	Elections–Polling Day	1859	Elections–Polling Day	1968
Dwyer. Michael	1946	Elections–Polling Day	1865	Elections–Polling Day	1972
Dwyer. Michael	1983	Elections–Polling Day	1868	Elections–Polling Day	1972
Dwyer. Michael	1992	Elections–Polling Day	1874	Elections–Polling Day	1972
Earthquake	1852	Elections–Polling Day	1874	Elections–Polling Day	1973
Earthquake	1984	Elections–Polling Day	1880	Elections–Polling Day	1974
East Coast Radio	2002	Elections–Polling Day	1885	Elections–Polling Day	1979
East Coast Radio	2002	Elections–Polling Day	1885	Elections–Polling Day	1979
Eaton. J	1755	Elections–Polling Day	1886	Elections–Polling Day	1979
Eaton. Thomas	1731	Elections–Polling Day	1886	Elections–Polling Day	1979
Eccles. Hugh	1698	Elections–Polling Day	1892	Elections–Polling Day	1983
Eccles. Isaac	1811	Elections–Polling Day	1892	Elections–Polling Day	1984
Eccles. Issac	1765	Elections–Polling Day	1895	Elections–Polling Day	1984
Eccles. Thomas	1754	Elections–Polling Day	1895	Elections–Polling Day	1985
Eccles. William	1801	Elections–Polling Day	1895	Elections–Polling Day	1985
Ecology Centre	1998	Elections–Polling Day	1899	Elections–Polling Day	1985
Economic Survey	1977	Elections–Polling Day	1900	Elections–Polling Day	1986
Education	1831	Elections–Polling Day	1900	Elections–Polling Day	1986
Education Inquiry	1806	Elections–Polling Day	1905	Elections–Polling Day	1987
Edwards. Col.	1783	Elections–Polling Day	1906	Elections–Polling Day	1987
Edwards. James	1759	Elections–Polling Day	1906	Elections–Polling Day	1989
Edwards. Richard	1668	Elections–Polling Day	1907	Elections–Polling Day	1990
Edwards. Richard	1702	Elections–Polling Day	1910	Elections–Polling Day	1992
Eisenhower. Gen	1962	Elections–Polling Day	1910	Elections–Polling Day	1992
Eksund	1987	Elections–Polling Day	1910	Elections–Polling Day	1992
Election	1634	Elections–Polling Day	1910	Elections–Polling Day	1992
Elections–Polling Day	1801	Elections–Polling Day	1910	Elections–Polling Day	1992
Elections–Polling Day	1802	Elections–Polling Day	1911	Elections–Polling Day	1994
Elections–Polling Day	1806	Elections–Polling Day	1914	Elections–Polling Day	1995
Elections–Polling Day	1807	Elections–Polling Day	1914	Elections–Polling Day	1996
Elections–Polling Day	1812	Elections–Polling Day	1918	Elections–Polling Day	1997
Elections–Polling Day	1816	Elections–Polling Day	1920	Elections–Polling Day	1997
Elections–Polling Day	1816	Elections–Polling Day	1925	Elections–Polling Day	1998

Section Three: Index

A–Z Reference	Year
Elections–Polling Day	1998
Elections–Polling Day	1999
Elections–Polling Day	2001
Elections–Polling Day	2001
Elections–Polling Day	2001
Elections–Polling Day	2001
Elections–Polling Day	2002
Elections–Polling Day	2002
Elections–Polling Day	2002
Elections–Polling Day	2002
Elections–Polling Day	2002
Elections–Polling Day	2002
Elections–Polling Day	2002
Elections–Polling Day	2002
Elections–Polling Day	2002
Elections–Polling Day	2004
Elections–Polling Day	2004
Elections–Polling Day	2004
Elections–Polling Day	2004
Elections–Polling Day	2004
Elections–Polling Day	2004
Electricity	1891
Electricity	1896
Electricity	1920
Electricity	1927
Electricity	1934
Electricity	1968
Electricity	1973
Elliott. Shay	1934
Elliott.Shay	1963
Elliott.Shay	1971
Ellis. R.F	1868
Elliston. Henry	1851
Elliston. Henry	1880
Elliston. Henry	1889
Elliston. Henry	1891
Elliston. Henry	1909
Employment	1847
Enniskerry	1783
Enniskerry	1815
Enniskerry	1818
Enniskerry	1830
Enniskerry	1843
Enniskerry	1860
Enniskerry	1925
Enniskerry	1930

A–Z Reference	Year
Enniskerry	1938
Enniskerry	1992
Enniskerry	2005
Enniskerry	2005
Enniskerry Bridge	1739
Enniskerry Dam	1925
Enniskerry Library	1911
Errity.Tom	1915
ESB	1937
ESB	1943
Esmond. Sir John	1875
Esplanade Hotel	1895
Esplanade Hotel	1951
Esplanade Hotel	1978
Eucharistic Congress	1932
Euro Coins	2001
Eustace. James	1613
Everett. James	1890
Everett. James	1954
Everett. James	1967
Exchequer	1817
Exhibition	1853
Failte Park	1965
Failte Park	1981
Fairbrother.William	1770
Falkener. Samuel	1788
Falkiner. Daniel	1759
Falkner.Thomas	1793
Farmed land	2002
Farrell	1798
Farrell. Kathleen	1641
Farrell. Margaret	1927
Fatima Hall	1940
FCA	1989
Feis	1903
Fenian Rebellion	1867
Ferghaile. Domnall Ua	1043
Fever hospital	1817
Fever hospital	1818
Film	1914
Film	1917
Film	1919
Film	1922
Film	1924
Film	1926
Film	1937
Film	1946

A–Z Reference	Year
Film	1947
Film	1957
Film	1957
Film	1960
Film	1960
Film	1961
Film	1962
Film	1962
Film	1963
Film	1964
Film	1964
Film	1965
Film	1968
Film	1969
Film	1971
Film	1972
Film	1973
Film	1977
Film	1978
Film	1979
Film	1983
Film	1984
Film	1984
Film	1986
Film	1986
Film	1988
Film	1988
Film	1988
Film	1989
Film	1990
Film	1990
Film	1990
Film	1990
Film	1990
Film	1990
Film	1991
Film	1992
Film	1992
Film	1993
Film	1993
Film	1994
Film	1994
Film	1994
Film	1995
Film	1995
Film	1995
Film	1995

A-Z Reference	Year	A-Z Reference	Year	A-Z Reference	Year
Film	1995	Fitzwilliam. 2nd Earl	1728	Flora-Fauna	1891
Film	1996	Fitzwilliam. 3rd Earl	1719	Flora-Fauna	1894
Film	1996	Fitzwilliam. 3rd Earl	1742	Flora-Fauna	1897
Film	1997	Fitzwilliam. 3rd Earl	1744	Flora-Fauna	1898
Film	1997	Fitzwilliam. 3rd Earl	1756	Flora-Fauna	1899
Film	1997	Fitzwilliam. 3rd Earl	1769	Flora-Fauna	1899
Film	1997	Fitzwilliam. 4th Earl	1748	Flora-Fauna	1899
Film	1998	Fitzwilliam. 4th Earl	1770	Flora-Fauna	1950
Film	1998	Fitzwilliam. 4th Earl	1822	Flower Festival	1992
Film	1998	Fitzwilliam. 4th Earl	1823	Flower Festival	2000
Film	1998	Fitzwilliam. 4th Earl	1837	Flusk. Michael	1946
Film	1998	Fitzwilliam. 5th Earl	1786	Foot & Mouth	1912
Film	1999	Fitzwilliam. 5th Earl	1806	Foot & Mouth Scare	2001
Film	1999	Fitzwilliam. 5th Earl	1830	Foot Regiment, Meath	1689
Findlater. Alex	1901	Fitzwilliam. 5th Earl	1857	Foot Regiment, Meath	1695
Fire Station	1991	Fitzwilliam. 6th Earl	1815	Forestry	2002
Fires	1785	Fitzwilliam. 6th Earl	1838	Forestry	2002
Fitz Walter, Theobald	1285	Fitzwilliam. 6th Earl	1895	Forestry	2002
Fitzgerald. Garret	1926	Fitzwilliam. 6th Earl	1902	Forestry	2002
Fitzgerald. Garret	1969	Fitzwilliam. 7th Earl	1872	Forestry	2002
Fitzgerald. Garret	1973	Fitzwilliam. 7th Earl	1896	Forestry	2002
Fitzgerald. Garret	1977	Fitzwilliam. 7th Earl	1943	Forestry	2002
Fitzgerald. Garret	1981	Fitzwilliam. 8th Earl	1910	Forestry	2002
Fitzgerald. Garret	1982	Fitzwilliam. 8th Earl	1933	Forestry	2002
Fitzgerald. Garret	1987	Fitzwilliam. 8th Earl	1935	Forestry	2002
Fitzgerald. John	1902	Fitzwilliam. 8th Earl	1948	Forestry	2002
Fitzgerald. John	1921	Fitzwilliam. 9th Earl	1853	Forestry	2002
Fitzgerald. John	1921	Fitzwilliam. 9th Earl	1952	Forestry	2002
Fitzgerald. Paul	1980	Fitzwilliam. W. 2nd	1671	Forestry	2002
Fitzimons	1753	Fitzwilliam. William	1795	Forestry	2002
Fitzpatrick. Hubert	2000	Fitzwilliam. W. 1st	1620	Forestry	2002
Fitzpatrick. John	1954	Fitzwilliam. W. 1st	1643	Forestry	2002
Fitzpatrick. Sean P.	1948	Fitzwilliam. W. 2nd	1638	Forestry	2002
Fitzsimons. C.	1861	Fitzwilliam. W. 2nd	1658	Forestry	2002
Fitzsimons. Richard	1648	Flannel Hall	1793	Forge Enniskerry	1855
Fitzsimons. Richard	1682	Flannery. Michael	1945	Forge Road Enniskerry	1807
Fitzsimons. Richard	1690	Flood. Francis	1970	Forge, Blessington	1852
Fitzsimons. Richard	1740	Flood. Francis	1993	Forsyth, Frederick	1938
Fitzwilliam Estates	1859	Flora-Fauna	1654	Forsyth, Frederick	1980
Fitzwilliam. 10th Earl	1904	Flora-Fauna	1802	Fortgranite House	1730
Fitzwilliam. 10th Earl	1979	Flora-Fauna	1832	Fortgranite House	1810
Fitzwilliam. 1st Earl	1643	Flora-Fauna	1832	Fortgranite House	1870
Fitzwilliam. 1st Earl	1669	Flora-Fauna	1838	Fownes. Kendrick	1713
Fitzwilliam. 1st Earl	1716	Flora-Fauna	1844	Fownes. Sir William	1707
Fitzwilliam. 1st Earl	1716	Flora-Fauna	1845	Fox. John	1991
Fitzwilliam. 1st Earl	1719	Flora-Fauna	1853	Fox. Mildred	1971
Fitzwilliam. 2nd Earl	1718	Flora-Fauna	1886	Frame. David	1925

Section Three: Index

A-Z Reference	Year
Free Mason's Hall	1903
French School Bray	1864
French School Bray	1960
French School Bray	1964
French. Percy	1890
French. Percy	1920
French. Robert	1841
French. Robert	1860
French. Robert	1862
French. Robert	1863
French. Robert	1863
French. Robert	1917
French. Susan	1891
Furlong	1881
Gaelscoil	1994
Gaelscoil	1996
Gaelscoil	1998
Gaffeney & Rice	1976
Gaffnet & Rice	2004
Gahan	1800
Galtrim House	1984
Galvin. Rev Richard	1878
Garland. Donald Edward	1918
Garland. Donald Edward	1940
Garland. Donald Edward	1940
Garvin. John	1945
Genealogy Service	1987
General Election	1992
GFS	1875
GFS	1877
GFS	1891
Gillis. Alan	1994
Gladstone. William	1877
Gladstone. William	1877
Gladstone. William	1877
Glanmore Castle	1928
Glass Factory	1950
Glen Mill Golf Club	1996
Glen of Imaal	1803
Glen of Imaal	1900
Glen of Imaal	1905
Glen of Imaal	1909
Glen of Imaal	1912
Glen of Imaal	1922
Glen of Imaal	1922
Glen of Imaal	1941
Glen of Imaal	1946

A-Z Reference	Year
Glen of Imaal	1955
Glen of Imaal	1977
Glen of Imaal	1979
Glen of Imaal Terrier	1933
Glen of Imaal Terrier	1934
Glen of Imaal Terrier	1975
Glen of Imaal Terrier	1987
Glen of Imaal Terrier	1994
Glen of the Downes	1552
Glen of the Downes	1905
Glen of the Downes	1906
Glen of the Downes	1996
Glen of the Downes	1998
Glen of the Downes	1999
Glenart Castle	1750
Glenart Castle	1869
Glenart Castle	1886
Glenart Castle	1921
Glenart Castle	1947
Glenbride Lodge	1970
Glencap	1557
Glencap	1557
Glencormac United F.C.	1999
Glencree	1244
Glencree	1280
Glencree	1296
Glencree	1305
Glencree	1849
Glencree	1858
Glencree	1945
Glencree	1959
Glencree	1998
Glencree	2005
Glencree	2005
Glencree Barracks	1803
Glencree Peace Centre	1974
Glendalough	617
Glendalough	618
Glendalough	1061
Glendalough	1084
Glendalough	1846
Glendalough	1849
Glendalough	1876
Glendalough	1876
Glendalough	1914
Glendalough	1957
Glendalough	1965

A-Z Reference	Year
Glendalough	1988
Glendalough Hostel	1935
Glendalough House	1880
Glendalough School	1836
Glendalough School	1850
Glenealy	1792
Glenealy	1799
Glenealy School	1867
Glenealy. St. Josephs	1869
Glenmalure	1599
Glenmalure	1934
Glenmalure Hostel	1955
Glenmalure, Battle of	1580
Glenmama. Battle of	998
Glenroe	1983
Glor na Gael	1968
Godkin. Edwin	1831
Golf Championship	1980
Goodwin. William	1741
Goodwin. William	1742
Goowdin. Simon	1720
Gordon Bennett Race	1903
Gore. Robert	1795
Gore. Robert	1798
Goulding. Basil Sir	1909
Goulding. Basil Sir	1982
Goulding. Valerie	1918
Goulding. Valerie	1951
Goulding. Valerie	1977
Goulding. Valerie	2003
Goulet. Yann Renard	1914
Goulet. Yann Renard	1947
Goulet. Yann Renard	1956
Goulet. Yann Renard	1959
Goulet. Yann Renard	1972
Goulet. Yann Renard	1982
Goulet. Yann Renard	1999
Goulet. Yann Renard	1999
Graham. Thomas	1672
Grand Hotel	1896
Grand Jury	1606
Grand Jury	1634
Grand Jury	1712
Grand Jury	1813
Grand Jury	1817
Grattan Harriet	1836
Grattan Harriet	1865

A-Z Reference	Year	A-Z Reference	Year	A-Z Reference	Year
Grattan Mary Anne	1834	Grey Fort	1934	Guinness. Anne	1899
Grattan Mary Anne	1853	Greystones	1855	Guinness. P. W	1875
Grattan. Catherine	1767	Greystones	1860	Guinness. P. W	1948
Grattan. Henry	1746	Greystones	1864	Guinness. R. W.	1837
Grattan. Henry	1772	Greystones	1870	Guinness. R. W.	1919
Grattan. Henry	1775	Greystones	1894	Gun. George	1818
Grattan. Henry	1782	Greystones	1895	Gypsy Moth III	1960
Grattan. Henry	1782	Greystones	1901	Hacketstown	1789
Grattan. Henry	1790	Greystones	1903	Hacketstown	1819
Grattan. Henry	1797	Greystones	1908	Hackett Hall	1889
Grattan. Henry	1800	Greystones	1909	Hackett. John	1663
Grattan. Henry	1800	Greystones	1910	Hagan. John	1874
Grattan. Henry	1805	Greystones	1922	Hagan. John	1904
Grattan. Henry	1806	Greystones	1936	Hagan. John	1919
Grattan. Henry	1817	Greystones	1940	Hagan. John	1930
Grattan. Henry	1820	Greystones	1947	Halpin. James	1847
Grattan. Henry	1820	Greystones	1950	Halpin. Robert	2003
Grattan. Henry	1822	Greystones	1964	Halpin.Robert Charles	1836
Grattan. Henry	1839	Greystones	1969	Halpin.Robert Charles	1869
Grattan. Henry	1875	Greystones	1983	Halpin.Robert Charles	1894
Grattan. Henry	1876	Greystones	1985	Halpin.Robert Charles	1897
Grattan. Henry	1880	Greystones	2001	Hamilton. Archibald	1787
Grattan. Henry Jnr	1789	Greystones	2002	Hamilton. Gladys Mary	1880
Grattan. Henry Jnr	1826	Greystones	2002	Hamilton. Gladys Mary	1902
Grattan. Henry Jnr	1859	Greystones	2002	Hamilton. Gladys Mary	1917
Grattan. James	1761	Greystones	2004	Handball	1930
Grattan. James	1766	Greystones Golf Club	1895	Handball	1931
Grattan. Lady Laura	1888	Greystones Golf Club	1985	Hanley. Daniel	1892
Grattan. Mary	1768	Greystones Golf Club	1990	Hanlon. Andrew	1966
Grattan. Rt.Hon.James	1847	Greystones Golf Club	1992	Harbour	1982
Grattan. Rt.Hon.James	1852	Greystones Golf Club	1995	Harmon	1866
Grattan. Rt.Hon.James	1854	Greystones Golf Club	1996	Harmon	1936
Gray. Sir John	1815	Greystones Rugby Club	1937	Harold. Thomas	1374
Gray. Sir John	1841	Greystones Rugby Club	1944	Harrington. Sir Henry	1574
Gray. Sir John	1863	Greystones Rugby Club	1999	Harristown	1768
Gray. Sir John	1868	Greystones School	1949	Hart, Henry C.	1847
Gray. Sir John	1875	Greystones United F.C.	1979	Hart, Henry C.	1908
Graydon. Robert	1703	Griffin. Victor	1924	Harty.H.H	1879
Green. Christy	1926	Griffin. Victor	1968	Harty.H.H	1894
Green. Christy	1997	Griffith's Valuation	1852	Harty.H.H	1901
Green. Harry Plunket	1865	Griffith's Valuation	1855	Harty.H.H	1904
Green. Harry Plunket	1936	Griffith's Valuation	1855	Harty.H.H	1920
Greenan Bottle Museum	1985	Griffith's Valuation	1855	Harty.H.H	1925
Grehan. Sir Richard	1618	Group Water Scheme	1958	Harty.H.H	1941
Grehan. Sir Richard	1619	Guinness	1876	Haskins. James	1843
Grehan. Sir Richard	1620	Guinness	1910	Haskins. James	1843
Grene. W.F	1804	Guinness	1936	Hassells. Dorothea	1643

Section Three: Index

A-Z Reference	Year
Hassells. Dorothea	1684
Hassells. Robert	1661
Hatton. Bridget	1898
Hatton. Jimmy	1962
Hatton. Jimmy	1963
Hatton. Jimmy	1964
Hatton. Jimmy	1965
Hatton. Jimmy	1966
Hatton. Jimmy	1966
Hatton. Jimmy	1966
Hatton. Jimmy	1967
Hatton. Jimmy	1970
Hatton. Jimmy	1970
Haughton's	1920
Hawkins. Sir William	1783
Hawkshead. Thomas	1730
Hayden. Alexander	1682
Hayes. John	1716
Hayes. John	1737
Hayes. Samuel	1773
Hayes. Samuel	1788
Hayes. Samuel	1788
Hayes. Samuel	1792
Hayes. Samuel	1794
Hayes. Seamus	1977
Health	1816
Health	1832
Health	1833
Health	1836
Health	1845
Health	1903
Health	1922
Health	1935
Health Association	1907
Healy. James	1824
Healy. James	1894
Healy. John	1873
Healy. John	1921
Healy. P.T	1942
Heaney. Seamus	1939
Heaney. Seamus	1972
Heaney. Seamus	1995
Heatley. Elizabeth	1977
Heighington. John	1729
Heighington. William	1803
Hempenstall. Edward	1766
Hempenstall. Edward	1797

A-Z Reference	Year
Hempenstall. Edward	1801
Hempenstall. Edward	1810
Henderson. Brian	1950
Henderson. Brian	1969
Henderson. Brian	1970
Hennessy. Henry	1826
Hennessy. Henry	1901
Henniker. Sir John	1800
Henniker. Sir John	1803
Henry. Grace	1868
Henry. Grace	1903
Henry. Grace	1953
Henry. Paul	1876
Henry. Paul	1953
Henry. Paul	1958
Henry. Paul	1974
Henry. Paul	1996
Henry. Paul	2002
Herbert Road	1856
Heritage Centre	1985
Heritage Centre	1993
Herman Molls Map	1714
Herrings	1754
Hewat. Richard	1940
Heyden. Alexander	1676
Hickey. John	1756
Hickey. John	1795
Higginbottam. Edward	1829
Higgins. Adian	1927
Higgins. John	1976
Hill. Arthur-3rd	1811
Hill. Trevor	1693
Hill. Trevor	1717
Hill. Willis	1718
Hill. Willis	1747
Hill. Willis	1768
Hill. Willis	1789
Hill. Willis	1793
Hill. Arthur-2nd	1753
Hill. Arthur-2nd	1786
Hill. Arthur-2nd	1801
Hill. Arthur-3rd	1788
Hill. Arthur-3rd	1845
Hill. Arthur-4th	1812
Hill. Arthur-4th	1837
Hill. Arthur-4th	1868
Hill. Arthur-5th	1844

A-Z Reference	Year
Hill. Arthur-5th	1870
Hill. Arthur-5th	1874
Hill. Arthur-6th	1871
Hill. Arthur-6th	1893
Hill. Arthur-6th	1918
Hill. Arthur-7th	1894
Hill. Arthur-7th	1953
Hill. Moyes	1573
Hime. Sir Albert H.	1842
Hime. Sir Albert H.	1886
Hime. Sir Albert H.	1899
Hime. Sir Albert H.	1900
Hime. Sir Albert H.	1902
Hime. Sir Albert H.	1902
Hime. Sir Albert H.	1919
Hinton. John	1695
Historical Society	1977
Historical Society	1985
Historical Society	1986
Historical Society	1990
Historical Society	2001
Historical Society	2004
Hodson	1686
Hodson	1713
Hodson	1721
Hodson	1740
Hodson	1750
Hodson	1757
Hodson	1759
Hodson	1768
Hodson	1780
Hodson	1789
Hodson	1799
Hodson	1802
Hodson	1806
Hodson	1809
Hodson	1809
Hodson	1815
Hodson	1831
Hodson	1839
Hodson	1852
Hodson	1853
Hodson	1854
Hodson	1856
Hodson	1859
Hodson	1863
Hodson	1879

A-Z Reference	Year	A-Z Reference	Year	A-Z Reference	Year
Hodson	1888	Homicide in Ireland	1991	Howard. Ralph	1749
Hodson	1892	Honan. Thomas	1993	Howard. Robert	1683
Hodson	1893	Honner. Thomas	2001	Howard. Robert	1726
Hodson	1895	Hopper. Nora	1871	Howard. Robert	1729
Hodson	1900	Hopper. Nora	1890	Howard. Robert	1740
Hodson	1900	Hopper. Nora	1901	Howard. Robert	1813
Hodson	1906	Hopper. Nora	1906	Howard. Sir Ralph	1853
Hodson	1911	Horndrige. Richard	1789	Hugo. Thomas	1796
Hodson	1915	Hornridge. George	1824	Hugo. Thomas	1823
Hodson	1921	Hornridge. John	1814	Hume. Dennison	1761
Hodson	1928	Hospital	1985	Hume. W.H.	1772
Hodson	1932	Hospital. Fever	1818	Hume. W.H.	1804
Hodson	1934	Housing	1860	Hume. W.H.	1815
Hodson	1934	Housing	1861	Hume. W.H.	1864
Hodson. George	1851	Housing	1861	Hume. William	1728
Hodson. Laurence	1681	Housing	1863	Hume. William	1747
Hodson. Laurence	1719	Housing	1863	Hume. William	1769
Hodson. Richard	1843	Housing	1897	Hume. William	1798
Hodson. Robert	1786	Housing	1909	Hume. William.H	1896
Hodson. Sir R.A	1891	Housing	1932	Hume. William. W.F	1805
Hodson. Sir Robert	1825	Housing	1935	Hume. William. W.F	1845
Hodson. Sir. G.F	1834	Housing	1935	Hume. William. W.F	1892
Hoey. Francis	1817	Housing	1939	Humewood Castle	1866
Hoey. John	1701	Housing	1948	Humewood Castle	1867
Hoey. Robert	1757	Housing	1962	Humewood Castle	1992
Hoey. W.P	1832	Housing	1977	Humphreys. C.F.	1818
Hoey. William	1684	Housing	1980	Humphreys. C.F.	1848
Hoey. William	1694	Housing	1980	Humphreys. C.F.	1895
Hollybrook House	1834	Housing	1985	Hussey. Gemma	1939
Hollybrooke House	1969	Housing	1989	Hussey. Gemma	1977
Hollywood	1640	Housing	1989	Hussey. Gemma	1982
Hollywood N.S.	1955	Housing	1997	Hussey. Gemma	1982
Holt. Ester	1827	Housing	2004	Hussey. Gemma	1986
Holt. Joseph	1762	Howard. Catherine	1831	Hussey. Gemma	1987
Holt. Joseph	1798	Howard. Catherine	1854	Hutchinsion, Sir. F.	1783
Holt. Joseph	1798	Howard. Catherine	1855	Hutchinson. Daniel	1657
Holt. Joseph	1826	Howard. Catherine	1864	Hutchinson. F.S	1830
Holy Redeemer, Bray	1824	Howard. Catherine	1882	Hutchinson. Sir. F.	1783
Holy Redeemer, Bray	1850	Howard. Hugh	1675	Hynes. Frank	1971
Holy Redeemer, Bray	1854	Howard. Hugh	1738	Hynes. Frank	1974
Holy Redeemer, Bray	1896	Howard. John	1636	Hynes. Frank	1980
Holy Redeemer, Bray	1914	Howard. John	1643	Hynes. Frank	1986
Holy Redeemer, Bray	1939	Howard. Katherine	1693	Hynes. Frank	1989
Holy Redeemer, Bray	1961	Howard. Katherine	1720	ICA	1951
Holy Redeemer, Bray	1980	Howard. Ralph	1668	IFI	1987
Holy Redeemer, Bray	1980	Howard. Ralph	1697	IFI	2002
Holy Redeemer, Bray	2003	Howard. Ralph	1710	Imports/Exports	1837

Section Three: Index

A-Z Reference	Year
Imports/Exports	1837
Industrial School	1902
Industrial Yarns	1958
Industrial Yarns	1998
Infirmary County	1766
Inglis. Henry D	1795
Inglis. Henry D	1820
Inglis. Henry D	1834
Inglis. Henry D	1835
Inquiry	1845
International Hotel	1862
International Hotel	1862
International Hotel	1865
International Hotel	1914
International Hotel	1919
International Hotel	1974
International Hotel	1990
INTO	1868
Iornworks	1638
Iredall. Benjamin	1706
Ireland	1741
Ireland	1816
Ireland	1835
Ireland	1916
Ireland	1941
Irish Mile	1826
Irish Naturalist	1896
Irish Penny Magazine	1841
Ironworks	1635
Ironworks	1641
Ironworks	1756
Ivers. M	1909
J. Pigot's Directory	1824
Jackman. Joseph	1916
Jackman. Joseph	1941
Jackman. Joseph	1942
Jackman. Joseph	1942
Jacob. Joe	1993
Jenney. C	1703
John Quin (Elder)	1852
Johnston. Brian	1984
Johnston. Jennifer	1979
Jones. George	1984
Jones. George	1987
Jones. George	1990
Jones. George	2000
Jones. Kenneth	1983

A-Z Reference	Year
Jones. Kenneth	1983
Jones. Kenneth	1984
Jones. Kenneth	1987
Jones. Kenneth	1991
Jones. Kenneth	1991
Jones. Owen	1700
Jones. Theophilus	1661
Jones. William	1864
Jones. William	1864
Jones. William	1864
Jones. William	1864
Jordan. Eddie	1948
Joyce, Eileen	1889
Joyce, Eva	1891
Joyce, Family	1887
Joyce, Family	1891
Joyce, George Alfred	1887
Joyce, George Alfred	1887
Joyce, Mary	1890
Joyce, James	1888
Joyce, James	1909
Joyce, James	1941
Kane. Daniel	1922
Kavanagh. Liam	1977
Kavanagh. Liam	1983
Kavanagh. Liam	1998
Kavanagh. Mark	1945
Kay. Dorothy	1866
Kay. Dorothy	1964
Keane. Joseph B	1859
Kearney. Teresa	1875
Kearney. Teresa	1898
Kearney. Teresa	1917
Kearney. Teresa	1923
Kearney. Teresa	1928
Kearney. Teresa	1935
Kearney. Teresa	1952
Kearney. Teresa	1954
Kearney. Teresa	1957
Kearon and Tyrrell	1873
Keegan. Charlie	1964
Keegan. Charlie	2003
Keegan. Claire	1969
Keenan. Tom	1985
Keenan. Tom	1988
Kelleher. John	1912
Kelleher. John	1937

A-Z Reference	Year
Kelleher. John	1989
Kelly. Alan	1936
Kelly. Alan	1955
Kelly. Alan	1956
Kelly. Alan	1956
Kelly. Alan	1957
Kelly. Alan	1958
Kelly. Alan	1972
Kelly. Alan	1980
Kelly. Alan	1983
Kelly. John	1948
Kemmis. William	1777
Kemmis. William	1806
Kemmis. William	1833
Kemmis. William	1864
Kemmis. William	1881
Kennedy. George	1590
Kennedy. Mrs. J.F.	1967
Kennedy. Rev	1926
Kennedy. Robert	1643
Kennedy. Robert	1686
Kenny. William	1981
Kiernan. Kitty	1892
Kiernan. Kitty	1925
Kiernan. Kitty	1945
Kiernan. Thomas	1855
Kilbride	1834
Kilbride, Bray	1857
Kilbride, Bray	1874
Kilbride, Bray	1893
Kilcaarra House	1888
Kilcommon Parish	1776
Kilcoole	1861
Kilcoole	1913
Kilcoole	1914
Kilcoole	1915
Kilcoole	1930
Kilcoole	1930
Kilcoole	1960
Kilcoole	1966
Kilcoole	1968
Kilcoole Golf Club	1992
Kilcroney	1650
Kilcroney	1890
Kilcroney	1927
Kilcroney	1949
Kilcroney	1955

The County Wicklow Database: 432 AD to 2006 AD

A-Z Reference	Year	A-Z Reference	Year	A-Z Reference	Year
Kilcroney	1956	Kippure	1959	La Touche	1788
Kildare	1296	Kippure	1961	La Touche	1789
Killincarrig	1649	Kippure	1961	La Touche	1791
Killincarrig	1833	Kippure	1961	La Touche	1792
Killiskey School	1857	Kish Lighthouse	1811	La Touche	1797
Killruddery	1645	Kish Lighthouse	1842	La Touche	1801
Killruddery	1651	Kish Lighthouse	1954	La Touche	1803
Killruddery	1830	Kish Lighthouse	1963	La Touche	1806
Killruddery	1848	Kish Lighthouse	1965	La Touche	1817
Killruddery	1852	Kish Lighthouse	1965	La Touche	1822
Killruddery	1868	Kish Lighthouse	1965	La Touche	1830
Killruddery	1890	Kish Lighthouse	1992	La Touche	1830
Killruddery	1978	Kish Lighthouse	1996	La Touche	1838
Killruddery	1982	Knockanarrigan	1884	La Touche	1845
Kilmacanogue	1824	Knocksink Wood	2005	La Touche	1857
Kilmacanogue	1864	Knocksink, Enniskerry	1992	La Touche	1860
Kilmacanogue	1950	Knox. Arthur	1791	La Touche	1861
Kilmacanogue	1967	Knox. Charles	1817	La Touche	1867
Kilmacanogue	1974	Knox. Edmond	1811	La Touche	1874
Kilmacanogue	1985	Knox. John	1809	La Touche	1882
Kilmacanogue	1987	Kyan. John Howard	1774	La Touche	1889
Kilmacoo N.S.	1933	Kyan. John Howard	1804	La Touche	1892
Kilmacurragh House	1697	Kyan. John Howard	1832	La Touche	1892
Kilmacurragh House	1848	Kyan. John Howard	1833	La Touche	1897
Kilmacurragh House	1944	Kyan. John Howard	1850	La Touche	1899
Kilpedder	1796	Kynoch of Arklow	1895	La Touche	1900
Kilquade	1802	Kynoch of Arklow	1917	La Touche	1902
Kilquade	1802	La Touche	1632	La Touche	1904
Kiltegan	1932	La Touche	1671	La Touche	1904
Kilternan	1904	La Touche	1690	La Touche	1906
Kilternan	1987	La Touche	1699	La Touche	1908
Kiltimon Castle	1550	La Touche	1704	La Touche	1913
Kinch. Michael	1950	La Touche	1716	La Touche	1920
King. Cecil	1921	La Touche	1725	La Touche	1922
King. Cecil	1986	La Touche	1729	La Touche	1925
King. Damiel M	1816	La Touche	1745	La Touche	1930
King. John	1674	La Touche	1747	La Touche	1935
King. John	1693	La Touche	1753	La Touche	1971
King. Thomas	1793	La Touche	1756	La Touche	1997
King. William	1792	La Touche	1761	La Touche	1998
Kinsella. Tommy	1906	La Touche	1762	La Touché	1764
Kinsella. Tommy	1917	La Touche	1766	Labourers Association	1917
Kinsella. Tommy	1998	La Touche	1785	Lackan	1811
Kinsella. Tommy	1999	La Touche	1785	Lacken School	1869
Kinsella. Tommy	2001	La Touche	1786	Lamb. Charles Vincent	1893
Kiosks	1935	La Touche	1788	Lamb. Charles Vincent	1964
Kippure	1959	La Touche	1788	Lamb. Charles Vincent	2001

Section Three: Index

A-Z Reference	Year
Land Commission	1881
Land League	1881
Land League	1881
Land League, Ladies	1881
Land Use	1840
Landscape Painting	1957
Laragh	1867
Laragh	1953
Laragh	1956
Laragh Church	1846
Laragh School	1840
Large. R.G	1971
Large. R.G	1985
Larkin. James	1969
Lawless. Hugh	1314
Lawlor. Hugh Jackson	1860
Lawlor. Hugh Jackson	1898
Lawlor. Hugh Jackson	1938
Lawlor. Michael	1994
Lawrence. William	1840
Lawrence. William	1865
Lawrence. William	1866
Lawrence. William	1880
Lawrence. William	1932
LDF/FCA	1941
LDF/FCA	1946
Le Brocquy. Louis	1916
Le Brocquy. Louis	2000
Le Fanu. William R.	1857
Le Fanu. William R.	1857
Le Fanu. William R.	1894
Le Fanu. Henry	1870
Le Fanu. Henry	1894
Le Fanu. Henry	1899
Le Fanu. Henry	1905
Le Fanu. Henry	1915
Le Fanu. Henry	1935
Le Fanu. Margery	1926
Le Faun. Henry	1904
Ledwidge. Peter	1950
Lee. Walter	1811
Lee. Walter	1861
Lee. Walter	1893
Lees. Kilcoole	1855
Leeson	1701
Leeson	1730
Leeson	1735

A-Z Reference	Year
Leeson	1756
Leeson	1760
Leeson	1763
Leeson	1783
Leeson	1799
Leeson	1801
Leeson	1807
Leeson	1835
Leeson	1837
Leeson	1866
Leeson	1871
Leeson	1890
Leeson	1891
Leeson. Anne	1814
LeFoy. Thomas	1860
Lefroy. Anthony Thomas	1839
Leigh. Edward	1623
Leland. Dr. Thomas	1722
Leland. Dr. Thomas	1767
Leland. Dr. Thomas	1773
Leland. Dr. Thomas	1773
Leland. Dr. Thomas	1785
Leland. Dr. Thomas	1865
Leland. Dr. Thomas	1913
Lemonstown	1818
Leslie. Charles	1766
Lewins. Phil	1818
Lewins. Phil	1818
Library. Bray	1911
Library. Bray	1911
Library. Bray	1945
Library. Bray	1953
Library. Bray	1984
Library. Bray	1986
Library. Bray	2000
Library. County	1927
Library. County	2000
Library. Greystones	1910
Life Saving	1888
Life Saving	1888
Life Saving	1893
Life Saving	1893
Life Saving	1899
Life Saving	1900
Life Saving	1905
Lifeboats	1826
Lifeboats	1830

A-Z Reference	Year
Lifeboats	1851
Lifeboats	1856
Lifeboats	1856
Lifeboats	1857
Lifeboats	1857
Lifeboats	1857
Lifeboats	1857
Lifeboats	1857
Lifeboats	1857
Lifeboats	1864
Lifeboats	1866
Lifeboats	1866
Lifeboats	1867
Lifeboats	1870
Lifeboats	1870
Lifeboats	1871
Lifeboats	1872
Lifeboats	1872
Lifeboats	1872
Lifeboats	1873
Lifeboats	1876
Lifeboats	1886
Lifeboats	1888
Lifeboats	1888
Lifeboats	1894
Lifeboats	1896
Lifeboats	1911
Lifeboats	1911
Lifeboats	1912
Lifeboats	1915
Lifeboats	1916
Lifeboats	1937
Lifeboats	1938
Lifeboats	1938
Lifeboats	1938
Lifeboats	1950
Lifeboats	1950
Lifeboats	1956
Lifeboats	1956
Lifeboats	1957
Lifeboats	1967
Lifeboats	1970
Lifeboats	1986
Lifeboats	1988
Lifeboats	1989
Lifeboats	1995
Lifeboats	1997

The County Wicklow Database: 432 AD to 2006 AD

A-Z Reference	Year	A-Z Reference	Year	A-Z Reference	Year
Lighthouse	1781	Lowe. Christopher	1740	Maguire. Thomas	1912
Lighthouse	1818	Lowe. Christopher	1771	Mail	1764
Lighthouse	1836	Lowe. Christopher	1803	Mail	1794
Lighthouse	1866	Lube. Andrew	1823	Mail Coach	1790
Lighthouse	1868	Lucas's Directory	1788	Mail Coach	1805
Lighthouse	1906	Luganure Mine	1807	Mail Coaches	1789
Lighthouse	1976	Luganure Mine	1825	Main Street	1850
Lighthouse	1994	Luganure Mine	1826	Malone. J.B.	1989
Lighting	1857	Luganure Mine	1834	Malynn. James Joseph	1920
Lightship	1865	Luganure Mine	1857	Malynn. James Joseph	1920
Lightship	1867	Luganure Mine	1857	Mangin. Edward	1800
Lightship	1867	Luganure Mine	1861	Manifold. Francis	1840
Lightship	1867	Luganure Mine	1890	Manor Kilbride	1833
Litographic	1997	Luganure Road	1826	Manor Kilbride	1836
Little Bray	2005	Luggala	1790	Manor Kilbride	1864
Little Flower Hall	1880	Luggala	1793	Map	1837
Liverpool Cathedral	1934	Luggala	1937	Maps	1610
Lloyd. Humphrey	1800	Luggala	1950	Maps	1760
Lloyd. Humphrey	1850	Luggala	1956	Maps	1760
Lloyd. Humphrey	1862	Lugnaquilla Walk	1886	Maps	1833
Lloyd. Humphrey	1865	Lugnaquilla Walk	1927	Maps	1838
Lloyd. Humphrey	1867	Lugnaquilla Walk	1976	Maps	1840
Local Government	1990	Lyon. John	1746	Maps	1853
Loftus. Edward	1645	M.P's	1918	Maps	1855
Loftus. John	1669	M.P's for Wicklow	1880	Maps	1858
Loftus. Samuel	1633	Mackintosh. C. Herbert	1843	Maps	1870
Loreto Convent Bray	1834	Mackintosh. C. Herbert	1864	Maps	1871
Loreto Convent Bray	1850	Mackintosh. C. Herbert	1865	Maps	1878
Loreto Convent Bray	1850	Mackintosh. C. Herbert	1868	Maps	1885
Loreto Convent Bray	1851	Mackintosh. C. Herbert	1871	Maps	1886
Loreto Convent Bray	1956	Mackintosh. C. Herbert	1873	Maps	1887
Loreto Convent Bray	1971	Mackintosh. C. Herbert	1873	Maps	1895
Loreto Convent Bray	2000	Mackintosh. C. Herbert	1882	Maps	1896
Loreto Convent Bray	2001	Mackintosh. C. Herbert	1882	Maps	1901
Loreto Convent Bray	2001	Mackintosh. C. Herbert	1893	Maps	1908
Lotto	1988	Mackintosh. C. Herbert	1908	Maps	1981
Lough Bray	1813	Mackintosh. C. Herbert	1931	Maps	1998
Lough Dan	1952	Mackintosh. C.H.	1820	Maps	2000
Lough Dan	1982	Mackintosh. C.H.	1843	Maps	2000
Loughlinstown	1837	Mackintosh. C.H.	1896	Marine Hotel. Wicklow	1859
Loughlinstown	1841	Mackintosh. C.H.	1896	Marine House	1842
Loughlinstown Hospital	1952	MacMahon. John	1982	Marino Clinic, Bray	1982
Loughlinstown Hospital	1980	Madden. Richard	1798	Marisco. Geoffery de	1260
Loughman. Joe	1999	Madden. Richard	1855	Marissa. Jordan de	1190
Louth Militia	1798	Madden. Richard	1886	Markets	1666
Lovett. John	1704	Maguire. Brian	1951	Marlborough Hall	1898
Lovett. Richard	1888	Maguire. Peter	1960	Marley Park	1972

Section Three: Index

A-Z Reference	Year
Marley Park	1975
Marriage Rate	1911
Marriages	2002
Marsden. William	1754
Marsden. William	1783
Marsden. William	1795
Marsden. William	1812
Marsden. William	1825
Marsden. William	1834
Marsden. William	1836
Martello	1804
Martello Terrace	1865
Martial Law	1798
Martin. Colbert	1980
Mason. G.H. Monck	1824
Mason. G.H. Monck	1842
Mason. G.H. Monck	1857
Masonic Lodge	1870
Masonic Lodge	1870
Masonic Lodge	1910
Massy. Anne L.	1867
Massy. Anne L.	1931
Mathew. John	1305
Matthew. Fr	1842
Matthew. Fr	1845
Matthews. William	1662
Matthews. William	1693
Maxtor	1990
Mc Alinden	1968
Mc Mahon J. H.	1890
Mc Mahon. Ella	1928
McAnally. Ray	1926
McAnally. Ray	1989
McCabe. Peter	1981
McCabe. Peter	1999
McCann. W.J.	1996
McCarthy. John	1977
McCarthy. Joseph	1817
McCoan. J. C.	1880
McCoan. J. C.	1880
McCormack. William	1947
McCormack. William	1947
McCormack. William	1970
McCormack. William	1976
McCormack. William	1982
McCormack. William	1983
McCormack. William	1985

A-Z Reference	Year
McCormack. William	1985
McCormack. William	1986
McCormack. William	1993
McCormack. William	1993
McCormack. William	1994
McCormick. William	1797
McCrea. John J.	1944
McCrea. John J.	1960
McDermott.J.E.	1933
McGuckian. Mary	1963
McHugh. Eugene	2003
McManus Liz	1947
McManus Liz	1990
McManus Liz	1994
McManus Liz	2002
McNaughton. Paul	1978
McShane. Paul	1986
McShane. Paul	2002
Meade. Anne	1788
Meade. Anne	1826
Meade. Joseph	1891
Meagan. Peter	1200
Meath Hospital	1770
Meath Hospital	1774
Meath Hospital	1822
Meath Hospital	1998
Meath Road	1883
Meath Road, Bray	1870
Meath. Lady	1881
Meceedy. Ralph	1912
Mecredy. Rev James	1820
Mecredy. Rev James	1874
Mecredy. Richard J.	1861
Mecredy. Richard J.	1882
Mecredy. Richard J.	1882
Mecredy. Richard J.	1887
Mecredy. Richard J.	1890
Mecredy. Richard J.	1890
Mecredy. Richard J.	1890
Mecredy. Richard J.	1891
Mecredy. Richard J.	1900
Mecredy. Richard J.	1924
Medical officer	1925
Melifont Hotel	1988
Messitt. Bertie	1960
Miami Showband	1975
Miley. Jim	1976

A-Z Reference	Year
Miley. Jim	1982
Miley. John J	1859
Miley. John J	1859
Miley. John J	1861
Military	1760
Military	1795
Military	1795
Military	1795
Military	1795
Military	1796
Military	1796
Military	1797
Military	1797
Military	1797
Military	1797
Military	1797
Military	1797
Military	1798
Military	1798
Military	1798
Military	1798
Military	1798
Military	1798
Military	1800
Military	1805
Military	1807
Military	1807
Military	1808
Military	1808
Military	1811
Military	1815
Military Road	1170
Military Road	1800
Military Road	1800
Military Road	1802
Military Road	1802
Military Road	1802
Military Road	1809
Military Road	1842
Militia Act 1809	1809
Millward Terrace	1864
Milne. Charles Ewart	1903
Milne. Charles Ewart	1987
Mining	1638
Mining	1756
Mining	1765
Mining	1837

A-Z Reference	Year	A-Z Reference	Year	A-Z Reference	Year
Mining	1930	Monck. Charles	1861	Moriarity. Andrew	1941
Mining	1956	Monck. Charles	1867	Moriarty. Andrew	1952
Mining Accident	1825	Monck. Charles	1870	Morrison. Sir Richard	1767
Mining Accident	1864	Monck. Charles	1881	Morrison. Sir Richard	1849
Mining Accident	1874	Monck. Charles	1894	Mortell. Mark	1961
Mining Co. of Ireland	1824	Monck. Emily	1818	Mound	1893
Mining Company	1950	Monck. Emily	1837	Mount Kennedy House	1710
Mitchelburne. Richard	1717	Monck. Henry	1746	Mount Kennedy House	1769
Molyneux. Sir Thomas	1661	Monck. Hon. Henry	1887	Mount Kennedy House	1772
Molyneux. Sir Thomas	1715	Monck. Viscount	1801	Mount Kennedy House	1782
Molyneux. Sir Thomas	1718	Moneystown	1888	Mount Kennedy House	1784
Molyneux. Sir Thomas	1733	Montague. Daniel	1867	Mount Kennedy House	1801
Molyneux. Thomas	1642	Montague. Daniel	1898	Mount Kennedy House	1928
Monck	1705	Montague. Daniel	1898	Mount Kennedy House	1930
Monck	1754	Montague. Daniel	1899	Mount Kennedy House	1938
Monck	1784	Montague. Daniel	1899	Mount Kennedy House	1971
Monck	1785	Montague. Daniel	1912	Mount Usher	1980
Monck	1791	Montigny	1994	Mountain Rescue	1960
Monck	1797	Moore. Fletcher	1894	Mountain Rescue	1985
Monck	1800	Moore. J.S	1865	Mountain Rescue	1997
Monck	1801	Moore. James	1673	Mountain Rescue	1999
Monck	1802	Moore. James	1933	Mountain Rescue	2000
Monck	1806	Moore. James	1956	Mountain Rescue	2002
Monck	1817	Moore. James	1957	Moyne Church	1815
Monck	1822	Moore. James	1995	Mozeen. Thomas	1744
Monck	1823	Moore. James	2005	Mozeen. Thomas	1768
Monck	1843	Moore. John	1798	Mr What	1958
Monck	1843	Moore. Seamus	1940	Mucklagh N.S.	1938
Monck	1844	Moore. Thomas	1779	Mulcare. P	1971
Monck	1848	Moore. Thomas	1803	Mulcare. P	1972
Monck	1849	Moore. Thomas	1811	Muldoon. John	1905
Monck	1849	Moore. Thomas	1852	Muldoon. John	1907
Monck	1866	Moorhead. Dr. Thomas G	1960	Muldoon. John	1911
Monck	1874	Moorhead. Dr. Thomas G.	1878	Mulligan. Rev	1986
Monck	1892	Moorhead. Dr. Thomas G.	1894	Mulso. Sir Edward	1450
Monck	1905	Moorhead. Dr. Thomas G.	1905	Mulso. Sir Edward	1463
Monck	1927	Moorhead. Dr. Thomas G.	1906	Murder	2003
Monck	1929	Moorhead. Dr. Thomas G.	1907	Murder	2005
Monck	1951	Moorhead. Dr. Thomas G.	1910	Murder	2005
Monck	1953	Moorhead. Dr. Thomas G.	1918	Murphy. Ciaran	1979
Monck	1982	Moorhead. Dr. Thomas G.	1926	Murphy. James	1839
Monck Family	1939	Moorhead. Dr. Thomas G.	1933	Murphy. James	1847
Monck Family Estates	1887	Moorhead. Dr. Thomas G.	1935	Murphy. James	1853
Monck Family Estates	1903	Moorhead. Dr. Thomas G.	1938	Murphy. James	1855
Monck. Baron	1797	Moorhead. Dr. Thomas G.	1960	Murphy. James	1864
Monck. Charles	1794	Moran. Joe	1991	Murphy. James	1913
Monck. Charles	1819	Morgan. Major	1567	Murphy. Matt	1983

Section Three: Index

A–Z Reference	Year
Murphy. Michael	1898
Murphy. William	1960
Murphy. William	1964
Murray. Andrew	1780
Murray. Daniel	1768
Murray. Daniel	1792
Murray. Daniel	1823
Murray. Daniel	1825
Murray. Daniel	1852
Nairne. Carolina	1766
Nairne. Carolina	1806
Nairne. Carolina	1830
Nairne. Carolina	1845
Nairne. William	1830
Napoleonic Wars	1815
National Archives	1738
National Archives	1822
National Archives	1831
National Archives	1843
National Archives	1847
National Archives	1922
National Archives	1927
National Archives	1930
National Archives	1930
National Archives	1934
National Archives	1934
National Archives	1934
National Archives	1934
National Archives	1934
National Archives	1935
National Archives	1936
National Archives	1937
National Archives	1938
National Archives	1940
National Archives	1950
National Archives	1953
National Archives 1846	1846
National Archives 1846	1846
National Archives 1846	1846
National Archives 1846	1846
National Archives 1846	1846
National Archives 1846	1846
National Archives 1846	1846
National Archives 1846	1846
National Archives 1846	1846
National Archives 1846	1846

A–Z Reference	Year
National Archives 1846	1846
National Archives 1846	1846
National Archives 1846	1846
National Archives 1846	1846
National Archives 1846	1846
National Archives 1846	1846
National Archives 1846	1846
National Archives 1846	1846
National Archives 1846	1846
National Archives 1846	1846
National Archives 1846	1846
National Archives 1846	1846
National Archives 1846	1846
National Archives 1846	1846
National Park	1990
National Park	2005
Naylor's Cove	1978
Needham. George	1862
Needham. Mary	1907
Nelsons Pillar	1808
Nelsons Pillar	1966
Nelsons Pillar	1966
Nevin. Catherine	2000
Nevin. Catherine	2000
Nevin. Tom	1996
New York	1843
Newcastle Barony	1841
Newcastle Barony	1851
Newcastle Barony	1861
Newcastle Barony	1871
Newcastle Barony	1891
Newcastle Hospital	1892
Newcastle Hospital	1894
Newcastle Hospital	1933
Newcastle Hospital	1964
Newcastle Hospital	1966
Newcastle Hospital	1972
Newcastle Mill	1228
Newcastle N.S	1983
Newrath	1756
Newrath Bridge	1839
Newspaper	1798
Newspapers	1763
Newspapers	1798
Newspapers	1834
Newspapers	1840

A–Z Reference	Year
Newspapers	1849
Newspapers	1849
Newspapers	1857
Newspapers	1861
Newspapers	1861
Newspapers	1872
Newspapers	1872
Newspapers	1873
Newspapers	1876
Newspapers	1876
Newspapers	1890
Newspapers	1893
Newspapers	1895
Newspapers	1900
Newspapers	1905
Newspapers	1916
Newspapers	1918
Newspapers	1924
Newspapers	1926
Newspapers	1927
Newspapers	1935
Newspapers	1936
Newspapers	1936
Newspapers	1939
Newspapers	1946
Newspapers	1958
Newspapers	1965
Newspapers	1974
Newspapers	1974
Newspapers	1978
Newspapers	1979
Newspapers	1983
Newspapers	1988
Newspapers	1989
Newspapers	1991
Newspapers	1991
Newtown F.C	1976
NewtownMountKennedy	1798
NewtownMountKennedy	1836
NewtownMountKennedy	1840
NewtownMountKennedy	1851
Nicol. Erskine	1825
Nicol. Erskine	1850
Nicol. Erskine	1904
Nicol. Erskine	1973
Nitrigin Eireann Teo.	1964
Nitrigin Eireann Teo.	1966

The County Wicklow Database: 432 AD to 2006 AD

A-Z Reference	Year	A-Z Reference	Year	A-Z Reference	Year
Nitrigin Eireann Teo.	1984	O'Connor. Joyce	2001	O'Kelly Edward Peter	1899
Nixdorf	1977	O'Connor. Peter J.	1874	O'Kelly Edward Peter	1914
Nixon. Abraham	1712	O'Connor. Peter J.	1901	O'Kelly. Sean T	1882
Nixon. Abraham	1740	O'Connor. Peter J.	1901	O'Kelly. Sean T	1918
Nolan. John	1955	O'Connor. Peter J.	1901	O'Kelly. Sean T	1934
Nolan. Winifride	1913	O'Connor. Peter J.	1906	O'Kelly. Sean T	1936
Nolan. Winifride	1953	O'Connor. Peter J.	1906	O'Kelly. Sean T	1939
Nolan. Winifride	1966	O'Connor. Peter J.	1957	O'Kelly. Sean T	1945
North Cork Militia	1800	O'Dalaigh. Aonghus	1580	O'Kelly. Sean T	1952
Nowlan. James	1939	O'Dalaigh. Cearbhall	1911	O'Kelly. Sean T	1957
Nowlan. James	1939	O'Dalaigh. Cearbhall	1918	O'Kelly. Sean T	1959
Nugent. Count Lavall	1777	O'Dalaigh.Cearbhall	1920	O'Kelly. Sean T	1966
Nugent. Count Lavall	1793	O'Dalaigh.Cearbhall	1946	O'Kelly. Sean T	1983
Nugent. Count Lavall	1816	O'Dalaigh.Cearbhall	1951	Old Conna	1931
Nugent. Count Lavall	1849	O'Dalaigh.Cearbhall	1953	Old Conna	1963
Nugent. Count Lavall	1862	O'Dalaigh.Cearbhall	1961	Old Conna Golf Club	1980
Nugent. Pat	1798	O'Dalaigh.Cearbhall	1972	Old Conna House	1957
Nun's Cross, Ashford	1817	O'Dalaigh.Cearbhall	1974	Old Conna House	1982
Nun's Cross, Ashford	1992	O'Dalaigh.Cearbhall	1975	Old Connaught	1600
Nursing Association	1896	O'Dalaigh.Cearbhall	1976	Old Connaught	1776
O'Brien. F.J	1973	O'Dalaigh.Cearbhall	1978	Old Connaught	1783
O'Brien. John	1796	O'Dalaigh.Cearbhall	1983	Old Connaught	1948
O'Brien. John	1814	O'Dea. Jimmy	1899	Old Connaught House	1776
O'Brien. John	1861	O'Dea. Jimmy	1965	Old Connaught House	2000
O'Brien. John	1935	O'Donnell. Hugh	1590	Old Connaught School	1630
O'Byrne clan	1374	O'Donnell. Hugh	1602	Oldcourt Castle, Bray	1774
O'Byrne Clan	1398	O'Dwyer. Thomas	1859	Oldcourt. Bray	1666
O'Byrne Clan	1428	O'Dwyer. Thomas	1887	Oldtown School	1862
O'Byrne Clan	1641	O'Faolain. Sean	1900	O'Mahony. Daniel	1869
O'Byrne Clan	1892	O'Faolain. Sean	1928	O'Meara. Francis	1687
O'Byrne. F	1597	O'Faolain. Sean	1930	O'Meara. Francis	1690
O'Byrne. Feagh McHugh	1544	O'Faolain. Sean	1932	O'Moore. Sean	1996
O'Byrne. Feagh McHugh	1606	O'Faolain. Sean	1940	O'Moore. Sean	1996
O'Byrne. Feagh McHugh	1997	O'Faolain. Sean	1991	O'Neill William	1927
O'Byrne. John	1884	O'Gorman. Tiomthy	1904	O'Neill William	1927
O'Byrne. John	1921	O'Halloran. P.J.	1896	O'Neill. Art	1591
O'Byrne. John	1924	O'Halloran. P.J.	1924	O'Neill. Henry	1798
O'Byrne. John	1954	O'Halloran. P.J.	1924	O'Neill. Henry	1835
O'Byrne. W.R	1823	O'Higgins. Brigid	1932	O'Neill. Henry	1880
O'Byrne. W.R	1849	O'Higgins. Brigid	1957	O'Neill. John	1927
O'Byrne. W.R	1872	O'Higgins. Brigid	1958	O'Neill/O'Donnell	1591
O'Byrne. W.R	1896	O'Keeffe. John	1747	Onge. Samuel	1748
O'Byrnes	1316	O'Keeffe. John	1796	O'Nolan. Shaun	1871
O'Callaghan. Rev	1823	O'Keeffe. John	1796	O'Nolan. Shaun	1945
O'Callaghan. Rev	1823	O'Keeffe. John	1796	Opera. Company Bray	1918
O'Connell. Daniel	1840	O'Keeffe. John	1833	Operation Shamrock	1945
O'Connell. John	1981	O'Kelly Edward Peter	1846	Orange Lodge	1798

Section Three: Index

A-Z Reference	Year
Orange Lodge	1949
Oranmore. Lord	1901
Oranmore. Lord	1925
Oranmore. Lord	2002
Order of Malta, Bray	2002
Ormsby. J.W	1796
Ormsby. J.W	1803
O'Rourke. Mary	1937
O'Rourke. Mary	1981
O'Rourke. Mary	1982
O'Sandair. Cathal	1922
O'Sandair. Cathal	1996
O'Shaughnessy. Jimmy	2001
O'Shea. Katherine	1921
O'Sullivan. Morgan	1945
Other Vehicles	1946
Other Vehicles	1947
Other Vehicles	1948
Other Vehicles	1949
O'Toole	1153
O'Toole	1939
O'Toole Art	1540
O'Toole Clan	1890
O'Toole. Garry	1968
O'Toole. Garry	1989
O'Toole. Garry	1991
O'Toole. Garry	1992
O'Toole. Garry	1998
O'Toole. Luke	1873
O'Toole. Luke	1913
O'Toole. Luke	1929
O'Toole. St Laurence	1128
O'Toole. St Laurence	1180
O'Toole. St Laurence	1226
O'Toole. St Laurence	1230
O'Tuairisc. Eoghan	1919
O'Tuairisc. Eoghan	1968
O'Tuairisc. Eoghan	1969
O'Tuairisc. Eoghan	1982
Owen. Nora	1945
Owen. Nora	1981
Owen. Nora	1994
Palladius	431
Parish Records	1655
Parish Records	1662
Parish Records	1663
Parish Records	1666

A-Z Reference	Year
Parish Records	1666
Parish Records	1666
Parish Records	1666
Parish Records	1666
Parish Records	1666
Parish Records	1677
Parish Records	1683
Parish Records	1683
Parish Records	1689
Parish Records	1695
Parish Records	1697
Parish Records	1698
Parish Records	1698
Parish Records	1698
Parish Records	1720
Parish Records	1720
Parish Records	1720
Parish Records	1720
Parish Records	1720
Parish Records	1720
Parish Records	1724
Parish Records	1727
Parish Records	1727
Parish Records	1729
Parish Records	1729
Parish Records	1739
Parish Records	1739
Parish Records	1739
Parish Records	1748
Parish Records	1748
Parish Records	1778
Parish Records	1785
Parish Records	1791
Parish Records	1793
Parish Records	1794
Parish Records	1795
Parish Records	1797
Parish Records	1800
Parish Records	1800
Parish Records	1804
Parish Records	1804
Parish Records	1807
Parish Records	1807
Parish Records	1808
Parish Records	1809
Parish Records	1810
Parish Records	1810

A-Z Reference	Year
Parish Records	1810
Parish Records	1812
Parish Records	1815
Parish Records	1815
Parish Records	1816
Parish Records	1818
Parish Records	1818
Parish Records	1818
Parish Records	1818
Parish Records	1818
Parish Records	1823
Parish Records	1823
Parish Records	1824
Parish Records	1824
Parish Records	1825
Parish Records	1825
Parish Records	1825
Parish Records	1825
Parish Records	1825
Parish Records	1826
Parish Records	1826
Parish Records	1827
Parish Records	1830
Parish Records	1830
Parish Records	1830
Parish Records	1831
Parish Records	1833
Parish Records	1833
Parish Records	1833
Parish Records	1836
Parish Records	1836
Parish Records	1838
Parish Records	1839
Parish Records	1841
Parish Records	1842
Parish Records	1843
Parish Records	1848
Parish Records	1852
Parish Records	1852
Parish Records	1858
Parish Records	1858
Parish Records	1864
Parish Records	1864
Parish Schools	1537
Parish Schools	1834
Parking	1997
Parnell	1777

The County Wicklow Database: 432 AD to 2006 AD

A–Z Reference	Year	A–Z Reference	Year	A–Z Reference	Year
Parnell Bridge	1860	Parnell. H.T.	1875	Peacock. Joseph	1783
Parnell Bridge	1946	Parnell. H.T.	1915	Peacock. Joseph	1813
Parnell Monument	1899	Parnell. Hayes	1838	Peacock. Joseph	1837
Parnell. Anna	1852	Parnell. Hayes	1854	Pearce. Thomas	1832
Parnell. Anna	1905	Parnell. J. H.	1842	Pearce. Thomas	1855
Parnell. Anna	1911	Parnell. J. H.	1923	Pearce. Thomas	1864
Parnell. Charles S	1780	Parnell. J.H.	1874	Pearce. Thomas	1871
Parnell. Charles S	1810	Parnell. J.H.	1892	Pearce. Thomas	1915
Parnell. Charles S	1811	Parnell. J.H.	1895	Pender. George	1735
Parnell. Charles S	1816	Parnell. J.H.	1903	Pennefather. Capt. C	1890
Parnell. Charles S	1835	Parnell. John	1727	People's Park	1881
Parnell. Charles S	1846	Parnell. John	1836	People's Park Bray	2003
Parnell. Charles S	1859	Parnell. Kitty	1921	Percy. Henry	1708
Parnell. Charles S	1874	Parnell. Rev Thomas	1705	Percy. Robert	1726
Parnell. Charles S	1874	Parnell. Rev Thomas	1716	Perkins. Deborah	1750
Parnell. Charles S	1875	Parnell. Rev Thomas	1717	Petty. William	1623
Parnell. Charles S	1880	Parnell. Sir H.B.	1766	Petty. William	1654
Parnell. Charles S	1880	Parnell. Sir H.B.	1801	Petty. William	1655
Parnell. Charles S	1881	Parnell. Sir H.B.	1842	Phone Number	1982
Parnell. Charles S	1881	Parnell. Sir J.A.	1775	Photo Collection	1860
Parnell. Charles S	1881	Parnell. Sir J.A.	1812	Photo Collection	1898
Parnell. Charles S	1881	Parnell. Sir John	1745	Photo Collection	1903
Parnell. Charles S	1882	Parnell. Sir John	1766	Photo Collection	1906
Parnell. Charles S	1884	Parnell. Sir John	1774	Photo Collection	1910
Parnell. Charles S	1884	Parnell. Sir John	1782	Photo Collection	1943
Parnell. Charles S	1889	Parnell. Sir John	1783	Pigott. John	1964
Parnell. Charles S	1890	Parnell. Sir John	1799	Pigott. John	1989
Parnell. Charles S	1891	Parnell. Sir John	1801	Pilsworth. Philip	1617
Parnell. Charles S	1891	Parnell. Sophia	1845	Pim. Joshua	1869
Parnell. Charles S	1891	Parnell. Sophia	1862	Pim. Joshua	1890
Parnell. Charles S	1898	Parnell. Sophia	1877	Pim. Joshua	1893
Parnell. Charles S	1911	Parnell. Street	1911	Pim. Joshua	1893
Parnell. Charles S	1986	Parnell. Theodosia	1853	Pim. Joshua	1894
Parnell. Charles S	1996	Parnell. Theodosia	1880	Pim. Joshua	1902
Parnell. Delia	1837	Parnell. Theodosia	1917	Pim. Joshua	1942
Parnell. Delia	1859	Parnell. Theodosia	1920	Pipe Band	1912
Parnell. Delia	1859	Parnell. Thomas	1625	Pipe Band	1927
Parnell. Delia	1873	Parnell. Thomas	1686	Ploughing	1931
Parnell. Emily	1841	Parnell. Tobais	1600	Ploughing	1932
Parnell. Emily	1867	Parnell. William	1795	Ploughing	1933
Parnell. Emily	1883	Parnell. William	1817	Ploughing	1935
Parnell. Emily	1918	Parnell. William	1821	Ploughing	1937
Parnell. Fanny	1848	Parnell. William	1836	Ploughing	1939
Parnell. Fanny	1880	Parsons. William	1778	Ploughing	1941
Parnell. Fanny	1881	Patrickson. William	1790	Ploughing	1942
Parnell. Frances	1814	Patterson. James	1849	Ploughing	1943
Parnell. H.T.	1850	Patterson. M	1887	Ploughing	1944

Section Three: Index

A–Z Reference	Year	A–Z Reference	Year	A–Z Reference	Year
Ploughing	1945	Plunket	1904	Police/Garda	1890
Ploughing	1946	Plunket	1920	Police/Garda	1920
Ploughing	1946	Plunket	1920	Police/Garda	1920
Ploughing	1946	Plunket	1922	Police/Garda	1920
Ploughing	1947	Plunket	1923	Police/Garda	1920
Ploughing	1948	Plunket	1925	Police/Garda	1920
Ploughing	1951	Plunket	1938	Police/Garda	1921
Ploughing	1952	Plunket	1951	Police/Garda	1921
Ploughing	1952	Plunket	1975	Police/Garda	1926
Ploughing	1953	Plunket.William	1630	Police/Garda	1930
Ploughing	1955	Plunket.William	1803	Police/Garda	1943
Ploughing	1956	Plunket.William	1825	Police/Garda	1947
Ploughing	1957	Plunket.William	1854	Police/Garda	1948
Ploughing	1959	Plunket.William	1857	Police/Garda	1952
Ploughing	1959	Plunket.William	1863	Police/Garda	1960
Ploughing	1959	Plunket.William	1876	Police/Garda	1965
Ploughing	1960	Plunkett.James	1920	Police/Garda	1967
Ploughing	1961	Plunkett.James	1969	Police/Garda	1974
Ploughing	1961	Plunkett.James	1980	Police/Garda	1977
Ploughing	1963	Plunkett.James	2003	Police/Garda	1999
Ploughing	1963	Plunkett.W.C	1825	Polo	1872
Ploughing	1965	Pobje.Bessie	1843	Polo	1874
Ploughing	1971	Pobje.Bessie	1905	Polo	1993
Ploughing	1974	Pobje.Charles	1806	Ponsonby.John	1655
Ploughing	1976	Pobje.Charles	1821	Pony Club	1970
Ploughing	1977	Pobje.Charles	1846	Pope John Paul II	1979
Ploughing	1978	Pobje.Henry	1771	Pope John Paul II	1979
Ploughing	1980	Pobje.Henry	1791	Population	1766
Ploughing	1984	Pobje.Henry	1820	Population	1821
Ploughing	1986	Pobje.Henry	1830	Population	1831
Ploughing	1986	Pobje.Henry Jnr	1806	Population	1831
Plunket	1765	Pobje.Henry Jnr	1821	Population	1831
Plunket	1791	Pobje.Henry Jnr	1879	Population	1836
Plunket	1792	Pobje.Mary	1845	Population	1838
Plunket	1793	Police/Garda	1795	Population	1901
Plunket	1819	Police/Garda	1802	Population	1946
Plunket	1821	Police/Garda	1814	Population	1961
Plunket	1824	Police/Garda	1822	Population	1981
Plunket	1830	Police/Garda	1822	Population	1981
Plunket	1864	Police/Garda	1837	Population	1981
Plunket	1866	Police/Garda	1839	Population	1981
Plunket	1871	Police/Garda	1839	Population	1986
Plunket	1886	Police/Garda	1840	Population	1986
Plunket	1893	Police/Garda	1840	Population	1991
Plunket	1894	Police/Garda	1842	Population	2002
Plunket	1897	Police/Garda	1861	Population Arklow	1821
Plunket	1899	Police/Garda	1876	Population Arklow	1831

The County Wicklow Database: 432 AD to 2006 AD

A-Z Reference	Year	A-Z Reference	Year	A-Z Reference	Year
Population Arklow	1841	Population Bray	1966	Population Enniskerry	1961
Population Arklow	1851	Population Bray	1971	Population Enniskerry	1966
Population Arklow	1861	Population Bray	1979	Population Enniskerry	1971
Population Arklow	1871	Population Bray	1981	Population Enniskerry	1979
Population Arklow	1881	Population Bray	1986	Population Enniskerry	1981
Population Arklow	1891	Population Bray	1991	Population Enniskerry	1986
Population Arklow	1901	Population Bray	1996	Population Enniskerry	1991
Population Arklow	1911	Population Bray	2002	Population Enniskerry	1996
Population Arklow	1926	Population County	1821	Population Enniskerry	2002
Population Arklow	1936	Population County	1831	Population Greystones	1821
Population Arklow	1946	Population County	1841	Population Greystones	1831
Population Arklow	1951	Population County	1851	Population Greystones	1841
Population Arklow	1956	Population County	1861	Population Greystones	1851
Population Arklow	1961	Population County	1871	Population Greystones	1861
Population Arklow	1966	Population County	1881	Population Greystones	1861
Population Arklow	1971	Population County	1891	Population Greystones	1871
Population Arklow	1979	Population County	1901	Population Greystones	1881
Population Arklow	1981	Population County	1911	Population Greystones	1891
Population Arklow	1986	Population County	1926	Population Greystones	1901
Population Arklow	1991	Population County	1936	Population Greystones	1911
Population Arklow	1996	Population County	1946	Population Greystones	1926
Population Arklow	2002	Population County	1951	Population Greystones	1936
Population Baltinglass	1986	Population County	1956	Population Greystones	1946
Population Baltinglass	1991	Population County	1961	Population Greystones	1951
Population Baltinglass	1996	Population County	1966	Population Greystones	1956
Population Baltinglass	2002	Population County	1971	Population Greystones	1961
Population Bray	1659	Population County	1979	Population Greystones	1966
Population Bray	1766	Population County	1981	Population Greystones	1971
Population Bray	1831	Population County	1986	Population Greystones	1979
Population Bray	1836	Population County	1991	Population Greystones	1981
Population Bray	1841	Population County	1996	Population Greystones	1986
Population Bray	1851	Population County	2002	Population Greystones	1991
Population Bray	1861	Population County	2002	Population Greystones	1996
Population Bray	1871	Population County	2006	Population Greystones	2002
Population Bray	1881	Population Enniskerry	1841	Population of Brockagh	1821
Population Bray	1891	Population Enniskerry	1851	Population of Brockagh	1831
Population Bray	1891	Population Enniskerry	1861	Population of Brockagh	1841
Population Bray	1901	Population Enniskerry	1871	Population of Brockagh	1901
Population Bray	1903	Population Enniskerry	1881	Population Rathdown	1986
Population Bray	1911	Population Enniskerry	1891	Population Rathdown	1991
Population Bray	1926	Population Enniskerry	1901	Population Rathdown	1996
Population Bray	1926	Population Enniskerry	1911	Population Rathdown	2002
Population Bray	1936	Population Enniskerry	1926	Population Rathdrum	1986
Population Bray	1946	Population Enniskerry	1936	Population Rathdrum	1991
Population Bray	1951	Population Enniskerry	1946	Population Rathdrum	1996
Population Bray	1956	Population Enniskerry	1951	Population Rathdrum	2002
Population Bray	1961	Population Enniskerry	1956	Population Roundwood	1996

Section Three: Index

A-Z Reference	Year
Population Shillelagh	1986
Population Shillelagh	1991
Population Shillelagh	1996
Population Shillelagh	2002
Population Wicklow (t)	1821
Population Wicklow (t)	1831
Population Wicklow (t)	1841
Population Wicklow (t)	1851
Population Wicklow (t)	1861
Population Wicklow (t)	1871
Population Wicklow (t)	1881
Population Wicklow (t)	1891
Population Wicklow (t)	1901
Population Wicklow (t)	1911
Population Wicklow (t)	1926
Population Wicklow (t)	1936
Population Wicklow (t)	1946
Population Wicklow (t)	1951
Population Wicklow (t)	1956
Population Wicklow (t)	1961
Population Wicklow (t)	1966
Population Wicklow (t)	1971
Population Wicklow (t)	1979
Population Wicklow (t)	1981
Population Wicklow (t)	1986
Population Wicklow (t)	1991
Population Wicklow (t)	1996
Population Wicklow (t)	2002
Population, Blessington	1891
Porter. John	1651
Porter. Rev. William	1719
Porter. William	1693
Post	1811
Post Office	1844
Post Office	1888
Post Office	1904
Post Office	1914
Post Office	1914
Post Office	1960
Post Office	1960
Post Office	1964
Post Office	1978
Post Office	1986
Post Office	1999
Post Office	2000
Post Office	2002
Potato	1775

A-Z Reference	Year
Potato	2003
Potts. John	1622
Pound	1762
Power. George	1849
Power. George	1879
Power. George	1931
Power. George	1935
Power. Jenny Wyse	1858
Power. Jenny Wyse	1893
Power. Jenny Wyse	1916
Power. Jenny Wyse	1922
Power. Jenny Wyse	1941
Power. John Wyse	1859
Power. John Wyse	1926
Power. Richard	1928
Power. Richard	1964
Power. Richard	1969
Power. Richard	1970
Powerscort Arms Hotel	1715
Powerscort Arms Hotel	2005
Powerscourt	1603
Powerscourt	1697
Powerscourt	1713
Powerscourt	1721
Powerscourt	1726
Powerscourt	1727
Powerscourt	1729
Powerscourt	1730
Powerscourt	1730
Powerscourt	1743
Powerscourt	1751
Powerscourt	1760
Powerscourt	1762
Powerscourt	1764
Powerscourt	1764
Powerscourt	1764
Powerscourt	1770
Powerscourt	1774
Powerscourt	1785
Powerscourt	1788
Powerscourt	1789
Powerscourt	1790
Powerscourt	1793
Powerscourt	1793
Powerscourt	1809
Powerscourt	1811
Powerscourt	1813

A-Z Reference	Year
Powerscourt	1815
Powerscourt	1820
Powerscourt	1820
Powerscourt	1821
Powerscourt	1823
Powerscourt	1831
Powerscourt	1836
Powerscourt	1836
Powerscourt	1841
Powerscourt	1843
Powerscourt	1844
Powerscourt	1844
Powerscourt	1846
Powerscourt	1849
Powerscourt	1854
Powerscourt	1857
Powerscourt	1857
Powerscourt	1860
Powerscourt	1860
Powerscourt	1860
Powerscourt	1861
Powerscourt	1864
Powerscourt	1869
Powerscourt	1870
Powerscourt	1873
Powerscourt	1875
Powerscourt	1880
Powerscourt	1884
Powerscourt	1894
Powerscourt	1897
Powerscourt	1899
Powerscourt	1900
Powerscourt	1903
Powerscourt	1904
Powerscourt	1905
Powerscourt	1908
Powerscourt	1922
Powerscourt	1931
Powerscourt	1931
Powerscourt	1932
Powerscourt	1932
Powerscourt	1935
Powerscourt	1943
Powerscourt	1947
Powerscourt	1961
Powerscourt	1962
Powerscourt	1963

The County Wicklow Database: 432 AD to 2006 AD

A-Z Reference	Year	A-Z Reference	Year	A-Z Reference	Year
Powerscourt	1973	Pub/Tavern	1835	Putland. George	1855
Powerscourt	1974	Pub/Tavern	1857	Queen of Peace, Bray	1945
Powerscourt	1974	Pub/Tavern/Inn	1691	Queen of Peace, Bray	1946
Powerscourt	1978	Publications	1938	Queen of Peace, Bray	1997
Powerscourt	1979	Putland	1650	Queen of Rumania	1890
Powerscourt	1981	Putland	1686	Queen Victoria	1881
Powerscourt	1997	Putland	1709	Quigley. D.B	1942
Powerscourt	2000	Putland	1719	Quigley. D.B	1990
Powerscourt	2005	Putland	1721	Quigley. D.B	1998
Powerscourt Golf Club	1996	Putland	1723	Quigley. D.B	2002
Powerscourt. Viscount	1744	Putland	1730	Quin	1761
Powerscourt/Religion	1620	Putland	1745	Quin	1776
Prandy. James	1911	Putland	1748	Quin	1807
Presentation	1921	Putland	1773	Quins Hotel	1823
Presentation Bray	1920	Putland	1777	Quinsborough Road	1854
Presentation Bray	1924	Putland	1778	Radio	1989
Presentation Bray	1960	Putland	1779	Radio Station	1978
Presentation Bray	1972	Putland	1782	Radio Station	1979
Presentation College	2001	Putland	1783	Railway	1900
Price. Cecil	1968	Putland	1785	Railways	1831
Price. Cecil	1989	Putland	1808	Railways	1834
Price. Evan	1697	Putland	1810	Railways	1836
Price. John	1691	Putland	1811	Railways	1837
Prince William Seat	1831	Putland	1811	Railways	1846
Printing Works	1950	Putland	1812	Railways	1846
Proby. Elizabeth	1844	Putland	1813	Railways	1846
Proby. Elizabeth	1900	Putland	1815	Railways	1846
Proby. G.L	1868	Putland	1816	Railways	1847
Proby. Hon. G.L	1816	Putland	1835	Railways	1847
Proby. Hon. G.L	1818	Putland	1836	Railways	1847
Proby. Hon. G.L	1831	Putland	1841	Railways	1848
Proby. Hon. G.L	1855	Putland	1842	Railways	1851
Proby. Hon. G.L	1857	Putland	1847	Railways	1853
Proby. Hon. G.L	1868	Putland	1849	Railways	1854
Proby. Hon. William	1860	Putland	1857	Railways	1854
Proby. Hon. William	1866	Putland	1859	Railways	1854
Proby. Hon. William	1872	Putland	1862	Railways	1854
Proby. Hon. William	1890	Putland	1864	Railways	1855
Proby. Hon. William	1909	Putland	1866	Railways	1855
Proby. John	1752	Putland	1870	Railways	1855
Proby. John	1772	Putland	1876	Railways	1855
Proby. John (2nd)	1780	Putland	1879	Railways	1857
Proby. John (2nd)	1855	Putland	1887	Railways	1859
Proby. John Joshua	1772	Putland	1902	Railways	1860
Proby. John Joshua	1789	Putland Road	2001	Railways	1860
Proby. John Joshua	1801	Putland. Charles	1864	Railways	1861
Pub/Tavern	1728	Putland. George	1776	Railways	1861

Section Three: Index

A–Z Reference	Year
Railways	1861
Railways	1862
Railways	1862
Railways	1862
Railways	1862
Railways	1863
Railways	1864
Railways	1865
Railways	1865
Railways	1865
Railways	1865
Railways	1866
Railways	1866
Railways	1867
Railways	1867
Railways	1868
Railways	1868
Railways	1868
Railways	1871
Railways	1872
Railways	1873
Railways	1873
Railways	1873
Railways	1876
Railways	1876
Railways	1876
Railways	1876
Railways	1877
Railways	1883
Railways	1884
Railways	1885
Railways	1886
Railways	1891
Railways	1893
Railways	1894
Railways	1894
Railways	1894
Railways	1895
Railways	1895
Railways	1895
Railways	1896
Railways	1896
Railways	1897
Railways	1897
Railways	1897
Railways	1898
Railways	1898

A–Z Reference	Year
Railways	1900
Railways	1900
Railways	1900
Railways	1903
Railways	1903
Railways	1905
Railways	1906
Railways	1907
Railways	1907
Railways	1908
Railways	1913
Railways	1914
Railways	1917
Railways	1922
Railways	1922
Railways	1923
Railways	1923
Railways	1924
Railways	1925
Railways	1927
Railways	1927
Railways	1931
Railways	1932
Railways	1944
Railways	1949
Railways	1952
Railways	1959
Railways	1960
Railways	1961
Railways	1964
Railways	1964
Railways	1966
Railways	1970
Railways	1976
Railways	1976
Railways	1979
Railways	1980
Railways	1980
Railways	1984
Railways	1996
Railways	2000
Railways	2000
Railways	2000
Railways	2001
Railways	2001
Railways	2004
Railways	2004

A–Z Reference	Year
Railways	2004
Railways	2004
Railways	2005
Railways	2005
Rates	1978
Rates	1980
Rathcoran	1934
Rathdangan	1847
Rathdangan	1920
Rathdangan	1923
Rathdown Barony	1841
Rathdown Barony	1851
Rathdown Barony	1861
Rathdown Barony	1871
Rathdown Barony	1891
Rathdown Union	1839
Rathdown Union	1841
Rathdrum	1794
Rathdrum	1837
Rathdrum	1856
Rathdrum	1860
Rathdrum	1940
Rathdrum Corn Mill	1860
Rathdrum Fair	1767
Rathdrum Workhouse	1837
Rathdrum Workhouse	1842
Rathmichael	1609
Rathmichael	1826
Rathmichael	1863
Rathmichael	1864
Rathmichael	1872
Rathmines	1830
Rathnew	1717
Rathnew	1753
Rathnew	2001
Rathnew	2001
Rathnew	2004
Rathnew A.F.C.	1986
Rathsallagh Golf Club	1995
Ravens well. Bray	1972
Ravenswell. Bray	1858
Ravenswell. Bray	1901
Ravenswell. Bray	1920
Ravenswell. Bray	1958
Rawson. George	1782
Reade. Richard	1724
Rebellion 1798	1798

The County Wicklow Database: 432 AD to 2006 AD

A-Z Reference	Year	A-Z Reference	Year	A-Z Reference	Year
Redmond. John E.	1856	Roads	1962	Roundwood Golf Club	1996
Redmond. John E.	1891	Roads	1969	Roundwood P.P.	1892
Redmond. John E.	1914	Roads	1984	Roundwood School	1820
Redmond. John E.	1918	Roads	1989	Roundwood School	1923
Redmond. John E.	1956	Roads	1989	Royal Hotel, Bray	1950
Reeves. Thomas	1714	Roads	1991	Royal Hotel, Bray	1973
Reeves. Thomas	1775	Roads	1993	Royal Hotel, Bray	1943
Reeves. William	1667	Roads	1998	Royal Hotel, Bray	1982
Reeves. William	1734	Roads	1999	Royal Hotel, Bray	1982
Reform Association	1901	Roads	2000	Royal Inn Glendalough	1902
Regan. T	1958	Roads	2002	Royal Marine Hotel	1916
Regulations	1925	Roads	2004	Royal Order	1661
Rents	1826	Roads	2005	Royal School	1629
Repeal Meeting	1843	Robbie. John	1955	Royal Visit	1821
Report	1856	Robbie. John	1976	Royal Visit	1849
Reynolds. B	1907	Robbie. John	1981	Royal Visit	1853
Rifle Contest	1875	Roberts. L	1750	Royal Visit	1853
Road Labourers Wages	1914	Roberts. L	1765	Royal Visit	1897
Road Labourers Wages	1939	Roberts. Lewis	1700	Royal Visit	1900
Road Labourers Wages	1946	Roche. Alexandra	1826	Royal Visit	1911
Road Safety	1966	Roche. Alexandra	1859	Royal Visit	1978
Road Tax Wicklow	1946	Roche. de la George	1308	Royal Visit	2002
Road Tax Wicklow	1946	Roche. Dick	2002	Royal Visits	2004
Road Tax Wicklow	1946	Roche. Dick	2004	Russborough House	1952
Road Tax Wicklow	1946	Rohan. K. C.	1944	Russborough House	1974
Road Tax Wicklow	1947	Rooney. Philip	1907	Russborough House	1986
Road Tax Wicklow	1947	Rooney. Philip	1946	Russborough House	2001
Road Tax Wicklow	1947	Rooney. Philip	1962	Russborough House	2002
Road Tax Wicklow	1947	Rossmore	1769	Ryan, Tony	1982
Road Tax Wicklow	1948	Rossmore. Lord	1796	Ryan. Kevin	1983
Road Tax Wicklow	1948	Rossmore. Lord	1801	Ryan. Tony	1987
Road Tax Wicklow	1948	Rotary Club of Bray	1972	Sacrobosco. Johannes	1150
Road Tax Wicklow	1948	Rotary Club of Wicklow	1988	Sacrobosco. Johannes	1235
Road Tax Wicklow	1949	Roundwood	1609	Sacrobosco. Johannes	1518
Road Tax Wicklow	1949	Roundwood	1780	Salkeld. Joseph	1858
Road Tax Wicklow	1949	Roundwood	1799	Sandford. Francis	1630
Road Tax Wicklow	1949	Roundwood	1800	Saul. Capt. P	1968
Road Tax Wicklow	1950	Roundwood	1823	Saul. Capt. P	1894
Roads	1802	Roundwood	1863	Saul. Capt. P	1930
Roads	1802	Roundwood	1863	Saunders Grove	1716
Roads	1802	Roundwood	1871	Saunders Grove	1923
Roads	1802	Roundwood	1875	Saunders Grove	1925
Roads	1856	Roundwood	1888	Saunders Newsletter	1798
Roads	1909	Roundwood	1966	Saunders. Maj.Gen J.S	1815
Roads	1928	Roundwood	1984	Saunders. Morley	1758
Roads	1930	Roundwood	2005	Saunders. Morley	1779
Roads	1939	Roundwood F.C.	2002	Saunders. R.J.P	1878

Section Three: Index

A–Z Reference	Year
Saunders. Robert	1722
Saunders. Robert	1822
Saunders. Robert	1908
Saurin. William	1757
Saurin. William	1799
Saurin. William	1807
Saurin. William	1839
Scalp	1832
Scannell. Brendan J.	1947
Scannell. Brendan J.	1953
Scannell. Brendan J.	1954
Scannell. Brendan J.	1955
Scannell. Brendan J.	1973
Scannell. Brendan J.	1975
Scannell. Brendan J.	1979
Scannell. Brendan J.	2003
Scharff. Robert F.	1858
Scharff. Robert F.	1887
Scharff. Robert F.	1890
Scharff. Robert F.	1934
School Medical Service	1930
School, Wicklow Town	1987
School, Wicklow Town	1996
School. Kilcoole	1898
Schoolhouse	1845
Scoil Chualann	1977
Scott. Charlotte	1951
Scott. G.D	1893
Scott. G.D	1901
Scott. G.D	1910
Scott. G.D	1943
Scott. G.D	1950
Scott. Hopton	1782
Scott. J.G.	1863
Scott. J.G.	1912
Scott. J.M	1805
Scott. Olive	1997
Scott. Walter	1825
Scott. Walter	1825
Scouting	1908
Scouting	1910
Scouting	1912
Scouting	1965
Scouting	1972
Scouting	1972
Scouting	1973
Scouting	1977

A–Z Reference	Year
Scouting	1979
Scouting	1983
Scouting	1985
Scouting	1990
Scouting	1990
Scouting	1996
Sea Baths	1880
Sea Park House	1860
Sea Park House	1958
Seaside Festival	1988
Seaside Festival	1992
Segrave. Capt. H	1893
Segrave. O'Neill	1870
Seminole County	1992
Servier (Ireland)	1972
Sexton. Pierse	1628
Seychelles	2003
Seymour. Mary	1547
Seymour. Mary	1560
Seymour. Mary	1570
Shanaganagh Castle	1800
Shanaganagh Castle	1818
Shanaganagh Castle	1919
Shee. Martin Archer	1769
Shee. Martin Archer	1783
Shee. Martin Archer	1850
Sheehy.Eddie	2001
Sheep	1907
Sheep	1907
Sheep	1968
Sheep	1997
Sheep Breeders	1926
Sheepwalk House	1727
Sheet/British Library	1689
Sheet/British Library	1725
Sheet/British Library	1728
Sheet/British Library	1875
Sheet/British Library	1891
Shelton Abbey	1697
Shelton Abbey	1770
Shelton Abbey	1830
Shelton Abbey	1947
Shelton Abbey	1951
Shelton Abbey	1972
Shilelagh Flower Show	1896
Shillelagh	1760
Shillelagh	1830

A–Z Reference	Year
Shillelagh Barony	1841
Shillelagh Barony	1851
Shillelagh Barony	1861
Shillelagh Barony	1871
Shillelagh Barony	1891
Shillelagh Courthouse	1860
Shillelagh Workhouse	1837
Shillelagh Workhouse	1842
Ships/Yachts	1679
Ships/Yachts	1694
Ships/Yachts	1750
Ships/Yachts	1755
Ships/Yachts	1765
Ships/Yachts	1766
Ships/Yachts	1771
Ships/Yachts	1771
Ships/Yachts	1776
Ships/Yachts	1782
Ships/Yachts	1784
Ships/Yachts	1784
Ships/Yachts	1785
Ships/Yachts	1787
Ships/Yachts	1787
Ships/Yachts	1788
Ships/Yachts	1789
Ships/Yachts	1791
Ships/Yachts	1795
Ships/Yachts	1797
Ships/Yachts	1799
Ships/Yachts	1799
Ships/Yachts	1799
Ships/Yachts	1801
Ships/Yachts	1802
Ships/Yachts	1802
Ships/Yachts	1802
Ships/Yachts	1804
Ships/Yachts	1804
Ships/Yachts	1805
Ships/Yachts	1807
Ships/Yachts	1807
Ships/Yachts	1807
Ships/Yachts	1812
Ships/Yachts	1812
Ships/Yachts	1820
Ships/Yachts	1821
Ships/Yachts	1824
Ships/Yachts	1824

A-Z Reference	Year	A-Z Reference	Year	A-Z Reference	Year
Ships/Yachts	1825	Ships/Yachts	1873	Ships/Yachts	1952
Ships/Yachts	1826	Ships/Yachts	1873	Ships/Yachts	1953
Ships/Yachts	1831	Ships/Yachts	1876	Ships/Yachts	1958
Ships/Yachts	1836	Ships/Yachts	1876	Ships/Yachts	1989
Ships/Yachts	1838	Ships/Yachts	1879	Ships/Yachts	1999
Ships/Yachts	1839	Ships/Yachts	1879	Ships/Yachts	2000
Ships/Yachts	1839	Ships/Yachts	1880	Ships/Yachts	2000
Ships/Yachts	1843	Ships/Yachts	1883	Short. Patrick	1940
Ships/Yachts	1844	Ships/Yachts	1885	Showbands	1960
Ships/Yachts	1844	Ships/Yachts	1885	Showbands	1960
Ships/Yachts	1846	Ships/Yachts	1885	Showbands	1960
Ships/Yachts	1846	Ships/Yachts	1886	Sidmonton Cottage	1855
Ships/Yachts	1848	Ships/Yachts	1888	Singapore	2003
Ships/Yachts	1849	Ships/Yachts	1892	Sinnott. Walter	1879
Ships/Yachts	1849	Ships/Yachts	1892	Sisters of Charity	1896
Ships/Yachts	1850	Ships/Yachts	1898	Skeletons	1835
Ships/Yachts	1850	Ships/Yachts	1901	Skinners Map	1778
Ships/Yachts	1851	Ships/Yachts	1902	Slater's Directory	1846
Ships/Yachts	1851	Ships/Yachts	1903	Slater's Directory	1856
Ships/Yachts	1851	Ships/Yachts	1906	Slater's Directory	1856
Ships/Yachts	1852	Ships/Yachts	1906	Slater's Directory	1870
Ships/Yachts	1852	Ships/Yachts	1907	Slater's Directory	1881
Ships/Yachts	1852	Ships/Yachts	1908	Slater's Directory	1894
Ships/Yachts	1855	Ships/Yachts	1909	Sliver Mines	1753
Ships/Yachts	1856	Ships/Yachts	1911	Smith. John	1741
Ships/Yachts	1858	Ships/Yachts	1914	Smith. John	1768
Ships/Yachts	1859	Ships/Yachts	1915	Smith. Mary	1798
Ships/Yachts	1861	Ships/Yachts	1916	Smith. Sir Michael	1740
Ships/Yachts	1861	Ships/Yachts	1918	Smith. Sir Michael	1765
Ships/Yachts	1861	Ships/Yachts	1918	Smith. Sir Michael	1808
Ships/Yachts	1861	Ships/Yachts	1919	Smith. Sir Michael	1988
Ships/Yachts	1861	Ships/Yachts	1925	Smith. Sir W.C.	1766
Ships/Yachts	1861	Ships/Yachts	1926	Smith. Sir W.C.	1794
Ships/Yachts	1861	Ships/Yachts	1931	Smith. Sir W.C.	1795
Ships/Yachts	1861	Ships/Yachts	1932	Smith. Sir W.C.	1800
Ships/Yachts	1861	Ships/Yachts	1934	Smith. Sir W.C.	1836
Ships/Yachts	1862	Ships/Yachts	1934	Smith. Sir W.C.	1988
Ships/Yachts	1863	Ships/Yachts	1935	Smith. Thomas	1753
Ships/Yachts	1865	Ships/Yachts	1936	Smithson. Annie	1873
Ships/Yachts	1865	Ships/Yachts	1939	Smithson. Annie	1890
Ships/Yachts	1867	Ships/Yachts	1940	Smithson. Annie	1944
Ships/Yachts	1871	Ships/Yachts	1940	Smithson. Annie	1948
Ships/Yachts	1872	Ships/Yachts	1941	Smuggling	1753
Ships/Yachts	1872	Ships/Yachts	1945	Smuggling	1766
Ships/Yachts	1873	Ships/Yachts	1947	Smuggling	1767
Ships/Yachts	1873	Ships/Yachts	1947	Smurfit. Victoria	1973
Ships/Yachts	1873	Ships/Yachts	1950	Smyth. Algernon	1884

Section Three: Index

A–Z Reference	Year	A–Z Reference	Year	A–Z Reference	Year
Smyth. Algernon	1914	St Patrick's School	1919	St. Mary's. Enniskerry	1859
Smythe. Emily	1837	St Patrick's School	1944	St. Mary's. Enniskerry	1859
Smythe. Emily	1842	St Patrick's School	1945	St. Mary's. Enniskerry	1861
Smythe. William	1808	St Patrick's School	1945	St. Mary's. Enniskerry	1861
Smythe. William	1832	St Patrick's School	2004	St. Mary's. Enniskerry	1996
Smythe. William	1837	St. Andrew's School	1887	St. Michael's N.S.	1940
Softball Club	1997	St. Andrew's School	1887	St. Patrick's Church	1865
Solus Teo	1935	St. Andrew's School	1888	St. Patrick's School	1975
Solus Teo	1961	St. Andrew's School	1942	St. Pauls. Bray	1816
Somerville-Large. P.	1901	St. Andrew's School	1943	St. Pauls. Bray	1818
Somerville-Large. P.	1959	St. Andrew's School	1943	St. Pauls. Bray	1869
Somerville-Large. P.	1991	St. Andrew's School	1971	St. Pauls. Bray	1892
Song	1928	St. Andrew's School	1991	St. Pauls. Bray	1910
Speed limit	1903	St. Anthony's F.C.	1977	St. Pauls. Bray	1912
Speed Limits	1968	St. Brendans College	1956	St. Pauls. Bray	1957
Speed Limits	1974	St. Brendans College	1970	St. Pauls. Bray	1972
Speed Limits	1978	St. Brendans College	1981	St. Pauls. Bray	1977
Speed Limits	2005	St. Brendans College	2003	St. Paul's. Bray	1609
Sport	1908	St. Bridgets	1866	St. Paul's. Bray	1770
Sport	1908	St. Colman's Hospital	1995	St. Paul's. Bray	1779
Sport	1922	St. Columba Church	1801	St. Paul's. Bray	1911
Sport	1928	St. Cronan's BNS Bray	1932	St. Paul's. Bray	1925
Sport	1942	St. Cronan's BNS Bray	1999	St. Paul's. Bray	1957
Sport	1945	St. Cronan's BNS Bray	2000	St. Peter's F.C.	2000
Sport	1961	St. Cronan's BNS Bray	2000	St. Peters School	1874
Sport	1976	St. Cronan's BNS Bray	2001	St. Peters School	1961
Sport	1986	St. Cronan's. Bray	1965	St. Peters School	1996
Sport	1989	St. David's School	1906	St. Peters. Bray	1830
Sport	1990	St. Gerard's School	1918	St. Therese of Lisieux	2001
Sport	1991	St. Gerard's School	1934	St. Therese of Lisieux	2001
Sport	1994	St. Gerard's School	1937	St. Thomas' College	1981
Sport	1999	St. Gerard's School	1963	St. Fergals Boxing Club	1997
Sport	1999	St. Gerard's School	1966	St. Fergal's. Bray	1976
Sport	1999	St. Gerard's School	1971	St. Fergal's. Bray	1980
Sport	1999	St. Gerard's School	1976	St. John Whitty, Sophia	1878
St Andrew's. Bray	1858	St. Gerard's School	1998	St. John Whitty, Sophia	1902
St Andrew's. Bray	1864	St. Joseph's Church	1868	St. John Whitty, Sophia	1924
St Andrew's. Bray	1983	St. Joseph's Church	1869	St. Joseph's Wicklow	1912
St Fergal's F.C	1978	St. Joseph's Newtown	1865	St. Kevin's N.S.	1934
St Kevin's Church	1680	St. Kevins Pipe Band	1966	St. Mary Convent. Arklow	1881
St Mary's Enniskerry	1940	St. Kiernan's Bray	1972	St. Mary Convent. Arklow	1999
St Mary's Enniskerry	1976	St. Kiernan's Bray	1976	St. Patricks Enniskerry	1859
St Matthwe's School	1883	St. L. O'Toole F.C.	2002	St. Patricks Enniskerry	1863
St Patricks School	1918	St. Mary's Blessington	1683	St. Patrick's. Wicklow	1844
St Patricks School	2000	St. Mary's Blessington	1683	St. Patrick's. Wicklow	1889
St Patrick's School	1864	St. Mary's, Wicklow	1887	St. Pauls N.S.	1904
St Patrick's School	1902	St. Mary's. Enniskerry	1857	St. Peters. Bray	1837

The County Wicklow Database: 432 AD to 2006 AD

A-Z Reference	Year	A-Z Reference	Year	A-Z Reference	Year
Stamps	1949	Sweeney. John	1988	Tansey & Co	1920
Stamps	1977	Sweetman. James	1844	Tarrant. Charles	1763
Stamps	2003	Swimming Club	1928	Tarrant. Charles	1771
Stats	2002	Symes. Mitchelburne	1767	Tarrant. Charles	1794
Stats	2002	Symes. Richard	1752	Tarrant. Charles	1802
Stats	2002	Synge	1804	Tarrant. Charles	1818
Steele. Laurence	1747	Synge	1847	Tarrant. Charles	1818
Stephens. John	1718	Synge	1871	Tate Gallery London	1972
Stephens. Sir John	1752	Synge	1880	Tate Gallery London	1996
Sterne. Laurence	1713	Synge	1884	Taylor. Katie	2002
Sterne. Laurence	1720	Synge	1888	TD's for Wicklow	1918
Sterne. Laurence	1768	Synge	1893	TD's for Wicklow	1921
Stewart. Robert	1710	Synge	1895	TD's for Wicklow	1922
Stillorgan	1862	Synge	1903	TD's for Wicklow	1923
Stockton. John	1685	Synge	1905	TD's for Wicklow	1927
Stratford on Slaney	1792	Synge	1906	TD's for Wicklow	1927
Stratford. Amelia	1831	Synge	1907	TD's for Wicklow	1932
Stratford. Edward	1706	Synge	1908	TD's for Wicklow	1933
Stratford. John	1698	Synge	1908	TD's for Wicklow	1937
Stratford. John	1721	Synge	1909	TD's for Wicklow	1938
Stratford. John	1736	Synge	1909	TD's for Wicklow	1943
Stratford. John	1736	Synge	1910	TD's for Wicklow	1944
Stratford. John	1776	Synge	1915	TD's for Wicklow	1948
Stratford. John	1777	Synge	1943	TD's for Wicklow	1951
Stratford. John	1777	Synge	1968	TD's for Wicklow	1953
Stratford. John	1777	Synge	1994	TD's for Wicklow	1954
Stratford. Robert	1677	Synge. Frances Mary	1842	TD's for Wicklow	1957
Stratford. Robert	1692	Synge. Frances Mary	1870	TD's for Wicklow	1961
Stratford. Robert	1699	Synge. Frances Mary	1883	TD's for Wicklow	1965
Stuart. Francis	1902	Synge. Frances Mary	1887	TD's for Wicklow	1968
Stuart. Francis	1920	Synge. Francis	1844	TD's for Wicklow	1969
Stuart. Francis	1920	Synge. John	1819	TD's for Wicklow	1973
Stuart. Francis	1924	Synge. John	1841	TD's for Wicklow	1977
Stuart. Francis	1930	Synge. John Hatch	1872	TD's for Wicklow	1981
Stuart. Francis	1949	Syria	2003	TD's for Wicklow	1982
Stuart. Francis	1951	Talbot. Bernard	1640	TD's for Wicklow	1982
Stuart. Francis	1953	Talbot. Richard	1685	TD's for Wicklow	1987
Stuart. Francis	2000	Talbotstown Lwr Barony	1841	TD's for Wicklow	1989
Stylebawn House	1773	Talbotstown Lwr Barony	1851	TD's for Wicklow	1992
Sugarloaf Common	1839	Talbotstown Lwr Barony	1861	TD's for Wicklow	1995
Sumbeam House Services	1977	Talbotstown Lwr Barony	1871	TD's for Wicklow	1997
Sunnybank	1402	Talbotstown Lwr Barony	1891	Tea & Coffee	1777
Sunnybank, Bray	2001	Talbotstown Upr Barony	1841	Teachers Salary	1836
Superquinn	1973	Talbotstown Upr Barony	1851	Templestown	1749
Survey	1636	Talbotstown Upr Barony	1861	The European G C	1992
Survey	1641	Talbotstown Upr Barony	1871	The Riordan's	1979
Survey	1837	Talbotstown Upr Barony	1891	The school house	1820

Section Three: Index

A-Z Reference	Year	A-Z Reference	Year	A-Z Reference	Year
The school house	1834	Tinahely	1798	Tourism	1966
The School house	1849	Tinahely	1843	Town Commissioners	1857
Thompson Dr C.	1870	Tinahely	1940	Town Hall. Bray	1881
Thompson Dr C.	1877	Tinahely	1996	Town Hall. Bray	1881
Thompson. Dr C.	1815	Tinakilly House	1870	Town Hall. Bray	1884
Thompson. Dr C.	1839	Tinakilly House	1883	Town Hall. Bray	1928
Thompson. Dr C.	1870	Tinakilly House	1949	Town Hall. Bray	1950
Thompson. Dr C.	1873	Tinakilly House	1959	Town Hall. Bray	1976
Thompson. Dr C.	1876	Tinakilly House	1962	Town Hall. Bray	1992
Thompson. Dr C.	1877	Tinakilly House	1978	Tozer. Mr	1872
Thompson. Dr C.	1877	Tinakilly House	1982	Tracey. Blaise	1985
Thompson. Henry	1861	Tinakilly House	1991	Tracey. Liam	1934
Tidy Towns	1958	Tinakilly House	1997	Tractors	1946
Tidy Towns	1978	Tinnehinch House	1782	Tractors	1947
Tidy Towns	1979	Tinnehinch House	1999	Tractors	1948
Tidy Towns	1980	Tinnehinch House	1999	Tractors	1949
Tidy Towns	1981	Tober House	1720	Trade	1850
Tidy Towns	1982	Tobin. James	1884	Trade	1945
Tidy Towns	1982	Tollemache. Laura	1807	Trade	1948
Tidy Towns	1986	Tombe. Gordon E	1879	Trade	1950
Tidy Towns	1986	Tomcork	1991	Trade	1950
Tidy Towns	1986	Tommnafinnoge	1444	Trade	1971
Tidy Towns	1986	Toole. King Mac	1010	Trade	1984
Tidy Towns	1986	Torrens. Thomas	1776	Trade	1985
Tidy Towns	1986	Tottenham. C.R.W	1845	Trade	1989
Tidy Towns	1986	Tottenham. C.R.W	1874	Trade	1989
Tidy Towns	1986	Tottenham. C.R.W	1903	Trade	1989
Tidy Towns	1986	Tottenham. Charles	1805	Trade	1990
Tidy Towns	1986	Tottenham. Charles	1812	Trade Union	1911
Tidy Towns	1986	Tottenham. Charles	1839	Traffic Lights	1937
Tidy Towns	1998	Tottenham. Charles	1846	Traffic Lights	1972
Tidy Towns	2001	Tottenham. Charles G	1881	Trams	1867
Tidy Towns	2001	Tottenham. Charles J.	1808	Trams	1878
Tidy Towns	2001	Tottenham. Charles J.	1839	Trams	1878
Tighe. James S	1876	Tottenham. Charles J.	1892	Trams	1888
Tighe. Mary	1772	Tottenham. Isabella	1878	Trams	1895
Tighe. Mary	1793	Tottenham. Lt Col C. G.	1863	Trams	1896
Tighe. Mary	1805	Tottenham. Lt Col C. G.	1874	Trams	1949
Tighe. Mary	1810	Tottenham. Lt Col C. G.	1878	Travellers Group	1992
Tighe. William	1771	Tottenham. Lt Col C. G.	1885	Tree Survey	2001
Tillage Barley	1997	Tottenham. Lt Col C. G.	1886	Tritschler. Robin	1977
Tillage Wheat	1997	Tottenham. Lt Col C. G.	1895	Troy. Aidan	1945
Timmins. Godfrey	1975	Tottenham. Lt.Col. C.J	1859	Troy. Aidan	2002
Timmins. Godfrey	1978	Tottenham. Maj.C.R.W	1888	Troy. Dermot	1927
Timmins. Godfrey	1981	Tottenham. Robert P.	1773	Troy. Dermot	1952
Timmins. Godfrey	1996	Tottenham. Robert P.	1850	Troy. Dermot	1962
Timmins. Godfrey	2001	Tourism	1964	Trudder House	1995

A–Z Reference	Year	A–Z Reference	Year	A–Z Reference	Year
Trudder Lodge	1840	VEC. Bray	1998	Weather	1933
Truell. Henry P	1871	VEC. Congress	1945	Weather	1947
Truell. Robert H	1824	VEC-Outdoor Centre	1987	Weather	1960
Tuberculosis	1913	Wade. Robert C	1847	Weather	1982
Tulfarris Golf Club	1989	Wakefield	1811	Weather	1982
Tulfarris House	1760	Walker. Joseph C.	1761	Weather	1989
Turkish Baths	1859	Walker. Joseph C.	1810	Weather	1990
Turkish Baths	1859	Walker. Robert	1621	Weather	2000
Turkish Baths	1859	Walking Routes	2004	Weather	2005
Turkish Baths	1867	Wall. Ambrose	1690	Weaver Thomas	1773
Turkish Baths	1946	Wall. James	1807	Weaver Thomas	1855
Turkish Baths	1980	Walpole	1868	Weaver. Thomas	1773
Turnpike Roads	1855	Walsh. Mary	1929	Weaver. Thomas	1807
Turnpike Trust	1855	Walsh. Mary	1969	Weaver. Thomas	1855
Twomey. John	1939	Walsh. Mary	1973	Wednesday	1913
Twomey. John	1946	Walsh. Mary	1976	Weld. Isaac	1774
Tynte. Joseph P.	1842	War Memorial	1919	Weld. Isaac	1813
Tynte. Lieut. Col.F.J	1892	Ward. Tony	1954	Weld. Isaac	1855
Tynte. Sir James S.	1785	Ward. Tony	1978	Weld. Isaac	1856
Tyrrell Shipping	1864	Ward. Tony	1978	Weld. Isaac	1856
Tyrrell Shipping	1960	Ward. Tony	1987	Wellesley. E.H	1895
Tyrrell. John	1864	Ward.J.J	1946	Wesley. John	1786
Tyrrell. Kate	1863	Ware. James	1632	Wesley. John	1786
Tyrrell. Kate	1921	Warren. John	1679	Wesley. John	1786
Unemployment	1982	Warren. John	1680	West Wicklow His. Soc.	1980
Unemployment	1982	Water – Vartry	1860	West. Tichbourne	1705
Unemployment	1984	Water – Vartry	1861	Westby. Edward	1806
Urban Renewal Scheme	1986	Water – Vartry	1862	Westby. Nicholas	1777
Usher. Christopher	1678	Water – Vartry	1865	Westby. Nicholas	1815
Usher. John	1764	Water – Vartry	1868	Westby. Nicholas	1860
Valleymount Church	1803	Water – Vartry	1870	Westby. Nicholas	1870
Valuation	1965	Water – Vartry	1908	Westby. W.J	1827
Vance & Wilson	1860	Water – Vartry	1990	Westby. William	1733
Vance. Pat	1997	Water Scheme	1986	Weston. Galen	1968
Vans & Lorries	1946	Water Treatment	1988	Weston. Galen	1983
Vans & Lorries	1947	Waters. T	1923	Wexford	1210
Vans & Lorries	1948	Watson. John	1786	Whale	1679
Vans & Lorries	1949	Wayman. P.A	1927	Whaley. R.C	1747
VEC. Bray	1901	Wayman. P.A	1992	Whaley. R.C	1791
VEC. Bray	1924	Wayman. P.A	1998	Whaley. Thomas (Buck)	1766
VEC. Bray	1926	WCEB	1995	Whaley. Thomas (Buck)	1785
VEC. Bray	1934	WDSL	1976	Whaley. Thomas (Buck)	1800
VEC. Bray	1977	Weather	1630	Wheatly. E.W	1857
VEC. Bray	1979	Weather	1839	Whelan. J.	1970
VEC. Bray	1980	Weather	1867	Whelan. J.	1973
VEC. Bray	1980	Weather	1905	White. J F de vere	1949
VEC. Bray	1997	Weather	1926	White. John	1723

Section Three: Index

A–Z Reference	Year
White. Larry	2002
Whiteside. James	1804
Whiteside. James	1851
Whiteside. James	1852
Whiteside. James	1858
Whiteside. James	1859
Whiteside. James	1876
Whitshead. John	1695
Whitshead. S.V.B.H	1867
Whitshed. E.A.F. H.	1861
Whitshed. E.A.F. H.	1886
Whitshed. E.A.F. H.	1892
Whitshed. E.A.F. H.	1900
Whitshed. E.A.F. H.	1907
Whitshed. E.A.F. H.	1928
Whitshed. E.A.F. H.	1934
Wicklow 200 Km	2001
Wicklow 200 Km	2002
Wicklow 200 Km	2003
Wicklow Ale	1244
Wicklow Ale	1788
Wicklow Ale	1805
Wicklow Ale	1840
Wicklow Castle	1566
Wicklow Coastguard	1831
Wicklow Coastguard	1831
Wicklow Coastguard	1835
Wicklow Coastguard	1839
Wicklow Coastguard	1888
Wicklow Corn Co. Ltd	1918
Wicklow County	1801
Wicklow County Council	1899
Wicklow County Shirred	1542
Wicklow County Shirred	1578
Wicklow County Shirred	1605
Wicklow County Shirred	1606
Wicklow County Show	2000
Wicklow Film Com.	1992
Wicklow Friary	1279
Wicklow Friary	1864
Wicklow GAA	1885
Wicklow GAA	1886

A–Z Reference	Year
Wicklow GAA	1886
Wicklow GAA	1886
Wicklow GAA	1896
Wicklow GAA	1898
Wicklow GAA	1901
Wicklow GAA	1902
Wicklow GAA	1904
Wicklow GAA	1905
Wicklow GAA	1906
Wicklow GAA	1907
Wicklow GAA	1910
Wicklow GAA	1910
Wicklow GAA	1919
Wicklow GAA	1920
Wicklow GAA	1921
Wicklow GAA	1927
Wicklow GAA	1929
Wicklow GAA	1931
Wicklow GAA	1934
Wicklow GAA	1936
Wicklow GAA	1936
Wicklow GAA	1940
Wicklow GAA	1947
Wicklow GAA	1949
Wicklow GAA	1953
Wicklow GAA	1954
Wicklow GAA	1955
Wicklow GAA	1956
Wicklow GAA	1957
Wicklow GAA	1958
Wicklow GAA	1964
Wicklow GAA	1965
Wicklow GAA	1966
Wicklow GAA	1967
Wicklow GAA	1967
Wicklow GAA	1967
Wicklow GAA	1967
Wicklow GAA	1968
Wicklow GAA	1969
Wicklow GAA	1969
Wicklow GAA	1970
Wicklow GAA	1971
Wicklow GAA	1971
Wicklow GAA	1971
Wicklow GAA	1974
Wicklow GAA	1974
Wicklow GAA	1974

A–Z Reference	Year
Wicklow GAA	1974
Wicklow GAA	1976
Wicklow GAA	1977
Wicklow GAA	1978
Wicklow GAA	1981
Wicklow GAA	1983
Wicklow GAA	1985
Wicklow GAA	1986
Wicklow GAA	1986
Wicklow GAA	1989
Wicklow GAA	1992
Wicklow GAA	1992
Wicklow GAA	1994
Wicklow GAA	1995
Wicklow GAA	1995
Wicklow GAA	1998
Wicklow GAA	2000
Wicklow GAA	2001
Wicklow GAA	2001
Wicklow GAA	2002
Wicklow GAA	2002
Wicklow GAA	2003
Wicklow GAA	2003
Wicklow GAA	2003
Wicklow GAA	2004
Wicklow Gaol	1702
Wicklow Gaol	1841
Wicklow Gaol	1848
Wicklow Gaol	1877
Wicklow Gaol	1900
Wicklow Gaol	1924
Wicklow Gaol	1985
Wicklow Gaol	1998
Wicklow Gas	1948
Wicklow Gas	1952
Wicklow Golf Club	1904
Wicklow Golf Club	1963
Wicklow Golf Club	1986
Wicklow Golf Club	1994
Wicklow Golf Club	2002
Wicklow Harbour	1753
Wicklow Harbour	1753
Wicklow Harbour	1842
Wicklow Harbour	1851
Wicklow Harbour	1855
Wicklow Harbour	1880
Wicklow Harbour	1884

408   The County Wicklow Database: 432 AD to 2006 AD

A-Z Reference	Year	A-Z Reference	Year	A-Z Reference	Year
Wicklow Harbour	1897	Wicklow Homicides	1876	Wicklow Infanticides	1865
Wicklow Harbour	1907	Wicklow Homicides	1877	Wicklow Infanticides	1866
Wicklow Harbour	1928	Wicklow Homicides	1878	Wicklow Infanticides	1867
Wicklow Harbour	1949	Wicklow Homicides	1879	Wicklow Infanticides	1868
Wicklow Harbour	1956	Wicklow Homicides	1880	Wicklow Infanticides	1869
Wicklow Harbour	1959	Wicklow Homicides	1881	Wicklow Infanticides	1870
Wicklow Harbour	1964	Wicklow Homicides	1882	Wicklow Infanticides	1871
Wicklow Harbour	1968	Wicklow Homicides	1883	Wicklow Infanticides	1872
Wicklow Harbour	1977	Wicklow Homicides	1884	Wicklow Infanticides	1873
Wicklow Harbour	1979	Wicklow Homicides	1885	Wicklow Infanticides	1874
Wicklow Harbour	1984	Wicklow Homicides	1886	Wicklow Infanticides	1875
Wicklow Harbour	1996	Wicklow Homicides	1887	Wicklow Infanticides	1876
Wicklow Hills Bus Co	1924	Wicklow Homicides	1888	Wicklow Infanticides	1877
Wicklow Hills Bus Co	1936	Wicklow Homicides	1889	Wicklow Infanticides	1878
Wicklow Homicides	1843	Wicklow Homicides	1890	Wicklow Infanticides	1879
Wicklow Homicides	1844	Wicklow Homicides	1891	Wicklow Infanticides	1880
Wicklow Homicides	1845	Wicklow Homicides	1892	Wicklow Infanticides	1881
Wicklow Homicides	1846	Wicklow Homicides	1893	Wicklow Infanticides	1882
Wicklow Homicides	1847	Wicklow Homicides	1894	Wicklow Infanticides	1883
Wicklow Homicides	1848	Wicklow Homicides	1895	Wicklow Infanticides	1884
Wicklow Homicides	1849	Wicklow Homicides	1896	Wicklow Infanticides	1885
Wicklow Homicides	1850	Wicklow Homicides	1897	Wicklow Infanticides	1886
Wicklow Homicides	1851	Wicklow Homicides	1898	Wicklow Infanticides	1887
Wicklow Homicides	1852	Wicklow Homicides	1899	Wicklow Infanticides	1888
Wicklow Homicides	1853	Wicklow Hotel	1858	Wicklow Infanticides	1889
Wicklow Homicides	1854	Wicklow Infanticides	1843	Wicklow Infanticides	1890
Wicklow Homicides	1855	Wicklow Infanticides	1844	Wicklow Infanticides	1891
Wicklow Homicides	1856	Wicklow Infanticides	1845	Wicklow Infanticides	1892
Wicklow Homicides	1857	Wicklow Infanticides	1846	Wicklow Infanticides	1893
Wicklow Homicides	1858	Wicklow Infanticides	1847	Wicklow Infanticides	1894
Wicklow Homicides	1859	Wicklow Infanticides	1848	Wicklow Infanticides	1895
Wicklow Homicides	1860	Wicklow Infanticides	1849	Wicklow Infanticides	1896
Wicklow Homicides	1861	Wicklow Infanticides	1850	Wicklow Infanticides	1897
Wicklow Homicides	1862	Wicklow Infanticides	1851	Wicklow Infanticides	1898
Wicklow Homicides	1863	Wicklow Infanticides	1852	Wicklow Infanticides	1899
Wicklow Homicides	1864	Wicklow Infanticides	1853	Wicklow Militia	1793
Wicklow Homicides	1865	Wicklow Infanticides	1854	Wicklow Militia	1793
Wicklow Homicides	1866	Wicklow Infanticides	1855	Wicklow Militia	1795
Wicklow Homicides	1867	Wicklow Infanticides	1856	Wicklow Militia	1796
Wicklow Homicides	1868	Wicklow Infanticides	1857	Wicklow Militia	1797
Wicklow Homicides	1869	Wicklow Infanticides	1858	Wicklow Militia	1802
Wicklow Homicides	1870	Wicklow Infanticides	1859	Wicklow Militia	1803
Wicklow Homicides	1871	Wicklow Infanticides	1860	Wicklow Militia	1810
Wicklow Homicides	1872	Wicklow Infanticides	1861	Wicklow Militia	1812
Wicklow Homicides	1873	Wicklow Infanticides	1862	Wicklow Militia	1814
Wicklow Homicides	1874	Wicklow Infanticides	1863	Wicklow Militia	1815
Wicklow Homicides	1875	Wicklow Infanticides	1864	Wicklow Militia	1822

Section Three: Index

A-Z Reference	Year	A-Z Reference	Year	A-Z Reference	Year
Wicklow Militia	1885	Wicklow. Earl of	1881	Woodbrook	1973
Wicklow Railway Stn.	1884	Wicklow. Earl of	1891	Woodbrook	1974
Wicklow Regatta	1878	Wicklow. Earl of	1902	Woodbrook	1975
Wicklow Regiment	1881	Wicklow. Earl of	1902	Woodbrook Golf Club	1926
Wicklow Regiment	1909	Wicklow. Earl of	1917	Woodbrook Golf Club	1943
Wicklow Rovers	1975	Wicklow. Earl of	1946	Woodbrook Golf Club	1982
Wicklow Rovers F.C.	1975	Wicklow. Earl of	1978	Woodbrook Golf Club	2000
Wicklow Rugby Club	1963	Wicklow. Earl of	1985	Woodbrook House	1840
Wicklow Rugby Club	1976	Wilde. Oscar	1878	Woodburn. William	1838
Wicklow Rural	1992	Wilde. Oscar	1900	Woodburn. William	1849
Wicklow Rural	1994	William Plunket	1897	Woodburn. William	1875
Wicklow Sailing Club	1951	Wilson. James	1876	Woodburn. William	1885
Wicklow Street	1837	Wind Farm	2003	Woodburn. William	1915
Wicklow Sub Aqua Club	1983	Windgates	1852	Woodenbridge	1767
Wicklow Town	1375	Windgates School	1954	Woodenbridge	1772
Wicklow Town	1578	Wingfield Estates	1859	Woodenbridge	1807
Wicklow Town	1641	Wingfield, Shelia	1992	Woodenbridge	1911
Wicklow Town	1799	Wingfield. Baron	1744	Woodenbridge Golf Club	1884
Wicklow Town	1834	Wingfield. Cromwell	1664	Woodenbridge Inn	1608
Wicklow Town	1950	Wingfield. Emily	1918	Woods. Michael	1935
Wicklow Town	2000	Wingfield. Hon. R.	1784	Woods. Michael	1977
Wicklow Town	2005	Wingfield. Hon. Richard	1762	Woods. Michael	1979
Wicklow Town Council	2001	Wingfield. Lewis S.	1842	Woods. Michael	1982
Wicklow Town F.C.	1939	Wingfield. Lewis S.	1868	Woods. Michael	1987
Wicklow Traffic	1976	Wingfield. Lewis S.	1891	Woods. Michael	1991
Wicklow Ward	1915	Wingfield. Maurice	1883	Woods. Michael	1992
Wicklow Way	1980	Wingfield. Maurice	1956	Woods. Michael	1993
Wicklow Way	1981	Wingfield. Richard	1721	Woods. Michael	1994
Wicklow. County	1834	Wingfield. Sir Richard	1603	Woods. Michael	1997
Wicklow. County	1846	Winston's	1988	Woods. Michael	1999
Wicklow. County	1846	Wolf Tone Youth Club	1973	Woodstock House	1770
Wicklow. County	1853	Wolfe Tone Sq	1954	Woodstock House	1780
Wicklow. County	1880	Wolfe. Charles	1791	Woodstock House	1827
Wicklow. Earl of	1755	Wolfe. Charles	1817	Woodstock House	1840
Wicklow. Earl of	1785	Wolfe. Charles	1823	Woodstock House	1946
Wicklow. Earl of	1788	Wolferston. John	1609	Woodstock House	1960
Wicklow. Earl of	1789	Wood Carving	1893	Woodstock House	1993
Wicklow. Earl of	1793	Woodbrook	1959	Woolworths. W.F	1953
Wicklow. Earl of	1793	Woodbrook	1963	Woolworths. W.F	1984
Wicklow. Earl of	1807	Woodbrook	1964	World War II	1941
Wicklow. Earl of	1815	Woodbrook	1966	WTDA	1950
Wicklow. Earl of	1815	Woodbrook	1967	Wynne. Edward	1883
Wicklow. Earl of	1839	Woodbrook	1968	Wynne. George	1859
Wicklow. Earl of	1842	Woodbrook	1969	Wynne. Gladys	1878
Wicklow. Earl of	1869	Woodbrook	1970	Wynne. Gladys	1907
Wicklow. Earl of	1877	Woodbrook	1971	Wynne. Gladys	1968
Wicklow. Earl of	1880	Woodbrook	1972		

A–Z Reference	Year
Yeats. Jack B.	1871
Yeats. Jack B.	1894
Yeats. Jack B.	1910
Yeats. Jack B.	1916
Yeats. Jack B.	1957
Young Scientist	2001
Young. Bernard	1870
Young. William	1822
Young. William	1822
Youth Group	1980
Youth Hostel	1999